F. Pichler R. Moreno-Díaz
R. Albrecht (Eds.)

Computer Aided Systems Theory – EUROCAST '95

A Selection of Papers from the
Fifth International Workshop on
Computer Aided Systems Theory
Innsbruck, Austria, May 22-25, 1995
Proceedings

Springer

Lecture Notes in Computer Science 1030

Edited by G. Goos, J. Hartmanis and J. van Leeuwen

Advisory Board: W. Brauer D. Gries J. Stoer

Lecture Notes in Computer Science

Edited by G. Goos, J. Hartmanis and J. van Leeuwen

Advisory Board: W. Brauer D. Gries J. Stoer

Springer

Berlin
Heidelberg
New York
Barcelona
Budapest
Hong Kong
London
Milan
Paris
Tokyo

Series Editors

Gerhard Goos, Karlsruhe University, Germany

Juris Hartmanis, Cornell University, NY, USA

Jan van Leeuwen, Utrecht University, The Netherlands

Volume Editors

Franz Pichler
Institute of Systems Science, Johannes Kepler University
Altenbergerstraße 69, A-4040 Linz, Austria

Roberto Moreno Díaz
Department of Computer Science and Systems
University of Las Palmas de Gran Canaria
P.O. Box 550, 35080 Las Palmas, Spain

Rudolf Albrecht
Institute of Informatics, University of Innsbruck
Technikerstraße 25, A-6020 Inssbruck, Austria

Cataloging-in-Publication data applied for

Die Deutsche Bibliothek - CIP-Einheitsaufnahme

Computer-aided systems theory : a selection of papers from the
Fifth International Workshop on Computer Aided Systems
Theory, Innsbruck, Austria, May 22 - 25, 1995 ; proceedings /
EUROCAST '95. F. Pichler ... (ed.). - Berlin ; Heidelberg ;
New York ; Barcelona ; Budapest ; Hong Kong ; London ;
Milan ; Paris ; Santa Clara ; Singapore ; Tokyo : Springer, 1996
  (Lecture notes in computer science ; Vol. 1030)
  ISBN 3-540-60748-X
NE: Pichler, Franz [Hrsg.]; EUROCAST <5, 1995, Innsbruck>; GT

CR Subject Classification (1991): J.6, I.6, I.2, J.7, J.3, C.1.m, C.3

ISBN 3-540-60748-X Springer-Verlag Berlin Heidelberg New York

© Springer-Verlag Berlin Heidelberg 1996
Printed in Germany

Typesetting: Camera-ready by author
SPIN 10512407   06/3142 – 5 4 3 2 1 0   Printed on acid-free paper

Sketches from EUROCAST'95

Excursion to the peak of the Hafelekar

Preface

This volume contains a selection of papers presented at the Fifth International Workshop on Computer Aided Systems Theory (CAST), which was held in Innsbruck (Tyrol/Austria) in May 1995.

Over the last years CAST research has become rather stable in the sense that the common paradigms to be followed are today generally accepted by the interested groups such as theoreticians, tool-makers, designers, or appliers. This we believe is reflected in this volume.

In section 1 (Systems Theory), new approaches for the development of systems theory, as required to provide theoretical frameworks for complex modelling tasks, are presented. Section 2 (Design Environments) gives an insight into different developments of method base systems and their architectures, which are crucial for the success of CAST in practical applications. Section 3 (Complex System Design) deals with methodological means to control complexity in engineering design tasks. Finally, section 4 (Specific Applications) presents some concrete examples of applied research, which can be embedded into the topics of CAST research.

EUROCAST'95 was organized by the Institute of Informatics, of the University Innsbruck, with administrative support from the Institute of Systems Science, Johannes Kepler University Linz, Austria, and the C.I.I.C., Universidad de Las Palmas de Gran Canaria, Spain.

The co-sponsorship of IFSR (International Federation of Systems Research) and IFIP (International Federation of Information Processing) is gratefully acknowledged.

Finally, the editors of this volume thank all contributors for providing the manuscript in due time and to the staff of Springer-Verlag in Heidelberg for their cooperation.

November 1995

Franz Pichler
Roberto Moreno-Díaz
Rudolf Albrecht

Contents

1   Systems Theory

2   Design Environments and Tools

3 Complex Systems Design

4 Specific Applications

1 SYSTEMS THEORY

On the Structure of Discrete Systems

Rudolf F. Albrecht

Institut für Informatik, Universität Innsbruck
A-6020 Innsbruck, Austria

Abstract. The intention of this article is to present a general, uniform and concise mathematical framework for modelling of systems, especially discrete systems. As basic structures families and relations, defined as families of families represented in parameterized form, are used, which allows the representation of dual and polymorphic relations. On these structures structors are applied to obtain higher level structures, parts of these, and lower level structures from higher level structures. Considered are the Π-product, selection of sub structures by properties, concatenations of relations subject to constraints. Treated are structures on index sets, topological structures, valuated structures, in particular fuzzy sets, sets of times as complete atomic boolean lattices with ordered atoms and induced orderings on the times, coarsenings of a time set, processes and their interactions, refinement and coarsenings of processes, and variables with their assignment operators. Most of our definitions are more general than those in literature. Relationships between various systems in applications are pointed out and illustrated by examples.
Keywords: System Theory, Modelling of Discrete Systems.

1 Families and Relations

For mathematical modelling of systems we use classical set theory and in particular the basic concepts of families and relations (see e.g. [6]).

Let M denote the "universe" of "objects" and I denote the "universe" of "indices" under consideration, with $M \cap I \neq \varnothing$ admitted. For $M \subset M$ and $I \subset I$ a function ind ("indexing") with ind: $I \to M$, $\wedge i \in I$ ($i \to m_{[i]} =_{def}$ ind(i)) defines a "family" $(m_i)_{i \in I} =_{def} \{(i, m_{[i]}) \mid i \in I\}$. We introduce a mapping "setof" : $(m_i)_{i \in I} \to \{m_{[i]} \mid i \in I\}$, setof $(m_i)_{i \in I} =$ ind(I) $\subseteq$ M. Setof affects the highest level index.

For $I = \varnothing \vee M = \varnothing$ $(m_i)_{i \in I} = \varnothing$. $\wedge$ denotes the universal, $\vee$ the existential quantifier.

Let be given $J \subset I$, $I \subset I$, $\varphi: J \to$ pow I such that $\wedge j \in J$ $(I_{[j]} =_{def} \varphi(j)) \wedge I = \bigcup_{j \in J} I_{[j]}$, and define $\wedge j \in J$ $(I_j =_{def} \{j\} \times I_{[j]}$. Further, let be given $\wedge j \in J$ $(\psi_j: I_{[j]} \to M)$ and define $\wedge j \in J(\wedge (j,i) \in I_j$ $(m_{[ji]} =_{def} \psi_j (i) \wedge m_{ji} =_{def} (j,(i,m_{[i]})_{[j]})))$. For notational convenience we write $m_{ji} = (ji, m_{[ji]})$.

Then a "relation parameterized by J" is given by $R =_{def} ((m_{ji})_{ji \in I_j})_{j \in J}$ and an unparameterized relation by setof $R = R' = \{(m_{[ji]})_{i \in I_{[j]}} \mid j \in J\}$. Define $\bigwedge i \in I$ ($J_{[i]}$ $=_{def} \{j \mid j \in J \wedge i \in I_{[j]}\} \wedge J_i =_{def} \{i\} \times J_{[i]} \wedge \bigwedge j \in J_{[i]} (m_{ij} =_{def} m_{ji}^T =_{def} (i,(j,m_{[ij]})) \wedge m_{[ij]} = m_{[ji]})$). Then the "transposed relation" to R is defined by $R^T =_{def} ((m_{ij})_{ij \in J_i})_{i \in I}$, and the unparameterized transposed relation by setof $R^T = R^{T'} = \{(m_{[ij]})_{j \in J_{[i]}} \mid i \in I\}$.

With $I_J =_{def} \bigcup_{j \in J} I_j \subseteq J \times I$ and $J_I =_{def} \bigcup_{i \in I} J_i \subseteq I \times J$ to R and R^T the double indexed families $\hat{R} =_{def} (m_{ji})_{ji \in I_J}$ and $\hat{R}^T =_{def} (m_{ij})_{ij \in J_I}$ are associated.

Expl. 1: Let $M = \{a,b,c,d,e\}$, $I = \{1,2,3\}$, $J = \{1,2\}$, $R = ((a_{11}, b_{12}, c_{13}), (d_{22}, e_{23}))$. $I_{[1]} = \{1,2,3\}$, $I_1 = \{1\} \times I_{[1]}$, $I_{[2]} = \{2,3\}$, $I_2 = \{2\} \times I_{[2]}$. $R^T = ((a_{11}), (b_{12}, d_{22}), (c_{13}, e_{23}))$, $J_{[1]} = \{1\}$, $J_1 = \{1\} \times J_{[1]}$, $J_{[2]} = \{1,2\}$, $J_2 = \{2\} \times J_{[2]}$, $J_{[3]} = \{1,2\}$, $J_3 = \{2\} \times J_{[3]}$. $I_J = \{(1,1), (1,2), (1,3), (2,2), (2,3)\}$. $J_I = \{(1,1), (2,1), (2,2), (3,1), (3,2)\}$. $\hat{R} = (a_{11}, b_{12}, ...e_{23}) = \{a_{11}, b_{12}, ...e_{23}\} = $ set of $((a_{11}), (b_{12}), ...(e_{23}))$. Setof $R = \{(a_1, b_2, c_3), (d_2, e_3)\}$, setof $(a_1, b_2, c_3) = \{a,b,c\}$, setof $(d_2, e_3) = \{d, e\}$.

The importance of families lies in the fact that in practice objects of a set are referenced by "indices", e.g. names, identifiers, addresses, labels, space - and time coordinates, or implicitly by descriptions or procedures to identify or to obtain them.

2 Structors

Structors are relations on sets and/or families of sets and/or families. Classical set theoretical structors are : union $\cup$, intersection $\cap$, difference $\setminus$, combinations of these, e.g. symmetrical difference Δ, selection of a subset $\subset$, aggregation of subsets to a set $\{.\}$, e.g. the power set pow. As important examples of relational structors we consider:

2.1 The $\prod$-product

Let be given $I \subset \mathbf{I}$, $(M_i)_{i \in I}$, $\bigwedge i \in I (\emptyset \neq M_{[i]} \subset \mathbf{M})$. Then
$$\prod_{i \in I} M_i =_{def} \{(m_i)_{i \in I} \mid \bigwedge i \in I (m_{[i]} \in M_{[i]})\}$$
is the product of the family $(M_i)_{i \in I}$, any $R \subseteq \prod_{i \in I} M_i$ is a conventional, not parameterized relation. Let $J \subseteq$ pow I, $\bigwedge j \in J (j \rightarrow R_{[j]} \wedge R_{[j]} \subseteq \prod_{i \in j} M_i)$, then $\tilde{R}$ $=_{def} \bigcup_{j \in J} R_j$ is a relation.

Special cases for card $I < \infty$:

(1) $R \subseteq M_i \ \pi \ M_k \ \pi ...$ with the product in infix notation,

(2) $I = \{i_{[1]}, i_{[2]}, ... i_{[n]}\}$, $\bigwedge k \in \{1,2,...n\}$ $(i_{[k]} \in \mathbf{N})$, the strict ordering of the naturals induces $i_{[1]} < i_{[2]} < ... < i_{[n]}$. Then the product is "cartesian" and

$$R \subseteq \overset{n}{\underset{k=1}{\times}} M_{i[k]} \text{ in prefix notation}, R \subseteq M_{i[1]} \times M_{i[2]} \times ... M_{i[n]} \text{ in infix notation.}$$

2.2 Selection by properties

If $m \in M$ and e is a "quality" of which we can decide, whether m has this quality or does not have it, we say "m has property e" or "m does not have property e". For example, if we know $m \in M$, then m has the property to be a member of M.

The following definitions give selections from relations by specifying properties on

(a) indices ("names"):

Let $C \subset I$, ind: $J \to$ pow C, $\wedge j \in J$ ($C_{[j]} =_{def} ind(i) \wedge C_j =_{def} \{j\} \times C_{[j]}$). Then "projection" $pr((C_j)_{j \in J}) R =_{def} ((m_{ji})_{i \in I(j)})_{j \in J'}$ with $I(j) =_{def} I_j \cap C_j$, $J' =_{def} \{j \mid j \in J \wedge I(j) \neq \varnothing\}$,

"coprojection" $cpr((C_j)_{j \in J})R =_{def} pr((I_j \setminus C_j)_{j \in J})R$,

"projection" $pr(C)R' =_{def} \{(m_{[ji]})_{i \in I[j]} \mid j \in J \wedge I[j] =_{def} I_{[j]} \cap C\}$,

"coprojection" $cpr(C)R' =_{def} \{(m_{[ji]})_{i \in I[j]} \mid j \in J \wedge I[j] =_{def} I_{[j]} \setminus C\}$,

for $V \subseteq C \times C$

"projection" $pr(V)\hat{R} =_{def} (m_{ji})_{i \in I_j \cap V}$, and "coprojection" $cpr(C)\hat{R} =_{def} (m_{ji})_{i \in I_j \setminus V}$.

The definitions for $pr((C_i)_{i \in I})R^T$, $cpr((C_i)_{i \in I})R^T$, $pr(C)R^{T'}$, $cpr(C)R^{T'}$, $pr(V)\hat{R}^T$, $cpr(V)\hat{R}^T$ follow from duality.

Any subfamily of a relation can be obtained by projections.

For $R \subseteq M_{i[1]} \times M_{i[2]} \times ... M_{i[n]}$ $pr(k) R =_{def} pr(\{i_{[k]}\})R$ ("k-th projection").

(b) objects ("values"):

Let $R = ((m_{ji})_{ji \in I_j})_{j \in J}$, $S = ((n_{lk})_{lk \in K_l})_{l \in L}$, $I_J =_{def} \underset{j \in J}{\bigcup} I_j$, $K_L =_{def} \underset{l \in L}{\bigcup} K_l$ and

$C =_{def} \{(ji,lk) \mid (ji,lk) \in I_J \sqcap K_L \wedge (m_{[ji]} = n_{[lk]})\}$,

$\wedge j \in J(I(j) =_{def} \{ji \mid ji \in I_j \wedge \vee c \in C(ji \in c)\}$, $J^* =_{def} \{j \mid j \in J \wedge I(j) \neq \varnothing\}$, we define "cut of R by S ": $cut(S) R =_{def} (m_{ji})_{ji \in I(j)})_{j \in J^*}$, and its extension to R :

$ext(R)cut(S)R =_{def} ((m_{ji})_{ji \in I_j})_{j \in J^*}$.

With $C(join) =_{def} \{(ji,lk) \mid (ji,lk) \in C \wedge (i=k)\}$, and

$\wedge j \in J(I(j) =_{def} \{ji \mid ji \in I_j \wedge \vee c \in C(join)(ji \in c)\}$, $J^* =_{def} \{j \mid j \in J \wedge I(j) \neq \varnothing\}$, we define "join cut of R by S ": $jcut(S)R =_{def} (m_{ji})_{ji \in I(j)})_{j \in J^*}$, and its extension to R:

$ext(R)jcut(S)R =_{def} ((m_{ji})_{ji \in I_j})_{j \in J^*}$.

Similar definitions apply to R^T.

For the unparameterized relations $R' = \{(m_i)_{i \in I[j]} \mid j \in J\}$, $S' = \{(n_k)_{k \in K[l]} \mid l \in L\}$, we have

$I =_{def} \underset{j \in J}{\bigcup} I_{[j]}$, $K =_{def} \underset{l \in L}{\bigcup} K_{[l]}$, for $C =_{def} \{ik \mid ik \in I \sqcap K \wedge (m_{[ji]} = n_{[lk]})\}$,

$\wedge j \in J(I(j) =_{def} \{i \mid i \in I_{[j]} \wedge \vee c \in C(i \in c)\})$, $J^* =_{def} \{j \mid j \in J \wedge I(j) \neq \varnothing\}$, cut $(S')R' =_{def} \{(m_i)_{i\in I(j)} \mid j \in J^*\}$, for $C(join) =_{def} \{ii \mid ii \in C\}$, $\bigwedge_{j\in J}(I(j) =_{def} \{i \mid i \in I_{[j]} \wedge \bigvee_{c\in C(join)}(i \in c)\})$, $J^* =_{def} \{j \mid j\in J \wedge I(j) \neq \varnothing \}$,

jcut$(S')R' =_{def} \{(m_i)_{i\in I(j)} \mid j \in J^*\}$.

Similar definitions apply to $R^{T'}$.

Given the families $\hat{R} = (m_u)_{u\in U}$, $U \subseteq J \times I$, $\hat{S} = (n_v)_{v\in V}$, $V \subseteq L \times K$, we define

$C =_{def} \{(u,v) \mid (u,v) \in U \Pi V \wedge (m_{[u]} = n_{[v]})\}$,

$C(join) =_{def} \{(u,v) \mid (u,v) \in C \wedge (m_u = n_v)\}$,

"cut of $\hat{R}$ by $\hat{S}$" : cut$(\hat{S})\hat{R} =_{def} (m_u)_{u\in C}$,

"join cut of $\hat{R}$ by $\hat{S}$" : jcut$(\hat{S})\hat{R} =_{def} (m_u)_{u\in C(join)}$.

Expl. 2: See Fig. 1. R like in Expl.1, $S = ((c_{23}, b_{24}))$, $J = \{1,2\}$, $I_J = \{11, 12, 13, 22, 23\}$, $L = \{2\}$, $K_L = K_l = \{23, 24\}$, $C = \{(12,24), (13,23)\}$, $I(1) = \{12, 13\}$, $I(2) = \varnothing$, $J^* = \{1\}$,

cut(S') $R' = ((b_{12}, c_{13}))$

$C(join) = \{(13,23)\}$, $I(1) = \{13\}$, $I(2) = \varnothing$, $J^* = \{1\}$,

jcut$(S')R' = ((c_{13}))$.

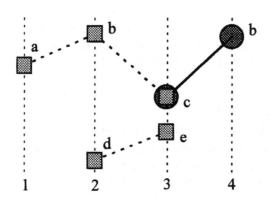

Fig. 1

2.3 Concatenations

Concatenations are functional structors and hence algebraic compositions. They are often combined with selections.

Let be given $(R_q)_{q\in Q}$ with $\varnothing \neq Q \subset I$, $\bigwedge_{q\in Q}(R_q =_{def} ((m_{qji})_{qji\in I_{qj}})_{qj\in J_q})$, with

$I_{qj} = \{q\}\times\{j\}\times I_{[qj]}$, $J_q = \{q\}\times J_{[q]}$. We define

$J_Q =_{def} \prod_{q\in Q} J_q$, and for $\bigwedge_{k\in J_Q}$:

$I_k =_{def} \bigcup_{qj\in k} I_{qj}$, $I_{[k]} =_{def} \bigcup_{qj\in k} I_{[qj]}$,

$\bigwedge_{i\in I_{[k]}} (D_i(k) =_{def} \{m_{[qj]i} \mid qj \in k\} \wedge E_i(k) =_{def} \{m_{qji} \mid qj \in k\})$,

$\hat{I}_{[k]} =_{def} \{i \mid i\in I_{[k]} \wedge \text{card } E_i(k) = 1\}$,

$\bigwedge i \in I_{[k]} (\varphi_i(k): D_i(k) \to s_i(k) \in M \land \text{card } D_i(k) = 1 \Rightarrow s_i(k) = m_{[qj]i})$.

$J_Q^* =_{def} \{k \mid k \in J_Q \land \bigwedge i \in I_{[k]} (\text{card } D_i(k) = 1)\}$,

$\hat{J}_Q =_{def} \{k \mid k \in J_Q^* \land \hat{I}_{[k]} \neq \varnothing\}$.

Important concatenations are:

$\mathbf{K}((R_q)_{q \in Q}) =_{def} ((m_{qji})_{qji \in I_k})_{k \in J_Q}$,

$\mathbf{K}_{join}((R_q)_{q \in Q}) =_{def} ((m_{[qj]i})_{i \in I_{[k]}})_{k \in J_Q^*}$,

$\mathbf{K}_\Delta((R_q)_{q \in Q}) =_{def} ((m_{[qj]i})_{i \in \hat{I}_{[k]}})_{k \in \hat{J}_Q}$,

$\mathbf{K}_\varphi((R_q)_{q \in Q}) =_{def} ((\varphi_i(k)(D_i(k)))_{i \in I_{[k]}})_{k \in J_Q}$.

For $\mathbf{K}, \mathbf{K}_{join}, \mathbf{K}_\Delta, \mathbf{K}_\varphi$ we use infix notations $\mathbf{k}, \mathbf{k}_{join}, \mathbf{k}_\Delta, \mathbf{k}_\varphi$.

$\mathbf{K}, \mathbf{K}_{join}, \mathbf{K}_\Delta, \mathbf{K}_\varphi$ are commutative and associative.

If $\bigwedge k \in J_Q (\bigwedge (qj, q'j') \in k \Pi k \ (qj \neq q'j' \Rightarrow I_{[qj]} \cap I_{[q'j']} = \varnothing))$ then $\mathbf{K}$ and $\mathbf{K}_{join}$ are isomorphic.

Expl. 3: See Expl. 2, set $R_{[1]} = R$, $R_{[2]} = S$, $M = \{a, b, c, d, e\}$.

$R_1 = (r_{11} = (a_{111}, b_{112}, c_{113}), r_{12} = (d_{122}, e_{123}))$, $R_2 = (r_{21} = (c_{213}, b_{214}))$, $J_{[1]} = \{1,2\}$, $J_{[2]} = \{1\}$, $I_{[11]} = \{1,2,3\}$, $I_{[21]} = \{3,4\}$, $I_{[12]} = \{2,3\}$, $J_Q = \{((1,1), (2,1)), ((1,2), (2,1))\}$.

$\mathbf{K}((R_1, R_2)) = ((a_{111}, b_{112}, c_{113}, c_{213}, b_{214}), (d_{122}, e_{123}, c_{213}, b_{214}))$,

$\mathbf{K}_{join}((R_1, R_2)) = ((a_1, b_2, c_3, b_4))$,

$\mathbf{K}_\Delta((R_1, R_2)) = ((a_1, b_2, b_4))$ (expresses transitivity),

let M be a set of real numbers, then φ_i can be for example the arithmetic mean:

$\mathbf{K}_\varphi((R_1, R_2)) = ((a_1, b_2, c_3, b_4), (d_2, ((c+e)/2)_3, b_4))$,

let M be a set of sets, then φ_i can be for example the union:

$\mathbf{K}_\varphi((R_1, R_2)) = ((a_1, b_2, c_3, b_4), (d_2, (c \cup e)_3, b_4))$.

Interpreting $(b_{112}, b_{214}) = (((112), (214)), ((b)))$ and $(c_{113}, c_{213}) = (((113), (213)), ((c)))$, then $\mathbf{K}_{join}$ yields $((112), (214), (b))$ and $((113), (213), (c))$. An important application of this distributivity is for example: if M is a set of files in a data base, then for the composed file (r_{11}, r_{21}) b and c need to be stored only once, $P(b) = ((112), (214))$ are pointers to b, $P(c) = ((113), (213))$ are pointers to c, deletion of r_{11} in R_1 results in deletion of the pointers (11), $P(b) := ((214))$, $P(c) := ((213))$.

Considering $(R_q)_{q \in Q}$, parts of the R_q may be selected by properties (membership in connecting relations) and then concatenated. We call the relations induced among the indices of the connecting relations "connectors". An example fundamental for networks of components with functional behaviour is:

$$C \subseteq \bigcup_{V \subseteq Q} \prod_{q \in V} I_q \text{ with } I_{[q]} =_{def} \bigcup_{qj \in J_q} I_{[qj]}, I_q =_{def} \{q\} \times I_{[qj]}, C \text{ set of connectors,}$$

$E(C) \subseteq \underset{c \in C}{\bigcup} \underset{qi \in c}{\prod} N_{qi}$ with $\varnothing \subset N_{[qi]} \subset M$, the connecting relation. We define

$K((R_q)_{q \in Q}, E(C)) =_{def} ((m_{qji})_{qji \in I_k})_{k \in K_Q}$ $(\subseteq K((R_q)_{q \in Q}))$ with for example

case (a): $K_Q =_{def} \{k \mid k \in J_Q \wedge (\vee c \in C \ (pr(c) \ (m_{q[ji]})_{qji \in I_k} \in E(C)))\}$ or

case (b): $K_Q =_{def} \{k \mid k \in J_Q \wedge (\wedge c \in C \ (pr(c) \ (m_{q[ji]})_{qji \in I_k} \in E(C)))\}$.

Selected are families of $K((R_q)_{q \in Q})$ with non-empty cuts with $E(C)$.

Expl. 4: Given $R \subset \{0,1\}^3$, written $R = \{(x_1, x_2, x_3)\}$ with variables $x_i : \{0,1\}$ for $i \in I$, $I = \{1,2,3\}$, functional $(x_1, x_2) \to x_3$, defined by $j = 1: (1,0) \to 0, j = 2: (0, 1) \to 1$. For $Q = \{1, 2, 3, 4, 5\}$ we consider $(R_q)_{q \in Q}$ with $R_{[q]} = R$. We have $I_q = \{(q1), (q2), (q3)\}$, $J_q = \{(q1), (q2)\}$, and choose $C = \{(13,41), (13,31), (23, 32), (23,42), (33,51), (43,52)\}$, and $E(C) = \{(x_{qi}, x_{q'i'})\}$ with the property $x_{[qi]} = x_{[q'i']}$ for $(qi, q'i') \in C$. Concatenation yields a composite relation N, visualized by the directed graph shown in Fig.2. Realized by physical objects, the R_q correspond to identical "processors", C corresponds to the connection network ("buses"). For the subrelation

$K((R_1,R_2)) = K((x_{11}, x_{12}, x_{13}),(x_{21}, x_{22}, x_{23})) = (x_{11}, x_{12}, x_{13}, x_{21}, x_{22}, x_{23})$,

"input" to it is $pr(\{11, 12, 21, 22\}) K((R_1,R_2))$, the input is not restricted,

"output" to it is $pr(\{13, 23\}) K((R_1,R_2))$.

If $x_{[12]} = x_{[21]} = x_{[1221]}$, then the input is $K_{join} ((x_{11}, x_{1221}), (x_{1221}, x_{22})) = (x_{11}, x_{1221}, x_{22})$.

$K((R_1,R_2,,R_3,R_4), E(C')) = \{(x_{11}, x_{12}, x_{13}, x_{21}, x_{22}, x_{23}, x_{31}, x_{32}, x_{33}, x_{41}, x_{42}, x_{43},)\}$ with $x_{[13]} = x_{[31]} = x_{[41]}$ and $x_{[23]} = x_{[42]} = x_{[32]}$, $C' = \{(13,41), (13,31), (23,32), (23,42)\}$. Admissible assignments

to

	x_{11}	x_{12}	x_{13}	x_{21}	x_{22}	x_{23}	x_{31}	x_{32}	x_{33}	x_{41}	x_{42}	x_{43}
are	1	0	0	0	1	1	0	1	1	0	1	1 ,
	0	1	1	1	0	0	1	0	0	1	0	0 .

$K((R_1,R_2,,R_3,R_4,R_5), E(C)) = \varnothing$. There are 2^5 decompositions of N which concatenated according C yield N. $C = \varnothing$ is admitted.

Equality of values on $c \in C$ is not binding: if for example the R_q are production units in a manufacturing system, only part of the output of R_q may be consumed as input to another $R_{q'}$.

If Q is ordered e.g. $1 < 2 < ...5$, then in the mathematical / physical model, Q can be considered a mathematical / physical "time" with time points $1,2,...5$, $(R_q)_{q \in Q}$ is a sequential "process". The "setof" operation maps $((R_q)_{q \in Q}, C)$ homomorphically onto a graph / network with cycles / feedback (see Fig.2), which has to be interpreted mathematical time parameterized / physical time parameterized with properly controlled switches (and eventual memories) in the connections.

$(K_1 =_{def} K((R_1,R_2,)), K_2 =_{def} K((R_1,R_2,,R_3,R_4)), K_3 =_{def} K((R_1,R_2,,R_3,R_4,R_5)))$ defines a parallel process in time $(1,2,3)$.

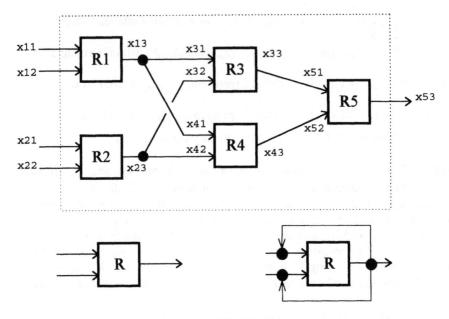

Fig. 2

Let be given a non-empty relation $R = ((r_{ji})_{ji \in I_j})_{j \in J}$, $Q \subset I$ with $1 < \text{card } Q < \infty$, and $\bigwedge j \in J(\text{card } Q \leq \text{card } I_{[j]} \wedge \text{ind}_j : Q \to \text{pow } I_{[j]} \backslash \emptyset \wedge \bigwedge q, q' \in Q(I_{[q]j} =_{\text{def}} \text{ind}_j(q) \wedge q \neq q' \Rightarrow I_{[qj]} \cap I_{[q'j]} = \emptyset) \wedge \bigcup_{q \in Q} I_{[q]j} = I_j)$. Define $\bigwedge q \in Q(R_q =_{\text{def}} ((r_{[q]ji})_{ji \in I_{[q]j}})_{j \in J}$, $C =_{\text{def}} \{I_j \mid j \in J\}$, $E(C) =_{\text{def}} R$. Then $\mathbf{K}((R_q)_{q \in Q}, E(C)) = R$.

3 Structures

3.1 Structures on index sets

The structors considered can be applied to sets / families of indices, as already done in the preceding. A structured index set induces its structure on the objects indexed. Important cases are:

1) hierarchical indexing of a family : $(m_i)_{i \in I} = \{(i, m_{[i]}) \mid i \in I\}$ indexed by $j \in I$ yields $(m_{ji})_{i \in I} = \{(j, (i, m_{[i]})_{[j]}) \mid i \in I\} = \{j\} \times \{(i, m_{[i]}) \mid i \in I\}$, by notational convention also written as $(m_{ji})_{ji \in I_j} = \{((j,i), m_{[ji]}) \mid (j,i) \in I_j\}$,

2) strictly or partially ordered index sets,

3) topological structures on index sets, treated in the next section,

4) structure preserving transforms (homomorphisms, isomorphisms) on sets of index sets :

Let I, K be non-empty index sets and ind: $K \to$ pow $I \setminus \varnothing$. For non-empty $W \subseteq K \times K$, we assume the existence of a family $(\tau (u,v) : I_u \leftrightarrow I_v)_{(u,v) \in W}$ of bijective mappings. Given a family $F = (o_{ui})_{ui \in I_u}$ of objects $o_{[ui]}$ of any complexity, and $\bigwedge ui \in I_u$ ($F \leftrightarrow F' = (o_{vj})_{vj \in I_v} \wedge vj = \tau (u,v)(ui) \wedge o'_{[vj]} = o_{[ui]}$), then F is transformed to F' by $\tau (u,v)$, F and F' are equivalent with respect to $\tau (u,v)$, are of the same "identity".
Note, in general $W \neq K \times K$, W is not symmetric, the $\tau's$ do not form a semi-group.

Expl. 5: $(I, \leq)$ the address space of a computer, $F = (o_{ui})_{ui \in I_u}$ a program located on $I_{[u]}$, $o_{[ui]}$ an instruction of F, $\tau (u,v)$ the order preserving relocation of F to $I_{[v]}$. F' and F are "identical".

Expl. 6: $I \subset \mathbf{R} \times \mathbf{R}$ ($\mathbf{R}$ the reals), $F = (o_{ui})_{ui \in I_u}$ a geometrical figure placed on I_u, $o_{[ui]}$ points of 2- dimensional euklidean space, $\tau (u,v)$ a euklidean motion (shift / rotation / symmetry operation) on F to give F' (see "Erlanger Programm" of F.Klein).

Expl. 7: $(I, <)$ a physical time, $F = (o_{ui})_{ui \in I_u}$ a physical process on $I_{[u]}$, $o_{[ui]}$ process states, $\tau (u,v)$ a time shift to later $I_{[v]}$. F' is the "same" process as F at later time.

3.2 Topological structures

Topology is the theory of neighborhoods of objects. The basic concept to define neighborhoods is a "filter base", or dual, an "ideal base" (see e.g. [5,7,12]).
Formulated for sets of sets, the definition of a filter base is: Given a set $I, I \neq \varnothing$, and an index set K. A set $F = \{F_{[k]} \mid k \in K \wedge F_{[k]} \subseteq I \wedge F_{[k]} \neq \varnothing \wedge \bigwedge k,k' \in K(F_{[k]} \in F$

$\wedge F_{[k']} \in F \Rightarrow \bigvee F_{[k'']} \in F (F_{[k'']} \square F_{[k]} \wedge F_{[k'']} \square F_{[k']})\}$ is a filter base for $\square = \subseteq$, and dual, an ideal base for $\square = \supseteq$. In the discrete case, $\lim F =_{def} \bigcap_{k \in K} F_{[k]}$ and $\bigcup_{k \in K} F_{[k]}$

respectively.
Considering instead of (pow I, $\subseteq$) a general complete lattice, $\square$ has to be replaced by $\sqcap, \sqcup$ (meet, join) for the definition of a filter / ideal base, respectively.

Let $S = (s_i)_{i \in I}$ be a family of (structured) objects s_i, consider (pow I, $\subseteq$), and a filter base $F = \{F_{[k]} \mid k \in K \subset I \wedge F_{[k]} \subset I\}$ on pow I with limit $F \subset I$ ($F \neq \varnothing$), and let be $s = (s_i)_{i \in F}$.
Then $N(s) = ((s_i)_{i \in F_{[k]}})_{k \in K}$ defines a neighborhood structure to s in the sense that an object s_i, $i \in F_{[k]}$, is in neighborhood $F_{[k]}$ (or for short k) to any element of s, and that s_j, $j \in F_{[n]}$, with $F_{[n]} \subset F_{[k]}$ is "closer" to the elements of s than s_i.
If $N(s') = ((s_i')_{i \in F_{[k]}})_{k \in K'}$ with filter base $F' = \{F_{[k]}' \mid k \in K' \wedge F_{[k]}' \subseteq I\}$ and limit F', and with $s' = (s_i')_{i \in F'}$, then s' may be in neighborhood $F_{[k]}$ to s, and s in

neighborhood $F'_{[n]}$ to s' without any further relationship between the $F_{[k]}$ and $F'_{[n]}$.

In this general form topological structures are applied for example in data bases or in "lattices of concepts" [13].

Expl. 8: $<$ given by 'is part of', denoted by $\longrightarrow$

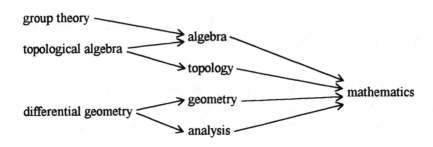

If a neighborhood system is defined for each element i of I and with further assumptions on these neighborhoods according the theory of topological spaces, we can arrive at "uniform" and in particular "metric" topological structures, employing "generalized" or conventional distance functions obeying the usual distance axioms , (see e.g. [7,12]).

Expl. 9: $S = (s_i)_{i \in N}$, $s_i \in B \times B \times B$, $B = \{0,1\}$.
A generalized uniform distance on S is defined by $d(s_i, s_k) = s_i$ "+" s_k , "+" component wise addition mod 2, a metric distance is given by $h(s_i, s_k) =$ $\sum_{n=1}^{3} pr(\{n\}) d(s_i, s_k)$ with ordinary addition of integers ("Hamming distance").

3.3 Valuated structures

Let $(B, \sqcup, \sqcap, O, 1)$ be a discrete complete lattice with join $\sqcup$, meet $\sqcap$, least element O , greatest element 1, and order relation $\sqsubseteq$ defined by $\sqcup$ or by $\sqcap$.
For $\varnothing \neq M \subset \boldsymbol{M}$, $\varnothing \neq I \subset \boldsymbol{I}$ an indexing ind: $I \to B \times M$ defines a family $(b_i, m_i)_{i \in I}$.
We say $\bigwedge i \in I ((m_i$ is "valuated" by $b_i) \wedge (\beta_i: m_i \to b_i$ defines a "B -valuation" of $m_i))$.
The definition can be extended to relations: $((b_{ji}, m_{ji})_{ji \in I_j})_{j \in I}$.

We define
$\bigwedge a, b \in B$ $(\Im(b) =_{def} \bigcup_{c \leq b} \{i \mid i \in I \wedge pr(1) \, ind(i) = c\})$ and $\Im(B) =_{def} \{\Im(b) \mid b \in B\}$.
Then $\Im(B) \subseteq (pow \, I, \cup, \cap, \varnothing, I)$, and $\bigwedge c, b, a \in B$ $(c \leq b \Rightarrow \Im(c) \subseteq \Im(b) \wedge \Im(c \sqcap b) \subseteq \Im(b) \cap \Im(c))$. Thus a filter base on B induces a filter base on $\Im(B)$ and this filter base induces a filter base on $(m_i)_{i \in I}$. For illustration see Fig.3.

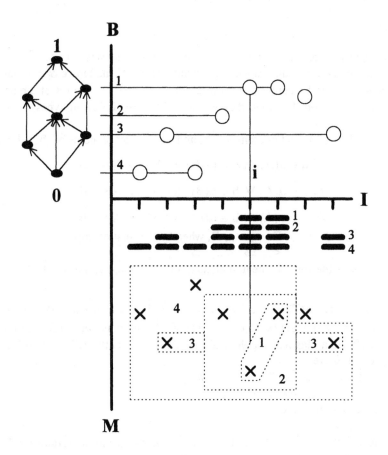

Fig. 3

$(b_i, m_i)_{i \in I}$ may be considered as object and valuated itself in dependence of its elements by any valuation β^*: $(b_i, m_i)_{i \in I} \rightarrow \beta^*((b_i, m_i)_{i \in I}) \in B$ to give $(\beta^*((b_i, m_i)_{i \in I}),$ $(b_i, m_i)_{i \in I})$. In particular, β^* need not depend on $(m_i)_{i \in I}$: $\beta^*((b_i, m_i)_{i \in I}) = \beta((b_i)_{i \in I})$.

Expl. 10: $B = \{O,1\}$, $I = \{0,1\}$, $((O, m_1) \sqcup (1, m_2)) = (1) ((O, m_1), (1, m_2))$.

Concatenation of relations with valuated elements:

For example consider $\mathbf{K}_{\varphi \beta}(\{(b_i, m_i)_{i \in I}\}, \{(b'_j, m'_j)_{j \in J}\}) = \{(b''_k, m''_k)_{k \in K}\}$ with
$K =_{def} I \cup J,$
$\bigwedge k \in I \setminus J((b''_k, m''_k) = (b_k, m_k)), \bigwedge k \in J \setminus I((b''_k, m''_k) = (b'_k, m'_k)),$
$\bigwedge k \in I \cap J((b''_k, m''_k) = (\beta_k(b_k, b'_k), \varphi_k(m_k, m'_k))).$
In particular, let $I = J = D$, $\bigwedge k \in D ((m''_{[k]} = m'_{[k]} = m_{[k]}) \wedge (\beta_k = \sqcup$ or $\beta_k = \sqcap))$.
This yields "union" or "intersection" of the "fuzzy sets" $(b_k, m_k)_{k \in D}$ and $(b'_k, m_k)_{k \in D}$, respectively. If B is boolean and $\bigwedge k \in D(b'_k = b_k)$, then the fuzzy sets are complementary, $\beta_k = \sqcup$ yields $(1, m_k)_{k \in D}$, $\beta_k = \sqcap$ yields $(O, m_k)_{k \in D}$.

3.4 Time

To model the time behaviour of systems we introduce "time sets" $(T, <, \sqcap, \sqcup)$ as complete atomic boolean lattices with two structures, first: the lattice operations join $\sqcup$ and meet $\sqcap$, and second: a strict ordering $<$ on $\alpha(T)$, the set of atoms, and partial orderings $<$ on T, induced by $<$ on $\alpha(T)$, of the following types:

For $A, B \in T$, $\alpha(A) = $ set of atoms of A, and $\alpha(B) = $ set of atoms of B, we define

$$\bigvee a \in \alpha(A) \bigwedge b \in \alpha(B) \, (a < b) \Leftrightarrow A <_{\vee\wedge} B$$

$$\bigwedge a \in \alpha(A) \bigvee b \in \alpha(B) \, (a < b) \Leftrightarrow A <_{\wedge\vee} B$$

$$\bigwedge a \in \alpha(A) \bigwedge b \in \alpha(B) \, (a < b) \Leftrightarrow A <_{\wedge\wedge} B$$

with $A <_{\vee\wedge\vee} B \Leftrightarrow A <_{\vee\wedge} B \wedge A <_{\wedge\vee} B$, whereby the relationship

$$<_{\wedge\wedge} \Rightarrow <_{\vee\wedge\vee} \Rightarrow <_{\vee\wedge} \wedge <_{\wedge\vee}$$

holds. $\mathbf{O}$ means the zero, $\mathbf{1}$ the unit element of T. Related to this is [4].

An "interval" I on $\alpha(T)$ is a subset $\varnothing \neq I \subseteq \alpha(T)$ such, that for $\bigwedge x, z \in I$ $(\bigwedge y \in \alpha(T) \, ((x < y < z) \Rightarrow y \in I))$. Let be $\Im(\alpha(T)) = $ set of all intervals on $\alpha(T)$. For all $c \in T$ let be defined a classical topological closure $\overline{c} \in T$ with $\alpha(\overline{c}) \in \Im(\alpha(T))$. The closure properties are:
$c \sqsubseteq \overline{c}$, $d \sqsubseteq c \Rightarrow \overline{d} \sqsubseteq \overline{c}$, $\overline{c} = \overline{\overline{c}}$, whereby
$c \sqsubseteq b \Leftrightarrow c = (b \sqcap c) \Leftrightarrow b = (b \sqcup c)$.
$\overline{c}$ defines the "length" of c.

From a given $(T^{(0)}, <, \sqcap, \sqcup)$ and $\alpha^{(0)}(T^{(0)})$ we can obtain hierarchies $(T^{(n)}, <, \sqcap, \sqcup)$, $\alpha^{(n)}(T^{(n)})$ of "coarser" time sets by induction:
Given $T^{(n)}$ for $0 \leq n < N$. If $T^{(N-1)} \neq \{ \mathbf{O}, \mathbf{1} \text{ of } T^{(N-1)} \}$, select a non-empty set $(\alpha^{(N)}(T^{(N)}), <_{\wedge\wedge}) \subset T^{(N-1)} \setminus U, \varnothing \neq U \subset \alpha^{(N-1)}(T^{(N-1)})$, then $T^{(N)} = \{\sqcup W \mid W \subseteq \alpha^{(N)}(T^{(N)})\}$.
$\Im(\alpha^{(N)}(T^{(N)}))$ is the set of all intervals on $\alpha^{(N)}(T^{(N)})$. $<, \sqcap, \sqcup$ on higher level are restrictions of those on lower level.
For $u \in T^{(N)}$, the complement of u with respect to $T^{(N)}$ is given by
$compl(T^{(N)})(u) = \sqcup \; compl(\alpha^{(N)} (T^{(N)}))(\alpha^{(N)} (u))$, join of the set theoretical complement of $\alpha^{(N)}(u)$ with respect to $\alpha^{(N)}(T^{(N)})$.

3.5 Processes

We consider :
Z_0 a non-empty set of objects z, named "primitive states", $Z = pow \, Z_0$.
$(T, <, \sqcap, \sqcup)$ a time set, $u \in T$, $\alpha(u)$ set of atoms of u, indexing: $\alpha(u) \to Z$.
Then $P = (z_t)_{t \in \alpha(u)}$ is a "process" ("time function") of "length" $\overline{u}$ with "state" $z_{[t]}$ at time point t. For discrete $\alpha(u)$, $t', t'' \in \alpha(u)$ and $t'' = succ \, t'$, $(z_{t'}, z_{t''})$ is a (first order) "event" (transition) of P.

If $P = (P_l)_{l \in L}$ is a family of processes $P_l = (z_{lt})_{t \in \alpha(u(l))}$, $u(l) \in T$, then $u(l)$ is the "local" time of P_l, $u = \bigsqcup \{u(l) \mid l \in L\}$ is the "global" time of P.

If for P_1, P_m, $1 \neq m$, $v = \bigsqcap \{u_l, u_m\} \neq \mathbf{O}$, then P_l, P_m are "concurrent" during v.

P can be concatenated by the connector $\alpha(u)$ and the property $E(\alpha(u)) = (z_t = (\bigcup_{l \in L} \{pr(t)P_l\}_{l \in L})_{t \in \alpha(u)}$ to give $\mathbf{K}(P, E(\alpha(u))) = (z_t)_{t \in \alpha(u)}$.

Considering two processes

$P' = (z'_t)_{t \in \alpha(u)}$ on $(T', <', \bigsqcap', \bigsqcup')$, $P'' = (z''_t)_{t \in \alpha(v)}$ on $(T'', <'', \bigsqcap'', \bigsqcup'')$ there is in general no relationship between T' and T", i.e. the local times u and v are independent. However, if $C \subseteq \alpha(u) \times \alpha(v) \cup \alpha(v) \times \alpha(u)$ is an acyclic non-empty connector, and if we define a partial ordering $<$ on $\alpha(u) \cup \alpha(v)$ by $< \mid \alpha(u) = <'$, $< \mid \alpha(v) = <''$ (| means "restricted to"),

$\wedge c \in C((c = (t_i, t_j) \in \alpha(u) \times \alpha(v) \Rightarrow t_i < t_j) \wedge (c = (t_j, t_i) \in \alpha(v) \times \alpha(u) \Rightarrow t_j < t_i))$,

then a maximal $<$ - chain $\alpha(w)$ on $\alpha(u) \cup \alpha(w)$ can be used to define a global time w for P' and P" by $<$ - homomorphisms $H(u): \alpha(u) \rightarrow \alpha(w)$ and $H(v): \alpha(v) \Rightarrow \alpha(w)$ compatible with C. Concatenation of P', P" yields $P = (\{z'_{H(u)^{-1}(t)}\} \cup \{z''_{H(v)^{-1}(t)}\})_{t \in \alpha(w)}$.

Expl. 11: Process $P' = (x_i)_{i \in I}$, $I = \{1,2,3,4,5,6,7; <'\}$ is local time for P', process $P'' = (y_k)_{k \in K}$, $K = \{a,b,c,d,e,f,g; <''\}$ is local time for P". I and K connected by connector $C = \{(2, d), (e, 5)\}$. Homomorphisms $H(I) = \{(1,b), (2,c), (3,d), (4,e), (5,5), (6,6), (7,7)\}$ and $H(K) = \{(a,a), (b,b), (c,c), (d,d), (e,5), (f,6), (g,7)\}$ on maximal chain $w = (a,b,c,d,e,5,6,7)$ are compatibel with C, w taken as global time for P', P" yields $P = (\{y_a\}, \{x_1, y_b\}, \{x_2, y_c\}, \{x_3, y_d\}, \{x_4, y_e\}, \{x_5\}, \{x_6, y_f\}, \{x_7, y_g\})$. See Fig.4.

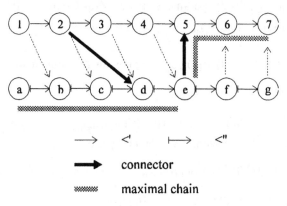

$$\longrightarrow \quad <' \quad \longmapsto \quad <''$$

$\blacktriangleright$ connector

$\text{\tiny{≋≋≋}}$ maximal chain

Fig. 4

Projections, coarsenings and refinements of processes:

Let be $u,v \in T$, T a time set, $P = (z_t)_{t \in \alpha(u)}$ a process. We define the "projection of P onto v" by $pr(v)P =_{def} (z_t)_{t \in \alpha(w)}$ with $w =_{def} v \bigsqcap u$.

Given two time sets T', T'', T'' coarser than T', with sets of atoms $\alpha'(T')$, $\alpha''(T'')$. Let be $v \in T''$, then v can be represented in T'' by $\alpha''(v)$, each element t'' of $\alpha''(v)$ has a representation $\alpha'(t'')$ in T'. Then $P'' =_{def} (z''_{t''})_{t'' \in \alpha''(v)}$ with $z''_{t''} =_{def} (z'_{t'})_{t' \in \alpha'(t'')}$ is a "coarsening" of P' and P' is a "refinement" of P''.

3.6 Variables

Let be given a non-empty relation $R = ((r_{ji})_{ji \in I_j})_{j \in J}$. We introduce a variable var $x \in V$, V the "universe of variables" under consideration, var x defined on the variability domain or "type" $D(\text{var } x) = \text{set of } R = R' = \{(r_{[ji]})_{i \in I_{[j]}} \mid j \in J\}$, together with the associated "assignment" or "control" function (or operator) val: $J \times \{\text{var } x\} \to D(\text{var } x)$ such that $\bigwedge j \in J(\text{val}(j, \text{var } x) = (r_{[ji]})_{i \in I_{[j]}})$, J being the set of assignment or control parameters for var x. Denotations are:

var $x : D$, var $x := (j)$ $(r_{[ji]})_{i \in I_{[j]}}$ for val$(j, \text{var } x)$, or in short $x := (r_{[ji]})_{i \in I_{[j]}}$.

Examples:

(1) A digital computer is a "processor variable" on a set of processors each performing one special operation, together with a "control processor". Given one particular control information ("instruction", "program" with "data") to the control processor, it assigns a particular processor to the variable, which then performs the specified computation.

(2) A mathematician substituting a "variable" in a "formula" by an admissible "constant", performs a val-function controlled by his mind.

(3) In λ-calculus, val corresponds to λ-abstraction.

Consider a family $(R_q)_{q \in Q}$ of parts R_q of R as described at the end of 2.3. Let be

var $x : R' = \{(r_{[ji]})_{i \in I_{[j]}} \mid j \in J\}$, parameter set J, $\bigwedge q \in Q(\text{var } x_q : R_q' = \{(r_{[ji]})_{i \in I_{[qj]}} \mid j \in J\})$, parameter set J, $(\text{var } x_q)_{q \in Q} : \prod_{q \in Q} R_q'$, parameter set J_Q .

An assignment var $x := (j)$ $(r_{[ji]})_{i \in I_{[j]}}$ implies an assignment to $(\text{var } x_q)_{q \in Q}$ by projection: $\bigwedge q \in Q$ $(\text{var } x_q := (j)$ $(r_{[ji]})_{i \in I_{[qj]}})$.

Assignments $\bigwedge q \in Q$ $(\text{var } x_q := (j(q))$ $(r'_{[qj(q)]ji})_{i \in I_{[qj(q)]}} \wedge j(q) \in J)$ imply an assignment to var x by concatenation if and only if property

$E((qj(q))_{q \in Q})$: $\bigvee j \in J(\bigwedge q \in Q ((r'_{[qj(q)]i})_{i \in I_{[qj(q)]}} = (r_{[ji]})_{i \in I_{[qj]}}))$ holds. Then

$K(((r'_{[qj(q)\, ii]})_{i \in I_{[qj(q)]}})_{q \in Q}, E((qj(q))_{q \in Q})) = (r_{[ji]})_{i \in I_{[j]}}$.

We express this property by saying $(\text{var } x_q)_{q \in Q} : \prod_{q \in Q} R_q'$ "restricted to" or "in" R',

and the equivalence for admissible assignments by var $x = (\text{var } x_q)_{q \in Q}$.

For partial assignments to $(\text{var } x_q)_{q \in Q}$ let $Q = S \cup T$ be a partition, $\bigwedge j \in J(I(S,j)$

$=_{def} \bigcup_{q \in S} I_{[qj]} \wedge I(T,j) =_{def} \bigcup_{q \in T} I_{[qj]}$) and $(var\ x_q)_{q \in S} : \prod_{q \in S} R_q'$ in $R'(S) =_{def} \{(r_{[ij]i})_{i \in I(S,j)}$

$| j \in J\}$.

If we assign $\wedge q \in S(var\ x_q := (j(q))\ (r'_{[qi(q)]i})_{i \in I_{[qi(q)]}}))$ with property $E((qj(q))_{q \in S})$:

$\vee j \in J\ (\wedge q \in S\ ((r'_{[qi(q)]\ ii})_{i \in I_{[qi(q)]}}) = (r_{[ji]})_{i \in I_{[qj]}}))$, then an equivalence $(qj(q))_{q \in S} \cong$

$(qj)_{q \in S}$ is defined. Let $J((qj(q))_{q \in S}) =_{def} \{j \mid j \in J \wedge (qj(q))_{q \in S} \cong (qj)_{q \in S} \}$. For admissible assignments complementary to $((r'_{[qi(q)]i})_{i \in I_{[qi(q)]}})_{q \in S}$ $(var\ x_q)_{q \in T} : \prod_{q \in T} R_q'$

is restricted to $R'(T, (qj(q))_{q \in S}) =_{def} \{(r_{[ji]})_{i \in I(Tj)} \mid j \in J((qj(q))_{q \in S}\}$.

If for all admissible assignments to $(var\ x_q)_{q \in S}$ card $R'(T, (qj(q))_{q \in S}) = 1$, then R' is functional from $R'(S)$ to $R'(T)$, defines a function, which we denote by $(var\ x_q)_{q \in T} = R'((var\ x_q)_{q \in S})$ with the meaning $K((var\ x_q)_{q \in T}, (var\ x_q)_{q \in S}) = (var\ x_q)_{q \in Q}$ on R'.

Notice: In general a function the way we have defined it has no fixed "n-arity", is multivalued and can be "polymorphic".

Use of variables makes it possible to express properties, shared by all elements of a relation, in a convenient way.

Expl. 12: **Z** the integers, $(var\ x, var\ y) : \mathbf{Z} \times \mathbf{Z}$ restricted to "less than" relation "<" $\subset \mathbf{Z} \times \mathbf{Z}$, represented by var x : **Z** , var y : **Z** , var x $<$ var y. Partial assignment var $x := 2$ results in var y : $\{a \mid a \in \mathbf{Z} \wedge 2 < a\}$, for var y := 3, $(2, 3) \in$ "<".

Consider the relation variable $((var\ R_q)_{q \in var\ Q}, var\ E\ (var\ C))$ with $\wedge q \in var\ Q(var\ R_q = ((var\ r_{qji})_{qji \in var I_{qj}})_{j \in var J_q}$, all variables defined on specified domains among which dependencies may exist.

Expl. 13:
var Q : pow **N** , **N** the natural numbers,
var R_q : functional boolean relations, the members of a relation parameterized by
var J_q : pow **N**,
set of argument indices var $I_{q[j]}'$: pow **N** , set of result indices var $I_{q[j]}''$: pow **N** ,
var $I_{q[j]}' \cap$ var $I_{q[j]}'' = \varnothing$, var $I_{q[j]}' \cup$ var $I_{q[j]}'' =$ var $I_{q[j]}$,
var C : pow ($\bigcup_{q \in var\ Q} var I'_{q[j]} \times \bigcup_{q \in var\ Q} var I''_{q[j]}$),

var $r_{[qji]}$: $\{0,1\}$
A possible assignment sequence to instantiate the composite relation of Expl. 4 is:
(1)   var Q := $\{1,2,...5\}$
(2)   var R_q := flip flop as in Expl. 4,
       follows card var $J_q = 2$, card var $I_q' = 2$, card var $I_q'' = 1$,
(3)   var $I_q' := \{q1, q2\}$, var $I_q'' = \{q3\}$, reduces
       var C : pow ($\bigcup_{q \in Q} \{(q1,q2)\} \times \bigcup_{q \in Q} \{(q3)\}$
(4)   var C := connector as in Expl. 4,
(5)   var E := equality on C,
(6)   var $r_{111} := 1$, var $r_{112} := 0$, var r $_{211} := 0$, var $r_{212} := 1$, follows var $r_{113} := 0$, etc.

Some other specification sequences are possible.

If the domains of the variables in a relation variable are reduced to subsets, the common properties inherit.

If the domains of the variables in a relation variable are disregarded, the relation variable is "abstract" with "abstract type". We may seek for any objects, which assigned to the respective variables make sense. Then they give a "model" or "interpretation" of the abstract relation.

Expl.14:
var M : non-empty sets,
var $\copyright$: var $M \times$ var $M \to$ var M, an abstract algebraic composition which defines an abstract property e_1 on var M,
var $\copyright$ (var m_1 , var m_2) = var $\copyright$ (var m_2 , var m_1), var m_i : var M, $i = 1,2,3$, defines abstract property e_2 of e_1 on var M,
var $\copyright$ (var m_1 , var $\copyright$ (var m_2 , var m_3)) = var $\copyright$ ((var $\copyright$ (var m_1 , var m_2), var m_3) defines abstract property e_3 of e_1 on var M,
(var M, $e_1 \wedge e_2 \wedge e_3$) specifies an abstract commutative semi-group.
A possible interpretation is var $M := \{$"true", "false"$\}$, var $\copyright := \wedge$.
Another choice for a structure could have been (var M, $e_1 \wedge (e_2 \vee e_3)$).

4 Remarks

The structures considered can be applied to model mathematical and physical systems on any hierarchical level. For example, we may have relations of relations, variables defined on sets of variables, variables on index sets. In case of physical systems, all objects have a physical time behaviour, are subject to causality and to physical constraints. For example, the physical realizations of data, functions, relations, control operators, assignments to variables, connecting relations among objects, are processes carried out by physical objects in physical time with non-zero duration.

This article contains modified parts of related publications of the author [1,2,3] which are application oriented. To give some references to related literature, a standard text book on system theory is [10], comprehensive representations are given in [8,13,15]. Out of the numerous publications on fuzzy sets I mention [9,11].

Acknowledgement: Thanks are due to Dr. H. Druckmüller and Prof. G. Németh for useful discussions.

References

1. Albrecht, R. F.: Some Basic Concepts of Object Oriented Databases. System Science 20, No. 1, Wroclaw, (1994)
2. Albrecht, R. F.: Modelling of Computer Architecures. Proc. Conf. on Massively Parallel Computing Systems, IEEE Computer Society Press, Los Alamitos, California (1994)

3. Albrecht, R. F.: Modelling of Discret Systems. Proceedings of the 1994 Human Interaction with Complex Systems Symposium, Greensboro (1994)
4. Allen, J. F.: Towards a General Theory of Actions and Time. Artificial Intelligence 23 (1984), 123-154
5. Birkhoff, G.: Lattice Theory. American Mathematical Society Colloquium Publications, Vol. XXV, Providence, Rhode Island (1973)
6. Bourbaki, N.: Théorie des Ensembles. In: Hermann & C^{de}. (eds.), Paris (1954)
7. Bourbaki, N.: Topologie Général. In: Hermann & C^{de}. (eds.), Paris (1951)
8. Fenton, N. E., Hill, G. A. F.: Systems Construction and Analysis: Mathematical and Logical Framework. London: McGraw-Hill 1993
9. Klir, G. J., Folger, T. A.: Fuzzy Sets, Uncertainty, and Information. State University of New York (1988)
10. Mesarovic, M. D., Takahara, Y.: Abstract Systems Theory: Berlin, Heidelberg: Springer 1989
11. Nauck, D., Klawonn, F., Kruse, R.: Neuronale Netze und Fuzzy-Systeme. Braunschweig: Vieweg 1994
12. Nöbeling, G.: Grundlagen der Analytischen Topologie. Berlin, Göttingen, Heidelberg: Springer 1954
13. Tremblay, J.-P., Manohar, R.: Discrete Mathematical Structures with Applications to Computer Science, McGraw-Hill 1975
14. Wille, R.: Bedeutungen von Begriffsverbänden. In: Ganter, B., Wille, R., Wolf, K. E. (eds.): Beiträge zur Begriffsanalyse. Mannheim, Wien, Zürich: B.I.-Wisschenschaftsverlag 1987, 161-211
15. Zeigler, B. P.: Multifacetted Modelling and Discrete Event Simulation. Academic Press Inc., London (1984)

Identification and Recognition through Shape in Complex Systems

Charles Rattray

Department of Computing Science, University of Stirling,
Stirling, Scotland FK9 4LA, UK
cr@cs.stir.ac.uk

Abstract. Categorical modelling is a useful tool in the study of systems. The basic idea of categorical shape theory is that, in any approximating situation, the approximations are what encode the only information that the system can analyse. Such approximations are very important in using time–varying complex systems to model system developments. Within this context, basic properties of categorical shape theory are introduced in order to better understand system approximation and construction.

A familiar process in mathematics and engineering is the creation of complex systems from given, more elementary, systems. The elementary systems can be considered as models of the process, and one usually says that the complex or *global* objects are formed from the elementary or *local* objects by "pasting together" models [2]. This provides a more *geometric* view of systems and allows us to consider the approximating shape [4] of such systems.

The basic idea of categorical shape theory is that, in any approximating situation, the approximations are what encode the only information that the system can analyse (Porter [11]). Such approximations are very important in using time–varying complex systems to model software developments. The strategy for constructing a new state is determined by the system approximation of the present state. That strategy is, in fact, a distortion of the true strategy applicable to the system state. This is interesting and it reflects what actually happens in practice in the development of complex systems. Having defined a time-varying complex system as a category, with the express purpose of modelling development processes, we can consider approximation in this category.

This leads to problems of *classification* (deciding whether two objects are the same) and *recognition* (deciding if it is possible to associate to a given object some definite model–object or archetype). Objects may be system components, system specifications, development processes, ...

In this paper, we extend our previous work on the application of categories of approximations and categorical shape theory in order to provide practical guidelines in dealing with the problems outlined above.

1 Objects and Categories

Approximation leads to problems of *classification* (deciding whether two objects are the same) and *recognition* (deciding if it is possible to associate to a given object some definite model–object or archetype). Objects may be system components, system specifications, development processes, ...

An *object*, in our sense, is considered to be a primitive concept (Ginali & Goguen [6]) and permits objects to represent almost anything. This freedom from the limiting effect of developing the approximation theory for a particular class of objects means that each application can be determined by a class of objects tailored to its needs, without the necessity of awkwardly identifying its objects with some standard class of given objects. Goguen points out that "this feature for general systems theory should not be underestimated".

Such a notion leads to another point. The only *structure* that an object has is by virtue of its interaction with other objects (Marti–Oliet & Meseguer [10], Porter [11]). That is, if a structured object is not interacting with others, if there are no relations between objects, then the structured object is no more than a black box and little can be said about it. The theme, then, is that "structure is only observable via comparison" (Porter [11]) and our objects of interest must come with suitable "comparison" mechanisms. Following this theme, we assume that our objects of interest and their comparisons form a category.

Definition 1. A *category* C is specified by a collection obC, disjoint sets $C(A, B)$ for $A, B \in obC$, and an associative operation $\circ$ of the members of $\bigcup_{A,B} C(A, B)$, such that

1. $f \circ g$ is defined for $g \in C(A, B)$, $f \in C(C, D)$ if and only if $B = C$;
2. for each $A \in obC$, there exists $1_A \in C(A, A)$ such that $1_A \circ f = f$ and $g \circ 1_A = g$, whenever the composition is defined.

Members of obC are called objects and members of $C(A, B)$ are called morphisms (or arrows) from A to B. We shall normally denote $f \in C(A, B)$ by $f : A \to B$ or $A \xrightarrow{f} B$; A is the source or domain of f and B is its target or codomain. Composition is usually denoted by

$$A \xrightarrow{g} B \xrightarrow{f} D.$$

A category $\mathbf{A}$ is a *subcategory* of category C if $ob\mathbf{A} \subset obC$, $\mathbf{A}(A, B) \subset C(A, B)$ for all objects A, B of $\mathbf{A}$, every $\mathbf{A}(A, A)$ contains $1_A \in C(A, A)$, the composition of $\mathbf{A}$ is the restriction of that of C to $\mathbf{A}$. If $\mathbf{A}(A, B) = C(A, B)$ for all objects A, B of $\mathbf{A}$ then $\mathbf{A}$ is said to be *full* in C. A morphism $f : A \to B$ in a category C is called

1. an isomorphism if there is a morphism $g : B \to A$ in C with $f \circ g = 1_B$, $g \circ f = 1_A$;
2. a retraction if there is a morphism $g : B \to A$ in C with $f \circ g = 1_B$.

Definition 2. A *functor* $F : \mathbf{A} \to \mathbf{B}$ for the categories $\mathbf{A}$ and $\mathbf{B}$ maps $ob\mathbf{A}$ into $ob\mathbf{B}$ and sets $\mathbf{A}(A, B)$ into $\mathbf{B}(FA, FB)$ such that it preserves

1. units, ie. $1_{FA} = F(1_A)$ for each object of $\mathbf{A}$;

2. composition, ie. $F(f \circ g) = Ff \circ Fg$ whenever $f \circ g$ is defined

Categories $\mathbf{A}$ and $\mathbf{B}$ are isomorphic if there exists functors $F : \mathbf{A} \to \mathbf{B}$, $G : \mathbf{B} \to \mathbf{A}$ with $F \circ G = 1_{\mathbf{B}}$ and $G \circ F = 1_{\mathbf{A}}$.

Definition 3. A *natural transformation* $\eta : F \to G$ between functors F, G : $\mathbf{A} \to \mathbf{B}$ is a collection of morphisms $\{\eta_A : FA \to GA\}$, indexed by objects $A \in ob\mathbf{A}$ such that, for every $f \in \mathbf{A}(A, A')$, the following diagram commutes:

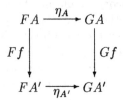

Definition 4. A subcategory $\mathbf{A}$ of category $\mathbf{C}$ is said to be *initial* if

1. for every object $C \in \mathbf{C}$ there exists a morphism $f \in \mathbf{C}(A, C)$ for some object $A \in \mathbf{A}$;
2. for every pair of morphisms $f_1 \in \mathbf{C}(A_1, C)$, $f_2 \in \mathbf{C}(A_2, C)$, there exists a finite sequence $\{g_i \in \mathbf{C}(A_i, C)\}_{i \leq 2n}$ with $g_0 = f_1$, $g_{2n} = f_2$, and a "zigzag" $\{m_j : 1 \leq j \leq 2n\}$ such that $g_{2i-1} \circ m_{2i-1} = g_{2i-2}$ and $m_{2i} \circ g_{2i-1} = g_{2i}$.

2 Shape Theory

Given the specification of a desired system component, several actual components which approximately satisfy the specification may exist. Some actual components will be better approximations than others. Of course, each actual component will satisfy some requirement exactly. If we measure how well this specification matches the given specification, then we will have some measure of how well the actual component satisfies the given system specification. Then again, it may be that every actual component specification is a poor match to the given system specification but that some combination of actual components form together a good match for the system specification. This type of situation in which information on system specifications is obtained by approximation has been studied, more abstractly, in category theory under the name of categorical shape theory [3, 5]. What follows has been influenced greatly by Cordier and Porter [4] and by Hušek [8].

In this context, the fundamental elements of categorical shape theory are:

1. a category $\mathbf{B}$ of objects of interest;
2. a category $\mathbf{A}$ of archetypes or model–objects;
3. a "comparison" of objects with archetypes, ie. a functor $K : \mathbf{A} \to \mathbf{B}$.

There is a level of uncertainty in labelling objects or assigning archetypes to objects. Taking the direction of the functor K from $\mathbf{A}$ to $\mathbf{B}$ makes the point that we may not be able to label all objects of interest, and this seems to reflect reality; by reversing K we need to add a "don't know" archetype to **A** in order to ensure every object of interest has a corresponding archetype. This seems less natural.

2.1 Categories of Approximations

To say that an archetype A "approximates" an object B means that there is some (specified) morphism $f \in \mathbf{B}(B, KA)$.

Definition 5. Given category **A** of archetypes, category **B** of objects of interest, and a comparison $K : \mathbf{A} \to \mathbf{B}$, an *approximation* to an object B in **B** is the pair (f, A), where A in **A** is an archetype and $f : B \to KA$.

An possible alternative is to proceed using a dual notion of approximation, namely $(f : KA \to B, A)$.

    A morphism between approximations $h : (f, A) \to (g, A')$ is a morphism $h : A \to A'$ of the underlying archetypes, such that $K(h) \circ f = g$, ie. the triangle

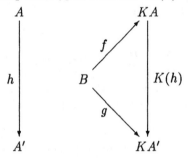

commutes. Approximations with their morphisms form a category $B {\downarrow} K$, the comma category [9] of K–objects under B.

    To describe the archetype A which most closely approximates B means that there exists an (f, KA), with $f : B \to KA$, such that for any other approximation (g, A'), with $g : B \to KA'$, and A' an archetype from **A**, there exists a morphism $K(h) : KA \to KA'$ in **A** such that $g = K(h) \circ f$, ie.

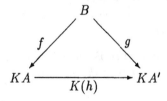

commutes.

    This concept is flawed in its present form for there may be reason enough to suppose that KA' is an equally good approximation to B. In such a case we have a morphism $K(h') : KA' \to KA$ such that $f = K(h') \circ g$; however, $K(h) \circ K(h)'$ and $K(h') \circ K(h)$ may not be identities and the two approximations may not be equivalent. Many optical illusions depend on these circumstances.

Associated with the category of approximations is a projection functor that picks out the archetype element of the approximation. This functor, the codomain functor, $pr_B : B{\downarrow}K \to \mathbf{A}$, assigns archetype A to approximation (f, A) and h to the approximation morphism $h : (f, A) \to (g, A')$ in $B{\downarrow}K$.

The cone–like form of the morphisms in $\mathbf{B}$ giving the approximations for some object B

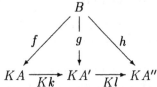

suggests that taking the limit of the diagram $pr_B : B{\downarrow}K \to \mathbf{A}$ would result in an archetype A^* "as near as possible" to B. That is, in considering the recognition problem for B, what we know about it is captured by the archetype A^* and A^* is the appropriate label to name B. Such limits are rare in practice for all objects of interest but we can identify some conditions that ensure the existence of the necessary limits which "are" the objects of interest. Earlier, the notion of "most closely approximates" led to an ambiguity in interpretation which may now be rectified.

Definition 6. Let $K : \mathbf{A} \to \mathbf{B}$ be a comparison functor. An archetype A of $\mathbf{A}$ is said to be K–*universal* for an object of interest B of $\mathbf{B}$ if there exists an approximation $(f : B \to KA, A)$ such that, for each approximation $(g : B \to KA', A')$, with $A' \in ob\mathbf{A}$, there exists a unique morphism $h : A \to A'$ in $\mathbf{A}$ with $g = K(h) \circ f$.

The "uniqueness" requirement implies that if there is an $h' : A' \to A$ satisfying $f = K(h') \circ g$, then $f = K(h'h) \circ f$ and $f = K(1_{A'}) \circ f$, and we have $h'h = 1_{A'}$. Similarly, $hh' = 1_A$. That is , there cannot be two non–isomorphic best approximations, the limit A^* of pr exists, and the recognition problem is solvable for objects of interest with best approximations. The recognition problem may be solvable up to a finite list of choices if $B{\downarrow}K$ has a finite subcategory of approximations, the initial subcategory, such that all approximations factor uniquely through one in the subcategory.

If every object of interest of $\mathbf{B}$ has a K–universal archetype in $\mathbf{A}$, then $\mathbf{A}$ is said to be K–universal in $\mathbf{B}$.

Theorem 7. *If $\mathbf{A}$ is K–universal in $\mathbf{B}$ then there exists a unique labelling functor $L : \mathbf{B} \to \mathbf{A}$ such that every LB is the K–universal object for B.*

2.2 Comparison of Objects

Recognising and understanding an object of interest B via a comparison $K : \mathbf{A} \to \mathbf{B}$ requires the identification of the corresponding archetype A which best represents B. The only "observations" on B are approximations (f, A) and, therefore, the only information available on B that can be used in labelling B by archetype A is the corresponding category of approximations $B{\downarrow}K$. To compare two objects of interest, say B and B', using only the information gained through the comparison functor $K : \mathbf{A} \to \mathbf{B}$, requires comparison of the corresponding categories of approximation, namely $B{\downarrow}K$ and $B'{\downarrow}K$ respectively.

If $h : B \to B'$ is a morphism in $\mathbf{B}$, any approximation $(g : B' \to KA, A)$ gives an approximation $(gh : B \to KA, A)$ by composition, ie

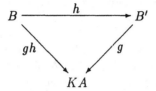

commutes. The morphism $h : B \to B'$ induces a functor

$$h^* : B'{\downarrow}K \to B{\downarrow}K$$

such that

$$h^*(g : B' \to KA, A) = (gh : B \to KA, A).$$

The functor h^* satisfies the condition that

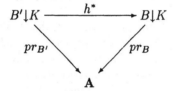

commutes and preserves the labelling for the approximations.

Definition 8. The *shape category* $\mathbf{Sh}(K)$ for comparison functor $K : \mathbf{A} \to \mathbf{B}$, $\mathbf{A}$ and $\mathbf{B}$ the categories of archetypes and objects of interest, respectively, has as objects the objects of $\mathbf{B}$, for morphisms $h : B \to B'$ the functors

$$h^* : B'{\downarrow}K \to B{\downarrow}K$$

satisfying $pr_B \circ h^* = pr_{B'}$.

Associated with the shape category $\mathbf{Sh}(K)$ is an obvious functor $S_K : \mathbf{B} \to \mathbf{Sh}(K)$ which is bijective on objects and maps h to h^*.

Definition 9. Two objects of interest, B and B', of the category $\mathbf{B}$ have the same K-*shape* if they are isomorphic in the shape category $\mathbf{Sh}(K)$.

Using the dual notion of approximation it is possible to consider two objects having the same K-*co-shape*.

Earlier, we equated "best" approximates with the concept of an archetype being K-universal for an object of interest. That is, such archetypes were the "labels" identifying the object of interest in terms of the information available through the comparison functor. That, in turn, suggests that if two objects of interest have equivalent labels, ie. have isomorphic K–universal archetypes, then the objects have the same K–shape since K is insufficiently refining to distinguish between them. Having the same K–shape is a generalisation of having isomorphic K–universal archetypes.

Theorem 10. *Let $K : \mathbf{A} \to \mathbf{B}$ be a comparison functor and objects of interest $B, B' \in \mathbf{B}$ have isomorphic K–universal archetypes in $\mathbf{A}$. Then B and B' have the same K–shape.*

The unique factorisation determined by the K–universality for the objects B and B', and the isomorphism $i : A \to A'$ in $\mathbf{A}$ preserved by the functor K in $\mathbf{B}$, determine an isomorphism between the categories of approximations $B{\downarrow}K$ and $B'{\downarrow}K$.

Theorem 11. *Let $K : \mathbf{A} \to \mathbf{B}$ be a comparison functor. An object of interest $B \in \mathbf{B}$ has a K–universal archetype $A \in \mathbf{A}$ if and only if $B{\downarrow}K$ has an initial subcategory consisting of a single morphism and a single object.*

2.3 Feature Comparison and Shape Invariance

The situations discussed so far are rather idealised. For example, the unique labelling functor (theorem 7) gives the archetype which best approximates an object as its label and ensures that two objects have the same shape if and only their labels are isomorphic. Such is rarely the case in reality. However, the fact that functors preserve certain properties of objects of interest and their archetypes, suggests that we may circumvent the difficulties of determining when two objects have the same shape by observing certain properties of the objects within a well–understood target category. Care must be taken in the choice of the target category since it may be so bereft of calculable discriminating features that objects of interest are not discernible, one from the other; alternatively, it may be that the important features being distinguished are as equally difficult to calculate in the target category as in the category of objects.

Since our knowledge of objects of interest is determined by the shape of the recognition system $K : \mathbf{A} \to \mathbf{B}$, the invariant properties are those that are preserved by functors from $\mathbf{Sh}(K)$ to some target category $\mathbf{C}$.

Definition 12. Given comparison functor $K : \mathbf{A} \to \mathbf{B}$, and shape functor $S : \mathbf{B} \to \mathbf{Sh}(K)$, a functor $F : \mathbf{B} \to \mathbf{C}$ is said to be *shape–invariant* if $F = \bar{F}S$ for some functor $\bar{F} : \mathbf{Sh}(K) \to \mathbf{C}$. Diagrammatically, that is

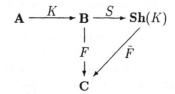

It may well be that archetypes are known through their "properties" or "features"; archetypes are comparable if their properties of features are comparable.

Suppose that a functor $F : \mathbf{A} \rightarrow \mathbf{C}$ is used to extract some property or collection of properties from archetypes. Now, we want to extend this to extraction of properties from objects of interest since we may only know archetypes and objects in terms of their properties or features. This requires that F be extended to a functor $\tilde{F} : \mathbf{B} \rightarrow \mathbf{C}$ in a shape–invariant way.

Recall that for $B \in \mathbf{B}$, the projection functor associated with the category of approximations $B{\downarrow}K$ is

$$pr_B : B{\downarrow}K \rightarrow \mathbf{A}.$$

Composition with $F : \mathbf{A} \rightarrow \mathbf{C}$ gives

$$F \circ pr_B : B{\downarrow}K \rightarrow \mathbf{C}.$$

Provided $\mathbf{C}$ has limits, calculate the limit of the diagram $F \circ pr_B$ and assign this limit to $\tilde{F}B$. This process defines a functor $\tilde{F}$ from $\mathbf{B}$ to $\mathbf{C}$ called the *right Kan extension of F along K* (MacLane [9]) which can be used to extract properties from objects of interest. The limits may or may not exist in real situations for all $B \in \mathbf{B}$. However, the existence of some limits may be useful in understanding the recognition system capabilities.

This approach is summed up in the following theorem [5].

Theorem 13. *For comparison functor $K : \mathbf{A} \rightarrow \mathbf{B}$ and shape functor $S : \mathbf{B} \rightarrow \mathbf{Sh}(K)$, let $F : \mathbf{A} \rightarrow \mathbf{C}$ be a functor and let $\tilde{F} : \mathbf{B} \rightarrow \mathbf{C}$ be the right Kan extension of F along K. Then $\tilde{F}$ is shape–invariant.*

This is proved by constructing an explicit functor $\bar{F} : \mathbf{Sh}(K) \rightarrow \mathbf{C}$ such that $\bar{F}S = \tilde{F}$. Diagrammatically, we have

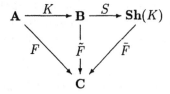

3 Shape in Complex Systems

For many existing complex systems, it is unlikely that any individual "knows the system"; at best, the individual has a view of the system and only understands certain aspects of it. Communicating individuals have their own systems views but can pass on aspects of their view to a colleague. "Composition" of individual views contribute to a better understanding of the system but such a composition is merely an approximation to, or distortion of, that system.

Each system component only has partial information about its environment, ie. it can only "know" about those other components to which it is linked. If every component, and every component to which it is linked, is known then obviously the whole system is known. But, in practice, the system is known solely through some particular components which interact with it.

The system is represented by the category $\mathbf{B}$, and a pattern of linked objects, called a Control Centre (CC), represented by a sub-category $\mathbf{C}$ of $\mathbf{B}$. The objects of $\mathbf{C}$ are what we call agents. In any representation, there will be a number of different kinds of control centres.

The information about any component B recognised by an agent C is represented by all the links b from B to C; each link b is a view that C has of B.

The fragment of the system $\mathbf{B}$ known to the agent C is the *slice* category $\mathbf{B} \downarrow C$, a special case of a comma category, defined to have as objects all C-views of system components, while an arrow in $\mathbf{B} \downarrow C$ from view $b : B \to C$ to view $c : B' \to C$ is a $\mathbf{B}$-arrow $f : B \to B'$ such that

$$B \xrightarrow{b} C = (B \xrightarrow{f} B' \xrightarrow{c} C).$$

Composition of arrows in $\mathbf{B} \downarrow C$ is determined by composition of arrows in $\mathbf{B}$, and the identity arrow of the object $c : B' \to C$ in $\mathbf{B} \downarrow C$ is just the identity $1_{B'}$. An interpretation of the identity arrow is that C knows itself!.

The projection functor from fragment $\mathbf{B} \downarrow C$ to $\mathbf{B}$ maps any view $c : B' \to C$ to its corresponding component B' and any link $f : b \to c$ to $f : B \to B'$ in $\mathbf{B}$. The projection functor is not an isomorphism except when C has only one view of each component, eg. if C is a terminal object in $\mathbf{B}$.

A link between agents in $\mathbf{C}$ induces a functor between corresponding system fragments; composition of links in $\mathbf{C}$ induces composition between corresponding functors between system fragments. This means that the information about the system fragment known to C can be communicated to an agent C' if C and C' are linked in $\mathbf{C}$. The collection of system fragments over the control centre CC is denoted by $\mathbf{B} \downarrow \mathbf{C}$.

A model or prototype for the control centre CC is a *colimit* of this collection: its objects are equivalences of views b linked by a zig–zag of communications between agents and its arrows are suitable equivalences of arrows in $\mathbf{B}$. The model is represented as a category $\mathbf{A}$ and supports a distortion functor to the system $\mathbf{B}$.

There are a number of ways to determine the shape of a complex system under this formulation of a system.

For example, take the dual category $\mathbf{B}^{op}$ of the system $\mathbf{B}$ as the category of objects of interest, model $\mathbf{A}$ as the category of archetypes, and the distortion functor as the comparison functor.

A more interesting idea has potential for the current interest in pattern–building systems. Within the object–oriented "world", a modification of the approach pioneered by Christopher Alexander [1], in architectural design, is the subject of considerable research in the design and implementation of software systems [7].

Let P be a pattern $(P_i)_{i \in \mathbf{I}}$ (ie. a diagram $P : \mathbf{I} \to \mathbf{B}$) in the system $\mathbf{B}$. To this pattern associate a subcategory $\mathbf{T}P$ of the comma category $P{\downarrow}K$, where $K : \mathbf{C} \to \mathbf{B}$, having for its objects the different views of P_i observables in the model $\mathbf{A}$ determined by $\mathbf{C}$. The pattern in $\mathbf{A}$ determined by the model–objects of $\mathbf{T}P$ is called the *trace* of P for $\mathbf{C}$.

One says that two patterns P and P' have the same $\mathbf{C}$–form ("shape" in our terminology) if $\mathbf{T}P$ and $\mathbf{T}P'$ are isomorphic. Whence we get a classification relative to $\mathbf{C}$ of the observable patterns in its model. A number of consequences flow from this connection, including the prospect of building systems around the notion of using patterns in the Alexander and Gomma approaches.

If we assume that models evolve into systems that meet user requirements, then the above describes the state of the system at some time t. The transition to a new (improved) state at time t', by application of suitable strategies and pattern–building, will result in an evolution of the system fragments and system models. System approximation through shape theory will now involve the category of models as archetypes and the category of states (ie. category of categories) as the objects of interest.

4 Conclusions

In this paper, the notion of categorical shape theory has been investigated. The theory in likely to be useful in determining frameworks within which to discuss image processing, software re–usability, and systems construction. An initial suggestion for the application of shape theory and the notion of system approximation are considered briefly.

References

1. C Alexander, S Ishikawa, M Silverstein: *A Pattern Language*, Oxford University Press, 1977.
2. H Appelgate, M Tierney: "Categories with Models", Lecture Notes in Mathematics, **80**, Springer–Verlag, 1969.
3. K Borsuk: *Theory of Shape*, Monografie Matematyczne, **59**, PWN Warsaw, 1975.
4. J-M Cordier, T Porter: *Shape Theory: categorical approximation methods*, Ellis Horwood Ltd., 1990.
5. A Deleanu, P Hilton: "On the Categorical Shape of a Functor", Fundamenta Mathematicae, **XCVII**, 3, 1977.
6. S Ginali, J Goguen: "A Categorical Approach to General Systems", in *Applied General Systems Research: recent developments and trends* (ed. GJ Klir), Plenum Press, 1978.
7. E Gomma, R Helm, R Johnson, J Vlissides: *Design Patterns: Elements of Reusable Object–Oriented Software*, Addison–Wesley Publ. Co., 1995.

8. M Hušek: "Introduction to Categorical Shape Theory, with Applications in Mathematical Morphology", in *Shape in Picture* (ed. O Ying–Lei, A Toet, D Foster, HJAM Heijmans, P Meer), Springer–Verlag, 1993.

9. S MacLane: *Categories for the Working Mathematician*, Springer-Verlag, 1971.

10. N Martí–Oliet, J Meseguer: "From Petri Nets to Linear Logic", Math. Struct. in Comp. Science, 1, 1991.

11. T Porter: "Can Categorical Shape Theory Handle Grey Level Images?", *Shape in Picture* (ed. O Ying–Lei, A Toet, D Foster, HJAM Heijmans, P Meer), Springer–Verlag, 1993.

12. C Rattray, D Price: "Sketching an Evolutionary Hierarchical Framework for Knowledge–Based Systems Design", EUROCAST'89, LNCS, **410**, Springer–Verlag, 1990.

13. C Rattray, M Marsden: "Object Identification and Retrieval in a CAST Library", EUROCAST'91, LNCS, **585**, Springer–Verlag, 1992.

14. C Rattray: "The Shape of Complex Systems", EUROCAST'93, LNCS, **763**, Springer–Verlag, 1994.

A Logical Approach to System Construction

Gillian Hill

Department of Computer Science, City University
and Department of Computing, Imperial College
of Science, Technology and Medicine,
London, Great Britain

Abstract. By taking a logical approach to the practical task of constructing complex engineering systems from their component parts, we achieve a precise semantics for our building operations. If the underlying logic has the Craig interpolation property we are also able to preserve the structure and properties of the system components that we build with. System construction, defined as systems configuration, is carried out by applying combinators to recursively defined system components, and the history of construction is recorded within the textual specification for that system. System configuration also provides for the reusability of system components by a new and simple definition of a module as an instance of a specification.

1 Introduction

A logical approach to systems theory, rigorously presenting the basic concepts of mathematical systems theory, is given by Takahashi and Takahara, [6]. Our own logical approach contrasts with this model-theoretic approach by focusing on a proof-theoretic view of the logic underlying systems theory and avoids the complexity of building a logical model during system configuration. We agree with Turski and Maibaum, [7], that the activity of specification in software engineering is one of theory-building. In this paper our logical view of systems theory underpins system configuration as a description of how system components, represented by theories, can be both structured and implemented to represent the architecture of a final executable system. The language for configuration, designed in [5], is at a meta-level to a specification language and describes the operations of the combinators on the logical objects that represent the parts of a system. The possible relationships between the component parts of systems have been identified at an intuitive level in [3] where extension, parameterisation and implementation are chosen as the appropriate high-level combinators for configuration. A categorical framework for configuration over first-order logic was initially described in [2]; a more powerful framework, based on a KZ-doctrine has been presented in [4].

The aim of the paper is to present the underlying logical framework for system configuration. In Section 2 we provide some simple examples for motivation before we present the logical concepts for configuration and define the extension and interpretation of many-sorted first-order theories in Section 3. The language component of each theory is defined by a many-sorted similarity type, as in [1]; the properties of the theory are given by a set of non-logical axioms expressed as formulae in the language of the theory. System components are then specified by first-order theories in Section 4 where we describe the configuration of our very simple example system. Our logical approach to configuration means that systems are built safely because parameterisation and implementation are defined only by conservative extensions. Because the Craig interpolation property holds in first-order logic, the structure of objects that are conservatively extended is preserved under subsequent interpretation. We draw conclusions in Section 5.

2 Motivating Examples

First we motivate our logical approach to the construction of systems from their component parts with the configuration of a simple system that we shall express in our configuration language. Using the informal diagrammatic notation developed in [3] we construct system components that express both the sharing and non-sharing of a queue between two users. By creating module instances from the specifications of these components we provide reusability for further configuration.

Example 1. The relationship of parameterization between components is part of the basic structure of a system. For example, a queue stores data, in a particular way, for another object. The queue that is used is also available for other objects to use. The object parameter formally represents a hole in the parameterized object's definition; in genericity this is filled by a suitable 'actual' object.

This informal diagram expresses the use of a queue, as the specification of a primitive system object, by configuring the specification form of the object structured as 'use-queue[queue]'.

Our simple module concept allows the sharing or non-sharing of a queue to be illustrated explicitly by use-hierarchies. Modules are represented within a box diagram and the interfaces that must be checked in the parameterization are identified in the diagrams as strips between the boxes.

Example 2. The configuration of two users that share a queue between them is given by the use-hierarchy

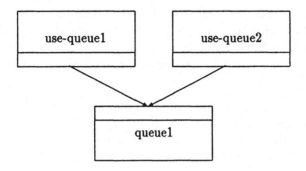

Parameterization by use relates a 'master' object to a 'slave' object. The matching of interfaces is then solely concerned with the minimal amount of information that is related to this use.

Example 3. The creation of an additional module from the specification of a queue is needed for the configuration of two users that use their own queues.

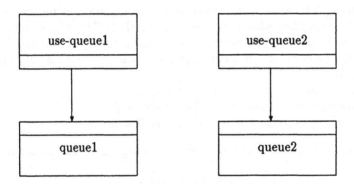

3 Logical Concepts for Configuration

We now present our own proof-theoretic approach to the logic underlying systems theory. In this paper we choose many-sorted first-order logic as the underlying logic for system configuration. We give some preliminary definitions of the language for this logic, before we define the extension and interpretation of many-sorted theories within a first-order linguistic system.

3.1 A First-Order Language

Definition 1. The *logical and non-logical symbols* of a language together define a family of first-order logical languages. The logical symbols are fixed in their meaning and use and are:

- *connectives* ¬, ∨, ∧, →, ↔, ∃ and ∀
- *punctuation* symbols (,) , and ,

The meaning of the non-logical symbols can be used to define, in a theory, the properties of a particular system object. For example, the following non-logical symbols will define a family of first-order languages, according to the choice of actual symbols, and would form the basis for classifying languages according to their *type*:

- n-place *predicate* symbols (relation symbols) $p, q, r, \ldots$ for each n
- *individual constant* symbols $c, d, e, \ldots$
- n-place *function* symbols $f, g, h, \ldots$ for each n
- *variable* symbols $x, y, z, x_1, y_1, z_1, \ldots$

The individual constant symbols are fixed symbols which are used to represent the objects in the system. The variable symbols will range over terms which are the expressions built up from the constant, variable and function symbols. The terms state the basic properties of objects and appear as arguments to the n-place predicate symbols of the language. The atomic formulae are similar to the propositions in propositional logic; they represent relations between objects and are built from the predicates with terms as arguments.

Definition 2. The *arity of relation and function symbols* is the value of n for which they are n-place relation and function symbols. The arity of relation symbols is given by the function denoted by ar_r and the arity of function symbols is given by the function ar_f. If a language L contains the non-logical symbols r, c and f where

r is an m-place relation symbol then $ar_r(r) = m$
c is an constant symbol $\qquad$ then $ar_f(c) = 0$
f is an n-ary function symbol $\quad$ then $ar_f(f) = n$

Definition 3. The *type* σ of a first-order language is defined as a pair of arity functions

$$\sigma = (ar_r, \ ar_f)$$

The concept of type defines a class of models on which the fixed relation and function symbols of the language syntax will be interpreted. Languages of 'similar' type are said to be of the same *similarity type*.

Definition 4. The *family of first-order languages* is classified according to the similarity type of the language and the set of well-formed formulae that can be constructed from the connectives of first-order logic. It is denoted by the pair L = (*Simtype, Form*) where

Simtype is the set of *similarity types*
Form is the set of *well-formed formulae* for all those similarity types.

Definition 5. A particular *first-order language* is a pair $L_\sigma = (\sigma, \ Form_\sigma)$ where $\sigma \in Simtype$ and $Form_\sigma$ is the set of *well-formed formulae* for σ. It is referred to as a σ-type language and is denoted by L_σ.

Definition 6. Let L be a family of first-order languages. A *first-order linguistic system* over L is the pair

$$LS = (L, \vdash)$$

where $\vdash$ is the *consequence relation* over the set *Form* for L such that for each $\sigma \in$ *Simtype* and *Form$_\sigma$* we have the binary relation $\vdash_\sigma \subseteq \mathcal{P}(Form_\sigma) \times Form_\sigma$. Here $\mathcal{P}(Form_\sigma)$ is the set of all subsets of *Form$_\sigma$*. Each consequence relation $\vdash_\sigma$ satisfies the usual properties of cut, weakening and inclusion.

Definition 7. A *first-order theory presentation* over a similarity type σ and in a linguistic system LS is the pair $T = (\sigma, \Gamma)$ where $\Gamma \subseteq Form_\sigma$ is a set of formulae called the non-logical axioms. The *theory* generated by T is the pair (σ, Γ°), where Γ° is the closure of the non-logical axioms under the consequence relation and is defined by $\{\varphi \in Form_\sigma \mid \Gamma \vdash_\sigma \varphi\}$.

3.2 A Many-Sorted First-Order Language

A logical approach to the construction of complex systems requires a many-sorted language. We therefore extend our definition of a similarity type to be many-sorted, before defining the terms and formulae of the language.

Definition 8. A *many-sorted similarity type* is the triple (S, ar_r, ar_f) where S is a non-empty set of *sorts* and ar_r and ar_f are *arity functions*. The elements in the domains of ar_r and ar_f are the *relation symbols* and the *function symbols* respectively. If the similarity type is called σ then we denote the domains by *rel* σ and *func* σ. The arity functions assign the sorts of the arguments to each symbol in *rel* $\sigma \cup$ *func* σ and, in addition, for symbols in *func* σ the result sort. If σ is a many-sorted similarity type,

$$
\begin{aligned}
sort\ \sigma &\rightleftharpoons S \\
rel\ \sigma &\rightleftharpoons dom\ ar_r \\
func\ \sigma &\rightleftharpoons dom\ ar_f \\
A^+ &\rightleftharpoons \textit{the set of all non-empty finite sequences of elements of } A \\
\langle s_1, s_2, \ldots, s_n \rangle &\rightleftharpoons \textit{sequence of elements of } A \textit{ of length } n \\
\lambda &\rightleftharpoons \textit{the empty sequence of length } 0 \\
A^* &\rightleftharpoons A^+ \cup \{\lambda\}
\end{aligned}
$$

where $\rightleftharpoons$ means 'is equal by definition'.

Definition 9. Let σ be a similarity type and let $t = \langle s_1, \ldots, s_n \rangle$ be a sequence, where $1 \leq n < \omega_0$ and $s_i \in S$ for $i = 1, \ldots, n$. Then $t \in S^+$ is a finite sequence of sort symbols of the similarity type σ. All the relations on the specific sequence, t, are described as being of the same *arity*. Similarly, any function symbols whose domains are the sequence t and whose ranges are a unique sort $s \in S$, are of the same arity. The *arity functions* for σ are defined so that

$$
\begin{aligned}
rng\ ar_r && &\subseteq S^* \\
rng\ ar_f && &\subseteq (S^* \setminus \{\lambda\}) = S^+ \text{ where } \setminus \text{ denotes set difference} \\
dom\ ar_r \cap dom\ ar_f && &= \emptyset \\
\text{If } r \in rel\ \sigma \text{ then } ar_r(r) && &= \langle s_1, \dots, s_n \rangle = t \text{ denoted by } r^t \\
\text{If } f \in func\ \sigma \text{ then } ar_f(f) && &= \langle s_1, \dots, s_n; s_{n+1} \rangle = t; s_{n+1} \text{ denoted by } f^{t; s_{n+1}}
\end{aligned}
$$

where $s_i \in sort\ \sigma$, $i = 1, \dots, n+1$, and $n + 1 < \omega_0$.

We use the notation ; to separate the ordered n-tuple of sorts in the domain of a function from the sort in its range. A function symbol c with $ar_f(c) = \langle s \rangle$ is called an s-sorted constant symbol.

Definition 10. Let L_σ be a language of many-sorted similarity type σ. The set of *variable symbols* for L_σ is $V = \bigcup \{V_s \mid s \in S\}$, where V_s is a denumerable set of *s-sorted variables* for each $s \in S$ and is disjoint from all other sets introduced up to now. The set V is the set of S-sorted variables.

Definition 11. The *sort* of a variable is defined by the function *sort*: $V \rightarrow S$ that assigns to each variable in V a unique sort $s \in S$ so that for $x \in V_s$, $sort(x) = s$. Subsets of the set of variables which are of identical sorts but differ in their names can be constructed by copying one subset in another.

Definition 12. Let L_σ be a many-sorted language of similarity type σ. Also let V be a set of S-sorted variables. For any $s \in S$, the set of s-sorted σ-type *terms*, denoted by $Term_s(\sigma, V)$, is the smallest set for which

1. $V_s \subset Term_s(\sigma, V)$
2. If $f \in func\ \sigma$ is such that $ar_f(f) = \langle s_1, \dots, s_n; s_{n+1} \rangle$ and $\tau_1, \dots, \tau_n$ are respectively of the sort $s_1, \dots, s_n$ so that $\tau_i \in Term_{s_i}(\sigma, V)$ then

$$
f(\tau_1, \dots, \tau_n) \in Term_{s_{n+1}}(\sigma, V)
$$

The set of σ-type terms is the set,

$$
Term(\sigma, V) = \bigcup \{ Term_s(\sigma, V) \mid s \in sort\ \sigma \}
$$

We write $\tau(x_1, \dots, x_n)$ to denote an n-ary term τ whose variables form a subset of $\{x_1, \dots, x_n\}$.

Definition 13. The *sort* of a term is defined by the function

$$
sort : Term(\sigma, V) \rightarrow sort\ \sigma
$$

that assigns to each term, $\tau \in Term_s(\sigma, V)$ its sort s. That is, $sort(\tau) = s$ iff $\tau \in Term_s(\sigma, V)$. For simplicity we use the notation *sort* for assigning both variables and terms to their sorts in a fixed similarity type σ.

For a many-sorted similarity type we assume the existence of a non-logical binary relation symbol for equality, $=_s$, for each $s \in S$. The usual equality axioms are assumed to be satisfied for $=_s$.

Definition 14. Let L_σ be a many-sorted language of similarity type σ. Also let V be a set of s-sorted variables. The set of σ-type *atomic formulae* is denoted by $Atom(\sigma, V)$ and defined by

$$Atom(\sigma, V) = \{r(\tau_1, \ldots, \tau_n) \mid r \in rel\ \sigma, \tau_1, \ldots, \tau_n \in Term(\sigma, V)$$
$$\text{and } ar(r) = \langle sort(\tau_1), \ldots, sort(\tau_n) \rangle\}$$
$$\cup \{\tau_1 = \tau_2 \mid sort(\tau_1) =_s sort(\tau_2)\}$$

Definition 15. Let L_σ be a many-sorted language of similarity type σ. The set of σ-type *well-formed formulae*, denoted by $Form(\sigma, V)$, is the smallest set such that

1. $Atom(\sigma, V) \subset Form(\sigma, V)$
2. If $\varphi, \psi \in Form(\sigma, V)$ and $x \in V$ then $\neg\varphi, \varphi \wedge \psi, \varphi \vee \psi, \varphi \rightarrow \psi, \varphi \leftrightarrow \psi, \forall x\ \varphi$ and $\exists x\ \varphi$ also belong to $Form(\sigma, V)$

The constants *true* and *false* can now be defined in terms of formulae in $Form(\sigma, V)$

$$true \rightleftharpoons (x = x)$$
$$false \rightleftharpoons \neg(x = x)$$

Definition 16. Let φ be a formula in $Form(\sigma, V)$. The set of *free variables* occurring in φ is denoted by $var(\varphi)$. If $var(\varphi) \subseteq X$ then the notation $\varphi(X)$ indicates that free variables of φ belong to the set X. If $var(\varphi) = \{x\}$ we write $\varphi(x)$.

3.3 Many-Sorted First-Order Theories

Definition 17. Let σ be a many-sorted similarity type and let $r \notin (rel\ \sigma \cup func\ \sigma)$. Then $\sigma \cup \{r\}$ denotes the new similarity type which *extends* σ *by the new symbol* r. If the arity of r is $\langle s'_1, s'_2, \ldots, s'_n \rangle$ then we define the extension of σ by

$$\sigma \cup \{r\} \rightleftharpoons (S \cup \{s'_1, s'_2, \ldots, s'_n\}, ar_r \cup \{r, \langle s'_1, s'_2, \ldots, s'_n \rangle\}, ar_f)$$

Here S is only extended if there is some $s_i \in \{s'_1, s'_2, \ldots, s'_n\}$ but $s_i \notin S$. We denote the *extension* of σ by $\sigma \cup \{r_1, r_2, \ldots, r_k\}$ where the new symbols are $r_1, r_2, \ldots, r_k$. If r is a function symbol we define the extension similarly by union with ar_f.

Definition 18. Let $\sigma_1 = (S_1, ar_r^1, ar_f^1)$ and $\sigma_2 = (S_2, ar_r^2, ar_f^2)$ be two many-sorted similarity types. Then σ_2 is an *extension* of σ_1 (or σ_1 is a *reduction* of σ_2), denoted by $\sigma_1 \subseteq \sigma_2$, iff

$$S_1 \subseteq S_2$$
$$ar_r^1 = ar_r^2 \upharpoonright (dom\ ar_r^1)$$
$$ar_f^1 = ar_f^2 \upharpoonright (dom\ ar_f^1)$$

Definition 19. Let $L_{\sigma_1} = (\sigma_1, Form(\sigma_1, V_1))$ and $L_{\sigma_2} = (\sigma_2, Form(\sigma_2, V_2))$ be many-sorted first-order languages. Then the *extension* of L_{σ_1} to L_{σ_2}, denoted by $L_{\sigma_1} \subseteq L_{\sigma_2}$, is characterised by $\sigma_1 \subseteq \sigma_2$ and $Form(\sigma_1, V_1) \subseteq Form(\sigma_2, V_2)$.

Definition 20. Let LS be a many-sorted linguistic system. Then a *many-sorted theory* in LS is the pair $T = (\sigma, \ \Gamma)$ where

1. $\sigma \in Simtype$ is a many-sorted similarity type
2. Γ is a set of formulae, such that $\Gamma \subseteq Form_\sigma$, called non-logical axioms
3. The formulae of T in $Form_\sigma$ are closed under $\vdash_\sigma$.

Our definition of a many-sorted theory gives a configured object in our configuration language and is based on that of a theory presentation in Definition 7. It allows sentences that are basic axioms to be distinguished from sentences that are derived theorems.

3.4   The Extension of a Theory

Definition 21. Let $\sigma_1 = (S_1, ar_r^1, ar_f^1)$ and $\sigma_2 = (S_2, ar_r^2, ar_f^2)$ be two many-sorted similarity types. Then σ_1 and σ_2 are *disjoint* similarity types, denoted by $\sigma_1 \cap \sigma_2 = \emptyset$, iff

$$S_1 \cap S_2 = \emptyset$$
$$(rel \ \sigma_1 \cup func \ \sigma_1) \cap (rel \ \sigma_2 \cup func \ \sigma_2) = \emptyset$$

Definition 22. Let $\sigma_1 = (S_1, ar_r^1, ar_f^1)$ and $\sigma_2 = (S_2, ar_r^2, ar_f^2)$ be two many-sorted similarity types. Let the many-sorted similarity type σ_3 be the extension of σ_1 denoted by $\sigma_1 \subseteq \sigma_3$. There are three possible ways in which the extension can be made:

1. If the extension σ_3 of σ_1 is made by σ_2 then σ_3 is the *sum* of σ_1 and σ_2, denoted by $\sigma_3 \rightleftharpoons \sigma_1 + \sigma_2$, such that $sort \ \sigma_3 \rightleftharpoons sort(\sigma_1 + \sigma_2)$. If $\sigma_1 \cap \sigma_2 = \emptyset$ then $+$ is defined by the *disjoint union* operation on sets.
2. If $\sigma_3 \rightleftharpoons \sigma_1 + \sigma_2, \sigma_1 \cap \sigma_2 \neq \emptyset$ and the symbols that are in both σ_1 and σ_2 belong to the minimal similarity type σ_0, then $+$ is defined by the *amalgamated sum* of two sets, and σ_3 is then defined by $\sigma_1 +_{\sigma_0} \sigma_2$. In this case σ_3 contains contains only one copy of those symbols in σ_0 that are in both σ_1 and σ_2.
3. If the symbols added to σ_1 do not form a similarity type, but extend σ_1 as in Definition 17 then the amalgamated sum is defined by $\sigma_1 +_{\sigma_1} \sigma_3$. In this case those symbols that are common to both the extension and the extended similarity type are in the minimal similarity type σ_1.

If the sum of similarity types were to be defined (more concretely) by union between two sets only one copy of any common symbols would be in the extension. However, different names that may be chosen for the same objects would be made distinct. By choosing to define the amalgamated sum abstractly within category theory we ensure that different symbols that may be used in the similarity types for the same objects will be identified. We define the amalgamated sum by the pushout construction within our configuration workspace in [4].

Definition 23. Let $T_1 = (\sigma_1, \Gamma_1)$ and $T_2 = (\sigma_2, \Gamma_2)$ be theories in a linguistic system LS. Then T_2 is an *extension* of T_1 if $\sigma_1 \subseteq \sigma_2$ and for every $\varphi \in Form(\sigma_1, V)$, $\Gamma_1 \vdash \varphi$ implies $\Gamma_2 \vdash \varphi$.

Definition 24. Let $T_2 = (\sigma_2, \Gamma_2)$ be an extension of the theory $T_1 = (\sigma_1, \Gamma_1)$. Then T_2 is a *conservative extension* of T_1 if for every $\varphi \in Form(\sigma_1, V)$, $\Gamma_2 \vdash \varphi$ implies $\Gamma_1 \vdash \varphi$.

Definition 25. Let $T_1 = (\sigma_1, \Gamma_1)$ and $T_2 = (\sigma_2, \Gamma_2)$ be theories. An *extension* of T_1 by T_2 is the theory $T_3 = (\sigma_1 + \sigma_2, \Gamma_1 \cup \Gamma_2)$.

3.5 Interpretation between Theories

Interpretation is the basic operation between theories. Extension and conservative extension of theories are a special case of interpretation that do not involve a change of language.

Definition 26. Let $\sigma_1 = (S, ar_r, ar_f)$ and $\sigma_2 = (S', ar'_r, ar'_f)$ be two similarity types of a many-sorted first-order language. Then an *interpretation* i *of* σ_1 *in* σ_2 is a morphism, denoted by $i : \sigma_1 \rightarrow \sigma_2$, that consists of four types of mapping. The first type maps the sorts of the similarity type, σ_1, to a sequence of the sorts of σ_2. The second type of mapping assigns to each predicate, constant and function symbol of σ_1 some non-empty sequence of symbols of σ_2. The length of the sequence of sort symbols of S that is assigned by the arity functions ar_r and ar_f in σ_1 is preserved under the interpretation to σ_2. The third type of mapping assigns each variable symbol over σ_1 a sequence of variable symbols of σ_2. Finally the fourth type of mapping assigns to each sort $s \in S$ a relativization predicate symbol $r \in rel\ \sigma_2$. The interpretation i is defined by the 4-tuple of interpretations $(i_S, i_{rel_{\sigma_1} \cup func_{\sigma_1}}, i_v, i_\rho)$ in [5].

In [5] we also define interpretation on the set of terms in $Term(\sigma, V)$ and the set of formulae in $Form(\sigma, V)$ by induction. We use a relativisation predicate to define a restriction on the range of values that are allowed in the terms constructed from the symbols of the target similarity type. This ensures that only terms which are themselves translations under the interpretation morphism are allowed to be substituted into formulae that are built from the target similarity type. As a result of the restriction, interpretation, when extended to configured objects, will reflect precisely the properties of the source object in the target object.

Definition 27. Let $\sigma_1 = (S, ar_r, ar_f)$, $\sigma_2 = (S', ar'_r, ar'_f)$ and $T_2 = (\sigma_2, \Gamma_2)$ be a theory. Then an *interpretation of a similarity type to a theory*, is denoted by $i : \sigma_1 \rightarrow (\sigma_2, \Gamma_2)$, and is an interpretation $i : \sigma_1 \rightarrow \sigma_2$ such that for each sort $s \in S$ of σ_1, where $i_\rho(s) = r_s^{t'}$ of arity $t' = \langle s'_1, s'_2, \ldots, s'_n \rangle$, the following properties hold in T_2:

1. There are free variables in the target similarity type for each of the restricted sorts that are the interpretation of the sorts in the source similarity type. That is

$$\Gamma_2 \vdash \exists x^{s'_1}, x^{s'_2}, \ldots, x^{s'_n} \; r^{t'}(x^{s'_1}, x^{s'_2}, \ldots, x^{s'_n})$$

2. A constant symbol for some sort in σ_1 is interpreted to a constant symbol in σ_2, that is of the restricted sort in σ_2 defined by the appropriate relativization predicate. The domain of values for the constant symbols is preserved in T_2. That is

$$\Gamma_2 \vdash r_s^{t'}(i_{C_s}(c^s))$$

where c^s is a constant in C_s.

3. Each function symbol of sort $\langle t; s \rangle$ in σ_1 is interpreted to a sequence of function symbols in σ_2, whose sorts are restricted by the appropriate relativization predicate; the domain of values for the function symbols in σ_1 must be preserved in σ_2.

$$\Gamma_2 \vdash r_{s_1}^{t'}(i_\nu(x^{s_1})) \wedge r_{s_2}^{t'}(i_\nu(x^{s_2})) \wedge \ldots \wedge r_{s_n}^{t'}(i_\nu(x^{s_n}))$$
$$\rightarrow r_s^{t'} \; (\; f'(i_\nu(x^{s_1})), \ldots, i_\nu(x^{s_n})),$$
$$g'(i_\nu(x^{s_1})), \ldots, i_\nu(x^{s_n})),$$
$$\vdots$$
$$m'(i_\nu(x^{s_1}), \ldots, i_\nu(x^{s_n}))$$

where $i_{func_{\langle t; s \rangle}}(f^{t;s}) = \langle f', g', \ldots, m' \rangle$ in σ_2.

Definition 28. Let $T_1 = (\sigma_1, \Gamma_1)$ and $T_2 = (\sigma_2, \Gamma_2)$ be theories. Then $i : T_1 \rightarrow T_2$ is an *interpretation* of T_1 in T_2 if both of the following conditions hold:

1. $i : \sigma_1 \rightarrow (\sigma_2, \Gamma_2)$ is an interpretation
2. For any $\varphi \in Form(\sigma_1, V_S)$ if $\Gamma_1 \vdash \varphi$ then $\Gamma_2 \vdash i_{Form(\sigma_1, V_S)}(\varphi)$.

Definition 29. Let $T_1 = (\sigma_1, \Gamma_1)$ and $T_2 = (\sigma_2, \Gamma_2)$ be theories. An interpretation $i : T_1 \rightarrow T_2$ is *conservative* iff for every $\varphi \in Form(\sigma_1, V_S)$, $\Gamma_2 \vdash i_{Form(\sigma_1, V_S)}(\varphi)$ implies $\Gamma_1 \vdash \varphi$. If i is conservative then T_2 is said to be a *conservative interpretation* of T_1.

4 Configuration over First-Order Logic

In our approach system components are represented by configured objects. The objects are defined by many-sorted first-order theories which can be both extended and interpreted in some new language. These logical operations on theories define the primitive operations on components within our framework for configuration. A requirement on the logic is that it should possess the Craig interpolation property. This ensures that the structure of objects that have been extended conservatively is preserved if subsequently operated on under interpretation.

Each object within a formal framework for configuration is one of two possible sorts: either specifications or their module instances. Either sort of object can be structured by the combinators of the configuration language. Our notion of modularization for a complex system is therefore at a meta-level to any specification theory or design methodology.

The original content of this section is both the use of an abstract similarity type as a syntactic structuring concept for specification that is paired with a minimal set of axioms, and the emergence of our simple module concept as the basis for the reusability of system components. The module is created as an instance of a specification and is not viewed as the realization of a specification, as in the algebraic approach.

4.1 Combinators Operate on Configured Objects

The primitive combinators between configured objects are the logical operations between theories: interpretation, extension and conservative extension, denoted by i, e and c . e respectively. The *primitive combinator* for creating a module from the specification of an object is denoted by cr.

Definition 30. Let O_1 be an object formed by naming the theory $T_1 = (\sigma_1, \Gamma_1)$, and let O_2 be formed by naming $T_2 = (\sigma_2, \Gamma_2)$. Then $i : O_1 \to O_2$ is an *interpretation* between O_1 and O_2 if i is an interpretation of T_1 in T_2.

Definition 31. Let O_1 be an object formed by naming the theory $T_1 = (\sigma_1, \Gamma_1)$, let O_2 be formed by naming $T_2 = (\sigma_2, \Gamma_2)$, and let O_3 be formed by naming $T_3 = (\sigma_3, \Gamma_3)$. Then the *extension* of O_1 to O_3, denoted by O_1 e to O_3, is defined by constructing (σ_3, Γ_3) as the extension of T_1. If O_1 is extended by some other object O_2 to form the structured object O_3 then O_3 is the named theory T_3 which is the extension of T_1 by T_2.

Definition 32. Let O_1 be an object formed by naming the theory $T_1 = (\sigma_1, \Gamma_1)$, The creation of a module from the specification of O_1 is defined by $cr(O_1) = module$ $(n + 1)$ where $n \geq 0$. The primitive combinator cr is defined as the function $cr : specification \times module^* \longrightarrow module_{n+1}$ where $n \geq 0$ and $module^*$ is the possibly empty string string formed by concatenating the names of the n modules that have been previously created as instances of O_1.

4.2 A Proof-Theoretic Approach to Specification

We choose a simple proof-theoretic basis for specification using a rule-based approach which is operational, rather than denotational in style. This approach does not require the interpretation of syntactic symbols by a model and the resulting separation between syntax and semantics. Renaming the symbols of a many-sorted similarity type achieves an intuitive and simple 'meaning' for the formal sort, function and relation symbols; the properties that express the 'use' of the object specified are then represented by axioms in first-order logic.

In a proof-theoretic style we therefore emphasize the properties of an object, in terms of the 'use' of the object, rather than the 'behaviour' of the object by interpretation in a model. An operational approach is, we believe, closer to the intuitions of software engineers. The 'use' of objects is emphasised rather than the mathematical mappings that are allowed between algebras and sets. Clearly model-theory has contributed much to the initial understanding of the specification process; the actual specification approach may be simplified by managing without models, however.

Specifications are Theories The specification form of a configured object is a theory that is expressed in some specification language and given a name. The theory itself is formed by first choosing the appropriate abstract similarity type; by expressing the required properties as axioms over the abstract similarity type; and finally by renaming the abstract similarity type and the symbols in the axioms to represent the application of the theory.

We suggest that both stacks and lists are linear structures and that at an intuitive level, their use is by the same discipline of access. We therefore build a theory for abstract 'first-in-last-out' structures by adding the appropriate axioms to the abstract similarity type that defines the syntactic structure of both stacks and lists. We define a minimal set of axioms for each specification and require:

Introduction axioms to define the grammar for elements of the type by building canonical elements and showing when two canonical elements are equal.

Reduction axioms to provide the key to defining how an element of the type is used by decomposing the element that has been built by the introduction axioms.

Induction axioms to state, as meta-level expressions, that the elements of the type are only those that have been built by the introduction axioms and used by the reduction axioms.

We identify a relation of 'inheritance' between some common specifications for abstract data types as descendents from the same abstract structure. Our aim for reusability in system construction can therefore be achieved during the initial stages of identifying the appropriate similarity type for a specification. The definition of the similarity type for a theory of abstract structures is based on Definition 8.

Definition 33. The *similarity type for an abstract structure*, denoted by σ, is the triple

$$\sigma = (S, ar_r, ar_f)$$

where

$$S \quad = \{s_1, s_2\}$$
$$rel \; \sigma \quad = \{p^{s_1}, q^{s_2}\}$$
$$func \; \sigma = \{c^{s_1}, f^{s_1, s_2; s_1}, g^{s_1; s_1}, h^{s_1; s_2}\}$$

Clearly the formal first-order language for this theory of a very general structure provides poor readability. By renaming, we obtain a more readable theory and present in addition a set of axioms that express the basic properties of any data structure which is used by the first-in-last-out property.

Definition 34. The *theory for an abstract structure*, denoted by $T_{structure}$ is the pair $(\sigma_{structure}, \Gamma_{structure})$ where

$$\sigma_{structure} = (S, ar_r, ar_f)$$

and

$$
\begin{aligned}
S &= \{s, e\} \\
rel\ \sigma_{structure} &= \{struct^s, elem^e\} \\
func\ \sigma_{structure} &= \{\lambda^s, add^{s,e;s}, delete^{s;s}, remove^{s;e}\}
\end{aligned}
$$

The introduction axioms are,

$struct^s(\lambda^s)$

$\forall x^s \forall y^e\ struct^s(add^{s,e;s}(x^s, y^e))$

$\forall x^s \forall y^e\ [\neg add^{s,e;s}(x^s, y^e) =_s \lambda^s]$

$\forall x_1^s \forall x_2^s \forall y_1^e \forall y_2^e\ [x_1^s = x_2^s \wedge y_1^e = y_2^e \rightarrow add^{s,e;s}(x_1^s, y_1^e) =_s add^{s,e;s}(x_2^s, y_2^e)]$

The reduction axioms telling us that the first element stored is the last element removed are,

$\forall x^s \forall y^e\ [delete^{s;s}(add^{s,e;s}(x^s, y^e)) =_s x^s \wedge struct^s(x^s)]$

$\forall x^s \forall y^e\ [remove^{s;e}(add^{s,e;s}(x^s, y^e)) =_s y^e \wedge elem^e(y^e)]$

The induction axiom schema is,
'for each formula $\mathcal{F}(x^s)$ in the theory, $T_{structure}$, the universal closure of the formula,

$$[\mathcal{F}(\lambda^s) \wedge \forall x^s \forall y^e\ (\mathcal{F}(x^s) \rightarrow \mathcal{F}(add^{s,e;s}(x^s, y^e)))] \rightarrow \forall x^s\ \mathcal{F}(x^s)$$

where y^e does not occur free in $\mathcal{F}(x^s)$, is an axiom'.

Now we have understood the meaning of the axioms in the more readable language of $\sigma_{structure}$, it is easy to construct the set Γ_{filo} in the language σ to complete the basic theory $T_{filo} = (\sigma, \Gamma_{filo})$.

Specifications of a Stack and a List The basic theory for abstract structures can be viewed as a reusable object for the specification of abstract data types with the first-in-last-out property. To illustrate this we specify first a stack and then a list. In order to save space we omit the full set of axioms in each specification.

spec stack is
stack[element]
by renaming of $T_{\text{filo}} = (\sigma, \Gamma_{\text{filo}})$ to $T_{\text{stack,filo}} = (\sigma_{\text{stack}}, \Gamma_{\text{stack,filo}})$ where

$$\sigma_{\text{stack}} = (S, ar_r, ar_f)$$

and

$$
\begin{aligned}
S \quad &= \{s, e\}\\
rel\ \sigma_{\text{stack}} &= \{stack^s, elem^s\}\\
func\ \sigma_{\text{stack}} &= \{\lambda^s, push^{s,e;s}, delete^{s;s}, top^{s;e}\}
\end{aligned}
$$

The set $\Gamma_{\text{stack,filo}}$ is a renaming of Γ_{filo}
endspec

The specification of a list inherits the same abstract theory as the specification of a stack.

spec list is
list[element]
by renaming of $T_{\text{filo}} = (\sigma, \Gamma_{\text{filo}})$ to $T_{\text{list,filo}} = (\sigma_{\text{list}}, \Gamma_{\text{list,filo}})$ where

$$\sigma_{\text{list}} = (S, ar_r, ar_f)$$

and

$$
\begin{aligned}
S \quad &= \{l, i\}\\
rel\ \sigma_{\text{list}} &= \{list^l, item^i\}\\
func\ \sigma_{\text{list}} &= \{\lambda^l, add^{l,i;l}, delete^{l;l}, head^{l;i}\}
\end{aligned}
$$

The set $\Gamma_{\text{list,filo}}$ is a renaming of Γ_{filo}
endspec

Our intention is to provide basic specifications that can be extended as required: in this way we provide reuse of both similarity types and specifications.

Specification of a Queue In contrast to stacks, lists and also strings, queues are used by a first-in-first-out property. Since this property must be expressed in the reduction axioms, we are unable to use our basic theory, $T_{\text{filo}} = (\sigma, \Gamma_{\text{filo}})$, for the specification of a queue. Although only the reduction axioms need to be changed to form Γ_{fifo} from Γ_{filo}, we define a new set of axioms Γ_{fifo} over σ to form an abstract theory denoted by

$$T_{\text{fifo}} = (\sigma, \Gamma_{\text{fifo}})$$

that is the basis for the specification of all data structures with a first-in-last-out access.

Two of the reduction axioms in Γ_{fifo} illustrate the decomposing operation 'jumping' over the operation that builds the type. The reduction ends when the decomposing operation is applied to the structure built from only one element. Two further axioms express the termination of the reduction of the value expression at this stage.

The axioms showing the reduction by 'jumping over' are,

$$\forall x^{s_1} \forall y_1^{s_2} \forall y_2^{s_2} \; [g^{s_1;s_1}(f^{s_1,s_2;s_1}(f^{s_1,s_2;s_1}(x^{s_1}, y_1^{s_2})), y_2^{s_2})) =_{s_1}$$

$$f^{s_1,s_2;s_1}(g^{s_1;s_1}(f^{s_1,s_2;s_1}(x^{s_1}, y_1^{s_2})), y_2^{s_2})]$$

$$\forall x^{s_1} \forall y_1^{s_2} \forall y_2^{s_2} \; [h^{s_1;s_2}(f^{s_1,s_2;s_1}(f^{s_1,s_2;s_1}(x^{s_1}, y_1^{s_2})), y_2^{s_2})) =_{s_2}$$

$$h^{s_1;s_2}(f^{s_1,s_2;s_1}(x^{s_1}, y_1^{s_2}))]$$

The axioms showing the termination of the reduction are,

$$\forall y^{s_2} \; [g^{s_1;s_1}(f^{s_1,s_2;s_1}(c^{s_1}, y^{s_2})) =_{s_1} c^{s_1}]$$

$$\forall y^{s_2} \; [(h^{s_1;s_2}(f^{s_1,s_2;s_1}(c^{s_1}, y^{s_2})) =_{s_2} y^{s_2} \wedge q^{s_2}(y^{s_2})]$$

The specification for a queue can now be based on T_{fifo},

spec queue is
queue[item]
by renaming of T_{fifo} to $T_{\text{queue,fifo}} = (\sigma_{\text{queue}}, \Gamma_{\text{queue,fifo}})$ where

$$\sigma_{\text{queue}} = (S, ar_r, ar_f)$$

and

$$S \qquad\quad = \{q, i\}$$
$$rel\ \sigma_{\text{queue}} \;\; = \{queue^q, item^i\}$$
$$func\ \sigma_{\text{queue}} = \{\lambda^q, add^{q,i;q}, delete^{q;q}, head^{q;i}\}$$

The introduction axioms are,

$$queue^q(\lambda^q)$$

$$\forall x^q \forall y^i \; queue^q(add^{q,i;q}(x^q, y^i))$$

$$\forall x^q \forall y^i \; [\neg add^{q,i;q}(x^q, y^i) =_q \lambda^q]$$

$$\forall x_1^q \forall x_2^q \forall y_1^i \forall y_2^i \; [x_1^q =_q x_2^q \wedge y_1^i =_i y_2^i \rightarrow add^{q,i;q}(x_1^q, y_1^i) =_q add^{q,i;q}(x_2^q, y_2^i)]$$

The reduction axioms express the addition of items to the back of the queue and the removal of items from the front of the queue. The first axiom states that using delete on a queue to which two items have previously been added is like adding the last item to the queue to which the first item was added and then deleted.

$$\forall x^q \forall y_1^i \forall y_2^i \; [(delete^{q;q}(add^{q,i;q}(add^{q,i;q}(x^q, y_1^i), y_2^i)) =_q$$

$$add^{q,i;q}(delete^{q;q}(add^{q,i;q}(x^q, y_1^i)), y_2^q)]$$

$$\forall x^q \forall y_1^i \forall y_2^i \ [(head^{q;i}(add^{q,i;q}(add^{q,i;q}(x^q, y_1^i), y_2^i) =_i head^{q;i}(add^{q,i;q}(x^q, y_1^i))]$$

$$\forall y^i \ [(delete^{q;q}(add^{q,i;q}(\lambda^q, y^i)) =_q \lambda^q]$$

$$\forall y^i \ [(head^{q;i}(add^{q,i;q}(\lambda^q, y^i)) =_i y^i) \wedge item^i(y^i)]$$

The induction axiom schema is,
'for each formula $\mathcal{F}(x^q)$ in the theory, T_{queue}, the universal closure of the formula,

$$[\mathcal{F}(\lambda^q) \wedge \forall x^q \forall y^i \ (\mathcal{F}(x^q) \rightarrow \mathcal{F}(add^{q,i;q}(x^q, y^i)))] \rightarrow \forall x^q \ \mathcal{F}(x^q)$$

where y^i does not occur free in $\mathcal{F}(x^q)$, is an axiom'.
endspec

Since naming conventions for the sorts and operations of abstract data types vary, we have aimed for flexibility by allowing specifications to be written by renaming appropriate basic theories. For example, a dequeue allows additions and deletions at either end of the structure; its specification would therefore be based on both T_{filo} and T_{fifo}. The similarity type, σ, provides the language; the specification is completed by the addition of an appropriate set of axioms, Γ.

4.3 Using the Configuration Language

Our primitive specification of a queue is now used to write configured specifications. We illustrate how our module concept enables the non-sharing of objects to be explicitly differentiated from the sharing of objects. Within our configured specification for the simple systems of Section 2 we express structuring by parameterisation, with modules of the primitive configured object 'queue' as parameters.

Example 4 (from Example 2). The specification for **obj sharingofqueue** is parameterized by two modules that each share a single queue module. The actual sharing of the queue is described by the text within the structured specification as a configuration from **obj use-queue** and **obj queue**.

spec sharingofqueue is
create(**spec use-queue**, λ) = **module use-queue1**;
create(**spec use-queue**, **module use-queue1**)= **module use-queue2**;
create(**spec queue**, λ) = **module queue1**;
spec use-queue[spec queue];
module use-queue1[module queue1];
module use-queue2[module queue1];
spec sharing[module use-queue1[module queue1],module use-queue2[module queue1]]

as $T_{sharingofqueue}$

$$= (\sigma_{sharingofqueue}, \Gamma_{sharingofqueue})$$
$$= (\sigma_{sharing} + \sigma_{use-queue1} + \sigma_{use-queue2} + \sigma_{queue1},$$
$$\Gamma_{sharing} + \Gamma_{use-queue1} + \Gamma_{use-queue2} + \Gamma_{queue1})$$

endspec

In spec sharingofqueue it is explicitly stated that the two parameters are modules, and also that these modules share a common module instance of a queue as a parameter.

Example 5 (from Example 3). Next we build an object structured from objects that each have their own queue. The queue owned by each object has been created as a unique module instance from the same specification of a queue. The specification for the object that represents the non-sharing of a queue is

spec nonsharingofqueue is
create(spec use-queue, λ) = module use-queue1;
create(spec use-queue, module use-queue1)= module use-queue2;
create(spec queue, λ) = module queue1;
create(spec queue, module queue1)= module queue2;
spec use-queue[spec queue];
module use-queue1[module queue1];
module use-queue2[module queue2];
spec non-sharing[module use-queue1[module queue1],
module use-queue2[module queue2]]

as $T_{\text{nonsharingofqueue}}$

$$= (\sigma_{\text{nonsharingofqueue}}, \Gamma_{\text{nonsharingofqueue}})$$
$$= (\sigma_{\text{nonsharing}} + \sigma_{\text{use-queue1}} + \sigma_{\text{use-queue2}} + \sigma_{\text{queue1}} + \sigma_{\text{queue2}},$$
$$\Gamma_{\text{nonsharing}} + \Gamma_{\text{use-queue1}} + \Gamma_{\text{use-queue2}} + \Gamma_{\text{queue1}} + \Gamma_{\text{queue2}})$$

endspec

We can use our simple systems as components for further configuration. From **obj** non-sharingofqueue, with its structure expressed by a specification, we can create module instances and use these to build even more structured objects that, in part, represent the non-sharing of queues. The module creation is expressed by,

$$create(\text{spec nonsharingofqueue}, \lambda) = \text{module nonsharingofqueue1}$$

The scope of the name of each queue module is *within* the structured specification that expresses its creation. Further configuration could construct an object allowing both sharing and non-sharing of queues in a system. This more complex object will express the operations of combinators on the simpler objects 'sharingofqueue' and 'nonsharingofqueue'. Within each of these simpler objects the names of the module instances of the queue specification will be in scope. If a further instance of a queue module were created from a queue specification, within the more complex object, its name would be in scope but would not clash with the names of the queue modules within the simpler objects. This is because names of modules created in new structured objects take precedence over names of modules previously created in the simpler objects.

5 Conclusions

Acknowledgments

The many discussions with Tom Maibaum, of Imperial College, have been both stimulating and valuable. He has also made useful comments on earlier drafts of this paper. Paul Taylor's macros were used for the diagrams.

References

1. T. Gergely and L. Ury. First order programming theories. In W. Brauer, G. Rozenburg, and A. Saloma, editors, *EATCS Monographs on Theoretical Computer Science, Volume 24*. Springer-Verlag, 1991.
2. G. Hill. Category theory for the configuration of complex systems. In T. Rus M. Nivat, C Rattray and G. Scollo, editors, *Algebraic Methodology and Software Technology, Entschede, 1993*, pages 193–200. Proceedings of the Third International Conference on Algebraic Methodology and Software Technology, University of Twente, The Netherlands, 21–25 June 1993, Springer-Verlag, 1994. Workshops in Computing series.
3. G. Hill. The configuration of complex systems. In T. Ören, editor, *CAST '94 Lecture Notes*. Fourth International Workshop on Computer Aided Systems Technology, University of Ottawa, Ottawa, Ontario, Canada, 16–20 May, 1994. to be published in 1995 by Springer-Verlag.
4. G. Hill. Constructing specifications and modules in a KZ-doctrine. In C. L. Hankin, I. Mackie, and R. Nagarajan, editors, *Theory and Formal Methods '94*. Proceedings of the Second Imperial College, Department of Computing, Workshop on Theory and Formal Methods, September 1994. to be published by IC-press, World Scientific Publishing.
5. G. Hill. *A Language for System Configuration*. PhD thesis, Department of Computing, Imperial College, University of London, 1994. draft.
6. S. Takahashi and Y. Takahara. Logical approach to systems theory. Technical report, Tokyo Institute of Technology, Japan, 1994.
7. W. M. Turski and T. S. E. Maibaum. *The Specification of Computer Programs*. International Computer Science Series. Addison Wesley, 1987.

Task Management System

Yasuhiko TAKAHARA

Tokyo Institute of Technology, Ookayama, Meguro, Tokyo, Japan

Xiaohong CHEN

Central South University of Technology, Changsha, Hunan, P. R. China

Abstract. A task which is supposed for our DSS (actDSS) consists of integrated models, solvers, graphical models for imput and output, various data models connected a data base and others. The organization of these subsystems is a task. A task management system (TMS) should take care of all aspects of a task construction and its operation. In this paper the concept of TMS is proposed and the structure and function are discussed.

1 Introduction

Our group has been working for development of a decision support system (DSS) which is called actDSS. The target of a DSS, in general, is a business system which is a complex system consisting of many submodels. The problem is so called semistructured. One of the current hot issues of the DSS research is, therefore, a realization of a model managememt system which can provide a satisfactory model integration environment and many efforts are being made on the study of it[1]. In this paper we will propose a concept of task management system (TMS) which is more than a model management. A satisfactory model integration mechanism is necessary for a practical DSS (and its implementation is not a trivial matter) but not sufficient for an effective DSS. What is really to be supported by a DSS or a computer-based system in general is a user's task processing itself.

Intuitively, a task which is supposed for our DSS consists of not only integrated models but also solvers, graphical models for input and output, various data models connected a data base and others. The organization of these subsystems is a task. A TMS should take care of all aspects of a task construction and its operation.

The TMS of our system consists of two subsystems, one for task definition and the other for task manipulation. The former is realized as a special graphical window called model space and the latter by a special menu system. The task construction and operation is supported by the two subsystems combined in an organic way.

Direct manipulation, real time manipulation and on-line manipulation are emphasized for their design. Since a task is just working image by a user which must change dynamically as he proceeds on his work, it must be able to be modified flexibly and his spontaneous thinking must not be interfered by the computer system.

In this paper the structure and the function of the TMS will be discussed in a formal way.

2 Task concept-functional model of a DSS

The combination of a DSS (or a specific DSS) and its user defines a goal-seeking system [2]. We will start our investigation from the combination or the total model so that the meaning of a task can be clarified.

According to MGST (mathematical general systems theory) a goal-seeking model is shown as Fig. 1. We will start from the representation. The first concept to be introduced is GSP (goal-seeking problem), GSP is given by:

$$\langle M, X, Y, P, G, \Theta_m, \Theta_x \rangle$$

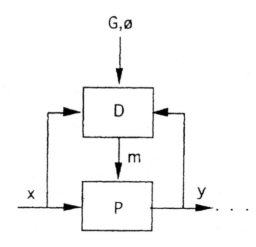

Fig. 1 Goal-seeking System

where

$M =$ *universal set of alternatives*
$X =$ *universal set of uncertainties*
$Y =$ *universal set of outcomes*
$P: M \times X \to Y$; *process*
$G: M \times X \times Y \to R$; *goal*
Θ_m: *unary predicate on M*
Θ_x: *unary predicate on X*.

$M' = \{m \mid \Theta_m(m)\}$ and $X' = \{x \mid \Theta_x(X)\}$ are an admissible alternative set and an admissible uncertainty set, respectively.

In order to solve a goal-seeking problem the concept of decision principle φ is to be introduced. That is,

$$\varphi: \{GSP\} \rightarrow \{\langle M, \leqslant \rangle\}.$$

φ is a map from the class of GSP to the class of ordered structure on M. A typical example of the decision principle is the max-min principle. Then, the concept of goal-seeking system GSS is given by

$$GSS = \langle GSP, \varphi \rangle.$$

Next, let us define the concept of solver.
Let the SLP (solver problem) with respect to a GSP be:

$$SLP = \langle M, X, g, \Theta_m, x_0 \rangle$$

where

$$g: M \times X \rightarrow R \text{ such that } g(m,x) = G(m,x,P(m,x))$$

and

$$x_o \in X.$$

Notice that the uncertainty is fixed in an SLP. Then, an SLS (solver system) is given by

$$SLS = \langle \{SLP\}, M, SLV \rangle$$

where

{SLP}=class of solver problems
SLV: {SLP}→M such that
$$SLV(M,X,g,\Theta_m,x_o) = m^* \Leftrightarrow$$
$$(i)\Theta_m(m^*)$$
$$(ii)(\forall_m \in M)(\Theta_m(m) \Rightarrow g(m,x_0) \leqslant g(m^*,x_0))$$

That is, a solver system is an input-output system which produces an optimum (maximization in this paper) solution for a given solver problem.

A DSS is supposed to deal with a semi-structured problem. The existence of the uncertainty input x reflects one aspect of ill-structuredness. At the same time mappings introduced above are not uniquely specified in general. Hence let us define the concept of a parameterized SLP. That is,

$$SLP(\omega,s,\gamma) = \langle M, X, g(d), \Theta_m(s,\gamma), x_0 \rangle$$

where $\omega \in W$, $s \in S$ and $\gamma \in \Gamma$ are parameters.

In the formulation of GSP the goal function G is assumed a scalar function. But in many of real DSS problems its goal is defined as multi-objective. The multi-objective situation, however, can be transformed into a single objective by introducing a weight vector of the multi-objective, that is, the linear weighted sum decision principle is used. The weight vector is an example of the parameter w of g.

The predicate Θ_m is usually called constraints condition. In a real situation we had better consider there exists a family of constraints, $\{\Theta_m^i | i \in I\}$ and some constraints are hard (they must be satisfied) while others are soft (they may be ignored depending on a situation). Suppose $\{\Theta_m^j | j \in J\}$ is a subfamily of the constraint family with an index set $J \subset I$ which is required to be satisfied on a given situation. Then, Θ_m of GSP is

$$\Theta_m = \bigwedge_j \{\Theta_m^j\}.$$

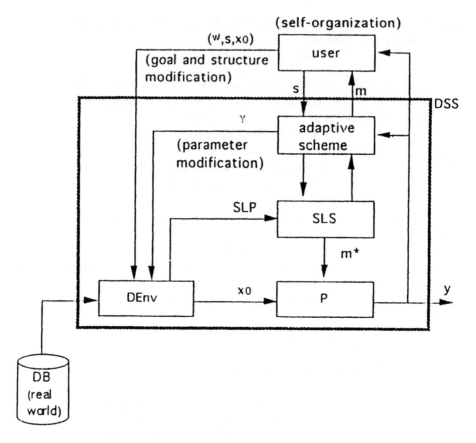

Fig.2 Hierarchical Functional Model of DSS

The index set J is an example of s of Θ_m. Notice that s is concerned with the structure of the constraint. There is another type of parameter of the constraint. Suppose Θ_m is given the following inequality:

$$\Theta_m(x) \Leftrightarrow f(x) \geqslant r.$$

Then, r is used as a parameter to modify the behavior of the constraint. The of the product mix problem is given by the following form:

Objective:

$$Total\ sales\ income = \sum_i c(1,i) \times x(i)\ i \in \{1\dots,5\}$$

$$Gross\ profit = \sum_i c(2,i) \times x(i)\ i \in \{1\dots,5\}$$

$$Total\ production\ output = \sum_i c(3,i) \times x(i)\ i \in \{1\dots,5\}$$

Constraint:

$$\sum_i a(k,i) \times x(i) \leqslant b(k)\ k \in \{1\dots5,\}\ i \in \{1\dots,5\}$$

The decision problem is a multi-objective. But in order to solve the problem by using an LP algorithm, the linear weighted sum method is adopted for the problem. Let the weight vector be $w = (w(1), w(2), w(3))$. Then,

Integrated objective:

$$\sum_j \sum_i w(j) \times c(j,i) \times x(i) \to max \quad j \in \{1,..,3\}, i \in \{1,..,5\}$$

All of the five constraints are not necessarily used for decision making. The choice depends on situations and is expressed by a vector $s = (s(1),...,s(5))$ where

$$s(i) = \begin{cases} 1 \ \text{if the i-th constraint is used} \\ 0 \qquad\qquad otherwise \end{cases}$$

Then,

Working constraint:

$$\{ \sum_i a(k,i) \times x(i) \leqslant b(k) \,|\, s(k) = 1, k \in \{1,..5\} \}$$

The user is supposed to have desired values for the three objectives which is specified by a vector $d = (d(1), d(2), d(3))$.

The three vector w, s and d are controlled by the user. The matrix $A = [a(k,i)]$, the vecor $b = (b(k))$ and the matrix $C = [c(k,i)]$ are not directly given by the user. There are six tables which are called databases and are given by aec. s, arm. s, apm. s, amd. s, apc. s and aop. s in Fig 3. For instance, aec. s $= (a(1,1),...,a(1,5),b(1))$. The first five databases specify A and b and the last one does C. Similarly, w, s and d are given by databases, ado. s, acc. s and adv. s, respectively. The family of the databases reflects the user's problem image of the real world. The user controls the problem through the image and not through the formulated problem. The databases and their transformation into the LP problem correspond to the DEnv of Section 2.

In actDSS every object is represented by a model which is conceptualized as an input output system following GST. Furthermore, models are managed on a special window called model space and are linked together on that space to yield one big model by the mechanism which will be discussed in Section 4.

Let us consider lpsolver. m of Fig. 3 as a typical model example. The model is defined by a model description language (MDL) of actDSS and is saved in the model base. In order to use the model it must be retrieved from the model base and transformed into an executable form. This operation is called model creation.

The model creation is done on the model space. Rectangle boxes with names on the model space of Fig. 3 represent created models. The creation can be done easily by " model" and "lable" menu commands of the model space using the mouse.

When lpsolver. m is defined on the model space, its MDL specification is transformed into an internal representation and at the same time an input output relation of it is produced. The relation is displayed in a table form on the screen which is called IORep. The IORep of lpsolver. m is shown in Fig. 3 where variables are classified into INPUT and OUTPUT and their current values are also displayed. An IORep is implemented on the spread sheet of parameter γ represents this type of parameter.

System's parameters are classified into two types, upper level parameters and lower level parameters. A upper level parameter is concerned with change of the goal or that of the structure of the system. It is usually difficult to specify its modification by a formalized rule. A lower level parameter

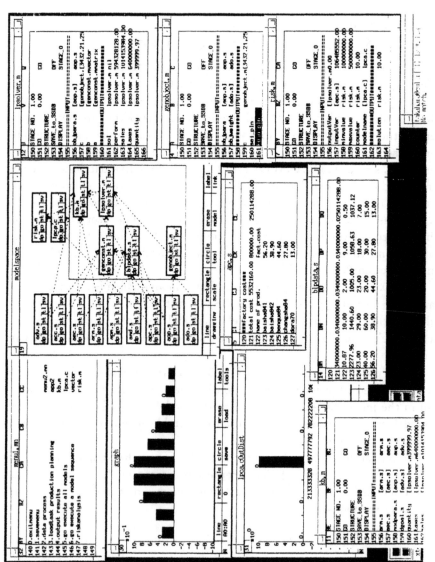

Fig.3 A task of the production planning of cigarettes

is, on the other hand, concerned with change of the behavior and its control may be given by a formalized rule. In this sense d and s are upper level parameters while γ is a lower level one. This classification corresponds to the hierarchy concept which will be discussed below [3,4].

Then, with respect to a parameterized SLP the concept of DEnv (decision environment) is introduced. That is,

$$DEnv: W \times S \times \Gamma \times X \to \{SLP\} \times X$$

such that $DEnv(w,s,\gamma,x_0) = (SLP(w,s,\gamma),x_0)$
where

$$W = set\ of\ parameter\ w$$
$$S = set\ of\ parameter\ s$$
$$\Gamma = set\ of\ parameter\ \gamma.$$

DEnv yields one specified SLP for a given (w, s, γ).

When the constraint is complicated or dynamically modified, it is quite possible that $\{m|\Theta_m(s,\gamma)(m)\}$ becomes empty, that is, the problem becomes infeasible. In that case the constraint may be modified by γ by using a formalized rule so that the problem can be feasible. Then, the concept of adaptive scheme is introduced.

Adaptive scheme:

$$Given\ s.\ Find\ \gamma \in \Gamma\ such\ that$$
$$\{m|\Theta_m(s,\gamma)(m)\} \neq \varnothing$$

The upper level parameters w, s and x_0 are usually adjusted by the user of a DSS. Then, integrating the concepts introduced above, we can have a hiearchical model of a DSS which is shown by Fig. 2.

The functional model of DSS, basically, consists of three components, DEnv, SLS and adaptive scheme. The model building problem of a DSS is exactly the problem of construction of the DEnv. Since the constraint Θ_m is usually complicated, the adjustment of γ is done heuristically, that is, an AI technique is used for the adaptive scheme. In the DSS community a working DSS is often called specific DSS. Then, the hierarchical model of Fig. 2 is a general model of a specific DSS and is the target of the TMS. It is clear that the hierarchical model is a special case of the multi-layer model of GST [3,4].

3 Illustration of task

Fig. 3 illustrates a task of some practical problem, production planning of cigarettes [5]. The problem is an extended product mix optimization problem.

Suppose we have five products of cigarette which will be indexed 1, 2,..,and 5. Let $x = (x(1),.. x(5))$ be a decision variable referring to the production quantity of the product 1 to the product 5. Then, the final form actDSS.

actDSS has several types of model. In Fig. 3 5 types are shown, m-model, s-model, g-model, c-model and mn-model. An m-model is a model specified by the MDL. Lpsolver. m is an example of the m-model. An s-model is a model defined on the spread sheet of actDSS. It is mainly used for a data storage area. The model aec. s is an example of the s-model. A g-model is a graph model which is used as a display of data as well as an input to a model. The window lpca. cInDist is a distribution input to a sheet model apc. s. A c-model and an mn-model are a composite model and a menu model, respectively. They will be discussed below. Models except composite and menu models are called atomic models.

In Fig. 3 the transformation of the DEnv is realized by the 3 models genobject. m, blpdata. s and genconst. m. The output of the DEnv, an LP problem, is sent to lpsolver. m. lpsolver. m solves the problem using an LP algorithm. The solution is sent to kb. m which corresponds to the adaptive scheme of Section 2.

kb. m, an knowledge base subsystem, is used to: (1)evaluate the obtained solution using the vector d; (2) amend the parameters of the databases to get a more satisfactory solution.

In Fig. 3 the submodels genobject. m, blpdata. s, genconst. m, lpsolver. m, and kb. m are integrated into one composite modle (c-model) whose name is lpca. c. This is indicated by the rectangle enclosing the submodels in the model space of Fig. 3. The c-model is created by "link" menu command of the modelspace. If a user executes lpca. c, the submodels are executed in the proper order, genobject. m → blpdata. s → genconst. m → lpsolver. m → kb. m. The order is found by the system on the link command execution.

In Fig. 3, the composite model lpca. c is linked to a risk analysis model risk. m which inputs a random input to apc. s and executes the whole system (lpca. c) and gets an output from lpsolver. m. The input distribution is given by the g-model lpca. cInDist and the output distribution is displayed on a g-model lpca. cOutDist in Fig. 3.

The task of Fig. 3 is controlled by a menu system. A submenu "menul. mn" is shown in Fig. 3 which is an example of the mn-model.

Although the menu system is discussed in Section 5, we will explain the meanings of the commands used in menul. mn in order to indicate how task operations are supported by the system.

The whole structure of the annual production planning system is saved as a task " app2" which is indicated by the menu statement "loadtask production planning app2" of menul. mn. The command "savetask" which is not shown in menul. mn is used to save the current task.

Suppose only menul. mn is displayed on the screen. When a user wants to use the system, he has to select "loadtask" from menul. mn. Then the whole configration of the production planning system, that is, Fig. 3 appears on the screen and he can analyze the system to get a satisfactory solution.

The command "go" is used to execute a model. A conditional execution is possible when a condition is assigned to the "go" statement.

The command "repeat" is used with a condition and as long as the condition is satisfied, the repeated execution of its argument is done. In menul. mn the statement "9. repeat while var (kb. m, eval) ≠ 0 [lpca. c]" which means that unless the variable eval of kb. m is equal to 0, the whole system is executed repeatedly..

4 Task definition by model space

In Section 3 we mentioned that a task is defined on the model space. In this section we will formalize the model space to make the meaning of a task clear.

The model space is a platform for model integration of various models, m-model, c-model, s-model, g-model, mn-model and others.

Let us consider an m-model first.

An m-model is an atomic model described by the MDL and the MDL is a functional language, that is , every variable is specified by a function of the other variables. Fig. 4 shows a model description by the MDL. Then ,let an m-model m be

$$m = \{v_i = f_i(V_{i1}, \ldots, V_{il} | i = 1, \ldots k\}.$$

In actDSS an m-model is transformed into an internal form $IntRep(m)$ $= \langle P_{RO}Rep(m), S_tRep(m) \rangle$ to be executed. $P_{RO}Rep(m)$ is a Prolog form representation of m, which is given by :

$$P_{RO}Rep(m) = \{v_i(Y) :- v_{i1}(X_1), \ldots, v_{il}(X_1), f_i^*(X_1, \ldots, X_l, X_0), Y = X_0 | i = 1, \ldots, k\}$$

where Y, $X_0, \ldots$, X_l are Prolog variables and

$$f_i^*(X_1, \ldots, X_l, X_0) \leftrightarrow X_o = f_i(X_1, \ldots, X_l).$$

When m is to be executed, actually, $P_{RO}Rep(m)$ is executed by the Prolog interpreter of actDSS. $S_tRep(m)$ represents the dependency relation among the variables and is biven by :

$$S_tRep(m) = \{node(v_i, [v_{i1}, \ldots, v_{il}]) | i = 1, \ldots, k\},$$

that is , each functional relation yields one node-predicate. Let

$$v \geq v' \leftrightarrow (\exists i)(\exists j)(node(v_i, [v_{i1}, \ldots, v_{il}]) \in S_tRep(m) \text{ and } v = v_i \text{ and } v' = v_{ij}).$$

It is assumed $\geq$ is a partially ordered relation.

Next let us define the IO representation of m, $IORep(m)$ (Refer to Fig. 3).

Suppose there are n models $m_1, \ldots, m_n$ on the model space which are assumed m-models for the sake of simplicity. Let

$N_i =$ set of variables (or variable names) of m_i.

$V_i =$ set of values which the variables of m_i take.

$N = \cup_i N_i$.

$varP = \{var(m_i, v_j) | v_j \in N_i, i = 1, \ldots, n\}$ where $var(m_i, v_j)$ will be called var function.

$F = \{f | f = \text{an arithmetic formula on } varP\}$.

$F_i^* = F \cup V_i$

Then, IORep(m_i) is given by :

$$IORep(m_i) \subset \{Ni \to (F_i^* \times Vi)\}.$$

where , for instance, if $(v, (var(m', v'), value)) \in$ IORep(m_i), then it means that the variable v is linked to a variable v' of a model m' and value is the current value of v' or the evaluation of var(m', v'). How a link is set up will be discussed below.

As mentioned in Section 3, an IORep is implemented on the spread sheet and displayed in a window and hence its display is specified by

$$IODisp(m) = \langle wp, mname, type, [X, Y, W, H] \rangle$$

where

wp = identification number of the window in which IORep(m) is displayed

mname = name of m,

type = type of m (currently m-model),

(X, Y) = location on the spread sheet where IORep(m) is displayed.

(W, H) = size of the spread sheet area used for IORep(m) where W = width and H = height.

Finally, the model representation of m, $M_dRep(m)$ is:

$$M_dRep(m) = \langle IODisp(m), IORep(m), IntRep(m) \rangle.$$

The above formulation is applicable to the other types of model with some modifications. For instance, let us consider an s-model datam. Since an s-model is implemented on the spread sheet, its variable (name) is a cell or is specified by $[i, j]$ which represents the location of the cell. Then, a model representation for datam is given by:

$$datam = \{cell\text{-}loc_i = f_i(cell\text{-}loc_{i1}, \ldots, cell\text{-}loc_{il}) \,|\, i = 1, \ldots, k\}$$

and a var-function takes the form:

var(mname, cell-loc)

where cell-loc $= [i, j]$ for some i and j. A spread sheet is, in general, used for building a model as well as for storing data. datam of the above expression is a formalization of a usual (spread) sheet model.

Since a sheet model can be executed by the calculation capability of the spread sheet, $P_{RO}Rep$(datam) is not needed and so defined as a dummy expression. As Fig. 3 shows, the IORep of an m-model is displayed as a mapping from a variable name to its value but since a variable of datam takes the form of $[i, j]$, its IORep is displayed as a matrix form, the usual spread sheet form. The M_dRep can be also defined for datam in the obvious way.

Using the above concepts we will formalize the model space.

Let M = set of models on the modle space.

Let mlink $\subset M \times M$ be such that

$(m, m') \in$ mlink $\leftrightarrow$ m depends on m',

that is, the value of some variable of m depends on some variable of m'.

Then, the model space is formalized by:

model space = $\langle \{MdRep(m) \,|\, m \in M\}, mlink \rangle$

In actDSS M is dynamically changing because a model can be created or deleted on the model space dynamically and so is the mlink. In this sense the model space is dynamically changing.

Then, finally, the concept of a task is given by:

task = ⟨model space, task status⟩

where task status is a process state of a task which will be discussed in Section 5 .

As the above formulation indicates, the model space corresponds to the structure of a task.

The most important concept of the model space is a link relation. As mentioned, a link relation from an m-model to another m-model is a relation between variables which is specified by a var-function on an IORep. If a variable v_1 of a model m_1 is linked to a variable v_2 of a model m_2, it is implemented as $(v_1, (var(m_2, v_2), value)) \in IORep(m_1)$ where value = evaluation of $var(m_2, v_2)$. Since $IORep(m_1)$ is implemented on the spread sheet, the formula $var(m_2, v_2)$ can be directly typed in value part cell of v_1 where, then, value is displayed. There is no problem to establish a link relation between m-models. A link relation between an s-model and an m-model is a little bit more complicated because a variable of an m-model is typeless (Notice that no type declaration exists in Fig. 4) and it may signify the whole data of an s-model. Let us consider the case of a link from an s-model datam to an m-model m. In this case, a variable v of m may be linked to one element of datam or to a portion of datam or to the whole data of datam. In order to deal with these situations the following convention of interpretation is used:

```
//genobject. m
//input=[objpara, objweight]; objpara=aop. s, objweight=ado. s
//output=new coefficients
//get weight vector; length of vector -weithts is not specified
-weights=vec(objweight, [4,2,1,-1])
//get para. vector; length of vector -objparas is not specified
-objpara1=vec(objpara. [1,2,-1,1])
-objpara2=vec(objpara. [1,3,-1,1])
-objpara3=vec(objpara. [1,4,-1,1])
-objpara4=vec(objpara. [1,5,-1,1])
-objpara5=vec(objpara. [1,6,-1,1])
//get scalor product of -weights and -objpara1
-cC1=sum(-weights * -objpara1)
-cC2=sum(-weights * -objpara2)
-cC3=sum(-weights * -objpara3)
-cC4=sum(-weights * -objpara4)
-cC5=sum(-weights * -objpara5)
c=[-cC1, -cC3, -cC4, -cC5]
```

Fig. 4 A model description (genobject. m) by MDL

var(datam, [i,j])＝(i,j) element of datam

var(datam, [−1,j])＝vector of the j-th column

var(datam,[i,−1])＝vector of the i-th row

var(datam,[−1,−1])＝the whole matrix.

Using this convention a flexible link relation can be established from an s-model to an m-model. The converse is also true.

5 Task manipulation by menu system

The structure of a task is given by the model space. The manipulation of a task is done by a menu system. A menu system consists of menu models. A menu model is really a program which gives a user a power to control execution of a task flexibly. Furthermore, the program of a menu model can be modified dynamically and so is the manipulation.

A menu model consists of a finite set of menu statements, which have the following structure:

⟨statement number⟩. ⟨commnd⟩[⟨condition/comment⟩]⟨argument⟩

- ⟨statement number ⟩ is the identification of a statement.
- ⟨command⟩ specifies how models are manipulated. Currently, we have 8 commands , exitmenu, savemenu, loadmenu, loadtask, savetask, load-model, go and repeat.
- ⟨condition⟩ specifies the condition how models are manipulated. Its structure is:

$$\begin{pmatrix} \text{while} \\ \text{on} \end{pmatrix} \langle \text{var name}\rangle \begin{vmatrix} < \\ \leqslant \\ = \\ \geqslant \\ > \end{vmatrix} \langle \text{var name}\rangle$$

- ⟨var name⟩includes constants (numeric or symbolic) as well as var-functions.
- ⟨argument⟩ is a list of model names or a list of statement numbers or a list of their combinations;for instance, [aec. s,4,aop. s] where 4 is a statement number, and executing sequence is aec. s→4→aop. s.

"menul. mn" of Fig. 3 is an example of the menu model.

Since a menu model is also implemented on the spread sheet, a user can write a statement freely on it as if it were a real blackboard. The written statements are saved by the command "savemenu" ,that is, when the menu model is called next time, it is displayed with the saved statements.

A task usually has more than one menu models and the family of them is organized as a menu system. The system is specified and managed by two commands, exitmenu and loadmenu. Suppose there is a family of menus $\{mn_1, \ldots, n_k\}$. Suppose the i-th menu mn_i has the following loadmenu commands:

st_1. loadmenu mn_{i1}

. .

. .

.

st_1. loadmenu mn_{il}

where st_j is a statement number.

If st_1 is selected, the menu mn_i is replaced by the new menu mn_{i1} (mn_i is unraised and mn_{i1} is raised). mn_{i1} is considered as a child menu of mn_i. This relation can be described by a node predicate as:

node(mn_i, $[mn_{i1}, \ldots, mn_{il}]$($i = 1, \ldots, k$)

The menu management system (MenMS) of actDSS assumes that {node (mn_i, $[mn_{i1}, \ldots, mn_{il}]$) | $i = 1, \ldots, k$} can be expanded as a tree structure and when "exitmenu" is selected in mn_{il}, MenuMS replaces mn_{il} by its parent mn_i, that is, mn_i is raised and mn_{il} is unraised.

If a new statement "stp. loadmenu mn_{ip}" ($p \geq 1$) is appended to mn_i and if it is selected, MenuMS opens an empty new menu model as mn_{ip} even if it has not been defined yet. The user, then, can write menu statements on it to manage his task. In this way the user can define the menu system dynamically.

A menu manipulation program can describe a special type of context free language of model execution sequences. If we recognize statement numbers correspond to nonterminal symbols of a context free language, we can understand that the family of go-statements (without a ⟨condition⟩ term) specifies a context free language. For instance, the following program specifies the model execution sequence $(m_1, m_2)^*$ for two models m_1 and m_2:

1. go$[m_1, 2]$
2. go$[m_2, 1]$

In the above program the execution cannot stop. The stop condition is given by a ⟨condition⟩ term as

2. go on ⟨boolean expression on variables⟩ $[m_2, 1]$.

Then, the execution will stop when the condition fails.

If we want to execute m_1, once, we can write, of course,

3. go $[m_1]$.

Since an iteration mechanism is often used for the adaptive scheme, the following statenent is useful:

4. repeat while ⟨stopping condition⟩$[m_1', \ldots, m_k']$

where $m_1', \ldots$ and m_k' are submodel names or statement numbers.

The status of a task consists of three component, directories of windows and models, asserted facts, and flags. Since models are executed after translated into Prolog forms, they produce various facts on their execution which are asserted facts. Asserted facts are used as common informations among models.

6 Conclusion

In this paper we introduced a framework of a task management system and its implementation. No one can argue against the saying that a task is more important than a model itself and what must be supported is user's task processing and not his model processing . Then, the question is what a task really means or what a useful task support is. The answer can be found only after doing many applications.

References

[1]D. R. Dolk: An introduction to model integration and integrated modeling environment. Decision Support System,No. 10(1993)

[2]M. Mesaroric and Y. Takahara: Abstract Systems Theory. Lecture Notes in Control and Information Sciences: Springer-Verlag 1989

[3]M. Mesaroric, D. Macko and Y. Takahara: Theory of Hierarchical, Multilevel system: Academic Press 1970

[4]H. Bossel: Modeling and Simulation: Vieweg 1994

[5]Xiaohong Chen and Li Yizhi: The Research of Enterprise Management DSS: J. CENT-SOUTH INST . MIN. METALL, Vol. 24, No. 5 (1993) (in chinese)

Toward a Unified Theory of Discrete Event Systems

Ryo SATO

Institute of Socio-Economic Planning, University of Tsukuba,
Tsukuba, Ibaraki 305, Japan

Abstract. Many man-made systems have discrete event mechanism. This paper first shows briefly a way how to construct a universal state space representations of a general discrete event system that is an input-output system with past-determinacy, stationarity, the discrete event input space, and discrete event-determinacy. The constructed state space representation for a discrete event system is minimal in a class of dynamical system representations of the system. This realization theory provides the fact that a reduced and reachable DEVS, which is originated by Zeigler[1], is unique up to isomorphism in the class of discrete event dynamical system representations. In this sense DEVS has concise information to describe discrete event dynamics. Since the Petri net formalism, that is a bit different from the DEVS formalism, is also used for the design and analysis of discrete event systems, some relation between DEVS and Petri nets is considered.

1 Introduction

Many man-made systems have discrete event mechanism. There are some models of discrete event systems accordingly. Discrete event systems are firstly formulated by Zeigler[1] from the systems theoretic view. The formalism is called discrete event system specification (DEVS). Petri net theory[3] is also widely used in modeling discrete event mechanisms. In both theories state variables are considered as one of the descriptive variables of discrete event models. That is, they are part of the definition of the systems itself.

Another understanding for state variable has been brought by [4, 5]. A general system is given as a set of input-output data (in the form of time functions) and then its state space representation (i.e., state transition mechanism) is constructed to describe the causal dynamic behavior of the system. From their point of view, state is not part of the definition of the system, but a derived, artificial variable.

In general one of possible variables can be used as a state variable of a state space representation of a system. We pose two different kinds of questions at this point.

(1) Assume there exists a discrete event system S. The system S is a set of input-output data in the form of time functions, which may be derived from a DEVS model or from a Petri net. There can be many state space representations of S. That is, the same S can be obtained by other DEVS specifications or Petri nets. Is the DEVS specification of a
system safe for the analysis and design of discrete event systems? Or, how about Petri nets? For example, if a DEVS specification or a Petri-net representation of S

had a kind of redundancy, then the use of other state representation probably lead to successful result. This situation is depicted in Fig. 1.

(2) How a DEVS specification and a Petri net are related? Which part is similar and how much they are different?

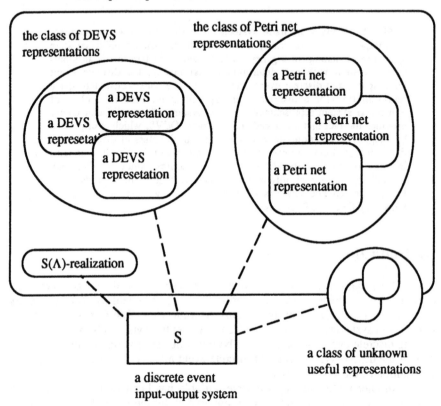

Fig. 1. Many state space representations of
a discrete event input-output system

What we have to show to answer these questions are as follows: Firstly, a general discrete event system is defined as an input-output system with certain conditions. We need this definition to make clear what a discrete event system really is. Because both the DEVS formalism and Petri nets are intended to describe discrete event systems, and there still exists gap between the DEVS formalism and Petri nets. Secondly, we can show that the input-output system obtained from a DEVS specification, which is called its state system, is a general discrete event system. Thirdly, a universal state space representation of a general discrete event system S is constructed, which is called the S(Λ)-realization. It can be shown that the S(Λ)-realization is minimal in the class of discrete event dynamical system representations. Fourthly, the state space representation of the state system S_D of a legitimate DEVS M is isomorphic to $S_D(\Lambda)$-realization, if the state space representation derived from M is reduced and reachable. In this sense a legitimate DEVS provides concise information of discrete event dynamics. Fifthly, we show a way to make possible DEVS representations for a certain general class of Petri nets.

In this paper we will look at these issues. For notation we refer [1, 4, 5].

2 Realization Theory of General Discrete Event Systems

The time set is the set of all non-negative real numbers in this paper. The same result is obtained without any modification for the set of all non-negative integers as a time set.

A discrete event system is a special time system defined as follows:

Definition 1: Discrete event system [6]

A time system $S \subseteq X \times Y$ is a discrete event system if satisfies the following conditions:

(i) S is strongly stationary[4, 5].

(ii) S is past-determined[4, 5] from $k \in T$.

(iii) The input space X is a discrete event input space. That is,

(iii-1) The input alphabet A for X is $P(A')$ which is the power set of A'.

(iii-2) The constant valued function $\bar{\Lambda}$ is in X, where $\bar{\Lambda}(t) = \Lambda$ for any $t \in T$ and Λ is the empty set.

(iv) S has the discrete event-determinacy: For any $(\bar{x}^k, \hat{y}^k) \in S^k$, $(x^k, y^k) \in S^k$,

$c \in S(\Lambda)$, $x' \in X$ and $y' \in Y$, if $(\bar{x}^k \bullet \Lambda_k, \hat{y}^k \bullet \sigma^k(c)) \in S$, $(x^k \bullet \Lambda_k, y^k \bullet \sigma^k(c))$

$\in S$ and $(\bar{x}^k \bullet \sigma^k(x'), \hat{y}^k \bullet \sigma^k(y')) \in S$ hold then $(x^k \bullet \sigma^k(x'), y^k \bullet \sigma^k(y')) \in S$.

In the rest of this paper $\bar{\Lambda}$ is simply denoted by Λ. The empty set Λ is called nonevent.

Definition 2: Dynamical system representation [5]

Let $S \subseteq X \times Y$ be a stationary system. A pair of families of mappings $<\varrho,$ $\phi>$ where $\varrho = \{\rho_t \mid \rho_t : C \times X_t \to Y_t$ and $t \in T\}$ and $\phi = \{\phi_{tt'} \mid \phi_{tt'} : C \times X_{tt'} \to C$ and $t, t' \in T, t \leq t'\}$ is a (time invariant) dynamical system representation of S if the following conditions are satisfied:

(i) ϱ is a response family of S.

That is, for each $t > 0$ and $(x_t, y_t) \in S_t$ there exists $c \in C$ such that $\rho_t(c, x_t) = y_t$ holds.

(ii) ϱ is time invariant.

That is, $\rho_t(c, x_t) = \sigma^t(\rho_0(c, \sigma^{-t}(x_t)))$ holds for each t, c and x_t.

(iii) Each function $\phi_{tt'}$ satisfies the following conditions:

(α) $\rho_t(c, x_t)|T_{t'} = \rho_{t'}(\phi_{tt'}(c, x_{tt'}), x_{t'})$ where $x_t = x_{tt'} \bullet x_{t'}$

(β) $\phi_{tt''}(c, x_{tt''}) = \phi_{t't''}(\phi_{tt'}(c, x_{tt'}), x_{t't''})$ where $x_{tt''} = x_{tt'} \bullet x_{t't''}$

(γ) $\phi_{tt}(c, x_{tt}) = c$

(iv) Each functions $\phi_{tt'}$ is time invariant.

That is, $\phi_{tt'}(c, x_{tt'}) = \phi_{0\tau}(c, \sigma^{-t}(x_{tt'}))$, where $\tau = t' - t$.

The family $\underline{\Phi}$ which satisfies the conditions (iii)-(β), (γ) and (iv) is called a family of time invariant state transition functions.

For a causal system we can decompose its dynamical system representation into a state space representation where the response family is decomposed. It is always possible to get a dynamical system representation from a state space representation.

Definition 3 State space representation [5]

Let $S \subseteq X \times Y$ be a stationary system with the input alphabet A and the output alphabet B. Let C be an arbitrary set. C is a state space for S if there exist a family of functions $\underline{\Phi} = \{\phi_{tt'} \mid \phi_{tt'} : C \times X_{tt'} \to C \text{ and } t, t' \in T, t \leq t'\}$ and a function $\mu : C \times A \to B$ such that

(i) $S = \{(x, y) \mid \text{there exists some } c \in C \text{ such that } y(t) = \mu(\phi_{0t}(c, x^t), x(t))$
for any $t \in T\}$

(ii) $\underline{\Phi}$ is a family of time invariant state transition functions.

The pair $<\underline{\Phi}, \mu>$ is called a (time invariant) state space representation of S.

In the case of a linear system S the linear space $S(0)$ of state responses is used as the canonical state space [5] , where $S(0) = \{y \mid (0, y) \in S \text{ and } 0 \text{ is the}$ constant function whose value is always $0\}$. Similar to this, for a discrete event system we will use the space $S(\Lambda)$ as a state space, where $S(\Lambda)$ is the set of all the response to the constant nonevent Λ. That is, $S(\Lambda)$ is the all possible behavior of the system without external event. Intuitively speaking, $S(\Lambda)$ holds all internal behavioral variety of the system.

In the following $S \subseteq X \times Y$ is an arbitrarily fixed discrete event system that is past-determined from k.

We have $S(\overline{X}) = S(\Lambda)$. Define the function $\rho_0 : S(\Lambda) \times X \to Y$ by the correspondence: $\rho_0(c, x) = y$ if and only if there exists $(\overline{x}^k, \hat{y}^k) \in S^k$ such that $(\overline{x}^k \cdot \Lambda_k, \hat{y}^k \cdot \sigma^k(c)) \in S$ and $(\overline{x}^k \cdot \sigma^k(x), \hat{y}^k \cdot \sigma^k(y)) \in S$ hold. The function ρ_0 is well-defined. The function ρ_0 defined above is an initial response function of S. That is, $(x, y) \in S$ if and only if there exists some $c \in S(\Lambda)$ such that $\rho_0(c, x) = y$. The function ρ_0 is reduced and causal.

Now we define the state space representation for a discrete event system. Let $t \in T$ be arbitrary. Define $\phi_{0t} : S(\Lambda) \times X_{0t} \to S(\Lambda)$ by $\phi_{0t}(c, x_{0\ t}) = \lambda^t(\rho_0(c, x^t \cdot \Lambda_t))$. Let $\underline{\Phi} = \{\phi_{tt'} \mid \phi_{tt'} : S(\Lambda) \times X_{tt'} \to S(\Lambda) \text{ and } t, t' \in T, t \leq t'\}$, where $\phi_{tt'}(c, x_{tt'})$ is defined as $\phi_{0\tau}(c, \sigma^{-t}(x_{tt'}))$ and $\tau = t'-t$. Define a function $\mu : S(\Lambda) \times A \to B$ as $\mu(c, a) = \rho_0(c, x)(0)$, where x is an arbitrary but $x(0) = a$. Since ρ_0 is causal, μ is well-defined. The pair $<\underline{\Phi}, \mu>$, that is called $S(\Lambda)$-realization, is a time invariant state space representation of S. The $S(\Lambda)$-realization is reachable. That is, for any c $\in S(\Lambda)$ there exist c' $\in S(\Lambda)$ and $x^k \in X^k$ such that $c = \phi_{0k}(c', x^k)$.

3 Uniqueness of DEVS Specification

We start this section by defining a way how to compare with two dynamical systems representations of a system.

Definition 4: Morphism [6]

Let $<\rho, \phi>$ and $<\rho', \phi'>$ be time invariant dynamical system representations of S. Then a mapping h: $C \to C'$ is called a morphism from $<\rho, \phi>$ to $<\rho', \phi'>$, if the diagrams in Fig. 2 are commute. That is, for any $t \in T$, $c \in C$ and $x \in X$, it holds that $\rho_t(c, x_t) = \rho'_t(h(c), x_t)$ and $h(\phi_{0t}(c, x^t)) = \phi'_{0t}(h(c), x^t)$. If h is bijective then $<\rho, \phi>$ is called isomorphic to $<\rho', \phi'>$.

A morphism h from $<\rho, \phi>$ to $<\rho', \phi'>$ is denoted by h : $<\rho, \phi> \to <\rho', \phi'>$.

We can have the dynamical system representation defined by $S(\Lambda)$-realization. In the following the dynamical system representation is also called $S(\Lambda)$-realization and is denoted by $<\rho^*, \phi^*>$. For discrete event systems the following property of dynamical system representations is imposed.

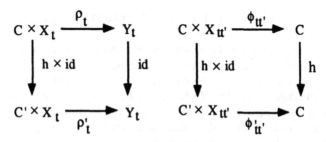

Fig. 2. Commutative diagram

Definition 5: Discrete event-response function

Let a function ρ_0: $C \times X \to Y$ be an initial response function of S. It is called a discrete event-response function of S if it satisfies the following condition: For any $c \in C$ and $x \in X$ there exist $c', c'' \in C$ and $\bar{x}^k \in X^k$ such that $\rho_0(c, \Lambda) = \lambda^k \rho_0(c', \bar{x}^k \cdot \Lambda_k)$, $\rho_0(c, x) = \lambda^k \rho_0(c'', \bar{x}^k \cdot \sigma^k(x))$ and $\rho_0(c', \bar{x}^k \cdot \Lambda_k)|[0, k) = \rho_0(c'', \bar{x}^k \cdot \sigma^k(x))|[0, k)$.

If ρ_0 of a dynamical system representation $<\rho, \phi>$ of S is a discrete event-response function then $<\rho, \phi>$ is called a discrete event dynamical system representation of S. It is easy to see for a dynamical system representation $<\rho, \phi>$ that ρ_0 is a discrete event-response function if and only if for any $c \in C$ and $x \in X$ there exists $(\bar{x}^k, \hat{y}^k) \in S^k$ such that $(\bar{x}^k \cdot \Lambda_k, \hat{y}^k \cdot \sigma^k[\rho_0(c, \Lambda)]) \in S$ and $(\bar{x}^k \cdot \sigma^k(x), \hat{y}^k \cdot \sigma^k[\rho_0(c, x)]) \in S$ hold.

The following theorem shows the uniqueness of $S(\Lambda)$-realization in the representations of discrete event systems.

Theorem 1 [6]

Let $<\rho, \phi>$ be a discrete event dynamical system representation of S and C its state space. Then there always exists a surjective morphism h : $<\rho, \phi> \to <\rho^*, \phi^*>$, which is defined by $h(c) = \rho_0(c, \Lambda)$.

We now will see that the state space representation for a legitimate DEVS and then the uniqueness of DEVS state space representation.

Since a legitimate DEVS specification can be extended to a state space representation $\langle \varrho, \phi \rangle$ as shown in [6],we can define the system S_D for a legitimate DEVS M, which shows the state transition of M.

$(x, y) \in S_D \subseteq X \times (Q_M)^T$ iff there exists $(s, e) \in Q_M$ such that $y(t) = \mu(\phi_{0t}(s, e, x^t), x(t))$ for any $t \in T$.

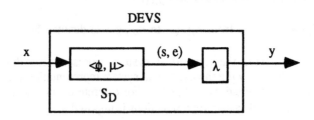

Fig. 3. The state system S_D of a DEVS specification

Since S_D represents the state transition mechanism of a legitimate DEVS M, it is called the state system of M. The pair $\langle \phi, \mu \rangle$ for S_D defined from a legitimate DEVS is called the DEVS state space representation (of M).

The state system S_D of a legitimate DEVS is stationary and past-determined from arbitrary positive time, and has a discrete event input space and the discrete event-determinacy. If the DEVS state space representation $\langle \phi, \mu \rangle$ for a legitimate DEVS M is reachable then S_D is strongly stationary.

The following theorem shows the minimality of the DEVS state space representation in the class of discrete event dynamical system representations.

Theorem 2 [6]

If the dynamical system representation that is defined by the DEVS state space representation for a legitimate DEVS is reduced and reachable then it is isomorphic to $S_D(\Lambda)$-realization, where S_D is the state system of the legitimate DEVS.

The result is interpreted as follows:
(1) If you find a real system which can be described as a (reachable and reduced) DEVS system, then you can manage it by working on the DEVS model. You do not miss important information on the discrete event dynamic mechanism of the real system, because the DEVS system provides universal representation.
(2) Similar to (1), many man-made discrete event systems can be engineered through DEVS models. Business processes are successfully investigated by multicomponent DEVS systems[6].

4 DEVS and Petri Net

A business transaction system is a model of routine processing in business functions such as order processing, inventory control, production control, financial aggregation and so forth. Business documents, slips, reports and note pads are common documents there, some of which are sometimes in a database. A business transaction system has two levels of description. Those are static and dynamic structures. The former consists of a file system, transaction names and the specification of interconnection between file names and transactions. The latter describes the dynamic behavior of a business system, which is a multicomponent DEVS.

The static structures have two kinds of transactions. They are external transactions and internal ones. Each activity causes modification of the corresponding data in the file. The description of the way these transactions are connected to corresponding file names are also in the static structure. Fig. 4 is an abstract simple example of a static structure of a business transaction system.

For example, in a sales department subsystem "issue order" is an external transaction whose record is added to the present file contents of "order" file. In Fig. 4, e_1 and e_2 are external transactions. If the box with e_1 were "issue order" then the oval with k_2 represents the order file. The arrow from el to k_2 shows this correspondence.

External transactions have no arrow that come into. If a box in a static structure has arrows that come into, then the box represents an internal transaction. The box al in Fig. 4 is an internal activity. Every internal transaction cannot start until some event arrives or appropriate data become available, such as orders from customers or the finish of a machine operation at the preceding stage in a assembly line. Since the arrival of any event can only be available through the records created by it, the start of any activity is decided by the incoming data.

The static structure of a business transaction system is defined as a combination of a file system, external transactions and internal transactions.

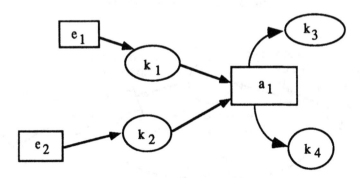

Fig. 4   Static structure of a business transaction system

The static structure is a description of a business system from the point of view that a business system is a transaction processing system based on a structured data(file).

It can be shown that the static structure actually defines static components of the dynamic mechanism of the business transaction system[7]. A dynamic mechanism of transaction processing is formulated as a multicomponent DEVS[2]. A file system and external and internal transactions are incorporated into a state space representation. The whole multicomponent DEVS is called a business transaction system, and is a DEVS which has its own state space representation.

In the following we show the resemblance between business transaction systems and Petri nets. The way how a Petri net is related to a DEVS is not made clear yet. Here we give a possible correspondence between a certain class of Petri nets graph and static structures of business transaction systems. This correspondence seems to provide a way how a Petri net is realized by a DEVS.

Petri nets consist of Petri net graphs and tokens in them[3]. Fig. 5 shows the components of Petri net. Fig. 6 a simple machine shop example modeled by a Petri net. In the example the machine shop waits until an order appears and then machine the ordered part and send it out for delivery.

```
|         Transition: This represetns an
|                     event ocurrence

◯         Place: This represents a
                 condition.

●         Token: This represents that
                 the condition holds.

↘         Arrow : State transition
                  mechanism
```

Fig. 5. Components of a Petri net

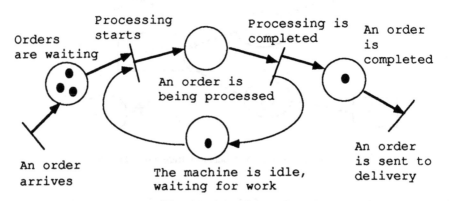

Fig. 6. Simple machine shop modeled by a Petri net

A relation between Petri nets and DEVS is given by a set of correspondence rules between static structures of business transaction systems and Petri nets graphs.

Some components in Petri net graph can be assigned to components of business transaction systems. In this sense a certain Petri net graph is realized by a multicomponent DEVS. The four correspondence rules are depicted in Fig. 7.

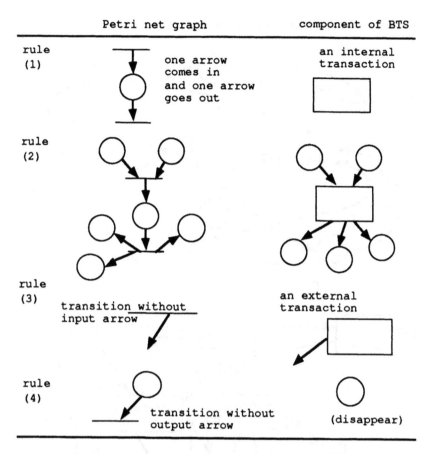

Petri net graph	component of BTS

rule (1) — one arrow comes in and one arrow goes out — an internal transaction

rule (2)

rule (3) — transition without input arrow — an external transaction

rule (4) — transition without output arrow — (disappear)

Fig. 7. Correspondense rules between Petri nets and DEVS

Fig. 8 is the correspondent business transaction system for the simple machine shop in Fig. 6.

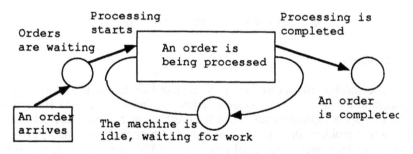

Orders are waiting — Processing starts — An order is being processed — Processing is completed

An order arrives — The machine is idle, waiting for work — An order is completed

Fig. 8. Simple machine shop modeled by a DEVS

The set of correspondence rules does not allow us to convert all of Petri net graphs into business transaction systems. Right now we can only show the fact that some of important discrete event mechanisms are modeled by both Petri net graphs and business transaction systems, which are "equal" under the correspondence rules.

A. Just-in-time inventory control (Kanban system)

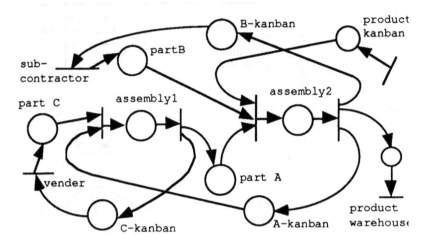

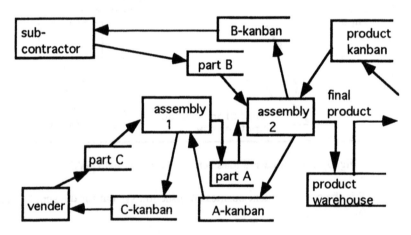

Fig. 9. Just-in-time system (Kanban system)

5 Conclusion

The construction shown here is an attempt how to construct a state space representation for discrete event systems defined as input-output data along time. Also the state space representation, called S(Λ)-realization, has provides a solution to the uniqueness problem for discrete event systems. Through the minimality of S(Λ)-realization we have seen a universal property of DEVS formalism. In this sense DEVS formalism is shown to be a fundamental framework in modeling discrete event systems.

In order to investigate a way how to relate Petri nets and the DEVS formalism, we have used the framework of business transaction systems. Since it has a static structure that is seemingly similar to Petri net graphs, some important discrete structures can be modeled both by Petri nets and by business transaction

B. The dining philosophers problem

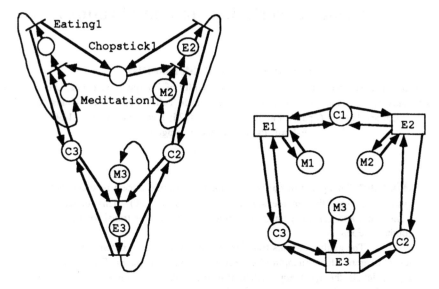

Fig. 10. The dining (three) philosophers

systems the latter of which is in a form of multicomponent DEVS. They are equivalent in the sense that we can provide a set of correspondence rules. It is a future research topic to establish wider correspondence between DEVS and Petri nets modeling facilities.

References

[1] B. P. Zeigler, *Theory of modelling and simulation.* John Wiley, 1976.

[2] ___, *Multifaceted modeling and discrete event simulation.* Academic, 1984.

[3] J. Peterson, Petri net theory and the modeling of systems, Prentice-Hall, 1981.

[4] M. D. Mesarovic and Y. Takahara, *Mathematical foundation of general systems theory.* Academic, 1975.

[5] ___, *Abstract systems theory.* (Lecture Notes in Control and Information Science 116), Springer, 1989.

[6] R. Sato, H. praehofer, F. Pichler: Realization theory of general discrete event systems and the uniqueness problem of DEVS formalism, Inst. of Socio-Economic Planning DP-625, University of Tsukuba, 1995.

[7] R. Sato and H. praehofer: A Discrete Event System Model of Business System - A Systems Theoretic Foundation for Information Systems Analysis: Part 1, submitted.

Intersensorial Transformations: General Systems Description and Implications

C. P. Suárez Araujo; R. Moreno-Díaz.

Department of Computer Sciences and Systems, Faculty of Computer Sciences, University of Las Palmas de Gran Canaria, Campus Universitario de Tafira, 35017 Las Palmas de G.C., Canary Islands (Spain). Phone: +34-28-458725; Fax: +34-28-458711/60
E-Mail: Paz@neurona.dis.ulpgc.es

Abstract. This paper has a theoretic nature. We introduce a new concept in systems theory, the intersensorial transformations (IT). This concept is transparent and general enough to include sensory-motor transformations for robotic actions.

The analysis of this transformations leads to the existence of various levels of generalized mapping between representation spaces. From lower to higher levels the most appropriate transformations are the artificial neural networks which cover from lineal transformations to diagnostic like transformations to go through automata transformations.

This concept allows to explain aspects of functional no specificity and reliability of complex systems. In the same way they supply an appropriate theoretic framework for developing integrated intelligent artificial systems having reasonable paradigmatic value for natural systems: the Generating Identifications Artificial System (GIAS), Reproductive Identifications Artificial System (RIAS), and for providing generalized sensory protheses.

1 Introduction

The principal goal of behaviour of natural systems is to provide identifications or diagnosis of a global situation, giving the possibility of planification and execution of and action. This requires to consider process of multinesorial integration because of the convergency in a diagnosis needs cooperative processing of the multisensorial information [1].

The process of the global identification has a multilevel structure, and it operates on data whose nature goes from the physical-chemical to non semantic sensorial data, low semantic content sensorial data, multisensorial with high semantic content and symbolic [2]. The preprocessed sensorial data feed a classifier which generates the local symptoms. Another classifier using this local symptoms and all previous information gives responses of differential nature, called the evolution symptoms. The last step uses together both kind of symptoms and an environment model in order to reach the global identification, Fig. 1.

From the behavioural point of view, multisensorial integration is directed towards three essentials goals: a) To increase the discriminant power of the sensory system because it will allow to separate classes of situations which are not separable by means of a single sensory modality, b) to accelerate and optimize the diagnostic and identification process, using intersensorial clues [3], c) to give reliability to the system by means of intersensorial information [1]. This last goal introduce the possibility to solve the problems caused by lesion of some neural/sensorial structure or by low flow of input information. From this point of view is necessary the existence of some neural or computational structure, in natural or artificial systems respectively, which allow handling this intersensorial information. This structure must perform a transformation such that the crossed sensorial information between different sensorial modalities can be translated by a sensorial modality as an "mental image" related to lesioned sensorial modality. A theoretical explanation and solution for this last capacity is provided by the Intersensorial Transformations [1, 4]. This is a new concept in systems theory, which will allow to explain aspects of functional no specificity and reliability of complex systems, as natural systems. In the same way the concept of IT supply an appropriate theoretic framework for developing artificial systems having reasonable paradigmatic value for central nervous systems, as a generalized robotic systems, and for providing generalized sensory protheses. We present a concept which is transparent and general enough to include sensory-motor transformations for robotic actions. The theoretical proposal permits fresh looks at fields like multisensorial integration, sensory-based decision and recognition.

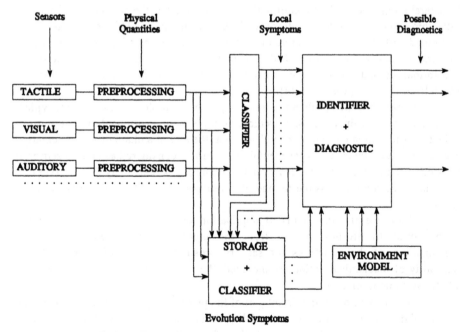

Fig. 1. Diagnostic scheme using multisensorial integration.

A fundamental aspect in the analysis of the IT is the level where they are present in the sensory-effector chain. In the natural systems they are present at medium and high level. This analysis will lead to the existence of various levels of generalized mapping between representation spaces. From lower to higher levels we will show that the most appropriate transformations are the artificial neural networks which cover from lineal transformations to diagnostic like transformations to go through automata transformations. This kind of transformation are the best since they present learning process which is vital so that specific computational structures can work without specificity and can supply functions which have been eliminated by lesions. An important potentiality of IT is in its implications artificial perception systems. They will permit to obtain intelligent artificial systems capable to generate identifications and to reproduce them. We will present two generalized schemes corresponding to: 1) *generating identifications artificial system*, 2) *reproductive identifications artificial system*, with an extended general structure for the integration of perception-planification-action. This schemes will be usefull for the synthesis of generalized robotic systems, as a paradigm of functional structure of natural system.

The concepts presented in this paper allow to propose a first scheme of a theoretical frame where said goals can be approached.

2 Intersensorial Transformations

In general an intersensorial transformation is understood as the conversion of sensory data from a sensory modality into data of another modality. This transformation is performed with the broad objective of recognizing properties of forms or patterns of the first modality by means of the second. The problem of the intersensorial transformation had its origin and inspiration in the analysis of the structure for generalized sensory prostheses [4].

In essence, such problem correspond, in their simplest cases, with the typical question of the transduction, which is more familiar in the instrumentation of physics. In fact, considering a normal human observer at the end of a chain of instrumentation in an experiment, the same experimental chain can be considered as an intersensorial transformation that transforms sensory data not directly perceived by the observer into other data which are accessible by one of his sensory modalities, typically visual or auditory.

Consequently, the fields of application of an appropriate theory of the intersensorial transformations go from the theory of instrumentation, to the formalization of the structures for sensory prosthesis. When effectors with the possibility of mechanical action are included, the field of the use of sensory data in robotic systems is involved.

The IT will be an important part of the process of pattern recognition, so the sensory data corresponding to a modality A are sensed by the transductors or corresponding sensors and, in general, they feed a system of property extraction, classification and recognition, that is, a complex system of pattern recognition in sad modality.

On the other hand, starting from the appropriate representation space of another sensory modality B, there exist rules of synthesis or generation of sensory data that can be perceived, through the corresponding effectors, by any system having sensors for said modality. The structure of the representation space for the modality B has to be logically in agreement with the nature of the analysis and perception that the exterior system is going to realize on these data. The differential question in a system of intersensorial transformation consists in establishing correspondence transformation between the representation spaces for the modalities A and B [4].

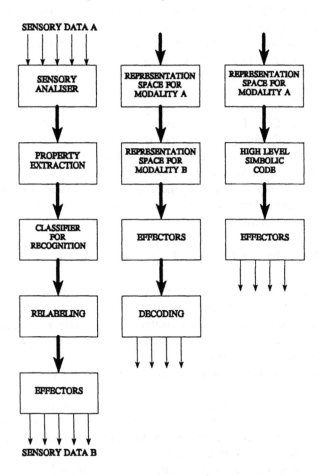

Fig. 2. General scheme for a system of Intersensorial Transformation.

These representation spaces are not, in principle, limited in their nature, and they can be spaces whose coordinates represent:

1) Physical quantities.

2) Functions of these quantities, as low-level properties of the input patterns.

3) Properties expressed at the semantic level and the same at the symbolic level.

Similarly, the nature of the representation space level in modality A has not, in principle, to coincide with the nature representation space level for modality B. That is, the space A can be represented in a level of physical properties, whereas the space B is at a symbolic level or viceversa.

The general scheme of a system that performs intersensorial transformation, according to the above, is shown in Fig. 2.

Consequently, the study of the intersensorial transformation, can be divided into three fundamental parts:

a) Generation of representation spaces, physical or abstract, for a sensory modality A, starting from the data sensed by a sensor or a mosaic of sensors. This problem coincides with the generation of representation spaces in pattern recognition.

b) Production of elementary sensory data, their sequences, elementary actions or sequences of them, for a different modality B starting from their own representation space. The generation of patterns, visual or auditory, as well as, in general, the generation of robotic chain reactions, fall into this area.

c) The establishment of the appropriate transformations or correspondences, which permit to go from representation space of the modality A to of the modality B. As indicated previously, these correspondences are peculiar and characteristic for the system of intersensorial transformation, and the operation c), are the most important to intersensorial transformation.

2.1 Production of Sensory Data from Representation Spaces

The typical situations in which it is necessary to generate sensory patterns from representation spaces or equivalent spaces are essentially two:

a) Reconstruction from a representation space, in the same sensory modality of the inputs, with the objective to determine similarity and discrepancy between the initial and the reconstructed stimuli.

b) Generation of sensory patterns from a basic alphabet, plus composition rules.

The situation a) appears in the schemes of recognition and classification of patterns. There, once property representation spaces are built, it is normal to realize a first test for the validity of the representation in said space, that logically have a very reduced information content. The test proceeds from descriptors corresponding to a point of said space, reversing the transformation that produced it and generating a new sensory pattern of the same modality. The new pattern will differ less from the original as more appropriate the reduced representation is. An simple example of a common situation of this type of reconstruction is the following: If the pattern had been characterized by a Fourier representation, the representation space corresponds to the terms of the series once truncated or band limited. The reconstruction, consequently, tries to generate a new pattern for the same modality, but built, in general, from much less terms. In this case, reconstruction consists in summing the corresponding terms, with their appropriates amplitudes and phases.

The second case of production of sensory data consists of their generation from a basic alphabet, which contains different sensory stimuli to can be considered as elementary units. For example in the visual case, the alphabet to generate white an black patterns consists in the different possible levels for each pixel. For generation of colour patterns, the alphabet can consist of the possible levels of intensity for each of the chromatic components. Note that in the first case there exists only one element of alphabet for each pixel, whereas in the second there are three symbols. This situation is so in general, that is to say, the symbols can appear simultaneously, all or in part.

The next component in this type of patterns is the existence of a rule or rules of composition, in such a way that to a point in the representation space there corresponds a group of elements of the selected alphabet which are composed according to the rule. Following with the previous example, the generation of random patterns in white and black will suppose the selection of an element of the alphabet according to some random dicision rule: Colour random patterns are generated similarly.

To project the representation space into the sensory space we can follow the options of:

b_1) Keep the rule fixed and change the elements of alphabet that are selected, according to the point being considered.

b_2) Keep the elements of alphabet and change the rule of composition.

b_3) Mixed situation of the previous.

In the generation of auditory patterns, if elements of alphabet are pure tones, the option b_1) will suppose to considerer a single tone, pairs of tones, triplets of tones, and so on, with a single composition rule, for example, to play them as a chord or in sequence [1,4].

The option b_2) will consist in taking always all the basic tones and play them in a type or other of sequences, according to the point being considered in the representation space (permutation of the elements of alphabet).

The option b_3) is, evidently, the mix of chords and sequences.
The more appropriate solution for a concrete application will have to be decided according to the discriminatory capacity of the receiver under consideration.

2.2 Correspondence Between the Representation Spaces

If we try to identify the concept of IT in natural systems we must referring to medium and high level in the sensorial pathways. A formal analysis leads to existence of various levels of generalized mapping between representation spaces. The main goal is to find the more appropriate transformations in order to cover all possibilities, and in the same time can explain its existence and behaviour in natural system. We propose a structured study starting from low level until high level. We present the formal framework corresponding to different levels of mapping between representation spaces.

In general a representation space is built taking as coordinates those significant parameters that can be measured in the input sensory configuration. In this sense, a group of values for such parameters, serves to characterize the corresponding input pattern.

To decide whether selected parameters to characterize the stimuli are or not significant, their utility in a recognitions normally considered. The typical way to determine what parameters are significant consists in the application of heuristic procedures, followed by the corresponding experimentation that determines the practical utility or signification of the selected parameters [4].

We consider initially representation spaces of medium-level, that they are continuous spaces of a dimension N, and that, for a sensory modality A, are given by coordinates $(\alpha_1, \alpha_2, \ldots \ldots \alpha_N)$. A point $(\alpha_1, \alpha_2, \ldots \ldots \alpha_N)$, in this space, corresponds to values of such parameters that characterize a concrete input sensory pattern. The nature of the α_1 has to be such that the distance between two points of representation spaces gives a measure of the similarity or discrepancy among the corresponding sensory pattern. This distance is any of the normally used in pattern recognition (Euclidian, Mahalanobis, etc.).

The representation space for the sensory modality B has a similar structure through of different dimension, M.

Let $(\beta_1, \beta_2, \ldots \ldots \beta_M)$ be the parameters that characterize this second representation space. In general, a correspondence between both spaces is any rule of transformation, such that:

$$\beta = \Gamma(\alpha) \tag{1}$$

Where α, β, are vectors in the corresponding spaces, and Γ, in principle, is an arbitrary transformation, including those of algorithmic nature, which work taking as data values of (α_i), to generate the values of (β_j). The differential question is to find the must appropriate Γ.

The simplest case corresponds to lineal transformations, that is:

$$\beta = \alpha \; C \tag{2}$$

If β and α are horizontal vectors, C, is a matrix M×N, of real or complex numbers according to the representation spaces A and B.

A requisite for this type of transformations is to keep the topology of the representation spaces, if in space A, two points corresponding to two patterns are close, this closeness is retained in the space B. This condition holds if the Euclidean distance between two initial points, d_A, and the distance between the transformed points, d_B, have a relation of the type:

$$d_B = \psi(d_A) \tag{3}$$

Where ψ is a monotonous increasing function, such that $\psi(0) = 0$.

The more simple example of monotonous increasing relation is:

$$d_B = K d_A \tag{4}$$

For this case, the conditions in the matrix are immediate:

$$d_B^2 = \beta\beta' = \alpha\ CC'\ \alpha' = \alpha\ \Gamma\ \alpha' \tag{5}$$

When

$$\Gamma = K'I \tag{6}$$

Where I is the identity matrix. Therefore:

$$d_B^2 = K'\ \alpha\ \alpha' = K'\ d_A^2 \tag{7}$$

That is, C has to be an orthogonal matrix, since such matrices be have like orthogonal vectors in Hilbert spaces:

$$HH' = H'H = I \tag{8}$$

The previous formulation permits an immediate generalization for the case of transformations given by:

$$\beta_i = F_1\ (\alpha_1, \alpha_2, \ldots, \alpha_N) \tag{9}$$

Where F_i is a derivable function up to order L, in point $(\alpha_1, \alpha_2, \ldots \alpha_N)$. In this case, it results:

$$\beta_i = F_1\ (0, \ldots, 0) + \left(\frac{\partial F_i}{\partial \alpha_i}\right) \alpha_i + \tfrac{1}{2} \left(\frac{\partial^2 F_i}{\alpha\partial_i\ \partial\alpha_j}\right) \alpha_i\ \alpha_j + \ldots \tag{10}$$

This expression, evidently, includes the lineal case.

One case of transformation F, which permits to link the above with the theory of actions in robotic systems, is to allow F to represent a finite automaton. In this case it is necessary to increase the content of the rule of transformation to include the new space of the possible states of the automaton. This operation is equivalent to insert a finite automaton between the representation spaces A and B which accepts the values of the parameters α as inputs and gives the values of space B as outputs. So, we will have that the corresponding transformation (with memory) can be expressed by the quintuple:

$$G = \{\alpha, \beta, S, S = g(\alpha, S), \beta = f(\alpha, S)\} \tag{11}$$

In the same way, the spaces β and S can coincide. The formulation is then simplify in the triplet given by Eq. (12).

This last formulation, corresponds to the formal neural networks.

$$G = \{\alpha, \beta, \beta = g(\alpha, \beta)\} \tag{12}$$

Other type of possible transformations, between representation spaces, are those used in diagnostic theory [2]. They relate parameters in representation spaces that cover all the range from the parameters of physical-chemical nature to behaviour, and even, high level stimuli-response by using natural languages.

From lower to higher levels the most appropriate transformations are the artificial neural networks (ANNs), whose neurodynamic and learning process are given by the following general formal expressions[5, 6].

$$\frac{d\beta_i}{dt} = \sum_{j=1}^{N} w_{ij}\,\alpha_{ij} - \Theta(\beta_i)$$

$$\tau\,\frac{dw}{dt} = -\frac{\partial}{\partial w}\,R\,(\boldsymbol{\alpha}(t),\,\delta(t),\,w(t)) \tag{13}$$

In the first expression w_{ij} are the synaptic weights between neurons i and j of ANN. β_i is the output of neuron i, α_{ij} are the input signals to neuron i. The term $-\Theta(\beta_i)$ stands for a non linear leakage effect that describes all nonideal properties such as saturation leakage, and shunting effects of the neuron [5], so Θ can be considered as a threshold function of the neuron. The second expression, which represents a general learning rule, δ can or not be present, depend on kind of learning and is defined as the teacher signal, R is a function called instantaneous learning potential [6], and $w(t)$ and $\alpha(t)$ are the synaptic weight and input vectors respectively.

They cover from lineal transformations to diagnostic like transformations to go through automata transformations, because an equivalent representation for ANNs are the finite automata and its activation function can be represented by whatever transformations mentioned before. This kind of transformation has a high paradigmatic value for the central nervous system because it has learning capacity which is vital because specific computational structures can work without specificity and can learn to perform functions which have been eliminated by lesions, so they can face whatever situation and to adapt oneself. Furthermore, these kind of transformations are biologically plausible, because along the sensor-effector chain in natural system are neural structures, into biological neural network, which perform such processes of intersensorial transformations giving reliability to the system.

3 Implications

Once we have done a general systems description of IT, we present its potentiality and implication in natural and artificial systems.

The most important implication refers to possibility both to understanding the behaviour of natural systems with innate and acquired sensorial pathologies and to obtaining artificial systems as paradigm of such natural systems. We will propose a generalized frame for architecture of intelligent artificial systems which will be capable to generate and reproduce global identifications and diagnostics: Generating Identifications Artificial System (GIAS), and the Reproductive Identifications Artificial System (RIAS).

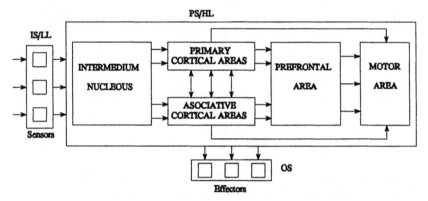

Fig. 3. Structural diagram of natural systems.

A General Robotic System (GRS) is understood as an intelligent artificial system capable to interact with the real world by employing their advances mechanism which allow sensing, perceiving and interpreting of the environment, capable also of computing appropriate strategies of action and planification in order to change the state of their environment by using the effectors [7, 8]. The design of such complex systems should be approached at different levels of abstraction. At a higher level one's interest is to propose an architecture for the system, this is our principal goal. In order to reach this objective we must be consider the main systemic requirements of GRS. These include system efficiency, modularity, flexibility, complexity, generality, man-machine interaction, portability [8], and two more, which should be taking into account in our general frame, because we are introducing the concepts of intersensorial transformations and multisensorial integration. These are reliability and natural flavour.

Important questions came up when we face this challenging action: a) How sensation-perception-action can be integrated?. b) How a GRS with all its systemic requirements can be obtained?. The only solution is to propose artificial systems biologically inspired.

Natural systems have a organizational/functional bottom-up structure which integrates perception-planification-action on sensed information. This structure is configured in three fundamental stages: a) Input Stage/Low Level (IS/LL), b) Processing Stage/High Level(PS/HL), c) Output Stage (OS), Fig. 3.

The natural systems use a set of cortical areas which perform a high level function by means parallel and cooperative processing [1]. The primary cortical areas perform, with the intermedium nucleus, **perception**, associative cortical areas realize the **interpretation** of the situation, and the prefrontal area cover the **planification**. In this last area is also performed and multicortical integration. Finally the motor area allow to execute the action by means the effectors of the system. The system proposed by us upholds this functional structure.

According with this an integrated intelligent robotic system can be consists of subsystems of sensory, perception, planning and control, and action. Our proposal is focused in perception stage based on previous development [1, 7, 9, 10, 11].

A simplified representation of various medium level cortical functions, as they are normally accepted in brain theory is typical process of sensory integration, whose goals are the diagnostics of an overall external sensory situation [3], by means a classification and labelling process performed on preprocessed sensory data by the primary sensory cortex (PSC). The messages being transmitted to the primary sensory cortex are already represented in a language which probably is much more complex than the usual pulse code normally accepted in neurophysiology [3].

This classification and labelling are a consequence of mapping in representation spaces and of applying classification and decision rules which are acquired either by learning or by instint.

This representation adscribs to PSC processors an almost total specifity, which is not true neither in PSC not in associative cortex. If we assume that a lesion in the specific pathways happens, the processors corresponding to the primary sensory cortex will became out of use. However, that is not strictly the case [3]. Also, the drawbacks which result from primary sensory cortex lesions can be diminished after training, such that the eliminated function is partly assumed by the remaining cortical structures.

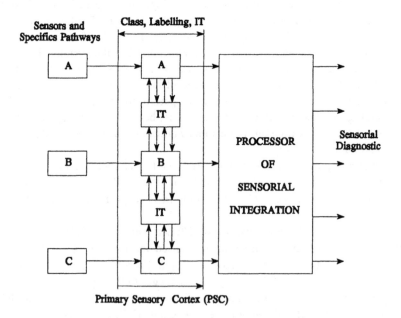

Fig. 4. Scheme of medium level cortical functions with IT.

The above can, in principle, be expressed in terms of a global behavioural goal, as it was done before for multisensorial integration. It is as follows: There exists an adaptive sharing of the specific structures of different sensory modalities, such that, after learning, intersensorial information can be utilized to increase reliability and to tend to optimize the use of the structures which remain after lesions or when there is a low information input in a sensory pathway, or when the "sensorial interpreter" is broken.

In terms of intersensorial transformations, there is a simple theoretical solution providing a new interpretation of this behaviour, Fig. 4.

According to this proposal, there are intersensorial transformations between the processors specific to each sensory modality. It is necessary to distinguish two questions related to the way in which these transformations operate. First, the transformation came into play: 1) When there is an overflow of sensory information from a sensory pathway (A) to their more central specific processors, and there are dimensions which are free in the representation spaces of other sensory modalities (B, C). This overflow may appear as a consequence of a traumatic reduction in the specific processors functionality of (A). The transformation proceeds from (A) to (B, C). 2) When, because a traumatic lesion or circumstantial effects, there is a low sensory flow from the sensory pathways of a modality (A), which has free dimensions in their representation space. These free dimensions can be occupied by data through transformation from other sensory modalities (B, C).

The second and important aspect is that the role on the new symbolic data which are present in a different representation space must be learned according to the total experience of the system. The subsequent labelling must take into account the heterosensory nature of the data was utilized to label points in the representation space.

Therefore, we can see that the IT can explain that the functional specifity is less dogmatic and more circumstantial as more central zones are considered in a sensory pathway. We can also deduce that should have computational and neural structures which can work without specifity and it also can learn to perform the functions of lesions structures. An essential capacity in order to reach all this potentiality, is the learning capacity which is solved using ANNs both in the IT and in the general architecture

According with these statements we can deduce that the IT will allow us to obtain paradigms of natural system with innate and acquired sensorial pathologies. In these systems the pattern recognition of a sensory modality (V) using the sensorial data of another sensorial modality (A) is considered as a global behavioural goal. The final identification will be generated or reproduced and they need a learning process using each one of them different specific knowledge. We propose a generalized frame for an architecture of an intelligent artificial system which presents integration of perception-planification-action with this potentiality, Fig. 5.

In this architecture the subsystem of perception, where the IT takes place, operates in accordance with the step by step scheme for representing multisensorial data, whereas the planning system operates according to integrated scheme. Is also important to note the existence of direct connection between sensors and effectors which can be equivalents to reflex signals in natural systems. This direct communication is not to much exact in the present stage of the nervous system of vertebrates. The direct perception-action is established at somatic level of our brain by means of "monosynaptic reflex arch" [12] . This neural circuit can be consider in our intelligent artificial system, as a reflected system of safety (RSS). This subsystem is appropriate for controlling motor actions. It will be capable to detect global errors which should produce an unsuccessful motor action generating a high spending of computational time. In this sense our safety system should balance the system. In general, the idea is that our subsystem avoids disharmony between perception-action.

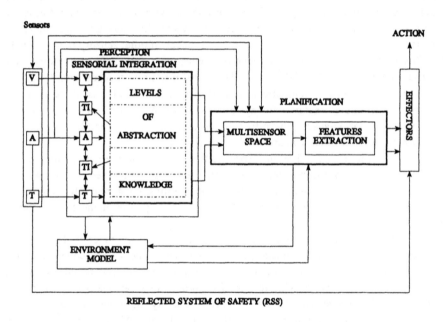

Fig. 5. General architecture for integration perception-planification-action in general robotic systems (GRS).

From this frame we can obtain both the Generating Identifications Artificial System (GIAS), and the Reproductive Identifications Artificial System (RIAS), capable to generate and reproduce identifications. These systems will represent a paradigm of natural systems previously mentioned. They will use different specific information for learning processing in order to reach the final diagnostic. The GIAS will handle the knowledge supplied by an environment model and the sensorial patterns. The RIAS will use abstractions from stored knowledge, built while the system has not pathology, and sensorial patterns too. The fundamental difference in the behaviour of these artificial systems is that in both cases the semantic global identification is the same but the real knowledge abstractions in RIAS, or lesioned modality, are different.

Conclusions

As conclusions we can say that we have introduced a new concept in system theory, the Intersensorial Transformations IT, proposing the artificial neural networks as the more appropriate transformation of correspondence between representation spaces. An important advantage of ANNs is its learning capacity, which provides important potentialities in intelligent artificial systems. The IT permit fresh looks at fields like sensory integration, sensory-based decision and recognition, they supplies a theoretical framework for generalized robotic systems, and provide systems with a reasonable paradigmatic value for natural systems. The name of these artificial systems are: Generating Identifications Artificial System (GIAS), and Reproductive Identifications Artificial System (RIAS). They also supply system architecture for generalized sensory prothesis. They provide new ideas on computational style of the brain. Their more appealing aspect is to handle both natural and artificial systems in a parallel way working like a reciprocal metaphor.

All this confirm that our developments gives a stepfordward not only in Systems Theory but in the field of Computational Neuroscience.

References

1. C.P. Suárez Araujo: Contribuciones a la Integración Multisensorial y Computación Neuronal Paralela. Aplicaciones. Doctoral Thesis. University of Las Palmas de Gran Canaria 1990.

2. J. Simoes Da Fonseca, R. Moreno-Díaz, J. Mira: Conditions for a theory of Diagnostics. In: Proc. Conf. on General Systems Research. Intersystems Pub. 1983, pp. 675-678.

3. J. Mira, R. Moreno-Díaz, A. Delgado, C.P. Suárez Araujo: Intersensory Communication in Machines as a Paradigm of Cortical Reliability. In: J. Rose (ed.): Cybernetics and Systems. Proc. 7th Int. Congress of Cybernetics and Systems Vol.1. England: Thales Publications (W.O.) 1987, pp. 432-438.

4. C.P. Suárez Araujo, R. Moreno-Díaz: New Concept in Systems Theory: Intersensorial Transformations. Orw. Symposium and Int. Conference on Systems Research Informatics. Germany 1984.

5. T. Kohonen: The "Neural" Phonetic Typewriter. Computer Vol. 21, N° 3, 11-24 (1988).

6. S. Amari: Mathematical Foundations of Neurocomputing. In: Neural Networks, I: Theory and modeling. Proceedings of the IEEE Vol.78, N° 9, 1443-1463, (1990).

7. R. Moreno-Díaz, J. Mira Mira: Architectures for Integrating Artificial Perception and Action. Proceedings of Interkibernetic'87. Tarragona. 1987.

8. Ch. Chen, M.M. Trivedi: Task Planning and Action Coordination in Integrated Sensor-Based Robots. IEEE Transactions on Systems, Man and Cybernetics Vol. 25, N° 4, 569-591 (1995).

9. L.L. Sutro, R.E. Warren, D. Moulton, C. Whitman, F. Zeise: Advance Sensor Investigations. R-470 Instrumentation Laboratory. Cambridge, MASS: MIT, 1964.

10. L.L. Sutro, W. Kilmer, W.S. McCulloch, R. Catchpole, D. Tweed, J. Blum, D. Peterson, R. Moreno-Díaz: Sensory Decision and Control Systems. R-548 Instrumentation Laboratory. Cambridge, MASS: MIT, 1966.

11. L.L. Sutro, W. Kilmer: Assembly of Computers to Command and Control a Robot. R-582 Instrumentation Laboratory. Cambridge, MASS: MIT, 1969.

12. W.J.H. Nauta, M. Feirtag: Organización del Cerebro. In: El Cerebro. Libros de Investigación y Ciencia. Prensa Científica. 1987, pp. 53-68.

Proving System Properties by Means of Trigger-Graph and Petri Nets

E. M. Thurner
Siemens AG, ZFE T SN 1
D - 81370 München

The formal description of hardware protocols allows system engineers to check these protocols for some important properties, such as completeness and consistency. In this paper, a methodology called trigger graph is introduced. It uses a notation that is similar to timing diagrams, but it strictly avoids their disadvantage of being ambiguous. In addition, the exact mathematical notation of the trigger graph gives the possibility to transform it into Petri nets. This gives the benefit to use methods developed for Petri nets also for the check of hardware protocols, for example to check them for security conditions. The trigger graph methodology is illustrated with three realistic examples: the control of traffic lights, the control of a railway-barrier, and the read-protocol for a DRAM.
Key Words: Formal description, verification, hardware protocol, bus protocol, timing diagram, trigger graph, Petri nets

Introducing the Problem

For hardware developers, timing diagrams are a widely-used description method for the functional behaviour, dependencies and timing specifications of hardware protocols. Examples for hardware protocols are the specification of a traffic light, the control of a lift, or the specification of a bus protocol. However, there is no formal definition for this method. Thus, it cannot be used for the formal specification and verification of hardware protocols – even if it is widely used as a basis for discussion and informal checks. On the other hand, some attempts to introduce a formal description method for timing diagrams were not very successful, because they considered only a part of their semantics.

In this paper, a formal description method is introduced that allows to represent the full semantics of timing diagrams. This method has the benefit of being similar enough to timing diagrams, to enable hardware engineers to use them without the effort of learning. What is even more important, is the possibility to check hardware protocols formally by this method for some interesting protocol properties like completeness and consistency. This method uses a class of directed acyclic graphs (DAG) with particular attributes of their points and edges to represent hardware protocols. We will call this DAG the *trigger graph (TG)* of a protocol. In addition, this trigger graph can be transformed into Petri nets in a formal way, and can also be used accordingly for the verification of hardware protocols.

Formal Specification of Hardware Protocols

In this chapter, the basic definitions for hardware protocols and trigger graphs are given. Furthermore, the way to transform trigger graphs into Petri nets is pointed out.

Hardware Protocols

The notion of hardware protocol is formulated in a precise way by analyzing all aspects of the semantics of a hardware protocol.

Convention (1a): Each signal is attributed with its *signal name*.
Examples for a signal name are RESET, ACK, DAT3.
Convention (1b): For signal bundles we use a common abbreviation:

> SIGNAL[from..to] :≡ SIGNALfrom, ... , SIGNALto

Example: ADR[0..7] ≡ ADR0, ADR1, ... , ADR7.

Definition (2): Each protocol signal is generated by at least one source. There are n concurrent talkers T and n concurrent listeners L, respectively. The *talkers* are characterized by starting the protocol (e.g. a bus operation). The *listeners* respond in compliance with the request of a talker. As an example, the address signals of a bus protocol are controled by the talker; data signals within read operations are controled by a listener. Furthermore, we introduce a particular data drain, marked by the suffix "f": At this class of signals, the output signals are led to the *same* bus agent. At last, a source called *Central Service Module* (CSM) is necessary, e.g. for system reset.
According to that, the set of sources in a protocol can be defined as a set

$$Source := \{ \; CSM \; , \; CSMf \; , \; T_1 \; , \; Tf_1 \; , \; L_1 \; , \; T_2 \; , \; Tf_2 \; , \; L_2 \; , \; ... \; , \; T_n \; , \; Tf_n \; , \; L_n \; \}$$

Note: The notions *talker* and *listener* have another meaning than the common *master* and *slave*. This is particularly clear at buses with interrupts: In a two-board-system with a CPU and an I/O-board, the controling CPU is called master-listener, the responding I/O-board is called master-talker. When the I/O-board sends an interrupt, it is called the slave-talker, the responding CPU is called the slave-listener.

Definition (3a): The set of *value changes of a signal* is determined by

$$\Xi_{bs} = \{ \; \xi_1 \; , \; \xi_2 \; , \; ... \; \} := \{ \; \langle \; \tau_\xi \; , \; val_\xi^- \; , \; val_\xi^+ \; , \; source_\xi \; \rangle \; , \; ... \; \}$$

In this definition τ_ξ describes the time (i.e. the moment) of the value change. val_ξ^- and val_ξ^+ mark the signal values before resp. after the change. $source_\xi$ is an element of the set *Source*.
Convention (3b): The *signal values* of a (bus) signal are part of the set

> $Val := \{ \; 0, 1, A, Z, U \; \}$

with

0	the signal *"Low"* (logically 0);
1	the signal *"High"* (logically 1);
A	the signal is *"High or Low" (activated);*
Z	the signal is *not driven;*
U	*undefined:* the signal is *irrelevant* for this particular protocol.

Note: The value Z means *not driven*; it is actually the idle value of the output driver. Therefore Z means "high resistance" at Tristate or "(weak) High" at Open Collector. The value A is often used for signal bundles. It describes a signal which is active and relevant for this protocol (i.e. "not U and not Z"). IN addition, the value A can be used to specify a *class* of signal behaviours, whose exact values must be delivered for each realization of this protocol.

Definition (4a): The temporal behaviour of a bus signal (*signal curve*) can be described by a pair

$$bs := \langle\ signal_{bs}\ ,\ \Xi_{bs}\ \rangle$$

where $signal_{bs}$ labels the signal name, and Ξ_{bs} is the set of value changes of the signal.
Definition (4b): bs is called *closed*, if

$$\exists x,y \in \Xi\ ,\ x \neq y : \tau_x \in min_\tau(\Xi) \wedge \tau_y \in max_\tau(\Xi) \wedge val^\Gamma_x = val^+_y$$

The signal value that can be measured before the first signal change and after the last one is called the *idle value* of this signal.
Now, we can define the notions of "particular protocol" and "entire protocol":
Definition (4c): A *particular protocol* π consists of m signal curves

$$\pi := \{\ bs_1\ ,\ bs_2\ ,\ ...\ ,\ bs_m\ \}$$

Definition (4d): A bus protocol π is called *valid*, if
- no signal curve is constant;
- all $bs \in \pi$ are closed (π is closed);
- the bus protocol π is complete, i.e. each action of a protocol has at least one cause
  - except   the   first   one.
  (A simple formulation for completeness can be given by means of the trigger graph.)

Definition (4e): The *entire protocol* Π of a bus is the set of its n particular protocols:

$$\Pi := \{\ \pi_1\ ,\ \pi_2\ ,\ ...\ ,\ \pi_n\ \}$$

According to that a particular protocol looks just like a well-defined timing diagram without dependencies between the signal curves. Therefore we have to extend our definitions to consider these dependencies. Afterwards, for better handling we will use a graph representation of the protocol, which is called its *trigger graph*.

Trigger-Graph

The trigger graph represents a hardware protocol as a sequence of signal changes and the dependencies that exist between these changes.
There are two types of signal dependencies:
- The dependencies "$\Rightarrow_u$": In most cases they carry timing intervals and specify timing contraints.
- The dependencies "$<_\xi$": In protocols, they are not specified explicitly, but they result from the linear order of the signal changes Ξ_{bs} of a bus signal.

Definition (5a): Let $bs = \langle\, signal_{bs}\,,\, \Xi_{bs}\,\rangle$ be a non-constant signal curve. According to that the signal changes for every bus signal can be defined as a set of tripels

$$U_{bs} := \{\, \langle a,b,c \rangle \in signal_{bs} \times \Xi_{bs} \mid (c \in \Xi \mid \tau_{min} \geq \tau_q \geq \tau_{max}) \wedge a = signal_{bs}\,\}$$

Definition (5b): Hence, we can define for a particular protocol: $U = \displaystyle\bigcup_{bs \in \pi} U_{bs}$

Definition (6): On the signal changes Ξ_{bs} we determine a relation "$<_\xi$" with

$$\xi_i <_\xi \xi_j :\Leftrightarrow \tau_{\xi i} < \tau_{\xi j} \qquad \text{for } i \neq j$$

Definition (7): There is a relation "$\Rightarrow_u$" between a cause u and an action w with

$$u \Rightarrow_u w :\Leftrightarrow \tau_{\xi u} < \tau_{\xi w} \qquad \text{with } u, w \in U$$

Agreement (8a): We call the *strong edges* of a protocol:

$$E_\Rightarrow (\pi) := \{\, \langle x,y \rangle \in U \times U \mid x \Rightarrow_u y\,\}$$

Convention (8a): The *weak edges* are:

$$E_< (\pi) := \{\, \langle x,y \rangle \in U \times U \mid x <_\tau y\,\} \setminus E_\Rightarrow (\pi)$$

Definition (9): Based on these definitions, we define the *trigger graph* of a hardware protocol as:

$$TG\,(\pi) = \langle\, V_{TG}\,,\, E_{TG}\,\rangle := \langle\, U\,(\pi)\,,\, E_\Rightarrow (\pi) \cup E_< (\pi)\,\rangle$$

The name of trigger graph indicates, that this kind of DAG specification covers all triggering and triggered signal changes of a protocol.

Transformation into Petri Nets

This section gives a transformation algorithm from the trigger graph into the Petri net class "synchronization graph". This transformation uses the circumstance, that hardware protocols have to be closed (see definition 4d). Accordingly, we can insert an additional "idle place" for every signal curve of the trigger graph. This idle place will be connected with the start transition $\rho l_T\,(V_{min})$ and the end transition $\rho l_V\,(V_{max})$ of the trigger graph. In each idle place is a token at the marking M_0.

Definition (10): Let $TG = \langle V_{TG}, E_{TG} \rangle$ be a trigger graph, $N° = \langle S_{N°}\,,\, T_{N°}\,,\, F_{N°}\,,\, M_{0,N°} \rangle$ be a marked synchronization graph.

Definition (10a): The set of signal names of the set of TG edges $X \subseteq V_{TG}$ is

$$Sig\,(X) := \{\, s \mid v \in X \wedge s = signal_v\,\}$$

According to that we define a mapping $\rho° : V_G \cup E_G \rightarrow S_{N°} \cup T_{N°} \cup F_{N°} \cup M_{0,N°}$ from a trigger graph into a marked synchronization graph:

$$T_{N°} := \rho°l_V\,(V_{TG})$$

$$S_{N°} := \rho°l_E\,(E_{TG}) \cup \rho°l_{Sig}\,(\,Sig\,(V_{TG})\,)$$

$$F_{N°} := \{\, \langle\, \rho l_V\,(x),\, \rho l_E\,(\langle x, y \rangle)\,\rangle\,,\, \langle\, \rho l_V\,(x),\, \rho l_E\,(\langle x, y \rangle)\,\rangle \mid \langle x, y \rangle\, E_{TG}\,\} \cup$$
$$\{\, \langle x, y \rangle \mid v \in V_{min} \wedge x \in \rho°l_V\,(v) \cup Sig\,(v) \wedge y \in \rho°l_V\,(v) \cup T_{N°}\,\} \cup$$
$$\{\, \langle x, y \rangle \mid v \in V_{max} \wedge x \in \rho°l_V\,(v) \cup T_{N°} \wedge y \in \rho°l_V\,(v) \cup Sig\,(v)\,\}$$

The marking M_0 is a mapping $m : S_{N°} \rightarrow \mathcal{N}_0$ with

$$M_0\,(s) := \begin{cases} 1 & \text{if } s \in Sig\,(V_{TG}) \\ 0 & \text{else} \end{cases}$$

Convention (10b): $\rho°\,(TG) = N°$

Proposition (10c): $\rho°$ *(TG)* is a marked synchronization graph with transitions at its border.

Proof: Therefore, we have to prove the following partial propositions:

(a) $\rho°$ *(TG)* is a Petri net.

(b) $\rho°$ *(TG)* fulfills the defintions for the calls of synchronisation graphs.

(c) $\rho°$ *(TG)* only has transitions at its border.

(d) The semantics of the trigger graph and the synchronisation graphs are similar.

(a)   (i) $S_{N°} \cup T_{N°} = \emptyset$ (elementary Petri net definition)

In accordance with def. (10a), we can say: $\rho°|_V (V_{TG}) \cup \rho°|_E (E_{TG}) = \emptyset$

Furthermore: *Sig* (V_{TG}) V_{TG}, due to *signal$_v$* $\neq v$

    (ii) $F_{N°}$ transforms either the edges of E_{TG}, which only generates edges $S \times T$ or $T \times S$. The connections from *Sig* (V_{TG}) and V_{min} resp. V_{max} only generates edges $S \times T$ or $T \times S$,

because $\rho°|_{Sig} ($ *Sig* $(V_{TG})) \subseteq S_{N°}$ and $\rho°|_V (V_{min} \cup V_{max}) \subseteq T_{N°}$.

(b) $\forall s \in S : |s| = 1 \wedge |s| = 1$

For all the placees of $\rho°|_E (E_{TG})$, a predecessor and a successor edge is generated. Analogously, for each place of $\rho°|_{Sig} ($ *Sig* $(V_{TG}))$ a predecessor and a successor edge is generated by the connection with $\rho°|_V (V_{min} \cup V_{max})$.

(c)   In $\rho°$ *(TG)* there are no absolute border nodes. Due to this, any set of nodes could be defined as border nodes. The following definitions makes sense for our purpose: *relRand* $(N, N') = relRand (\rho° (TG), \rho (TG)) \subseteq \rho°|_V (V_{min} \cup V_{max})$.

(d)   (i) The computing rules for the trigger graph are: The effective length of a path through the graph is the sum of the *maximums* of all the partial paths.

(ii) The firing rule for Petri nets is wellknown: a transition fires, when it is activated; it is activated, if

     ① $\forall s \in •t : M (s) \geq W (s, t)$ *and* ② $\forall s \in t• : M (s) \leq K (s) - W (t, s)$

(iii) The nodes of *TG* correspond to the transitions of $\rho°|_V$ *(TG)*. Now, part ① of the rule is fulfilled, if *all* the proconditions are fulfilled. That corresponds to the *max*-rule in the trigger graph. Part ② respects contact situations: There is no correspondence at the trigger graph. We can solve this problem (a) if we think, that a trigger graph is only run once. Or (b) we have to consider contact situations explicitly, as a speicification deficiency. (This will be done at the lights example.) ∎

Examples for Using the Trigger Graph Methodology

The usefulness of the trigger graph methodology, that has been defined above, will be shown considering three examples. These examples are chosen to demonstrate the verification of hardware protocols and discovering typical specification deficiencies in them:

1. *Control of traffic lights for pedestrians:*

This example shows the specification of timing constraints and the reduction of the trigger graph.

2. *A simple control of a railway-barrier:*
   This example shows how the trigger graph can be used for safety checks of a hardware protocol using Petri nets.
3. *A DRAM read protocol:*
   The protocol of a commercial DRAM is used to show deficiencies and inconsistencies in a timing diagram specification.

Control of traffic lights for pedestrians

In this section, the specification of a simple traffic lights control for pedestrians is considered. Using this protocol we will demonstrate the trigger graph methodology in detail, while the following sections will only care for the results, that can be gained by this methodology.

Timing Diagram. Fig. 1 shows the timing diagram of the traffic lights control. The signals for the car drivers are named C_red, C_yellow and C_green, the respective signals for the pedestrians P_red and P_green. The requesting button is called button; it is the only input signal of this protocol. The moments of signal changes are numbered from 1 to 8.

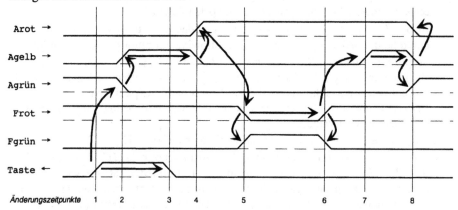

Fig. 1: Timing diagram of a traffic lights control for pedestrians

The functionality of the timing diagram is the following: When button is pressed, the traffic lights for drivers have to switch from green (C_green) to yellow (C_yellow) and to red (C_red). Afterwards, the traffic lights for pedestrians change from red (P_red) to green (P_green). After the switch from P_green to P_red, the drivers' lights become red and yellow, and then green again. button is assumed to be pressed only once and to be released before the end of the protocol. According to that, we formulate a protocol

$\pi_{Bsp1} = \{ bs_1 , \dots , bs_6 \} = \{ \langle signal_{bs1} , \Xi_{bs1} \rangle , \dots \}$

$\quad bs_1 = \langle signal_{bs1} = $ C_red$; \Xi_{bs1} = \{ \langle \tau = 4, val^- = 0, val^+ = 1, source_{bs1} = \rightarrow \rangle, \langle 8,1,0, \rightarrow \rangle \}$

$\quad bs_2 = \langle $ C_yellow$; \{ \langle 2,0,1, \rightarrow \rangle, \langle 4,1,0, \rightarrow \rangle, \langle 7,0,1, \rightarrow \rangle, \langle 8,1,0, \rightarrow \rangle \} \rangle$

$\quad bs_3 = \langle $ C_green$; \{ \langle 2,1,0, \rightarrow \rangle, \langle 8,0,1, \rightarrow \rangle \} \rangle$

$\quad bs_4 = \langle $ P_red$; \{ \langle 5,1,0, \rightarrow \rangle, \langle 6,0,1, \rightarrow \rangle \} \rangle$

$bs_5 = \langle$ P_green; $\{\langle 5,0,1,\rightarrow\rangle,\langle 6,1,0,\rightarrow\rangle\} \rangle$

$bs_6 = \langle$ button; $\{\langle 1,0,1,\leftarrow\rangle,\langle 3,1,0,\leftarrow\rangle\} \rangle$

Its dependencies are:

$E_{\_} \cap E_K = \{ \textcircled{1} \}$

$E_{\_} \cap E_T = \{ \textcircled{2}, \textcircled{3}, \textcircled{4}, \textcircled{5}, \textcircled{6}, \textcircled{7} \}$

$E_< \cap E_K = \{ (\langle$ C_red$,\rightarrow,t_4\rangle, \langle$ C_red $,\rightarrow,t_8\rangle), (\langle$ C_yellow $,\rightarrow,t_4\rangle, \langle$ C_yellow $,\rightarrow,t_7\rangle),$
$(\langle$ C_green $,\rightarrow,t_2\rangle, \langle$ C_green $,\rightarrow,t_8\rangle), (\langle$ P_green $,\rightarrow,t_5\rangle, \langle$ P_green $,\rightarrow,t_6\rangle) \}$

$E_< \cap E_T = \varnothing$

In this timing diagram the events $\{3,7\}$, $\{1,4\}$, $\{9,11\}$, $\{10,12\}$, and $\{2,6,8\}$ are coincident.

The timing specification for this protocol is given in Table 1 (the unit of measure is seconds). For the evaluation the timing of the weak edges is specified as $(0, \infty)$.

Table 1: Timing specifications for the traffic lights control

$\tau_x \rightarrow \tau_y$	name	$\vartheta_{min} .. \vartheta_{max}$
$1 \rightarrow 2$	ϑ_1 ①	5 s .. 40 s
$2 \rightarrow 4$	ϑ_2 ②	3 s .. 7 s
$4 \rightarrow 5$	ϑ_3 ③	2 s .. 5 s
$5 \rightarrow 6$	ϑ_4 ④	30 s .. 40 s
$6 \rightarrow 7$	ϑ_5 ⑤	20 s .. 30 s
$3 \rightarrow 8$	ϑ_6 ⑥	3 s .. 7 s
$1 \rightarrow 3$	ϑ_7 ⑦	1 s .. 40 s

It is simple to show, that π_{Bsp1} is a valid hardware protocol (according to definition 4):

(a) No $bs_i \in \pi_{Bsp1}$ is constant: no $\Xi_{bsi} = \varnothing$.

(b) All $bs_i \in \pi_{Bsp1}$ are closed.

(c) The hardware protocol is complete:

There is only one signal change without cause, namely the activation of button.

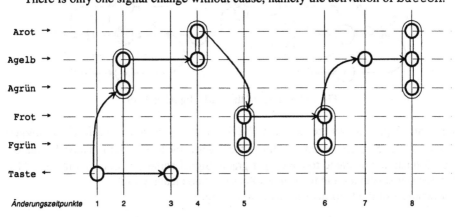

Fig. 2: Trigger graph for the traffic lights control

Trigger Graph. Now we are able to construct the trigger graph of this protocol (Fig. 2); the only starting edge $v_s = \{v_{13}\}$ is marked with a broad arrow. The trigger graph has *no loops*. All nodes are *reachable from* v_s. From v_s to all the end nodes $V_E = \{v_{2,6,8}, v_{14}\}$ there is at least one path that consists of strong edges only.

There is no strong edge that starts from the nodes, which are marked with the signal P_green. The explanation for that is, that one of the signals P_red and P_green is redundant – but for traffic lights, this redundancy is intended. Considering the coincidences (circeled nodes), we can derive the *reduced trigger graph* (Fig. 3):

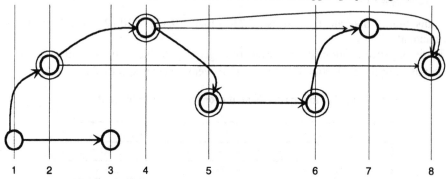

Fig. 3: Reduced Trigger graph of the traffic lights control for pedestrians

The timing from the starting nodes to the end nodes can be computed easily:

$$\text{I } (v_{13}, v_{14}) = (0, 40); \text{ I } (v_{13}, v_{2,6,8}) = (63, 129).$$

Due to the consistency of every timing specification, and because there is only one path $v_s \rightarrow v \in V_E$, this trigger graph is *consistent*.

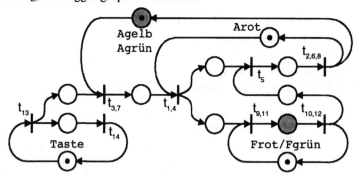

Fig. 4: Petri net of the traffic lights control

Petri net. Fig. 4 shows the Petri net ρ° (*TG*), that has been derived from the trigger graph of Fig. 5.5. This example shows the significant loss of information by the ρ-transformation, compared to the trigger graph: Signal names are only comments in the net, the signal sources and the signal values have no meaning in it.

The analysis of the Petri net shows the following:

- The critical situation, i.e. the traffic lights for car drivers and pedestrians show green lights simultaneously (P_green=1 and C_green=1; the respective places are marked as grey) will never happen according to the specification of Fig. 2.
- However, a *contact situation* may occur. To show this, we consider the behaviour of transition t_{13} more exactly: When t_{13} fires the first time, the protocol is started. When t_{13} fires the second time within this protocol – and there is no means to avoid this –, then a token is fired into the place between t_{13} and $t_{3,7}$. The contact situation occurs, when t_{13} is going to fire the third time; this is prevented by the token, that is still in this place. But this token makes the protocol start again, as soon as there is a token in the place between $t_{2,6,8}$ and $t_{3,7}$.

  Let us consider now, what the occuring of a contact situation means to the traffic light control, which we want to describe by this net. The multiple fireing of t_{13} basically represents a usage error – but, considering realistic systems, this error occurs rather often. The error consists in button being pressed, before the protocol has been terminated. The traffic light system decribed in the timing diagram of table 1 *stores* this request erroneously and processes it after the end of the protocol. Due to that, the traffic lights show in case of erroneous usage P_green=1 and C_red=1 for a second time, even if the pedestrians have already crossed the passage.

  The trivial solution for this case is the respective embedding. But there is another possibility to exclude this contact situation: Constructing a dependency between the end transition $t_{2,6,8}$ and the transition t_{13}. By this measure, a new start of the protocol cannot be requested, before the previous request has been treated.

According to that, the Petri net analysis has two important results: The protocol garantees, that the dangerous situation P_green=1 *and* C_green=1 cannot occur. Furthermore, the contact situation gives a hint at a specification deficiency, that can hardly be found by other methods.

A simple control of a railway-barrier

To get data about the reliability and the performance of protocols, the trigger graph turned out to be a suitable method. For many protocols however, another questions are even more important, e.g.:
- Does the protocol guarantee the sequence of signal changes, that is intended?
- Do the protocol specifications prevent the system to get into not-allowed or dangerous states?

Examples for dangerous states are, if the traffic lights show green in two directions, or when a lift door is able be opened during its running.

For questions like these, Petri nets are highly suitable. Therefore, we can take a trigger graph as basis and use the transformation $\rho°$ (*TG*):
- In the timing diagram, for further evaluation protocol values resp. phases are marked, that must not appear simultaneously. These values represent purely temporal (weak) edges in a trigger graph. They are mapped into a place in $\rho°$ (*TG*).
- Afterwards, the reachability graph $\rho°$ (*TG*) is examined for a marking, in which more than one critical place carries a token.

– The reachability graph also shows, if the *sequence* of the signal changes is not unique, i.e. if it is splitted into more than one sequential marking.

That proceeding will be pointed out by using an example by [Leveson, Stolzy 87]. The names of TG nodes and changing moments have been taken from there.

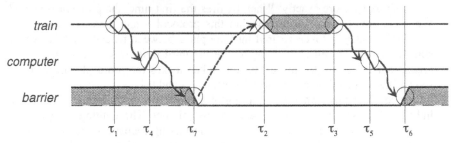

Fig. 5: Timing diagram of a railway-barrier control

This example models the following situation (Fig. 5): A train approaches a railway-barrier. At a moment τ_1 the train transmits a signal to the controlling computer (τ_4). The computer makes the railway-barrier go down at τ_7. Between the moments τ_2 and τ_3 the train passes the passage, which has been secured – hopefully – in the meantime by the railway-barrier. After that, the passage of the train (τ_3) is transmitted to the controlling computer, which lifts the railway-barrier again. In this example the situation of an open railway-barrier during the train passage has to be avoided. These situations, which must not occur simultneously, are marked as grey in the timing diagram.

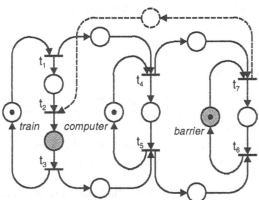

Fig. 6: Petri net of the railway-barrier control of fig. 5

Fig. 6 shows the Petri net $\rho°$ (*TG*), which has been derived from the timing diagram. The critical places $s_{2,3}$ and $s_{6,7}$ are marked as grey. A critical state appears, iff both places carry a token. The reachability graph of this net is sketched in Fig. 7. The markings M_2 and M_5 appear as critical, which means, that critical situations are not excluded by this specification.

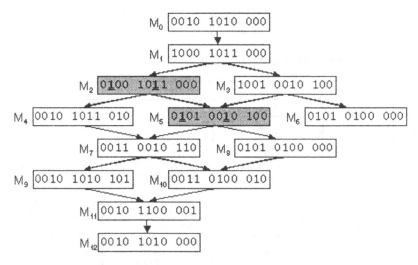

Fig. 7: Reachability graph of the net of fig. 6

By making a slight change to that specification, the dangerous situation of the railway-barrier being open during the train passage can be avoided: If an additional dependency $⑦⇒_u②$ is introduced (painted with points), then there are no situations like these, because t_2 cannot fire before t_7 has fireed and a token is in the place between t_7 and t_2. Now, the trigger graph can be used to determine the resulting timing of the specification: For this purpose, f_E $(⑦,②)$ is considered as braking time of the train, f_E $(①,④)$ as reaction time of the controlling computer, f_E $(④,⑦)$ the time to bring down the railway-barrier. Accordingly, the sensor moment τ_1 needs at least a temporal distance of

$$|\tau_1 - \tau_2| = f_E\ (①,②) \le f_E\ (①,④) + f_E\ (④,⑦) + f_E\ (⑦,②).$$

A DRAM read protocol

The last example uses the trigger graph method for a DRAM read protocol (TC514100AP-80, vgl. [Toshiba 91], pp. 462 ff.). In this case the wires A[0..10] are multiplexed for row-address and column-address. In addition, no acknowledge signal is specified.

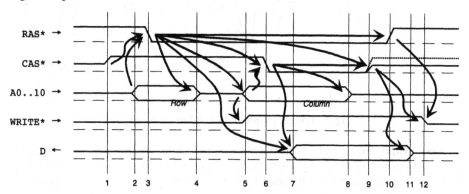

Fig. 8: DRAM read cycle

Timing diagram. Fig. 8 shows the timing diagram of a read cycle of the DRAM described above. Table 2 lists its timing constraints.

Table 2: Timing constraints for the DRAM read protocol

$\tau_x \rightarrow \tau_y$	name	$\vartheta_{min} .. \vartheta_{max}$	corrections
$\tau_1 \rightarrow \tau_3$	t_{CRP}	5 ns .. ∞	–
$\tau_2 \rightarrow \tau_3$	t_{ASR}	0 .. ∞	–
$\tau_3 \rightarrow \tau_4$	t_{RAH}	10 ns .. ∞	10 ns .. < 40 ns
$\tau_3 \rightarrow \tau_5$	t_{RAD}	15 .. 40 ns	–
$\tau_3 \rightarrow \tau_6$	t_{RCD}	20 .. 60 ns	–
$\tau_3 \rightarrow \tau_7$	t_{RAC}	0 .. 80 ns	–
$\tau_3 \rightarrow \tau_9$	t_{CSH}	80 ns .. ∞	20 .. 80 ns
$\tau_3 \rightarrow \tau_{10}$	t_{RAS}	85 .. 10 000 ns	–
$\tau_5 \rightarrow \tau_6$	t_{RCS}	0 .. ∞	–
$\tau_5 \rightarrow \tau_7$	t_{AA}	0 .. 40 ns	–
$\tau_6 \rightarrow \tau_7$	t_{CAC}	0 .. 20 ns	–
$\tau_6 \rightarrow \tau_8$	t_{CAH}	15 ns .. ∞	–
$\tau_6 \rightarrow \tau_9$	t_{CAS}	20 .. 10 000 ns	–
$\tau_9 \rightarrow \tau_{11}$	t_{OFF}	0 ..20 ns	–
$\tau_) \rightarrow \tau_{12}$	t_{RCH}	0 .. ∞	–
$\tau_{10} \rightarrow \tau_{12}$	t_{RRH}	0 .. ∞	–

The protocol begins with the activation of the signal CAS; then the bundle A[] is activated with the column address and the signal CAS is set to 0. Afterwards the data wire D is activated. At last, all signals are de-activated. CAS is not closed: the signal starts with value Z and ends with 1. Accordingly we change the signal end to Z (the specification given by the manufacturer is drawn with dotted line).

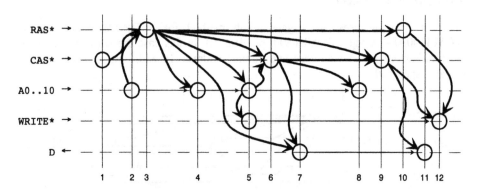

Fig. 9: Trigger graph of the DRAM read cycle

Trigger graph. Now, the respective trigger graph can be constructed (Fig. 9). There are paths consisting of strong edges to all of the end nodes. v_s is the only starting node; all the end nodes can be reached from v_s using strong edges. The moments

{2,3}, {5, 6}, {9, 10, 12} can – in conformity with the protocol's timing contraints – be interpreted as coincident. By means of path analysis an error can be found at t_{RAH} $(3\rightarrow4) = (10,\infty)$: Due to t_{RAD} $(3\rightarrow4) = (15,40)$ and "$v_4 <_\tau v_5$", the time interval ϑ_{max} of t_{RAH} has to be specified as "< 40 ns". This error seems to be simple, but to see its serious consequences, we have to look at its realization (Fig. 10): The EN input (*enable*) is intended to be active between τ_2 and τ_4 and the respective EN input of column address between τ_5 and τ_8. If there is an intersection between the end of column address and the beginning of row address, then there may occur bus collisions with tristate drivers and erroneous addresses with open collector drivers may be generated.

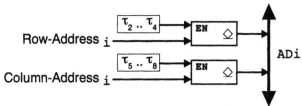

Fig. 10: Realization of the time multiplexing at bundle A[0..10]

The signals A and WRITE have no sending nodes. According to that, this specification is not sufficient to construct the DRAM protocol. (But presumably that is not intended. The description rather has the task to give enough information to be able to construct a DRAM controller.)

Petri net. The Petri net $\rho°$ (*TG*) of the trigger graph of Fig. 9 is shown in Fig. 11. We can observe, that the overlapping of column and row address cannot be seen with this representation: The reason is, that an edge in the trigger graph is generated by the relation "$v_7 <_\tau v_8$". But we could already find this error by the trigger graph analysis, which notes an inconsistency about this edge.

Considering the reachability graph we can observe, that it is not clear – from a non-temporal point of view –, if t_7 (D = A), t_8 (A[] = A) or $t_{9,10,12}$ (CAS = Z, RAS = 1, WRITE = Z) is first. The timing analysis however shows, that the protocol has been specified correctly: D = A and A[] = A overlap for 5 ns (ϑ_{max} (6,7) = 20ns, ϑ_{min} (6,8) = 20ns); the same with D = 0 and RAS = 0 ($\vartheta_{min}(3,10)$ = 85ns, ϑ_{max} (3,7) = 80ns).

Conclusion and Further Work

To get a formal notion of hardware protocols, we described them as a set of signals, with signal names, signal changes and some dependencies between them. This representation we transformed into a directed acyclic graph, called *trigger graph*, with the node-attributes signal names and signal changes and the edge-attributes timing intervals. In the next step, the trigger graph was transformed into a Petri net (ρ-Transformation).

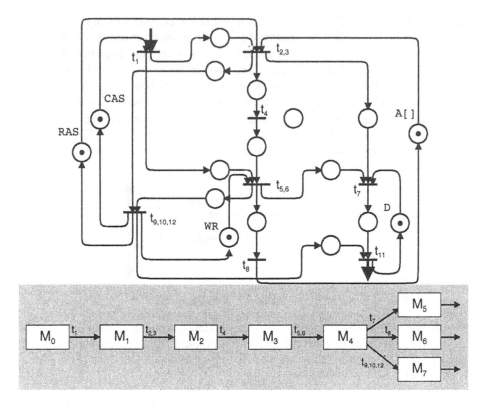

Fig. 11: Petri net and reachability graph of fig. 9

Afterwards we considered three hardware protocol examples, to show how important protocol properties like completeness or consistency of a specification can be proven by means of this method. In addition, checks like safety-conditions of the protocol can be done by means of the ρ-transformation.

The trigger graph, which has been introduced in this paper, builds a bridge between formal description methods, e.g. Petri nets, and the common (informal) specification methods of hardware developers: On the one hand the trigger graph is rather similar to well-known timing diagrams, on the other hand the developer is enabled by the "formal part" to use established methods of graph theory and net theory for the automatic proving of important protocol properties.

This methodology has been implemented as a program, that is based on an intermediate representation of the trigger graph and transforms it into an intermediate representation of Petri nets. As the next step we will connect a graphical editor as the tool's "frontend"; this editor should be able to display protocol errors graphically. Furthermore we will implement a "backend", which transforms the Petri net inter-mediate representation into the input language of a Petri net tool called TOMSPIN (see e.g. [Thurner, Wincheringer 95]). At last, we are preparing the hardware syn-thesis of the protocol, which is also based on the trigger graph.

Bibliographie

[1] André, C.: *Delays in Synchronized Elementary Net Systems*. In: Rozenberg, G.; Goos, G.; Hartmanis, J. (Eds.): Advance in Petri Nets, 1991, LNCS, Vol. 524. Springer-Verlag: Berlin 1991, pp. 1-28

[2] Thurner, E.M.; Wincheringer, C.: TOMSPIN – A Tool for Modelling With Stochastic Petri Nets. Proceedings EUROCAST '95

[3] Leveson, N. G.; Stolzy, J. L.: *Safety Analysis Using Petri Nets*. IEEE Trans. Software Engineering, Vol. SE-13, No. 3, March 1987, pp. 386-397

[4] Reisig, W.: *Petrinetze. Eine Einführung*. Springer-Verlag: Berlin [2]1986

[5] Toshiba: *Databook MOS Memory (DRAM)*. Tokyo, Jan. 1993

Refinement Mapping for
General (Discrete Event) Systems Theory

P. Blauth Menezes[†], J. Félix Costa[††] and A. Sernadas[†]

† Departamento de Matemática, Instituto Superior Técnico
Av. Rovisco Pais, 1096 Lisboa Codex, Portugal - {blauth, acs}@raf.ist.utl.pt

†† Departamento de Informática, Faculdade de Ciências, Universidade de Lisboa
Campo Grande, 1700 Lisboa, Portugal - fgc@di.fc.ul.pt

Abstract. A categorial semantic domain for general (discrete event) systems based on labeled transition systems with full concurrency is constructed, where synchronization and hiding are functorial. Moreover, we claim that, within the proposed framework, a class of mappings stands for refinement. Then we prove that refinement satisfies the diagonal compositionality requirement, i.e., refinements compose (vertical) and distribute over system composition (horizontal).

1   Introduction

We construct a semantic domain for interacting systems which satisfies the diagonal compositionality requirement, i.e., refinements compose (vertically), reflecting the stepwise description of systems, involving several levels of abstraction, and distributes through combinators (horizontally), meaning that the refinement of a composite system is the composition of the refinement of its parts.

Taking into consideration the developments in Petri net theory (mainly with seminal papers like [17], [11] and [15]) it was clear that nets might be good candidates. However, most of net-based models such as Petri nets in the sense of [14] and labeled transition systems (see [12]) lack composition operations (modularity) and abstraction mechanisms in their original definitions. This motivate the use of the category theory: the approach in [17] provides the former, where categorical constructions such as product and coproduct stand for system composition, and the approach in [11] provides the later for Petri nets where a special kind of net morphism corresponds to the notion of implementation. Also, category theory provides powerful techniques to unify different categories of models (i.e., classes of models categorically structured) through adjunctions (usually reflections and coreflections) expressing the relation of their semantics as in [15].

We introduce the concept of (nonsequential) automaton as a kind of automaton structured on states and transitions. Structured states are "bags" of local states like tokens in Petri nets and structured transitions specify a concurrency relationship between component transitions in the sense of [3] and [7]. In [9] we show that nonsequential automata are more concrete then Petri nets (in fact, categories of Petri nets are isomorphic to subcategories of nonsequential automata) extending the approach in [15], where a formal framework for classification of models for concurrency is set.

The resulting category is bicomplete where the categorial product and coproduct stand for (system) composition. Synchronization and hiding are functorial operations. A synchronization restricts a (system) composition according to some given interaction specification. A view of a system is obtained through hiding of transitions introducing an internal nondeterminism. A hidden transition cannot be used for interaction.

A refinement mapping maps transitions into transactions reflecting an implementation of a system on top of another. It is defined as an automaton morphism where the target object is enriched with all conceivable sequential and nonsequential computations. Computations are induced by an endofunctor tc (transitive closure) and composition of refinements φ: $N_1 \rightarrow tcN_2$, ψ: $N_2 \rightarrow tcN_3$ is defined using Kleisli categories as illustrated in the Figure 1.

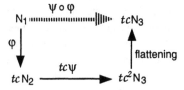

Fig. 1. Composition of refinements

Therefore, refinements compose, i.e., the vertical compositionality requirement is achieved. Moreover we find a general theory of refinement of (discrete) systems which also satisfies the horizontal compositionality requirement. i.e., for refinements φ: $N_1 \rightarrow tcM_1$, ψ: $N_2 \rightarrow tc\,M_2$, we have that:

$$\varphi N_1 \times \psi N_2 = \varphi \times \psi(N_1 \times N_2)$$

where $\varphi N_1 \times \psi N_2$ and $N_1 \times N_2$ are composed systems and the refinement $\varphi \times \psi$ is (uniquely) induced by φ and ψ.

Note that, while the vertical compositionality is easily achieved in several models, they lack horizontal compositionality (see [9] for Petri nets and [10] for transition systems).

2 Nonsequential Automata

A nonsequential automaton is a reflexive graph (a graph with an endoarc for every node) labeled on arcs such that nodes, arcs and labels are elements of commutative monoids. A reflexive graph represents the *shape* of an automaton where nodes and arcs stand for states and transitions, respectively, with endoarcs interpreted as *idle* transitions. The labeling procedure allows the occurrence of more then one transition with the same label. A structured transition specify a concurrency relation between component transitions. Comparing with asynchronous transition systems (first introduced in [3]), the independence relation of a nonsequential automaton is explicit in the graphical representation. A structured state can be viewed as a "bag" of local states where each local state can be viewed as a resource to be consumed or produced, like a token in Petri nets.

Nonsequential automata and its morphisms constitute a category which is complete and cocomplete with products isomorphic to coproducts. A product (or coproduct) can be viewed as (system) composition. In what follows $\mathcal{CMon}$ denotes the category of commutative monoids and suppose that k is in $\{0, 1\}$.

Definition 2.1 Nonsequential Automaton. A nonsequential automaton $N = \langle V, T, \partial_0, \partial_1, \iota, L, \text{lab} \rangle$ is such that $T = \langle T, \|, \tau \rangle$, $V = \langle V, \oplus, e \rangle$, $L = \langle L, \|, \tau \rangle$ are $\mathcal{CMon}$-objects of transitions, states and labels respectively, ∂_0, ∂_1: $T \rightarrow V$ are $\mathcal{CMon}$-morphisms called source and target respectively, $\iota\colon V \to T$ is a *CMon*-morphism such that $\partial_k \circ \iota = \mathrm{id}_V$ and lab: $T \to L$ is a *CMon*-morphism such that $\mathrm{lab}(t) = \tau$ whenever there is v in V where $\iota(v) = t$. ❑

We may refer to a nonsequential automaton $N = \langle V, T, \partial_0, \partial_1, \iota, L, \mathrm{lab}\rangle$ by $N = \langle G, L, \mathrm{lab}\rangle$ where $G = \langle V, T, \partial_0, \partial_1, \iota\rangle$ is a reflexive graph internal to *CMon* (i.e., V, T are *CMon*-objects and $\partial_0, \partial_1, \iota$ are *CMon*-morphisms).

In an automaton, a transition labeled by τ represents a hidden transition (as we will see later, a hidden transition is encapsulated and therefore, can not be triggered from the outside). Note that, all idle transitions are hidden. The definition above is not extensional in the sense that two distinct transitions with the same label may have the same source and target states. In this paper we are not concerned with initial states.

A transition t such that $\partial_0(t) = X$, $\partial_1(t) = Y$ is denoted by $t\colon X \to Y$. Since a state is an element of a monoid, it may be denoted as a formal sum $n_1 A_1 \oplus \dots \oplus n_m A_m$, with the order of the terms being immaterial, where A_i is in V and n_i indicate the multiplicity of the corresponding (local) state, for $i = 1 \dots m$. The denotation of a transition is analogous. We also refer to a structured transition as the *parallel composition* of component transitions. When no confusion is possible, a structured transition $x \| \tau\colon X \oplus A \to Y \oplus A$ where $t\colon X \to Y$ and $\iota_A\colon A \to A$ are labeled by x and τ, respectively, is denoted by $x\colon X \oplus A \to Y \oplus A$. For simplicity, in graphical representation, we omit the endotransitions. A state $n_1 A_1 \oplus \dots \oplus n_m A_m$ and a labeled transition $n_1 t_1 \| \dots \| n_m t_m$ are graphically represented as in the Figure 2.

Fig. 2. Graphical representation of structured states and transitions

Example 2.2 The graphical representation of an automaton $N = \langle \{X, Y\}^\oplus, \{a, b, \iota_X, \iota_Y\}^\|, \partial_0, \partial_1, \iota, \{x, y\}^\|, \mathrm{lab}\rangle$ with free monoids determined by the local transitions a: $2X \to Y$, b: $2X \to Y$ and with labeling given by $a \mapsto x$, $b \mapsto y$ is illustrated in the Figure 3. ❑

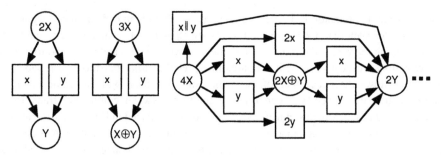

Fig. 3. Graphical representation of a nonsequential automaton

Considering the monoidal structure of nonsequential automata and since in this paper we are not concerned with initial states, the schema above has an infinite number of distributed diagrams. If an initial state is considered, only the corresponding diagram may be drawn. For instance, in the example above, if the initial state is $4X$ then the schema could be reduced to the rightmost diagram in the Figure 3.

Comparing the graphical representation with the one for Petri nets (see, e.g., [14]), in a nonsequential automaton all possible states are explicit while in Petri nets the reachable markings are implicit. Also, the concurrency relation between transitions in Petri nets is implicit. Both models, categories of Petri nets and categories of nonsequential automata can be unified through adjunctions. For details, see [9].

Remark 2.3 Non-Reflexive Automata. If we define the category of non-reflexive automata (with source, target and labeling preserving morphisms) the product construction reflects a composition operation with (total) synchronization in the sense that each transition of the first automaton is synchronized with all transitions of the second. This construction has very few practical applications. ❑

Remark 2.4 Structured Transition × Independence Square. Consider the Figure 4. Let a: A → B, x: X → Y be two transitions of some automaton. Then, a‖x: A⊕X → B⊕Y, a: A⊕X → B⊕X, a: A⊕Y → B⊕Y, x: A⊕X → A⊕Y, x: B⊕X → B⊕Y are also labeled transitions of the same automaton. This leads to the "independence square" associated to the structured transition a‖x, i.e.:

a) if two transitions can fire independently from the same source state, then they should be able to fire concurrently and doing so, reach the same target state;
b) if two independent transitions can fire, one immediately after the other, then they should be able to fire with interchanged order. ❑

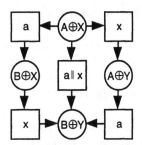

Fig. 4. Independence square

Definition 2.5 Nonsequential Automaton Morphism. A nonsequential automaton morphism h: $N_1 \rightarrow N_2$ where $N_1 = \langle V_1, T_1, \partial_{01}, \partial_{11}, \iota_1, L_1, lab_1 \rangle$ and $N_2 = \langle V_2, T_2, \partial_{02}, \partial_{12}, \iota_2, L_2, lab_2 \rangle$ is a triple h = $\langle h_V, h_T, h_L \rangle$ such that h_V: $V_1 \rightarrow V_2$, h_T: $T_1 \rightarrow T_2$, h_L: $L_1 \rightarrow L_2$ are *CMon*-morphisms, $h_V \circ \partial_{k1} = \partial_{k2} \circ h_T$, $h_T \circ \iota_1 = \iota_2 \circ h_V$ and $h_L \circ lab_1 = lab_2 \circ h_T$. ❑

Nonsequential automata and their morphisms constitute the category *NAut*.

Proposition 2.6 The category *NAut* is complete and cocomplete. Moreover products and coproducts are isomorphic.
Proof: See [9]. ❑

A categorical product (or coproduct) of two automata $N_1 = \langle V_1, T_1, \partial_{01}, \partial_{11}, \iota_1, L_1, lab_1 \rangle$, $N_2 = \langle V_2, T_2, \partial_{02}, \partial_{12}, \iota_2, L_2, lab_2 \rangle$ is as follows:

$$N_1 \times_{NAut} N_2 = \langle V_1 \times_{CMon} V_2, T_1 \times_{CMon} T_2, \partial_{01} \times \partial_{02}, \partial_{11} \times \partial_{12}, \iota_1 \times \iota_2,$$
$$L_1 \times_{CMon} L_2, lab_1 \times lab_2 \rangle$$

where $\partial_{k1} \times \partial_{k2}$, $\iota_1 \times \iota_2$ and $lab_1 \times lab_2$ are uniquely induced by the product construction. Intuitively, the product in *NAut* is viewed as a composition of component automata.

Example 2.7 Consider the nonsequential automata $N_1 = \langle \{A, B, C\}^{\oplus}, \{a, b, \iota_A, \iota_B, \iota_C\}^{\|}, \partial_{01}, \partial_{11}, \iota_1, \{u\}^{\|}, lab_1 \rangle$ and $N_2 = \langle \{X, Y\}^{\oplus}, \{x, \iota_X, \iota_Y\}^{\|}, \partial_{02}, \partial_{12}, \iota_2, \{v\}^{\|}, lab_2 \rangle$ (free monoids) where source and target morphisms are determined by the local transitions a: A → B, b: B → C, x: 2X → Y and with labeling given by a ↦ u, b ↦ u, x ↦ v. Then, $N_1 \times N_2 = \langle \{A, B, C, X, Y\}^{\oplus}, \{a, b, x, \iota_A, \iota_B, \iota_C, \iota_X, \iota_Y\}^{\|}, \partial_0, \partial_1, \iota, \{u, v\}^{\|}, lab \rangle$ with ∂_0, ∂_1, ι, lab uniquely induced by the product construction is represented in the Figure 5. ◻

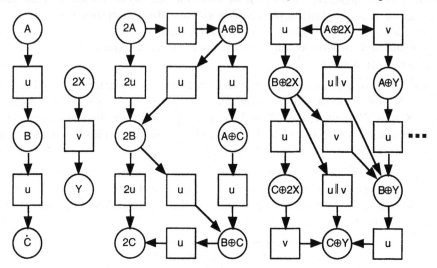

Fig. 5. Resulting nonsequential automaton of a product

3 Synchronization and Hiding

Synchronization and hiding of transitions are functorial operations defined using fibration and cofibration techniques. Both functors are induced by morphisms at the label level.

The synchronization operation erases from the product all those transitions which do not reflect some given table of synchronizations. The approach for synchronization is inspired by [8] and is as follows (see the Figure 6):

a) let N_1, N_2 be nonsequential automata with L_1, L_2 as the corresponding commutative monoids of labels;

b) let $Table(L_1, L_2)$ be a table of synchronizations determined by the pairs of labels to be synchronized and sync: $Table(L_1, L_2) → L_1 \times L_2$ be the synchronization morphism which maps the table into the labels of a given automaton;

c) let $u: \mathcal{N}\!\mathcal{A}ut → \mathcal{C}\mathcal{M}on$ be the obvious forgetful functor taking each automaton into its commutative monoid of labels. The functor u is a fibration and the fibers $u^{-1}Table(L_1, L_2)$, $u^{-1}L_1 \times L_2$ are subcategories of $\mathcal{N}\!\mathcal{A}ut$;

d) the fibration u and the morphism sync induce a functor *sync*: $u^{-1}L_1 \times L_2 → u^{-1}Table(L_1, L_2)$. The functor *sync* applied to $N_1 \times N_2$ provides the automaton reflecting the desired synchronizations.

Traditionally, in concurrency theory, the concealment of transitions is achieved by resorting to labeling and using the special label τ (cf. [17]). Such hidden transitions cannot

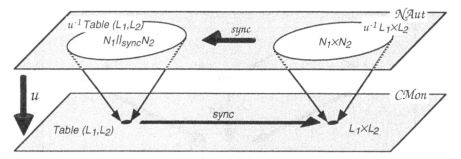

Fig. 6. Induced synchronization functor

be used for synchronization since they are *encapsulated*. The steps for hiding are the following:

a) let N be a nonsequential automaton with L_1 as the commutative monoid of labels;
b) let hide: $L_1 \to L_2$ be a morphism taking the transitions to be hidden into τ;
c) let u: $\mathcal{N}\mathcal{A}ut \to \mathcal{C}\mathcal{M}on$ be the same forgetful functor used for synchronization purpose. The functor u is a cofibration (and therefore, a bifibration) and the fibers $u^{-1}L_1$, $u^{-1}L_2$ are subcategories of $\mathcal{N}\mathcal{A}ut$;
d) the cofibration u and the morphism hide induce a functor *hide*: $u^{-1}L_1 \to u^{-1}L_2$. The functor *hide* applied to N provides the automaton reflecting the desired encapsulation.

3.1 Synchronization

In what follows, we show a categorial way to construct tables of synchronizations for event calling and event sharing and the corresponding synchronization morphism.

Table of Synchronizations. The table of synchronizations for interaction is given by a colimit of a "twin peaks" or "M" diagram (i.e., a diagram with the shape •←•→•←•→•). We say that a shares x if and only if a calls x and x calls a. In what follows, we denote by a | x a pair of synchronized transitions.

Definition 3.1 Table of Synchronizations. Let N_1, N_2 be nonsequential automata with L_1, L_2 as the corresponding commutative monoids of labels and let i be in {1, 2}:

a) let Channel(L_1, L_2) be the least commutative monoid determined by all pairs of transitions to be synchronized;
b) let L_i' be the least commutative submonoid of L_i containing all transitions of N_i which call a transition of the other automaton;
c) the morphisms $call_i$: $L_i' \to$ Channel(L_1, L_2) are such that, for a in L_i', if a calls x then $call_i(a) = a \,|\, x$.

Let M(L_1, L_2) be the twin peaks diagram represented in the Figure 7 where inc_i: $L_i' \to L_i$ are the canonical inclusion morphisms. The table of synchronizations Table(L_1, L_2) is given by the colimit of M(L_1, L_2). ❑

From the definition above, we can infer that: (from c) $call_i$ are monomorphisms.

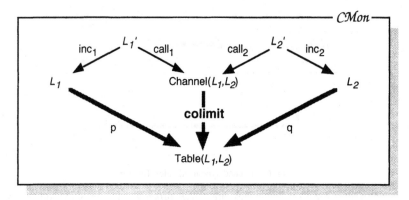

Fig. 7. Table of synchronizations

Example 3.2 Consider the free commutative monoids of labels $L_1 = \{a, b, c\}^\|$, $L_2 = \{x, y\}^\|$. Suppose that a calls x, b calls y and y calls b (i.e., b shares y). Then, Channel(L_1, L_2) = {a|x, b|y}$^\|$, $L_1' = \{a, b\}^\|$, $L_2' = \{y\}^\|$ and Table(L_1, L_2) = {c, x, a|x, b|y}$^\|$. ❑

Let M(L_1, L_2) be a twin peaks diagram whose colimit determines Table(L_1, L_2) and p: $L_1 \to$ Table(L_1, L_2), q: $L_2 \to$ Table(L_1, L_2). Then there are retractions for p and q denoted by p^R and q^R respectively as follows:

for every b in Table(L_1, L_2),

if there is a in L_1 such that p(a) = b then $p^R(b)$ = a else $p^R(b)$ = ✔;
if there is a in L_2 such that q(a) = b then $q^R(b)$ = a else $q^R(b)$ = ✔.

Definition 3.3 Synchronization Morphism. The synchronization morphism sync: Table(L_1, L_2) $\to L_1 \times L_2$ is uniquely induced by the product construction as illustrated in the Figure 8. ❑

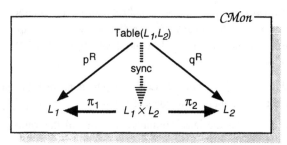

Fig. 8. Synchronization morphism

Synchronization Functor. First we show that the forgetful functor which takes each nonsequential automaton into its commutative monoids of labels is a fibration and then we introduce the synchronization functor.

Proposition 3.4 The forgetful functor u: $\mathcal{N}\mathcal{A}ut \to \mathcal{C}\mathcal{M}on$ that takes each nonsequential automaton onto its underlying commutative monoid of labels is a bifibration. ❑

Proof: Let $\mathcal{R}Gr(CMon)$ be the category of reflexive graphs internal to $CMon$ and let $id: \mathcal{R}Gr(CMon) \to \mathcal{R}Gr(CMon)$, $emb: CMon \to \mathcal{R}Gr(CMon)$ be functors. Then, $\mathcal{N}Aut$ can be defined as the comma category $id \downarrow emb$. Let $f: L_1 \to L_2$ be a $CMon$-morphism and $N_2 = \langle G_2, L_2, lab_2 \rangle$ be a nonsequential automaton where $G_2 = \langle V_2, T_2, \partial_{02}, \partial_{12}, \iota_2 \rangle$ is a $\mathcal{R}Gr(CMon)$-object. Consider the $\mathcal{R}Gr(CMon)$-pullback represented in the Figure 9. Define $N_1 = \langle G_1, L_1, lab_1 \rangle$ which is an automaton by construction. Then $u = \langle u_G, f \rangle: N_1 \to N_2$ is cartesian with respect to f and N_2. $\qquad\square$

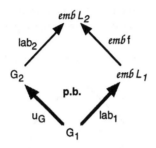

Fig. 9. Pullback

Definition 3.5 Functor sync. Consider the fibration $u: \mathcal{N}Aut \to CMon$, the nonsequential automata $N_1 = \langle V_1, T_1, \partial_{01}, \partial_{11}, \iota_1, L_1, lab_1 \rangle$, $N_2 = \langle V_2, T_2, \partial_{02}, \partial_{12}, \iota_2, L_2, lab_2 \rangle$ and the synchronization morphism sync: $Table(L_1, L_2) \to L_1 \times L_2$. The synchronization of N_1, N_2 represented by $N_1 \|_{sync} N_2$ is given by the functor sync: $u^{-1}(L_1 \times L_2) \to u^{-1}(Table(L_1, L_2))$ induced by u and sync applied to $N_1 \times N_2$, i.e.:

$$N_1 \|_{sync} N_2 \quad \text{is} \quad sync(N_1 \times N_2). \qquad\square$$

Example 3.6 Consider the nonsequential automata **Consumer** and **Producer** (with free monoids) determined by the following labeled transitions:

Producer: prod: $A \to B$, send: $B \to A$
Consumer: rec: $X \to Y$, cons: $Y \to X$

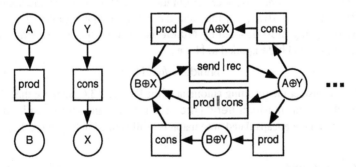

Fig. 10. Synchronized automaton

Suppose that we want a joint behavior sharing the transitions **send** and **rec** (a communication without buffer such as in CSP [6] or CCS [12]). Then, Channel$(L_1, L_2) = \{$send$|$rec$\}^{\|}$ and Table$(L_1, L_2) = \{$prod, cons, send$|$rec$\}^{\|}$. The resulting automaton is illustrated in the Figure 10. Note that the transitions **send**, **rec** are erased and send$|$rec is included. $\qquad\square$

3.2 Hiding

For encapsulation purposes, we work with *hiding morphisms*. A hiding morphism is in fact an injective morphism except for those labels we want to hide (i.e., to relabel by τ). In what follows, remember that a monoid with only one element, denoted by e, is a zero object.

Definition 3.7 Hiding Morphism. Let L_1 be the commutative monoid of labels of the automata to be encapsulated, L be least commutative submonoid of L_1 containing all labels to be hidden and inc: $L \to L_1$ be the inclusion morphism. The hiding morphism hide: $L_1 \to L_2$ is determined by the pushout illustrated in the Figure 11 where the morphism ! is unique. ❑

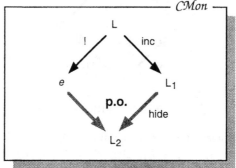

Fig. 11. Hiding morphism

Proposition 3.8 The forgetful functor u: $\mathcal{N}\!Aut \to \mathcal{C}Mon$ that maps each automaton onto its underlying commutative monoid of labels is a cofibration.

Proof: Let f: $L_1 \to L_2$ be a $\mathcal{C}Mon$-morphism and $N_1 = \langle V_1, T_1, \partial_{01}, \partial_{11}, \iota_1, L_1, \mathrm{lab}_1 \rangle$ be an automaton. Define $N_2 = \langle V_1, T_1, \partial_{01}, \partial_{11}, \iota_1, L_2, \mathrm{f} \circ \mathrm{lab}_1 \rangle$. Then $u = \langle \mathrm{id}_{V_1}, \mathrm{id}_{T_1}, \mathrm{f} \rangle$: $N_1 \to N_2$ is cocartesian with respect to f and N_1. ❑

Definition 3.9 Functor hide. Consider the fibration u: $\mathcal{N}\!Aut \to \mathcal{C}Mon$, the nonsequential automata $N = \langle V, T, \partial_0, \partial_1, \iota, L_1, \mathrm{lab} \rangle$ and the hiding morphism hide: $L_1 \to L_2$. The hiding of N satisfying hide denoted by N\hide is given by the functor $\widehat{hide}$: $u^{-1}L_1 \to u^{-1}L_2$ induced by u and hide applied to N, i.e.,

$$\text{N\textbackslash hide} = \widehat{hide}\,\text{N}$$

❑

Example 3.10 Consider the resulting automata of the Example 3.6. Suppose that we want to hide the synchronized transition send|rec. Then, the hiding morphism is induced by send|rec $\mapsto \tau$ and the encapsulated automaton is as illustrated in the Figure 12. ❑

4 Refinement

A refinement mapping is defined as a special automaton morphism where the target object is closed under computations, i.e., the target (more concrete) automaton is enriched with all the conceivable sequential and nonsequential computations that can be split into permutations of original transitions, respecting source and target states. This transitive closure is easily performed in Category Theory:

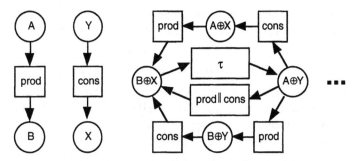

Fig.12. Encapsulated automaton

a) a reflexive graph plus a composition operation on transitions determines a category;
b) there exists a (obvious) functor forgetting the composition operation;
c) this functor has a left adjoint: a functor that freely generates a category from a reflexive graph;
d) the composition of both functors determines an endofunctor taking each reflexive graph onto its transitive closure;
e) the generalization of the above approach for nonsequential automata leads to the envisaged transitive closure.

Therefore, a refinement of an automaton N on top of an automaton M is a morphism φ: N → tcM, where tc is the transitive closure functor. Automata and refinement morphisms constitute a category (defined as a Kleisli category - see [2]) and thus, refinements compose. Then we show that refinement distributes over (system) composition and therefore, the resulting category of automata and refinements *satisfies the diagonal compositionality.*

In what follows, let *CMonCat* be the category of small strictly symmetric strict monoidal categories which is complete and cocomplete with products isomorphic to coproducts. Consider the functor $id_{CMonCat}$: *CMonCat* → *CMonCat* and the comma category $id_{CMonCat} \downarrow id_{CMonCat}$ denoted by *CMC↓CMC*. Note that the objects of *CMC↓CMC* are functors.

Definition 4.1 Functor u: CMC↓CMC → NAut. The functor *u: CMC↓CMC → NAut* is such that for each *CMC↓CMC*-object $l: M → L$ we have that:

a) for $M = \langle\langle V, T, \partial_0, \partial_1, \iota, ;\rangle, \otimes, e\rangle$, uM is the *RGr(CMon)*-object $M = \langle\langle V, \otimes, e\rangle, \langle T^a, \otimes^a, \iota_e\rangle, \partial_0^a, \partial_1^a, \iota\rangle$ where T^a is T subjected to the equational rule below and $\partial_0^a, \partial_1^a$, $\otimes^a$ are $\partial_0, \partial_1, \otimes$ restricted to T^a;

$$\frac{t: A \to B \in T^a \quad t': A' \to B' \in T^a \quad u: B \to C \in T^a \quad u': B' \to C' \in T^a}{(t;u) \otimes (t';u') = (t \otimes t');(u \otimes u')}$$

b) for $L = \langle\langle V, T, \partial_0, \partial_1, \iota, ;\rangle, \otimes, e\rangle$, uL is the *CMon*-object $L = \langle L, \otimes^a, \iota_e\rangle$ where $L = T^a - \{t \mid$ there is v in V such that $\iota(v) = t\}$ and $T^a, \otimes^a$ are as defined above;
c) lab: M → L is the labeling morphism canonically induced by $l: M \to L$. □

Besides forgetting about the composition operation, the functor *u: CMC↓CMC → NAut* has an additional requirement about concurrency:

$$(t;u) \| (t';u') = (t\|t');(u\|u')$$

That is, the parallel composition of two computations t;u and t';u' has the same effect as the computation whose steps are the parallel compositions t∥t' and u∥u'. As an illustration, let t: A → B and u: C → D be two computations. Then, for t∥u: A⊕C → B⊕D, we have that (in the following, we do not identify an endotransition by its label τ):

$$t\|u = (\iota_A;t)\|(u;\iota_D) = (\iota_A\|u);(t\|\iota_D) = u;t$$
$$t\|u = u\|t = (\iota_C;u)\|(t;\iota_B) = (\iota_C\|t);(u\|\iota_B) = t;u$$

Therefore, the concurrent execution of two transitions is equivalent to their execution in any order. As a consequence, any computation $t = t_1\|t_2\|...\|t_n$ can be split as the sequential composition of its local transitions, i.e. (suppose $t_i: A_i \to B_i$):

$$t = t_1\|t_2\|...\|t_n = (t_1\|\iota_{A_1});(t_2\|\iota_{A_2});...;(t_n\|\iota_{A_n}) = t_1;t_2;...;t_n$$

Definition 4.2 Functor f: $\mathcal{N}Aut \to CMC\downarrow CMC$. The functor $f: \mathcal{N}Aut \to CMC\downarrow CMC$ is such that:

a) for each $\mathcal{N}Aut$-object $N = \langle M, L, lab\rangle$ where $M = \langle V, T, \partial_0, \partial_1, \iota\rangle$, $V = \langle V, \oplus, e\rangle$, $T = \langle T, \|, \tau\rangle$, $L = \langle L, \|, \tau\rangle$ we have that:

    a.1) fM is the $CMonCat$-object $M = \langle\langle V, T^c, \partial_0^c, \partial_1^c, \iota, ;\rangle, \langle\oplus, \|\rangle, e\rangle$ where the composition is a partial operation and $T^c, \partial_0^c, \partial_1^c$ are defined by the following rules of inference:

$$\frac{t: A \to B \in T}{t: A \to B \in T^c} \qquad\qquad \frac{t: A \to B \in T^c \quad u: B \to C \in T^c}{t;u: A \to C \in T^c}$$

$$\frac{t: A \to B \in T^c \quad u: C \to D \in T^c}{t\|u: A\oplus C \to B\oplus D \in T^c}$$

    subject to the following equational rules:

$$\frac{t: A \to B \in T^c}{\iota_A;t = t \text{ and } t;\iota_B = t}$$

$$\frac{t: A \to B \in T^c \quad u: B \to C \in T^c \quad v: C \to D \in T^c}{t;(u;v) = (t;u);v}$$

$$\frac{t \in T^c}{t\|\tau = t} \qquad\qquad\qquad \frac{t \in T^c \quad u \in T^c}{t\|u = u\|t}$$

$$\qquad\qquad\qquad\qquad\qquad \frac{t \in T^c \quad u \in T^c \quad v \in T^c}{t\|(u\|v) = (t\|u)\|v}$$

$$\frac{}{\iota_A\|\iota_B = \iota_{A\oplus B}}$$

    a.2) fL is the $CMonCat$-object $\langle\langle\{e\}, L^c, !, !, \iota, ;\rangle, \|, e\rangle$ where L^c is defined as above, $!$ is unique and ι is such that $\iota(e) = \tau$;

    a.3) the functor freely generated by $N = \langle M, L, lab\rangle$ is $flab: fM \to fL$;

b) for each $\mathcal{N}Aut$-morphism $h = \langle h_V, h_T, h_L\rangle$ where $\langle h_V, h_T\rangle$ is a $\mathcal{R}Gr(CMon)$-morphism and h_L is a $CMon$-morphism we have that:

    b.1) $f\langle h_V, h_T\rangle$ is the $CMonCat$-morphism $\langle h_V, h_T^c\rangle: fM_1 \to fM_2$ where h_T^c is inductively defined as follows (suppose A, B in V and t, u in T):

        $h_T^c(t) = h_T(t)$ $h_T^c(\iota_A) = \iota_{h_V(A)}$

        $h_T^c(t\|u) = h_T^c(t) \| h_T^c(u)$ $h_T^c(t;u) = h_T^c(t) ; h_T^c(u)$

    b.2) fh_L is the $CMonCat$-morphism $\langle !, h_L^c\rangle: fL_1 \to fL_2$ where h_L^c is defined as above. □

Proposition 4.3 The functor f is left adjoint to u.

Proof: Consider η: $id_{\mathcal{N}\mathcal{A}ut} \to u \circ f$ a natural transformation which is an embedding on transitions (and corresponding labels). Thus, for each $\mathcal{N}\mathcal{A}ut$-object $N = \langle M, L, lab \rangle$, for each $CMC{\downarrow}CMC$-object $\mathcal{N} = \langle M, L, l \rangle$, for each $\mathcal{N}\mathcal{A}ut$-morphism f: $N \to u \mathcal{N}$, there is only one $CMC{\downarrow}CMC$-morphism g: $fN \to \mathcal{N}$ such that $f = ug \circ \eta N$. In fact g is just like ff except that its target is $\mathcal{N}$ instead of $f \circ u \mathcal{N}$. By duality, ε: $f \circ u \to id_{CMC{\downarrow}CMC}$ is a natural transformation which takes each freely composed transition (label) $\langle t \rangle;\langle u \rangle$ and $\langle t \rangle \| \langle u \rangle$ onto the transition (label) $\langle t;u \rangle$ and $\langle t \| u \rangle$, respectively. Thus, $\langle f, u, \eta, \varepsilon \rangle$: $\mathcal{N}\mathcal{A}ut \to CMC{\downarrow}CMC$ is an adjunction. □

Let $\langle f, u, \eta, \varepsilon \rangle$: $\mathcal{N}\mathcal{A}ut \to CMC{\downarrow}CMC$ be the adjunction defined in the proposition above. Then, $T = \langle tc, \eta, \mu \rangle$ is a monad on $\mathcal{N}\mathcal{A}ut$, where $tc = u \circ f$: $\mathcal{N}\mathcal{A}ut \to \mathcal{N}\mathcal{A}ut$ is an endofunctor and $\mu = u\varepsilon f$: $tc^2 \to tc$ is a natural transformation where $u: u \to u$, $f: f \to f$ denote the identity natural transformations and $u\varepsilon f$ is the horizontal composition of natural transformations. A monad is useful to understand the computations of an automaton: for an automaton N, tcN reflects the computations of N, i.e., the transitive closure of N, η_N: N $\to$ tcN maps N into its computations and μ_N: tc^2N $\to$ tcN flattens computations of computations into computations.

Example 4.4 Consider the nonsequential automaton N_1 with free monoids on states, transitions and labels determined by the labeled transitions a: A $\to$ B and b: B $\to$ C. Its transitive closure is represented in the Figure 13 (the transactions added by the transitive closure are dashed). Note that transactions with "$\|$" are in fact classes of transactions. For instance, for a;2b: A⊕B $\to$ 2C we have that a;2b = $(\iota_B \| a);(b \| b) = (\iota_B;b) \| (a;b)$ = b$\|$(a;b) = (b;ι_C)$\|$(ι_A;(a;b)) = (b$\|\iota_A$);($\iota_C \|$(a;b)) = b;a;b = ... □

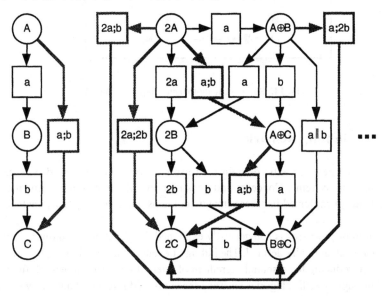

Fig. 13. Transitive closure of a nonsequential automaton

Definition 4.5 Category $\mathcal{R}ef\mathcal{N}\mathcal{A}ut$. Let $T = \langle tc, \eta, \mu \rangle$ be a monad on $\mathcal{N}\mathcal{A}ut$ induced by the adjunction $\langle f, u, \eta, \varepsilon \rangle$: $\mathcal{N}\mathcal{A}ut \to CMC{\downarrow}CMC$. The category of nonsequential automata and refinement morphisms is the Kleisli category determined by T, denoted by $\mathcal{R}ef\mathcal{N}\mathcal{A}ut$. □

Therefore, a refinement between two nonsequential automata N_1 and N_2, denoted by φ: $N_1 \Rightarrow N_2$, is a $\mathcal{N}\!Aut$-morphism φ: $A_1 \to tc A_2$ and the composition of given refinement morphisms is the composition in $\mathcal{R}ef\mathcal{N}\!Aut$.

Example 4.6 Consider the nonsequential automaton N_1 (previous example) and the automaton N_2 with free monoids on states, transitions and labels determined by the local labeled transitions x: X $\to$ Y and y: Y $\to$ X. The refinement morphism φ: $N_1 \Rightarrow N_2$ is given by A $\mapsto$ 2X, B $\mapsto$ 2Y, C $\mapsto$ 2Y, a $\mapsto$ x$\|$x and b $\mapsto$ 2y;x;y;2x. $\square$

In the next proposition, we prove that this construction also satisfies the horizontal compositionality: refinement of systems distributes through system composition.

Proposition 4.7 Let $\{\varphi_i\colon N_i \Rightarrow M_i\}_{i \in I}$ be a family of refinement, with I a set. Then $\times_{i \in I} \varphi_i$: $\times_{i \in I} N_i \Rightarrow \times_{i \in I} M_i$.

Proof: For simplicity, we abbreviate $\times_{i \in I}$ and $+_{i \in I}$ by $\times_i$ and $+_i$, respectively Consider the morphism $\times_i \varphi_i$: $\times_i N_i \to \times_i tc M_i$ uniquely induced by the product construction as illustrated in the Figure 14. Now, we have only to prove that $\times_i \varphi_i$: $\times_i N_i \to \times_i tc M_i$ is a $\mathcal{R}ef\mathcal{N}\!Aut$-morphism. Since $tc = u \circ f$ and u is right adjoint we have that $\times_i \varphi_i$: $\times_i N_i \to u(\times_i f M_i)$. Moreover $\times_i f N_i'$ is isomorphic to $+_i f N_i'$. Thus, up to an isomorphism, $\times_i \varphi_i$: $\times_i N_i \to u(+_i f M_i)$. Since f is left adjoint (and so, preserves colimits) we have that $\times_i \varphi_i$: $\times_i N_i \to u \circ f(+_i M_i)$. Since $\times_i M_i$ is isomorphic to $+_i M_i$, then $\times_i \varphi_i$: $\times_i N_i \to tc(\times_i M_i)$ and thus, is a $\mathcal{R}ef\mathcal{N}\!Aut$-morphism. $\square$

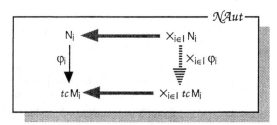

Fig. 14. Refinement morphism uniquely induced

5   Concluding Remarks

We introduced a new semantic domain for (discrete event) system based on structured labeled transition systems. Concepts and constructions like interaction, refinement and hiding, not (fully) explained in other semantic domains, have now a precise mathematical semantics.

Interaction of processes is categorically explained, by fibration techniques. Tables for interaction are categorically defined. The hiding of events is also dealt with, by cofibration techniques, introducing the essential ingredient of internal non-determinism. Refinement is explained through Kleisli categories ensuring the envisaged levels of diagonal (vertical and horizontal) compositionality.

With respect to further work, it should be clear that this may be the starting point of a rather fruitful line of research on the semantics of discrete event systems around transition systems and graph based models.

Acknowledgments

This work was partially supported by: UFRGS - Universidade Federal do Rio Grande do Sul and CNPq - Conselho Nacional de Desenvolvimento Científico e Tecnológico in Brazil; CEC under ESPRIT-III BRA WG 6071 IS-CORE, HCM Scientific Network MEDICIS, JNICT (PBIC/C/TIT/1227/92) in Portugal.

References

1. M. A. Arbib, E. G. Manes, *Arrows, Structures and Functors - The Categorial Imperative*, Academic Press, 1975.
2. A. Asperti, G. Longo, *Categories, Types and Structures - An Introduction to the Working Computer Science*, Foundations of Computing (M. Garey, A. Meyer Eds.), MIT Press, 1991.
3. M. A. Bednarczyk, *Categories of Asynchronous Systems*, Ph.D. thesis, technical report 1/88, University of Sussex, 1988.
4. H. D. Ehrich, A. Sernadas, *Algebraic Implementation of Objects over Objects*, Stepwise Refinement of Distributed Systems: Models, Formalisms, Correctness (J. de Bakker, W. -P. de Roever, G. Rozenberg Eds.), pp. 239-266, Springer-Verlag, 1990.
5. R. Gorrieri, *Refinement, Atomicity and Transactions for Process Description Language*, Ph.D. thesis, Università di Pisa, 1990.
6. C. A. R. Hoare, *Communicating Sequential Processes*, Prentice Hall, 1985.
7. A. Mazurkiewicz, *Basic Notion of Trace Theory*, REX 88: Linear Time, Branching Time and Partial Orders in Logic and Models for Concurrency (J. W. de Bakker, W. -P. de Roever, G. Rozenberg, Eds.), pp. 285-363, LNCS 354, Springer-Verlag, 1988.
8. P. B. Menezes, J. F. Costa, *Synchronization in Petri Nets*, preprint IST/DM/2-94, IST, Lisbon, 1993. Revised version accepted for publication in Fundamenta Informaticae.
9. P. B. Menezes, J. F. Costa, *Compositional Refinement of Concurrent Systems*, preprint IST/DM/26-94, IST, Lisbon, 1994. Revised version accepted for publication in the Journal of the Brazilian Computer Society - Special Issue on Parallel Computation.
10. P. B. Menezes, J. F. Costa, *Object Refinement*, preprint IST/DM/24-94, IST, Lisbon, 1994.
11. J. Meseguer, U. Montanari, *Petri Nets are Monoids*, Information and Computation 88, pp. 105-155, Academic Press, 1990.
12. R. Milner, *Communication and Concurrency*, Prentice Hall, 1989.
13. C. Rattray, *The Shape of Complex Systems*, EUROCAST 93: Computer Aided Systems Theory (F. Pichler, R. M. Díaz, Eds.), pp. 72-82, LNCS 763, Springer-Verlag, 1994.
14. W. Reisig, *Petri Nets: An Introduction*, EATCS Monographs on Theoretical Computer Science 4, Springer-Verlag, 1985.
15. V. Sassone, M. Nielsen, G. Winskel, *A Classification of Models for Concurrency*, CONCUR 93: 4th International Conference of Concurrency (E. Best, Ed.), pp. 82-96, LNCS 715, Springer-Verlag, 1993.
16. M. E. Szabo, *Algebra of Proofs*, Studies in Logic and the Foundations of Mathematics, vol. 88, North-Holland, 1978.
17. G. Winskel, *Petri Nets, Algebras, Morphisms and Compositionality*, Information and Computation 72, pp. 197-238, Academic Press, 1987.

A System-Theoretic Approach to Planning and Programming*

Ireneusz Sierocki

Institute of Technical Cybernetics
Technical University of Wrocław
50-370 Wrocław, Poland

Abstract. This paper deals with a multiple planning problem, which is a collection of planning problems defined for the same partial transition system and have the same set of goal states. It is shown that a solution to the multiple planning problem can be written in procedural (imperative) languages like Pascal. The formal definition of the syntax and semantics of conditional-iterative actions is provided. It is proven that a multiple plan can be generated by a conditional-iterative action. A language of formal representation of partial transition systems with a vector-state space is proposed.

1 Introduction

The planning problem [6], [7], [8] for a partial transition (sequential) system is determined by an initial state and a set of goal states. A solution to a planning problem, called also a sequential plan is a sequence of atomic actions that maps the initial state to one of the goal state.

In this paper, we are concerned with a multiple planning problem, which is a collection of planning problems defined for the same partial transition system and have the same set of goal states. A solution to a multiple planning problem is called a multiple plan. (It is worth noting that the planning and multiple planning problem are, to a certain extent, similar to the control and regulation problem.)

The direct and natural strategy for solving a multiple planning problem consists in solving every component-planning problem. To solve a component-planning problem one can apply search methods like backtracking algorithm, depth-first, iterative deepening algorithm, algorithm A* and decomposition methods like GPS, STRIPS, ABSTRIPS and DCMOP [15]. This strategy is methodologically and computationally justified only in a case of a finite, multiple planning problem having a small number of initial states. Otherwise, one way to obtain a multiple plan is to write a program in rule-based programming languages, known also as production systems. Typical examples of this class of A.I. programming languages are OPS5, PLANNER and PROLOG [3], [4]. A production system is a program consisting of conditional statements, called production

---

* This research was supported by KBN Grant "Design of intelligent robotic system based on knowledge engineering"

rules, which have the following interpretation: *if* the condition ϕ *then* the action a. In general, the syntax of rule-based programming languages is based on a predicate language. AI literature provides two general tools for predicate-representation of partial transition systems, namely: situational calculus and STRIPS formalism. Roughly speaking, they assume that a world state consists of a number of objects together with various relations and functions over those objects.

The main objective of this paper is to show that a solution to the multiple planning problem can be written in procedural (imperative) languages like Pascal. In Section 2, the formal definition of the syntax and semantics of conditional-iterative actions is provided. It is proven that a multiple plan can be generated by a conditional-iterative action. In order to transform a conditional-iterative plan into a procedural program, an appropriate representation of the partial transition system is needed. For this reason, it is assumed that a world state can be modelled by a finite numbers of attributes or state variables, where each attribute can take a value from some finite or infinite domains. It should be pointed out that the specification of a state-space as a vector-space is a standard technique used in system theory. A language of formal representation of partial transition systems with a vector-state space is proposed (see, Section 3). It can be regarded as a special case of the Z language and the VDM language.

Finally, one can say that this paper can be treated as a system-theoretic approach to a new paradigm of artificial intelligence, which views plans as programs [6], [11], [18].

2 The Syntax and Semantics of the Conditional and Iterative Plans

We begin with recalling some basic notions from system theory and artificial intelligence.

Definition 2.1 The *partial (incompletely specified) transition system* M is a two-sorted partial algebra $M = (S, Act, do)$, where:

- S is a set of *states*, called also a *state space*,
- Act is a finite set of *atomic actions*,
- $do : S \times Act \longrightarrow S$ is a partial function, called *one-step transition function*, if $do(s, a)$ is defined then we will say that the atomic action a *is applicable to the state* s. The set of all states for which the atomic action a is applicable will be called the *applicability domain of* a . If do is a function then M is called the *transition system*. M is said to be a *finite*, partial transition system if the set S is finite.

The structure $(S, Act, do, S^o, G) =_{def} (M, S^o, G)$ is said to be a *multiple planning problem for* M, where $S^o \subseteq S$ is called a set of *initial states* and $G \subseteq S$ is called a set of *goal states*. If $S^o = \{s^o\}$ and $S^o = S$ then the multiple planning problem is called the *planning problem* and the *global planning problem*, denoted (M, s^o, G) and (M, G), respectively.

Act^* and Act^ω denotes a set of all finite and infinite strings over Act, respectively. The elements from Act^* and Act^ω are called the *finite* and *infinite actions*, respectively. ϵ denotes the empty action. The concatenation of finite actions α, β is denoted by $\alpha.\beta$. The inductive extension of the function do is denoted by $do^* : S \times Act^* \longrightarrow S$ and is called the *transition function*.

Definition 2.2 A finite action $\alpha \in Act^*$ is said to be the *solution to* $(M, s^o, G) = P$ or the *sequential plan for* P if and only if α is applicable to s^o and $do^*(s^o, \alpha) \in G$. A finite action $\alpha \in Act^*$ is said to be the *optimal solution to* P or the *optimal, sequential plan for* P if and only if it is the shortest solution to P. P is *solvable* if and only if there exists a solution to P.

Definition 2.3 Let $(M, S^o, G) = Q$ be a multiple planning problem. A multiset $\{\alpha(s^o) : s^o \in S^o\}$ of finite actions is said to be the *solution to* Q or the *multiple plan for* Q if and only if $\alpha(s^o)$ is the solution to (M, s^o, G). A multiset $\{\alpha(s^o) : s^o \in S^o\}$ of finite actions is said to be the *optimal solution to* Q or the *optimal, multiple plan for* Q if and only if, for every $s^o \in S^o$, $\alpha(s^o)$ is the optimal solution to (M, s^o, G). Q is *solvable* if and only if (M, s^o, G) is solvable, for every $s^o \in S^o$.

Proposition 2.4 [16] If a finite, multiple planning problem is solvable then there exists a semantically correct, deterministic and complete production system.

It has also been shown that the Macro Problem Solver can be viewed as a method for automatic design of a production system [16]. It should be pointed out that the Macro Problem Solver requires a partial transition system to be serially decomposable [13]. Otherwise, the construction of a production system is a creative activity.

As mentioned in the Introduction, our goal is a show that a multiple plan has the structure of a conditional-while program. This will be done by showing that a production system is a specific form of a conditional-iterative action. In order to define the syntax and semantics of conditional-iterative actions we needed some additional definitions and conventions. Let $M = (S, Act, do)$ be a partial transition system. A subset $T \subseteq S$ is called a *situation*. Let L denote a state description language. Let ϕ be a formula of L and s be a state of M. Then $s \models \phi$ means that the formula ϕ is satisfied in the state s under an intended interpretation for the nonlogical symbols appearing in L. We will say that a formula ϕ is a *situation formula for* T or a *description of* T if and only if $T = \{s \in S : s \models \phi\} =_{def} Mod(\phi)$. ϕ_s denotes a state formula.

Definition 2.5 The syntax of the set Act^{ci} of *conditional- iterative actions* is defined recursively as follows:

(i) an atomic action is a conditional-iterative action,

(ii) if ϕ is a situation formula and α, β are conditional-iterative actions then $if(\phi, \alpha, \beta)$ is a conditional-iterative action,

(iii) if ϕ is a situation formula and α is a conditional-iterative action then $while(\phi, \alpha)$ is a conditional-iterative action,

(iv) if α and β are conditional-iterative actions then $\alpha.\beta$ is a conditional-iterative action.

We will apply the following, well-known and useful abbreviations: $repeat(\phi, \alpha)$ stands for $\alpha.while(\neg\phi, \alpha)$ and $if(\phi, \alpha)$ stands for $if(\phi, \alpha, \epsilon)$. Note that if $\alpha \in Act^*$ then $if(\phi, \alpha)$ is a production rule. This means that a production system, which is a sequence (concatenation) of production rules (see, [6], [19]), is a special case of a conditional-iterative action.

Definition 2.6 The semantics of conditional-iterative actions is described by a partial function $do^{ci} : S \times Act^{ci} \longrightarrow S$, which is defined recursively as follows:

(i) if $do(s, a)$ is defined then $do^{ci}(s, a)$ is also defined and $do^{ci}(s, a) = do(s, a)$,

(ii1) if $s \models \phi$ and $do^{ci}(s, \alpha)$ is defined then $do^{ci}(s, if(\phi, \alpha, \beta))$ is also defined and $do^{ci}(s, if(\phi, \alpha, \beta)) = do^{ci}(s, \alpha)$,

(ii2) if $s \models \neg\phi$ and $do^{ci}(s, \beta)$ is defined then $do^{ci}(s, if(\phi, \alpha, \beta))$ is also defined and $do^{ci}(s, if(\phi, \alpha, \beta)) = do^{ci}(s, \beta)$,

(iii1) if $s \models \neg\phi$ then $do^{ci}(s, while(\phi, \alpha))$ is defined and $do^{ci}(s, while(\phi, \alpha)) = do^{ci}(s, \epsilon) = s$

(iii2) if $s \models \phi$ and $do^{ci}(s, \alpha)$ is defined then $do^{ci}(s, while(\phi, \alpha))$ is also defined and $do^{ci}(s, while(\phi, \alpha)) = do^{ci}(do^{ci}(s, \alpha), while(\phi, \alpha))$,

(iv) if $do^{ci}(s, \alpha)$ and $do^{ci}(do^{ci}(s, \alpha), \beta))$ are defined then $do^{ci}(s, \alpha.\beta)$ is also defined and $do^{ci}(s, \alpha.\beta) = do^{ci}(do^{ci}(s, \alpha), \beta))$.

With the above definitions, one can easily construct an auxiliary, partial function: $f : S \times Act^{ci} \longrightarrow Act^* \cup Act^\omega$, which will be called an *action-generating function*.

Definition 2.7 The conditional-iterative action γ is said to be *applicable* to the state s if and only if $do^{ci}(s, \gamma)$ is defined and an action generated by s and γ is finite, i.e., $f(s, \gamma) \in Act^*$.

Definition 2.8 The conditional-iterative action γ is said to be an *if-while plan for the multiple planning problem* $Q = (M, S^o, G)$ (written $M \models \phi(o)\{\gamma\}\psi(g)$, where the formulas $\phi(o)$ and $\psi(g)$ are the situation formulas for S^o and G, respectively) if and only if, for every $s^o \in S^o$, whenever the planning problem $P = (M, s^o, G)$ is solvable and γ is applicable to s^o then $do^{ci}(s^o, \gamma) \in G$.

This definition can be also expressed as follows: $M \models \phi(o)\{\gamma\}\psi(g)$ if and only if, for every $s^o \in S$, if $s^o \models \phi(o)$, $P = (M, s^o, G)$ is solvable and γ is applicable to s^o then $do^{ci}(s^o, \gamma) \models \psi(g)$. Note that if γ is an if-while plan then $f(s^o, \gamma)$ is a solution to the planning problem $P = (M, s^o, G)$. This means that an if-while plan generates a solution to a multiple planning problem. From this observation and Proposition 2.4 follows that:

Theorem 2.9 If a finite, multiple planning problem is solvable then there exists an if-while plan.

3   A Vector-Representation of a Partial Transition System

In general, the partial transition system M can be represented either *explicitly* or *implicitly*. In an explicit representation, the partial function *do* is displayed in a tabular form, referred to as the *transition table*, or in a graph form, called the *transition graph*. Obviously, an explicit representation is impractical for large, finite transition systems and impossible for infinite transition systems. For this reason, an implicit representation is required. An implicit representation of the states relies on defining a state description language together with a set of state-constraints axioms, which should describe the laws of the world being modelled. However, an implicit representation of an atomic action has a form of a procedure, which should be viewed as a mechanism allowing to check whether an atomic action is applicable to a current state and allowing to generate (compute) the next state.

The AI literature provides two general tools for the implicit representation of a partial transition system, namely: situation calculus and STRIPS formalism. [5], [6], [7]. They are based on a very general model of states that can be formulated as "states are many-sorted algebras". Consequently, they employ a first-order predicate language to describe the states of the system. In turn, the atomic actions are modelled with the help of a modified version of the pre- and postcondition technique. The verification of atomic action precondition is performed by a resolution theorem prover. A description of the effects of atomic actions in the situation calculus gives rises to the so-called *frame problem*, which relies on indicating a large number of facts that do not change when the atomic actions are performed. This is the main disadvantage of the situation calculus. On the other hand, the STRIPS representation provides an effective solution to the frame problem. This is done by describing the effect of an atomic action in terms of add list (the list of formulas that must be added to the current state description) and delete list (the list of formulas that may no longer be true and therefore must be deleted from the current state description). The next state description is produced by first deleting all formulas given in the delete list and then adding all formulas in the add list. It should be pointed out that the STRIPS representation allows to describe only the context-independent actions, i.e., the actions which effects do not depend on the state in which they are applied. This is the main limitation of the STRIPS representation. Finally, it is worth noting that the STRIPS representation and the situation calculus can be directly implemented in LISP and PROLOG, respectively.

In order to transform an if-while plan into a procedural program, an appropriate representation of the partial transition system is needed. We will show that a sufficient condition for a partial transition system to be represented in imperative programming languages is a vector-representation of the state set. In order to provide a formal description of partial transition systems with a vector-state space, we must recall some basic definitions from the first-order logics.

The *alphabet L of the first-order language* is defined as follows: $L = (X, C, REL, FUN)$, where X is a set of variables, C is a set of constant symbols, REL is a set of relation symbols (predicates), FUN is a set of function symbols (functors). Each function and relation symbol has a fixed arity, that is a number of arity. In the standard way, one can define a set of formulas and terms over L. The *L-relational algebra (system, structure)* A is 3-tuple $A = (D, Rel, Fun)$, where D is a domain of A, Rel and Fun is a set of relations and functions (operations) on D, respectively. It is assumed that each n-ary predicate R corresponds to the n-ary relation $r \subset D^n$, each n-ary functor F corresponds to the n-ary function $f : D^n \longrightarrow D$, and each constant symbol c corresponds to $d \in D$. The typical examples of the relational algebras are the simple data types consisting of quantitative (numeral) types like *Integer*, *Real*, *Boolean* and qualitative (symbolic) types like *Char*, *String*, *Symbol*. Let A be an L-relational algebra. The *variable valuation* η, written $\eta \in Val(Y, D)$ is a function from Y to D, where $Y \subseteq X$. The fact that the formula ϕ is satisfied by A and η is written $A, \eta \models \phi$.

A formal representation of a partial transition system begins with conceptualization. This process relies on determining the relevant parameters (attributes, properties). These parameters are called the *state variables* and denoted $X(S) = \{x[1], ..., x[m]\}$. Next, to every state-variable $x[i]$ one should assign the appropriate data type, i.e., the L_i-relational algebra $A_i = (D_i, Rel_i, Fun_i)$. Then the relation $S \subseteq D_1 \times ... \times D_m$ will be called a *vector-state space*. If $S = D_1 \times ... \times D_m$ then S is called a *cartesian* vector-state space. The state $s \in S$ will be written as $s = (s_1, ..., s_m)$. For the sake of brevity, we will consider the case of a *homogeneous* vector-state space, i.e. it will be assumed that $D_1 = ... = D_m = D$. Additionally, we assume that D is the domain of the simple data type A. A partial transition system satisfying these requirements will be called a *homogeneous, first-order* system. Next, we will say that a homogeneous, first-order, partial transition system is *quantitative* and *qualitative* if a simple data type, associated with state variables, is quantitative and qualitative, respectively. The typical examples of quantative, finite transition systems are the linear and boolean automata, which are a subject of computer engineering [12]. On the other hand, artificial intelligence deals with the qualitative, partial transition systems.

Recall that the operational semantics of imperative, sequential programs is described by a partial transition systems, which states, called computation states, are the variable valuations [14], [1]. (Below, we will show that a computation state corresponds to a vector state.) Software engineering proposes two formal languages for an implicit representation (specification) of partial transitions systems, namely: the Z language [18] and the VDM language [10]. Both languages are independent of program code, because they use an abstract data type to represent a state variable. On the other hand, the homogeneous, first-order, partial transition system is specified by concrete, simple data types. For this reason, we will design a simplified version of these languages. More specifically, our language will be a combination of a first-order predicate language and a Pascal-like language. Consequently, the language we want to propose can be treated an implementation-oriented language.

Definition 3.1 Let $S \subseteq D^m$ and $A = (D, Rel, Fun)$ be a simple data type associated with the set $X(S)$ of state variables. The alphabet $L = (X, C, REL, FUN)$ is said to be the *alphabet of the state description language* if $X(S) \subseteq X$ and $C = D$, $REL = Rel$ and $FUN = Fun$, i.e. it is assumed that the names denoting the elements of a domain, the relations and the functions are not distinguished from the constant symbols, the relation symbols and the function symbols, respectively.

Definition 3.2 The *logical specification of the vector-state space* S is the pair (L, Σ) with $\Sigma = \Sigma(S) \cup \Sigma(A) \cup \Sigma(L)$, where:

- $\Sigma(S)$ is a set of *specific axioms*, called also a set of *state-constraints axioms*, $\Sigma(S)$ is a set of free formulas with variables from $X(S)$, (a state-constraint axiom plays the same role as an invariant in VDM),
- $\Sigma(A)$ is a set of *algebraic axioms*, called also an *algebraic specification* of the simple data type A, $\Sigma(A)$ is a set of sentences with variables from $X - X(A)$,
- $\Sigma(L)$ is a set of *logical axioms*, $\Sigma(L)$ is a set of sentences with variables from $X - X(A)$.

Let $s = (s_1, ..., s_m) \in D^m$. Then the variable valuation $\eta(s) : X(S) \longrightarrow D$, defined as follows: $\eta(s)(x[i]) = s_i$, for $i = 1, ..., m$, will be called the *variable valuation associated with* s. With this definition, one can easily verify that there exists an one-to-one relationship between the set D^m of m-tuples (vectors) and the set $Val(X(S)), D)$ of variable valuations from the set of states variables into the domain D. This observation allows to define the semantics of the state description language as follows:

Definition 3.3 Let ϕ be a free formula with variables from $X(S)$ and $s = (s_1, ..., s_m)$ be a tuple from D^m. Then $s \models \phi$ if and only if $A, \eta(s) \models \phi$.

Let $s = (s_1, ..., s_m) \in D^m$. Then it is obvious that the formula $\phi_s = (x[1] = s_1 \wedge ... x[m] = s_m)$, called a *simple, complete* formula, is a description of s. If $s \in S$ then ϕ_s is called the *state formula* or the *logical state*. Assume that $T \subseteq D^m$ is finite. One can easily observe that the formula ϕ defined as follows: $\bigvee_{s \in T} \phi_s$ is a description of T. Hence, we have shown that:

Proposition 3.4 Every finite situation can be described by a formula of the state description language.

Definition 3.5 The logical specification of the vector-space S is *sound* if and only if the set $\Sigma(S)$ of state-constraints axioms is satisfiable, i.e., $Mod(\Sigma(S)) \neq \emptyset$, and $\Sigma(S)$ is a description of S.

Recall that if a set of formulas is satisfiable then it is consistent. The next corollary provides a syntactic characterization of situations and states.

Corollary 3.6 Let (L, Σ) be a sound specification of S. The free formula ϕ with variables from $X(S)$ is a situation formula if and only if $\Sigma \cup \{\phi\}$ is consistent.

We will now proceed to the description of atomic actions. To this end, we will apply and modify a notion of an *action (operator) scheme*, which plays a crucial role in the *STRIPS* formalism. Roughly speaking, the action scheme $a(\overline{v})$ describes a collection of atomic actions by taking into account the sequence $\overline{v}$ of variables. An instance of an action scheme, obtained from an action scheme by replacing each occurrence of a variable by a constant, is a description of an individual, atomic action. An action scheme will be represented as a parametric procedure of the following form:

procedure $a(\overline{v} : E)$; **begin** *the description of* $a(\overline{v})$ **end**

- $\overline{v} = v_1, .., v_l$ is a sequence of auxiliary variables (formal parameters) and $E \subseteq D \cup 1..m$,
- the description of action scheme $a(\overline{v})$ is expressed in terms of preconditions and effects and it looks as follows:

$$\textbf{if } \phi_a(\overline{v}) \wedge \phi_{1a}(\overline{v}) \textbf{ then begin } \rho_{1a}(\overline{v}) \textbf{ end};$$

- -

$$\textbf{if } \phi_a(\overline{v}) \wedge \phi_{ka}(\overline{v}) \textbf{ then begin } \rho_{ka}(\overline{v}) \textbf{ end};$$

- $\phi_a(\overline{v})$ and $\phi_{ia}(\overline{v})$, for $i = 1, ..., k$, are free formulas with index variables,
- $\rho_{ia}(\overline{v})$, for $i = 1, ..., k$, is a sequence of assignment instructions: $x[w_{i1}(\overline{v})] := \tau_{i1}(\overline{v}); ...; x[w_{ip}(\overline{v})] := \tau_{ip}(\overline{v})$, where: $\tau_{ij}(\overline{v})$, for $j = 1, ..., p$, is a term of type D and $w_{ij}(\overline{v})$, for $j = 1, ..., p$, is a term of type *Integer*.

Let $\overline{e} = e_1, ..., e_l$ be a sequence of elements from E, i.e. a sequence of current parameters. Then the atomic action $a(\overline{e})$ is an instance of action scheme $a(\overline{v})$. In other words, the atomic action $a(\overline{e})$ is represented as a procedure instruction.

Definition 3.7 Let $a(\overline{e})$ be an atomic action. The formula $\phi_a(\overline{e})$, which is a substitution instance of $\phi_a(\overline{v})$, is called the *precondition of* $a(\overline{e})$ if and only if it is a description of the domain applicability of $a(\overline{e})$.

The next definition provides a syntactic and semantic criterion for testing whether an atomic action is applicable to a given state.

Definition 3.8 The atomic action $a(\overline{e})$ is applicable to the state s if and only if $\Sigma \cup \{\phi_s\} \vdash \phi_a(\overline{e})$ or $s \models \phi_a(\overline{e})$

Recall that Pascal-like programming languages are equipped with a semantic mechanism for testing whether a formula is satisfied in a computation state. Hence, the representation of a partial transition system in imperative programming languages does not require a construction of an action applicability testing procedure.

Let the atomic action $a(\overline{e})$ be applicable to the state s. Additionally, we assume that there exists exactly one $i \in \{1, .., k\}$ such that $s \models \phi_{ia}(\overline{e})$. The formula $\phi_{ia}(\bar{e})$, which is a substitution instance of $\phi_{ia}(\bar{v})$, will be called the *sub-precondition of $a(\bar{e})$*. Take into account the assignment instruction $x[w_{ij}(\bar{e})] := \tau_{ij}(\bar{e})$. Then, according to a semantic interpretation of an assignment instruction, a procedure for computing a next state is constructed as follows: for every $j = 1,..,p$, $\eta(do(s, a(\bar{e}))(x[w_{ij}(\bar{e})]) = \tau_{ij}(\bar{e})\eta(s)$ and, for every $x[k] \in X(S) - \{x[w_{i1}(\bar{e})], ..., x[w_{ip}(\bar{e})]\}$, $\eta(do(s, a(\bar{e})))(x[k]) = x[k])$. The last rule can be expressed as follows: if a state variable does not appear on the right side of the assignment instruction then the state variable is not affected by the execution of the assignment instruction. This statement can be regarded as the frame axiom for imperative programming languages [10]. In other words, one can say that our representation of partial transition systems provides an obvious solution to the frame problem.

The next definition provides a formal classification of atomic actions.

Definition 3.9 The atomic action $a(\bar{e})$ is said to be:

(i) *context-independent* if and only if, for every $i = 1, ..., k$ and $j = 1, ..., p$, the term $\tau_{ij}(\bar{e})$ does not contain any state variable; otherwise, it is called *context-dependent*,

(ii) *ordinary* if and only if the description of $a(\bar{e})$ consists of only one conditional statement with the sub-precondition being equal to the precondition; otherwise, it is called *branching*.

Observe that our definition is compatible with the general notion of context-dependent action. It is clear that our language allows to represent context-dependent actions.

As a summary of this part of our consideration, we will propose the following, general form of a system description:

> **program** *Partial Transition System*
> **type** D=*Simple data type*; **var** x : **array**$[1..m]$ **of** D;
> $\{\Sigma(S)$ - *a set of state-constraints axioms* $\}$
> **procedure** $a_1(\bar{v}_1 : E_1)$; **begin** *the description of $a_1(\bar{v})$* **end**
> -
> **procedure** $a_k(\bar{v}_m : E_m)$; **begin** *the description of $a_k(\bar{v})$* **end**

Our next task is to determine an expressive power of the language for the system representation. Let $M = (S, Act, do)$ be a finite, partial transition system and $a \in Act$ be an arbitrary atomic action. Next, assume that a is applicable to the state $s = (s_1, ..., s_m)$ and $do(s, a) = t = (t_1, ..., t_m)$. Because S is finite then from Proposition 3.4 it follows that there exists the situation formula ϕ_a, which is the precondition of a. It is obvious that the transition $do(s, a) = t$ can be described as follows:

$$\text{if } \phi_a \wedge \phi_s \text{ then begin } x[1] := t_1; ...; x[m] := t_m \text{ end};$$

Note that every atomic action of a finite, partial transition system can be represented as a context-independent and branching atomic action. So, we have shown that:

Theorem 3.10 Every finite, homogeneous, first order and partial transition system can be modelled in our language of the system description.

4 An Example

For a more complete understanding of our formal approach it might be helpful to consider a multiple planning problem for the blocks world [6]. The blocks world consists of several numbered blocks resting on the table or on each other and a robot with moving arm able to change positions of these blocks. Let us assume that a manipulation ability of the robot is described by three action schemata: $move(i, j, k)$ denotes the atomic action of moving block i from block j to block k, $unstack(i, j)$ denotes the atomic action of unstacking block i from block j and placing it on the table, $stack(i, j)$ denotes the atomic action of picking up block i and stacking it on block j. It is clear that the blocks world can be described as a finite, partial transition system. Usually, predicate language is used to describe a state of the blocks world. An alphabet of a predicate language includes the following predicates: $on(x,y)$, $ontable(x)$, $clear(x)$. A state of the blocks world is described as a conjunction of the ground atomic formulas. We will show that a state can also be represented as a m-tuple. Assume that the blocks world consists of n blocks. Then $m = 2 * n$ and $D = 0..n + 2$. A vector-state is constructed as follows:

(b1) $x[i] = j$ iff $on(i,j)$, for $i = 1, ..., n$,
(b2) $x[i] = 0$ iff $clear(i)$, for $i = 1, ..., n$,
(b3) $x[i] = n + 1$ iff $ontable(i)$, for $i = n + 1, ..., 2 * n$,
(b4) $x[i] = n + 2$ iff $\neg ontable(i)$, for $i = n + 1, ..., 2 * n$.

Using our language of a system description, the blocks world can described as follows:

program *Blocks World*
type $D = 0..n + 2$;**var** x : **array**$[1..2 * n]$ **of** D;
$\{1.\ x[i] = k \wedge x[j] = k \wedge k \neq 0 \Longrightarrow i = j$, for $i, j = 1, ..., n$,
$2.\ x[i] = k \wedge k \neq 0 \Longrightarrow x[k * 2] = n + 2\ \}$
procedure *stack(i,j: 1..n)*; **begin if** $x[2 * i] = n + 1 \wedge x[i] = 0 \wedge x[j] = 0$ **then**
begin $x[j] := i$; $x[2 * i] := n + 2$ **end end**
procedure *unstack(i,j: 1..n)*; **begin if** $x[i] = 0 \wedge x[j] = i$ **then**
begin $x[2 * i] := n + 1$; $x[j] := 0$ **end end**
procedure *move(i,j,k: 1..n)*; **begin if** $x[i] = 0 \wedge x[j] = i \wedge x[k] = 0$ **then**
begin $x[j] := 0$; $x[k] := i$ **end end**

The first state-constraints axiom asserts that an object can be at most one other object. The second state-constraints asserts that an object is not on the table if it is on other object.

Now, consider a global planning problem $Q = (M, G)$ for the blocks world specified as follows: $G = \{(2, 3, ..., n, 0, n + 1, n + 2, ..., n + 2\}$, i.e., the goal is to build the stack of blocks in increasing order of numbers. In order to find a solution to the global planning problem, we apply the following problem decomposition strategy:

(a) first, clear all blocks,

(b) next, stack the blocks according to the goal pattern.

Remark It has been shown [1], [5] that an optimal planning problem for the blocks world is NP-complete. Note that the above strategy allows to find a sequential plan in a polynomial time.

An if-while action , based on this strategy, has the following form:

$$\textbf{repeat}$$
$$\textbf{for } i=:1 \textbf{ to } n \textbf{ do}$$
$$\textbf{for } j=:1 \textbf{ to } n \textbf{ do}$$
$$\textbf{procedure } unstack(i,j) \textbf{ until } x[n+1] = n+1 \wedge ... \wedge x[2*n] = n+1$$
$$stack(2,1); ...; stack(n, n-1)$$

It is intuitively clear that this if-while action is an if-while plan, i.e., $M \models \phi(o)\{\gamma\}\psi(g)$ (see, Definition 2.8). In general, in order to show that $M \models \phi(o)\{\gamma\}\psi(g)$, i.e., to show that if γ terminates then the resulting multiple plan is correct w.r.t. its specification, one should apply the Hoare logics [9], [1], [14].

References

1. Alagic, S.and Arbib, M.A., *The Design of Well-Structured and Correct Programs*, Springer-Verlag, 1978.

2. Bylander, T., Complexity results for planning, in: *Proceedings of International Joint Conference on Artificial Intelligence (IJCAI-91)*, 274-279, 1991.

3. Bratko, I., *Prolog Programming for Artificial Intelligence*, Addison-Wesley Publ. Co., Massachusetts; Menlo Park, California, 1986, 1987.

4. Brownston, L., Farrell, R., Kant, E. and Martin, N., *Programming Expert Systems in OPS5*, Addison-Wesley Publ. Co., Massachusetts; Menlo Park, California, 1985.

5. Chenoweth, S.V., On the NP-hardness of blocks world planning, in: *Proceedings of AAAI-91: Ninth National Conference on Artificial Intelligence*, 623-628, 1991.

6. Genesereth, M.R. and Nilsson, N.J., *Logical Foundations of Artificial Intelligence*, Morgan Kaufmann Publishers, 1987.

7. Georgeff, M.P., Planning, *Ann. Rev. Comput. Sci.*,2, 359-400, 1987.

8. Hendler, J., Tate, A. and Drummond, M., AI planning: systems and techniques, *AI Magazine* 11(2), 61-77, 1990.

9. Hoare, C.A.R., An axiomatic basis for computer programming, *Com.ACM*, 12, 576-580, 1969.

10. Jones, C.B., *Systematic Software Development using VDM, Second Edition* Prentice- Hall International, 1989.

11. Kautz, H.A., Planning within first-order logic, in: *Proceedings of the CSC-SI/SCEIO*, 19-26, 1982.
12. Kohavi, Z., *Switching and Finite Automata Theory*, McGraw-Hill, New York, 1970.
13. Korf, R.E., Macro-operators: a weak method for learning, *Artificial Intelligence*, 26, 35-77, 1985.
14. Mirkowska, G. and Salwicki, A., *Algorithmic Logic*, Warszawa, PWN, Dordrecht, Reidel Publ. Comp. 1987.
15. Nilsson, N., *Principles of Artificial Intelligence*, Tioga Publishers, Palo Alto, CA, 1980.
16. Sierocki, I., Algebraic structure of Macro Problem Solver, *Cybernetics and Systems: An International Journal, to appear*
17. Spivey, J., *Understanding Z: A Specification Language and its Formal Semantics*, volume 3 of Cambridge Tracts in Theoretical Computer Science, Cambridge University Press, 1988.
18. Stephan, W. and Biundo S., A new logical framework for deductive planning, in: *Proceedings of the 13 th International Joint Conference on Artificial Intelligence*, 32-38, 1993.
19. Winston, P.H., *Artificial Intelligence*, Addison-Wesley Publ. Co., Massachusetts; Menlo Park, California, 1984.

Equality of Functions in CAST

Josep Miró, Margaret Miró-Juliá

Universitat de les Illes Balears. Ed A. Turmeda . Campus Universitari.
07071 Palma de Mallorca, SPAIN

Abstract This paper deals with the systematical checking of the possible equality of two functions or what is the same, of two expressions. The nature of the problem is first considered. The concept of Universe is reexamined. The concepts of Object Attribute Power Table, Prime Universe, Prime Table and Canonical Expression, unique for each class of equivalent functions, are introduced. A procedure to determine the Canonical Expression is presented.

1 Introduction

Computer use has become very fashionable, and at present is being used for all kinds of tasks. Speed and convenience are the main reasons behind it, although sometimes one is led to the suspicion that the computer has become a status symbol. Unfortunately, computer's popularity has concealed the fact that its power as a tool has allowed not only to solve problems that before were considered hopeless, but to outline new approaches to them.

When looking for a solution to a proposed problem, its solver uses the best technique available. However, the capability of the tools used in finding a solution imposes modifications on the techniques and this is specially true when the tool is the computer.

In particular, this has happened in the development of Computer Aided System Theory. CAST has been developed as an independent branch of thought. With the use of the computer, solutions to systems of great complexity can be found, but peculiarities and new concepts appear continuously. Without a doubt, CAST represents a set of intellectual developments, that has been increasing over time. New needs or new equipment has promoted new implementations, in what has been called explorative software engineering, trying to solve specific problems for complex systems, for example feasibility, prototyping, or testing. But CAST has also placed on the table problems that were once considered trivial, imposing again a change in the approach, and therefore in its formulation.

This paper has been motivated by one of such problems. In the development of prototypes, the aim of testing is not only detecting design flaws, but also directing the prototype evolution, toward better performances. Normally the decision of what is *better* is taken by a human being. It usually involves the comparison of at least two functions, deciding when one is better than the other or when they are equal. It was at this point the problem dealt with in this paper appeared.

1.1 The problem.

Let's consider two functions:

$$y_1 = f: D - V$$
$$y_2 = f: D - V$$

where $D = \{d_1, d_2, ...d_m\}$ is a finite domain and $V = \{v_1, v_2, ... v_k\}$ is a finite set of values the function takes over the different elements of the domain. Consider the following question:

Is $y_1 = y_2$?

Apparently the question is trivial. Each function is described by a graph or relation of the type

$$y_1 = G_1 \subseteq D \times V$$

$$y_2 = G_2 \subseteq D \times V$$

where $\times$ is the symbol for the Cartesian product. If the ordered pairs $<d_i, v_j>$ of G_1 and G_2 are the same, then the two functions are equal. In order to check for equality, the function values for every domain element d_i must be determined, and all resulting pairs $<d_i, v_j>$ must be compared. This means that for every domain element d_i the equality of the values of the functions must be checked. This task is conceptually trivial. The job size depends upon the difficulty of obtaining the corresponding values for every domain element. When the values are known, then it will depend upon the size of domain.

So far the problem has been extensionally formulated, but occasionally it may be formulated by means of a declaration or sentence. When this occurs, y_1 and y_2 may be expressed in terms of a set of attributes R_b , called *basis* . In this case the decision upon the equality of the two functions must be made by comparing the two *expressions*.

In the case that — is a set of v distinct values, then it is known that a v -valued function may be described by a set of v binary boolean functions of at most m binary attributes, where $m-1 < \log_2 |D| \leq \mu$

Then every one of the v boolean function may be analytically described in terms of the same m attributes, and the problem reduces to determine the equality of two binary boolean functions v times.

The problem to determine whether two binary boolean functions are equal is conceptually very simple whether approached extensionally from truth table point of view, or from its analytical description. However, it may become a bit involved computationally . An example will illustrate.

1.1.1 Example

Let the basis be $R_b = \{a, b, \dots c\}$ and let the functions $y_1 = f_1 (a, b, \dots c)$ and $y_2 = f_2 (a, b, \dots c)$. Is $y_1 = y_2$?

If the expressions for y_1 and y_2 were indeed equal, then equality may be ascertained by a simple examination. But if the expressions are not equal, the test may not be made by inspection.

A first possible way to test for equality is by means of the truth table. It is the extensional test. A second possible way to test for equality is by transforming the expressions into a sum of minterms. If the resulting minterms are the same for the two expressions then the two functions are equal too. A third possible test is by using the following well known logical equivalence

$$(y_1 \leftrightarrow y_2) \rightarrow f_1 f_2" + f_1" f_2 = 0$$

where " is the symbol for boolean complementation. Both the expansion and complementation may be quite laborious procedures for a reasonably sized DB. Something as trivial as the determination of function equality can turn into a problem of considerable complexity. In order to improve its solution, this paper modifies the "classical" approach, introducing concepts and techniques to deal with this problem with only one multivalued declarative expression.

2 The concept of OAT

2.1 Extensional descriptions

The data structures of conventional relational data bases have been described from different points of view depending upon the treatment and and the results aimed at by the study. The most usual methods [1] [2] are equivalent [3] in the sense that from one kind of a description the other may be constructed and conversely. This is reasonable since data bases contain the same information independently of how they are referred to. For convenience we start this discussion using the well known finite Object Attribute Table (OAT) concepts, outlined below, for the convenience of the reader.

D is the symbol for the *domain*, of elements d_i $i = 1, 2, ...$ m. representing the *objects*, m in number

$$D = \{ d_1, d_2, ... d_m \}$$
$$R = \{ r_1, r_2, ... r_n\}$$

R is the symbol for the set of the names of attributes, characteristics or properties of the objects.

Examples of possible attributes are: *age, date, height, hair color* etc. In general attributes may be multivalued. The set of values of attribute r_j is represented by $\nabla_j = \{\rho_{j1}, \rho_{j2}, ... \rho_{jv}\}$. In relational data base theory, ∇_j is usually called the *domain of r_j*. Here, the term "domain" is reserved for D and ∇_j is referred to as the *range of r_j*. The cardinal of ∇_j is represented by $|\nabla_j| = v_j$. When no confusion is expected it will be represented by a simple v as in ρ_{jv}. For each attribute there is a column in the table, describing the values of the attribute for each of the elements of the domain. The values of the column of attribute r_j, written lr_j, constitute a *function* whose domain is D and whose codomain is ∇_j : $lr_j = f: D \rightarrow \nabla_j$. The whole OAT may be considered as a set of functions on the same D, assumed in the same order, or what is the same the n functions lr_j are defined on the elements of $< d_1, d_2, ... d_m>$. It can be written:

$$OAT = \{ lr_j, j = 1, 2, ... n\}$$

or as a unique function

$$OAT = f: D \rightarrow \nabla_1 \times \nabla_2 \times ... \times \nabla_n,$$

Two OAT's are equal if they are defined by equal functions lr_j, $j = 1, 2, ... n$

OAT's, as considered above, describe a *full* extensional knowledge, in the sense that no data cell is empty, undefined or unknown. For the purpose of this paper, this concept will suffice.

Two OAT's are considered equal if they are identical or one may be obtained from the other by permutation of rows (with their headings) or columns (with their headings) or both.

In the case of binary attributes, the column functions $lr_i = f: D \rightarrow \{0, 1\}$, have the structure of a characteristic function, therefore the concepts of *binary attribute* and *subset of D* are equivalent. Or, in other words, *for every binary attribute, there is a subset of the domain, made up by those elements exhibiting it.* This is an old belief that is easy to justify in a *finite* OAT. An OAT may also be considered a part of a *conceptualization* [4]. All these concepts can also be introduced from another approach,that will illustrate other aspects usually not considered

For a given attribute r_j, the set of its values may be established in three steps.

1.- The names of the attributes and their values either must be previously defined, or borrowed from a previous language. The *initial* set of values are the values that are initially considered. For example, consider an arbitrary data base, and *distance* and *hair color* two of its attribute. The initial range of *distance* might be $\nabla_{init\,d} = \mathbb{R}$, the set of real numbers. For the attribute *hair color* the elements of an initial range $\nabla_{init\,c}$ might be all the colors one can imagine the hair of a person can be, as well as all the names used as colors in cosmetic dyes.

2.- The range of *possible* values, that is the values one is willing to consider. Possible range for *distance* and *hair color* could be:

$$\nabla_{poss\,d} = [\text{from } 0 \text{ to } 10^{30} \text{ km}]$$
$$\nabla_{poss\,c} = \{ \text{white, grey, black, brown, red, blond}\}$$

3.- The set of actual values appearing in the considered OAT. For example in the particular OAT, the range for the attribute *hair color* could be

$$\nabla_{act\,c} = \{ \text{white, grey, black, brown, }\}$$

since in the particular OAT there is neither a red haired person nor a blond one.

For every attribute r_j it must happen that

$$\nabla_{act\ j} \subseteq \nabla_{poss\ j} \subseteq \nabla_{init\ j}.$$

For convenience OAT's will be denoted or named by the symbol A, with or without a subscript.

A given subset of attributes $R_j = \{r_1, r_2, ... r_k\} \subseteq R$, of ranges $\{\nabla_1, \nabla_2, ... \nabla_k\}$, determines a *universe* defined as follows

$$U = \nabla_1 \times \nabla_2 \times ... \times \nabla_k$$

In other words: Given a set of attributes and their value ranges, their universe is the set of all possible tuples made of one value of each attribute, in same order as in the OAT. Since only full OAT's are considered, if $\nabla_i = \emptyset$, then U is also empty, represented again by $U = \emptyset$.

Definition Given two universes

$$U_x = \nabla_{1x} \times \nabla_{2x} \times ... \times \nabla_{kx} \text{ and } U_y = \nabla_{1y} \times \nabla_{2y} \times ... \times \nabla_k\ y$$

$U_x \subseteq U_y$ if and only if $\nabla_{ix} \subseteq \nabla_{iy}$; $i = 1, 2, ... k$

Of course one may distinguish different universes to start with. First, an *initial universe*, U_{init}. Second, a *possible universe*, U_{poss}. Considering the *lines* of an OAT as *n-tuples*, then a given A may be or may not be a Cartesian product of ranges. In general A will not be called a universe, but it will be a part of a *factual* universe U_{fact} determined by the values actually appearing in the OAT.

There is another universe that deserves a comment. It is the *semantically constrained* universe, U_{sem}. It may be obtained from the possible universe U_{poss} by removing all the elements of $\nabla_1 \times \nabla_2 \times ... \times \nabla_k$ that are impossible on account of the *meaning* of the attributes and their values. For example, consider that two binary attributes in a given OAT are "to be a father" and "to be a mother". The Cartesian product of the two ranges are:

$$\nabla_i \times \nabla_i = \nabla_p \times \nabla_p = \{0,1\} \times \{0,1\} = \{<0,0>,<0,1>, <1,0>,<1,1>\}$$

That is, $<1.1>$ is an element of the possible universe, but no normal person may be both a father and a mother, therefore the element $<1,1>$ may be removed on account of semantic impossibilities. Of course the relation between the different universes is $A \subseteq U_{sem} \subseteq U_{fact} \subseteq U_{poss} \subseteq U_{init}$.

The difference $U_{poss} - U_{sem} = U_{cons}$ is the set of impossible cases because of semantic *constraints*. Every subset of U_{sem} is one possible OAT, that is, a *possible world*. Every OAT is one of the possible worlds. *The difference* $U_{sem} - A = A_m$ is the set of *missing* cases, not existent in a particular OAT but totally possible in another possible world.

2. 2 Declarative expressions.

As mentioned above, an OAT is an extensional description of a portion of reality, made up by the description of each of its elements in terms of their attributes. A *declaration* is an expression (typically a function f (R)) describing an aspect of this reality made not in terms of its elements but in terms of a set R of their attributes. Since the concept of attribute is equivalent to that of subset, it follows that declarative expressions describe aspects of a whole OAT, in terms of specific subsets D_s, described by the binary attributes r_s that define them as follows.

$$D_s = \{ d_k \in D \mid r_s(d_k) = 1 \}.$$

The OAT aspects that can be declaratively expressed are:
1), D ; 2) , all $D_i \subseteq D$; 3), *relations* among subsets of D; 4), *functions* of subsets; 5), *operations* on subsets, depending upon the possibilities offered by the particular language used in the declarations. Even though languages normally used are be mathematically oriented (for example statistical), they are usually strongly related to the first order logic language, whose structure relies on a well known Boolean Algebra.

A set of attributes $R_b \subseteq R$ such that some subsets D_i $i = 1, 2, \ldots k$ may be defined by declarations f_i in terms of R_b, (written $f_i(R_b)$),

$$D_i = \{ d_k \in D \mid f_i(R_b) = 1 \}; \ i = 1, 2, \ldots k,$$

is said to be the *basis* for $(P(D))_i = \{D_i \ ; i = 1, 2, \ldots k\} \subseteq P(D)$, where $P(D)$ is the symbol for the power set of D, that is, the set of all the subsets of D. A basis allowing the definition of every subset of $P(D)$ of a given OAT, is referred to as *universal basis*.

The problem referred to in the introduction stems from the fact that given

$$D_i = \{ d_k \in D \mid f_i(R_b) = 1 \}$$

$$D_j = \{ d_k \in D \mid f_j(R_b) = 1 \}$$

where f_i and f_j are expressed in the declarative language,

$$(f_i = f_j) \Rightarrow (D_i = D_j)$$

but not otherwise. Therefore the un-equivalence of declarations cannot be inferred from the fact that the expressions are different.

3   Object Attribute Power Tables (OAPT)

3.1   Introduction.

Definition. A *sub-universe*, $U_x \subseteq U_{poss}$, is a subset of a possible universe

$$U = \nabla_1 \times \nabla_2 \times \ldots \times \nabla_k$$

that is a universe of its own because

$$U_x = \nabla_{1x} \times \nabla_{2x} \times \ldots \times \nabla_{kx}, \quad \nabla_{ix} \subseteq \nabla_i, \quad i = 1, 2 \ldots k$$

Lemma .   Let A_o be an arbitrary OAT. If $\nabla_{1x} \times \nabla_{2x} \times \ldots \times \nabla_{kx} \subseteq A_o$, then there is a $D_x \subseteq D$ such that

$$D_x = \{ d_j \in D \mid < \rho_{x1}, \rho_{x2}, \ldots \rho_{xk} > \in U_x \}$$

or simply

$$D_x = \{ d_j \in D \mid U_x \}$$

Proof: The proof is immediate. By assumption all elements (lines) of U_x are in A_o, and D_x is the name granted to the subset of D showing these lines in A_o.

Definition.   A is *complete* OAT if and only if is a sub-universe: $A = U_x$

Definition.   An Object Attribute Power Table (OAPT) is a function

$$OAPT = f: (P(D))_i - P(\nabla_1) \times P(\nabla_2) \times \ldots \times P(\nabla_k)$$

In other words, it can be considered as a table with a domain (headings of rows) and a range (headings of columns). Every row is headed by a subset of D. The columns can be considered headed by the attributes or their ranges, $\nabla_1, \nabla_2, \ldots \nabla_k$ and the elements of column j are subsets of ∇_j. Table-wise it may be depicted as in Fig 1.

	∇_1	∇_2	......	∇_k
D_x	∇_{1x}	∇_{2x}	......	∇_{kx}
D_y	∇_{1y}	∇_{2y}	......	∇_{ky}
D_z	∇_{1z}	∇_{2z}	......	∇_{kz}

Fig 1.- An Object Attribute Power Table

For convenience an OATP will be represented by the character T . Subscripts will be used when necessary. A T may also be described by its lines as follows: $T = D_x - U_x, D_y - U_y \ldots D_z - U_z$.

Since the table is a set (union) of rows and each row is equivalent to a complete sub-universe, it follows that a T may be considered a description for a whole A, given by

$$A = U_x \cup U_y \cup \ ... \ \cup U_z$$

On the other hand, since subsets may be singletons it follows that:

•   Given an arbitrary A, an equivalent trivial T_{triv} may be found by simply substituting the corresponding singletons for both the domain elements and the column elements, this may be symbolically written $T_{triv} = \sigma(A)$

From the above considerations it follows that T's may be considered descriptions of A's in a $P(\nabla)$ - language and the following conclusions may be inferred:

•   *Every T_i describes a unique A.j. Or $T_i \rightarrow A_j$*
•   *An arbitrary OAT may be described by different OATP's.*
•   *A lattice (the conventional $P(\nabla)$ boolean algebra) is induced on every column of a T*

3.2   Equivalence.

A relation ρ may be defined on the set of possible T's as follows

Definition. *Let $T_i \rightarrow A_i$ and $T_j \rightarrow A_j$; $\rho(T_i, T_j) = 1$ if and only if $A_i = A_j$.*

It is immediate that ρ is reflexive, symmetric and transitive, therefore it is an equivalence relation. A classification A/ρ is induced on the set of A's. For the purposes of this paper this relation will be represented by the symbol =. Thus $\rho(T_i, T_j) = 1$ will be simply written $T_i = T_j$. In this concern several problems may be remarked:

Problem 1.   Given T_i and T_j, is $T_i = T_j$?

Problem 2. Given $T_i \in (A/\rho)_i$ find a computing process Π such that $\Pi(T_i) = C_i$, where C_i represents a unique *canonical T* for the class $(A/\rho)_i$.

Problem 3   Given A, find C_i.

It is clear that a solution of Problem 2 would provide indirectly the solution to problems 1 and 3, since

$$T_i = T_j \quad \text{if and only if} \quad \Pi(T_i) = \Pi(T)_j$$

and $$C_i = \Pi(\sigma(A))$$

3.3   Prime universes.

Definition An universe U_x is prime with respect to A if and only if:
        1) $U_x \subseteq A$ and
        2) There is no U_y such that $U_x \subseteq U_y \subseteq A$

Definition. Let $T = D_x - U_x$, $D_y - U_y$ ... $D_z - U_z$. T is said to be *prime* if and only if $U_x, U_y, ... U_z$ are prime universes

Lemma 3.3.1. *If a T has only one line $D_x - U_x$, then U_x is prime and therefore T is prime.*

Theorem 3.3.2. *If two lines of a given T are:*

$$D_x - U_x$$
$$D_y - U_y$$

and $U_x \subseteq U_y$ then after suppressing the line $D_x - U_x$ the new T belongs to the same equivalence class .

Proof: If $U_x \subseteq U_y$ then $D_x \subseteq D_y$, therefore $D_x \cup D_y = D_y$, and $D_x - U_x$, $D_y - U_y$ describe the same A than only $D_y - U_y$.

Theorem 3.3.3. *Let U_x , U_y , given below, be universes with respect to A*

$$U_x = \nabla_{1x} \times \nabla_{2x} \times ... \times \nabla_{kx}$$

$$U_y = \nabla_{1y} \times \nabla_{2y} \times ... \times \nabla_{ky}$$

then

$$U = (\nabla_{1x} \cap \nabla_{1y}) \times (\nabla_{2x} \cup \nabla_{2y}) \times ... \times (\nabla_{kx} \cup \nabla_{ky})$$

is also a universe included in $\acute{A}$.

Proof: $\qquad U \subseteq U_x \cup U_y \subseteq A$

If U_x and U_y are prime, then as far as they are concerned, U could be prime also. It will be or will not be depending *only* upon its $\subseteq$ relation with respect to every other $U_z \subseteq A$.

Corollary 3.3.4 An immediate consequence of Theorem 3.3.3 is that

$$U_2 = (\nabla_{1x} \cup \nabla_{1y}) \times (\nabla_{2x} \cap \nabla_{2y}) \times ... \times (\nabla_{kx} \cup \nabla_{ky}) \subseteq A$$

$$.........$$

$$U_k = (\nabla_{1x} \cup \nabla_{1y}) \times (\nabla_{2x} \cup \nabla_{2y}) \times ... \times (\nabla_{kx} \cap \nabla_{ky}) \subseteq A$$

Another immediate consequence of Theorem 3.3.3. is

Corollary 3.3.5 *Let a prime T be given by $T = D_x - U_x , D_y - U_y$, where*

$$U_x = \nabla_{1x} \times \nabla_{2x} \times ... \times \nabla_{kx}$$

$$U_y = \nabla_{1y} \times \nabla_{2y} \times ... \times \nabla_{ky}$$

then the results of Theorem 3.3.3. and Corollary 3.3.4 are also prime.

Let U' be the set of *all* prime universes in (A_i / ρ); and T', the set of all prime T's in (A_i / ρ) . $< U \cap U >$ is a sub-algebra and every prime T is the union of several sub-universes. The meet of all the elements of a lattice belongs to the lattice and both $\vee$ and $\wedge$ are unique. For similar reasons *the union of all prime T's in T'* is also a prime T, and it *is unique.*

Procedure. Let $T = D_x - U_x , D_y - U_y , ..., D_z - U_z$. Let π represent the application of Theorem 3.3.3. and its corollaries to two universes, adding the resultant not empty universes to the table T. The procedure consists of the following steps:

Step 1 Apply π to all possible couples of universes.

Step 2 Delete all universes included in other universes in the table.

Step 3 Repeat Steps 1 and 2 until its application does not introduce a change in the table.

The end result is the set of all prime universes included in T. A complete formal proof falls beyond the scope of this paper, although it can be understood that : 1) if a universe in the table is not prime, Theorem 3.3.3 is still applicable, producing a new result, and 2) if one prime universe is missing, the procedure has not finished.

4 Algebraic declarative expressions

Given a T table, it is possible to represent it completely and exactly by means of an algebraic expression. In the same fashion that a boolean sum of products can represent a set of minterms, a universe of the table can be represented by an algebraic product of subsets of range values that define it, and the whole table as the sum of as many products as lines. Thus the algebraic declaration of the content of the table is

$$T = \nabla_{1x} \bullet \nabla_{2x} \bullet ... \bullet \nabla_{kx} + \nabla_{1y} \bullet \nabla_{2y} \bullet ... \bullet \nabla_{ky} + ... + \nabla_{1z} \bullet \nabla_{2z} \bullet ... \bullet \nabla_{kz}$$

Of course, the operations $\bullet$ and $+$ are commutative

The structure of this algebra and that of the sub-algebra generated by the prime products (sub-universes) are mentioned here for reference purposes, but a thorough discussion is beyond the scope of this paper.

4.1 Function declarations.

As discused above, an OAT is a subset of a possible universe. A subset of D is described by a characteristic function $f: D - \{0,1\}$. this function induces a subset of the OAT, which is also a subset of the possible universe. Therefore all the concepts introduced here apply directly to the description of functions with multivalued language.

Definition. The canonical expression CT of an OAT or of an OAPT is the algebraic expression describing the unique prime T made up of all its prime universes.

From the above discussion it follows that for every function there is a CT, that is a unique analytic description. Therefore it may be stated that

Theorem 4.1.1. *Let f_i and f_j be two functions, inducing two subsets of a domain in a possible world extensionally or declaratively introduced. Let CT_i and CT_j be the corresponding canonical expressions.*

$$f_i = f_j \text{ if and only if } CT_i = CT_j$$

5 Significance and future work

At first sight there is reason to hope that the concepts and techniques introduced here may become important, because they allow to diagnose the equality of two functions, without having to perform laborious function complementations or extensional checking. On the other side they allow a very compact analytical descriptions of large OAT's, provided that they are made up of sub-universes. Of course there will always be unmanageable DB's, even with power tables.

A number of important questions remain to be studied.

• The numeric decimal equivalent formulation for computer use, and real test on practical cases

• A detailed formulation of the procedure, considering several possible different implementations

• A formal presentation of the mathematical structure of the power table emerging algebra.

Acknowledgements: The helpful suggestions of Mercè Llabrés in the final draft are gratefully acknowledged.

References

[1]   Scot, D. Domains for Denotational Semantics. A connected and expanded Version of a paper prepared for ICALP, 1982, Aarhus, Denmark 1982.

[2]   Pawlak Z., Systemy Informacyjne, ANT, Warzawa, 1983

[3]   Vakarelow D. Consequence Relations and Information Systems in Slowinski, R Intelligent Decision Support, Kluwer A. Publ. Dordrecht 1992

[4]   Genesereth M. R., N.J. Nilsson Logical Foundations of Artificial Intelligence Morgan Kauffman Inc..- Los Altos, Calif. 1987

Basins of Attraction Estimation Through Symbolic Graphical Computing Techniques

Jesús Rodríguez-Millán

Universidad de Los Andes - Facultad de Ingenieria
Escuela de Sistemas - Dept. de Sistemas de Control
Apartado 11 - La Hechicera, Mérida 5251-A, VENEZUELA
Fax: 58-74-402846, E-mail: jrmillan@ing.ula.ve

Abstract. In the present paper an elementary symbolic method for the estimation of basins of attraction in second order nonlinear dynamical systems is formulated and its implementation using Mathematica® is shown. The estimation algorithm is based upon the construction of positively invariant compact boxes that trap the trajectories with unbounded initial conditions. We obtain such boxes through a Lyapunov function whose orbital derivative is bounded by a bounding function that can be represented as the addition of two scalar functions. The detection of persistent oscillating behaviors deserves a prominent place between all possible applications of our tool, as it will be shown by considering Fitzhugh Equations as a case study.
Keywords: Dissipative Dynamical Systems, Basins of Attraction, Lyapunov Functions, Nonlinear Oscillations, Symbolic Computing

Contents

1 Introduction

The origin of the present paper can be traced back [RM2] to an attempt to count and classify the nontrivial periodic patterns of behavior in Fitzhugh Equations, our case study at the end of the paper, and other physically motivated models. This kind of problems is usually approached through a twofold strategy: first we try to prove the very existence of nontrivial periodic orbits to proceed afterwards to count and classify them. However, what it seems to be a simple, straightforward and reasonable strategy to attack a problem very frequently leads to challenging technical problems.

Dissipativity and stability are two of the main properties we have to take advantage of when we try either to demonstrate that a second order system exhibits nontrivial periodic orbits or, in a more general context, to characterize attractors and repellors, because this two concepts are deeply related to the long term behavior of the trajectories of dynamical systems.

138

To be dissipative means that as time goes by, a system looses part of its own energy and "warm up" its environment by transferring the lost energy to it. Thus, dissipativity could be geometrically modeled by the converge of the trajectories of the system to a compact region of the phase space where they will remain trapped forever [H-C]. This mental image was the starting point to develop our symbolic computing tool, because every compact set might be enclosed by a family of big enough nested boxes, in such a way that were the system dissipative their trajectories would have to inwardly cross the borders of the boxes on their way to the trapping compact set. Thus, to think about Lyapunov functions as a tool to construct the family of nested boxes was quite natural, and so they appeared on scene.

People do not use to think of mathematics as an experimental science, but dynamicists happen to discover it very early when, on their first course on dynamical systems, they are asked to design a Lyapunov function to solve some stability problem. For there are no other way but to make (symbolic) experiments to calculate Lyapunov functions. Perhaps this might be the most valuable contribution of symbolic computing to applied mathematics: to help on speeding up the experimental stages leading to mathematically proved theorems.

It is within this context that we would like to introduce PICBox, a symbolic graphical computing tool for the construction of Positively Invariant Compact Boxes, because it is nothing else but a tool to perform symbolic graphical experiments to construct radially unbounded positive defined functions to study stability problems. The Flow Diagram 1 resumes the internal structure of PICBox and how it works.

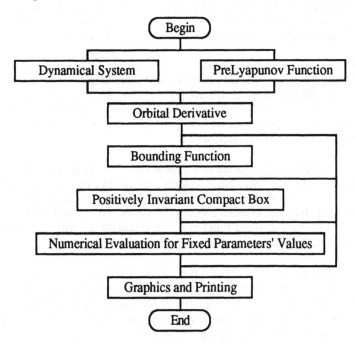

Flow Diagram 1. Functional Description of PICBox.

As it can be seen on Flow Diagram 1 given a dynamical system x' = f(x) and a positive defined function V(x), PICBox automatically calculate the orbital derivative of V, which can be used for whatever purposes: to study asymptotical stability or estimate the basin of attraction of equilibrium points, for instance. Afterwards, PICBox proceeds to calculate a bounding function for the orbital derivative that might be useful for estimating the basin of attraction of an attracting equilibrium point or to study the existence of nontrivial periodic orbits, as we will show in this paper. In this second case the bounding function must be rewritten in such a way that it can be used to construct positively invariant trapping compact boxes i.e., to prove that x' = f(x) is dissipative. Finally, it is possible to numerically evaluate the borders of the positively invariant compact boxes for fixed values of the parameters of the system, either to exhibit or to print them.

In the sequel we will always assume that vector fields are at least Lipschitz continuous to assure the existence and uniqueness of the trajectories for a given initial condition.

2. Dissipativity and Lyapunov Stability

In this section we will implicitly develop the symbolic algorithm that supports our computing tool for constructing positively invariant compact trapping boxes for second order multiparameter dynamical systems. Such algorithm admits a straightforward extension to nth order dynamical systems and might be used, either by hand or through a symbolic manipulator, to study whether a particular dynamical system is dissipative or not. In the case of second order dynamical systems, this algorithm will prove to be of great help on detecting periodic patterns of behavior.

Roughly speaking we could rephrase the definition of dissipativity [H-C] to say that a dynamical systems x' = f(x) is dissipative if there exists a compact set B that eventually traps all the trajectories of the system. Such a compact set B is dipheomorphic to a disc [H-C], and will contain all the relevant features about the global dynamics of the systems as well. In particular, the unique global attractor of the system will be located at the interior of B.

Lyapunov stability theory appears as a natural way [PlV] to approach the study of dissipativity in nonlinear dynamical systems. With this purpose in mind it is sufficient, however, to consider radially unbounded positive defined functions V as candidates to Lyapunov functions i.e., $V(x) > 0$ for every $|x| > X$ and $V(x) \to \infty$ as $|x| \to \infty$, instead of positive defined functions. For shortness we will refer to radially unbounded positive defined functions as preLyapunov functions.

It is possible to assure there exists a preLyapunov function for every dissipative system [PlV], but this result does not help us to exhibit a preLyapunov function for a particular dynamical system. Thus we have to rely upon experience, intuition and long and involved symbolic calculations when we search for preLyapunov functions to construct positively invariant trapping compact sets.

The proof of next theorem implicitly contains an algorithm for the construction of positively invariant compact boxes, which might eventually trap all the trajectories with unbounded initial conditions of the dynamical systems under study, provided the proposed preLyapunov function is appropriate. We will give some hints about how to propose preLyapunov functions for polynomical dynamical systems at the end of the paper. Given that this symbolic algorithm can be fully implemented through a symbolic manipulator, it might help us on speeding up the necessarily iterative searching process for appropriate preLyapunov functions.

Theorem. Let us consider a second order polynomical dynamical system

$$x' = p_1(x,y), \; y' = p_2(x,y) \tag{1}$$

where $d_i = \text{Degree}[p_i(x,y)]$, $i = 1,2$ and $d = \max\{d_1, d_2\}$. Let $V(x,y)$ be a preLyapunov function such that $\text{Degree}[V(x,y)] \geq 2d$, and let $V'(x,y) = \langle \text{grad}V(x,y), (x',y') \rangle$ be the derivative of V along the trajectories of (1). Suppose there exist an upper bounding function W for V' with the following structure:

$$
\begin{aligned}
W(x,y) = {}& - \alpha x^n + \sum_i |\alpha_i| |x|^{n_i} + \sum_{k;l} \frac{|\gamma_{kl}|}{\mu} |x|^{k\mu} \\
& - \beta y^m + \sum_j |\beta_j| |y|^{m_j} + \sum_{k;l} \frac{|\gamma_{kl}|}{\eta} |y|^{l\eta}.
\end{aligned}
\tag{2}
$$

If $\alpha, \beta \in \Re_+$, n, m are even positive integers, n_i, $k\mu < n$ and m_j, $lh < m$, then there exists a positively invariant compact neighborhood of the origin that traps all the trajectories of (1) with unbounded initial conditions.

Proof. Given the dynamical system (1) and the preLyapunov function V, calculate $V'(x,y) = \langle \text{grad}V(x,y), (x',y') \rangle$, and express it as follows:

$$V'(x,y) = V_1(x) + V_2(y) + h(x,y), \tag{3}$$

where V_1, V_2 and h merely collect the x-terms, y-terms and cross xy-terms of V', respectively, i.e., V_1, V_2 and h can be represented as

$$V_1(x) = - \alpha x^n + \sum_i |\alpha_i| |x|^{n_i}, \quad n_i < n \tag{4}$$

$$V_2(y) = - \beta y^m + \sum_j |\beta_j| |y|^{m_j}, \quad m_j < m \tag{5}$$

$$h(x,y) = \sum_{k;l} \gamma_{kl} x^k y^l, \quad k < n, \, l < m \tag{6}$$

where k, l, m, n, n_i and m_j are all positive integers and α, α_i, β, β_j, $\gamma_{kl} \in \Re$. After Jensen inequality [RuW], $uv \leq \dfrac{u^\mu}{\mu} + \dfrac{v^\eta}{\eta}$, for every real numbers μ, η such that $\mu + \eta = \mu\eta$. Then,

$$|x|^k|y|^l \leq \frac{|x|^{k\mu}}{\mu} + \frac{|y|^{l\eta}}{\eta} \text{ if and only if } \mu + \eta = \mu\eta, \Rightarrow \tag{7}$$

$$h(x,y) \leq \left| \sum_{k;l} \gamma_{kl} x^k y^l \right| \leq \sum_{k;l} |\gamma_{kl}||x|^k|y|^l \leq \sum_{k;l} \frac{|\gamma_{kl}|}{\mu}|x|^{k\mu} + \sum_{k;l} \frac{|\gamma_{kl}|}{\eta}|x|^{l\eta} \tag{8}$$

and therefore,

$$V(x,y) \leq -x^n \left[\alpha - \sum_i |\alpha_i|\frac{|x|^{n_i}}{x^n} - \sum_{k;l} \frac{|\gamma_{kl}|}{\mu}\frac{|x|^{k\mu}}{x^n} \right] +$$

$$- y^m \left[\beta - \sum_j |\beta_j|\frac{|y|^{m_j}}{y^m} - \sum_{k;l} \frac{|\gamma_{kl}|}{\eta}\frac{|y|^{l\eta}}{y^m} \right] = W(x,y). \tag{9}$$

This inequality is obviously the same than (2), but (9) is more convenient for the rest of the proof. Let us now choose k in such a way that $k\mu < n$ also holds. Then, given that $n_i < n$ it follows that:

$$\lim_{|x|\to\infty} \frac{|x|^{n_i}}{x^n} = \lim_{|x|\to\infty} \frac{|x|^{k\mu}}{x^n} = 0 \text{ and } \lim_{|x|\to 0} \frac{|x|^{n_i}}{x^n} = \lim_{|x|\to 0} \frac{|x|^{k\mu}}{x^n} = \infty. \tag{10}$$

Moreover, $\dfrac{|x|^{n_i}}{x^n}$ and $\dfrac{|x|^{k\mu}}{x^n}$ are continuous positive strictly decreasing functions of $|x|$, and hence so are $\sum_i |\alpha_i| \dfrac{|x|^{n_i}}{x^n}$ and $\sum_{k;l} \dfrac{|\gamma_{kl}|}{\mu} \dfrac{|x|^{k\mu}}{x^n}$. Then, there exists a unique $X \in \Re^+$ such that

$$\alpha - \sum_i |\alpha_i|\frac{|X|^{n_i}}{X^n} - \sum_{k;l} \frac{|\gamma_{kl}|}{\mu}\frac{|X|^{k\mu}}{X^n} = 0, \tag{11}$$

and

$$\alpha - \sum_i |\alpha_i|\frac{|x|^{n_i}}{x^n} - \sum_{k;l} \frac{|\gamma_{kl}|}{\mu}\frac{|x|^{k\mu}}{x^n} > 0, \tag{12}$$

for every x > X. Analogously, there exists a $Y \in \Re^+$ such that

$$\beta - \sum_j |\beta_j| \frac{|Y|^{mj}}{Y^m} - \sum_{k;l} \frac{|\gamma_{kl}|}{\eta} \frac{|Y|^{l\eta}}{Y^m} = 0 \tag{13}$$

and

$$\beta - \sum_j |\beta_j| \frac{|y|^{mj}}{y^m} - \sum_{k;l} \frac{|\gamma_{kl}|}{\eta} \frac{|y|^{l\eta}}{y^m} > 0, \tag{14}$$

for every y > Y. Thus, V(x,y) < 0 for every (x,y) such that |x| > X and |y| > Y simultaneously hold. See Figure 1.

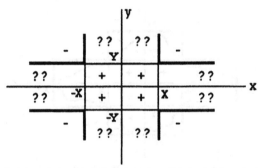

Figure 1. Map of signs of the bounding function for the orbital derivative of V(x,y).

To get a positively invariant compact box it still remains to study the sign of V(x,y) in {(x,y): |x| > X and |y| < Y} and {(x,y): |x| < X and |y| > Y}.

If |y| < Y, the term $- y^m \left[\beta - \sum_j |\beta_j| \frac{|y|^{mj}}{y^m} - \sum_{k;l} \frac{|\gamma_{kl}|}{\eta} \frac{|y|^{l\eta}}{y^m} \right]$ is positive and

bounded, whereas the term $- x^n \left[\alpha - \sum_i |\alpha_i| \frac{|x|^{ni}}{x^n} - \sum_{k;l} \frac{|\gamma_{kl}|}{\mu} \frac{|x|^{k\mu}}{x^n} \right]$ is negative and

diverges as |x| → ∞. Let

$$M_y = \max_{y \in [-Y;Y]} \left\{ -\beta y^m + \sum_j |\beta_j| |y|^{mj} + \sum_{k;l} \frac{|\gamma_{kl}|}{\eta} |y|^{l\eta} \right\} > 0. \tag{15}$$

Then, for every (x,y) such that |y| ≤ Y and |x| > X,

$$V(x,y) \le M_y - \alpha x^n + \sum_i |\alpha_i| |x|^{n_i} + \sum_{k;1} \frac{|\gamma_{k1}|}{\mu} |x|^{k\mu}. \tag{16}$$

Let X^* be the unique value of x such that

$$M_y - \alpha(X^*)^n + \sum_i |\alpha_i| |X^*|^{n_i} + \sum_{k;1} \frac{|\gamma_{k1}|}{\mu} |X^*|^{k\mu} = 0. \tag{17}$$

Then, for every $|y| < Y$ and $|x| > X^*$, $V(x,y) < 0$. Analogously, there exists a Y^*, such that for every $|x| < X$ and $|y| > Y^*$, $V(x,y) < 0$, as it is shown in Figure 2. Therefore, $V(x,y) < 0$ for every (x,y) such that $|x| > X^* + \varepsilon$ and $|y| > Y^* + \varepsilon$.

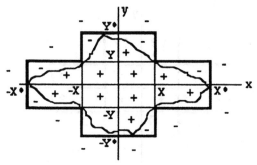

Figure 2. Positively Invariant Compact Box for Dynamical System (1). ♦

3. PICBox: A Symbolic Graphical Computing Tool for Constructing Positively Invariant Compact Boxes

From the aesthetic point of view it is possible to prove Theorem 1 in a nicer way. However, we decided ourselves for the proof above, because it is based upon a very simple constructive algorithm leading to the construction of Positively Invariant Compact Boxes. We used nearly the same symbolic algorithm to develop PICBox.

Even though we have only implemented the algorithm for second order systems, with some additional effort it would be possible to develop an n-dimensional version of PICBox. Calculations would obviously take longer as the order of the systems increases, but would not be necessarily more complicated.

The symbolic algorithm supporting PICBox can be resumed in the following 13 steps:

Step 1   (*First input*) Consider a second order dynamical system as in (1).

Step 2   (*Second Input*) Consider a preLyapunov function V: $\Re^2 \to \Re$.

Step 3   Calculate the orbital derivative of V: $V'(x,y) = <\text{grad}V(x,y), (x',y')>$.

Step 4.   Represent V' as $V'(x,y) = V_1(x) + V_2(y) + h(x,y)$, where V_1, V_2 and h are the functions described in (3), (4) and (5), respectively.

Step 5.   Construct an upper bounding function $W(x,y)$ for $V'(x,y)$ as in (9).

Step 6.   Calculate X for (11) to hold.

Step 7   Calculate Y for (13) to hold.

Step 8.   Calculate $M_x = \max\limits_{x \in [-X;X]} \left\{ -\alpha x^n + \sum\limits_j |\alpha_i||x|^{n_i} + \sum\limits_{k;l} \frac{|\gamma_{kl}|}{\mu} |x|^{k\mu} \right\} > 0$.

Step 9   Calculate Y^* such that

$$M_x - \beta(Y^*)^m + \sum\limits_j |\beta_j||Y^*|^{m_j} + \sum\limits_{k;l} \frac{|\gamma_{kl}|}{\eta} |Y^*|^{l\eta} = 0. \tag{18}$$

Step 10   Calculate $M_y = \max\limits_{y \in [-Y;Y]} \left\{ -\beta y^m + \sum\limits_j |\beta_j||y|^{m_j} + \sum\limits_{k;l} \frac{|\gamma_{kl}|}{\eta} |y|^{l\eta} \right\} > 0$.

Step 11   Calculate X^* such that

$$M_y - \alpha(X^*)^n + \sum\limits_i |\alpha_i||X^*|^{n_i} + \sum\limits_{k;l} \frac{|\gamma_{kl}|}{\eta} |X^*|^{l\eta} = 0. \tag{19}$$

Step 12   Draw the lines

$L_{Y^*} = \{(x, Y^* + \varepsilon): x \in \Re, \varepsilon > 0\}$

$L_{-Y^*} = \{(x, -Y^* - \varepsilon): x \in \Re, \varepsilon > 0\}$

$\qquad\qquad\qquad\qquad\qquad\qquad\qquad\qquad\qquad (20)$

$L_{X^*} = \{(X^* + \varepsilon, y): y \in \Re, \varepsilon > 0\}$

$L_{-X^*} = \{(-X^* - \varepsilon, y): y \in \Re, \varepsilon > 0\}$

Step 13   The closed rectangular box $C = \{(x,y) \in \Re^2: |x| < X^* + \varepsilon, |y| < Y^* + \varepsilon, \varepsilon > 0\}$ is a positively invariant trapping compact box.

Remark. The previous algorithm can be improved to get non symmetrical (more realistic) boxes, if we firsts substitute |x| = x for x > 0 in (19) to get X^*, and then substitute |x| = - x for x < 0 in (19) to get X^{**}, because in general $X^{**} \neq X^*$. PICBox actually generates non symmetrical boxes with respect to both the x and y variables. Furthermore, it would be possible to remove the corners of box C as well, as Figure 2 suggests, to get a smaller positively invariant compact box because in these regions W(x,y) < 0.

4. Detection of Nontrivial Periodic Orbits

One amongst others possible applications of PICBox is to combine it with Poincaré-Bendixon Theorem to detect NonTrivial Periodic Orbits (NTPO) in second order dynamical systems. The general strategy for such applications is implicitly formulated in the next Theorem, that rephrases Poincaré-Bendixon Theorem.

Theorem 2. Consider a second order nonlinear dynamical systems x' = f(x) with a unique repelling equilibrium point. If the system is dissipative then it exhibits at least one nontrivial periodic orbit.

Proof. If the system is dissipative, there exists a positively invariant compact set C whose boundary ∂C is eventually inwardly crossed by all trajectories of the system with unbounded initial conditions. Suppose the origin is the unique repelling equilibrium point of the system (otherwise move it to the origin). Then, there exists a small enough negatively invariant neighborhood of the origin, $B_\delta(0)$, whose boundary $\partial B_\delta(0)$ is eventually outwardly crossed by every trajectory with initial condition at the interior of $B_\delta(0)$. Let A = Closure(C - $B_\delta(0)$). Then A is a positively invariant compact topological annulus without equilibrium points in its interior, whose boundary is eventually inwardly crossed by every trajectory with non zero initial condition in $\Re^2$ - A. Hence, after the Poincaré-Bendixon Theorem, A contains at least one NTPO. ♦

Thus, a possible general strategy to detect NTPO in second order dynamical systems could be resumed in three steps

Step 1.   Given a second order polynomical nonlinear dynamical system, proceed to exhaustively topologically classify their equilibrium points, to determine under what conditions it exhibits a unique repelling equilibrium point. PAH could be helpful for this purpose [RM3].

Step 2.   Use PICBox to study whether the system is dissipative or not.

Step 3   Use Theorem 2 to detect NTPO.

5. Fitzhugh Equations: A Case Study

In this section we show how PICBox can be used to study the existence of NTPO in second order dynamical systems by applying it to Fizthugh Equations (FE), a simplified model for the generation of action potentials in nerve membranes [FiR], [RM1], [RM2], [Troy].

PICBox helped us, after a couple of experiments, to obtain a preLyapunov function to prove that FE are dissipative for all values of their parameters. On this basis we can demonstrate first that NTPO persist for big ranges of values of the parameters, and second that FE have at least two NTPO when their Poincaré-Andronov-Hopf (PAH) bifurcations are subcritical.

In an appropriate system of coordinates FE can be represented as:

$$x' = (1 - x_0^2)x + y - x_0 x^2 - \frac{1}{3} x^3, \ x_0 \in \Re$$

$$y' = - \mu(x + by), \ \mu, b \in \Re \ . \tag{21}$$

The next two theorems [RM2], [Troy] describe all possible local dynamics around the origin and x_0-depending PAH bifurcations .

Theorem 3. For $b \in [0,1]$ the origin is the unique equilibrium point of FE, and all its possible dynamics are described on the map of Figure 3.

Theorem 4. Suppose $b \in [0,1]$ and $\mu \geq 0$ in (21). Then $x_{01} = - \sqrt{1 - \mu b}$ and $x_{02} = \sqrt{1 - \mu b}$ are PAH bifurcation points for (21). Moreover, PAH bifurcations are supercritical when $\mu > \frac{2b-1}{b}$, and subcritical when $\mu < \frac{2b-1}{b}$.

According to next theorem FE are dissipative for all values of the their parameters. The Lyapunov function appearing in the proof was obtained by way of PICBox after a couple of experiments.

Theorem 5. Fitzhugh Equations are dissipative for all values of their parameters.

Proof. Consider the preLyapunov function $V(x,y) = b(\mu x^6 + y^4)$. After running the PICBox algorithm we obtain the following results:

$$V'(x,y) = \langle (6\mu b x^5, 4by^3); (x', y') \rangle = V_1(x) + V_2(y) + h(x,y) \tag{22}$$

$$= \mu b \ \{[- 2x^8 + 6(1 - x_0^2)x^6 - 6x_0 x^7] + [- 4by^4] + [6x^5 y - 4xy^3] \ \} \tag{23}$$

$$\leq - 2\mu b \, x^8 \left[1 - \frac{3|1 - x_0^2|}{x^2} - \frac{3|x_0|}{|x|} - \frac{2}{\sqrt{|x|}} - \frac{2}{7|x|} \right]$$

$$- 2\mu b \, y^4 \left[2b - \frac{1}{|y|} - \frac{12}{7\sqrt{|y|}} \right]. \tag{24}$$

(24) obviously satisfy the hypothesis of Theorem 1 and therefore Fitzhugh Equations are dissipative for all μ, b, $x_0 \in \Re$. ♦

In Figure 4 we show the positively invariant compact box generated by PICBox when $x_0 = 0.5$, b $= 0.25$ and $\mu = 1$.

Corollary 1. Suppose b $\in [0,1]$ and $\mu \geq 0$ in FE. Then for every $x_0 \in [x_{01}, x_{02}]$ there exist at least one NTPO, and all these NTPO are uniformly bounded with respect to x_0.

Proof. For every $x_0 \in [x_{01}, x_{02}]$ the origin is a repelling spiral point. Hence, by Theorem 2 there exists at least one NTPO for each value of x_0 is this interval. The uniform boundedness of the NTPO is a direct consequence of the compactness of $[x_{01}, x_{02}]$. ♦

Remark. It is worth to mention that the global existence of NTPO for $x_0 \in [x_{01}, x_{02}]$ is absolutely independent of the existence of attracting bifurcating families of NTPO associated to supercritical PAH bifurcations occurring at x_{01} and x_{02}.

Corollary 2. Let us suppose that b $\in [0,1]$, $\mu \geq 0$ and that PAH bifurcations at x_{01} and x_{02} are subcritical. Let $(x_{01} - \varepsilon_1, x_{01})$ and $(x_{02}, x_{02} + \varepsilon_2)$ be the maximal intervals of persistence of the repelling connected families of NTPO collapsing to x_{01} and x_{02}, respectively. Then for every $x_0 \in (x_{01} - \varepsilon_1, x_{01}) \cup (x_{02}, x_{02} + \varepsilon_2)$, there exist at least two NTPO.

Proof. Suppose $x_0 \in (x_{02}, x_{02} + \varepsilon_2)$ and let Γ_{x_0} be the repelling NTPO associated to x_0 in the family of subcritical bifurcating orbits collapsing to x_{02}. Given that Γ_{x_0} is a repellor, there exists a negatively invariant annulus $A_\delta(\Gamma_{x_0})$ of width δ around Γ_{x_0}, for small enough $\delta > 0$, whose boundary $\partial \Gamma_{x_0}$ is eventually outwardly crossed by every trajectory with initial condition in the interior of $A_\delta(\Gamma_{x_0})$. Hence, the unbounded connected component of $\Re^2 - \Gamma_{x_0}$ must contain at least another NTPO, because it contains the outer boundary of $A_\delta(\Gamma_{x_0})$ and FE are dissipative. ♦

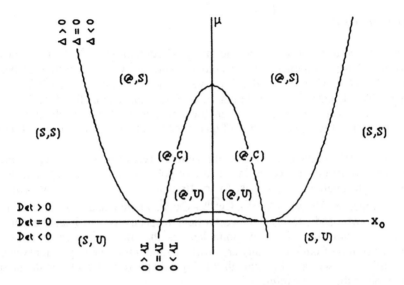

Figure 3. (μ, x_0)-Topological Classification Map of the origin in Fitzhugh Equations.

The topological classification map is qualitatively invariant for $b \in (0,1)$. Tr = 0, Det = 0 and $\Delta = 0$ denote the zero level curves of the trace, the determinant and the discriminant of the linearization matrix of FE around the origin. Possible local dynamics are denoted by $(@,S)$ = Spiraling Attractors, $(@,U)$ = Spiraling Repellors, $(@,C)$ = Center, (S,S) = Stable Nodes, (U, U) = Unstable Nodes , (S,U) = Saddle Points.

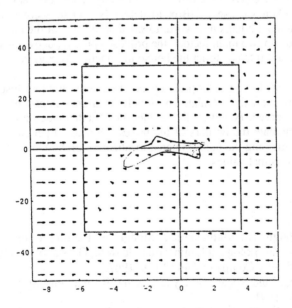

Figure 4. Positively Invariant Compact Boxes for Fitzhugh Equations when $x_0 = 0.5$, $b = 0.25$ and $\mu = 1$. Closed curves correspond to some negative level curves of V'.

6. Discussion

In this paper we introduced a symbolic graphical computing tool: PICBox, for the estimation of basins of attraction (repulsion) in nonlinear dynamical systems. Given a dynamical system $x' = f(x)$ and a positive defined function $V(x)$, PICBox can automatically calculate the orbital derivative of V, generate a bounding function $W(x)$ for $V'(x)$ and construct positively invariant trapping compact boxes for the flow of the system. We apply PICBox to Fitzhugh Equations to study the persistence of NTPO.

As it is well known, there are no general rules to propose appropriate preLyapunov functions. However, in the case of polynomical dynamical systems we suspect are dissipative, we suggest to try first preLyapunov functions with the following structure: $V(x,y) = Ax^{2n} + By^{2m} + Cx^k y^l$, where n and m are the maximal exponents of the x and y terms in the vector field, respectively. The k and l exponents have to be found later. The key point here is that in dissipative systems the trajectories coming from the infinity are nearly parallel lines that might transversally and inwardly intersect any big enough topological sphere that encloses the unique global attractor they are traveling to.

The main advantages of the algorithm behind PICBox are its simplicity, the uniqueness of the generated positively invariant compact box for each preLyapunov function, and the possibility of a straightforward extension to $\Re^n$.

PICBox is not an optimal algorithm in the sense of generating minimal trapping boxes, but we have to pay some price for simplicity. This drawback is, however, not so important when we use PICBox to detect NTPO in second order nonlinear dynamical systems. Perhaps it is worth to say that the size of the boxes generated by PICBox depends on two main factors: the proposed preLyapunov function $V(x,y)$ and the choice of μ and η to construct the bounding function $W(x,y)$ in (9).

To help the user to search for preLyapunov functions, and for illustration purposes too, PICBox can show the calculated positively invariant compact boxes, as in Figure 4. We have observed, however, that sometimes Mathematica® has difficulties to numerically calculate the borders of the boxes. This could perhaps be attributed to difficulties on guessing the approximated localization of X, X*, Y, Y* as a previous step to find their actual values.

References

[FiR]   Fitzhugh, R., Mathematical Models of Excitation and Propagation in Nerve, in Biological Engineering, Schwan, G. (Editor), 1-85, McGraw-Hill Publishing Company, New York, 1969.

[H-C]   Hale, J. and Koçak, H., Dynamics and Bifurcations, Springer-Verlag, New York, 1991.

[PlV]   Pliss, V., Nonlocal Problems of the Theory of Oscillations, Academic Press, New York, 1966.

[RM1] Rodríguez-Millán, J., Multiparameter Hopf Bifurcations in Fitzhugh Equation, Proceedings of the Eleventh International Conference on Nonlinear Oscillations, 479-481, Budapest, August 17-23, 1987.

[RM2] Rodríguez-Millán, J., A Topological Approach to the Global Dynamics of Fitzhugh Equation Without Diffusion, MSc Dissertation, Facultad de Ciencias, Universidad Central de Venezuela, Caracas, 1992. (In Spanish)

[RM3] Rodríguez-Millán et al, PAH, A Symbolic-Graphical Tool for the Study of Nonlinear Oscillations in Second Order Dynamical Systems, Program and Abstracts of the First European Nonlinear Oscillations Conference, Hamburg, August 16-20, 1993.

[RuW] Rudin, W., Real and Complex Analysis, Second Edition, McGraw-Hill Publishing Company, New York, 1979.

[Troy] Troy, Bifurcation Phenomena in Fitzhugh's Nerve Conduction Equations, J. Math. Anal. Appl. 54, 678-690, 1976,

Acknowledgments

It is with gratitude that we acknowledge the financial support of the Science Research Council of Los Andes University (CDCHT-ULA) to the Dynamical Systems Laboratory (DSLab) of the Control Systems Department, where this work was developed. The code of PICBox was written by Richard Márquez during his research assistantship at the DSLab in 1994. The final version of this paper was written during my stage at SZTAKI in Budapest in June 1995. I hearty thank Prof. Jozseph Bokor for his invitation and support during my stage at SZTAKI.

Temporal and Functional Verification of a Symbolic Representation of Complex Systems

Mireille LARNAC, Janine MAGNIER, Eric VANDERMEULEN,
Gérard DRAY, Vincent CHAPURLAT

LGI2P
EMA / EERIE
Parc Scientifique Georges Besse
30000 - NIMES
France

Phone : (33) 66 38 70 25 - Fax : (33) 66 38 70 74
e-mail : larnac@eerie.fr

Abstract. The complexity of systems requires that validation methods are set in the designing phase as well as during their use or maintenance. We propose a modelling approach of the system which allows us to bring into play some methods for the validation of temporal and functional properties. The model that we have defined, called Interpreted Sequential Machine, is based on the concept of Sequential Machine and avoids the main limitation (combinatorial explosion of the number of states when introducing any new data) by separating the purely sequential part of the system from the data and the operations on the data. The validation of the complex system thus modelled consists in :

- expressing the behaviour of the system by a set of symbolic, logico-temporal formulæ,
- carrying out automatic proof procedures on these formulæ.

1 Introduction

The most widely-spread validation methods applied on complex systems are based on the use of simulation techniques. Unfortunately, unless an exhaustive simulation of all the cases which can occur is carried out, this technique does not allow us to prove the absence of any dysfunctioning. For this reason, we are developping a methodology to formally verify some properties of the system. The process is the following :

- the system is modelled by a set of Interpreted Sequential Machines (ISM),
- the behaviour of the system is then described by a set of symbolic, logico-temporal formulæ,
- the properties of the systems are formally proved by formal manipulation of these formulæ.

We explain, in the first part of this paper, the starting point of our work, that is the methodology which handles the formal proof of temporal properties of a

Finite State Machine. In the second part, we present the ISM model ; we then show, in the third part, how it will be possible to verify temporal or functional properties of a system which is modelled by one or several ISM.

2 Proof of temporal properties of a Finite State Machine

During the last years, we have carried out a set of work on the proof of properties of systems modelled by Finite State Machines (FSM) [MAG90]. First of all, the behaviour of the system is expressed in a symbolic way by the means of temporal logic formulae ; then, starting from this representation of the machine, it is possible either to generate symbolic input sequences in order to verify the behaviour of the system for some situations (by simulation), or to formally prove some properties.

2.1 Temporal logic

We use linear temporal logic (LTL) [MAN82] which is well-known and has been widely used for the verification of programs [AUD90]. The suitability of this tool lies in its expresiveness power, and in its properties (completeness and decidability). LTL is defined by :

- a set of propositional variables : $V_p = \{p, q, r, \ldots\}$
- the classical logical operators : $\neg$ (not), $\wedge$ (and), $\vee$ (or), $\supset$ (implication)
- temporal operators :
  - $\star$ unary : $\bigcirc$(next), $\square$(always), $\Diamond$(sometimes)
  - $\star$ binary : $\mathcal{U}$(until)
- True, False

The building rules of formulæ are :

(i) - Every propositional variable of Vp, True, False are formulæ,
(ii) - If A and B are formulæ, then
  - $\star$ ¬A, A∧B, A∨B, A⊃B
  - $\star$ $\bigcirc$A, $\square$A, $\Diamond$A
  - $\star$ A$\mathcal{U}$B
  are formulæ,
(iii) - Any formula is obtained by application of rules (i) and (ii).

Interpretation :

- $\bigcirc$A (next A) means that "A will be true in the next (1-future) instant"
- $\square$A (always A) means that "A is true for all future instants (including the present one)"
- $\Diamond$A (sometimes A) means that "A will be true for some future instant (possibly the present one)"
- A$\mathcal{U}$B (A until B) means that "there is a future instant where B holds, and such that until that instant, A continuously holds"

Remark : We denote by $\bigcirc^n$ the n-future instant.

2.2 Representation of the behaviour of a FSM

A FSM is usually represented by a 5-tuple [KOH78]

$$M = <S, I, O, \delta, \lambda> \text{ where}$$

- S is a non-empty, finite set of states
- I is a non-empty, finite set of inputs
- O is a finite set of outputs
- $\delta : S \times I \to S$ is the state transition function
- $\lambda : S \times I \to O$ is the output function

To each state $s_i \in S$, we associate a propositional variable $\mathbf{s_i}$ as follows :

$$\mathbf{s_i} \text{ is True iff the state of } M \text{ is } s_i$$

In the same way, we associate a propositional variable $\mathbf{i_j}$ (respectively $\mathbf{o_l}$) to each input vector (output vector) built on the input variables of I (output variables of O).

Let $(s_i, s_k) \in S^2$, $i_j \in I$ and $o_l \in O$ be two states, an input vector and an output vector of M. We have :

If $\delta(s_i, i_j) = s_k$ and $\lambda(s_i, i_j) = o_l$ (which means "if s_i is the present state, and i_j is the present input, then the present output is o_l and the next state will be s_k"), then we establish an equivalent symbolic formula on the propositional variables, called **Elementary Valid Formula** (EVF) :

$$EVF ::= \Box(\mathbf{s_i} \wedge \mathbf{i_j} \supset \bigcirc\mathbf{s_k} \wedge \mathbf{o_l})$$

The expression of all the EVFs gives a complete, equivalent description of the machine M which presents several advantages :

- the EVFs express the **temporal behaviour** of M,
- this behaviour appears in a logico-temporal fashion,
- these formulæ are symbolic and can be easily manipulated through formal procedures.

We only deal here with deterministic machines. Therefore, we can establish a set of formulæ which express this property. For example, the state determinism is expressed in the following way :

$$DF1 ::= \Box\neg(\mathbf{s_i} \wedge \mathbf{s_j}) \text{ for all } (i, j) \text{ such that } i \neq j.$$

Identically, at a given time, one and only one input vector is present. This property is expressed as follows :

$$DF2 ::= \Box\neg(\mathbf{i_j} \wedge \mathbf{i_k}) \text{ for all } (j, k) \text{ such that } j \neq k.$$

The complete list of these determinism formulæ is given in [MAG90]. The analysis of the behaviour of M may require a more global approach. This is the reason why we have defined the concept of **Temporal Event** (E_t) as either a next state ($\bigcirc\mathbf{s_k}$), or an output function ($\mathbf{o_l}$).

A **Universal Valid Formula** (UVF) gathers all the conditions which involve a temporal event E_t :

$$UVF(E_t) = \bigvee_{(p,q):\mathbf{s_p \land i_q} \supset E_t} \mathbf{s_p \land i_q}$$

This means that an UVF is obtained by performing a "logical OR" of the right parts of the EVFs which contain the temporal event E_t in their left part.

Remark : It is possible to extend the notion of temporal event to a n-future state, n-future output, as well as a sequence of states or outputs.

2.3 Verification of properties

The properties of the system that one may wish to verify concern the dynamic behaviour of the system. The most useful of these properties are "safety" (i.e. nothing bad will happen) and "liveness" (i.e. good things will always happen). Unfortunately, real systems do not always possess these properties. It is therefore very important to know the conditions which lead the system into "bad" states. In other words, it is necessary to highlight :

- some structural properties of the Finite State Machine which represents the system, in order to identify source states and sink states, cycles, etc.
- the conditions which make the system reach a sink state, evolve according to a given sequence of states, or generate a given output sequence. This is what we call "temporal" properties.

Verification of structural properties. Saying that a state S_i is a source state means that there is no path in the state-graph which goes into state S_i (except a loop from S_i to S_i). It is therefore equivalent to verify that the UVF of $\bigcirc \mathbf{S_i}$ is either empty, or reduced to a combination of $\mathbf{S_i}$ with some input sequences. In the same way, verifying that S_i is a sink state is equivalent to show that for any state S_j (where $i \neq j$), $\mathbf{S_i}$ does not appear in UVF($\bigcirc \mathbf{S_j}$).

Verification of temporal properties. The key idea of this process is to study the "sensitivity" of a temporal event E_t with respect to a variable $\mathbf{v}$ (a propositional variable associated with an input vector or a state). Saying that E_t is sensitive to $\mathbf{v}$ means that changing the truth-value of $\mathbf{v}$ "has an influence" on the truth-value of E_t. This process is handled by a mathematical tool which is based on the concepts of **Temporal Boolean Derivative**. The result of the application of the temporal boolean derivative on UVF(E_t) with respect to $\mathbf{v}$ is a symbolic formula which expresses the "sensitivity" of E_t with respect to $\mathbf{v}$. See [MAG90], [MAG94] for details.

2.4 Example

Let us consider a sequential system made up of four states with a single input variable, called i and a single output variable o. The state graph representing this sequential machine is given in Figure 1. The labels (i/o) on the edges represent the input sequence which generates the state changes (transitions), and the output associated with it.

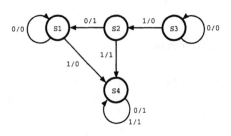

Fig. 1. State graph

Let :

- i_0 be the propositional variable associated to the input vector $(i=0)$
- i_1 be the propositional variable associated to the input vector $(i=1)$
- o_0 be the propositional variable associated to the output vector $(o=0)$
- o_1 be the propositional variable associated to the output vector $(o=1)$
- s_1 be the propositional variable associated to the state S1
- s_2 be the propositional variable associated to the state S2
- s_3 be the propositional variable associated to the state S3
- s_4 be the propositional variable associated to the state S4

Each transition is expressed by an EVF :

$$EVF ::= \Box(s_1 \wedge i_0 \supset \bigcirc s_1 \wedge o_0)$$

$$EVF ::= \Box(s_1 \wedge i_1 \supset \bigcirc s_4 \wedge o_0)$$

$$EVF ::= \Box(s_2 \wedge i_0 \supset \bigcirc s_1 \wedge o_1)$$

$$EVF ::= \Box(s_2 \wedge i_1 \supset \bigcirc s_4 \wedge o_1)$$

$$EVF ::= \Box(s_3 \wedge i_0 \supset \bigcirc s_3 \wedge o_0)$$

$$EVF ::= \Box(s_3 \wedge i_1 \supset \bigcirc s_2 \wedge o_0)$$

$$EVF ::= \Box(s_4 \wedge i_0 \supset \bigcirc s_4 \wedge o_1)$$

$$EVF ::= \Box(s_4 \wedge i_1 \supset \bigcirc s_4 \wedge o_1)$$

It is then possible to establish the UVFs. For instance, the following formula expresses all the conditions which generate the output o_1 :

$$UVF(o_1) ::= (s_2 \wedge i_0) \vee (s_2 \wedge i_1) \vee (s_4 \wedge i_0) \vee (s_4 \wedge i_1)$$

In the same way, the UVFs which contain the conditions showing when s_i will be the next state are the following :

$$UVF(\bigcirc s_1) ::= (s_1 \wedge i_0) \vee (s_2 \wedge i_0)$$

$$UVF(\bigcirc s_2) ::= (s_3 \wedge i_1)$$

$$UVF(\bigcirc s_3) ::= (s_3 \wedge i_0)$$

$$UVF(\bigcirc s_4) ::= (s_1 \wedge i_1) \vee (s_2 \wedge i_1) \vee (s_4 \wedge i_0) \vee (s_4 \wedge i_1)$$

We can immediately see here some structural properties of the system :

- S3 is a source state : it is impossible to reach S3 as a next state unless if the current state is already S3,
- S4 is a sink state : when the current state of the system is S4, the next state will be S4 whatever the input vector is.

2.5   Conclusion

The method presented herewith is very powerful to verify structural and temporal properties of systems which are represented by Finite State Machines. In addition, the concepts of Temporal Boolean Derivative can also be used to generate input sequences for functional testing of the system (thanks to simulation). This validation framework has been implemented successfully for systems which manipulate up to 200,000 transitions. Unfortunately, this method needs that the data which are manipulated are boolean. So the use of this method remains quite difficult in the case of complex systems whose inputs are not boolean, or which handle a very large number of data. In this case, it is necessary to define some extension of the FSM model. This is the reason why we have defined the Interpreted Sequential Machine model.

3   The Interpreted Sequential Machine

The **Interpreted Sequential Machine** (ISM) is a representation model for discrete complex systems. The concepts of this method are based on the work of Chang and Krishnakumar [CHA93] on Extended Finite State Machines. The key idea is to consider that the core of the system (some kind of sequential system) evolves into an environment (made up of data) ; this environment influences the evolution process of the core, and is modified when it changes state. After a brief formal definition of the model, we will see how the method presented before was adapted to verify some properties on ISMs.

3.1 Formal representation

Externally, an *ISM* is defined by the following 3-tuple :

$$ISM =< \mathcal{I}, \mathcal{O}, \mathcal{M} >$$

The internal view of an *ISM* model is defined by a 4-tuple :

$$ISM =< \mathcal{I}, \mathcal{O}, \mathcal{CP}, \mathcal{DP} > \text{ where :}$$

- $\mathcal{I}$ is a finite, non-empty set of input variables,
- $\mathcal{O}$ is a finite set of output variables,
- $\mathcal{CP}$ is the Control Part of the system,
- $\mathcal{DP}$ is the Data Part of the system.

The set $\mathcal{I}$ of input variables is partitioned into two distinct sets : $\mathcal{I}_C$ and $\mathcal{I}_D$. We have :

$$\mathcal{I} = \mathcal{I}_C \cup \mathcal{I}_D \text{ and } \mathcal{I}_C \cap \mathcal{I}_D = \emptyset$$

$\mathcal{I}_C$ is the set of control input variables, as $\mathcal{I}_D$ is the set of data input variables. In the same way, the set $\mathcal{O}$ of output variables is partitioned into two distinct sets : $\mathcal{O}_C$ and $\mathcal{O}_D$. We have :

$$\mathcal{O} = \mathcal{O}_C \cup \mathcal{O}_D \text{ and } \mathcal{O}_C \cap \mathcal{O}_D = \emptyset$$

$\mathcal{O}_C$ is the set of control output variables, as $\mathcal{O}_D$ is the set of data output variables. The Control Part $\mathcal{CP}$ is defined as follows :

$$\mathcal{CP} =< \mathcal{I}_C, \mathcal{G}, \mathcal{O}_C >, \text{ where :}$$

- $\mathcal{I}_C = \{i_{C_1}, \ldots, i_{C_n}\}$ (respectively $\mathcal{O}_C = \{o_{C_1}, \ldots, o_{C_p}\}$) is the set of control input (resp. output) variables,
- $\mathcal{G}$ is a state-graph defined by an 8-tuple :

$$\mathcal{G} =< S, I_C, O_C, F, U, \delta, \lambda, \beta > \text{ where :}$$

- S is a set of symbolic states
- I_C is the set of symbolic control input vectors made up on the control input variables. Let $D_{i_{C_j}}$ be the definition set of i_{C_j}.
  $I_C = \{v_{C_j} \ / \ v_{C_j} = (i_{C_1}, \ldots, i_{C_n}), i_{C_k} \in D_{i_{C_j}}\}$
  The function which makes an input vector i_{C_j} correpond to a configuration of the input variables is called the **control input function.**
- O_C is the set of symbolic control output vectors made up on the control output variables Let $D_{o_{C_k}}$ be the definition set of o_{C_k}.
  $O_C = \{w_{C_j} \ / \ w_{C_j} = (o_{C_1}, \ldots, o_{C_p}), o_{C_k} \in D_{o_{C_k}}\}$
  The function which makes an output vector o_{C_k} correpond to a configuration of the output variables is called the **control output function.**
- F is a set of enabling functions
- U is a set of updating functions
- $\delta : S \times I_C \times F \to S$

- $\lambda : S \times I_C \times F \rightarrow O_C$
- $\beta : S \times I_C \times F \rightarrow U$

    A transition t of $\mathcal{G}$ is defined as follows :

    $$t : (s_i, i_{C_j}, f_k) \rightarrow (s_l, o_{C_m}, u_n) \text{ where :}$$

    * $s_i \in S$ is a symbolic state
    * $i_{C_j} \in I_C$ is an input vector
    * $f_k \in F$ is an enabling function
    * $\{s_l\} \subset \delta(s_i, i_{C_j}, f_k)$
    * $\{o_{C_m}\} \subset \lambda(s_i, i_{C_j}, f_k)$
    * $\{u_n\} \subset \beta(s_i, i_{C_j}, f_k)$

The Data Part $\mathcal{DP}$ is defined as follows :

$$\mathcal{DP} = < I_D, O_D, F, U, \mathcal{D} >, \text{ where :}$$

- I_D is the set of symbolic data input vectors made up on the data input variables : $I_D = \{v_{D_j} / v_{D_j} = (i_{D_1}, \ldots, i_{D_q}), i_{D_k} \in \mathcal{I}_D\}$
- O_D is the set of symbolic data output vectors made up on the data output variables : $O_D = \{w_{D_j} / w_{D_j} = (o_{D_1}, \ldots, o_{D_r}), o_{D_k} \in \mathcal{O}_D\}$
- $\mathcal{D}$ is the set of internal variables
- $F : \mathcal{D} \times I_D \rightarrow \{True, False\}$ is the set of enabling functions
- $U : \mathcal{D} \times I_D \rightarrow \mathcal{D}$ is the set of updating functions

The external and internal representations of the ISM are shown in Figure 2.

3.2 Evolution process and interpretation

A transition $t : (s_i, i_{C_j}, f_k) \rightarrow (s_l, o_{C_m}, u_n)$ of $\mathcal{G}$ is interpreted as follows : if s_i is the current state of the system and if the control input vector is i_{C_j} and if the evaluation of the enabling function f_k returns $True$, then the current control output is o_{C_m}, the updating function u_n is activated and the next state of the control part $\mathcal{CP}$ will be s_l.

The interaction between the dynamic part of the system (state-graph in the Control Part) and the environment (the variables of the Data Part) clearly appears here. The modelling methodology therefore consists in identifying :

- the data which really define the state of the system, and the data which only influence its evolution ; the first class defines the states, as the second one contains the internal data (set $\mathcal{D}$)
- the partition of the input variables is then straightforward : the inputs which lead the state-graph to evolve when changing value are control input variables ; on the other hand, the inputs whose value changes do not imply a state change, are data inputs.
- the criterion to decide if an output is a control output or a data output is the following : a control output directly depends on the states, and its value is assigned without any calculation ; a data input is the result of a function involving some internal variables of the Data Part.

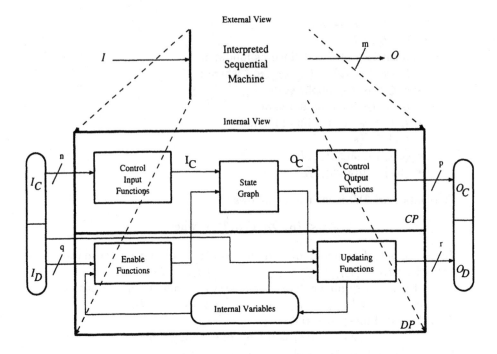

Fig. 2. External and internal view of the ISM

3.3 Logico-temporal description of an ISM

It is possible to express the behaviour of the Control Part of an ISM in a symbolic, logico-temporal fashion, similarly as for a FSM. The formalism just takes the enabling and updating functions into account when expressing a transition. An **Elementary Valid Formula** (EVF_{ISM}) manipulates the propositional variables associated with the variables which are involved into the transitions of the state-graph. Its general form is therefore the following :

$$EVF_{ISM} ::= \Box(s_i \wedge i_j \wedge f_k \supset \bigcirc s_l \wedge om \wedge un)$$

As stated in the case of a FSM, the list of all the EVFs gives a symbolic, equivalent description of the dynamic behaviour of the system.

Similarly, an **Unified Valid Formula** (UVF_{ISM}) gathers all the conditions which generate a **temporal event** (E_t). Here, the notion of temporal event must be extended not only to a next state or an output, but also to an update function. The general form of an UVF_ISM is the following :

$$UVF(E_t) = \bigvee_{(p,q,r):\mathbf{sp} \wedge \mathbf{iq} \wedge \mathbf{fr} \supset E_t} \mathbf{sp} \wedge \mathbf{iq} \wedge \mathbf{fr}$$

The main difference with the FSM model lies in the expression of determinism. Indeed, saying that the system is deterministic and completely specified does no longer mean that for a given state, there exists one and only one transition corresponding to a given input configuration. The completeness and determinism of the system now involves not only the input configuration, but also the enabling functions which come from the Data Part. So, an ISM is completely specified and deterministic iff for each state of the graph, there exists one and only one transition which takes into account the input configuration **and** the state of the Data Part (through the evaluation of an enabling function).

We can then establish a new formula which expresses this property :

Let $\mathbf{s_i}$ be the propositional variable associated with a state of $\mathcal{G}$, E_{t_1} and E_{t_2} two distinct temporal events,

$$DF_{ISM}1 ::= \Box((\mathbf{i_j} \wedge \mathbf{f_k}) \supset \neg(\mathbf{i_l} \wedge \mathbf{f_m})) \text{ for all } (j, k, l, m) \text{ such that}$$

$$\exists(E_{t_1}, E_{t_2}) \, / \, \Box(\mathbf{s_i} \wedge \mathbf{i_j} \wedge \mathbf{f_k} \supset E_{t_1}) \text{ and } \Box(\mathbf{s_i} \wedge \mathbf{i_l} \wedge \mathbf{f_m} \supset E_{t_2})$$

3.4 Modelling complex systems with ISMs

A complex system can be viewed as a hierarchy and an interconnection of simpler systems. This is the reason why we have added some features in the formal model of the ISM in order to describe the decomposition/aggregation process. The key idea for tackling complexity, is that it is possible to prove some properties of the simple elements which make up the system ; the verification of properties on the global system does not involve to build the complete ISM associated with it, but to study the properties of the elementary ISMs, and then to describe how these properties behave at a higher level.

4 Verification of properties

The validation of an ISM model addresses the proof of some properties ; In addition to structural or temporal properties, it is also possible to establish functional properties.

4.1 Structural properties

Basically, the structural properties of an ISM are the same as for a FSM. They concern the structure of the state-graph, like :

- source states,
- sink states,
- cycles, ...

The proof of this kind of properties follows the same process as for FSMs. The only difference is that the formulæ which are manipulated (EVFs and UVFs) contain some information about the Data Part (by the way of enabling and updating functions) ; but the important point here is that these functions have no influence on the existence of the structural properties.

4.2 Temporal properties

The verification of temporal properties is based on the use of the temporal boolean derivative of a temporal event with respect to a propositional variable, as well. The main difference here lies in these two points :

- a temporal event is either a next state, an output or an updating function
- the variable with respect to which the temporal boolean derivative is applied, can be a state, an input, or an enabling function ; furthermore, one can define a new variable which represents a couple (input, enabling function). This approach allows us to search temporal properties with respect to both the inputs of the Control Part, but also the state of the Data Part.

4.3 Functional properties

Considering a complex system, one may like to verify some properties on the data, or be able to control the influence of the data on the evolution process of the system. We call this class of properties **functional properties**.
Two distinct verification processes appear : the first one consists in verifying that a given constraint (on the data) is fulfilled ; the second one consists in expressing the conditions on the data which imply some properties on the state-graph.

Verification of constraints on the data. This process consists in establishing that a constraint the user gives is verified by the Data Part, either when the system remains in a given state, or whatever the state of the system is.
This implies to be able to express, in a symbolic fashion, the evolution of the data through the bringing into play of the updating functions.

Influence of the data on structural properties. We have already seen that the state-graph of an ISM owns structural properties. Nevertheless, the data can modify some of these properties (not all of them). For instance, a state which, structurally, is not a sink state, can actually **functionally** be a sink state in some situations - when the enabling functions standing on the transitions which leave the state cannot be true -. This kind of properties is very interesting, in the sense that one may ask for the conditions on the data which will functionally make the system remaining into a given state.

5 Conclusion

We have defined a formal model, the Interpreted Sequential Machine, which allows us to represent discrete systems. This modelling methodology considers the interaction of an environment containing any type of data, with a kind of sequential machine which expresses the dynamic evolution of the system.

We have also established a method for the verification of properties of the model, by the means of formal manipulation of symbolic, logico-temporal formulæ which represent the behaviour of the system.

In order to deal with the complexity of real systems, the process of interconnection and hierarchical organization has been defined. We are now studying how to prove properties of a such a complex system, considering the properties of the elements which make it up.

At the present time, we are applying this modelling and validation approach on a real industrial manufacturing system [1] ; a software implementing the method is therefore under development.

References

[AUD90] Audureau, E., Enjalbert, P., Farinas del Cerro, L.: Logique Temporelle - Sémantique et validation de programmes parallèles. Masson, Paris (1990)

[CHA93] Chang, K.T., Krishnakumar, A.S. : Automatic functional test generation using the Extended Finite State Machine Model. 30th ACM/IEEE Design Automation Conference, USA (1993)

[KOH78] Kohavi, Z. : Switching and Finite Automata Theory. Tata McGraw Hill, Computer Science Series (1978)

[MAG90] Magnier, J. : Représentation symbolique et vérification formelle de machines séquentielles. PhD Thesis, University of Montpellier II, France (July 1990)

[MAG94] Magnier, J., Pearson, D., Giambiasi, N. : The Temporal Boolean Derivative Applied to Verification of Sequential Machines. European Simulation Symposium, Istanbul, Turkey (1994)

[MAN82] Manna, Z., Pnueli, A.: How to cook a temporal proof system for your pet language. Report No STAN-CS-82-954, Department of Computer Science, Stanford University (1982)

[VAN95] Vandermeulen, E., Donegan, H.A., Larnac, M., Magnier, J. : The Temporal Boolean Derivative Applied to Verification of Extended Finite State Machines. Computers and Mathematics with Applications, Vol.30, N. 2 (January 1995)

---

[1] This project is supported by Merlin Gérin-Schneider, the Ecole des Mines d'Alès, FIBA and FEDER-Objectif 2

Modelling Differential Equations by Basic Information Technology Means

Maria Brielmann

Cadlab, Fürstenallee 7, 33094 Paderborn, Germany
maria@cadlab.de

Abstract. Current systems are no longer pure physical systems or information systems but tend to consist of elements from both of these areas. Thus, one modelling technique which considers the behaviour of all the different system elements is elaborated within this paper. Extended Predicate/Transition nets often used for information technology serve as a basis for this modelling. It is shown how differential equations as used for the description of the physical elements can be modelled by this technique. Linear and nonlinear systems are regarded as well as the coupling of these systems. For continuous modelling of the equations a continuous Predicate/Transition net is presented.

1 Introduction

Information technology is more and more used within complex systems also containing a lot of partially physical subsystems. In order to design such complex systems it is necessary to consider the behaviour of both the physical system components and the information technology components. Here the problem arises that physical systems are typically handled quite differently compared to information technology. For example, they are described by system theoretical means (e.g. continuous differential equations) whereas the description of information technology is event based. Within this paper a modelling technique is developed which allows the handling of system theoretical aspects by the same means as used for the specification of information technology. This technique is based on the state-space representation of physical systems. It is shown how this representation can be used for the construction of Predicate/Transition nets, a basic means for describing information technology behaviour. Thus, a specification of the entire system including the information system parts and the physical system parts is developed. This specification can be used for simulation and analysis of the entire system and for additional steps during the design process, that is partitioning and synthesis.

2 Extended Predicate/Transition Nets as Underlying Modelling Technique

Predicate/Transition nets are extensions of Petri nets [Pet62] which are well suited for describing event based concurrent behaviour and have been proven to be applicable for information systems modelling. They consist of places, transitions and directed arcs connecting places and transtions. A place may contain markings or tokens. If there are sufficient tokens in the predecessing places of a transition the transition is enabled or may fire. The enabling tokens are removed and new tokens are produced which are added to the successing places.

To reduce the complexity of the description of larger systems we use Predicate/Transition nets [Gen86]. Within these nets the tokens are identifyable and the net structure is annotated by a predicate logic language. The predicate annotating a place is fulfilled for the individual tokens currently inside the place. A transition may be annotated by conditions and actions. The conditions have to be fulfilled by the tokens enabling the transition, the actions are executed during firing of the transition.

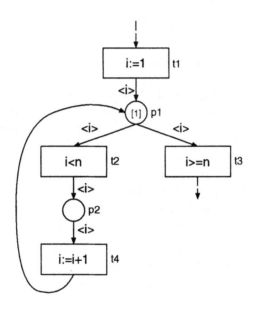

Fig. 1. Predicate/Transition net of a for–loop.

Figure 1 shows the modelling of a for–loop as an example of a Predicate/Transition net. When transition $t1$ fires the variable i is initialized and its value is put into place $p1$. The value of i can then be tested by the two transitions $t2$ and $t3$. If i is less than the constant n the body of the loop is executed and i is incremented. If i is greater or equal n the loop is exited and the rest of the net is executed.

For complex systems Predicate/Transition net models tend to be rather difficult to survey. Thus, we have introduced two concepts of hierarchy, hierarchical transitions and hierarchical places. Hierarchical transitions are similar to subroutine calls of any programming language. Their firing terminates when the subnet firing terminates. Hierarchical places can be compared to the activation of processes. The subnet firing terminates when the corresponding token at the higher level is removed.

For the handling of real time aspects a concept of time had to be introduced [Mer74, Sac94]. Therefore, transitions can be annotated by timing intervals determining the enabling and firing delay. For example, let transition $t4$ of Figure 1 be annotated by the firing delay $fd(t4) = [2, 3]$. In this case, firing of $t4$ is as follows: the marking of $p2$ is removed, the action $i = i + 1$ is executed, and the new marking i is put into place $p1$ after 2 to 3 time steps. In addition to that, the interval denoting the enabling delay ed determines how long a marking has to be within all predecessing places of a transition t before t can fire. During the enabling time of t the corresponding marking may be removed by other transitions whereas during the firing time they are reserved. Thus, the enabling time can be used e.g. for handling timeouts.

3 The Modelling Approach

Physical systems are usually described by the means of systems theory e.g. differential equations. In [BK93] a modelling approach for linear differential equations with Predicate/Transition nets has already been presented. The approach is based on the Z–transform.

In this paper a different approach will be discussed using the state–space representation. This representation is very common for physical systems and used within mechatronic description languages like DSL [Sch91]. The state–space representation calculates the output of the system and the derivation of the new state by the following equations:

$$\dot{x} = f(x, u, p, t)$$
$$y = g(\dot{x}, x, u, p, t) \tag{1}$$

The vector x denotes the state, $\dot{x}$ its derivative, u is the input, y the output, p are parameters and the scalar t denotes the time. g and f are functions which generally show nonlinear behaviour. In the following sections it will be shown how systems in state–space representation can be modelled by extended Predicate/Transition nets.

3.1 Modelling of Linear Systems

For linear systems the general state–space representation as shown in Equation 1 can be simplified as follows ($A, B, C,$ and D are linear matrices):

$$\dot{x} = A * x + B * u$$
$$y = C * x + D * u \tag{2}$$

Since Predicate/Transition nets are a discrete modelling technique a discretization of the equations has to take place before a net representation can be derived. Here some methods common in systems theory e.g. the backward difference method are used (cf [AW84]). These methods transform the continuous signals into signals sampled with a specific sampling interval. Furthermore, also the matrices for the calculation have to be adapted to the sampling interval. Thus, the sampled system is described by the following equations:

$$x(t+h) = A(h) * x(t) + B(h) * u(t)$$
$$y(t) = C(h) * x(t) + D(h) * u(t) \tag{3}$$

Based on this discretized state–space representation a Predicate/Transition net can be constructed. This Predicate/Transition net is shown in Figure 2. The input vector u sampled at a specific time point t is fed to two transitions, $t1$ for the calculation of the output and $t2$ for the determination of the new state. For the calculation of the output vector the old state determined at the previous time point (expressed by the marking $init$) is stored in place $p4$. After the calculation the old state is put into place $p5$. Transition $t2$ removes the tokens from place $p5$ and $p3$ and puts the new state into place $p4$ delayed by sampling time h (expressed by the annotation $fd = (h, h)$).

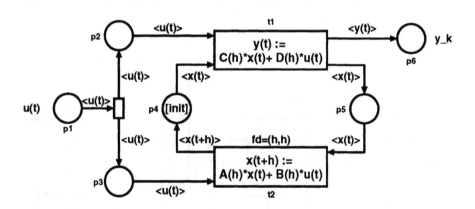

Fig. 2. Predicate/Transition net of discretized state–space representation.

3.2 Coupling of Linear Systems

The technique shown in the previous section allows the modelling of single systems described by linear differential equations. For the coupling of several systems the problem of feed back loops has to be solved. These feed back loops are important if outputs of the coupled system are used as input signals of the coupled system without any delay. As a solution there are algorithms [Sch94] which calculate new matrices for the coupled system disregarding the modularity. For this calculation a so called coupling matrix K has to be determined which depends on the D matrices of the coupled systems. The following equation holds [Sch94] for the coupling of two systems:

$$K = \begin{pmatrix} k11 & k12 \\ k21 & k22 \end{pmatrix}$$
$$= \begin{pmatrix} I & -D_{1CC} \\ -D_{2CC} & I \end{pmatrix}^{-1} \tag{4}$$

where D_{1CC} and D_{2CC} contain those rows of the two D matrices which affect the coupling signals. With the help of the matrix K the values of the feed back signals yc can be determined:

$$yc = K * C_c * x + K * D_c * u \tag{5}$$

where C_c and D_c contain those elements of the C and D matrices of the two systems which determine the contribution of the state x and the system input u to the feed back signals. In order to maintain the modularity of the coupled system this calculation can be introduced into the net modelling of the coupled system. Figure 3 shows the coupling of the two systems $L1$ and $L2$.

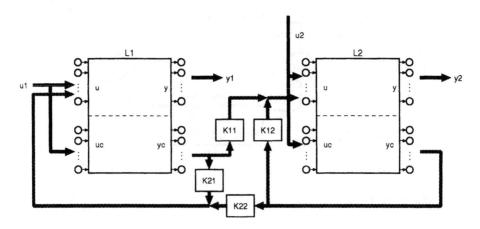

Fig. 3. Modelling of coupled systems.

In the lower part of the two systems the input signals are connected to the states and the relevant elements of the C and D matrices. The output of these two parts are multiplied with the relevant elements of the coupling matrix K. The result of this together with the system input is used in the higher part of the two systems which are realized as shown in Figure 2. The principles of this modelling can be easily extended for the coupling of several systems.

3.3 Modelling of Nonlinear Systems

For nonlinear systems a matrix based formula as in Equation 3 does not exist. Two kinds of nonlinearities have to be distinguished: nonlinearities caused by discontinuities in the result values and nonlinearities caused by nonlinear functions.

Nonlinearities Caused by Discontinuities Discontinuities are points of the functions f and g where the result values cannot be connected by a continuous line. Thus, the function can be divided into continuous subfunctions. If these subfunctions show linear behaviour they can be modelled as described in Section 3.1. If they are nonlinear the modelling techniques of the following two sections can be used. For the modelling of the entire function the subfunction models have to be combined and share one state. This is shown in Figure 4 for a function with one discontinuous point and thus two subfunctions (the new net elements are highlighted).

The input $u(t)$ of the system is tested by the transitions $t1$ and $t2$. Depending on the constant k denoting the discontinuous point and the input value, $t1$ or $t2$ puts the input stored in $p1$ and the state stored in $p7$ into the corresponding subnet which does the necessary calculations. If $u(t) > k$ the matrices $A1, B1, C1$ and $D1$ (the loop at the top of the figure) and otherwise the matrices $A2, B2, C2$ and $D2$ are used. After the calculation of the new state in transition $t4$ or $t5$ respectively the state is put back into place $p7$ where it can again be used by the input transitions $t1$ and $t2$ of the two subnets.

Nonlinearities Caused by Nonlinear Functions If the nonlinearities of the function are not caused by discontinuities but by the function itself the problem is much more difficult. Here, no simple selection of linear subfunctions is possible. Thus, the modelling of linear systems cannot be used directly. For this case two solutions are possible: the introduction of the integration algorithm into the Predicate/Transition net model and the piecewise linearization of the involved functions.

Piecewise Linearization

As one possibility for the handling of nonlinear functions the linearization of the function can be considered which allows the construction of linear functions with nearly the same behaviour as the nonlinear function in the area close to a specified operation point. The Taylor linearization (cf [FF82] P. 70) applied to the general formula for nonlinear systems (cf Equation 1) leads to the following formula:

$$\Delta \dot{x} = A(x_0, u_0, t, p) * \Delta x + B(x_0, u_0, t, p) * \Delta u$$
$$\Delta y = C(x_0, u_0, t, p) * \Delta x + D(x_0, u_0, t, p) * \Delta u \qquad (6)$$

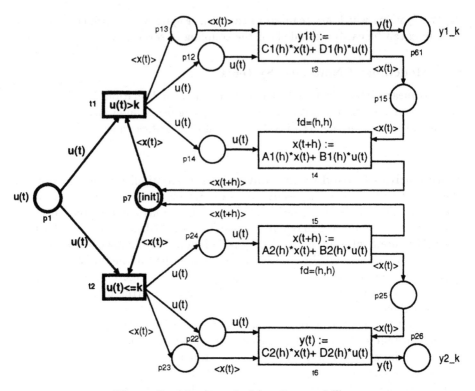

Fig. 4. Combination of subfunction modelling

where the matrices are constructed by the following equations:

$$A = \frac{\partial f}{\partial x}, \qquad B = \frac{\partial f}{\partial u}, \qquad C = \frac{\partial g}{\partial x}, \qquad D = \frac{\partial g}{\partial u}.$$

Thus, a linear description of the nonlinear system is constructed. But Formula 6 is only valid for small deviations of the operation point. Thus, the nonlinear function has to be splitted into several parts and each of these parts has to be separately linearized. The linear descriptions of the system parts can be modelled as shown in Section 3.1 and combined as shown in Section 3.3. The part to be used can be selected by evaluating the current state and the input.

Introduction of the Integration Algorithm

The piecewise linearization of a nonlinear function and the additional discretization necessary for the modelling leads to some errors in the calculation of the results. Sometimes these results are not sufficiently close to the exact values. In these cases another modelling technique with smaller errors is required. Therefore, we investigatedd the integration algorithms which are usually used for simulation of differential equations. These algorithms are based on the approximation of the original function by small pieces of straight lines. Thus, the integration of the function can be approximated by the summation of the space below of these pieces of straight lines. For example, for the Euler integration the differentiation is approximated by the following formula:

$$\dot{x}(t) \approx \frac{x(t+h) - x(t)}{h} \tag{7}$$

With $\dot{x}(t) = f(x,t)$ this leads to the formula for the integration (Equation 8) which is illustrated in Figure 5.

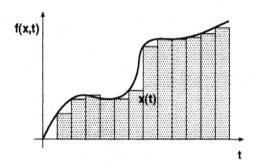

Fig. 5. The Euler integration.

$$x(t+h) \approx h * \dot{x}(t) + x(t) = h * f(x,t) + x(t) \tag{8}$$

The quality of the result of this approximation depends on the distance h between two calculations. A small h leads to good results but requires a lot of calculations.

For the modelling of nonlinear differential equations it is also possible to model the integration algorithm with Predicate/Transition nets. This is shown in Figure 6. The current value of x is stored in place $p2$. When a new input arrives in place $p1$ the transition is enabled. It removes the new input from $p1$ and the value of x from $p2$ and calculates the new value according to Equation 8. The new value is put into $p2$ and $p3$ after a delay of h.

With this model of the integration nonlinear differential equations can be modeled as shown in Figure 7. This modelling is very similar to the one of Figure 2. But the calculations executed by the transitions are not based on matrices but on the functions themself. Furthermore, the integration algorithm is introduced for the determination of the new state.

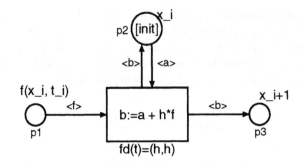

Fig. 6. Modelling of Euler integration.

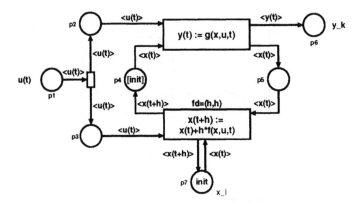

Fig. 7. Modelling of nonlinear differential equations.

3.4 Continuous Modelling

Predicate/Transition nets are in their nature a discrete modelling technique. Thus, all the modelling concepts described in the previous sections are also discrete. But regarding the definition of integration it is possible to define some kind of continuous Predicate/Transition nets for the description of differential equations. As shown in Section 3.3 for integration the function is approximated by pieces of straight lines. The integration itself is calculated by summing up the space below these pieces of straight lines. The quality of the result depends on the length of the pieces, that is on the sampling time h. A smaller h leads to a less difference between the result and the correct integration value. Thus, for the definition of integration a limes calculation for $h \to 0$ is done. The same can be done on Predicate/Transition net level. For the modelling of the integration algorithm the length of the pieces is explicitly mentioned at two points: within the calculation of the new value of x and as firing delay of the transition. When introducing the limes calculation this has to be done at both places simultaneously.

With this mechanism a transition is created which fires continuously if enabled continuously. Thus, as a next step the continuous enabling of the transition has to be assured. This is only possible if the markings in the predecessing places are not consumed by the transition. This can be solved by putting the markings back into the corresponding places. Thus, the continuous modelling of the integration algorithm can be done as shown in Figure 8.

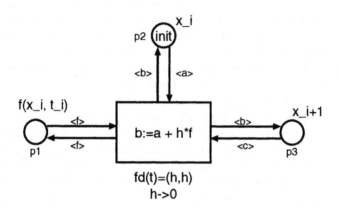

Fig. 8. Continuous modelling of the integration algorithm.

Here, the arcs connecting the places and the transition are bidirectional so that a valid marking can be found in the places at any time. The continuous modelling of the whole differential equation as shown in Figure 7 can be solved by the same means. Again the markings of all places must not be consumed. Therefore, each arc connecting a place and a transition has to become bidirectional.

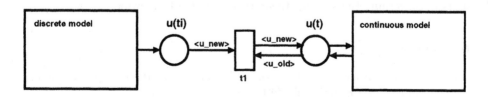

Fig. 9. Connecting discrete and continuous model parts.

The connection to a discrete model part can be realized as shown in Figure 9. The discrete model delivers a new input $u(ti)$ at time ti. This new input has to replace the old one $u(t)$. Therefore, the input transition $t1$ removes the old value via the arc annotated by u_old and replaces it by the new one via the arc annotated by u_new. For the connection of a discrete model part to the output of the continuous model a transition of the discrete model has to read the output without removing the marking.

4 Conclusion

Within this paper it has been shown how continuous differential equations usually used for the description of physical systems and their control can be modelled by extended Predicate/Transition nets. This modelling is especially valuable if a system consisting of physical system parts as well as information technology shall be handled. The use of only one modelling technique allows the simulation and analysis of the entire system. Furthermore, the model can be used for subsequent design steps, e.g., partitioning and synthesis.

For the modelling of nonlinear differential equations several different techniques have been elaborated, e.g. with or without linearization or discretization. The selection of the modelling technique for a special differential equation depends on its application. If it is applied to a system with hard real time conditions the calculation time is especially important thus requiring a more simple modelling whereas other systems might require a more accurate modelling. Furthermore, the final realization of the system part has to be considered. If the differential equation describes a real time control of some physical part, the realized integration algorithm has to be as simple as possible. Thus it does not make sense to use complicated calculations for the modelling because the results of the realized system part might differ too much.

Acknowledgements

The author wants to thank her colleagues from the Process and System Modelling Group, Cadlab, Paderborn, especially Bernd Kleinjohann, Rainer Milczewski and Joachim Stroop, for their support and the fruitful discussions leading to some of the solutions presented in this paper. Special thanks to Jobst Richert and his colleagues from MLaP (University of Paderborn) and for their support concerning the systems theoretical aspects of the work.

References

[AW84] Karl J. Åström and B. Wittenmark. *Computer Controlled Systems: Theory and Design*. Prentice Hall, 1984.

[BK93] Maria Brielmann and Bernd Kleinjohann. A formal model for coupling computer based systems and physical systems. In *Proceedings of the EURO–DAC*, pages 158–163, 1993.

[FF82] Otto Föllinger and Dieter Franke. *Einführung in die Zustandsbeschreibung dynamischer Systeme*. Oldenbourg Verlag, 1982.

[Gen86] Hartmann J. Genrich. Predicate/transition nets. In G. Rozenberg, editor, *Advances in Petri Nets*, pages 207–247. Springer–Verlag, 1986.

[Mer74] P. Merlin. *A study of the recoverability of computing systems*. PhD thesis, University of California, Department of Information and Computer Science, 1974.

[Pet62] C.A. Petri. Kommunikation mit Automaten. Schriften des IIM 2, Institut für Instrumentelle Mathematik, Bonn, 1962. English translation: Technical Report RADC-TR-65-377, Griffiss Air Force Base, New York, Vol. 1, Suppl. 1, 1966.

[Sac94] Krzysztof Sacha. Real-time software specification and validation with transnet. *Real-Time Systems*, 6:153–172, 1994.

[Sch91] Joachim Schröer. A short description of a model compiler/interpreter for supporting simulation and optimization of nonlinear and linearized dynamic systems. In *5th IFAC/IMACS Symposium on CADCS*, Swansea, UK, 1991.

[Sch94] Joachim Schröer. *Eine Modellbeschreibungssprache zur Unterstützung der Simulation und Optimierung von nichtlinearen und linearisierten hierarchischen Systemen*. PhD thesis, Universität Paderborn, 1994.

System Theoretic Aspects of Software Architectures

Franz Kapsner

Siemens Corporate Research and Development

D - 81730 Munich

1 Introduction

In our world software-based systems become more and more important. Although we live in the so called „software crisis" with all its difficulties and problems, we are able to realise more complex applications than ever before. Methods and principles help us to control all the processes of development of software systems from problem analysis via realisation to maintenance of existing systems. But the biggest problem of today is to produce and to maintain software-based systems very quickly, with low costs and high quality. Only under these preconditions is a company able to be and remain competitive on the market.

New, more complex software-based solutions cause much greater effort during development and use (analysis, design, implementation, test and maintenance). So we are looking for possible support to reduce the time for development and costs in all phases of the software life cycle.

Recently the aspects of software architecture as a method for structuring the systems has gained increased importance. The aspect of architecture in former times included all topics of a system and mostly the hardware components stood in the foreground. In the meantime, the software archi-tecture becomes more and more important, because the role of software architecture is of utmost importance for the success of a software project.

An approach for developing software architecture in a systematic way is described in the following sections.

2 System architecture - Software architecture

In the area of system development, the aspects of hardware, operating systems, databases and user interfaces play an important role. The interoperability of all these components is a precondition for a successful system. Common interfaces must fit together to allow information exchange (data flow, control flow).

Standardised components are available today. Hardly anyone is willing to develop a new operating system or a data base for a specific application. User interfaces are constructed based on prefabricated kits. After some decisions concerning the hardware platform (e.g. processor, operating system, language), it is possible to select suitable components as a base for the application. These components fix a specific system architecture as a precondition for the development on the system level.

In general, the realisation of a new application requires the production of new code and this code has a specific structure (architecture). In the following the focus lies on the software architecture for specific applications.

A definition for the term "Software Architecture" is: *The software architecture specifies the system structure in form of components and the relationships between them.*

In addition to the functional properties of a software system one must also consider the non-functional properties (see section 3). The software architecture has great influence on both aspect. Specific software architectures have specific properties and characteristic features. One very important approach for the development of a software architecture considering these aspects is the design pattern approach (see section 4).

All of the best methods are necessary to optimize the process of producing software architecture. The knowledge of system theory has very useful aspects for developing software architectures

3 System Theoretic Aspects

Within system theory, knowledge about a problem, specification, realisation, and production is put into a systematic order. One goal of system theory is to divide the process of development into clearly defined steps, each step having its own specific tasks and milestones.

The following steps can be defined using system theory:

-       selection of a formal method for the development of an abstract model

-       composition and decomposition for the development of a system architecture

-       optimisation of the system architecture

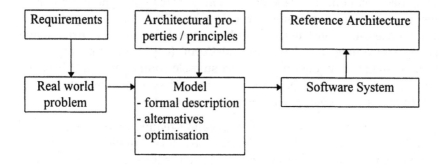

Fig. 1. Environment of the architectural design process

The real world problem is formulated in terms of requirements. There are functional requirements and non-functional requirements. Both types of requirements are important and have to be fulfilled. In the past, normally the software architecture was based mostly on the needed functions. A required function "A" caused the existence of an element "A" in the architecture. Each element can be a module, a class, or an other structural element.

Different applications need different architectures but mostly similar applications don't necessarily lead to similar architectures. Each developer / group of developers produce in his / its own style "ad hoc" a specific software architecture in their own way. To enhance this situation, it makes sense to use the knowledge of system theory.

Many aspects have influence on an architecture. As mentioned there are the functional requirements. Beside them there are the non-functional requirements such as:

-       performance
-       flexibility
-       adaptability
-       reusability
-       testability
-       maintainability
-       robustness

To be aware of all these points, it is necessary to use suitable structuring mechanisms. Each of architecture has its own properties (see Fig. 1). Principles of realisation (e.g. the object-oriented paradigm) can be installed more or less, depending on the structuring style used. To develop a model of the real world (functional and non-functional requirements, e.g. powerplant control) these principles and properties of different types of architecture have to be considered for fulfilling the requirements.

The system theory applied to software architecture delivers methods, principles and support to control the process of development of complex systems. The software architecture as mentioned before specifies the system structure in form of components and the relationships between them. Installing a software architecture is a process of structuring (e.g. divide et impera) a system. Input for the realisation of the software architecture is an abstract model of the real world (e.g. a power plant). This model reflects the real needs for some additional components like data base components (e.g. for storing the data of the power plant in a software specific manner) or user interfaces (e.g. for representation of the status of the abstract software model). After this extension we have a complete software architecture as a basis for the implementation.

The process of software architecture design is a vehicle to transform the real world problem into a software-specific structure (see Fig. 2).

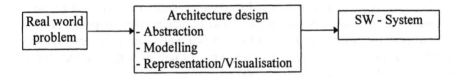

Fig. 2. Process of architectural design

The main steps of the transformation are:

- Abstraction

- Modelling

- Representation / Visualisation

During <u>abstraction</u> the real world problem has to be analysed (identification of the objects and the relationships between them). For example, in the object-oriented design process the first question during analysis is: „How to find the proper objects?" Thus, we find the basis of our system design. Aggregates within the set of objects having a strong connection among each other are defined as subsystems. Finally, decisions are necessary to fix the levels of design.

In the phase of <u>modelling</u> the structuring process concerning specific paradigms (e.g. design pattern) follows. The components of this structuring process should be the objects found in the first phase. In the past the functionality was the basis of the design. Now - in contrast to that - the basis basement of the design are the objects with services. Services realise the requested functionality. Such a design makes the structure more stable. Objects are not so volatile in comparison to functions, because functions often change. This principle to install a software architecture based on objects (real world or abstract objects) has a very positive effect on the behaviour of a system during the phase of operation (e.g. maintenance, adaptation or extension).

Aspects of realisation on the available platform (system components in hard- and software) must be considered. Decisions concerning operating systems, databases, or user interface are necessary. A stable base for the realisation is the final output of this step.

For <u>representation /visualisation</u> the results are documented in several diagrams (control flow, data flow, scenarios, ...) and formal specifications (description of semantics, ...).

4. Design patterns

Design patterns (1, 3, 4) can be used to develop software architectures in a systematic way. They describe a particular recurring design problem that arises in specific design contexts and presents a well-proven generic scheme for its solution. The descriptions are semi-formal and they make these „architectural frames" available for reuse.

New architectural structures will not be defined but existing well-proven structures from existing applications are documented, classified, and added to a catalogue of patterns. Each pattern has its specific principles and properties. These principles and properties are described in a formal and systematic manner and made available via a handbook. So the developer has the possibility to find a appropriate architecture for the needed functional and non-functional requirements.

In (3) the fundamental properties of patterns are described. A schema is given describing the different patterns. The kind of properties presented are normally concerned with non-functional requirements. As an example: the problem of consistency is solvable with the design pattern „publisher subscriber" (2). After a proper functional decomposition to fulfill the functional requirements, the non-functional requirements are the basis for the selection of the best software architecture. The listed properties of design patterns in the handbook give valuable hints for fixing the final appropriate architecture.

5 Outlook

The first goal in software development is the implementation of the functional requirements for fulfilling the requests of the customer. But as important as that goal is, is the way to reach the goal. During the operation phase changes are often necessary. Failures have to be corrected or new functions have to be added. Decisions made during the development phase determine the necessary maintainance effort.

It is obvious that the software architecture plays a decisive role during the realization as well as the maintenance phases. According to the importance of this aspect, all support in form of principles, methods or tools coming from all disciplines should be used to produce a stable, flexible, adaptive, reusable, and easily testable software system.

References

1. F. Buschmann, R. Meunier: Software-Konstruktion mit Entwurfs-muster. In: OBJEKTspektrum 5/95, pp 48 - 58

2. F. Buschmann, R: Meunier: A System of Patterns. In: Pattern Languages of Program Design. Herausgeber: J. Coplien und D. Schmidt, Addison-Wesley, 1995

3. E. Gamma, R. Helm, R. Johnson, J. Vlissides: Design Patterns: Elements of Reusable Object-Oriented Software, Addison-Wesley, 1995

4. F. Buschmann, R. Meunier, H. Rohnert, P. Sommerlad, M. Stal: Pattern-Oriented Software Architecture: A System of Patterns, John Wiley and Sons, 1995 (in preparation)

A Language for Describing Complex-Evolutive Software Systems.

José Parets, Juan Carlos Torres

Dept. de Lenguajes y Sistemas Informáticos. Universidad de Granada
ETS Ingeniería Informática. 18071 - GRANADA (Spain)
e-mail: jparets@ugr.es

Abstract. Software systems are conceived by the developers in an iterative, recursive and evolutive way. Traditional software development methods avoid the modelling of this evolutive conception. Three years ago we began the development of a method (MEDES) which tries to model and represent this important characteristic of all the human conception activities. The main objective of this paper is to present a language which allows the description of software systems in an evolutive way, based on a model of software system which incorporates evolutive features in its structure and functioning. The language is used to make prototypes of software systems in a tool (HEDES) which implements the method.

1 Introduction

In previous papers we presented a representation of the evolution of software systems [4] based on the Theory of the General System [2] and starting from a criticism of the software development methods [5]. This paper has the objective of presenting a brief summary of a refined version of our conception of software systems and a description language which we use as a base to make prototypes of these kinds of systems. Both are developed in the context of MEDES (SSDEM - "Software Specification Design and Evolution Method") and represent important improvements in the development of the method. The main contributions of this version derive from establishing a framework to conceive evolution based on Piaget, Morin and Le Moigne [6] and from the use of dynamic classification as conceived in the branch of object-oriented programming which works with delegation mechanisms [1,3].
In the sections which follow we will comment on how we conceive the three main viewpoints of a system in the case of software systems, i.e. how we conceive their structure, functioning and evolution. After, we will describe the main features of the language and an architecture for its implementation. The syntax of the language is summarized in the appendix. The reader can find a more detailed exposition of the concepts in [6].

2 A Basic Structure of a Software System

Figure 1 shows our model of the minimal structure of a software system (SS). We distinguish the following interrelated components:

- An action interface: through this interface it is possible to request actions from the SS and the SS can also request actions from the Information System in which it is included.

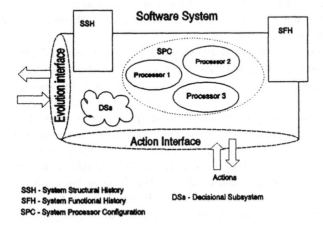

SSH - System Structural History
SFH - System Functional History
SPC - System Processor Configuration

DSs - Decisional Subsystem

Fig. 1. A minimal structure of a software system.

- An evolution interface: this allows the SS to evolve through structural actions carried out by the developer which is represented as a special software system called Metasystem.
- A processor configuration: the set of processors which works inside or for the system.
- A System Functional History (SFH): the memory of the functional actions (represented by functional events) developed by the system or by its processors.
- A System Structural History (SSH): the memory of the structural actions (represented by structural events), carried out by the Metasystem, which determine the current structure of the SS.
- A Decision distributed Sub-system: this is capable of taking decisions which are involved in the activation, suspension and termination of the actions. It is attached to each processor by the system in which the processor works and consists in pre, during and post conditions for each processor action. We introduce a System Decisional History (SDH) to memorize the decisions carried out.

These elements interact, determining the cinematics (functioning) and the dynamics (evolution) of the SS through time.

3 Functioning of a Software System: Action and Decision

Because the main functional element in this representation is the processor carrying out actions, it is decisive to explain how actions are conceived. Traditionally a processor is represented as a black box with inputs and outputs, the outputs being a result of the transformation of the inputs. This conception presents us with two important problems:

- It makes the interruption of an action difficult to represent.
- It does not allow us to conceive actions in a bidirectional way: the action exerted and the action suffered.

An input/output pattern would be adequate for continuous and indivisible actions without a waiting process, but when a processor needs to suspend an action because it is waiting for the result of an action carried out by another processor, a *stimulus/elaboration/response* pattern based on biological analogy is more interesting[1]. Using this pattern, the software system can be stimulated by a stimulus event which it memorizes in its SFH. This event will activate, through the decision subsystem, the actions of the processors involved. The termination of the action will be detected by a decision (DE_END) over the SFH. At this moment the result of the action will be reconstructed and answered. This form of conceiving actions allows a very complex and concurrent action pattern. Figure 2 shows the structure of an action of an isolated processor, and figure 3, the process of carrying out an action inside a system.

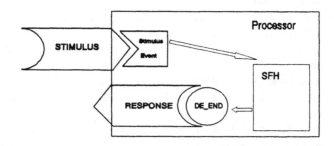

Fig. 2. Action of an isolated processor.

With this action pattern, decision plays a definite role. Except for the decision of ending an action (DE_END) which is inherent to each processor action, the system imposes three kinds of decisions onto the processor actions:

---

[1]This pattern derives from the widely used model of the animal Nervous System, which distinguishes aferent structures (sensorial nerves), elaborative structures (Central Nervous System) and eferent structures (motor nerves). The reader can find this model in any handbook of pshysiology or neurology.

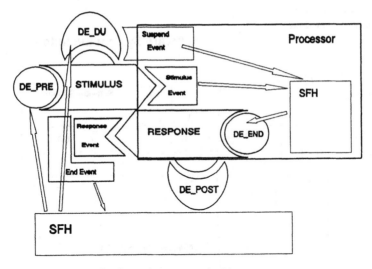

Fig. 3. Action patttern inside a system.

- a precondition (DE_PRE): a condition of activation of the action.
- a during condition (DE_DU): a condition which monitors the development of the action.
- a post condition (DE_POST): a condition which determines if the result of the action is adequate.
This decision presents two aspects:
- the conditions: DE_PRE, DE_DU, DE_POST.
- the events of decision, i.e. the events generated when a condition is evaluated and memorized in the SDH (DE_PREEvent, DE_DUEvent, DE_POSTEvent).

4 Evolution of a Software System

Evolution actions are carried out by a Software Metasystem which represents the structural actions performed by the development system onto the system structure. Software Metasystems may be associated with every software system. The Metasystem is isomorphic with the SS, i.e. its structure, functioning and evolution have the same characteristics of a SS. Each software system has a special kind of processor, called the Genetic Subsystem, which knows how to carry out the evolution actions. The pattern of these actions is also one of stimulus/elaboration/response and the actions are stimulated through the evolution interface using events memorized in the SSH.

The model also allows some evolution actions of the processors to be stimulated during the functional activity, that is to say, events of the SFH of a SS can stimulate actions of the evolution interface of its processors. For the moment only reproduction and some kind of classification actions can be stimulated in this way. We hope that this mechanism can be extended to allow self-evolution.

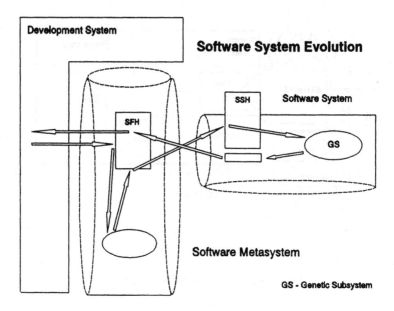

Fig. 4. Evolution of a software system through its metasystem.

Figure 4 shows how an action stimulated by the Development System through the Metasystem produces an evolution action carried out by the Genetic Subsystem of the software system. Figure 5 reflects a functional stimulus which can be interpreted by the Genetic Subsystem of a processor allowing its evolution.

Software System Evolution through functional events

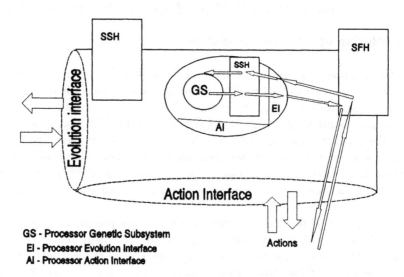

Fig. 5. Evolution of a software system processor during the functional activity of the SS.

From the structural, functional and evolutionary point of view, a system and a processor are equivalent. In fact the word *processor* is used to denominate the functional (active) aspect of a system.

5 The System Description Language (SDL)

We conceive a software system as shown in the previous paragraphs, but this conception would be useless if we cannot describe real software systems and resolve how SFH, SDH, SSH and decision can be represented. To do this, a formalization of the structure and functioning of a Software System [6] and a language which allows us to describe it are used.

The most important features included in this SDL are:
- Addition, deletion and replacement of processors.
- Addition, deletion, replacement and description of events associated to system and processor actions.
- Decision imposed onto the processor actions.
- Reproduction (cloning).
- Delegation of actions.
- Description of action events.
- Description of decision events.

In the following paragraphs the implications of these features are explained. In order to avoid repetition of the language sentences in the text, we will make references to the appendix, which is divided into five main sections, using the following notation: {see *sectionNumber[. subsectionNames]*; ...}. In section 1 of the appendix some general characteristics of the syntax used are explained.

5.1 Elemental Processors and Systems

Because our goal is to implement the previous conception in a programming language, the SDL distinguishes between Elemental Processors and Systems {see 2, 3}. Elemental Processors (EP) have actions implementable in a programming language (Smalltalk message to an object with delegation and concurrence) and they lack SFH and DE_END. The rest of the processors are Systems with the features previously described. This purely instrumental distinction has no repercussions on the evolutive capacities of a system because, from the functional point of view, an Elemental Processor and a Processor are equivalent.

Stemming from this distinction, the SDL is evolution-oriented, that is to say, it contains evolution actions on systems and processors in a way that the action interface of a system/processor will be described using these evolution actions by the developer. In this way, the Action Interface of a system/processor will be described by the developer using Evolution Actions.

5.2 Action and Decision: the Code of Events

Actions of a system/processor can be added, deleted, replaced {see 2.4.Actions; 2.5.System Actions} and described {see 2.4.Action description; 2.5.SystemActions}. The description of an action includes the definition of the events associated with the action. These events are described using an Action Event Code which has a different form depending on their type {see 4}.

Decision is, in general, imposed by the system on the processor actions in the form of pre, during and post conditions {see 3.3.Processor Actions}. When a processor is included in a system these forms of decision should be described. Because decision implies the evaluation of some condition over the SFH and the generation of a decision event memorizable in the SDH, it is necessary to describe these conditions and to assign a composition to the decision events. The former, i.e. the conditions, have a different structure depending on the type of decision, but always imply a condition on the SFH expressed in first order temporal logic {see 5}. The latter has a uniform composition including: the processor involved in the realization of the action, the stimulus of the action, the action events pertinent[2] in taking the decision, the result of the decision and its type.

5.3. Reproduction

The main mechanism which modifies the configuration of processors in a software system is reproduction (cloning). Reproduction is considered as a structural action carried out through stimulus on the evolution actions {see 2.4.Reproduction; 3.3.System Reproduction}, but some kind of processors will need to be reproduced during the normal functional activity of the system (for instance, patients in a Hospital will be created during the admission activity). This reason leads us to include the possibility of describing decision on the cloning action to activate it depending on functional events {see 3.3.Decision and events imposed...on...structural actions}.

5.4 Delegation

Delegation implies that a system, or processor, can delegate a part of its actions in another processor or system. The mechanism was introduced in some object oriented languages without classes to allow sharing of behaviour and state between objects (a revision can be found in [1,8]). The use of delegation at the level of abstraction of processor allows it to behave as other processors without modifying its own action capabilities. In the SDL, delegation is a structural action which can be linked to the activity of the system through a condition on the SFH {see 3.3.Delegation of the processor actions; 3.3.Delegation of the system actions}.

---

[2]We will say that an event, X, is a *pertinent stimulus* for another event, Y, iff X appears in the DE_PRE condition of Y and is needed to produce Y. X will be a *pertinent response* for Y, iff X appears in the DE_END condition of Y and is needed to produce Y.

5.5. Structuring a Software System: Collaboration Actions

So far we have considered a HIERARCHICAL structure of a system, i.e. a processor is *a part* of a software system and it only has sense inside a system. Yet we can conceive a COLLABORATIVE structure where a processor has a *working for* relationship with the system. Because this conception of software systems allows autonomy and the possibility of a processor/systems working for more than one system (simultaneously), we introduce direct communication between the processor interfaces, as figure 6 shows.

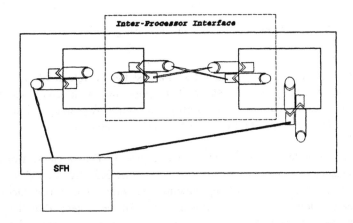

Fig. 6. Direct communication between processors without memorizing events.

The use of collaborative actions is a powerful mechanism in modelling evolution because a software system can be derived from one processor using reproduction and collaboration [6]. In addition it allows us to model autonomy and complex relationships between the software system and: its processors, its environment and its Metasystem {see 3.3.Collaboration Actions}.

5.6 Dynamic Classification

In our initial work, largely influenced by the classical object-oriented approach, we tried to introduce classes of processors and inheritance between processors. For different reasons, we now propose to put the notions of EVOLUTION and REPRODUCTION before those of classification and hierarchy, in order to transform them into processes, i.e. into dynamic features in a system.
This dynamicity of the classification process can be represented as in figure 7, which reflects the possibilities of transformation between four primitive categories: individual (phenomenic or conceptual), class, property and value. A class is a representation of a set of individuals, and a property is a characteristic which allows us to classify individuals depending on different values. There are no direct transformations of an individual into a property because this transformation implies that the individual is a class (at least the class of the values of the property).

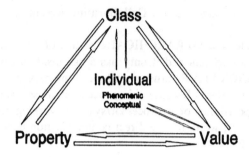

Fig. 7. Transformations between primitive categories of classification.

It is probably not always reasonable to travel across the triangle in all directions, but there are many examples that show it is possible. With this conception of classification, nothing guarantees the stability of an entity. We can conceive something as various things. The sole stability is that of the four categories used to classify the universe [6].

The SDL allows us to describe an individual (a processor) as a class, a property, a value, an instance of a class or a subclass of a class {see 3.3.Structural Categorization of processors}. As in the case of reproduction, instantiation of processors can be a very common action during the functional activity of the system, thus the language allows us to instantiate a processor when an action is carried out {see 3.3.Functional Categorization of processors} and to categorize a processor depending on a condition over the SFH {see 3.3.Structural Categorization of processors}.

6. Implementation: HEDES

An automated tool which "understands" these descriptions and allows us to make rapid prototyping of software systems is being developed. This tool, a second and refined version of HEDES (SSDET - Software Specification, Design and Evolution Tool) [4], is being implemented in Smalltalk/80 using delegation facilities which we have introduced into the language [7].

The elemental structure of HEDES is based on the following assumptions:

- HEDES will be the name of a unique system capable of understanding the System Description Language and capable of generating all the software systems and metasystems. HEDES will have a SFH and an action interface which can interpret the System Description Language.
- At the beginning, HEDES has an elemental core (CORE) capable of creating systems and elemental processors. This core will be constituted by a SFH and an Elemental System which has all the features of a system: SFH, SSH, GS. HEDES will be the metasystem of this Elemental System.

- All the evolution actions of a system will be actions of the interface action of its metasystem.

Figure 8 shows this primitive structure for HEDES.

Primitive HEDES Structure

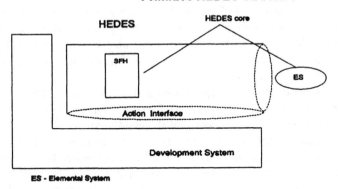

Fig. 8.

7. Conclusions and Further Research

A System Description Language in the context of MEDES has been described which allows us:

- To define and structure evolutive software systems composed of collaborative, autonomous processors.
- To include the description of action and decision.
- To incorporate features dispersed in the programming languages and difficult to incorporate in the design of software systems: delegation, dynamic classification and concurrence.
- To incorporate the role of the developer through the Metasystem which works as a Software Development Tool.

Future works will focus on:

- The *implementation of HEDES*: it will allow us to approach the design and implementation of real examples in a dynamic way. These examples will allow us to refine the concepts, the language and the applicability of the method.
- The use of *temporal logic* to represent decision and the influence between action and decision.
- The *conceptual framework* to include the finalities of the modeller and the possibilities of self-evolution of software systems.

References

1.   C. Dony, J. Malefant, P. Cointe: Prototype-based languages: From a new taxonomy to constructive proposals and their validation. Proc. OOPSLA'92. ACM SIGPLAN Notices 27, 12, 201-207 (1992)

2. J.L. Le Moigne: La théorie du système général. Thórie de la modélisation. Paris: Presses Universitaires de France 1977-1983-1990

3. O. Nierstrasz: A survey of object-oriented concepts. In: W. Kim, F. Lochowsky (eds.): Object-oriented concepts, applications and databases. Reading MA: Addison-Wesley 1989.

4. J. Parets, A. Anaya, M.J. Rodriguez, P. Paderewski: A Representation of Software Systems Evolution Based on the Theory of the General System. In: F. Pichler, R. Moreno Díaz (eds.): Computer Aided Systems Theory - EUROCAST'93. Lecture Notes in Computer Science 763. Berlin: Springer-Verlag 1994, pp.96-109

5. J. Parets-Llorca: On some epistemological challenges of Object-Oriented Software Engineering: If Objects were Systems. 2ème. Congrès Européen de Systemique (CES2). Prague 1993, vol II, pp.447-456

6. J. Parets-Llorca: Reflexiones sobre el proceso de concepcion de sistemas complejos. MEDES: un método de especificación, desarrollo y evolución de sistemas software. Doctoral Thesis. Universidad de Granada 1995

7. G. Sanchez, J. Parets: Estudio de alternativas a la herencia en lenguajes orientados a objetos. Working paper 94-1. Dept. LSI 1994

8. G. Sánchez, J. Parets: Mecanismos alternativos en lenguajes orientados a objetos. Novatica 114, 51-58 (1995)

Appendix. The System Description Language Syntax

Section 1 **** GENERAL SYNTAX

A Smalltalk-like syntax is used. The message arguments in bold are terminal symbols. The terms preceded by # are variables which should be substituted by Smalltalk symbols. Variables beginning with *a, an, another, other* can be substituted by an object of the class pointed out (for instance, anEProcessor, anotherEProcessor refer to an elemental processor).

EProcessorId: elemental processor identifier.
    EProcessorId ::= anEProcessor | #EProcessorId
SystemId: system identifier.
    SystemId ::= aSystem | #SystemId
ProcessorId: processor identifier.
    ProcessorId ::= EProcessorId | SystemId
ProcessorAction: action identifier.
    ProcessorAction ::= #EProcessorAction | #SystemAction
SFHCondition: condition on SFH
SSHCondition: condition on SSH
SDHCondition: condition on SDH
SYSTEMCondition: system condition
    SYSTEMCondition ::= SFHCondition | SSHCondition | SDHCondition

Section 2 **** ELEMENTAL PROCESSOR DESCRIPTION

2.1 ELEMENTAL PROCESSOR: #EProcessorId.

2.2 KIND: [**sequential** | **parallel**].

2.3 ACTION INTERFACE
(* It is created using evolution interface actions *)

2.4 EVOLUTION INTERFACE
(* ---------------------------- Actions ----------------------------------*)
    EProcessorId   add: #EProcessorAction. "Add an action to an El. Processor"
    EProcessorId   delete:#EProcessorAction.
    EProcessorId   replace: #EProcessorAction
               by: #AnotherEProcessorAction.

(* ---------------------------- Action description ----------------------*)
    EProcessorId   describes: #EProcessorAction
                   with: [aCollectionOfEProcessors |
                            aCollectionOfClassesOfEProcessors
                   execution: #ActionEvent
                   stimulus: **nil**
                   character: [**public** | **private**]
                   reponseCausedBy: **nil**.

(* ---------------------------- Reproduction (cloning) ------------------------- *)
    EProcessorId   cloneTo: AnotherEProcessorId.

2.5 ACTION EVENTS
    ActionEvent :: = EPEventCode
    EPEventCode :: = anEventForm | anSmalltalkMessage

(* EventForm will be forms which represent the information associated with an event *)

Section 3 **** SYSTEM DESCRIPTION

3.1 SYSTEM: #SystemId.

3.2 ACTION INTERFACE
(* It is created using evolution interface actions *)

3.3 EVOLUTION INTERFACE

```
(* ------------------------------ Processors ------------------------------*)
      SystemId  add: ProcessorId
                as: [subsystem | collaborator].        "Add a processor"
      SystemId  delete: ProcessorId.
      SystemId  replace: ProcessorId
                by: AnotherProcessorId.
      SystemId  get: ProcessorId.
      SystemId  put: ProcessorId.
      SystemId  changeStatusOf: EProcessorId
                to: [subsystem | collaborator].


(* ------------------------ Processor Actions ------------------------ *)

      (* ----- Decision and events imposed by the system on processor functional
      actions ----- *)
      SystemId  to: ProcessorId
                action: ProcessorAction
                addDE_PRE: aDE_PRE
                addDE_DU: aDE_DU
                addDE_POST: aDE_POST
                addEndEvent: anEndEvent
                addSuspendEvent: anSuspendEvent.

      (* ----- Decision and events imposed by the system on processor structural
      actions ----- *)
      SystemId  to: ProcessorId
                action: cloneTo
                addDE_PRE: aDE_PRE
                addDE_DU: aDE_DU
                addDE_POST: aDE_POST
                addEndEvent: anEndEvent
                addSuspendEvent: aSuspendEvent

      (* --- Delegation of the processor actions ---- *)
      SystemId  a: ProcessorId
                canBe: AnotherProcessorId
                for: [life | aSFHCondition ]
                toDo: [ AnotherProcessorAction | all ]
                effect: [additive | annulative].

      SystemId  a: ProcessorId
                canNotBeMore: AnotherProcessorId
                toDo: [ AnotherProcessorAction | all ].
```

(* ------------------------ System Actions ------------------------- *)

(* --- Action interface ------ *)
SystemId   add: #SystemAction. "Add a system action to the interface"
SystemId   delete:#SystemAction.
SystemId   replace: #SystemAction
           by: #AnotherSystemAction.

(* ---- Delegation of the system actions ---- *)
SystemId   canBe: AnotherProcessorId
           for: [life | aSFHCondition]
           toDo: [AnotherProcessorAction | all]
           effect: [additive | annulative].

SystemId   canNotBeMore: AnotherProcessorId
           toDo: [AnotherProcessorAction | all].

(* -------------- Action description ------------ *)
SystemId   describes: #SystemAction
           priority: aPriority
           stimulus: anStimulusEvent
           response: aResponseEvent
           character: public
           reponseCausedBy: aDE_ENDEvent

(* ----------------------- Collaboration Actions ----------------------- *)

(* ----- Between the System and Processors ------- *)
SystemId   systemAction: #SystemAction
           withSystemDE_PRE: aDE_PRE
           collaboratesWith: #ProcessorAction
           of: ProcessorId
           withProcessorDE_PRE: anotherDE_PRE
           withEND_EV: anEndEvent.

(* ----- Between the System and an Environment -----*)
SystemId   systemAction: #SystemAction
           withSystemDE_PRE: aDE_PRE
           collaboratesWith: environment
           withEND_EV: anEndEvent.

(* ----- Between a MetaSystem and its systems -----*)
SystemId   metaSystemAction: #MetaSystemAction
           withMetaSystemDE_PRE: aDE_PRE
           collaboratesWith: #EvolutionSystemAction

```
            of: SystemId
            withSystemDE_PRE: anotherDE_PRE
            withEND_EV: anEndEvent.
```

(* -------------------------- System Reproduction ------------------- *)
```
      SystemId   cloneTo: #AnotherSystemId
```

(*---------------- Structural Categorization of processors ----------- *)

```
      (* ------- Classes ------- *)
      SystemId   a: ProcessorId
              isClassFor: [life | SYSTEMCondition].

      SystemId   isNotMoreClass: #ProcessorId.

      (* ------ Properties ------- *)
      SystemId   a: ProcessorId
              isPropertyFor: [life | SYSTEMCondition].

      SystemId   isNotMoreProperty: #ProcessorId.

      (* ------ Values ----------- *)
      SystemId   a: ProcessorId
              isValueFor: [life | SYSTEMCondition]
              ofProperty: ProcessorId.

      SystemId   isNotMoreValue: #ProcessorId.
              ofProperty: ProcessorId.

      (* ----- Instantiation ----- *)
      SystemId   a: ProcessorId
              isInstanceFor: [life | SYSTEMCondition]
              ofClass: ProcessorId.          "Should be a class"

      SystemId   isNotMoreValue: #ProcessorId.
              ofClass: ProcessorId.

      (* ----- Subclassification --- *)
      SystemId   a: ProcessorId
              isSubclassOf: AnotherProcessorId
              onCriterion: ProcessorId          "Should be a property"
              withValue: ProcessorId            "Should be a value"
              for: [life | SYSTEMCondition]
              toDo: [AnotherProcessorAction | all].
```

SystemId a: ProcessorId
          isNotMoreSubclassOf: #AnotherProcessorId

(* ------------- Functional Categorization of Processors ----------- *)
SystemId theAction: ProcessorAction
          ofProcessor: ProcessorId
          transformsAsInstance: aProcessedProcessor
          ofASubclassOf: anotherProcessorId.   "Should be a class"
          usingProperty: aSecondProcessorId.

SystemId theAction: ProcessorAction
          ofProcessor: ProcessorId
          suppressesAsInstance: aProcessedProcessor
          usingProperty: aSecondProcessorId.

3.4 ACTION EVENTS

SystemActionEvent ::= ResponseEvent | StimulusEvent | EndEvent
ResponseEvent ::= ActionResponseCode
StimulusEvent ::= ActionStimulusCode
EndEvent ::= ActionEndCode
(* see Action Event Code in section 4)

3.5 DECISION EVENTS

SystemDecisionEvent ::= DE_ENDEvent | DE_PREEvent | DE_POSTEvent
                  | DE_DUEvent | SuspendEvent
DE_ENDEvent ::= DecisionENDCode
DE_PREEvent ::= DecisionPRECode
DE_POSTEvent ::= DecisionPOSTCode
DE_DUEvent ::= DecisionDUCode
SupendEvent ::= SuspendCode
(* see Decision Code in section 5*)

Section 4 **** ACTION EVENT CODE

EPEventCode
  - Smalltalk message to an object with delegation + concurrence

ActionResponseCode ::= SFHEvent | ARC + SFHEvent
  WHERE SFHEvent ⊨ SFHCondition

ActionStimulusCode
  - Action id + arguments

ActionEndCode
    Adapts the ResponseEvent

Section 5 **** DECISION CODE

```
(* ----------------- DE_PRE: DecisionPRECode ------------------------------- *)
    IF SFHCondition
       THEN action
       ELSE suspend
    ENDIF
(* ----------------- DE_DU: DecisionDUCode ------------------------------- *)
    WHILE NOT EXIST ResponseEvent
       IF SFHCondition
           THEN generate DE_DUEvent and SuspendEvent
       ENDIF
    END WHILE
(* ---------------- DE_POST: DecisionPOSTCode --------------------------- *)
    CASE
       SFHCondition1 on ResponseEvent: nil
       SFHCondition2 on ResponseEvent: suspend action
       SFHCondition3 on ResponseEvent: restart action
       .........
    OTHERWISE
       [nil | suspend action | restart action]
    END CASE
(* ----------------- DE_END: DecisionENDCode --------------------------- *)
    WHILE NOT SFHCondition
       nil
    END WHILE
    generate a ResponseEvent
```

2 DESIGN ENVIRONMENTS AND TOOLS

An Architecture for Process Modelling and Execution Support

Christine Kocourek

Siemens AG, Corporate Research and Development,
81730 Munich, Germany

Abstract. This paper discusses concepts and techniques supporting modelling, planning and execution of design activities in distributed design environments. The task of planning, executing, and supervising the design processes has become so complex that it itself requires advanced computer support facilities. We propose extended planning facilities exploiting old design projects. The planning functions form a basis for a larger framework for decision and execution support. In what follows, we discuss the phases of a design process, especially planning including process model generation using history based planning techniques. Finally, we present our prototype of an architecture for a design process management system (DPMS). The DPMS architecture promotes highly autonomous execution of system designs. The system has been used in the electronic design automation area. The concepts described here, however, are also applicable to other design domains.

1 Introduction

Modern engineering design is a highly complex process involving considerations about a variety of objectives, constraints, materials and configurations. Despite great strides in computational tools, such as high performance workstations, intended to help in coping with this rising complexity, the design process remains error prone. The working hypothesis of this paper, however, is that advanced computational tools are of limited effectiveness without a reliable decision support methodology to induce a systematic handling of the multitude of goals and constraints impinging on a design process.

Design processes are very complex; users need support for producing the design quickly and efficiently. Especially in recent times great emphasis has been placed on the reduction of time-to-market and cost-reduction in the engineering design process. We analyze design process phases in section 2. In section 3 we present an architecture for planning facilities. Section 4 explains in detail, how history-based planning can be applied to design process. The section 5 presents the execution support of our DPMS architecture. In section 6 we present our prototype system. We close by looking at future research goals and extensions to the current prototype.

2   Design Process Phases

The design process can be divided into four different phases, which are necessary for controlling the process, supporting the production of a design, and achieving an optimal result (Figure 1).

In the first stage, the specification phase, the design process is initiated. This includes the definition of requirements and constraints on the design as well as the first specifications of design features. During this phase, the users exert the greatest influence on the outcome of the design process.

In the next stage, the planning phase, the already-gathered information is used to define the process model for the design process. This task is mainly performed by system managers or system designers, who are responsible for the initial layout of the design and the design process. Details of the planning phase can be found in section 3.

After collecting the design information and setting up the design process, the execution phase controls the design production, using the process model developed during the planning phase. In this stage the designers produce the actual design object. The design production is carefully monitored and a diagnosis process is started in case any deviation from the original process model is detected. In section 5, the functions of the execution phase is explained in detail.

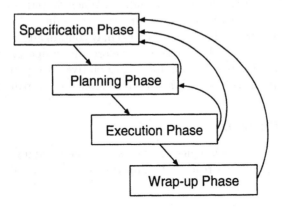

Fig. 1. Design Process Phases

Finally, during the wrap-up phase, data on the design and the corresponding design process is collected and evaluated. Here, system managers, responsible for the proper working of the proposed system architecture, check the collection and evaluation of the design. The design history is gathered, analyzed, and prepared for later reuse. Reuse can take place on parts of the finished design or only the design process. Details of the wrap-up phase can be found in section 4.

The partitioning of the design process into four phases, as proposed here, is especially relevant for large design projects, where a large number of activities and resources has to be coordinated.

3   Planning

This section describes planning techniques, which support the planning phase of a design project, as described above. Starting with the motivation for planning, each planning task is presented, leading to Section 4 on history-based planning.

3.1   Overview and Motivation

Since management requires strict control over the design process and progress, any design should only be started after a verified process has been defined. The process model emulation, presented in Section 3.2, allows verification for correctness and feasibility. Design flow management [1] requires a validated process model for executing the design process quickly and effectively. As deviations between the planned process model and the actual design process can be monitored, the process can be controlled and time delays are recognized early. Further, the process status can be checked against the predicted project end. This information allows management to determine the actual project status easily.

Concurrencies and alternatives of tasks, tools, and tool-sets are implicitly defined in the process model. These concurrencies and alternatives in the process model can be detected early and evaluated by their impact on design time, risks and quality. For novice users the system might provide help for tool selection and handling of concurrencies and alternatives. When detecting concurrencies in the process model, the system architecture can determine a fastest throughput configuration of the tools. The process model may contain alternatives, for which the optimal choice cannot be determined before the design process is started. The system may delay the decision for an alternative until more information is available, but still provide a complete process model for starting the design.

3.2   Process Planning

The following different techniques can be used in the planning phase, where an optimal result will only be reached by applying a sensible combination of all of them:

- Process Model Planning,
- History-Based Planning,
- Execution Planning,
- Emulation, and
- Replanning

Figure 2 demonstrates the interaction and the coordination of the planning components, each representing a different planning task. The Design Flow Manager, presented in detail in Section 5, takes care of the process execution.

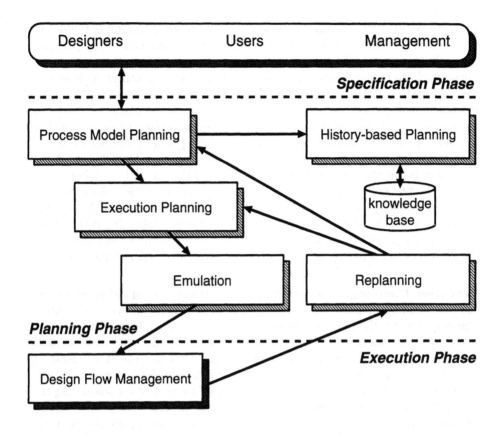

Fig. 2. Process Planning

As a result of the process planning, the Design Flow Manager receives a scheduled process model for execution. We chose the Petri net representation for the process model, proven to be very efficient for modelling and executing the process. In the following, we describe the process modelling and each planning task in detail, as shown in Figure 2.

Process Models. High level Petri net models provide a representation of design process dependencies [1], [9]. High Level Petri nets [6] are directed, bipartite graphs consisting of places and transitions. Being compact in size, Petri Nets express various relations between objects - such as conflicts, sequences or concurrencies among activities - and process steps. Supporting a correct and fast design production, we introduced so called "decision nodes" in the Petri net based process model. By executing a decision node, the invoked design decision support mechanism helps users determine the subsequent design step correctly [7, 1]. With respect to a given specification, the correct behavior of a Petri net can be tested by simulation and verified to some extent by formal methods [1, 9].

Process Model Planning. The goal of process model planning is the definition of a process model plan. This is the fundamental activity of the planning phase. In process model planning all available information from the specification phase, such as requirements, constraints and strategies, is collected. Based on this information, the main tasks of the design process are identified, using a product model definition. Parallel to this activity, history-based planning, described in section 4, is started in order to find and reuse old design projects stored in a knowledge base. Results from the history-based planning are fed back into process model planning, if a similar design project is detected. The similarity can either be on the level of the design object and the product model or at the level of the process model and the structure for design execution. As a last step in process model planning, effectiveness measurements for later analysis of the project's success are defined. The result of process model planning is the aggregation of objects and tasks, a process structure, a process model and milestones. This information is passed as input to the following execution planning step.

Execution Planning. Based on the results of the process model planning, execution planning prepares the process model for execution by users. Execution planning receives the process structure, the process model, first milestones and resources being available for the project, as input. This information allows identifying dependencies between activities and tools. These are used for generating an execution sequence, guiding the user in executing the design project. At this level concurrencies in the planned process can be recognized for scheduling the best plan. Based on the current knowledge of the process, execution planning proposes a preselection of alternatives for the process model plan. So, all workpackages are determined within the process model. Now, using the available resources, all task activities are scheduled. This process includes the definition of a cost and time schedule. These results are presented to management for approval. The emulator receives these results for simulating and validating the process model plan.

Emulation. The emulator receives its input data, the process model plan, from execution planning. It checks the planned process model for correctness and for feasibility by running the process model without producing real design data using simulation techniques. It only verifies the data transfer between tools and activities using interface definitions. Further, the emulator checks the process against the requirements. Using Petri nets for determining the process model, deadlock detection can be performed. The process monitor (described in section 5) later requires the simulation results for detecting deviations between the process model and the actual design process.

Finally, the emulator sends the validated process model plan to the Design Flow Management (see section 5) for executing the project.

Replanning. Replanning is invoked if a process model plan fails to achieve the desired design goal during the execution phase. It starts a modification of the process model based on the failure diagnosis, the current state of the design process including the state of the process execution and the state of the design artifact. Some of the replanning functions may be delegated to execution planning or process model planning, where a design task may be substantially altered or modified. Thus, new goals may emerge that possibly require a new design methodology, models, and a new set of tasks. Here, the scheduling function is again required for generating the revised time boundaries during which design actions should be executed. Further, the new resource assignments are also required for these replanning actions [8]. Since the now available information can be exploited, replanning can present better plans and plan corrections than the first planning at the planning phase, based only on the specification.

4 History-based Planning

As mentioned in section 3 history-based planning represents an important task in the planning phase. History-based planning supports the process planning task by searching in a knowledge base for previous designs. Hence, knowledge forms the basis for history-based planning by reusing successfully completed design projects, which have similarities with the current design problem. The identification of similarities is achieved by applying case-based reasoning techniques. Therefore, a similarity measurement has to be defined, allowing the finding of successfully finished design projects that are similar to the characteristics of the new project. The criteria used during the search are based on a limited amount of information available at this early stage of the project.

In order to allow this flexibility in finding reusable design processes or artifacts, the repository for finished design projects needs to be defined for storing all relevant information of a design project, e.g. design data, requirements, specification, the process model, design traces, i.e. the representation of an executed design model process [1, 4], including all design decisions. It is also necessary to provide indices to all of this information, allowing access it from different viewpoints.

If the search is successful, a successfully finished design project is retrieved from the knowledge base. The reuse of previous design projects can also be extended to the level of the actual design artifact. In this case design objects or parts of them have to be identified, which have similarities with requirements for the current design. Related to the design artifact is also the design process, used for its production. So the executed process forms a basis for reusing it in the process model. This process model requires further refinement and adaptation to the current design problem, because the process is only similar but not identical to the current design project.

A history-based planner consists of two different components:

- case storage, collecting all case information structured for a later reuse
- case access, retrieving stored cases for adaptation to the current design problem.

First, we describe the case storage component, which is the basis for the later retrieval of cases. Second, we propose the functionality for the case access component.

4.1 Case storage

The case storage takes place in the wrap-up phase of the design project after finishing the design. At this state of the design project, the system manager gathers all information, regarding project data, design data, documentation, process and trace data, being now available for evaluation. This allows extracting the relevant information, used for later storage in a knowledge base. Also, each module of the case is indexed with search keys for later retrieval.

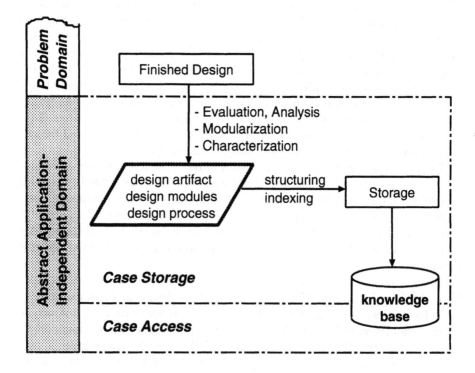

Fig. 3. Case storage component

Allowing an efficient retrieval and successful reuse of process data, the design process has to be carefully analyzed before it can be used in the case storage. Here, we describe the analysis functionality for the case storage component by splitting it up into four phases (Figure 3):

Evaluation of the project. As a first action, the finished design project is evaluated for later reuse. Depending on the customer requirements, the designed artifact may contain many components, based on atypical features. These special customer requirements may also lead to an atypical design process, including additional design activities or the use of special tools. Also the operation of the design object may reveal problems or instabilities which prohibit later reuse of the design. In all of these cases the design process should not be stored as a reference case in the knowledge base.

Analysis of specification and documentation. In order to reuse a design process or the design object it is necessary that consistent documentation is maintained during the complete design processes. This also implies that the design artifact is compliant with the specification in all areas or deviation from the specification are clearly documented. This step checks these requirements.

After these two first steps, the system manager can decide if the design process is potentially valuable for storing in the knowledge base. The storage requires more analysis steps for input into the knowledge base.

Modularization and Indexing of the design artifact. The reuse of design objects or parts thereof require an analysis of the design artifact, including modularization. For representing the case, first the structural features are captured. Then, the functional description allows the first indexing step for characterizing the design artifact. Modularization is performed, clearly identifying the components of the design object and their interactions. Modularization allows a causal description of the module behavior, using module interfaces. Causal relationships describing the behavior of design artifacts refer to specific modules. Now, the indexing procedure characterizes each module by its specific features, including quality, interfaces and relation to other modules and cost. Additionally, the relevance of the module for certain applications is defined. All this information leads to specific attributes, such as importance or cost-intensiveness, attached to the module as an index for later retrieval. Finally, by analyzing the design artifact, a structure for storing the design artifact of this case in the knowledge base is determined.

Characterization of the project. As a last step in the case storage procedure, the project itself and the process is characterized by analyzing the design trace containing all design decisions. It is checked whether the users executed the proper tasks for reaching the design goal in the design trace which describes the executed design process. For all concurrencies and alternatives having occurred during the design process, the design trace is analyzed to verify that the correct decisions were taken or if deadlocks were introduced into the process. For storage in the knowledge base, these detected problems are fixed, so that for later reuse, an optimal process will be executed.

Knowledge Storage. A design project knowledge base should contain all the information shown in figure 4, characterizing the project, the process and the design objects itself. All this information is indexed for finding an analog solution to a given design problem.

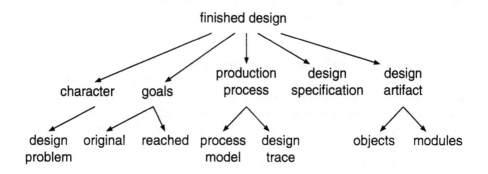

Fig. 4. Characterization of a Design Project

A finished design is described by its characteristics, the underlying design problem, the original and the finally reached goals, and the design specification. In this area, the production process includes the setting up of the process model, using the process model for producing the design artifact and evaluation of the design trace. So, the production process includes all four design phases, defined in section 2. The design trace also contains all design decisions, taken during design production. The design artifact includes all design objects and modules produced during the project and revised by the system manager, i.e. reduced to the relevant information for the knowledge base as described above. After all this data for one single design process has been collected and structured, the system manager has to place this case in the framework of the other design projects, stored in the knowledge base. Therefore, an overall structure for the cases has to be provided, which allows indexing and identifying a specific case. The structure of the knowledge base largely depends on the application area of the design processes.

The knowledge base contains also a module library that enables organized creation, storage and retrieval of the modules. This library maintains all module information and storage, e.g. locations of the related CAD plans. Also included are rules regarding constraints and usage of the modules and configuration rules for the library components.

This information forms the basis for searching relevant cases of successfully finished designs. Applying case based reasoning techniques, the system can look for previous designs during the planning phase.

4.2 Case Access

The major problem when accessing the knowledge base is the mapping of already stored cases to the new developing design project. Therefore, the components of an old design project, such as the structure of the project, the design objects and the individual design steps are indexed using their characteristics. Indexing requires an abstraction from the actual problem domain to a more general, application independent description of each index, so that cases from different application domains can be mapped to the current problem.

The only available basis for the current design problem is design specification, describing the required features of the design artifact mainly from the customer's point of view. Specification represents the input to the first step of the case access component, trying to identify the indices for the search looking for a solution from similar design problems in the knowledge base.

Using reasoning by reference techniques to past experiences, stored in a knowledge base [3], the system attempts to model the current design problem with design steps used in previous design projects. Case retrieval strategies are also described in [11] by index transformation for finding a stored case, that can not be found using the first determined indices. Case access is performed by the following steps (Figure 5):

Anticipating problems in achieving a given set of goals. Based on customer requirements or specifications, the recognition process identifies some indices, given a set of goals, which represent the design problem in an abstract notation. Using these indices, it is attempted to anticipate problems in the design project. The solutions to these problems represent the key issues in solving the current design problem, therefore the knowledge base is browsed for solutions in previous design projects, which have been successfully applied to similar problems.

Retrieval of cases from the knowledge base. For the retrieval of cases from the knowledge base, search techniques on the following levels of abstraction can be used:

- general goals mapping:
  Here the mapping is done on the level of the general goals of the design problem, using indices of the available specifications.
- module mapping:
  The mapping of different modules of the design project or the design artifact to the problem, requires knowing the characteristics of the modules. The indices of the problem can be compared to the defined indices determining modules stored in the knowledge base for reuse. Therefore, a detailed knowledge of the problem domain is required.
- process mapping, tools, procedures and structures:
  In case specific tools, procedures or structures of the design project are already known, the mapping can be performed on this detailed level. As this

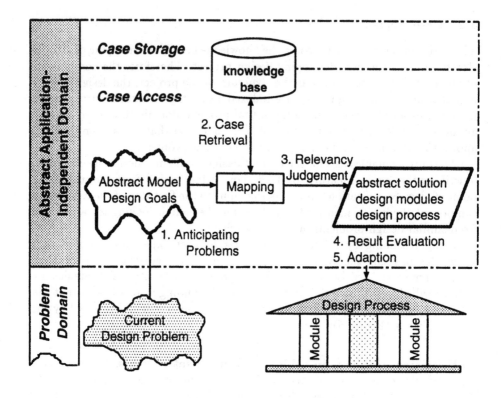

Fig. 5. Case access component

method requires the most detailed knowledge of the design process, it can also be expected that a successful search in the knowledge base will provide the most detailed support for the planning process.

Relevancy judgment. After the search process is completed, the quality of the retrieved cases matches the given problem has to be determined. Those cases, which satisfy the goals the best, are selected for further analysis.

Mapping for detecting similarity. Here we determine the degree of similarities between the found case and the design problem. Now, we check, if the case proposed by the system maps to the problem. Using a predefined similarity rating, we determine the degree of difference between the problem and the proposed case.

Adapting the case to the problem. The search in the knowledge base has produced a number of cases that are similar to the current design problem or parts of it, e.g. the process, used tools, parts of the design artifact or procedures.

The description of these cases, derived from the knowledge base, is still on an abstract level. The next step in the process, therefore is to adapt the retrieved cases to the problem domain of the current design project. With this step, it is possible to identify all parts of the project that can be mapped to existing solutions from the knowledge base and those parts that have to be developed additionally.

Results evaluation. The results from the case access component provided a number of reusable design components mapped to the current problem domain. These results have to be evaluated for their usability and effectiveness. This will lead to a structuring of the results into three levels.

- When finding many similarities between design objects and modules, it seems feasible to reuse the design process as well as the design objects. Only those modules which do not map to a case stored the knowledge base have to be produced and developed. This case provides the greatest benefit from the use of the knowledge base, because an already verified design process as well as existing design objects can be reused. The adaptations and additions necessary to the existing design artifacts can be performed in a sound process environment and with defined interfaces. Here, we found a mapping in a causal structure, as we can reuse most of the design artifact.
- If similarities can be detected in only a few modules, these are normally not sufficient to form the basis for a complete design process. Therefore, the design process and most of the modules have to be developed anew. This means that there is higher risk and higher costs involved. In this case, we use a mapping in a causal structure.
- If the search in the knowledge base determines that only the design process may be reused, this implies that all modules have to be newly created. This case matches only in the used principle by applying the process.

When applying history based planning techniques, e.g., at the bidding phase, the first search in the knowledge base can produce a cost evaluation, in which of the three above determined categories this design may fall.

4.3 Planner: Methodology-based versus History-based

Planning based on methodology knowledge operates on the knowledge defined once. The methodology knowledge is static and defined by expert users and system managers. A history based planner operates on knowledge being revised constantly. New design cases influence and form the knowledge base. Using the history-based planning techniques, new cases modyify the knowledge, always revising the knowledge base slightly and keeping the accessible knowledge up-to-date. Every new project entered in the knowledge base increases either the chance to find similarities in later searches or the reliability of the cost and schedule estimates. This also emphasizes the importance of a careful analysis of past projects in the wrap-up phase.

When system environments are created, they only contain methodology knowledge for planning, because past experience for history based planning is not available. A procedure for setting up a very first process model is based only on the methodology or has to be set up manually. So, the process model planner starts using methodology knowledge, later revising it with history knowledge, if available. Both alternatives have to be supported by a good planning module.

The major advantage of the case based planning techniques are retrieval and adaptations of successfully finished designs. This procedure is not only cheaper, but also more reliable than planning from scratch.

5   Execution Support

This section focuses on supporting the execution phase within the proposed architecture for a Design Process Management System (DMPS). The architecture fosters a high level view of intelligent design support and planning, intended to make design environments more autonomous. This architecture was designed using the principles of autonomous acting and decision making. Autonomy is defined here as the ability of a system and system components to function independently, subject to its own laws and control principles. Whereas achieving full and complete autonomy in artificial systems is not yet possible, we develop decision support mechanisms that would facilitate a highly autonomous operation of a design environment. If the system has more decision making capabilities and abilities to "chart its own course of action," it also has a higher degree of autonomy. Thus, we can incorporate a means for doing some of the design tasks automatically in the architecture, and we can claim that a design process that is executed within the architecture has a degree of autonomy [2].

Figure 6 demonstrates the mechanisms of the architecture for process modelling and execution support. All components are connected by communication interfaces, controlling the information and data exchange between the components of the DPMS architecture. The central module of the DPMS architecture is a knowledge base, with all information about successfully completed designs and the corresponding tools for planning, decision making and execution support.

Users invoke the planner for creating the design process model, which is then checked by the Emulator for feasibility and correctness. These first two steps are described in detail in Section 3. After setting up the design process, the Design Flow Manager (DFM) supervises the execution of the design process. The DFM operates on Petri net based process models, defined by the Planner, for controlling the flow of the design process, and supervises all constraints among design steps contained in the process model. It also determines the current design state and the design actions that can be taken next, e.g. tool invocations. The DFM checks all constraints between design steps that are defined in the process models and provides additional services: gathering of design history information, supporting of backtracking for the investigation of design alternatives, automating restoration of design data and the enforcement of design policies [2, 1]. Additionally, the DFM makes decisions regarding the progress of the design process and

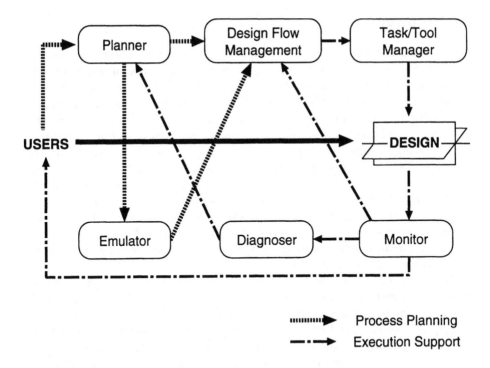

Fig. 6. DMPS Architecture for Execution Control

invocations of various tools. For this purpose, the DFM invokes the Task/Tool manager for starting the tools or tool environments for performing the design task.

The Task/Tool Manager is responsible for invoking individual tools as directed by the DFM having the knowledge of the process model, the current state of the design process, and the state of the design object on which the process and the tools operate. As design tools are invoked, the states of the process and design objects are updated. Optimization and inferencing procedures should support the DFM in its actions at two levels: reasoning about the design process and reasoning about the system being designed.

The Monitor checks the proper execution of the design process flow and the design artifact by comparing the actual process with the simulated process data from the Emulator. Minor deviations are reported directly to the DFM. In case of major deviations, the Monitor reports the problem to the Diagnoser for analyzing the state and the problem space. Hence, the Diagnoser has to identify the reasons for these anomalies in design production. Normally, the Diagnoser sends a replannig request to the Planner for fixing the problem, reaching the design goal and repairing plan failures, using model based reasoning techniques.

All these components provide execution support for design production. In the following section, we describe our prototype for the DPMS architecture.

6 Prototype

The design process management system prototype system has been implemented using OPS83 and the C programming language in the UNIX environment. The system architecture, including the Petri net process model, is a domain independent system not only suited for VLSI design, but also used as major support architecture for a comprehensive Hardware/Software co-design framework. Our prototype, implemented on a Sun workstation, provides execution support by incorporating facilities for design trace recording, retrieval, and selection. The prototype has been applied to various design processes consisting of a very large number of design trace steps. Apart from a slight delay when activating and completing a design step (due to the communication overhead), there is no measurable performance decrease since the evaluation of rule sets and restoration of design process states is extremely fast. The superior performance of the system allows us to handle all graphical requests (such as redrawing of windows) elegantly through the OPS83 rules.

To create a process model, users invoke a graphical editor, offering a predefined set of symbols to form a process net. A checking program automatically supervises the compliance of the process model with the extended Petri net syntax [1]. A process model can consist of any number of partial nets which are semantically joined by the checker through the identification of nodes having the same type and name. After the process model has been completely defined, the rule generator is started, which creates OPS83 production rules [5] for the process nets. The resulting rule set is linked together with the flow manager, the design decision rules, and the planning rules to provide an executable design flow for the given process.

The design process management system is capable of controlling the correct execution of hierarchical PrT-nets, of invoking the design tools associated with the net transitions when they are fired, and of providing restoration and recreation services for the tokens. Traces, which can be represented graphically, are collected automatically. The hierarchy of the process net is exploited to distinguish between partial traces representing net executions at different levels.

7 Summary and Conclusions

In this paper we analysed the design process phases, especially the process planning phase, where we investigated the requirements and functionality for history-based planning. As solution to the problems indicated in the analysis, we presented our prototype of the DPMS architecture, promoting process planning and highly autonomous execution of design processes. The system has been used in the electronic design automaton area. Hence, the framework can be used as well in the systems design area, in the Hardware/Software Co-Desgin or the control of engineering processes.

Our future work will focus on the automatic knowledge acquisition from finished design traces. A design consulting tool exploiting the knowledge of previous designs to support users will be investigated and developed. The concepts of design trace will be the basis for defining the operational aspects of such a tool.

References

1. F. Bretschneider: A Process Model for Design Flow Management and Planning, PhD Thesis, University Kaiserslautern, VDI Verlag, **Reihe 9, No. 157** (1993)
2. F. Bretschneider, C. Kocourek, S. Mittrach, J. Rozenblit: Design Decision Support, Planning, and Data Management of Complex Discrete Event Systems. Proc. Artificial Intelligence, Simulation, and Planning in High Autonomy Systems, IEEE Computer Society Press, (1993) 245–251
3. L. Birnbaum, G. Collins, M. Brand, M. Freed, B. Krulwich, L. Pryor: A Model-Based Aproach to the Construction of Adaptive Case-Based Planning Systems. Procedings of the 1991 DARPA workshop on case-based reasoning, Morgan Kaufmann Publishers (1991) 215–224
4. A. Casotto: Automated Design Management Using Traces, Ph.D. Dissertation, University of California, Berkeley (1991)
5. C. Forgy: The OPS83 User's Manual - System Version 3.0, Production Systems Technologies Inc (1993)
6. G. Gernich: Predicate / Transition Nets. Springer Publishing Company, Lecture Notes in Computer Science 254, (1987)
7. C. Kocourek: A Petri Net Based Design Decision Support System. Proceedings of IASTED International Conference Applied Modelling and Simulation (1993) 108–114
8. C. Kocourek: Planning and Execution Support for Design Processes. Proceedings of the 1995 International Symposium and Workshop on Systems Engineering of Computer Based Systems, IEEE (1995) 177–183
9. C. Kopf, F. Bretschneider: Systems Modeling and Process Control. Computed Aided systems Theory - EUROCAST '91, Lecture Notes in Computer Science 585, Berlin: Springer Verlag, (1991)
10. A. Pagnoni: Project Engineering: Computer Oriented Planning and Operational Decision Making, Springer Verlag, Berlin (1990)
11. K. Sycara, D. Navinchandra: Index Transformation and Generation for Case Retrieval. Procedings of the 1989 DARPA workshop on case-based reasoning, Morgan Kaufmann Publishers (1989) 324–328

A Formal Semantics for a Graphical Model Representation in System Design

Stefan Kahlert, Thomas Kruse, Dieter Monjau

Department of Computer Science, Technical University of Chemnitz
09107 Chemnitz, Germany

Abstract. This paper describes a formal semantics for a graphical model representation in the hardware/software codesign. The approach to the specification and design of heterogeneous hardware/software systems defines a strict sequence of transformations that begins with an implementation-independent specification on the system level using graphical tools. It leads to an implementation description on the register-transfer level using VHDL or C code.

1 Introduction

Today, specification and automated hardware synthesis starting from algorithmic or register-transfer level VHDL description is well established. For system-level specification and design, however, other formal description techniques than VHDL have been considered. These include SDL [1], StateCharts [3], Structured Petri Nets [4] or SpecCharts [5]. Many of these approaches use graphical descriptions and provide a link to simulation, synthesis, or formal hardware verification through appropriate VHDL interfaces. Our approach differs from all others in the dynamic description of the system to be developed. So the designer is able to describe not only a statical view of the system but also the behavior (dynamic view) of the particular processes and the temporal and causal order of communication and task processing.

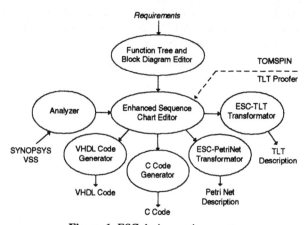

Figure 1: ESC design environment

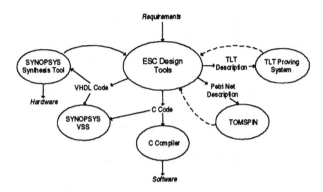

Figure 2: Connections between the design environment and available tools

The design of heterogeneous systems has to be based on a formal approach. We use models on every level of abstraction in the design process. In our view, hardware/software systems are usually complex, operate in real time and consist of concurrent components that are related to each other [6][7]. The design process is defined as a sequence of transformations between individual models, while every model in turn is the subject to a gradually refinement process. Here we consider only the two phases requirement system specification and design.

Our approach is based on Function Tree Diagrams (FTD) and Function Block Diagrams (FBD) for the requirement specification and Message Sequence Charts (MSC) as well as Enhanced Message Sequence Charts (ESC) for the system design. Figure 1 shows the structure of the ESC Design Environment and figure 2 the connections between the ESC Design Environment and commercial tools for simulation, verification, analysis, and hardware synthesis.

2 An Algebra Based Semantics

The first model in the design process is the conceptual model represented by one FTD (figure 3) and a set of FBD (figure 4). The FTDs, FBDs, MSCs and ESCs showed in this paper are part of the description of an air-conditioning system. Every FBD shows the data flows between all functions of a certain level of abstraction within a subtree.

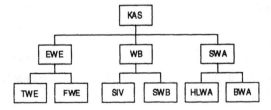

Figure 3: Example FTD

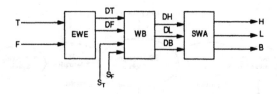

Figure 4: Example FBD

The semantics for these graphical representations of the system may be defined by algebras.

FunctionTreeAlgebra =

    Sorts: Function
            Tree

    Operations:

$$f_1, \dots, f_m: \qquad \rightarrow \text{Function}$$
$$\text{leaf: Function} \quad \rightarrow \text{Tree}$$
$$\text{ins: Tree Tree} \quad \rightarrow \text{Tree}$$

    Equations:

$$F, f_1, \dots, f_n \in \text{Function}$$
$$t_1, t_2, t_3 \in \text{Tree}$$
$$t_1 = f_1$$
$$t_2 = \text{ins}(t_1, t_2)$$
$$F \equiv h(f_1, \dots, f_n)$$

FunctionBlockAlgebra =

    Sorts: Data
            Function
            Arc
            Dataflow

    Operations:

$$d_1, \dots, d_n: \qquad\qquad\qquad\qquad\qquad \rightarrow \text{Data}$$
$$f_1(d_{1,1}, \dots, d_{1,n}), \dots, f_m(d_{m,1}, \dots, d_{m,k}): \qquad \rightarrow \text{Function}$$
$$a_1(s_{i,j}, s_{k,l}), \dots, a_n(s_{i,j}, s_{k,l}): \qquad\qquad \rightarrow \text{Arc}$$
$$\text{Connection: Function Arc Function} \qquad\qquad \rightarrow \text{Dataflow}$$

Equations:

$$i_1, ..., i_n, o_1, ... , o_n, c_1, ... , c_n, a_1, ... , a_n \in \text{Data}$$
$$F, f_1, ... , f_n \in \text{Function}$$

$I = \{i_1, ..., i_n\}$; input values of the root of the subtree

$O = \{o_1, ... , o_n\}$; output values of the root of the subtree

$C = \{c_1, ... , c_n\}$; connections between functions

$A = \{a_1, ... , a_n\}$; arcs within this level of abstraction

$O = F(I)$; functionality of the whole system

The functionality of the system is divided into a set of subfunctions $f_1, ..., f_n$, with $O_i = f_i(I_i)$.

$$I_i \subseteq I \cup \bigcup_j f_j(I_j) , j = 1, ..., n$$
$$O \subseteq \bigcup_j f_j(I_j) , j = 1, ..., n$$
$$\forall i_i \in I : i_i \in A \quad ; \text{all input values are used}$$
$$\forall o_i \in O : o_i \in A \quad ; \text{all output values are generated}$$
$$\forall a_i \in A : a_i \in (C \cup I \cup O)$$

All arcs in a certain level of abstraction are input or output values or connections between the subfunctions within this level of abstraction.

The transition from the specification to the design of the system is connected with a change of the kind of graphical representation. Starting with the first behavioral model MSCs [2] are used for system description (figure 5).

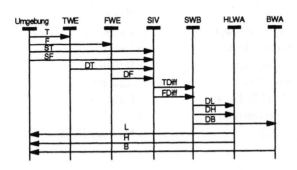

Figure 5: Example MSC

The initial MSC is produced automatically by the following rules:

(1)   Every function at the lowest level of abstraction (basic function = leaf in the FTD) is translated into a process.

(2)   Every arc between these basic functions is translated into one message.

The temporal order of the messages has to be added by the designer manually. There is the possibility to refine messages by processes as shown in figure 6.

The message between the processes A and B becomes an additional process M. M is connected with the source and target process of the original message through the new messages a_to_M and a_from_M. A reason for this kind of message refinement is for example the necessity of a data translation from serial to parallel performed by the new process.

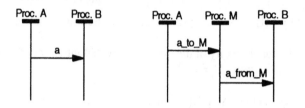

Figure 6: Refinement of a Message

The MSC represents a process model of the system which is defined by the algebra:

ProcessModelAlgebra =

Sorts: Message
      Process
      Event
      Relation

Operations:

$m_1, \ldots, m_n$	$\rightarrow$ Message
$p_1, \ldots, p_n$:	$\rightarrow$ Process
!: Process Message	$\rightarrow$ Event
?: Process Message	$\rightarrow$ Event
{ }: Event Event	$\rightarrow$ Relation
$\prec$: Event Event	$\rightarrow$ Relation
{ }: Event Relation	$\rightarrow$ Relation
$\prec$: Event Relation	$\rightarrow$ Relation
#: Message	$\rightarrow$ Message Process Message

Equations:

$e, e_1, e_2, e_3, e_4 \in$ Event; $p, p_1, p_2 \in$ Process;
$r, r_1, r_2, r_3 \in$ Relation; $m \in$ Message
$e = p\ !\ m,\ e = p\ ?\ m$
$r = e_1 \prec e_2$; events in a certain order
$r = \{e_1, e_2\}$; events in an arbitrary order
$r_2 = e_1 \prec r_1, r_2 = \{e_1, r_1\}$

if $r_1 \prec r_2$ and $r_2 \prec r_3$ then $r_1 \prec r_2 \prec r_3$

if $\{r_1, r_2\}$ and $\{r_2, r_3\}$ then $\{r_1, r_2, r_3\}$

$\#m = new\_m_1\ new\_p\ new\_m_2$

with $\quad e_1 = p_1!m$, $e_2 = p_2?m$

$new\_e_1 = p_1!new\_m_1$, $new\_e_2 = new\_p?new\_m_1$

$new\_e_3 = new\_p!new\_m_2$, $new\_e_4 = p_2?new\_m_2$

$new\_Event =$

$(Event \setminus \{e_1, e_2\}) \cup \{new\_e_1, new\_e_2, new\_e_3, new\_e_4\}$

$new\_Message = (Message \setminus \{m\}) \cup \{new\_m_1, new\_m_2\}$

$new\_Process = Process \cup \{new\_p_1\}$

The relation $new\_e_1 \prec new\_e_2 \prec new\_e_3 \prec new\_e_4$ replace the relation $e_1 \prec e_2$.

The total order of all events within a system is called the process model (PM). This process model may be expanded by event-prefixing and event-postfixing:

$$PM_{neu} = e \prec PM_{alt} \qquad\qquad PM_{neu} = PM_{alt} \prec e$$

There is also a possibility to concatenate different PMs:

(1) in certain order: $PM_{neu} = PM_1 \ll PM_2 \in PM \times PM \rightarrow PM$

(2) in an arbitrary order: $PM_{neu} = PM_1 \diamondsuit PM_2 \in PM \times PM \rightarrow PM$

(3) parallel: $PM_{neu} = PM_1 \parallel PM_2 \in PM \times PM \rightarrow PM$

In the next step the process model will be transformed into an initial automata model of the system. This transformation may be done total automatically by the following scheme:

(1) Every process becomes an automata.
(2) Every message becomes a trigger (message input event). Trigger means that the message input event leads to a state transition.
(3) An unique local state is placed before every trigger.

But states cannot only be local to an automata, there are also two other kinds of states used for synchronization: shared states and global states. Shared states belong to more than one and less than all automatas, global states belong to all automatas. Figure 7 shows the result of the automatic transformation of the ESC presented in figure 5. The next steps in the refinement of the automata model, which have to be done manually by the designer, are

(1) unification of states,
(2) addition of actions, decisions and local memories, and
(3) composition or decomposition of processes.

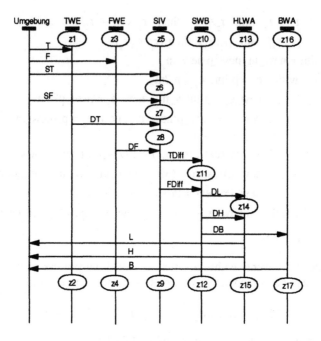

Figure 7: Example for an ESC representing an Automata

A refined ESC for the air-conditioning system is shown in figure 8. Furthermore the tasks may be enriched with VHDL or C statements and decisions may contain VHDL or C expressions. So the whole system description may be translated into VHDL and C code which can be simulated with the VHDL Simulation System by SYNOPSYS (figure 1 and 2).

Behavioral models based on automatas with these features can be defined with the following algebra:

AutomataAlgebra =

      Sorts: State
              Triggers
              Memory
              Action
              Transition
              Automata

      Operations:

$s_1, \dots, s_n$:	$\rightarrow$ State
$t_1, \dots, t_n$:	$\rightarrow$ Trigger
$v_1, \dots, v_n$	$\rightarrow$ Memory
$a_1, \dots, a_n$	$\rightarrow$ Action

      (): State Trigger Memory Action Trigger Memory State $\rightarrow$ Transition

*: Transition Transition $\rightarrow$ Automata

*: Automata Transition $\rightarrow$ Automata

*: Automata Automata $\rightarrow$ Automata

Equations:

$s_1, s_2 \in$ State; $t_1, t_2 \in$ Trigger; $v_1, v_2 \in$ Memory;

$a_1 \in$ Action; $tr_1, tr_2 \in$ Transition; $au_1, au_2, au \in$ Automata

$tr = (s_1, t_1, v_1, a_1, t_2, v_2, s_2)$

$\in$ State $\times$ Trigger $\times$ Memory $\times$ Action $\times$ Trigger $\times$ Memory $\times$ State

$au = tr_1 * tr_2$

$au = au_1 * tr_1$

$au = au_1 * au_2$

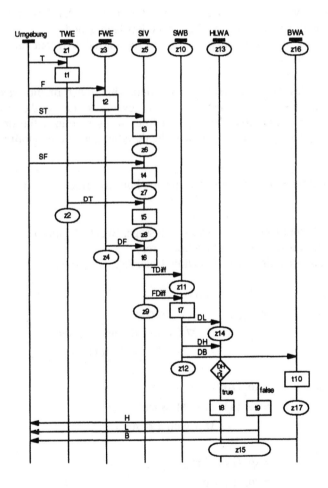

Figure 8: Refined ESC for the air-conditioning system

A decision will be described as two or more different transitions depending on the value of the triggering message or one or more local variables.

3 Algebra Transformation

Now the models at every level of abstraction are well defined trough algebras. But it is also nessessary the define functions for the sem- automatic transformation from an algebra at a higher level of abstraction into an algebra at a lower level of abstraction. This transformation can only be semi-automatic because a lower level of abstraction contains more detail informations which have to be added by the designer during the refinement of the model.

Because of the three levels of abstraction we need two transformation functions:

-    a function for the transformation of the FunctionTreeAlgebra and the FunctionBlockAlgebra into the ProcessModelAlgebra, and
-    a function for the transformation of the ProcessModelAlgebra into the AutomataAlgebra.

The following function describes the first transformation. This transformation needs additional informations about the temporal order of events to create the event relation. These information can either be obtained from an user defined file or an arbitrary order will be given from the system and the designer gets the possibility to change this order.

$$\text{ProcessModelAlgebra} = \Phi \text{ (FunctionTreeAlgebra, FunctionBlockAlgebra)}$$

with

$$\text{ProcessModelAlgebra} = \text{(Process, Message, Event, Relation)}$$
$$\text{FunctionTreeAlgebra} = \text{(Function, Tree)}$$
$$\text{FunctionBlockAlgebra} = \text{(Function, Data, Arc, Dataflow)}$$

$$\text{Process} = \phi_1 \text{ (Function)}$$
$$p_i = \phi_1(f_i) \qquad p_i \in \text{Process}$$
$$\forall f_i \text{ with } f_i \in \text{Function and}$$
$$f_i \in \text{leaf(Tree)}$$

$$\text{Message} = \phi_2 \text{ (Arc)}$$
$$m_i = \phi_2 (a_i) \quad m_i \in \text{Message}$$
$$\forall a_i \text{ with } a_i \in \text{Arc}$$

$$\text{Event} = \phi_3 \text{ (Dataflow)}$$
$$e_j = \phi_3 (d_i) = p_1 ! \, m$$
$$e_{j+1} = \phi_3 (d_i) = p_2 ? \, m$$

$$e_j, e_{j+1} \in \text{Event}; \; p_1, p_2 \in \text{Process}$$
$$f_1, f_2 \in \text{Function}; \; a \in \text{Arc}$$
$$p_1 = \phi_1 \, (f_1); \; p_2 = \phi_1 \, (f_2)$$
$$m = \phi_1 \, (a_1)$$
$$\forall \, d_i \; \text{with} \; d_i = (f_1, a, f_2) \in \text{Dataflow}$$

Relation	$= \phi_4 \, (\text{Event})$
r_i	$= \phi_4 \, (e_i) \qquad r_i \in \text{Relation}$
	$\text{with} \; i < j \rightarrow e_i \prec e_j$

The function for the transformation of the ProcessModelAlgebra into the AutomataAlgebra does not need additional informations. The transformation occurs in two steps: a full automatic part, described below, and a manual part, carried out by the designer. In the automatic part the processes are transformed into automatas by the insertion of states before every incomming message. All inserted states are unique. The section between two states is a transition, messages become triggers of these transitions.

$$\text{AutomataAlgebra} = \Phi \, (\text{ProcessModelAlgebra})$$

with

ProcessModelAlgebra	$= (\text{Process, Message, Event, Relation})$
AutomataAlgebra	$= (\text{State, Triggers, Memory, Action,}$
	$\text{Transition, Automata})$

Aktion	$= \varnothing$
Speichervektor	$= \varnothing$

Triggers	$= \phi_1 \, (\text{Message})$
t_i	$= \phi_1 \, (m_i) \qquad t_i \in \text{Trigger}$
	$\forall \, m_i \; \text{with} \; m_i \in \text{Message}$

Transition	$= \phi_2 \, (\text{Process, Message, Event, Relation})$
$(s_i, t_i, v, a, t_j, v, s_j) = \phi_2 \, (p_i, m_i, m_j, e_i, e_j, r)$	
	$t_i, t_j \in \text{Triggers}; \; s_i, s_j \in \text{State}$
	$v = \varnothing; \; a = \varnothing$
t_i	$= \phi_{21} \, (m_i)$
t_j	$= \phi_{21} \, (m_j) \qquad m_i, m_j \in \text{Message};$
	$e_i = p_i ? n_i \wedge e_j = p_i ! n_j \wedge e_i \prec e_j$

The second step is an optimisation step. States will be combined. If states in the same automata are combined, cycles are created. But it is also possible to combine states from different automatas. So global or shared states are created which are used for the synchronisation of the automatas.

4 Conclusions

In this paper we presented our new approach for the design of heterogeneous systems and defined a formal semantics for it. We introduced our approach for the description of a system with the Function Tree Diagrams, the Function Block Diagrams, the Message Sequence Charts, and the Enhanced Message Sequence Charts. For every description method we defined a formal semantics by algebras. Lastly we showed transformation functions for the algebras starting from the FunctionTreeAlgebra/FunctionBlockAlgebra (the highest level of abstraction) over the ProcessModelAlgebra leading to the AutomataAlgebra (the most detailed level of abstraction in our system).

References

[1]   CCITT: *Functional Specification and Description Language (SDL)*, Recommendation Z.100-Z.104, Blue Book, October 1989.

[2]   CCITT: *Message Sequence Charts (MSC)*, Recommendation Z.120, September 1992.

[3]   Harel, D.: *State Charts: A Visual Formalism for Complex Systems*, Science of Computer Programming, 8:231-274, 1987

[4]   Kotov, V.E.; Cherkasova, L.A.: *Structured Nets*, in proc. of MCSF, Springer LNCS 118, 1981

[5]   Vahid, F.; Narayan, S.; Gajski, D.D.; *SpecCharts: A Language for System Level Synthesis*, in Proc. of the IFIP Tenth Internat. Symposium on Computer Hardware Description Languages and their Applications, pages 145-154, April 1991

[6]   Buchenrieder, K.; Kahlert, St.; Monjau, D.; Veith, Ch.: *A new Model-based Approach to the CoDesign of Heterogeneous systems*, in Proc. of the Eurocast'93, Springer LNCS 763, 1994

[7]   Kahlert, St.; Knäbchen, J.-U.; Monjau, D.: *Design and Analysis of Heterogeneous Systems Using Graphically Oriented Methods: A Case Study*, in Proc. of the SASIMI'93, Nara, Japan, Oct. 1993

A User-Interface for a Microsystems High-Level Simulator

E. Meyer zu Bexten and C. Moraga

University of Dortmund

Department of Computer Science and Computer Engineering

44221 Dortmund, Germany

Abstract:

This paper presents a descriptive specification of the user interface for a microsystems simulator at the highest level of abstraction in a hierarchical design environment. A new design paradigma WYSIWYS "What You See Is What You Simulate" is disclosed.

1 Introduction

Microsystems consist basically of one or more sensors, signal processing circuitry and one or more actuators, which are integrated on a single chip. The development of microsystems is becoming a key-technology for industrial progress [Mokw 95] as well as for future ambitious goals like, for instance, medical micro-robotics.

The design of microsystems is a complex problem, that cannot be realised without support of CAD-tools. Furthermore it should be seen as a special VLSI-Design problem and as such, it should take advantage of the rich experiences of the last decade. It is a well established strategy in VLSI to realise a hierarchical design and to use appropriate CAD-tools for each level of abstraction. Among these, simulators play a very important role. A stable trend of the last years is that of using simulation already at the highest level of abstraction [Gajs 93, Ramm 89] to have a fast turnaround check on preliminary designs.

This paper discusses a high-level simulator for microsystems, called MISIM, which is based on the Computer Aided Symbolic Simulation SYstem CASSY [MzBe 92, MzBM 92] and exhibits the most relevant features of the later. The figure 1 shows the main window of MISIM in the CASSY environment.

2 CASSY-System

The CASSY-System [MzBM 93] was developed at the Fraunhofer-Institute for Microelectronic Circuits and Systems in cooperation with the University of Dortmund. This system is a CAD-tool with the following main features:

- Support of early design stages of mixed analog/digital signal processing systems

- Operation at a high level of abstraction in an interactive way

- Use of symbolic simulation methods

- Possesion of a powerful user friendly interactive graphic user-

  interface following ergonomical requirements as:

  - support of common practice in engineering design work

  - compliance with existing guidelines

  - integration of supporting tools for the users work

  - operation mainly under direct manipulation [Shne 92]

  - orientation after the "WYSIWYS" principle

  ("*What you see is what you simulate*")

3 System Description

In what follows, the system will be described *from the user's point of view*. The system environment, as seen by the user, consists of a main working window (see Fig. 1), several communication windows and a display window.

The main working window (see Fig. 1 and 2) supports the interactive assembly of microsystems by selecting and placing appropriate icons for microcomponents - sensors, signal processing-circuits and actuators - as well as drawing the required connections among them. Moreover, a connection may be marked as "visible" if the user wants to "see" the (simulated) signal at this point of the microsystem. The user is given support in the following different ways during the various steps required to simulate a microsystem:

1. Special menu-options enable the selection of components by opening a communication window with a list of components.

2. Placement of components is achieved by dragging with the mouse. Placed components may be fully specified if taken from a library or empty in case of a new component.

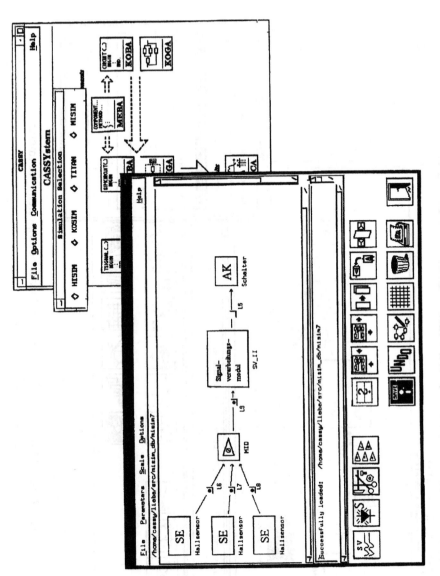

Fig. 1: MISIM in the CASSY Environment

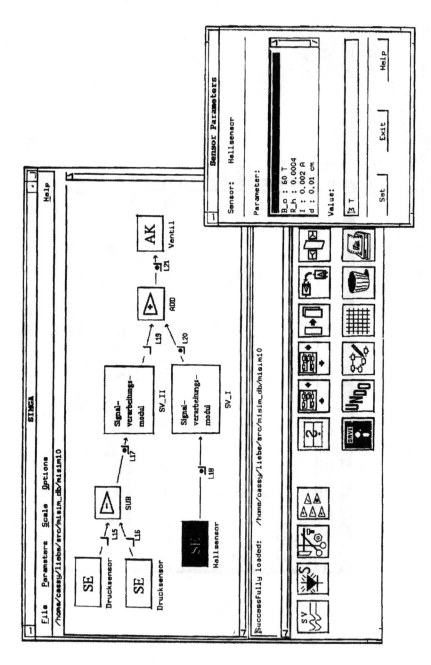

Fig. 2: MISIM main window and window for component parameters

3. Double-clicking a component, e.g. on the Hallsensor as shown in figure 2, opens a new communication window to specify (or possibly modify) its parameters. For example in the case of a temperature sensor the parameters could be the temperature range, the type of response within that range (linear or logarithmic) the polarity (positive or negative) and specific coefficients of the materials of the sensor.

4. Linking components is done by simply selecting the two corresponding icons and pressing a pre-defined mouse key.

5. Most frequently used menu-options are also available in a special row of buttons with adequate graphical encriptions to facilitate the work with the system. (This row may however be optionally hidden to provide a larger area for assemblying the microsystem. An entry of the menu "Options" allows the user to do this.)

6. Communication windows serve the following purposes: Selection of components and specification of their parameters (as mentioned above) (see Fig. 2), as well as definition of simulation parameters (see Fig. 3). These windows are controlled by the user.

7. A communication window controlled by the system is a constituent part of the main working window and displays error messages or status messages of the system.

8. As soon as a simulation request is processed the system opens the display window of the CASSY-System [MzBH 93] to show the graphic representation of the selected signals of the microsystem (see Fig. 4).

4 System Core

The MISIM prototype is object-oriented and basically consists of a class-hierarchy of components linked to the class-hierarchy of CASSY. This means that every component in MISIM has associated a collection of methods to compute its behaviour when driven by an allowed signal. Signals correspond to messages, which the objects (components) may exchange. By linking two components, the user is thus defining a channel to send a message. In summary, when the user assembles a microsystem in the working window as explained above, he is also assembling the corresponding instance of the simulator, which begins the processing when the user activates the option to start the simulation after specifying the appropriate simulation parameters, like number of requested simulation steps, a reference voltage value and selection of report files for sensors and actuators (see Fig. 3).

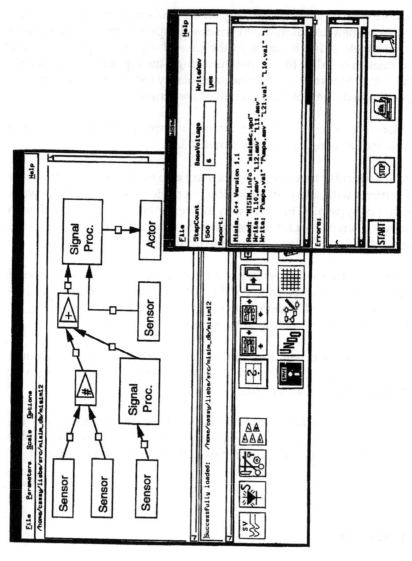

Fig. 3: MISIM main window and window for simulation parameters

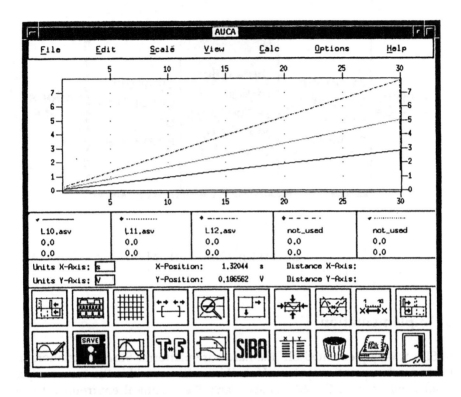

Fig. 4: Display window showing the output signal of a linear
sensor under different parameter values

The system core of MISIM consists of three functional blocks as shown in
figure 5. The blocks at the left and right side support the simulation of sensors
and actuators respectively meanwhile the grey bock in the middle is taken
from the CASSY-system and is devoted to the simulation of signal processing
circuits.

One of the accepted interpretations of the concept "Visual Programming"
refers to the construction and control of programs by means of graphic objects
[PoVM 94]. From this point of view, a user of MISIM who graphically
constructs a representation of a microsystem, as explained above, assembles a
Visual Program which is executed after the simulation is started. This is the
basis of the new paradigma mentioned above WYSIWYS: "*what you see is what
you simulate*".

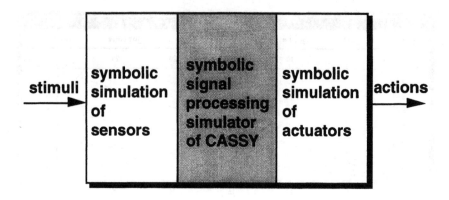

Fig. 5: System Core of MISIM

5 Implementation

MISIM was implemented on the hardware platforms Sun workstation and PC under the operating systems Unix/Linux. It runs within the same environment conditions as CASSY. That means, the graphical environment is X-Windows and OSF/Motif (X11 R5, OSF/Motif 1.2). The implementation language is C++.

Acknowledgement

The authors thank the student Mr. Markus Liebe for the implementation of a prototype of the simulator MISIM [Lieb 94], which allowed the evaluation and verification of the leading concepts supporting this project.

References

[Gajs 93]   D.D. Gajski: *Design Process Beyond ASICs*, Proceedings of the IEEE, EDAC, pp. 3-5, February 1993

[Lieb 94]   M. Liebe: *Simulation von Mikrosystemen unter Einbindung in das CASSY-System*, Diplomarbeit, Universität Dortmund, Fachbereich Informatik, 1994

[MzBe 92]   E. Meyer zu Bexten: *Eine Simulationsumgebung für signalverarbeitende Systeme*, Dissertation, Universität Dortmund, Fachbereich Informatik, Shaker Verlag, Aachen, 1992

[MzBH 93]   E. Meyer zu Bexten, D. Heinen, C. Moraga: *AUCA: A Tool for Presentation and Analysis of CAD-Simulation Results*, Proceedings of the HCI International 93, Orlando FLA, USA, Elsevier Science Publishers, pp. 267-272, 1993

[MzBM 92]   E. Meyer zu Bexten, C. Moraga, J. Büddefeld: *A High-Level Interactive Design Environment for Complex Systems*, in: Computer Aided System Theory - EUROCAST '91, Lecture Notes in Computer Science, Vol. 585, Springer-Verlag, Berlin, pp. 442 - 459, April 1992

[MzBM 93]   E. Meyer zu Bexten, C. Moraga: *Simulation für die Systemebene (Elektronik-Cad: Werkzeuge zur Unterstützung der frühen Phasen des Schaltungsentwurfs)*, Elektronik Journal, Europa-Fachpresse-Verlag, München, 28. Jahrgang, Ausgabe 12, S. 16-23, September 1993

[Mokw 95]   W. Mokwa: *Mikrosystemtechnik - Entwicklung und Marktumsetzung*, 9. Fachtagung Mikroelektronik, Baden-Baden, März 1995

[PoVM 94]   J. Poswig, G. Vrankar, C. Moraga: *VisaVis: A Higher-order Functional Visual Programming Language*, Journal of Visual Languages and Computing, 5, pp. 83-111, 1994

[Ramm 89]   F. Rammig: *Systematischer Entwurf digitaler Systeme*, Teubner Verlag, Stuttgart, 1989

[Shne 92]   B. Shneiderman: *Designing the User Interface: Strategies for efficient Human-Computer Interaction*, Addison-Wesley Publishing Company, New York, 1992

CAST Extensions to DASME to Support Generalized Information Theory

Cliff Joslyn[1] and Scott Henderson[2]

[1] Code 522.3, NASA Goddard Space Flight Center
Greenbelt, MD 20771, USA
joslyn@kong.gsfc.nasa.gov
http://groucho.gsfc.nasa.gov/joslyn
[2] Senior Scientist, Cambridge Research Associates
1430 Spring Hill Rd. Suite 200, McLean, VA 22102, USA
scott@cambridge.com

Abstract. The Data Analysis and System Modeling Environment (DASME) is a computer-assisted modeling environment, currently under development at NASA's Goddard Space Flight Center, designed to support ground-based mission operations with a mixed discrete/continuous modeling capability. This paper describes planned CAST-based extensions to DASME to support a broader range of systems theoretical computing models, and in particular models utilizing concepts from Generalized Information Theory (GIT) such as fuzzy systems, possibilistic measurement, and possibilistic processes. Support for model-based diagnostics and trend analysis of spacecraft systems is targetted.

1 Introduction

This paper describes a software systems development project ongoing in the Software and Automation Systems Branch (Code 522) of NASA's Goddard Space Flight Center in Greenbelt, Maryland. Code 522's role—within the overall Goddard mission of Earth and space science research with earth-orbiting satellites—is to conduct research and development to support mission operations and data systems. Code 522 provides systems engineering, development, and operation tools, and prototypes demonstrating new technologies and advanced systems architectures. Their areas of technology expertise span from systems modeling and human-computer interaction to software engineering and knowledge-based systems.

The overall thrust of Code 522 research is to move towards increasing autonomy and automation of both spacecraft platforms and their ground-based control and support systems. The foreseen development path moves from rule- and object-based approaches, characteristic of expert systems; through model-based approaches, typical of enhanced knowledge-based systems; and aiming towards sophisticated agent-based AI approaches.

One of the important research areas of Code 522 is the development of methods for trend analysis of spacecraft systems and components. In trend analysis, mathematical representations of spacecraft health are developed from telemetry analysis. These analysis methods are then employed to reveal any long-term trends indicating degradation in system health, or any incipient threat of failure.

The initial focus of the trend analysis program is the battery subsystem for the Small Mission EXplorer (SMEX) family of missions. Batteries provide a particular challenge for trend analysis because of the complexity of their environments (loads and charges) and the complexity and inherent limitations in our knowledge of their electrochemical dynamics. These conditions have resulted in great difficulties in battery quality assurance, and a number of spacecraft platforms are at risk for failure.

Existing Code 522 facilities for trend analysis provide only basic visualization and rudimentary statistical analysis of telemetry. More sophisticated approaches to supplement these methods are under development, including a Model-Based Diagnostic (MBD) approach.

In addition, due to the many forms of uncertainty inherently present in complex engineering systems like spacecraft, and especially in their battery subsystems, Qualitative Modeling (QM) methods for MBD are especially appropriate [10]. To support qualitative MBD, we plan to use the Generalized Information Theory (GIT) computational paradigm, and especially its possibilistic modeling techniques. GIT is the synthesis of modern mathematical theories of uncertainty, including fuzzy systems, random sets, evidence theory, and possibility theory [9, 16, 17]. GIT promises to provide a key generalizing technology for QM methods in systems theory [9, 11].

This paper describes the Data Analysis and Systems Modeling Environment (DASME), which is being used as the development environment for this approach, and our proposed CAST-based extensions to DASME to support a broader range of computational models (for example finite automata, petri nets, or neural nets), and especially a qualitative approach to MBD using possibility theory and possibilistic processes.

2 The Data Analysis and Systems Modeling Environment (DASME)

DASME is a computer-assisted modeling platform developed by Henderson to support ground-based mission operations. It has the dual capacities of telemetry analysis and systems modeling using a mixture of discrete-event and discrete-time methods. DASME's general and flexible architecture allows it to be easily adapted to fulfill multiple tasks, although it will be first applied in model-based trend analysis of spacecraft battery subsystems.

2.1 DASME Design

DASME is a collection of behavioral components, input components, output components, a graphical model editor, and a run-time executive.

Behavioral components simulate specific elements within the domain (currently satellite power systems) and were implemented as a library of C++ classes. Input components were derived from this same class hierarchy to feed the simulation with file-based data streams or direct user input. Output components (also a part of the class library) produce dynamic plots of their inputs, or transmit those values to a CLIPS environment for processing by expert systems.

The X-Windows based graphical model editor allows the synthesis of complex hierarchical models by connecting the input and output ports of behavioral components, input/output components, or other models. This editor also allows "zooming" into sub-models for inspection or adjustment of parameters. Completed models can be stored to and retrieved from disk through this editor.

The run-time executive provides scheduling and time management for a heterogeneous mix of discrete-time and discrete-event components with an X-Windows interface for starting, pausing, resuming, and stopping execution. Support for other computational paradigms, including causal, state, and qualitative modeling, is planned for the future, and is partially the focus of this paper. Additional future capabilities include a neuro-fuzzy machine learning component for model adaptivity.

2.2 DASME Model Architecture

DASME provides a general black box architecture. Nodes are called "components", and each contains distinct input and output ports and initial state variables called "parameters". It is also strictly hierarchical, with each component containing a number of sub-components whose ports are accessible to the parent and to each other, but not outside the containing component. Atomic components are independently compiled C++ modules, and non-atomic components are aggregates of either atomic or other aggregate components. An aggregate DASME component is shown in Fig. 1. The children **Component A** and **Component B** may either be atomic or themselves aggregates.

Data are passed among components in structures called "polyvalues", which are heterogeneous, hierarchical lists of C++ primitive data elements. For example, **float**, **str**, **(int int)**, and **((char float) int)** are polyvalue types. Type-checking is done at run-time.

Time values are either scalar (a relative duration), or absolute (microseconds from January 1, 1970). Component state transitions (execution of C++ code for atomic components, or propagation to children for aggregate components) can be triggered by means of an elegant mixture of discrete-event and discrete-time methods, as summarized in Table 1.

Events (component executions) are scheduled in either absolute or relative time, and according to one of three timing modifiers. By using the **NotBefore** modifier, components can schedule their own execution at the indicated time and no other. By using the **OrBefore** modifier, components indicate that execution should also occur if one or more of the component's inputs change. By using the **PreferBefore** modifier, components indicate that execution before the indicated time (even in the absence of new inputs) is desirable. The executive is then

Temporal Modifier	Method	When a component updates
NotBefore	Discrete Event	At scheduled time
OrBefore	Discrete Event	At scheduled time, or if input changes
PreferBefore	Discrete Time	At scheduled time, or if input changes, or if desired by executive

Table 1. Temporality in DASME.

allowed to increase the frequency of evaluation to be no greater than a minimal time step, as configured by the user.

This **PreferBefore** method adds a discrete-time modeling capability to DASME. This is crucial to support components whose behaviors are best modeled as continuous functions. For example, a component with piecewise-continuous behavior can guarantee its evaluation at landmark points (such as inflections or discontinuities), while simultaneously allowing the executive to trigger intermediate evaluations. Placing this responsibility in the executive, rather than solely with the component itself, allows the executive to determine an appropriate tradeoff between fidelity of the simulation and its time to compute. The benefit of this approach is that this configuration is achieved without having to modify the model.

2.3 Comparison to DEVS

DASME took substantial initial design inspiration from Zeigler's powerful Discrete EVent Systems (DEVS) modeling formalism. Only a brief summary is provided here; for full details see [24, 25].

Define a DEVS system as

$$\mathcal{D} := \langle X, Y, S, t, \delta_{\text{int}}, \delta_{\text{ext}}, \lambda \rangle, \tag{1}$$

where:

- X is a set of external events;
- Y is a set of outputs;
- S is a set of sequential states;
- $t: S \mapsto \mathbb{R}^+ \cup \{\infty\}$ is the time advance function;
- $\delta_{\text{int}}: S \mapsto S$ is the internal transition function;
- $\delta_{\text{ext}}: Q \times X \mapsto S$ is the external transition function, where

$$Q := \{(s, e) : s \in S, 0 \leq e \leq t(s)\} = \bigcup_{s \in S} [0, t(s)] \tag{2}$$

  is the total state set; and

- $\lambda: S \mapsto Y$ is the output function.

These functions are interpreted as follows. Assume that $\mathcal{D}$ is in state $s \in S$. If an event $x \in X$ arrives after a duration $e \leq t(s)$, then $\mathcal{D}$ transits to state $\delta_{\text{ext}}(\langle s, e \rangle, x)$. Otherwise $\mathcal{D}$ transits to state $\delta_{\text{int}}(s)$. Finally, at all times, if $\mathcal{D}$ is in state s, then it produces output $\lambda(s)$.

It is clear that DASME components can be generally interpreted as DEVSs, and in general that DASME has much in common with the DEVS implementation in Scheme called DEVS-Scheme [26]. This relation is specified as follows:

- The overall hierarchical structure, including atomic and aggregate components and input and output ports, is essentially identical.
- X and Y are the joint state spaces of the polyvalue types of the input and output ports.
- Depending on whether the component is atomic or aggregate, S is either the states achievable in virtue of the C++ code of the module, or recursively the joint state spaces of the child components.
- Each component has two methods `ClockMeAfter()` and `ClockMeAt()` for scheduling at relative and absolute times respectively. Together these determine t and δ_{int}, which is the maximum elapsed time before the component is updated; in particular, the `ClockMeAfter()` method establishes the *sigma* variable in DEVS-Scheme.
- The `NotBefore` temporal modifier sets

$$\delta_{\text{ext}}(\langle s, e \rangle, x) \equiv s, \qquad \forall s \in S, e \in [0, t(s)], x \in X, \tag{3}$$

so that external events are essentially ignored.
- The `OrBefore` temporal modifier effectively establishes the component as a regular DEVS. δ_{ext} is fired if an input event occurs by the scheduled time, otherwise δ_{int} is triggered.
- Each component has a `Sleep()` method, which calls `ClockMeAt()` with `EndOfTime` (maximal absolute time) and the `OrBefore` method. This sets $t(s) = \infty$, so that the component will not be updated until an external event occurs, essentially ignoring δ_{int}.

Where DASME departs from the classical DEVS formalism is in the use of the `PreferBefore` modifier. It allows the model executive (basically, the DASME operating environment for the highest level component of the hierarchy) to "reach down" and intervene, triggering component updating before scheduled times, and in the absence of any external events from within the hierarchy. It is this facility which allows the executive to evaluate continuous functions at discrete times. The modeler then has the flexibility to adjust evaluation step size depending on the analytical properties of the continuous functions in question, without modifications to the model itself.

It is this capability which adds a discrete-time component, in order to better handle continuous-time functions, to an otherwise discrete-event modeling environment. Thus it is similar in outlook to the approach of Praehofer and his colleagues [20, 21].

Another difference between DASME and the DEVS approach is at the engineering level. DEVS as a modeling methodology is a completely analytical, mathematical formalism. DEVS platforms have typically been implemented in a highly constrained subset of a very high level artificial intelligence language like Scheme [26].

DASME's reliance on C++ means that it can escape from the strict DEVS formalism. For example, input DASME components can be positioned at any level of the hierarchy. As these rely on external inputs (from disk files or the terminal), there can be no *a priori* knowledge about the possible states of these components. Thus no purely analytical model of a DASME system is possible.

This creates an engineering tradeoff when considering DASME in the context of the wider DEVS world. On the one hand, DASME components have a greater flexibility, and will be generally much more efficient than implementations in higher level languages. But on the other hand, since DASME departs from the formal DEVS model, verification and formal design will be more difficult.

3   Application to Model-Based Trend Analysis

The MBD approach [5] is based on the premise that knowledge about the internal structure of a system can be useful in diagnosing its failure. In MBD, a software model of the system, given inputs from the real system, generates and tests various failure hypotheses.

A typical MBD approach (derived from some of the standard literature [1, 3, 4]) to diagnosing a spacecraft is shown in Fig. 2. The overall MBD system involves two distinct spacecraft models. The Fault Generation Model (FGM) takes inputs from telemetry, alarms (reports of departures from nominal behavior), and errors (reports of departures from predicted behavior), and either produces new, or modifies existing, fault hypotheses. The behavior model takes inputs from telemetry and fault hypotheses, and outputs predictions. These are then corroborated against telemetry to produce errors.

The fault hypotheses act to modify the behavior model so that it predicts system behavior as if the hypothetical system components had actually failed. If the prediction of the behavior model as modified by a particular fault hypothesis produces errors, then that fault hypothesis is not retained. As the system is monitored over time, further observations narrow the class of viable fault hypotheses. Achieving the null set indicates model insufficiency. But if the overall MBD system stabilizes to a non-empty set of fault-hypotheses, then these are advanced as possible causes of the failure.

Model-based trend analysis is similar to MBD, but with some differences:

- Trend analysis is typically done over a longer time-frame.
- In addition to being purely diagnostic, trend analysis attempts to be predictive. By diagnosing certain components to be failing or otherwise trending in a particular direction, potential future failures can be anticipated.
- Trend analysis is especially appropriate for modeling systems where gradual degradation leads to catastrophic failure, as is the case with batteries.

In the context of trend analysis, detection of anomalous component states, even though they may not be in a failed condition, is extremely important. Within the overall model-based approach, a variety of methods are available for signature matching of a time-varying telemetry signal against model predictions, including statistical techniques, neuro-fuzzy adaptive approaches, and possibilistic measurement (discussed below).

4 CAST Extensions to DASME

It is our intention to use DASME as a CAST-based platform for modeling within Code 522. While DASME is generally adherent to the DEVS paradigm, there is a desire for DASME to support a wider range of computational models—for example neural nets, finite automata, or fuzzy reasoning—if possible. DASME as it exists now already has many advantages for this effort, including its generality and flexibility, but some significant enhancements will be required.

The ultimate necessary extension to DASME is the introduction of weights on the links among the children of aggregate components. Similar to the data values passed among components, weights will also be PolyValues. These weights can be used generally as elements of a wide class of computational modeling methods, for example, weights in a neural network, conditional possibilities in a possibilistic network (discussed below), or entire fuzzy sets in a more traditional fuzzy system.

In order to facilitate the introduction of weighted aggregates, strict data typing of the components' ports, and thus of the types of the links between components, must be introduced. At model construction time, only links between ports of equivalent types will be allowed, thus eliminating the need for model run-time type checking and error recovery. An example of a DASME component with typed links is shown in Fig. 3.

Two weight data types are introduced for each component. The internal weight type is held in common by all weights on the links between the children of the component (if null, the aggregate is unweighted). The external weight type is the type of weight acceptable to a component on its inputs (if null, the component need not be a child of a weighted aggregate). An example of a DASME component with weighted links is shown in Fig. 4.

5 Possibilistic Qualitative Modeling

Possibility theory [2] is an alternative information theory to that based on probability. It was originally developed in the context of fuzzy systems theory [23], and was thus related to the kinds of cognitive modeling that fuzzy sets are usually used for. More recently, possibility theory is being developed as a new form of mathematical information theory complementing probability theory [12]. The details of mathematical possibility theory will not be introduced here (see [9, 10]), but will be described only very cursorily, and its role as a QM method briefly outlined.

5.1 Possibility Theory

A possibility distribution π over a given space or set Ω is similar to a probability distribution, but whereas a probability distribution p is additive,

$$\int_\Omega dp(\omega) = 1, \qquad \sum_{\omega \in \Omega} p(\omega) = 1, \tag{4}$$

in the continuous and discrete cases respectively, π is "maxitive"

$$\sup_\Omega \pi(\omega) = 1, \qquad \bigvee_{\omega \in \Omega} \pi(\omega) = 1, \tag{5}$$

in the continuous and discrete cases, where $\vee$ is the maximum operator. Similarly, a possibility measure Π based on π is maxitive, in that

$$\forall A, B \subseteq \Omega, \quad \Pi(A \cup B) = \Pi(A) \vee \Pi(B). \tag{6}$$

Superficially, possibility theory is broadly similar to probability theory with $\langle +, \times \rangle$ algebra replaced by $\langle \vee, \sqcap \rangle$ algebra, where $\sqcap$ is a t-norm function: a monotonic, associative, commutative operator with identity 1. The minimum operator $\wedge$ and $\times$ are both t-norms, but there are many others. Concepts of marginal, joint, and conditional possibility have all been defined, as have possibilistic correlates to stochastic entropy, called nonspecificities.

Although possibility theory is logically independent of probability theory, they are related: both arise in Dempster-Shafer evidence theory as fuzzy measures defined on random sets; and their distributions are both fuzzy sets. So possibility theory is a component of a GIT, which includes all of these fields [9, 16, 17].

But at a semantic level, probability and possibility are radically different. Probability represents division of knowledge among a distinct set of point outcomes. Possibility, on the other hand, is inherently *non-additive*. Possibility represents *coherence* of knowledge *around* a central core of certainty: the region on which $\pi(\omega) = 1$, which is guaranteed to be non-empty by normalization.

And so while probability is related to *dispersive* concepts like frequency, chance, and likelihood, possibility is related to *ordinal* concepts like capacity, ease of attainment, distance, and similarity. Furthermore, unlike probability, possibility places very weak constraints on the representation of information: the maximum relation is a very weak operator, and there is a choice of many norms to use, some of which are strong, and others of which, like $\vee$, are also weak.

So possibilistic models are appropriate where stochastic concepts and methods are inappropriate, including situations where long-run frequencies are difficult if not impossible to obtain, or where small sample sizes prevail. This is true, for example, in trend-analysis, where even though observations are made over a long time, the trending state variables of concern change only very slowly, and new domains of behavior are only very rarely seen. In these cases the weakness of the possibilistic representation is matched by the weak evidence available.

Mathematical possibility, in both theory and applications, is still in the basic research phase, just out of its infancy. For example, the axiomatic basis for possibility theory and the properties of possibility distributions on continuous spaces are still being defined, and the semantics of possibility in physical systems has been considered only by very few. Joslyn is developing mathematical possibility theory on the basis of consistent random sets, general possibilistic modeling methods (including possibilistic measurement and interpretation procedures), and an empirical semantics for possibility [9].

5.2 Possibility Theory for Qualitative Modeling

There are many reasons why it can be expected that possibility theory can come to play an important role in QM in general, and in the application of QM to MBD in particular. Two of the most important reasons for this are that possibility theory is the appropriate and direct generalization of two of the key methods used in QM: interval analysis and nondeterministic processes.

Interval analysis [19], and in particular interval-valued processes [18], are an important component of general QM methodology. A crisp real interval $I = [a, b] \subseteq \mathbb{R}$ can be represented by its characteristic function $\chi_I \colon \mathbb{R} \mapsto \{0, 1\}$, where

$$\chi_I(x) = \begin{cases} 1, x \in I \\ 0, x \notin I \end{cases}. \tag{7}$$

χ_I is a special kind of possibility distribution called "crisp", where $\forall \omega \in \Omega, \pi(\omega) \in \{0, 1\}$. Generalizing (7) from $\{0, 1\}$ to $[0, 1]$, and keeping some simple convexity requirements, results in "fuzzy intervals" or "fuzzy numbers". Fuzzy arithmetic [14] defines mathematical operations such as addition and multiplication on fuzzy intervals and numbers, and directly generalizes interval arithmetic. Probability theory, on the other hand, does not.

A non-deterministic process [6] can be characterized by its transition network. Each state $\omega \in \Omega$ can transit to any number of other states. If the value 1 is assigned to a possible transition, and 0 to one which is not allowed, then a boolean $n \times n$ transition matrix can be constructed, where $n := |\Omega|$. Given an initial state $\omega_i \in \Omega$, then future states are represented as subsets $\sigma(\omega_i) \subseteq \Omega$.

Similarly, nondeterministic processes generalize to possibilistic Markov processes in a way which is much more natural than stochastic Markov processes. Possibilistic processes provide an ideal medium for causal modeling using a graduated, nondeterministic representation of causal relatedness. The transition graph of a possibilistic process can essentially be regarded as a possibilistic network, similar to Bayesian networks in stochastic systems theory.

An example is shown in Fig. 5 for $\Omega = \{x, y, z\}$. The arcs indicate possible state transitions, each of which is non-additively weighted with the conditional possibility of the transition. This results in the possibilistic transition matrix

$$\Pi = \begin{bmatrix} 0.0 & 0.8 & 0.0 \\ 1.0 & 0.0 & 0.0 \\ 0.2 & 1.0 & 1.0 \end{bmatrix}. \tag{8}$$

Each column of $\boldsymbol{\Pi}$ plays the role of $\sigma(\omega)$ in a nondeterministic process. Given an initial state possibility distribution, future possibilistic states are calculated by $\langle \vee, \sqcap \rangle$ matrix composition. Joslyn has also developed possibilistic Monte Carlo methods [9], which are required to select a specific final outcome given a possibility distribution on the state variables of the process at any given time.

6   Possibilistic Modeling with CAST-Extended DASME

We intend to use CAST-extended DASME in a number of different ways to support qualitative model-based trend analysis of spacecraft.

6.1   Data Analysis

The most immediate application of DASME to possibilistic modeling, even before the addition of weighted links, is the development of possibilistic representations of telemetry through possibilistic measurement procedures [7, 8]. The essential requirement is the collection of the frequency of occurrence $m(A_j)$ of subsets or intervals $A_j \subseteq \Omega$, yielding what is called an "empirical random set" [15]. If any of the observed intervals are overlapping, then such a representation cannot be reduced to a traditional point-valued random variable, and thus no traditional point-valued probability distribution can be forthcoming [13]. If the core of the observed intervals is nonempty, so that $\bigcap_j A_j \neq \emptyset$, then

$$\pi(\omega) := \sum_{A_j \ni \omega} m(A_j). \tag{9}$$

is an empirical possibility distribution, called a possibilistic histogram, with the same core.

An example is shown in Fig. 6. On the left, four observed intervals are shown. The bottom two occur with frequency 1/2, while each of the upper two have frequency 1/4. Together they determine an empirical random set. The step function on the right is the possibilistic histogram derived from (9).

There are a variety of well-justified continuous approximations to a possibilistic histogram. Two examples are shown in the figure. The rising diagonal on the left is common to both. The two falling continuous curves on the right are distinct to each. The trapezoidal form marked π^* is one of the most commonly used continuous approximations, but it must be noted that this is only one possibility among many, including smooth curves. This approach to possibilistic measurement generalizes to n intervals and to the continuous case.

So possibilistic measurement is distinguished from measurement in probability theory by its reliance on interval-based observations. There are a number of different ways in which intervals result from measurement [9]. The method of most immediate interest for spacecraft modeling derives from local extrema of a telemetry stream.

A simple example is shown in Fig. 7. Given a time-varying telemetry signal, each time the curve turns marks a local extrema. The segments of the ordinate between these local extrema produce a statistical collection of intervals, and thus an empirical random set and possibilistic histogram. It should be noted that this method is sensitive to noise, since each non-signal fluctuation generates two spurious local extrema, and thus interrupts the "real" interval being observed.

In the context of trend analysis, possibilistic histograms of telemetry promise to provide a novel and significant new representation of the long-term trending of the data. The core is the central region of purely nominal behavior, while the support (the larger region on which the possibility distribution is positive at all) represents the domain of observed behavior, and is thus similar to a concept of a "yellow limit". Comparison, through possibilistic distance measures [22], between possibilistic histograms at different times reveals trending information.

The data path for possibilistic measurement in DASME is shown in Fig. 8. Each node indicates a different DASME component. In the context of spacecraft systems modeling, measurements are typically desired of such variables as voltages and temperatures. The noisy telemetry signal requires smoothing. Intervals are typically observed between orbital periods, yielding one data interval approximately every 45 minutes. Data sets on the order of months are required.

6.2 Systems Modeling

Finally, CAST-extended DASME provides a rich modeling environment within which to implement possibilistic causal network models. Fig. 9 shows how the three-state possibilistic process shown in Fig. 5 would be implemented in a CAST-extended aggregate DASME component.

The three inputs to the component represent the initial possibility values of the three automata states, each of which in turn is represented by the three child components. These are atomic components, which take the initial possibility value as input, and calculate the current possibility value as output. They also take as input the values of any other state which can transition to them, that is, which have a non-zero conditional possibility.

The internal data type of the weights on the links between the components are called fits, for "fuzzy digit", a float in $[0, 1]$. The weights represent the conditional possibility of transition between states, and together comprise Π. The external weight type is null, indicating that the whole possibilistic process does not participate in a higher level systems model. Finally, the aggregate process component outputs the current possibility value of each state.

References

1. Davis, R and Hamscher, W: (1992) "Model-Based Reasoning: Troubleshooting", in: *Readings in Model-Based Diagnosis*, ed. W Hamscher *et al.*, pp. 3-24, Morgan Kaufman, San Mateo CA

2. Dubois, Didier and Prade, Henri: (1988) *Possibility Theory*, Plenum Press, New York

3. Dvorak, D and Kuipers, B: (1992) "Model-Based Monitoring of Dynamic Systems", in: *Readings in Model-Based Diagnosis*, ed. W Hamscher *et al.*, pp. 249-254, Morgan-Kaufmann, San Mateo CA

4. Hall, Gardiner A; Schuetzle, James; and La Vallee, D *et al.*: (1992) "Architectural Development of Real-Time Fault Diagnositc Systems Using Model-Based Reasoning", in: *Proc. 1992 Goddard Conf. on Space Applications of AI*, ed. Steve Rash, pp. 77-86, NASA Goddard, Greenbelt MD

5. Hamscher, W; Console, Luca; and Kleer, Johan de, eds.: (1992) *Readings in Model-Based Diagnosis*, Morgan-Kaufman

6. Hopcroft, John E and Ullman, Jeffery D: (1979) *Introduction to Automata Theory Languages and Computation*, Addison-Wesley, Reading MA

7. Joslyn, Cliff: (1992) "Possibilistic Measurement and Set Statistics", in: *Proc. NAFIPS 1992*, v. **2**, pp. 458-467, Puerto Vallerta

8. Joslyn, Cliff: (1993) "Some New Results on Possibilistic Measurement", in: *Proc. NAFIPS 1993*, pp. 227-231, Allentown PA

9. Joslyn, Cliff: (1994) *Possibilistic Processes for Complex Systems Modeling*, PhD Dissertation, Binghamton University, UMI Disseration Services, Ann Arbor MI

10. Joslyn, Cliff: (1994) "Possibilistic Approach to Qualitative Model-Based Diagnosis", *Telematics and Informatics*, v. **11**:4, pp. 365-384

11. Joslyn, Cliff: (1995) "An Object-Oriented Architecture for Possibilistic Models", in: *Proc. 1994 Conf. Computer-Aided Systems Technology*, to appear

12. Joslyn, Cliff: (1995) "Towards an Independent Possibility Theory with an Objective Semantics", in: *Proc. 1995 Int. Workshop on Foundations and Applications of Possibility Theory*, to appear

13. Joslyn, Cliff: (1995) "Strong Probabilistic Compatibility of Possibilistic Histograms", in: *Proc. 1995 Int. Symposium on Uncertainty Modeling and Analysis*, to appear

14. Kaufmann, A. and Gupta, M.M.: (1985) *Introduction to Fuzzy Arithmetic*, Reinhold, New York

15. Kendall, DG: (1974) "Foundations of a Theory of Random Sets", in: *Stochastic Geometry*, ed. EF Harding and DG Kendall, pp. 322-376, Wiley, New York

16. Klir, George: (1993) "Developments in Uncertainty Based Information", in: *Advances in Computers*, v. **36**, ed. M. Yovitz, pp. 255-332, Academic Press

17. Klir, George and Yuan, Bo: (1995) *Fuzzy Sets and Fuzzy Logic*, Prentice-Hall, New York

18. Kuipers, BJ: (1994) *Qualitative Reasoning: Modeling and Simulation with Incomplete Knowledge*, MIT Press, Cambridge MA

19. Moore, RM: (1979) *Methods and Applications of Interval Analysis*, in: *SIAM Studies in Applied Mathematics*, SIAM, Philadelphia

20. Praehofer, Herbert: (1991) "Systems Theoretic Formalisms for Combined Discrete-Continuous Systems Simulation", *Int. J. of General Systems*, v. **19**, pp. 219-240

21. Praehofer, Herbert and Zeigler, Bernard P: (1995) *Automatic Abstraction of Event-Based Control Models*, in preparation

22. Ramer, Arthur: (1990) "Structure of Possibilistic Information Metrics and Distances: Properties", *Int. J. of General Systems*, v. **17**, pp. 21-32

23. Zadeh, Lotfi A: (1978) "Fuzzy Sets as the Basis for a Theory of Possibility", *Fuzzy Sets and Systems*, v. **1**, pp. 3-28

24. Zeigler, BP: (1976) *Theory of Modeling and Simulation*, Wiley, New York

25. Zeigler, BP: (1985) *Multifacetted Modeling and Discrete Event Simulation*, Academic Press, San Diego

26. Zeigler, BP: (1990) *Object-Oriented Simulation with Hierarchical Modular Models*, Academic Press, San Diego

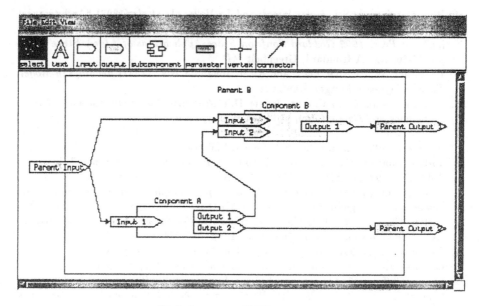

Fig. 1. An aggregate DASME component.

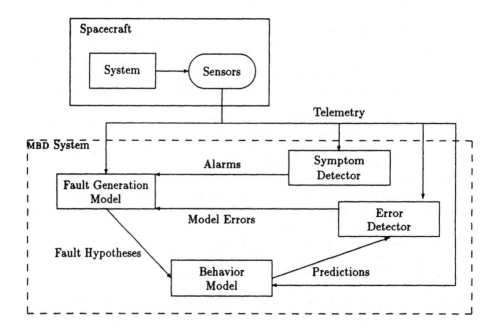

Fig. 2. A typical model-based diagnostic system.

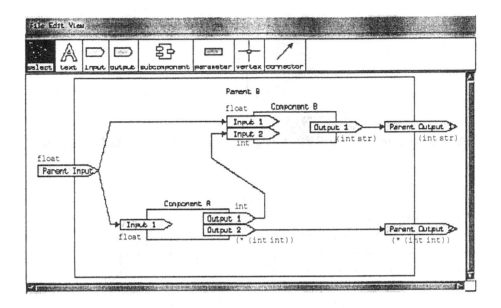

Fig. 3. A DASME component with typed links.

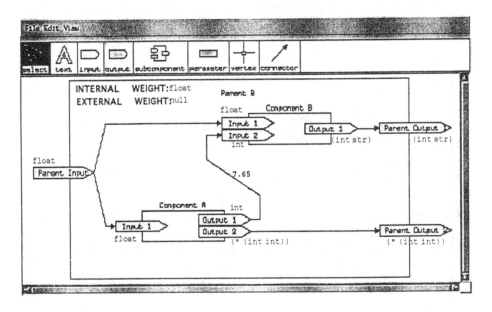

Fig. 4. A DASME component with weighted links.

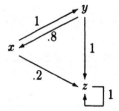

Fig. 5. Weighted state transition diagram for a possibilistic Markov process.

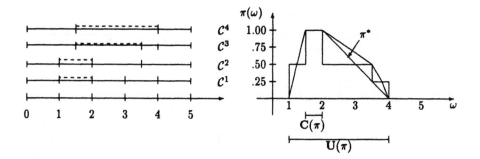

Fig. 6. (Left) Four example observed intervals. (Right) The possibilistic histogram and two continuous approximations.

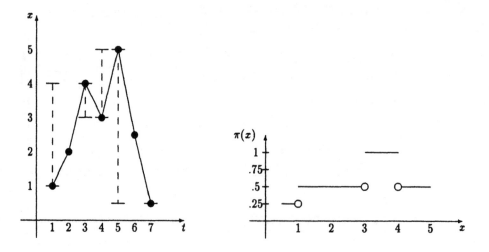

Fig. 7. Observed intervals and resulting possibilistic histogram from local extrema.

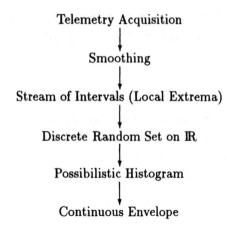

Telemetry Acquisition

↓

Smoothing

↓

Stream of Intervals (Local Extrema)

↓

Discrete Random Set on ℝ

↓

Possibilistic Histogram

↓

Continuous Envelope

Fig. 8. Possibilistic measurement in DASME.

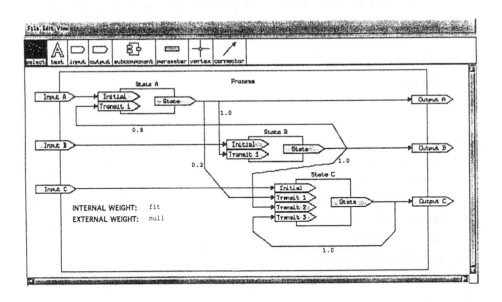

Fig. 9. A possibilistic process implemented in a CAST-extended DASME component.

Symbolic Computing Aided Design of Nonlinear PID Controllers

Jesús Rodríguez-Millán and Juan Cardillo

Universidad de Los Andes - Facultad de Ingeniería

Escuela de Sistemas - Dept. de Sistemas de Control

Apartado 11 - La Hechicera, Mérida 5251-A, VENEZUELA

Fax: 58-74-402846, E-mail: jrmillan@ing.ula.ve

Abstract. In this paper we introduce a symbolic computing tool, denoted by NLPID in the sequel, for the automatic design of linear and nonlinear PID controllers for nth order nonlinear control systems. The nonlinear design algorithm is based upon Rugh's Extended Linearization Technique, and it was implemented using Mathematica® as symbolic computing platform. At its present stage of development NLPID uses Ziegler-Nichols tables to synthesize linear PID controllers, and therefore its ability to deal with first and second order plants could be limited.

Keywords: Nonlinear PID Controllers, Jacobian and Extended Linearization, Symbolic Computing.

Contents

1 Introduction

NonLinear Control Systems (NLCS) are dynamical systems defined through (i) a *state equation*, i.e., an ordinary differential equation:

$$x' = f(x,u), x \in \Re^n, u \in \Re^k \qquad\qquad (1\text{-}a)$$

where f is at least Lipschitz continuous to assure the initial value problem has a unique solution, and (ii) an algebraic *output equation*:

$$y = h(x), y \in \Re^m. \qquad\qquad (1\text{-}b)$$

An *operating point* of the NLCS (1) is a point $(U, X(U), Y(U))$ in $\Re^k x \Re^n x \Re^m$ such that $f(X(U),U) = 0$ and $Y(U) = h(X(U))$. We will assume in the sequel that $k = m = 1$, and that the output function h is continuous.

One of the main problems of control theory is the stabilization problem, which might be mathematically formulated as follows: Does it exist a control law u capable of asymptotically stabilize the NLCS (1) to a specified operating point $(U, X(U), Y(U))$?. From the engineering point of view, however, the actual question is: Is it possible to exhibit, by way of a designing algorithm, a control law u that asymptotically stabilized the NLCS (1) to a desired operating point $(U, X(U), Y(U))$?. The answer to this question is generically affirmative provided the usual controllability conditions hold, and that we think of stabilization only in the restricted, local sense, i.e., of stabilization in small enough neighborhoods of the desired operating point.

Local stabilization of control systems can be approached through different control strategies: state feedback controllers, PID controllers, lead-lag compensators, amongst others. In this paper we will focus our attention unto the PID-family of control strategies, and our main purpose is to develop a symbolic computing tool for the automatic design of nonlinear PID controllers by using the extended linearization technique.

2. The Jacobian Linearization Method

The most frequently used local stabilization strategy is Jacobian Linearization Method (JLM), according to which we must firstly stabilize the linearization of the NLCS (1) around the desired operating point $(U, X(U), Y(U))$ with a linear control law $u = G(x,y)$, to proceed, secondly, to locally stabilize the NLCS (1) with the very same linear controller. After the Hartman-Grobman theorem (Hartman 1982, Perko 1991) the dynamic of the closed loop linearized system:

$$\xi' = D_x f(X(U),U)\xi + D_u f(X(U),U)\upsilon = A(U)\xi + B(U)\upsilon \qquad\qquad (2\text{-}a)$$

$$\upsilon = G(x,y) \tag{2-b}$$

$$\psi = D_x h(X(U))\xi = C(U)\xi \tag{2-c}$$

is generically homeomorphically equivalent to the local dynamics of the closed loop NLCS

$$x' = f(x,G(x,y)), \ y = h(x) \tag{3}$$

in small enough neighborhoods of the operating point $(U, X(U), Y(U))$.

JLM is a strictly local design technique and, in principle, it does not allow to stabilize a NLCS when its initial conditions are far away from the desired operating point. Thus, to improve the stabilization capabilities of NLCSs, nonlinear controllers must be introduce.

3. The Extended Linearization Method

The Extended Linearization Method (ELM), developed by Rugh and coworkers (Rugh 1986 & 1987) proposes a twofold strategy to solve the stabilization problem in LNCSs:

(i) Firstly, design a stabilizing linear controller according to the JLM to locally satisfy the design specifications, and proceed

(ii) Secondly, to synthesize a nonlinear controller in such a way that its linearization coincides with the JLM previously designed controller.

Thus, in the ELM nonlinear controllers are conceived as nonlinear extensions of previously designed JLM linear controllers.

In a more precise way, the general ELM design algorithm can be resume as follows:

Step 1   Consider a NLCS $x' = f(x,u), y = h(x)$, and its desired operating point $(U, X(U), Y(U))$.

Step 2   Translate the operating point to the origin by way of the coordinates transformation

$$x = \xi + X(U), \ y = \psi + Y(U), \ u = \upsilon + U, \tag{4}$$

and obtain the representation of the NLCS in the new coordinates:

$$\xi' = f(\xi + X(U), \upsilon + U)$$

$$\psi = -Y(U) + h(\xi + X(U)) \tag{5}$$

Step 3   Linearize the NLCS (5) around the origin:

$$\xi' = D_x f(X(U),U)\xi + D_u f(X(U),U)\upsilon = A(U)\xi + B(U)\upsilon$$

$$\psi = D_x h(X(U))\xi = C(U)\xi \tag{6}$$

Step 4   Stabilize the linearization $(A(U), B(U), C(U))$ through a linear controller described by

$$\zeta' = P(U)\zeta + Q(U)\varepsilon$$

$$\upsilon = R(U)\zeta + T(U)\varepsilon, \tag{7}$$

where $\varepsilon(t) = s(t) - \psi(t)$ is the error signal, and suppose that for any set point U, $\varepsilon(U) = 0$. Then, the closed loop linear system would be:

$$\xi' = A(U)\xi + B(U)\upsilon \tag{8-a}$$

$$\zeta' = P(U)\zeta + Q(U)\varepsilon \tag{8-b}$$

$$\upsilon = R(U)\zeta + T(U)\varepsilon \tag{8-c}$$

$$\psi = C(U)\xi \tag{8-d}$$

Step 5   Introduce a nonlinear controller described by

$$\zeta' = p(\zeta + Z(U), \varepsilon)$$

$$\upsilon = r(\zeta + Z(U), \varepsilon), \tag{9}$$

where $\zeta = z - Z(U)$.

Step 6   The closed loop NLCS would then be:

$$\xi' = f(\xi + X(U), \upsilon + U)$$

$$\zeta' = p(\zeta + Z(U), \varepsilon)$$

$$\upsilon = r(\zeta + Z(U), \varepsilon)$$

(10)

$$\psi = -Y(U) + h(\xi + X(U))$$

Step 7 Linearize the closed loop NLCS around the desired operating point:

$$\xi' = A(U)\xi + B(U)\upsilon$$

$$\zeta' = D_z p(Z(U), 0)\zeta + D_e p(Z(U), 0)\varepsilon$$

(11)

$$\upsilon = D_z r(Z(U), 0)z_\delta + D_e r(Z(U), 0)\varepsilon$$

$$\psi = C(U)\xi.$$

Step 8 The nonlinear controller will then be the solution of the following set of partial differential equations (PDE):

$$D_z p(Z(U), 0) = P(U)$$

$$D_e p(Z(U), 0) = Q(U)$$

(12)

$$D_z r(Z(U), 0) = R(U)$$

$$D_e r(Z(U), 0) = T(U).$$

Step 9 Return to the original coordinates through the inverse coordinates transformation

$$\xi = x - X(U), \psi = y - Y(U), \upsilon = u - U, \zeta = z - Z(U).$$

(13)

Remark 1. For the simplicity of the design algorithm, Steps 4 and 6 are, perhaps, the most important ones, because they allow to obtain the PDE leading to the desired control law in the easiest possible way.

Example 1. Let $x' = f(x,u)$, $y = h(x)$ be a NLCS, and let $(U, X(U), Y(U))$ be the desired operating point. After applying the coordinates transformation (4) the NLCS adopts the standard form (5), and its linearization around the origin is given by (6).

The simplest example of stabilization techniques is state feedback stabilization, i.e., $\upsilon = - K(U)\xi$. Such a linear controller can be modelled by:

$$\zeta' = \xi'$$

$$\upsilon = - K(U)\zeta.$$

(14)

Thus, the full model for the linearization of the NLCS with state feedback is

$$\xi' = A(U)\xi + B(U)\upsilon$$

$$\zeta' = 0\zeta + \xi'$$

$$\upsilon = - K(U)\zeta$$

$$\psi = C(U)\xi.$$

(15)

Consider a nonlinear controller with the following structure:

$$\zeta' = \xi'$$

$$\upsilon = - k(\zeta).$$

(16)

Then, the full model for the NLCS with the controller (16) will be

$$\xi' = f(\xi + X(U), \upsilon + U)$$

$$\zeta' = \xi'$$

$$\upsilon = - k(\zeta)$$

$$\psi = -Y(U) + h(\xi + X(U)),$$

(17)

where at equilibrium $U = k(Z(U)) = k(X(U))$. The linearization of (17) around the origin is:

$$\xi' = A(U)\xi + B(U)\upsilon$$

$$\zeta' = 0\zeta + \xi'$$

$$\upsilon = D_z k(X(U))\zeta \tag{18}$$

$$\psi = C(U)\xi,$$

and therefore, from (15) and (18) it follows that the solution of the PDE

$$D_z k(X(U)) = -K(U), \, k(X(U)) = U \tag{19}$$

is the desired control law $k(z)$, which as it is shown in (Rodríguez-Millán & Serrano, 1995) can be iteratively calculated. ♦

4. Linear PID Controllers

Linear proportional-integral-derivative (PID) controllers conform a whole family of controllers satisfying the control law

$$u(t) = K_1 e(t) + K_2 \int_0^t e(s)ds + K_3 \frac{de(t)}{dt} \tag{20}$$

where $e: \Re \to \Re$ and $u: \Re \to \Re$ denote the input and output signals of the controller, respectively. When $K_2 = K_3 = 0$ controllers are called proportional (P) controllers, whereas when $K_3 = 0$ we speak about proportional-integral (PI) controllers.

To define the state of a PID controller as

$$z(t) = K_2 \int_0^t e(s)ds \quad z' = K_2 e(t) \tag{21}$$

allow to model a PID controller as in Step 4 of the general ELM design algorithm:

$z' = K_2 e(t)$

$$u(t) = z(t) + K_1 e(t) + K_3 \frac{de(t)}{dt} . \tag{22}$$

In stabilization problems constants K_1, K_2 and K_3 will obviously depend on the desired operating point $(U, X(U), Y(U))$ of the system, i.e., $K_i = K_i(U)$, $i = 1, 2, 3$. From the physical point of view K_1, K_2 and K_3 represent the proportional, integral and derivative gains, respectively.

In the sequel we will assume $K_2(U)$ is never zero, to assure that the error $e(U) = s(U) - Y(U) = 0$ for every seting point U.

There exist several techniques (Aström & Hägglund 1988, Ogata 1992) for calculating the gains $K_i(U)$, $i = 1, 2, 3$ in linear PID controllers. However, what we actually need to develop a symbolic computing tool for the automatic design of nonlinear PID controllers is a symbolic algorithm leading to linear PID gains. Such an algorithm (Rugh 1987 & Sira-Ramírez 1994) can be resumed in five steps:

Step 1   Given a linear control system parametrized by U:

$$\xi' = A(U)\xi + B(U)\upsilon, \; A(U) \in M_n, B(U) \in \Re$$

$$\psi = C(U)\xi, C(U) \in \Re, \tag{23}$$

calculate its transfer function:

$$G_c(s) = C(U)[sI - A(U)]^{-1}B(U). \tag{24}$$

Step 2   Calculate the phase-crossover frequency $w_0(U)$:

$$\mathrm{Im}G_c(jw_0(U)) = 0 \; \text{with} \; w_0(U) \neq 0 \; \text{and} \; w_0(U) \neq \infty. \tag{25}$$

Step 3   Calculate the ultimate gain $K_0(U)$:

$$K_0(U) = \frac{1}{|G_c(jw_0(U))|} \tag{26}$$

Step 4   Calculate the PID gains by way of the Ziegler-Nichols in Table 1:

Controller	$K_1(U)$	$K_2(U)$	$K_3(U)$
P	$0.5\,K_o(U)$	0	0
PI	$0.45\,K_o(U)$	$\dfrac{0.27K_o(U)w_o(U)}{\pi}$	0
PID	$0.6\,K_o(U)$	$\dfrac{0.6}{\pi}K_o(U)w_o(U)$	$\dfrac{0.15\pi K_o(U)}{w_o(U)}$

Table 1. Ziegler-Nichols gains for linear PID Controllers

Step5   Construct the linear PID controller

$$\zeta' = K_2\varepsilon$$

$$\upsilon(t) = \zeta(t) + K_1\varepsilon(t) + K_3\frac{d\varepsilon(t)}{dt} \ . \tag{27}$$

From now on we will refer to the algorithm above as the ZN-algorithm. As Step 2 clearly shows, the ZN-algorithm structurally depends on the existence of a phase-crossover frequency different from both zero and infinity.

5. Nonlinear PID Controllers.

On searching for nonlinear extensions of the linear PID controller (22) it is natural to consider nonlinear dynamical systems with the following structure:

$$z' = k_2(z)e$$

$$u(t) = z + k_1(z)e + k_3(z)\frac{de(t)}{dt} \ , \tag{28}$$

because $k_i(z)$, i = 1, 2, 3 coefficients would correspond to nonlinear extensions of the linear PID gains $K_i(U)$, i = 1, 2, 3. The operating point of this nonlinear controller is $e(U) = 0$ and $U = Z(U)$.

The linearization of (28) around its operating point is

$$z' = k_2(U)e$$

$$u(t) = z + k_1(U)e + k_3(U)\frac{de(t)}{dt} \tag{29}$$

and from the comparison of (29) with (22) it follows that

$$k_i(z)_{|z=U} = K_i(U), \quad i = 1, 2, 3. \tag{30}$$

Thus, nonlinear gains are given by $k_i(z) = \left[K_i(U)\right]_{U=z}$, where the operator $[.]_{U=z}$ formally substitute the operating point coordinate U by the controller state variable z.

6. Functional Description of NLPID

As it has been shown in the previous sections, the general design algorithm of nonlinear controllers by way of ELM has two main parts: first that all we have to design a linear controller through JLM and second we synthesize a nonlinear extension of the previously designed linear controller.

In the particular case of nonlinear PID controllers, the design algorithm has been resumed in the Flow Diagram 1.

7. Examples

In this section we consider three examples, the first two of which illustrate how NLPID can be used to design nonlinear PID controllers for a Boost continuous current converter and a cascade of three identical tanks. The third example shows that for systems with trivial phase-crossover frequencies NLPID does not allow to calculate the desired stabilizing nonlinear PID controller.

Example 2. Let us consider the average model of a Boost continuous-current converter

$$x1' = -\omega_1(u - 1)x2 + b$$

$$x2' = \omega_1(1 - u)x1 - \omega_2 x2 \tag{31}$$

$$y = x2$$

where $x1$ and $x2$ are the states of the system, $0 \le u \le 1$ is the control signal and b, ω_1 and ω_2 are positive parameters (Sira-Ramírez, 1994). Except from transcription and headings' translation into English, NLPID provides next results:

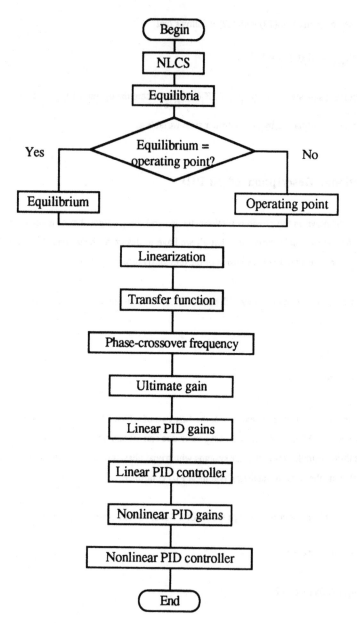

Flow Diagram 1. Functional decomposition of NLPID.

PID CONTROLLER DESIGN

****

DYNAMICAL SYSTEM

x1' = b - w1 x2 + u w1 x2

x2' = w1 x1 - u w1 x1 - w2 x2

y = x2

Control variable: u

System parameters: {w1, x2, b}

****

EQUILIBRIUM POINTS

$$\{u \to U, x1 \to \frac{b\ w2}{(-1 + U)^2\ w1^2}, x2 \to \frac{b}{w1 - U\ w1}\}$$

OPERATING POINT

$$\{u \to U, x1 \to \frac{b\ w2}{(-1 + U)^2\ w1^2}, x2 \to \frac{b}{w1 - U\ w1}\}$$

A(U) MATRIX

matA [1,1] : 0

matA [1,2] ; (-1 + U) w1

matA [2,1] : (1 - U) w1

matA [2,2] : -w2

B(U) MATRIX

matB [1,1] : $\dfrac{b}{1 - U}$

matB [2,1] : $- \left(\dfrac{b\ w2}{(-1 + U)^2\ w1} \right)$

C(U) MATRIX

matC [1,1] : 0

matc [1,2] : 1

TRANSFER FUNCTION Gu(s):

$$\frac{b\ (w1^2 - 2\ U\ w1^2 + U^2\ w1^2 - s\ w2)}{(-1 + U)^2\ w1\ (s^2 + w1^2 - 2\ U\ w1^2 + U^2\ w1^2 + s\ w2)}$$

TRANSFER FUNCTION EVALUATED AT $s = i*w$, Gu(i*w):

$$\frac{b\ (w1^2 - 2\ U\ w1^2 + U^2\ w1^2 - i\ w\ w2)}{(-1 + U)^2\ w1\ (i^2\ w^2 + w1^2 - 2\ U\ w1^2 + U^2\ w1^2 + i\ w\ w2)}$$

IMAGINARY PART OF Gu(i*w):

$\{(b\ w\ (w^2 - 2\ w1^2 + 4\ U\ w1^2 - 2\ U^2\ w1^2)\ w2) / ((-1 + U)^2\ w1\ (w^4 - 2\ w^2\ w1^2 + 4\ U\ w^2\ w1^2 - 2\ U^2\ w^2\ w1^2 + w1^4 - 4\ U\ w1^4 + 6\ U^2\ w1^4 - 4\ U^3\ w1^4 + U^4\ w1^4 + w^2\ w2^2))\}$

PHASE-CROSSOVER FREQUENCY wo:

1.- $wo = - (\ Sqrt[2 - 4\ U + 2\ U^2]\ w1)$
2.- $wo = Sqrt[2 - 4\ U + 2\ U^2]\ w1$

ULTIMATE GAIN Ko:

$$\frac{1}{Sqrt[\dfrac{b^2}{(-1 + U)^4\ w1^2}]}$$

LINEAR PID CONTROLLER:

$$z' = \{\{\frac{0.6 \text{ Sqrt}[2] \text{ Sqrt}[(-1 + U)^2]w1}{\text{Pi Sqrt}[\dfrac{b^2}{(-1 + U)^4 \ w1^2}]}\}\} * e$$

$$u = z + \{\{\frac{0.6}{\text{Sqrt}[\dfrac{b^2}{(-1 + U)^4 \ w1^2}]}\}\} * e +$$

$$\{\{\frac{0.075 \text{ Sqrt }[2] \text{ Pi}}{\text{Sqrt}[(-1 + U)^2] \text{ Sqrt}[\dfrac{b^2}{(-1 + U)^4 \ w1^2}] \ w1}\}\} * e'$$

NONLINEAR PID CONTROLLER

$$z' = \{\{\frac{0.6 \text{ Sqrt }[2] \text{ Sqrt }[(-1 + z)^2] \ w1}{\text{Pi Sqrt }[\dfrac{b^2}{(-1 + z)^4 \ w1^2}]}\}\} * e$$

$$u = z + \{\{\frac{0.6}{\text{Sqrt }[\dfrac{b^2}{(-1 + z)^4 \ w1^2}]}\}\} * e +$$

$$\{\{\frac{0.075 \text{ Sqrt }[2] \text{ Pi}}{\text{Sqrt }[(-1 + z)^2] \text{ Sqrt }[\dfrac{b^2}{(-1 + z)^4 \ w1^2}] \ w1}\}\} * e'$$

******************************** END ************************* ◆

Example 3. Let us consider a cascade of three identical, noninteracting tanks (Rugh, 1987):

$$x1' = -\frac{c}{A}\sqrt{x1} + \frac{1}{A}u$$

$$x2' = -\frac{c}{A}\sqrt{x2} + \frac{c}{A}\sqrt{x1}$$

$$x3' = -\frac{c}{A}\sqrt{x3} + \frac{c}{A}\sqrt{x2}$$

(32)

$$y = x3,$$

where $u(t) \geq 0$ is the flow into the first tank, $x_i(t)$ is the height in the ith tank, $A > 0$ is the cross-sectional area of the tanks, and $c > 0$ is the outflow resistance. We assume in the sequel that $u(t) = U$.

After running NLPID we get the following main results:

PID CONTROLLER DESIGN

****

DYNAMICAL SYSTEM

$$x1' = \frac{u}{A} - \frac{c \; Sqrt \; [x1]}{A}$$

$$x2' = \frac{c \; Sqrt \; [x1]}{A} - \frac{c \; Sqrt \; [x2]}{A}$$

$$x3' = \frac{c \; Sqrt \; [x2]}{A} - \frac{c \; Sqrt \; [x3]}{A}$$

$$y = x3$$

Control variable: u

System parameters: $\{c, A\}$

****

OPERATING POINT

$$\{u \to U, x1 \to \frac{U^2}{c^2}, x2 \to \frac{U^2}{c^2}, x3 \to \frac{U^2}{c^2}\}$$

- -

TRANSFER FUNCTION Gu(s):

$$c^4 / (3 s A c^4 + 4 s^3 A^3 U^2 + 6 s^2 A^2 c^3 \; Sqrt \; [\frac{U^2}{c^2}] + \frac{c^7 \; Sqrt \; [\frac{U^2}{c^2}]}{2 U^2})$$

- -

PHASE-CROSSOVER FREQUENCY wo:

$$1.- wo = \frac{-(Sqrt\ [3]\ c^2)}{2\ A\ U}$$

$$2.- wo = \frac{Sqrt\ [3]\ c^2}{2\ A\ U}$$

- -

ULTIMATE GAIN Ko:

$$\frac{4}{Sqrt\ [\frac{U^2}{c^4}]}$$

- -

LINEAR PID CONTROLLER:

$$z' = \{\{\frac{1.2\ Sqrt\ [3]\ c^2}{U\ A\ Sqrt\ [\frac{U^2}{c^4}]\ Pi}\}\} * e$$

$$u = z + \{\{\frac{2.4}{Sqrt\ [\frac{U^2}{c^4}]}\}\} * e + \{\{\frac{1.2\ U\ A\ Pi}{Sqrt\ [3]\ Sqrt\ [\frac{U^2}{c^4}]\ c^2}\}\} * e'$$

- -

NONLINEAR PID CONTROLLER:

$$z' = \{\{\frac{1.2\ Sqrt\ [3]\ c^2}{z\ A\ Sqrt\ [\frac{z^2}{c^4}]\ Pi}\}\} * e$$

$$u = z + \{\{\frac{2.4}{Sqrt\ [\frac{z^2}{c^4}]}\}\} * e + \{\{\frac{1.2\ z\ A\ Pi}{Sqrt\ [3]\ Sqrt\ [\frac{z^2}{c^4}]\ c^2}\}\} * e'$$

************************************* END ******************************

Straightfoward calculations probe that these results are exactly the same reported in (Rugh, 1987). ◆

Last example shows that the phase-crossover frequency is not well defined for some second order NLCS, and therefore the ZN-algorithm cannot be used to design stabilizing PID controllers for them.

Example 4. Consider the NLCS

$$\theta' = \phi$$

$$\phi' = u \ \text{sen}\theta \ \cos\theta - g/a \ \text{sen}\theta \tag{33}$$

$$y = \theta$$

and suppose the desired operating point is $(U, \Theta, \Phi, Y) = (\frac{g}{a \cos\Theta}, \Theta, 0, \Theta)$. The linearization of (33) around the operating point is given by:

$$A(\Theta) = \begin{pmatrix} 0 & 1 \\ -\frac{g}{a} \ \text{sen}\Theta \ \text{tg}\Theta & 0 \end{pmatrix}, B(\Theta) = \begin{pmatrix} 0 \\ \frac{\text{sen}2\Theta}{2} \end{pmatrix}, C(\Theta) = (1 \ \ 0) \tag{34}$$

and then

$$G_\Theta(s) = \frac{\text{sen}2\Theta}{2} \frac{1}{s^2 + \frac{g}{a} \ \text{sen}\Theta \ \text{tg}\Theta} . \tag{35}$$

It is obvious that $\text{Im}G_\Theta(s) = 0$, which implies that $\omega_0(\Theta)$ is not well defined, and therefore the ZN-algortihm cannot be used to synthesize K_i, $i = 1, 2, 3$. ♦

8. Discussion

In this paper we introduced a symbolic computing tool, NLPID, for the automatic design of nonlinear PID controllers, which is based upon Rugh's Extended Linearization Method and uses Mathematica® as symbolic computing platform.

Because of the symbolic nature of the ZN-algorithm, it is perhaps the best design algorithm from the symbolic computing point of view. It has to be kept in mind, however, that this algorithm depends, in an essential way, on the existence of a nontrivial, i.e., neither zero nor infinity, phase-crossover frequency. When the phase-crossover frequency only assumes the trivial values, as it is usually the case in first and second order NLCS, the linear PID gains $K_1(U)$, $K_2(U)$, $K_3(U)$ cannot be calculated through the ZN-algortihm. In this case another design algorithm must be used. The development of a complementary tool to cover this case is currently in progress.

In the ZN-algorithm it is assumed that we have at hand a good analytical model of the NLCS to be stabilized. When this is not the case, the linear PID gains must be obtained by another means.

Given that calculations leading to the nonlinear PID gains do not involve integration algorithms, as it is the case in state-feedback stabilization for instance (Rodríguez-Millán & Serrano 1995), the main limitation of NLPID is the ability of Mathematica® to simplify complex expressions. Hence, it could happen that nonlinear PID gains, or whatever other intermediate results, generated by the NLPID tool appear under very involved forms that could still be simplified (by hand).

References

Aström, K. and Hägglund, T. 1988, Automatic Tuning of PID Controllers, Instrument Society of America, USA.

Hartman, P. 1982, Ordinary Differential Equations, Birkhäuser, Basel.

Ogata, K. 1992, Modern Control Theory, 6th Edition, Prentice-Hall, Engelwood Cliffs.

Perko, P. 1991, Differential Equations and Dynamical Systems, Springer-Verlag, New York.

Rodríguez-Millán, J. and Serrano, S. 1995, Symbolic Computing Aided Design of Nonlinear Controllers by Jacobian and Extended Linearization, International Congress for Industrial and Applied Mathematics: ICIAM' 95, Hamburg, 3-7 July.

Rugh, W. 1987, Design of Nonlinear PID Controllers, AIChE Journal, Vol. 33, No. 10, 1738-1742.

Rugh, W. 1986, The Extended Linearization Approach, in Nonlinear Control and Systems, M. Fliess and M. Hazewinkel, Editors, D. Reidel Publishing Company, Dordrecht.

Sira-Ramírez, H. 1994, Nonlinear Control by Extended Linearization, Cuadernos de Control Vol. 2-94, Postgrado de Control, Facultad de Ingeniería, ULA, Mérida. (In Spanish)

Acknowledgments

It is with gratitude that the authors acknowledge the support of the Science Research Council (CDCHT) to the Universidad de Los Andes under the grant I-458-94-S. The final version of this paper was written during the stage of the first author at the ICTP in Trieste and SZTAKI in Budapest. I specially thank Prof. J. Bokor for his invitation and support during my stage at SZTAKI.

Discrete Event Simulation in an Environment for Temporal Expert Systems

Ramón P. Otero, Alvaro Barreiro, Pedro Cabalar and David Lorenzo

Dept. Computación, Fac. Informatics, University of A Coruña,
E-15071, A Coruña, Spain
email: otero@udc.es

Abstract. The relationship between *Generalized Magnitudes* (a Temporal Reasoning Scheme) and Discrete Event Systems Specifications is examined, revisiting a previous work of translation between both formalisms. As a result of this study, the Generalized Magnitudes Scheme is extended by adding autonomous activation — the system determines the next instant in which it must be re-evaluated. This new feature allows using the Generalized Magnitudes for representing and simulating Discrete Events models directly, which contributes several interesting representational properties. Finally, the computing process of the next activation instant is described.

1 Introduction

Temporal Reasoning in Artificial Intelligence is first understood as the ability to reason with temporal expressions, making inferences with temporal relations. Following this point of view, there are well known temporal formalisms, almost all of them, presented as extended logics that incorporate temporal features. However, we are interested in other Temporal Reasoning schemes – needed for Expert Systems – that are focused on reasoning about the evolution of the domain, rather than on reasoning about time itself. The formalisms used under this focusing can be related to classical Systems Theory formalisms, like the DEVS formalism [Zeigler76, Zei84]. A previous work [Otero94] has shown the possibility to represent DEVS structures in the temporal formalism called *Generalized Magnitudes* (GMs) focused on the domain evolution.

In this paper, we revisit the translation made between the two formalisms and we present a new approach that resolves open questions and increments the representational power of the GMs Scheme, taking concepts from Systems Theory. This new approach implies incorporating autonomous activation by deducing the instant, implicitly represented in the knowledge expressions, in which the knowledge must be evaluated. Autonomous activation would correspond to the concept of internal transition in the DEVS formalism.

As a consequence of incorporating autonomous activation, the resulting extended GMs scheme can be used for representing directly Discrete Event Systems, without a previous step of modeling using DEVS formalism. We will comment the differences between modeling and simulation in the GMs formalism versus classical Systems Theory approaches [Pichler92].

We also describe how to compute the next activation instant (what we have called *next evaluation time point*) making an incremental study of the possible knowledge expressions. After this, several complex expressions are examined considering a more formal description of this computation.

Finally, we get the conclusions and introduce some open topics.

2 Previous work: the translation oriented approach

DEVS	GMs Scheme
State Variables Input Variable Output Variable	Generalized Magnitude
State Transition Functions Output Functions	Knowledge Expression
State Transition Output	Knowledge Expression Evaluation (application of knowledge)

Table 1. Proposed equivalence between basic concepts

The incorporation of autonomous activation to the GMs Scheme has been already treated in [Otero94]. That work was intended for representing Discrete Events models by following a two steps procedure: first, representing the model in DEVS, and then translating it to GMs. The translation consisted in defining GMs for each DEVS element (inputs, outputs, state variables, transition functions and time advance function). Equivalences between basic concepts from boths formalisms are shown in table 1.

The whole work rested on two important features of the GMs formalism: the special temporal identifier **now** and the property of *pertinence*.

In the GMs scheme, the **now** identifier can be referred in the *Knowledge Expression* (KE) used to determine the value of a GM. When a reference to **now** occurs, it is evaluated returning the current time value in the continuous base time. On the other hand, a GM is said to be *pertinent* when, in a particular moment, it offers outstanding knowledge, i.e. it is capable of providing the system with new facts. One kind of pertinence is due to input changes whereas another one is due to references to **now**. When translating DEVS into GMs, the former has been used to represent DEVS *external transitions*, whereas the last allows representing *internal transitions*.

Using these two features (pertinence and references to **now**), a GM called **tnext** was defined. Such GM, that was evaluated after a certain elapsed time, was used to implement an internal transition, which can be seen as an autonomous activation of the system. Of course, it became necessary providing that GM with a special behavior: its value pointed out directly the instant in which the system would be automatically re-evaluated.

As we can notice, the study of the DEVS translation has not provided a general solution from the GMs point of view, since it forces to a previous modeling step in DEVS and needs the unnatural introduction of a GM with a special behavior. This has led us to take into account an extension to the formalism that includes *per se* autonomous activation.

3 The embedded autonomous activation

As we have seen before, we are looking for a way of adding autonomous activation to the GMs Scheme but, at the same time, we try to get such feature from the basic properties of the formalism. This implies that we must get an implicit way of representing autonomous activations and deduce when they will take place.

As a starting point, we can suppose that the system is continuously evaluated at any moment of time. Of course, evaluation of an infinite set of time points would be impossible at all. However, given the kind of models we are dealing with, we know that only several discrete time points are actually outstanding for knowledge evaluation. Therefore, the knowledge representation structure must be analyzed for finding out those outstanding time points.

Once the system has made a knowledge evaluation, it must predict the next evaluation time point. Since external inputs will always cause a knowledge activation, we only need to determine if an activation due to time changing by itself may occur during the interval comprised between two external inputs. The only GM that could change its value during such interval is **now**. Therefore, the next evaluation time point will be the next outstanding value for **now**, that is, a moment that causes that a condition that refers to **now** changes from true to false or vice versa.

The computing process of the next evaluation time point will be described later. For the present, we can notice several interesting consequences from this approach.

First of all, the time advance function does not need to be explicitly represented. It can be moved and distributed into each transition function, that is, each knowledge expression for the GM. The system will deduce the evaluation time points from references to **now**. Notice that, in fact, the **tnext** solution was a particular case of such analysis, that limited the possible references to **now** to those obtained from the DEVS translation.

Another result is getting a more natural representation (from the GMs Scheme point of view), since we have not introduced any formal change, but a semantical one, that is, a change of the meaning of the knowledge expressions. This involves a great advantage for the Temporal Expert Systems developers that already know the GMs Scheme, and even for migrating existing Temporal Expert Systems to the extended GMs Scheme.

As a consequence of the two preceding results, Discrete Events models can be directly represented using the extended GMs Scheme. Thus, we can override the previous phase of DEVS modeling and the following translation that was necessary in the first approach. If we do so, the equivalences between basic concepts of both formalisms are not as clear as before. For instance, one important outcome is that a knowledge expression can be seen now, from the DEVS point of view, as a mixture of external and internal transition function. This means that transition functions can mix indifferently references to external and internal events and, furthermore, a same condition of the transition function will even be able to behave dynamicly as an external or an internal transition.

The following section shows an example of representation of a DEVS system translated to GMs Scheme, but using an implicit time advance function.

4 A DEVS example

Figure 1 shows an example from [Zei89] of a generic control system. A system moves through several checkstates (denoted as Pi) in concert with the input received from a sensor. There is a time window (tmin) for the reception of that input and a generic function (expected) that decides if an input is expected for the current checkstate. Transitions are denoted as:

hold in <NEXT_PHASE_VALUE> <NEXT_SIGMA_VALUE>

where sigma is a state variable that determines directly the time advance function.

In figure 2 we have represented the translation of this DEVS example into the GMs formalism. Equivalences of table 1 have been applied , excepting for the time advance function. We have defined GMs phase and chstate that corresponds to the states variables of the DEVS specification, and GM output that corresponds to the output of the system.

The GM tlast is used for converting the absolute time reference represented by now into a relative reference to the last transition instant. For clarity reasons, we have also used a GM called received that will be true only when an input occurs.

The most important part of the example is the way in which we have represented the internal transitions. Notice that no sigma variable nor time advance function have been used. Instead of that, we have represented the temporal conditions – using references to now – that must hold for a given transition. Of course, the system will have to compute which is the next value of now that activates a transition (the next evaluation time point).

5 Computing the next evaluation time point

We have seen that, since the time advance function is given in an implicit way, the system must deduce which is the next evaluation time point. The general process is described by figure 3.

The graph shows the behavior of the system in absence of external inputs. An external input would assign directly a value for now (the instant in which the input occurred) and would jump to the knowledge application phase.

```
------- initial conditions -------

initial phase: WAIT
initial sigma: tmin(P1)
initial checkstate: P1

------- external transition -------

when receive value on sensor-port
        case of: phase
        WAIT    :       hold-in EARLY 0
        WINDOW  :       if value = expected (Pi)
        then hold-in SEND-COMMAND 0
        else hold-in ERROR 0

------- internal transition -------

case of: phase
        WAIT    :       hold-in WINDOW window (Pi)
        WINDOW  :       hold-in LATE 0
        SEND-COMMAND: set checkstate = next (checkstate)
                hold-in WAIT tmin (next(Pi))
        ERROR   :       passivate

------- output function -------

case of: phase
        EARLY   :       send "(Pi) input arrived too early" to error-port
        SEND-COMMAND:   send control command(Pi) to command port
        ERROR   :       send "(Pi) error in sensor value" to error-port
        LATE    :       send "(Pi) input arrived too late" to error-port
        else    :       send null message
```

Fig. 1. DEVS specifications of a generic control system

The interesting part of the process is the computation of the next evaluation time point for each GM. The minimum of those values will be the next evaluation time point for the whole system. When computing each time point, only the values for now that make true an expression will be interesting. The values for the rest of the GMs do not need to be computed, since they have just been evaluated in the knowledge application phase.

We will make an incremental study of knowledge expression cases. We will assume that Ei are the assignment expressions and that Ci and Fi are expressions that do not contain any reference to now.

```
GM phase (Initial Value: WAIT)
Knowledge Expression:
WINDOW        if previous(phase) = WAIT and timeof(now)=
                                   tmin(previous(chstate))+tlast;
LATE          if previous(phase) = WINDOW and timeof(now)=
                                   twindow(previous(chstate))+tlast;
WAIT          if previous(phase) = WINDOW and received and
                                   expected(value);
PASSIVE       if previous(phase) = WINDOW and received and
                                   unexpected(value);
EARLY         if previous(phase) = WAIT and received;

GM chstate (Initial Value: P1)
Knowledge Expression:
next(previous(chstate)) if phase = WAIT;

GM Output
Knowledge Expression:
"send command"    if phase = WAIT;
"error message"   if phase = PASSIVE;
"late message"    if phase = LATE;
"early message"   if phase = EARLY;

GM tlast (Initial Value: initial-absolute-time)
// time of the previous phase change
Knowledge Expression:
timeof(previous(phase));

GM received (Initial Value: false)
// indicates if there is input
Knowledge Expression:
true        if timeof(now)=timeof(value);
false;
```

Fig. 2. Translation into GMs formalism

5.1 No references to now

This would be the most trivial case. It would consist of a list of **if** clauses without any reference to **now**:

```
E1 if C1;
E2 if C2;
...
```

This kind of knowledge expression would not produce future activations caused by internal transitions. It would be equivalent to have only external transitions.

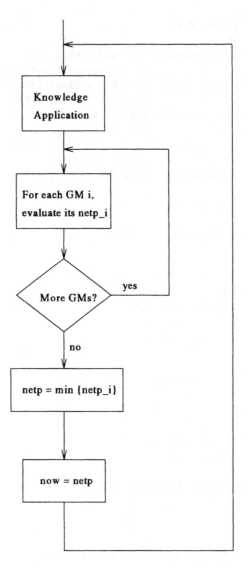

Fig. 3. General process

5.2 Only references to now

In order to simplify the calculus of the next evaluation time point, we will assume that references to **now** are always cleared in relational expressions (they do not occur, for instance, at both sides of an equals sign). The shape of a knowledge expression for this case would be:

E1 if timeof(now)=F1;

```
E2 if timeof(now)=F2;
...
```

and the resulting time point would be the minimun of `Fi`.

5.3 Conditions with now and conditions without it

This case is a mixture of the two preceding ones. For instance, it could look like:

```
E1 if timeof(now)=F1;
E2 if C2;
E3 if timeof(now)=F3;
E4 if C4;
E5 if C5;
E6 if timeof(now)=F6;
E7 if timeof(now)=F7;
...
```

The next time point will depend on the truth values of conditions `Ci`. It will be the minimum of those `Fi` preceding the first condition `Cj` that is true. If all the `Ci` are false, it will be directly the minimum of all the `Fi`.

In case of simultaneous true conditions, there is no conflict, since the conditional clauses are executed as an *if-then-else* structure. Because of this same reason, when a `Cj` is true we can ignore all the conditions with references to now below.

5.4 A reference to now mixed with other expressions

```
E1 if timeof(now)=F1 and C1;
```

If we use the logical operator **and**, it will depend again on the truth value of the other conditions (`C1` in this case): if `C1` is false, it will not be any activation, whereas if it is true, the next time point will be `F1` (this would take the same behavior as case 5.2). The use of **or** operator would be analogous.

5.5 Use of order relation operators

```
E1 if timeof(now)>F1
E2 if timeof(now)<F2
```

Both cases would mean continuous evaluation, that is, we cannot specify a discrete instant in which the condition will change to true. This would make no sense in a Discrete Events Systems study and so, it would not yield any activation.

5.6 Mixing several references to now

Disjunctions of expressions with now would take as next evaluation time point the minimum of all the values, whereas conjunctions would only yield a value if all the referred values are the same. Mixing both operators would imply handling sets of values for evaluating a complex expression. The next activation would be taken at the minimum of the final set of values. Anyway, we will see in the following section a more general way of treating this kind of expressions.

6 A more formal treatment

The two last cases of the previous study have showed that complex expressions require a more formal analysis. For instance, the expression:

```
E1 if not (timeof(now)>F1) and not (timeof(now)<F2);
```

would not yield, at a first sight, any future activation. Nevertheless, when F1 is equal to F2, the expression would be equivalent to:

```
E1 if timeof(now)=F1;
```

and should yield an activation at moment F1.

Type of Condition	Corresponding Interval
true condition	all possible values
false condition	$\emptyset$
timeof(now) $= x$	single point $\{x\}$
timeof(now) $> x$	(x, ∞)
timeof(now) $< x$	(t_{app}, x)

Table 2. Interval calculus for single expressions

Logical Operator	Corresponding Operation
and	intersection
or	union
not	complementary set

Table 3. Interval calculus for logical operators

This leads us to take into account all the values – expressed as intervals – that describe the truth temporal range of each condition. Table 2 describes how to obtain these intervals from single subexpressions, whereas table 3 shows how to combine them using logical operators.

Using both tables, we can always get a final set of values expressed as a union of disjoint intervals. Besides, since we are only interested in those future instants in which the condition is true, the final set of values must be truncated by the interval $(-\infty, t_{app})$, where t_{app} is the instant in which the knowledge is applied. The result will be what we can call *future truth range* of the condition.

The next evaluation time point of a GM must be determined from the future truth ranges of all the conditions contained in its knowledge expression. At a first sight, we could just take the minimum left end point of all those intervals. However, this is not always possible, since it may be the case in which the lower interval of all the future truth ranges is left open. In such case, we would not have a minimum value.

This left open interval problem can be seen as the formalization of the continuity problem that arose when studying expressions with order relation operators (case 5.5). When we face this exception, we can take two different decisions:(1) ignoring left open intervals; or (2) extending knowledge application for being executed in an interval instead of a discrete instant. However, only the first approach is applicable, since the second one would imply transitions that do not occur in an exact instant, which cannot happen when dealing with Discrete Event Systems.

Therefore, we can make the following:

Definition 1 *The* next evaluation time point *is the minimum left end point of all the left closed intervals contained in the future truth ranges.*

When there are not left closed intervals, there does not exist a next evaluation time point, and the GM does not cause a future activation.

Figure 4 shows two examples of computation of the next evaluation time point (netp).

In the first case, there is a knowledge application at instant $t = 2$ due to a change to value 3 of the GM C, and being the value of B different from 2. In such situation, GM A takes the value 8, and the future truth ranges of each condition are shown in the first column on the right of the knowledge expression. There is only one left closed interval, $[15, \infty)$, and its left end point is the next evaluation time point.

The following knowledge application takes place at moment $t = 15$ (we are assuming that no external input has occurred). At that situation, there is not a left closed interval and so, there is no future activation.

The second case is another example of absence of future activation. Notice that there is no transition of A to value 8, since we cannot determine the exact instant in which the change of value occurs.

Note also that, though conditions that yield left open intervals do not cause future activations, they can be normally used in a knowledge application caused by any other event. In that sense, we can distinguish two meanings of references

Example 1
GM A
Knowledge expression:

7 if B=2;	∅	∅
8 if C=3 and timeof(now)<15;	$(2, 15)$	∅
9;	$[15, \infty)$	$(15, \infty)$

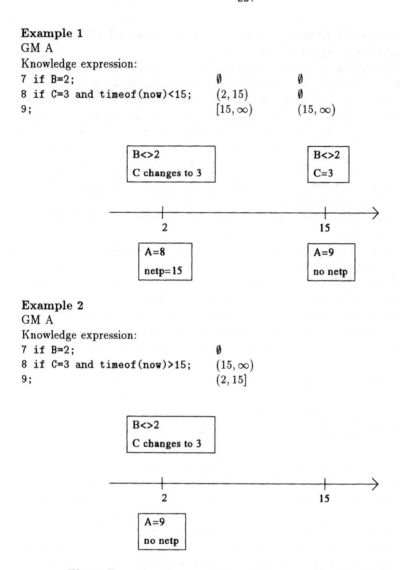

Example 2
GM A
Knowledge expression:

7 if B=2;	∅
8 if C=3 and timeof(now)>15;	$(15, \infty)$
9;	$(2, 15]$

Fig. 4. Examples of computation of the next evaluation time point.

to now: as a temporal condition in a knowledge application (this was the traditional meaning) or as a future activation of knowledge. These two meanings of time also appear in the DEVS formalism. The first one corresponds to the elapsed time (when used in external transitions) and the second one corresponds to the time advance function.

7 Conclusions

The extension made to the GMs formalism involves a generalization of the former solution for the DEVS translation, with the advantage of preserving the basic properties of the scheme. Moreover, it is clear that autonomous activation can become a useful tool for implementing some typical temporal tasks that may appear when defining Temporal Expert Systems and where not treated before.

Another advantage is that a uniform specification of temporal expressions is achieved. The same representation is used for time in knowledge activations and for time as a temporal condition (like any other state variable).

Representing Discrete Event Systems directly with the GMs Scheme appears as an interesting possibility. From a Systems Theory point of view, the extended GMs formalism presents a different approach whose main features are: (1) only one transition function for internal and external events — even mixing both kind of events in the same transition function is possible; (2) the transition function is partitioned and attached to the associated state and output variable; and (3) the time advance function is integrated implicitly into the transition function expression.

Finally, the study has outlined several interesting open topics. Particularly, the possibility of treating knowledge applications in an interval of time, instead of an exact instant. This could lead to a different line of research that, although it does not fit exactly with the field of study of Discrete Events Systems, could cover more general models without implying necessarily continuous evaluation.

Another open topic would be the optimization of the computing process, trying to define those cases in which previous computations of the next evaluation time point can be reused for the whole system or a part of it.

Acknowledgements This investigation was supported in part by the Government of Galicia (Spain), grants XUGA10502A/92 and XUGA10503B/94.

References

[Otero94] R.P. Otero, A. Barreiro, H. Praehofer, F. Pichler, and J. Mira. Stimsmedtool: Integration of expert systems with systems modelling and simulation. *Lecture Notes in Computer Science*, (763):347–356, 1994.

[Pichler92] F. Pichler and H. Schwärtzel (Eds.). *CAST, Methods in Modelling*. Springer Verlag, 1992.

[Zeigler76] B. P. Zeigler. *Theory of Modelling and Simulation*. John Willey, 1976.

[Zei84] B. P. Zeigler. *Multifaceted Modelling and Discrete Event Simulation*. London: Academic Press, 1984.

[Zei89] B. P. Zeigler. Devs representation of dynamical systems: Event-based intelligent control. *Proceedings of the IEEE*, 77(1):72–80, 1989.

TOMSPIN - A Tool for Modelling with Stochastic Petri Nets

E. M. Thurner, Ch. Wincheringer
Siemens AG, ZFE T SN 1
D - 81370 München

Petri nets have become a wide-spread method to model the behaviour of computing systems. One drawback of standard Petri nets however is the absence of constructs for the notion of time and conflict-probabilties. Generalized Stochastic Petri Nets (GSPNs) have been developed to deal with these constructs.

The program TOMSPIN (Tool for Modelling with Stochastic Petri Nets) supports the full descriptive power of GSPNs. It has been developed to model and to evaluate complex computing systems, such as multiprocessor machines and communicaton systems. In this paper, the structure of TOMSPIN is pointed out, and some examples for its usage in commercial environment are given.

Key words: *Modelling, performance, realiabilty, Generalized Stochastic Petri Nets, TOMSPIN*

Revision: Standard Petri nets

Petri nets were introduced by C.A. Petri in 1962 (see [Petri]). Petri nets have turned out to be an intuitive approach to represent the structure of computing systems as well as their dynamic behaviour. What is even more important: Petri nets are well defined in a strict mathematical sense. Due to this, they give an exact representation of notions like

- causality,
- concurrency, and
- synchronisation.

Typical examples for the usage of standard Petri nets are:

- proving the *liveness* of systems, resp. to find *deadlocks* in them,
- proving their *boundedness (safety).*

These system properties can be found out by *analytical* evaluation. This means, that statements about the system's behaviour have no restrictions that are typical for simulation-based evaluation, i.e. the modeler needs not to care for the completeness of the "simulation" or to find out confidence intervalls, because this completeness is inherently given by the analytical approach. An introduction to semantics and usage of Petri nets is given in [Reisig].

Let us consider one of the evaluation methods, namely the construction of the so-called *reachability graph*. The states of the reachability graph (the *markings*) represent the complete system state. Fig. 1 gives a very simple Petri net, in which the token is wandering cyclically, i.e. starting from the place p_1 through the transition t_1 to the next place p_2 and so on. On the right side of fig. 1, the respective reachability graph is shown: In the so-called *initial marking* M_0 there is only one token in p_1, in the next marking M_1 there is one token in p_2 etc.

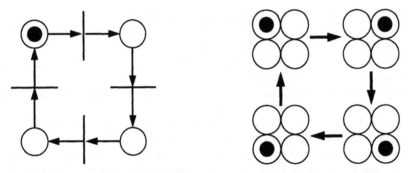

Fig. 1: A simple Petri net and its reachability graph

Generalized Stochastic Petri Nets

Unfortunately, standard Petri nets are not able to represent time within a system. To deal with this problem, *Generalized Stochastic Petri Nets (GSPNs)* were introduced by [Marsan]. In this class of nets, there are two kinds of transitions:

- *Immediate transitions*, which fire immediately after their activation.
- *Timed transitions*, which fire at an exponentially distributed random time after their activation.

While immediate transitions use the same firing rule as standard Petri nets do, timed transitions are a key to represent time in a system: To each timed transition a delay time $1/\lambda$ is assigned; The value λ is called the *firing rate* of this transition.

Furthermore, in GSPNs *conflict probabilities* can be assigned to every transition that participates in the conflict. At last, marking-depending functions, e.g. the arc-weight or the firing rate as a funtion of the number of tokens in a place can be expressed.

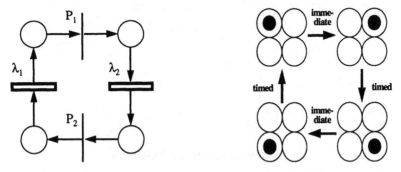

Fig. 2: A simple GSPN and its reachability graph

An example for a simple GSPN and its reachability graph is given in fig. 2: The immediate transitions are depicted by thin bars, and timed transitions are depicted by thick bars. The respective transitions in the reachability graph are timed or immediate. Due to the notion of time, GSPNs have the most of the evaluation capabilities of standard Petri nets and can be used in addition to get performance measures of a computing system. The evaluation process for GSPNs consists of the following steps:

1. Construct the complete reachability graph of the GSPN.
2. Test, whether each state of the reachability graph is part of a cycle, i.e. if each state can be reached by every other state (*ergodicity*).
3. Reduce the reachability graph by eliminating the so-called *vanishing states*. These are produced by immediate transitions.
4. Transform the reduced reachability graph into a time continuous, state discrete Markov chain.
5. Compute the stationary state probabilities by solving a system of linear equations, containing the transition rates of the Markov chain.
6. Derive typical results of the GSPN from the state probabilities. Examples are the mean number of tokens in a certain place, the firing frequency of a transition, or the probability of a certain marking.
7. Compute the system measures as a function of the results related to the GSPNs.

The GSPN-tool TOMSPIN

The program TOMSPIN has been developed for the practical use of GSPN models within commercial environment. Due to this, the evaluation process decribed in the upper section can be found in its software structure as well as some extensions that are necessary for industrial use (see fig. 3).

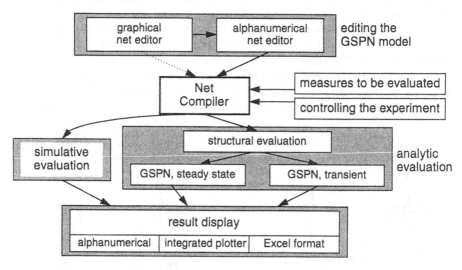

Fig. 3: Software structure of TOMSPIN

Roughly spoken, TOMSPIN consists of the modules net editor, net compiler and experiment control, structural evaluation, simulative evaluation, and result display. The modules are controlled by the graphical user interface shown in fig. 4.

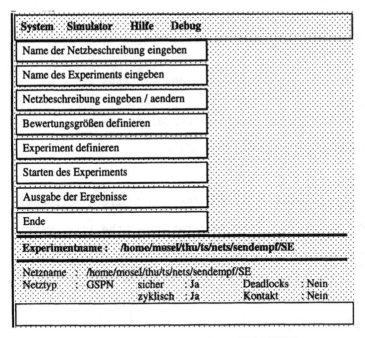

Fig. 4: Graphical user interface of TOMSPIN

Net Editor

TOMSPIN has two modelling interfaces to enter the net model in a textual and in a graphical way. Indeed, the graphical net editor LoGraph is configured as a pre-processor to the alphanumerical editor. The net description language of TOMSPIN supports the full descriptive power of GSPNs:

- Transitions can be defined as immediate or with an exponentially distributed firing rate.
- A firing probability can be assigned to every transistion within a conflict.
- Inhibitior arcs can be used.
- The firing rates of transitions can be defined as marking-dependent, i.e. as a function of the numvers of token in an arbitrary place. The arc-weights in the model can also be defined as marking-dependent.
- Furthermore, auxiliary variables and cpp preprocessor statements can be used to allow model-structuring based on software-engineering concepts.

Fig. 5 shows an example for a module using the TOMSPIN net description lnuguage. There are no subnets, only the net MAIN. Auxiliary variables can be defined after the key word VARIABLEN. Places are defined after STELLEN; without an capacity number, they are considered having infinite capacity. The transistions either are defined as immediate, with a firing probability (DIRE WAHR); or they can be defined with an exponentially distriibuted firing rate (EXPO RATE). The marking dependabiltity is expressed by the #-sign (e.g. #SenderIdle). After the arcs (KANTEN), which can also be marking-dependent, the initial marking is assigned (MARKIERUNG).

```
NETZ MAIN
TYP GSPN
VARIABLEN          /*** variable declaration ***/
FLOAT Pfail = 0.05
STELLEN            /*** place declaration ***/
SenderIdle, SenderBusy, SendBuffer KAPA = 5,
...
TRANSITIONEN       /*** declaration of transitions ***/
SenderStart EXPO RATE #SenderIdle*SendRate,
SenderFinished EXPO RATE #SenderBusy/SendTime,
Transmit EXPO RATE 1/TransTime,
Erroneous DIRE WAHR Pfail,
...
KANTEN             /*** declaration of arcs ***/
Senderfinished -> SendBuffer; SendBuffer -> Transmit;
...
MARKIERUNG         /*** declaration of the init. marking ***/
SenderIdle = 2, ReceiverIdle = 2
ENDNETZ
```

Fig. 5: Example for the TOMSPIN net description language

Net Compiler and Experiment Control

After transforming the net into an internal structure, the variation of system parameters (experiment control) and the measures that are to be evaluated can be defined. Fig. 6 shows an example for an experiment control file.

```
[number of runs]
   4
[initial markings]
   sender_idle      2 3 7 9
   sender_ready     0 ++1
[place capacities]
   sender_idle      -1
   sender_ready     9 --2
[variables]
   Pfail            DOUBLE 4.0E-02 --0.005
   Ttrans           DOUBLE 1.5E+00 1.56 1.89 2.07
```

Fig.6 : Example for an TOMSPIN experiment control file

First of all, the number of experiments that are to run is defined. Then, the initial markings, place capacities, and auxialiary variables are defined. The values can be written explicitly, or they are given in an incremental way.

Furthermore, the result variables have to be defined. This can be done by using arbitrary arithmetic expressions, based on the values of the net evaluation. Examples are:

        diff = 100 * (Rt_transmit - Rt_send) / Rt_transmit
where a difference (in percent) caused by Rt_send is found.

        Pidle = P { p1:3 | p2:4 & p3:8 }

where the idle probability is expressed by the probability that either in place p1 are 3 tokens or in p2 are 4 and in p3 are 8 tokens.

Structural Evaluation

The structural evaluation begins with an analysis for structural errors. In this phase, e.g. deadlocks and contact situations are found, and the net is examined for boundedness and ergodicity.

In the steady state analysis, the equation $\pi\,Q = 0$ is solved (see [Marsan]). We implemented several algorithms for the soolving of this linear equation, e.g. Gauß-Seidel or Gauß-elimination. In addition, we developed a very fast solution method, called Method 100, that can also be used for very big models. To give an example, we need about 8 CPU hours for a GSPN model with 5 millions of states.

Result Display

The last phase for the use of TOMSPIN is the result display. Basically, three ways are given to display the computed results:
- An alphanumerical output, which can be used for arbitrary (e.g. graphical) post-processing.
- The integrated result display *plotp*, that offers several ways of curve interpolation and oher display options.
- An input file for the PC program Excel, whose display capabilities can be used to write reports.

Examples for the usage of TOMSPIN and Further Work

TOMSPIN has been used widely to evaluate complex commercial systems. Typically, the *all-over performance* of computing systems was evaluated. By modelling with TOMSPIN, for example predictions of the performance of a multiprocessor system could be given in an early design phase. Furthermore, by varying several architectural parameters systematically, the hardware could be optimized in a very efficient way.

Another area that was examined by TOMSPIN are the *reliability and availability* of computing systems. For these areas, also a quantitative analysis was made. In the next steps, different redundancy structures of the system components and their interconnections were examined in order to find out the optimal price-performance-ratio for the considered use. Another wide range is the consideration of the effect of some redundancy strategies on the system performance.

References

[1] Ajmone Marsan, M.; Balbo, G.; Conte, G.: Performance Models of Multiprocessor Systems. The MIT Press: Cambridge (Mass.), 1986
[2] Petri, C. A.: Kommunikation mit Automaten. Dissertation, Universität Bonn, 1962
[3] Reisig, W.: Petrinetze. Eine Einführung. Springer-Verlag: Berlin [2]1986

Hybrid Evolutionary Programming: the Tools for CAST *

Witold Jacak and Stephan Dreiseitl

Research Institute for Symbolic Computation
Johannes Kepler University Linz, A-4040 Linz, Austria
email: wj@shannon.sea.uni-linz.ac.at
email: dreiseitl@risc.uni-linz.ac.at

Abstract. With the development of new computing paradigms, such as neural networks and genetic algorithms, new tools have become available in computer-aided systems theory. These tools can be used to tackle problems that are considered "hard" in traditional systems theory, like *the modeling and identification* of nonlinear dynamical systems.

We present a general methodology based on neural networks and genetic algorithms that can be applied to a wide range of problems. The main emphasis is on using the approximation capabilities of neural networks to model systems based on their input-output behavior.

We first show how the inverse problem of a static system can be solved by two feedforward neural networks in a feedback loop.

We then present a general methodology for modeling nonlinear systems with known rank (i.e., state space dimension) by feedforward networks with external delay units.

We further show how genetic algorithms can be employed to find neural networks to model dynamical systems of unknown rank. Two genetic algorithms are presented for this case: one that determines the best feedforward network with external delay, and one that searches for a network with arbitrary topology and memory cells within each neuron.

1 Introduction

One of the main research topics in systems theory is the modeling and control of nonlinear dynamical systems. In contrast to linear systems, for which there is a large and well-established theoretical background, nonlinear systems lack such a foundation. Control methods generally have to be established on a case-by-case basis.

There are several methods for constructing the model of an unknown system, such as analytical and statistical methods, as well as methods based on identification and experiment theory. In this paper, we present a general method that is based on neural network modeling. Some results that were published on this topic in recent years include [9, 6, 8]. Determining the best network to model

---

* This work was supported by the RWC Partnership project "Hybrid Evolutionary Programming".

a system is either done by training the network with a pattern set, or by using genetic algorithms to find the best network. The pattern sets needed for both approaches can be constructed from input-output observations of the system with the help of a computer algebra system.

In this paper we show how genetic algorithms and neural networks can be used as tools to quickly approximate a given system, without regard to theoretical considerations. We first present an approach to modeling static systems by using neural networks as general function approximators. We show how we can use symbolic computation to construct a feedback system that solves the inverse problem for this static system.

Moving on to dynamical systems, we show how they can be modeled by neural networks with external delay units that feed back to the inputs of the network. This method is based on knowing the *rank* of the system, i.e., the dimension of the state space. We present a symbolic computation approach to calculating the pattern set used to training these networks. Since this approach requires knowledge of the rank of the system (which need not be known in general), we propose two variation of this method that do not need this information.

Both alternative methods use genetic algorithms to find the neural network that can best model a nonlinear system without knowledge of the rank of that system. Employing genetic algorithms to find "good" neural networks for a specific task has been studied in the past (e.g., [10, 7, 1, 2]). Most of these publications were concerned with encoding schemes and restricting networks to certain topologies. Of the two methods we propose in this paper, the first considers feedforward networks with fixed (fully connected) topology and external delay units. The genetic algorithm is used to determine which of the inputs to the system is actually relevant to calculating the output, and to find the correct weight settings in the process.

The second approach uses different neurons, and a different topology. The neurons employed in this method each contain a memory cell that stores the previous activation of the neuron. There is also no restriction on the topology of the network (except that the number of neurons be fixed), and the genetic algorithm finds the connections (and their strengths) between the neurons. The feedback in this method is accomplished by evolving recurrent links in the network.

This paper is structured as follows: Sect. 2 presents the algorithm for calculating the inverse of a static system. Sect. 3 shows how neural networks can be used to model nonlinear dynamical systems of known rank. Sect. 4 points out the shortcomings of the previous method when the rank of the system is not known, and how genetic algorithms can be used to find networks that model dynamical systems. Two approaches using genetic algorithms are presented: Sect. 4.1 introduces a method for finding networks with external memory cells, and Sect. 4.2 deals with a different genetic algorithm that evolves more general networks for the same problem. Concluding remarks are given in Sect. 5.

2 The Inverse Problem of Static Systems

It has been established that neural networks can function as universal function approximators ([4, 3, 5]). We use this capability to train a network to represent a static function, given an observation of its input-output behavior.

More precisely, we consider N input-output pairs $(\hat{u}_i, \hat{y}_i)$ that were obtained as observations of a static function $f : U \rightarrow Y$. This data is approximated by a network with one layer of hidden neurons. The hidden neurons all use the logistic activation function $net_i = 1/(1 + \exp(-net))$ to calculate an output from the weighted sum of its inputs net. We then train the network with a standard back-propagation algorithm to approximate the given pattern set, obtaining a function ψ. The quality of this approximation is dependent on a number of parameters, such as choice of observation points, training times, step size in training, network topology, and so on. We like to point out that finding a sufficiently close approximating function to a given data set can require some experimentation with these parameters.

The inverse problem is stated as:

given y^*, find a u^* such that $f(u^*) = y^*$.

Considering that $f^{-1} \subset Y \times U$ is generally a relation, the solution u^* obtained need not be the *only* solution. Our approach is neural network-based, meaning that we solve the inverse problem for the approximating function ψ. If the approximation ψ is sufficiently close to f, the solution to the inverse problem will be as well.

To solve the inverse problem, we introduce an error function

$$e(u) = [y^* - \psi(u)].$$

The inverse problem can be transformed to an optimization problem by introducing a Lyapunov function

$$V(u) = \frac{1}{2}e(u)^T e(u) \tag{1}$$

that can be minimized by a gradient descent method. A u^* with $V(u^*) \rightarrow \min$ satisfies the inverse problem.

It can be shown that for Lyapunov functions (1), isolated minima are asymptotically stable; i.e., a solution can always be found. We can satisfy the criterion of Lyapunov function by observing that the time derivative of V is

$$\frac{dV}{dt} = e^T \frac{de}{dt} = -e^T J(u) \frac{du}{dt} \ .$$

where $J(u) = [\frac{\partial \psi(u)}{\partial u}]$ is the Jacobian matrix.

To obtain $dV/dt < 0$, it suffices to set

$$\frac{du}{dt} = \alpha\, J^T(u)\, e = \alpha\, J^T(u)\, (y^* - \psi(u)) \ , \tag{2}$$

as then

$$\frac{dV}{dt} = -\alpha\, e^T\, J(u) J^T(u)\, e \ < 0$$

for positive α.

These theoretical considerations are the basis for the feedback loop that solves the static inverse problem. The discrete form of (2) is

$$u(k+1) = u(k) + \alpha\, J^T(u(k))\,(y^* - \psi(u(k)))\ . \tag{3}$$

This updating process for u can be implemented as a simple feedback loop around two neural networks, one implementing the function ψ and one implementing the Jacobian matrix J. Fig. 1 shows the process of obtaining the two neural networks in the feedback loop, as well as the loop itself. The network for ψ has to be training with the use of a pattern set. The Jacobian matrix can be computed from ψ in a purely *symbolic manner*. For this, the network implementing ψ has to be transformed back to a symbolic format. Partial derivatives are taken with the help of a computer algebra program. The resulting expressions (that again contain only sums and products of the logistic function) can be mapped back to a neural network without further training.

Example. Consider the static function $f : \mathbb{R}^2 \to \mathbb{R}$, given by $y = -3u_1 u_2^3 + 5u_1^3 + 4u_2^2 - 6u_1 u_2 + 1$, scaled to $[0,1]^2 \to [0,1]$ for neural network computations. We used a network with 10 hidden sigmoid neurons and trained it with 225 patterns until the error was less than 1%. The trained network was converted to a symbolic expression, from which the Jacobian neural network was constructed. For a desired value of $y^* = 0.7$, the feedback loop found a solution $(u_1, u_2) = (0.978, 0.311)$ within 15 executions of the loop (Fig. 2).

3 Neural Networks based Modeling of Dynamical Systems with Known Rank

In this section, we show how standard feedforward networks with external memory cells can be used to model any nonlinear system of known rank.

The general format of a dynamical system with input $u(t)$ and output $y(t)$ is a differential equation

$$F_1\left(\frac{d^m y(t)}{dt^m}, \ldots, \frac{dy(t)}{dt}, y(t), \frac{d^\nu u(t)}{dt^\nu}, \ldots, \frac{du(t)}{dt}, u(t)\right) = 0\ , \tag{4}$$

or, alternatively,

$$y(t) = F_2\left(\frac{d^m y(t)}{dt^m}, \ldots, \frac{dy(t)}{dt}, \frac{d^\nu u(t)}{dt^\nu}, \ldots, \frac{du(t)}{dt}, u(t)\right)\ . \tag{5}$$

In the discrete case, this equation has the form

$$y(k) = F_3(y(k-m), \ldots, y(k-1), u(k), u(k-1), \ldots, u(k-\nu))\ . \tag{6}$$

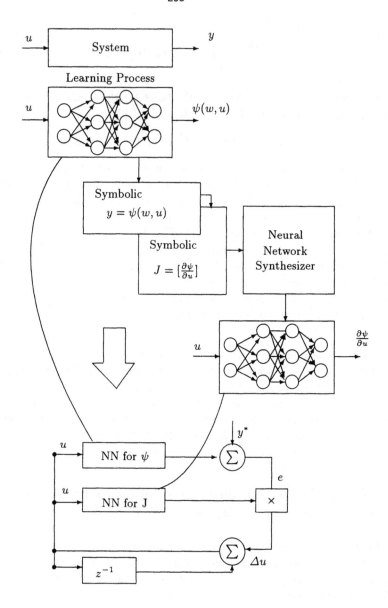

Fig. 1. Obtaining the feedback loop for calculating the inverse of a static system.

The functions y and u can be vector-valued. The values of the parameters m and ν determine the rank of the system and therefore also the dimension.

The structures of neural networks that use external memory cells to compute the functions in (5) and (6) are given in Fig. 3. The central block of this figure represents the feedforward network approximation to the static transition func-

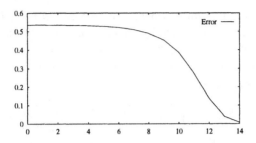

Fig. 2. Convergence of inverse solution

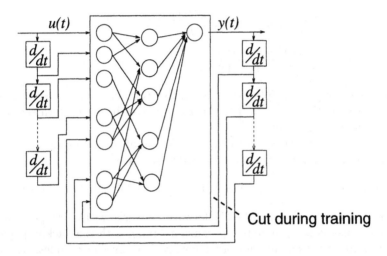

Fig. 3. Network with external memory (delay) units for modeling a continuous system.

tions F_2 and F_3, respectively. During the training phase, for which we again use a standard backpropagation algorithm, the feedback loop around the network is disabled, with the corresponding input coming from the training pattern.

The training pattern sets have to be constructed from an observation set of input/output pairs $\{(\hat{u}(k), \hat{y}(k) \mid k = 1, \ldots, N\}$, with $N > m$. We further assume that $m \geq \nu$.

The values of $\hat{u}(k)$ and $\hat{y}(k)$ are realizations of u and y at times $t = t_k$. For simplicity, we assume that these observation times are equidistant, i.e., $t_k = t_0 + k\,\delta T$.

In the continuous case, we can construct a training pattern set P from the observation set as

$$P = \left\{ \left(\left\langle \hat{u}(k), \frac{d\hat{u}(k)}{dt}, \ldots, \frac{d^\nu \hat{u}(k)}{dt^\nu}, \frac{d\hat{y}(k)}{dt}, \ldots, \frac{d^m \hat{y}(k)}{dt^m} \right\rangle, \hat{y}(k) \right) \mid k = 1, \ldots, N \right\}.$$

Pattern preparation: The unknown derivative terms $d^i \hat{y}(k)/dt^i$ and $d^i \hat{u}(k)/dt^i$ that appear in P can be calculated by solving equations obtained from the Taylor series expansion of $\hat{u}(k)$ and $\hat{y}(k)$. For example, the Taylor series expansion around $\hat{y}(1)$ can be written as the following set of linear equations (disregarding higher-order terms):

$$\hat{y}(2) = \hat{y}(1) + \frac{d\hat{y}(1)}{dt} \delta T + \frac{d^2 \hat{y}(1)}{dt^2} \frac{\delta T^2}{2!} + \cdots + \frac{d^{m-1}\hat{y}(1)}{dt^{m-1}} \frac{\delta T^{m-1}}{(m-1)!}$$

$$\hat{y}(3) = \hat{y}(1) + \frac{d\hat{y}(1)}{dt} 2\delta T + \frac{d^2 \hat{y}(1)}{dt^2} \frac{(2\delta T)^2}{2!} + \cdots + \frac{d^{m-1}\hat{y}(1)}{dt^{m-1}} \frac{(2\delta T)^{m-1}}{(m-1)!}$$

$$\vdots$$

$$\hat{y}(m) = \hat{y}(1) + \frac{d\hat{y}(1)}{dt} (m-1)\delta T + \frac{d^2 \hat{y}(1)}{dt^2} \frac{(((m-1)\delta T)^2}{2!} + \cdots +$$
$$+ \frac{d^{m-1}\hat{y}(1)}{dt^{m-1}} \frac{((m-1)\delta T)^{m-1}}{(m-1)!}.$$

We can use a computer algebra system to solve this set of $m-1$ equations for $d\hat{y}(1)/dt$ through $d^{m-1}\hat{y}(1)/dt$. The other derivatives in the pattern set can be calculated in the same way.

Obtaining the pattern set for the discrete function of (6) is considerably easier; this can be done directly from the observation set as

$$P = \{(\langle \hat{u}(k), \hat{u}(k-1), \ldots, \hat{u}(k-\nu), \hat{y}(k-m), \ldots, \hat{y}(k-1)\rangle, \hat{y}(k)) \mid k = m+1, \ldots, N\}.$$

As mentioned before, training the feedforward networks with these pattern sets can take a considerable amount of parameter-tuning with the backpropagation algorithm and adjusting the network topology. For simple examples, we found that hidden layer sizes of 5 to 10 neurons and a step size parameter of about 0.2 were achieved good results.

In our experiments, we obtained good results using this approach for modeling simple nonlinear systems.

Example. We consider the discrete system $y(k+1) = \cos(3 \cdot y(k)) \cdot \sin(u(k))$, again scaled to $[0,1] \to [0,1]$. For this simple system, $m = 1$ and $\nu = 1$. We randomly generated a series of 80 input values $\hat{u}(k)$, and took $\hat{y}(0) = 0.5$. From these values, we generate the values for $\hat{y}(1)$ through $\hat{y}(80)$ from the definition of $y(k+1)$. Of the input/output patterns, the first 50 were used to train the neural network approximating the static transfer function. The network used 10 hidden logistic neurons, and was trained until the error was less than 1%.

The performance of the network modeling the nonlinear system is shown in Fig. 4. The first 50 patterns were used for training, the second 30 for testing the network. The error of the network does not increase over the testing patterns. The network in this example used a linear output neuron; this makes the output values of less than 0 (between patterns 70 and 80) possible. The average error in this simulation was about 0.8%, with the maximal error being less than 3%.

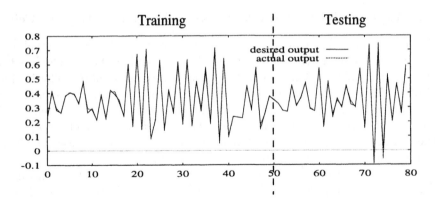

Fig. 4. Desired and actual outputs for a network with external memory cells.

4 Using Genetic Algorithms to Find Neural Networks for the Dynamical System Modeling Problem with Unknown System Rank

Although the above example shows that neural networks can obtain good results for modeling nonlinear systems, there are still some drawbacks of this method. These are:

- The size of the network can quickly become large, as $u(t)$ and $y(t)$ are generally vector-valued functions;
- the Taylor series approximations in the continuous case are not exact;
- the rank of the system has to be known in advance.

The last drawback is the one that often prevents the use of the methodology introduced in Sect. 3, since the state-space dimension (the rank) of a system cannot be determined from an observation set. The best one can do in this case is to use the algorithm with guessing the values for m and ν.

In the remainder of this paper, we introduce two possibilities to circumvent this problem by using genetic algorithms to determine the best networks for modeling a given observation set. The first approach (in Sect. 4.1) uses feedforward networks with external memory cells, just as the networks in Sect. 3. The second approach, given in Sect. 4.2, places no restriction the network topology, and uses internal memory cells associates with each hidden neuron.

To shorten the presentation of the methods, we now restrict the dynamical systems that we consider to the discrete case. The continuous form can be constructed from the discrete form.

4.1 Evolving Feedforward Networks with External Memory Cells

The methodology presented here uses feedforward networks with external memory cells to model a dynamical system. The method described here differs from the approach presented above in the fact that it is centered on the following idea: Without knowing the rank of the system, we set an upper limit on m and ν and let the genetic algorithm determine which inputs to the network are relevant for computing the output. These inputs are the terms $d^i\hat{y}(k)/dt^i$ and $d^i\hat{u}(k)/dt^i$ for the continuous case, and $\hat{u}(k-i)$ and $\hat{y}(k-i)$ for the discrete case. The length of the input vector to the network is $m+\nu+1$ (as before).

We want to point out again the motivation for using genetic algorithms in this context is that they offer a possibility to find out which of the $m+\nu+1$ inputs is actually relevant to modeling the system.

Network Encoding for the Genetic Algorithm. We consider the number of neurons in the network fixed. For simplicity, we also assume that the dimension of u and y is one, so that each input is represented by only one neuron.

The whole network is encoded as a string of weight vectors. The kth weight vector holds the connection strengths between the kth neuron and all the neurons that *receive* activation signals from it. For the input neurons (i.e., with $1 \leq k \leq m+\nu+1$), we also store a boolean flag with each weight vector. This flag signals whether activation signals from this input neurons will be propagated or not.

This encoding scheme is shown in Fig. 5. The w_{ij} denote the weight from neuron i to neuron j, and α_i is the boolean activation flag for the input neurons. With this encoding scheme, it is possible to "turn off" the kth input neuron

Input neurons   **hidden neurons**

| w_{11} w_{12} $\cdots$ α_1 | w_{21} w_{22} $\cdots$ α_2 | $\cdots$ | w_{k1} w_{k2} $\cdots$ w_{kn} |

Fig. 5. Encoding a network with external memory cells.

by setting α_k to false. This is done on purpose in some members of the initial population, and can be propagated through crossover. The flag can also be toggled by the mutation operation, or switched to false when all entries in the corresponding weight vector fall below a threshold value.

Fitness Calculation. The network output ψ depends on the network encoding $\bar{w}$ as a parameter. We use the notation $\psi(\cdot, \bar{w})$ to denote this dependency. The error of a network encoding $\bar{w}$ for an observation set

$$OB = \{(\hat{u}(k), \hat{y}(k)) \,|\, k = 1, \ldots, N\}$$

is the mean square error

$$E(\bar{w}) = \frac{1}{N} \sum_{k=m+1}^{N} (\psi(\hat{u}(k), \ldots, \hat{u}(k-\nu), \hat{y}(k-1), \ldots, \hat{y}(k-m); w) - \hat{y}(k))^2 \; .$$

The fitness f of an individual $\bar{w}$ is then the negative relative error

$$f(\bar{w}) = -\frac{E(\bar{w})}{\bar{f}},$$

where $\bar{f}$ is the average error over the population set P : $\bar{f} = \frac{1}{|P|} \sum_{\bar{w} \in P} E(\bar{w})$.

Generating an Initial Population. The aim of using a genetic algorithm in this context is to find the relevant inputs to a neural network that models a dynamical system. We therefore construct the initial population in the following way: The first element of the initial population has only α_1 and $\alpha_{\nu+1}$ set to true. These are the flags of the input neurons representing the input function u and the first derivative of the output y, the simplest case of a dynamical system.

The second element of the initial population has, additionally, $\alpha_{\nu+2}$ set to true; the third, $\alpha_{\nu+3}$ as well, and so on. The $(\nu + m + 1)$th element has α_1 and all flags between $\alpha_{\nu+2}$ and $\alpha_{\nu+m+1}$ set to true.

Next, we set α_1 and α_2 to true and again, in increasing order, additionally set one more flag from the neurons between $\nu + 1$ and $\nu + m + 1$ to true.

We continue this process until we reach the last member of the initial population, the network encoding that has all the flags between neuron 1 and neuron $\nu+m+1$ set to true. Using this procedure, there are $(\nu + 1) \times m$ elements in the initial population. The other entries in the network encoding (the weight values) are all set to small random numbers, a usual procedure for preparing networks before training. The initial population is shown in Fig. 6.

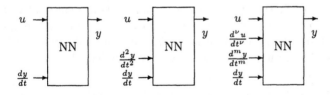

Fig. 6. Initial population set

Calculating a New Population. In the process of generating a new population from an old one, we use only the standard mutation and crossover operators. The mutation operator randomly changes the flags α_k from true to false and vice versa, and changes the entries in the weight vector by small amounts $\pm \delta w$. The crossover operator takes two network encodings and splices them at arbitrary locations, combining the head of the first with the tail of the second and the head of the second with the tail of the first. The resulting new individuals have, in some locations, different weight and flag value entries.

A new generation of size M is obtained as follows: First, we copy the $M-m$ fittest individuals into an auxiliary pool, and add m randomly chosen individuals from the rest of the population. In this auxiliary pool, we randomly pick individuals to perform the mutations and crossover operations. This process is repeated until the fitness of the best individual does not increase over some time. At this point, the genetic algorithm has either found a network that can model the given dynamical system, or it has gotten stuck in a local minimum of the search process.

The network that was obtained as the result of the genetic algorithm search is able to model the dynamical system with some small error (depending on the quality of the solution that was found). We can further post-process this solution by training the network with the backpropagation algorithm to achieve an even better solution.

Discussion. The approach described above used genetic algorithms to find a neural network that can model a dynamical system. The subgoals of using a genetic algorithm for this task were twofold: to find the weights of the network, and, more importantly, to determine which of the inputs to the network are relevant for computing the output.

The feedforward network found by the genetic algorithm uses external memory cells to feed the output back to the input neurons (as shown in Fig. 3). The only difference to the network shown in this figure is the fact that now, some of the inputs are not processed by the network, since they were found not to contribute to the output of the network.

Based on the methods presented in Sect. 3 and above, we have found that feedforward networks with external memory cells are capable of approximating dynamical systems. To further pursue the question of how genetic algorithms can be used to find networks with these approximation capabilities, we applied a genetic algorithm to finding recurrent networks with internal memory cells for the modeling task. The results of this work are given in Sect. 4.2.

4.2 Evolving Recurrent Networks with Internal Memory Cells

The networks presented in this section can have arbitrary connections between neurons, and are not restricted to the feedforward activation propagation of the networks presented in Sect. 3 and Sect. 4.1. This means that in particular, a neuron can have a recurrent connection to itself. Furthermore, we place the memory cells *inside* the network, i.e., we associate a memory cell with each hidden neuron. The structure of such networks is shown in Fig. 7.

For a fixed number of hidden neurons, we use genetic algorithms to find the best network topology and weight settings to model a given nonlinear system.

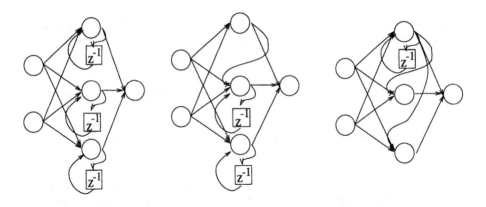

Fig. 7. Sample topologies for networks with internal memory cells.

Network Encoding for the Genetic Algorithm. We fix the number of neurons in the network and set m and ν to some upper bounds. We then place a linear ordering on the neurons, with the input neurons first, then the hidden neurons in arbitrary order, followed by the output neuron. The encoding of the network is a string of the encodings of hidden and output neurons (input neurons aren't encoded).

Each hidden and output neuron is encoded as a string of real-valued parameters and boolean flags. These parameters are the weight values of connections *leading* to the neuron and, for the hidden neurons, the value of the internal memory cell.

The weight vector of a hidden neuron contains the weights of connections from the input neurons to that hidden neuron *and* the weights of connections from other hidden neurons. There are three boolean flags for each real-valued parameter: Flag 1 determines whether the parameter, or some default value, is used; flag 2 determines whether to allow changes (by mutation) to the parameter; and flag 3 is a "meta-flag" that controls whether flag 1 can be toggled or not.

This encoding scheme is shown in Fig. 8. The weight w_{ij} is the connection strength from neuron j to neuron i. The ordering of neurons in this figure is from top to bottom. This network encoding is much more general than that of the feedforward networks in Sect. 3 and Sect. 4.1 , because there can be arbitrary connections within the hidden layer.

The activation propagation through the network is performed in the order in which the neurons are encoded in the chromosome. Forward connections, i.e., connections from a neuron i to a neuron j with $j > i$, are treated as in a regular feedforward network. Recurrent connections (from i to j with $j \leq i$) propagate the activation stored in the memory cell. This memory cell is updated with the new activation of the corresponding neuron as soon as that activation is calculated.

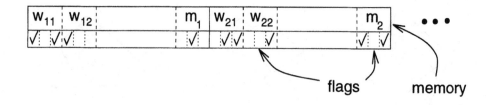

Fig. 8. Encoding a network with internal memory cells.

Fitness Calculation. The fitness of an individual $\bar{w}$ with respect to an observation set $\{(\hat{u}(k), \hat{y}(k)) \mid k = 1, \dots, N\}$ is calculated as the sum of absolute errors

$$E(\bar{w}) = \sum_{k=m+1}^{N} | \psi(\hat{u}(k), \dots, \hat{u}(k-\nu), \hat{y}(k-1), \dots, \hat{y}(k-m); \bar{w}) - \hat{y}(k) | \ ,$$

where $\psi(\cdot; \bar{w})$ is the output of a network with encoding $\bar{w}$.

The fitness f of an individual $\bar{w}$ is its negative scaled error

$$f(\bar{w}) = -\frac{E(\bar{w})}{\bar{s}},$$

with the scaling factor $\bar{s} = \sum_{k=1}^{N} |\hat{y}(k)|$.

Generating an Initial Population. The process of setting up an initial population is considerably easier than the process described in Sect. 4.2, because we are not interested in determining relevant inputs. It therefore suffices to fix a number of hidden neurons, set values of m and ν (to determine the size of the input layer), and randomly pick initial values for the weights, memory cells, and flags.

Calculating a New Population. We again use only the standard mutation and crossover operators to calculate a new population from an old one. The mutation operator changes the values of the real parameters by small amounts, if flag 2 of this parameter allows such a change. The values of the flags 1 and 2 themselves can also be toggled by the mutation operation. The crossover operation can splice and recombine two network encodings at arbitrary locations.

These two operators are applied in the following form: we randomly choose two individuals from the population and calculate their fitness. The fitter of the two individuals is allowed to reproduce, by either copying this individual or by performing a crossover operation with this and another randomly chosen individual. With a small likelihood, the resulting new individual is subject to a mutation operation as well, and again placed into the population pool.

This process of applying the genetic operators to the population is continued until no increase in fitness of the individuals chosen for crossover are observed for some time period. At this point, the search process is terminated with an individual that can model the dynamical system (unless the genetic algorithm search got stuck in a local minimum).

Example. We and tested the genetic algorithm described above on the dynamical system $y(k+1) = \cos(3 \cdot y(k)) \cdot \sin(u(k))$, scaled to the range $[0, 1]$, that was introduced as the example in Sect. 3. We again generated a random sequence of input data points $\hat{u}(k), k = 1, \ldots, 80$, and a random value for $\hat{y}(0)$. We then used the definition of $y(k)$ to generate a sequence $\hat{y}(k), k = 1, \ldots, 80$ of output data.

Of these patterns, the first 50 were used as evaluation data for the genetic algorithm. The network in our simulation used two input neurons and five hidden neurons. After the genetic algorithm had terminated, we tested the network that was found on all 80 patterns. The result of this testing is shown in Fig. 9 and Fig. 10. Because we used different random input sequences and initial values

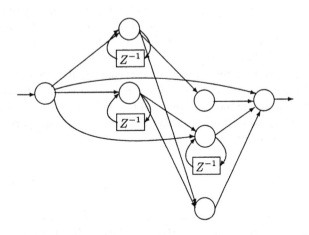

Fig. 9. Neural network generating by GA.

$\hat{y}(0)$ for the examples here and in Sect. 3, the two graphs are not the directly comparable. The maximal difference between desired and actual outputs in this simulation was less than 2%, with the average being about 0.5%. There was no difference in error on the patterns belonging to the training set and those that only belonged to the testing set.

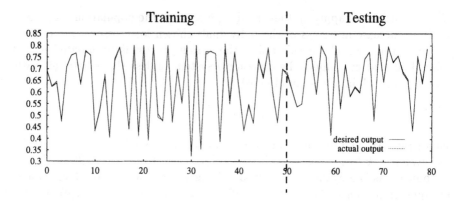

Fig. 10. Desired and actual outputs for a network with internal memory cells.

5 Conclusion

In this paper, we presented a general approach to using neural networks as tools in computer-aided system theory. We showed how the approximation capabilities of the network can be used in a different application areas, such as solving the inverse problem for the static system or modeling nonlinear dynamical systems. For the modeling problem, we investigated the use of neural networks with external memory cells, and obtained good results when the rank of the system to be modelled is not known.

In this case, genetic algorithms can be used to find networks to model the systems. Two different network topologies were considered: feedforward networks with external memory units, and recurrent networks with internal memories. Simulation results show that all the networks presented in this paper are capable of modeling nonlinear dynamical systems.

References

1. H. Braun and J. Weisbrod. Evolving neural feedforward networks. In J. D. Schaffer, editor, *Proceedings of the Third International Conference on Genetic Algorithms (ICGA)*, pages 25–32, San Mateo (CA), 1989. Morgan Kaufmann Publishers.
2. J. Heistermann. Learning in neural nets by genetic algorithms. In R. Eckmiller et al., editor, *Proceedings of Parallel Processing in Neural Systems and Computers (ICNC)*, pages 165–168, Elsevier, 1990.
3. K. Hornik. Approximation capabilities of multilayer feedforward networks. *Neural Networks*, **4**(2):251–257, 1991.
4. K. Hornik, M. Stinchcombe, and H. White. Universal approximation of an unknown mapping and its derivatives using multilayer feedforward networks. *Neural Networks*, **3**(5):551–560, 1990.

5. V.Y. Kreinovich. Arbitrary nonlinearity is sufficient to represent all functions by neural networks: A theorem. *Neural Networks*, 4(3):381–383, 1991.

6. A.U. Levin. *Neural Networks for Dynamical Systems*. PhD thesis, Yale University, 1992.

7. K. Lindgren, A. Nilsson, M. G. Nordahl, and I. Rade. Evolving recurrent neural networks. In J. D. Schaffer, editor, *Proceedings of the Third International Conference on Genetic Algorithms (ICGA)*, pages 55–62, San Mateo (CA), 1989. Morgan Kaufmann Publishers.

8. R. Murray-Smith, D. Neumerkel, and D. Sbarbaro-Hofer. Neural networks for modelling and control of a non-linear dynamic system. In *IEEE International Conference on Intelligent Control*, 1992.

9. K.S. Narendra and K. Parthasarathy. Identification and control of dynamical systems using neural networks. *IEEE Transactions on Neural Networks*, 1(1):4–27, 1990.

10. D. Whitley and T. Hanson. Optimizing neural networks using faster, more accurate genetic search. In J. D. Schaffer, editor, *Proceedings of the Third International Conference on Genetic Algorithms (ICGA)*, pages 391–396, San Mateo (CA), 1989. Morgan Kaufmann Publishers.

Automatic Induction of DEVS Structures

Ramón P. Otero, David Lorenzo and Pedro Cabalar

Dept. Computación, Fac. Informatica, University of A Coruña,
E-15071, A Coruña, Spain
email: otero@dc.fi.udc.es

Abstract. Machine Learning methods seem to help for model-building in the field of Systems Theory. In this work, we present a study on a method for automatically inducing a *discrete event structure* (DEVS) from descriptions of behaviours of a system. To this end, both inductive learning and DEVS formalisms have been made compatible in order to translate input data into a form usable by the inductor. Morover, the language used in classical inductive learning algorithms must be enhanced to cope with the temporal characteristics of input data.

1   Introduction

Machine Learning methods have been used successfully for the analysis and design phases in the field of Systems Theory. In this work, we present a study on the application of machine learning to the automatic modelling of Discrete Event Systems [1, 2] (**DEVS**). Given some or all the behaviours exhibited by a particular system, a DEVS model that reproduces those behaviours is induced.

This study is particularly useful when the real system to be modelled is available, so that input data could be taken directly from that system. If this is not possible, the input data would consist of the desired behaviour of the system to be modelled.

On the other hand, inductive learning obtains a set of symbolic rules from an initial set of examples that are used to train the system. These rules classify each example into a set of categories or classes based on the values an example takes in a set of domain descriptors.

Due to the complexity of DEVS modelling, a previous work of *data-enginee-ring* must be carried out to fit a set of requirements needed to apply inductive learning. Besides, *constructive induction* techniques must be used to obtain more powerful domain descriptors from the initial ones.

Morover, the variable *time* is present on the input data, and consequently, the examples are time-ordered. The internal working of the model at each state is be based on the external events and on the previous behaviour of the system. Therefore, we need to bring the system's past behaviour into present as new descriptors (or state variables) constructed from the initial ones, and consequently the inductive algorithm will obtain rules including time-dependent relationships,

The final model will be expressed with the *Generalized Magnitudes formalism* [3], that has been used previously for the modelling and simulation of DEVS in previous works [4, 5].

2 Inductive learning

Inductive learning obtains a set of symbolic rules that are the membership conditions of a set of entities to a set of classes. These rules are induced from a set of pre-classified entities that are used as a training set. In classical inductive learning an example describes the characteristics of an entity by means of a set of domain descriptors and the rules classify univoquely each entity into a class on the basis of the values of the descriptors in that example.

$$\text{Class=}c_1 \text{ if A=}a_2 \text{ and } \dots$$

The induced rules are intensional descriptions of each class that are used to predict the classification of a new example, not considered during the training phase, and so they must be general enough to correctly classify every example presented to the system. Obviously, the set of examples used as a training set must be big enough, and ideally should describe all possibilities of the domain.

The success of Inductive learning depends greatly on the descriptors used, because they will influence the expresiveness of the induced rules. Sometimes, the initial set of descriptors is not enough to obtain a complete and correct set of rules. Constructive induction allows the construction of new descriptors from the initial ones by applying a set of operators, eg. arithmetical operators like $A + B$ and so on. These new descriptors make explicit a kind of knowledge that was in some way "hidden" in the input data.

Inductive learning uses a heuristic search of complete and correct rules covering all the examples through a set of generalization operators. The internal working of the inductive algorithm is not essential to our purpose and consequently it will not be treated here. Therefore, we are not subjected to a concrete algorithm, on the contrary, a set of existing algorithms could be used with similar results.

Finally, the way at which the classes and the examples are selected influences greatly the quality and the meaning of the induced rules.

3 Related work

In this section we will see some previous related works that apply machine learning techniques to the field of Systems Theory. Mladenic in her work [6] applies inductive learning to the analysis of DEVS simulation data and obtains a set of rules that contains regularities about the behaviour of a system, which contributes to a better understanding of that system.

Below, a typical rule obtained from the simulation of a supermarket can be seen that relates the performance of the model to a set of input parameters as the number of cashiers and so on.

if $Cashs * Arriv < 5$ or $Cashs * Arriv < 6$ and $QWSize = 1$
then $CustomerUtil < 90\%$

On the other hand, Kuipers [7] abduces a qualitative model of a system from descriptions of behaviours of the system, that reproduces those behaviours. Input data consist of a temporal sequence of quantitative values for a set of input parameters that must be translated into a set of qualitative values consisting of a qualitative magnitude, eg. a landmark, and a direction of change, ie. increasing, decreasing, stable.

From these data, the system generates a set of constraints, ie. a set of relationships among parameters that assert functional, ie. correlations, and arithmetical relations among the values associated with those parameters at a given time and also among the values associated with a single parameter at different time points. There exists a set of rules that create each constraint from the input data.

The complete search space is explored, ie. all possible constraints are tested on data. Below, some typical constraints about a system consisting of two cascaded tanks can be seen.

```
(constant inflow_a)
(add outflow_a netflow_a inflow_a)
(d/dt amount_b netflow_b)
(M+ amount_b outflow_b)
```

4 Inductive learning in DEVS

In order to apply Inductive Learning in DEVS modelling, several steps must be carried out (figure 1). Firstly, the formalism of DEVS and Inductive Learning must be compatibilized in order to translate input data into a form usable by the inductor, ie. a set of classes, examples and descriptors.

Secondly, inductive learning obtains a set of rules for each class. If these rules *cover* the whole training set, then the model can be constructed. If not so, the initial set of attributes can be not descriptive enough to completely model the system, ie. some essential state variables are missing, and so we need to generate new descriptors of a better quality from the initial ones.

On the other hand, inductive learning schemes are not, in general, suited to deal with *time-dependent data*. The typical form of input data for such algorithms is a simple two dimensional table of attribute-value pairs for each entity in the training set. In *induction from time-dependent data*, temporally-dimensioned data for an entity is presented to the learner. This is the case of DEVS, where input data will consist of a system's behaviour, ie. a time-ordered sequence of states, so each entity becomes now the state of the system at a time point.

Besides, the classical language at which the hypotheses are expressed is not the most appropriate, because it only allows to express relations comparing the attributes and a set of constants and it does not allow to express time-dependent relations. So, the hypothesis language needs to be enhanced to be able to describe some characteristics about the behaviour of a descriptor along time. To do it, some new operators will be used, eg.:

– duration, time-of, number-of, previous, ...
– max, min, $\sum$, ...

which obtain the duration of a state, the time point at which an event occurred, the number of times an event occurred, the previous event and so on.

Finally, inductive and constructive steps are iterated until a complete set of rules are obtained or until there is no a significant improvement in the rules. This last case is mostly due to the absence of essential descriptors on input data or to the presence of noise in data.

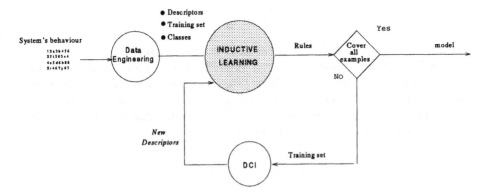

Fig. 1. General scheme

4.1 Data Engineering

The complexity of Discrete Event models makes unfeasible the direct application of inductive learning algorithms. On the one hand, a DEVS specification consists of a set of elements, namely a set of inputs, outputs and states, as well as a set of functions, namely the internal and external transition functions, the output function and the next activation time function.

$$(X, Y, S, \delta_i, \delta_e, t_a, \lambda)$$

On the other hand, inductive learning has a set of requirements, ie. a set of classes, a set of examples and a set of domain descriptors. Therefore, we must compatibilize both formalisms. First of all, classes are, in some way, the goals of inductive learning, because they are used to classify the input examples, whereas, in DEVS the goals are each of the functions in the model's specification.

Then, each of these functions will identify the classes, so that their values will become the classes, and so there will be several learning phases, one for each function. The induced rules will determine the current value of the function at each state, ie. the output of a function f at the state represented by the example

E is f_1 (the class), if the values of the descriptors in E match those in the right-hand side of the rule.

But the different nature of each function entails several considerations in selecting a training set and a set of descriptors for each of them. With regard to the *next activation time function* t_a, we cannot use each of its values as a class, because we are restricted to discrete classes. In this case, we must obtain one or more mathematical expressions that compute the next activation time for each example. Each expression, if there are more than one, will become a class for induction and the induced rules will establish which expression is the right one at each state.

$$t_a = A - 1 \; \textbf{if} \dots$$
$$t_a = 5 \qquad \textbf{if} \dots$$

But, we are not provided with the next activation time for each example, and then it must be obtained from input data. To this purpose, we will compute the time elapsed from each example or "state" to the nearest *detected* internal transition. We will assume that an example is due to an internal transition if there is not an external event. We will not consider the case when an internal and an external transition occur simultaneously.

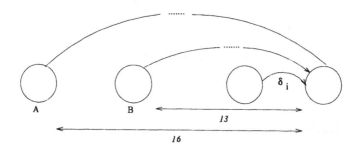

Fig. 2. Next activation time

The *output function* λ, establishes which of the elements in the output set corresponds to each state. At this point, we must distinguish two cases regarding the output set:

- When the output set consists of a limited number of elements, eg. error messages and so on
- When the output set consists of an unlimited number of elements

The latter would correspond for example to the set of clients of a supermarket. In this case we are not interested in knowing when the client A leaves the system but in those conditions that must be hold for every client to leave the system. That is, there is not an especial meaning or behaviour of each client.

Whereas in the first case, each output element would become a class, in the second one, there will be two classes:

- Those elements leaving the system at each state.
- Those elements not leaving the system at each state

Consequently, the induced rule will be like this:

$$\lambda = x \quad \textbf{if } P(x) \wedge \ldots$$

On the other hand, we must obtain an expression for each *state variable* provided to us in the input data that explains the behaviour of the variable at each state. Hence, each value of the variable's domain will become a class for induction. For those numerical state variables, we must apply a similar methodology as with the t_a function.

The internal and external transition functions move the system to a different state by modifying some state variables. Hence, they will be obtained indirectly in the description of the state variables, in order to obtain a rule directly usable in the Generalized Magnitudes formalism, ie.:

$$S = s_1 \textbf{ if } \delta_e \ldots \text{ instead of } \delta_e \Rightarrow S = s_1 \textbf{ and } \ldots$$

where δ_e means "there is an external event at the current state". Finally, the *set of states* of a system will come determined by the values of a set of *state variables* that includes both initial and constructed descriptors.

5 An example: Process scheduling

The example we present, consists of a system consisting of a processor (**CPU**) that executes one process at a time (figure 3). There exists an input queue where the processes wait to enter CPU. A process is allowed to stay in CPU for a time τ (*time slice*), and once elapsed this time, it must leave CPU and the next process on the input queue will enter CPU. The processes leaving CPU are positioned at the end of the input queue. Finally, a process leaves the system when it has completed its required CPU time.

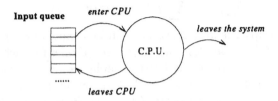

Fig. 3. Process scheduling

The input data will consist of the input queue and the output of the system at each state, ie. the set of processes waiting for entering CPU and the process that leaves the system. A state variable that identifies the process currently in

CPU is also provided and a constant with the time slice τ of the processor. With these elements we can know what the system is doing at each time point.

On the other hand, we have some variables particular of DEVS, like e that records the time elapsed from the previous state to the current one and b/i that describe the system's state (busy or idle). Besides, each process is described through its name, its required CPU time and its position on the input queue.

I	O	b/i	τ	CPU	e	name	t_{cpu}	queue	name	t_{cpu}	queue
-	-	i	5	-	-						
a	-	b	5	a	∞	a	3	1			
-	a	i	5	-	3				a	10	1
b	-	b	5	b	∞	b	15	1			
-	-	b	5	b	5	b	15	1			
c	-	b	5	b	2	b	15	1			
						c	12	2			
-	-	b	5	c	3	b	15	1			
						c	12	2			

Table 1. Training set

Process scheduling needs an essential variable in order to be modelled, that is not initially provided to the system. At each state, we need to know how much processing time needs a process to leave the system. This descriptor summarizes, in some way, the process's history and so it is a clear example of how essential is the ability of inducing rules from time-dependent data.

The remaining CPU time can be obtained from the difference between the initial CPU time required, and the time that a process has already been in CPU. The first one is one of the initial descriptors and the second one can be constructed by adding the length of the time intervals during which a process is in CPU, ie. when $CPU = x$.

$$t_{cpu}(x) - \sum duration(CPU = x)$$

Once this descriptor is available (that will be denoted as tr), the inductive machinery can obtain a complete and correct set of rules for each class (below).

First of all, with regard to the CPU variable, we are not interested in the particular process that enters CPU at each state, but in those general conditions that must be held for a process to enter CPU. Therefore, we will distinguish two classes, one containing the processes that enter CPU at each example and a second one that contains the remaining processes. This can also be applied to the output function.

Each disjunct explains a different situation in the system's behaviour, eg. when the input queue is empty, when the time slice has elapsed, when a process leaves definitively the system and when a new process enters the input queue.

CPU=x if $queue(x) = 1 \wedge \#X = 1$
$\qquad \vee \; queue(x) = queue(prev(CPU)) + 1 \wedge e = 5$
$\qquad \vee \; queue(x) = 1 \wedge queue(prev(CPU)) = prev(max(queue(x))) \wedge e = 5$
$\qquad \vee \; queue(x) = 1 \wedge queue(prev(CPU)) = prev(max(queue(x))) \wedge output = yes$
$\qquad \vee \; queue(x) = prev(queue(prev(CPU))) \wedge output = yes$
$\qquad \vee \; prev(CPU) = x \wedge e < 5 \wedge input = yes$

On the other hand, a process leaves the system if it has been executing in CPU for exactly the remaining CPU time required for that process.

$$\lambda = x \text{ if } prev(CPU) = x \wedge e = prev(tr(x))$$

And finally, the next activation time function, that needs a previous work of discovery in order to find a set of mathematical expressions that calculate t_a for each example. In this case, the constructed descriptor *remaining CPU time* also plays an essential role: an internal transition always occurs every τ time units, excepting when the remaining CPU time required for the process currently executing in CPU is less than τ.

$$t_a = \tau \qquad \text{if } tr(CPU) \geq 5 \wedge (output = yes \vee e = 5)$$
$$t_a = \text{prev}(t_a)\text{-e if } input = yes \wedge CPU = prev(CPU) \wedge e < prev(t_a)$$
$$t_a = \text{tr(CPU)} \qquad \text{if } tr(CPU) \leq 5 \wedge (output = yes \vee e = 5)$$

6 Conclusions

Machine learning methods have been used successfully in the field of Systems Theory. The work presented here, will be of help in the design phase of Discrete Event systems because it automatically induces a model from descriptions of behaviours of the system. A previous data engineering work has had to be done in order to compatibilize DEVS and machine learning formalisms.

On the other hand, the temporal characteristics of data in DEVS has supposed significant changes in inductive learning, eg., the examples are now time-ordered and so, the interesting knowledge must include time-dependent relations. Hence, the hypothesis language has had to be enhanced with some operators that allow to describe the behaviour of a descriptor along time.

This study is also useful for the application of machine learning methods in the field of Temporal Expert Systems, where the relevant knowledge includes many time-dependent relationships that describe a patient's evolution along time.

Acknowledgements This research was supported in part by the Government of Galicia (Spain), grant XUGA10503B/94.

References

1. B. P. Zeigler. *Multifaceted Modelling and Discrete Event Simulation*. London: Academic Press, 1984.
2. F. Pichler and H. Schwärtzel (Eds.). *CAST, Methods in Modelling*. Springer Verlag, 1992.
3. R.P. Otero. *MEDTOOL, una herramienta para el desarrollo de sistemas expertos*. PhD thesis, Universidad de Santiago, 1991.
4. R.P. Otero, A. Barreiro, H. Praehofer, F. Pichler, and J. Mira. Stims-medtool: Integration of expert systems with systems modelling and simulation. *Lecture Notes in Computer Science*, (763):347–356, 1994.
5. R. Otero, A. Barreiro, P. Cabalar, and D. Lorenzo. Discrete event simulation in an environment for temporal expert systems. *EUROCAST 95*, 1995.
6. D. Mladenic, I. Bratko, R.J. Paul, and M. Grobelnik. Knowledge adquisition for discrete event systems using machine learning. *ECAI 94. 11th European Conference on Artificial Intelligence*, 1994.
7. B. L. Richards, I. Kraan, and B. J. Kuipers. Automatic abduction of qualitative models. *Proceedings of the Fifth International Workshop on Qualitative Reasoning about Physical Systems*, pages 295–301, 1991.

3 COMPLEX SYSTEMS DESIGN

Systems Engineering and Infrastructures for Open Computer Based Systems

Engineering of Computer Based Systems (ECBS) and Open System Architecture - Platform with Universal Services (OSA-PLUS)

Gerhard Schweizer   Markus Voss

Universität Karlsruhe, Institut für Mikrorechner und Automation (IMA)
Haid-und-Neu-Straße 7, D-76131 Karlsruhe, Germany
e-mail: mvoss@ira.uka.de

Abstract. ECBS (Engineering of Computer Based Systems) provides frameworks of architecture principles to model perceived environments in which CBS (Computer Based Systems) must be embedded and the functionality of CBS as discrete event systems and to model physical CBS as service-oriented systems. In addition it contains frameworks for process models with precise guidelines to perform all engineering steps required to build these models and to integrate and operate CBS as well as frameworks for information models with precise guidelines what information has to be captured within an ECBS process to establish the documentation for a complete and consistent information base.

OSA-PLUS (Open System Architecture - Platform with Universal Services) provides frameworks with precise guidelines to architect system platforms as basic building blocks for a base-line physical component infrastructure. In addition it contains frameworks with precise and generalised guidelines to architect services conform with the architecture in terms of both basic services for intelligent actuation, measurement, and feedback control, men/machine interaction, and data storage and retrieval for a base-line functional component infrastructure, as well as specific application services. It also contains guidelines to architect general tools to support the ECBS processes and dedicated tools which must go along with all services to support CBS integration, test, validation, operation.

Together, ECBS and OSA-PLUS form one coherent framework for open CBS development and operation.

1.   Introduction

1.1   Scope of ECBS

ECBS (Engineering of Computer Based Systems) as promoted by the IEEE Technical Committee on ECBS provides precise guidance on the development of CBS (Computer Based Systems) which fit the user needs and purposes with respect to functionality and performance as well as delivery time and cost budget. ECBS therefore defines all steps for the life cycle (see Fig. 1) process to produce CBS, the interfaces between the processes and all management activities required to ensure that CBS are developed to the right quality.

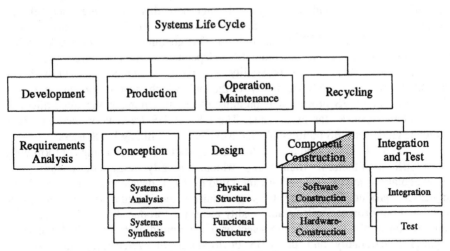

Fig. 1. CBS Life Cycle

The guidelines for the management activities and the CBS processes are linked together into one harmonised framework. Its guidelines comprise a set of precise rules for both the customer and the developer of CBS. ECBS hereby fits all needs for the user and customer by emphasising the role of CBS acquisition as well as CBS development and delivery.

ECBS aims to provide everyone involved in CBS projects (CBS analysts and designers, component developers and vendors, CBS integrators and suppliers, CBS customers and operators, and manegement) with a common framework, built on a well proven system theory and on sound experience. This framework provides reference guide to CBS engineers, to be applied in a rigid manner and with common sense. This gives users, developers, managers and administrators a platform for their work and a vocabulary that allows concurrent engineering and the discussion of problems and experience in a precise manner. The knowledge acquired can be re-applied across different CBS projects.

The discipline of ECBS in general was reported on in e.g. [1,2,3]. One major characteristic of ECBS as it is perceived here however is its systems theoretical foundation [4,5,6]. That aspect will be talked about in more detail later.

1.2 Scope of OSA-PLUS

OSA-PLUS (Open System Architecture - Platform with Universal Services) as promoted by the OSA-PLUS research network related to the IEEE TC on ECBS provides precise guidance on the architecture principle for the design of building blocks needed to integrate CBS and for components by which building blocks can be integrated. The building blocks fit the needs for the production of CBS with open system architecture properties. Furthermore concrete OSA-PLUS products so far provide a substantial infrastructure of components by which basic building blocks can be integrated for CBS in various ways and with different performance measures.

OSA-PLUS guidelines in detail define the generalised interfaces between the building blocks and its functional interoperability and interchangeability independent from their implementation. Building blocks that meet these requirements are called OSA-PLUS conform. This guarantees building blocks which can be plugged together to integrate CBS independent of their supplier. The OSA-PLUS principles thus allows portability and reuse of components. OSA-PLUS guidelines also define the functionality for the tools which must accompany an OSA-PLUS conform ECBS process and building blocks to automate the integration of CBS and the tests as far as possible. The OSA-PLUS framework therefore is a reference guide for CBS building block developers and building block users.

OSA-PLUS is based on a systems theory for CBS design being conform with the ECBS architectural frameworks which naturally does not contain any implementation details. This allows the building block developers and suppliers to implement products according to a generalised specification scheme but with individual performance criteria and quality measures (product lines). The managers and developers of CBS are able to select or replace building blocks which meet the required functionality and the CBS environment in which they must fit in, independent of the vendor. Furthermore the OSA-PLUS framework represents a uniform vocabulary. Problems and experience can be discussed between vendors and customers. The knowledge can be re-applied across all building block initiatives. This principle leads to CBS with open system architectures.

1.3   Benefits of ECBS/OSA-PLUS

For contractors the frameworks clearly spell out what is expected from a CBS under consideration. The CBS manager can handle all required steps in a consistent proven way. No essential activities in CBS management will be forgotten or erroneously performed. They all will be done at the right time.

The success of a CBS project on one side depends heavily on the use of proven building blocks. CBS delivery time and cost on the other side is determined to a large degree by the use of tools mainly to assist the whole management process and the integration and test of CBS. Therefore even with a methodological framework like ECBS the availability of building blocks and tools to fit the framework is essential for CBS project success. This again shows, that ECBS and OSA-PLUS are two sides of the same coin.

Experience indicates, that by the use of ECBS/OSA-PLUS productivity producing CBS increases considerably with respect to delivery time and cost. The work flow of the engineering activities can be managed with respect to the control of the results, quality assurance, and configuration control. The customer has insight into the contractors work in a way which can be individually defined. Prerequisite however is an adequate training of engineers.

The ECBS/OSA-PLUS framework used by vendors of building blocks guides the building block design and leads to products which can be widely used for CBS production. This allows the vendors to tailor their market. The same applies to vendors of tools which fit the needs to manage and produce CBS.

The guidelines of the OSA-PLUS framework are applicable for the design of all kind of building blocks, independent of the intended individual function and implementation. The use of the guidelines leads to a OSA-PLUS comform component infrastructure which covers a baseline of products by which building blocks with different performance criteria can be integrated. The functionality and the interfaces of it fit into all CBS with open system architecture.

Because ECBS/OSA-PLUS has the character of a reference standard a few words about standards are necessary. A variety of standards related to ECBS/OSA-PLUS do exist. Some of the given process standards only cover the software engineering aspect, others like e.g. IEEE P 1220, MIL-STD 499 B or ISO 9000 the system engineering aspects as well. Product standards are mostly quasi standards set by important product producers and architecture standards for open system architectures are only beginning to develop. The relation of ECBS/OSA-PLUS to all these other standards is that of ECBS/OSA-PLUS intended to be an 'umbrella methodology', that, if applied satisfies the CBS requirements with the items of different standards met. One major difference between ECBS/OSA-PLUS and other standards is its system theoretical foundation, a fact that was also discussed in [7].

Summerizing all this, the ECBS/OSA-PLUS approach could lead to sound engineering infrastructures of methods, components, tools, and trained personnel fit to really change the way CBS products are built and marketed to the better.

2. Contects of ECBS

2.1 ECBS models

The scope of ECBS is to provide a framework for CBS production which is short but complete, consistent and precise, readable, covers the whole life cycle and is applicable with common sense, creativity and experience.

The framework covers guidelines to execute the processes as defined for the CBS life cycle to produce required CBS and guidelines to manage the ECBS processes. The management part includes guidance and control for the execution of the ECBS processes, for the quality assurance of the ECBS processes and the accompanying results and for the configuration control of the results. This part of the framework is called the *ECBS process model* (see e.g. [8]).

Furthermore the framework contains guidelines which precisely describe in all necessary details the information to be captured when executing the ECBS processes independent of their specific presentation. This allows a comprehensive, complete and qualified documentation, which is understandable and allows the tracing of the performed ECBS processes. Languages to be used for presentation which are formal, applicable and understandable in practice are proposed. This part of the framework is called the *ECBS information model*.

The third part of the ECBS framework contains architecture principles for the CBS and the different models to be built during the ECBS process called *ECBS architecture models*. These are first needed to model the structure and the behaviour of the environment into which CBS should be embedded for automation. The activities to build a model to represent the environment in which a CBS must be embedded are part of the work to be done within the ECBS process and are subsumed under the name of *systems analysis*. Environment in that context can mean physical systems to be automated or organisational systems with information processing to be automated.

Next, architecture principles must be given which guide model building to represent the functionality of some CBS to be built to meet the requirements set by the CBS environment and the specified operational scenario. These activities also belong to the ECBS process and are subsumed under the name of *systems synthesis*.

Within the ECBS process towards CBS design a model must be built which represents the physical architecture of the CBS to be built determined by both the arrangement of the physical components and subsystems to form the CBS and its required behaviour. Functions to determine this behaviour which must meet the requirements set in systems synthesis in design is allocated to the physical components. Therefore architectural principles which guide the steps to establish a CBS design model describing physical structure and functional allocation are prerequisite for the ECBS design processes. The engineering activities to create such a CBS design model are subsumed under the neme of *systems design*.

Because both, the ECBS process and information models, follow from these architectural principles, these are described in more detail. It shows that a theory of hierarchical discrete event systems is adequate for systems analysis and synthesis while systems design can be based on a theory of so called service-oriented systems.

2.2 Concepts for system analysis and synthesis

The concept of the discrete event system is a theoretical basis for the architecture principles needed for ECBS processes towards system analysis and system synthesis. Environments in which CBS should be embedded and the functionality of CBS which are required to automate the environment can both be perceived as discrete event systems independent of the application domain. The theory presented hereafter differs from well known time discrete systems and discrete event systems theories (e.g. [9,10]) mostly by its more flexible perception of system coupling allowing for state aggregation and different levels of abstraction.

A discrete event system as a whole is described by its identity, its time invariant describing properties here called its frame, its (internal) state, its effecting events perceived as input events, and its observable states (changes) perceived as output events. This is illustrated in Fig. 2.

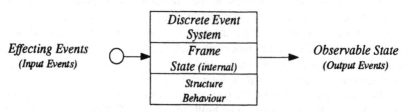

Fig. 2. Discrete Event System as a Whole

The architecture effort to model something which can be perceived as an aggegated discrete even system comprises the conception of the system as a whole as well as the conception of its hierarchy, structure, and behaviour. To conceive a systems hierarchy is to recursively decompose the system into its parts. The component hierarchy is illustrated in Fig. 3.

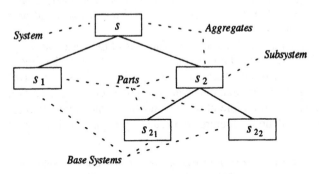

Fig. 3. Component Hierarchy

To conceive a systems structure is to conceive how the parts are arranged, so that their aggregation represent the system. The frame attached to a composite system are defined by a function which maps the frames of the parts and the properties of the arrangement relations into the frame of the aggregate. This 'theorem' of systems theory is on basic architecture principle to be applied in modeling and is illustrated in Fig. 4.

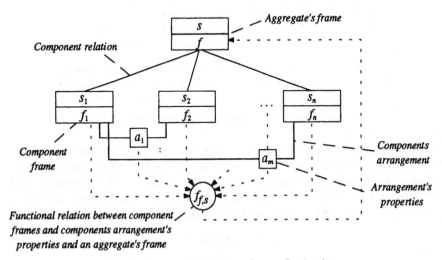

Fig. 4. Aggregated System Frame Deduction

The architecture principles to model the behaviour of something which is perceived as a discrete event system (with the structure of it known) results from the conception of its function which maps the inputs, called effecting events into the outputs, called the systems observable states. The input/output function of a composite hierarchical system can be recursively defined as follows:

One recursively defines functions which map the actual effecting events of the aggregate and the state changes of its parts into the events effecting the parts called internal effecting events. The outputs of an aggregate's parts are to be perceived as its internal states, the output of itself is some abstraction of its internal state called its observable state. For base systems internal states and observable states are defined as identical.

If one assumes the input/output functions of the basic parts, which must not decomposed further, to be known, one can recursively define the states of the aggregates from the states of their parts. To do this, one must recursively, beginning with the basic parts, define functions which map the states of the parts into the states of the aggregate. This principle of moving 'down the hierarchy' by internal effecting events definition and 'up the hierarchy' by state aggregation is illustrated in Fig. 5.

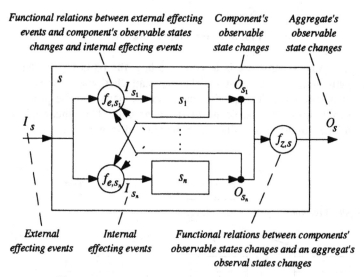

Fig. 5. Aggregated System Behaviour Deduction

The engineering steps and the encompassing rules to build discrete event system models can also be perceived as a process model for discrete event system modeling. The architecture principles altogether being used to perceive something which can be conceived as a discrete event system leads to a model which describes the class of systems to which a discrete event system under consideration belongs by a 4-tuple

$$M := \{A,K,R,F\}$$

where

A represents a set of sorts or classes to which the systems, its parts, the describing properties, the effecting events and the enforced states belong.

K represents a set of constants or objects which comprise the elements of the sorts belong which describe the systems under consideration.

R represents a set of relations which define the relevant relationships between the elements of the sorts.

F represent a set of functions which define the relevant functionalities between the elements of the sorts.

Different syntactical forms can be used to represent the model of a discrete event system like algebraic or predicate logic-based formalisms or graphical presentations, which are especially adequate for communication purposes. Independent of the presentation syntax however the architecture principles of discrete event systems precisely specify the semantics of the information represented. The 4-tuple from above can therefore be identified with the information model of a discrete event system.

2.3   Concepts for systems design

The concept of the *service* is the theoretical foundation of the architecture principles for physical CBS which are called service-oriented systems. A service represents a conception of an information processing unit onto which prescriptions can be soft- or hardwired and executed. Processing units as parts of service-oriented CBS must be interfaceable with each other via communication networks. Their functionality must allow the allocation of prescriptions, service accesses to the configured services via service access protocols, the interconnection between the allocated services, the control of the services and the execution of the services which includes the intercommunication between the services and the synchronisation of the service execution. Information processing units which meet these general requirements are called *system platforms*. They are the backbones of every CBS. Their functionality and interconnectivity is defined in detail within the OSA-PLUS framework.

     System platforms interconnected via communication systems, with services and service accesses allocated to them represent the basic architecture principles for the structure of CBS as illustrated in Fig. 6.

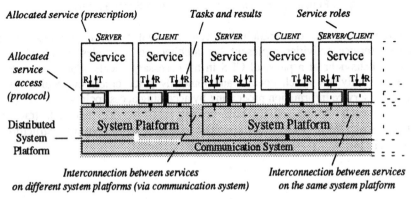

Fig. 6. Physical Structure of a service-oriented CBS

The architecture principles applied to model the behaviour of CBS are as follows: The concept of the service allows the configuration of service activities which are attached to a service. A service activity, sometimes called an agent, operates autonomously and processes information according to the service prescription and renders the result if it is in the operation mode and if necessary is assigned with an order. Service configuration allows to create required service activities and to define protocols for service activity access points, sometimes called ports. Defined service activity access points can be interconnected so service activities can communicate. Possible ways of communication with respect to who is responsible for information aquisition are writing, reproting and reading. Connecting service activities leads to a (with respect to responsibility hierarchic structured) net of service activities which the CBS has to execute. This is illustrated in Fig. 7.

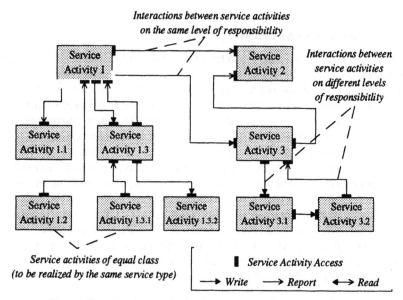

Fig. 7. Functional Structure of cooperating Service Activities

The definition of the cooperation between the configured, interconnected and initialised service activities represent the architecture principles which allow to model the behaviour of a physical CBS in all necessary details. Cooperation takes place when activities which operate autonomously place orders or receive results required for service information processing by accessing access points.

As each service activity now belongs to a service, one can trace the functional structure of a CBS as illustrated in Fig. 7 to the physical structure as illustrated in Fig. 6. This is illustrated in Fig. 8.

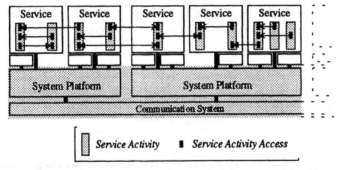

Fig. 8. Behaviour of a service-oriented CBS given by Activity Allocation

The architecture principles of service-orineted systems and service activity networks lead to a CBS-specific specialization of component types and their arrangements compared to the general concept of a discrete event system. But still service-oriented CBS are discrete event systems. The guidelines for the engineering steps to architect CBS according to these architecture principles can therefore be based on the notion of this specialization and comprise the process model for the design of service-oriented CBS.

The information model of service-oriented CBS related to the design process is a 4-tuple like above only with more concrete component classes namely system platforms, services, service activities, communication systems, related properties, orders, results and attributes which define the service activities access protocols. A variety of syntactical forms can be used to present models of service-oriented CBS. The presentations can be formally or graphically based. The architecture principles specify precisely independent of the syntax the semantics of the information to be captured within the design process.

3. Contents of OSA-PLUS

OSA-PLUS provides a framework to define and specify building blocks needed to aggregate CBS with open system architectures independent from the application functionality and an implementation. Based on this framework infrastructure of building blocks have been developed which can be used to integrate system platforms and basic services for intelligent actuation measurement and feedback control (IAMF) intelligent data storage and retrieval (IDSR) and intelligent men machine control (IMMC). Both system platform and service functionality in general and the basic services in particular will be presented in this chapter. OSA-PLUS conventions on tools will not be talked about here.

3.1 Functionality of System Platforms

System platforms as outlined above are the basic physical building blocks on which all CBS services are based. OSA-PLUS provides the architecture principles for the structure and the functionality of system platforms independent of their implementation and performance details. A system platform's general functionality (called the OSA-PLUS system interface) is illustrated in Fig. 9.

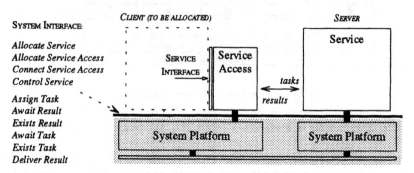

Fig. 9. Functionality of a System Platform

The functionality of the system platforms comprises

- functions to integrate services by the allocation of service prescriptions onto system platforms
- functions to interconnect services by attaching service access protocols to services which need access to defined services already integrated
- functions to control (start, stop, suspend,resume) the service operation
- functions to transfer information between interconnected services and to synchronise parallel service information processing.

According to the ECBS framework communication there is hierarchical with different responsibilities. Therefore the communication functionality of the system platform is organized around tasks and results rather than just messages.

3.2 Structure of System Platforms

Each implementation of a system platform takes care of how the allocation of the service prescriptions (soft/or hardwired) is done and how the required performance is achieved, which is determined by underlying hardware platform, operating systems used, and basic communication means. For heterogeneous systems construction capability the OSA-PLUS system platform guidelines define uniform process and communication layers realized by extended process operating system and message transport services to be mapped to standardized process and communication facilities like UNIX (POSIX standard) or TCP/IP e.g. or others. On top of this uniform interface OSA-PLUS system platform functionality conform services are realized. Fig. 10 illustrates the basic structure and functionality of system platforms as defined in OSA-PLUS.

Dependent on the hardware and standard software environment used a special system platform's functionality comprises specific instruction sets and operating system services besides the uniform OSA-PLUS systems interface.

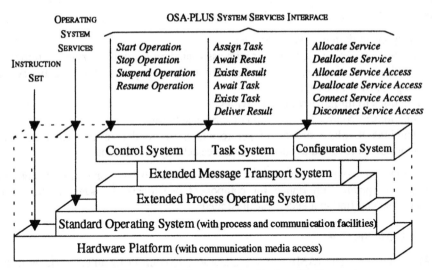

Fig. 10. General Structure of a System Platform

3.3 Functionality of Services

In addition to the guidelines for the generalised structure and functionality of the system platforms which allow to distribute services and to operate them as required OSA-PLUS provides a generalised framework which defines the (meta-)functionality a service must provide independent of its application domain and its implementation. This generalised functionality of a service is illustrated in Fig. 11.

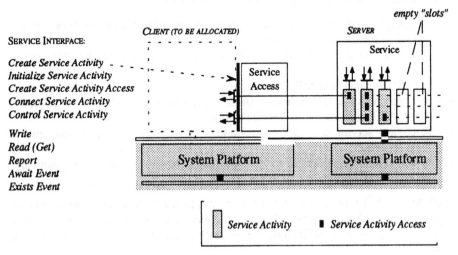

Fig. 11. (Meta-)Functionality of a Service

The (meta-)functionality of a service comprises

- functions to define service activities
- functions to define access points with associated protocols for service activities.
- functions to interconnect service activity access points for a network of cooperating service activities
- functions to initialize service activities
- functions to control the operation of service activities
- functions to place orders, to get results or to render results according the protocols as required to coordinate service activity cooperation

This definition serves to ensure that interfaces to services have one uniform outlook which is of prime importance for component developers. Looking at the basic services one can find that statement illustrated.

3.4   Basic Services

IAMF Services. The IAMF services allow to interconnect technical systems to be automated and CBS for automation by intelligent actuation (control), measurement (data acquisition) and feedback control of physical variables.

They comprise system platforms with allocated IAMF service prescriptions (soft- or hardwired) extended by converters, signal conditioning devices, actuators, sensors. The actual configuration of an IAMF device depends on the functions the services should perform, e.g. an IAMF device based on a micro controller can serve only for distributed measurements of analogue physical variables whereas a PC based IAMF service can serve for actuation, measurement and feedback control at the same time.

The functionality of the IAMF services comprise in accordance with the OSA-PLUS conventions from 3.3 knows six functions which serve:

- to configure analogue in, digital in, analogue out, digital out, feedback control, and surveillance service activities
- to define access points with related access protocols for created IAMF service activities
- to initialize created IAMF service activities
- to interconnect access points of IAMF service activities with access points of other IAMF and non-IAMF service activities
- to control service activities by beginning, suspending, resuming, and ending their operation
- to place explicitly orders to service activities to be carried out and to commands get results like get measured or put control values

Feedback control loop service activities are composed by associated measurement, actuator and feedback controller service activities. The operations of the feed back control loop services are defined on the feedback control loop as a composite service activity.

All service activity functions can be used as programmable interfaces within an implementation environment. The explicit programming of the configuration, including access points and corresponding protocols of the interconnection and initialisation of the IAMF service activities is tedious. Therefore tools which allow men/machine dialogue oriented configuration, test and simulation of IAMF service activities must accompany all IAMF services.

IMMC Services . The IMMC services allow to interface the human operator with service-oriented information processing systems. Men/machine interfaces serve to visualise information for the human operator and to acquire information about the interactions which human operators carry out.

The surface by which a set of windows can be grouped together, the window which comprise a frame and a set of planes to which coordinate systems can be attached and graphical symbols which can be placed into the planes for presentation are the basic concepts of the IMMC services and yield service activity types.

The prescriptions for IMMC services can be soft- or hardwired on system platforms which are extended by the adequate hardware needed for visual presentation. High performance men/machine interfaces can be built by system platforms which are extended by special hardware devices which support the execution of the men/machine service activities, e.g. graphic controllers.

According to 3.3 the functionality of men/machine services must encompass functions

- to configure IMMC service activities for operations on surfaces, windows, planes and symbols
- to define access points to configured IMMC service activities with access protocols
- to initialise configured IMMC service activities
- to interconnect access points of IMMC service activities with access points of other IMMC and non-IMMC service activities
- to control the operation of IMMC service activities
- to place orders on IMMC service activities e.g. to handle windows, visibility, scrolling and zooming of symbol attached to planes and commands to read results from men/machine interactions carried out

Within a service-oriented CBS environment all functions can be used as programmable interfaces. The explicit programming of the configuration of IMMC service activities is tedious. Therefore tools are provided which allow to configure IMMC service activities.

IDSR Services. The IDSR services allow to store and retrieve information from information bases. An information or database comprise a set of sequences of tuples which are called relations. Functions allow to insert tuples into the relations and to retrieve tuples out of the relations. The relations are ordered according one or more attributes in a descending or ascending mode.

The IDSR services belongs to a system platform on which the IDSR service prescriptions are allocated. IDSR services can be distributed as required within the frame of a CBS. The functionality comprises functions

- to configure data bases and to open, close and save them

- to configure relations as set of tuples with operations which allow data retrieval and to set access protocols and locks on it
- to insert, replace and delete tuples

4. Resumé

Above we have talked about selected characteristics of the systems engineering and infrastructure framework of ECBS/OSA-PLUS.

Although space limitations for this contribution does not allow to illuminate all interesting aspects one most important thing was at least clearly stated. This is that no methodological framework (like ECBS) is of any real value unless it is complemented with concrete architectural definitions and product interface specifications (like OSA-PLUS) that fit. On the other hand architecture and product standards alone do not help either. It is the combination (like ECBS/OSA-PLUS) that makes the difference .

References

[1]   Lavi, J.Z., et.al.: *Formal Establishment of Computer Based Systems Engineering Urged.* IEEE Computer, 24 (3), pp. 105-107, 1991
[2]   White, S., et.al.: Systems Engineering of Computer-Based Systems. IEEE Computer, 26 (11), pp. 54-65, 1993
[3]   Schweizer, G., Thomé, B., Voss, M.: *A Systems Engineering Approach for Computer Based Systems.* In: Systems Engineering in the Global Market Place. Proceedings of the 5th annual intern. Meeting of NCOSE, 1995
[4]   Schweizer, G., Voss, M.: *Managing the ECBS Process - Towards a System Theory for ECBS.* In: Lawson, H.W. (Ed.): 1994 Tutorial and Workshop on Systems Engineering of Computer-Based Systems. IEEE Computer Society Press, 1994
[5]   Voss, M., Schweizer, G.: *A Development Methodology for Systems Engineering of Computer-Based Systems and its Environmental Support.* In: Ören, T., Klir, G. (Eds.): Computer Aided Systems Technology. Proceedings of CAST '94, Springer, 1995
[6]   Schweizer, G., Thomé, B., Voss, M.: *A Systems Theory Based Approach to Systems Engineering of Computer Based Systems and its Consequences.* In: Melhart, B., Rozenblit, J. (Eds.): 1995 Intern. Symposium and Workshop on systems Engineering of Computer Based Systems, 1995
[7]   Voss, M., Hummel, H. and Wolff, T.: *The Role of Process Standards within ECBS Work.* In: Lawson, H.W. (Ed.): 1994 Tutorial and Workshop on Systems Engineering of Computer-Based Systems. IEEE Computer Society Press, 1994
[8]   Oliver, D.W., *A Tailorable Process Model for CBSE,* Draft, GE Research & Development Center, February 1993.
[9]   Wymore, A.W.: *Model-Based Systems Engineering.* CRC Press, 1993
[10]   Zeigler, B.P.: *Multifacetted Modeling and Discrete Event Simulation.* Academic Press, 1984.

Object–Oriented High Level Modeling of Complex Systems

Karlheinz Agsteiner, Dieter Monjau, Sören Schulze

Department of Computer Science
Technical University of Chemnitz–Zwickau
Chemnitz, Germany

Abstract. We present an object–oriented method to represent knowledge about a set of digital systems. Based on this representation, concrete systems can easily be specified, their implementations in various models such as VHDL or Petri-nets can be derived automatically from a specification by a knowledge based configuration system. In this paper, we focus on the set–theoretic foundations of our model.

1 Introduction

In the last years, several methods for the design of digital systems at the system level have been proposed [9]. Most of these methods, like SpecCharts [11], Statecharts [3], speedCHARTS [10], SDL [4], or Extended Sequence Charts [7], use a graphical representation for their systems. The formal basis of these approaches is formed by communicating concurrent processes, extended finite state machines, and hierarchical descriptions. The methods for system level design with these concepts usually follow a top–down approach: Starting with an initial graphical representation of a certain system, a sequence of refinement steps is executed. The intermediate representations are attributed by VHDL annotations. This refinement process lasts until a complete description of the system's behavior is built that can be compiled into VHDL code which in turn serves as a foundation for a simulation or synthesis.

Our approach is different: Instead of forcing the designer to specify details of the intended system each time a new unit is designed, all properties and dependencies involved in all the systems of a certain domain (eg. all RISC processors) have to be put together only once for building an object oriented domain model.

The basic building blocks of this model are a set of types and a set of relations connecting these types. The types describe concepts met when dealing with systems in the particular domain. To keep our model simple we use only two relations — an *is-a*–relation forming a taxonomical hierarchy which allows to represent specialization and a *has-parts*–relation which builds a decompositional hierarchy. The domain representation is divided into three consecutive levels that cover different aspects of the domain knowledge (how to specify a system, how to decompose it into different functions, and how to implement these functions by hardware or software components). Basically, these levels are connected by $n : m$ relations. Every level contains a *constraint net* devoted to modeling dependencies between classes that cannot be described with our relations.

After a domain model is developed, systems from the domain can be designed easily by converting a specification to a set of classes and constraints in the function level and building a complete tree consisting of instances of these classes using a knowledge based *configuration system* [8]. This tree represents the structure of the system. *Model generators* derive a VHDL or Petri–net description of the system from this tree which can be simulated or synthesized.

2 Representing Domains

Our approach bases on a representation of all the knowledge about a whole domain of digital systems that is needed to specify and implement such a system. Basically, this model consists of three disjoint sets of classes that are connected by certain relations. In order to gain all advantages of the object–oriented paradigm we add the concepts of inheritance and abstract base class.

2.1 A Conceptual Hierarchy

The basic notion in our domain model is a *conceptual hierarchy*. One single hierarchy builds a model of all systems in the domain.

Definition 1 (Conceptual Hierarchy). A *conceptual hierarchy* is defined by a tuple $(S, \text{is-a}, \text{parts}, A_g, A_a)$ where S is a finite set of classes and $\text{is-a} \subseteq S \times S$, $\text{has-parts} \subseteq S \times \mathbb{N} \times S$, $A_g : S \longmapsto (\text{string} \mapsto \mathbb{N})$, $A_a : S \longmapsto (\text{string} \mapsto \mathbb{N} \times \text{string})$ with

- *is-a* is the inverse relation of a "father map" from S to S. Furthermore, *is-a* has to be acyclic,
  $\forall X, Y \in S : X \text{ is-a } Y \Rightarrow \forall n \in \mathbb{N} : \neg(Y \text{ is-a}^n X)$. Notation: $X \overset{is-a}{\longrightarrow} Y$
- In $\text{has-parts}(X, n, Y)$, $n \in \mathbb{N}$ holds the number of parts of type Y an X must have. In contexts where this number is not relevant we write $\text{has-parts}(X, Y)$ as an abbreviation for $\exists n > 0 : \text{has-parts}(X, n, Y)$. $\text{has-parts}(X, 0, Y)$ is defined as equal to $\neg \text{has-parts}(X, Y)$. Using this notation, *has-parts* has to be an acyclic relation like *is-a*. We write $X \overset{n \text{ parts}}{\longrightarrow} Y$.
- A_g maps the name of a generic attribute onto the default value of this attribute. Generic attributes describe parameters of the class that have to be set to certain values in an instance of the class. In the case of a domain model of RISC processors, such an attribute could be the width of a word in this processor, or the size of a cache.
- A_a maps the name of an analysis attribute onto the product of a default value and a string identifying the method used to compute the real value. Analysis attributes, in contrast to generic attributes, describe (physical) properties of a concrete instance (including its parts). For example, physical components of a RISC processor like pipeline registers or ALUs are provided with properties like size or mean response time.

A hierarchy should contain exactly one topmost element. The following definition guarantees this property:

Definition 2 (Well–Defined Hierarchy). A *conceptual hierarchy* $(S, is\text{-}a, has\text{-}parts, A_g, A_a)$ is *well–defined* iff it contains exactly one root class X_{top},

$$\exists_1 X_{top} \in S \; \forall X \in S \setminus \{X_{top}\} \; \exists Y \in S : X \xrightarrow{is-a} Y \vee Y \xrightarrow{parts} X.$$

Graphically, a conceptual hierarchy can be depicted as a directed graph with nodes that represent classes and two different kinds of arcs, one for each relation. Fig. 1 shows an extract of our hierarchy for RISC processors, The root class REGD represents a register file with two read ports and one write port. The figure shows two specializations of a REGD, a REGB that consists of banks, and a REGFD that does not. A closer look at REGB_1, a register with the same behavior as REGB that consists of n =REGBANKS parts of class REGFD reveals that it defines no new attributes or ports but inherits (see 2.3) several of them. The behavior is described as a VHDL architecture body and a Petri–net.

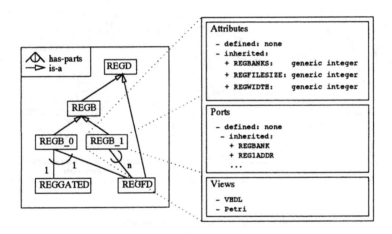

Fig. 1. An example hierarchy

2.2 An Instance Tree

The purpose of a domain model is to implicitly represent a large set of systems. To represent concrete systems, the notion "instance tree" is introduced.

Definition 3 (Instance Tree). An *instance tree* $T = (I, C, has\text{-}parts_i, A_{gi}, A_{ai})$ of a hierarchy H as defined above consists of

− a finite set of instances I,

- a map $C : I \mapsto S$ that represents, of which class every instance is,
- a relation *has-parts$_i$* depending on *has-parts*,
- attribute functions A_{gi}, A_{ai} defined exactly as in the hierarchy.

T is only a valid instance tree if it is fulfills the properties

- presence of a root instance: Let X_{top} be the root class of H. Then $\exists_1 x_{top} \in I$: $C(x_{top}) = X_{top}$.
- correctness of parts: if $x \in T$ with $C(x) = X$ and *has-parts*(X, n, P), then

$$\exists p_1, \ldots, p_n \in I : \forall 1 \leq k \leq n : \textit{has-parts}_i(x, p_k) \wedge \exists m \in \mathbb{N} : \textit{is-a}^m(C(p_k), X)$$

and if I and *has-parts$_i$* are minimal with these properties.

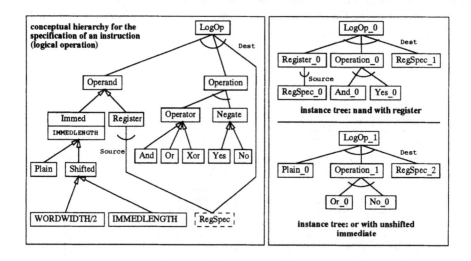

Fig. 2. Conceptual hierarchy and instance tree

Fig. 2 shows an extract of our conceptual hierarchy and possible instance trees. The hierarchy describes the variants of instructions of a RISC CPU that perform boolean operations that are available in our system. A logical operation consists of three parts. Operand specifies how one source operand looks like, Operation represents what operation should be performed (a boolean operation together with an optional negation of the result). RegSpec describes the target register where the result will be placed in. A fourth part which specifies the other source operand of the instruction is inherited from a class not visible in this figure.

The first instance tree represents the instruction *register=register* nand *register* that takes the contents of two registers, performs a negated and on them, and places the result in the target register. The second one describes the instruction *register=register* or *immediate*. Not visible in the figure is that the attribute IMMEDLENGTH is available in instance `Plain_0` and set to a reasonable value that can differ from the default. The two instance trees are compatible to the conceptual hierarchy and differ only by the specializations they use.

Using a conceptual hierarchy as a model of a certain domain and an instance tree as a description of a system in this domain it is possible to represent a broad range of domains. However, for reasons given in [2] it is useful to adopt ideas presented in [6] and [5] to introduce a domain model consisting of three distinct conceptual levels, each of them containing a single hierarchy:

- a specification level which allows the designer to specify a unit informally in a convenient manner. In the case of RISC CPUs this description of the intended system could be the desired instruction set and restrictions concerning performance, size, costs, number and width of CPU's registers. The appearance of this level strongly depends on the respective domain, therefore it is necessary to develop this level from the scratch each time a new domain is analyzed. When the whole domain model is completed and concrete units have to be developed, interaction with the designer usually takes place at this level, so tools should be supplied to assist in this activity. In designing RISC processors, for example, an "instruction set editor" could provide a convenient way to select the instructions and addressing modes the processor should have. Fig. 3 shows the top classes of a specification hierarchy for RISC processors. Classes marked by an underlined square are incomplete.

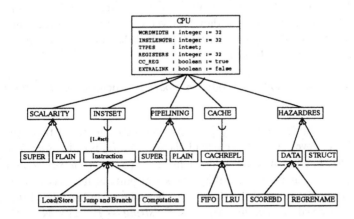

Fig. 3. Top classes of a specification hierarchy

- A *function level* which consists of *classes* representing the different functions that a unit from the domain can implement and relations between them. In addition to attributes, function classes contain a set of ports that describe the interface of the class and a set of views modeling the behavior of a class instance using different models like VHDL, Petri–nets, or temporal logic. This level contains a complete model of each possible system function but still doesn't care about how this function is realized, i. e. if it is implemented as hardware or software, or if one hardware component is used to implement several functions.The top classes of our function hierarchy for RISC processors with a pipeline of five stages are shown in Fig. 4.

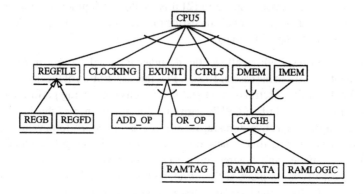

Fig. 4. Function hierarchy for RISC processors

– A *component level* has to provide implementations for the classes in the function level. This level can be seen as an object–oriented component library, therefore no specializations are permitted within this level. For every class at the function level, there exists a set of "key components" (cf. [8]) that are necessary in any case to implement the classes' behavior.

Definition 4 (Domain Model). A *domain model* is a defined as $(H_s, H_f, H_c, M_{sf}, M_{fc})$, where

– $H_s = (S_s, \text{is-}a_s, \text{has-parts}_s, A_{g_s}, A_{a_s})$ is a conceptual hierarchy that represents the specification level. An instance tree of classes from H_s is called *specification*.
– $H_f = (h_f, P, V)$ is an extended hierarchy: $h_f = (S_f, \text{is-}a_f, \text{has-parts}_f, A_{g_f}, A_{a_f})$ is a conceptual hierarchy. P defines the set of ports of this class. Ports are used to specify the interface of the class — the behavior of an instance of the class can only be observed by examining its ports. $P : string \mapsto \mathbb{B} \times \mathbb{B} \times \mathbb{N}$ specifies a map from a port name to a tuple (i, o, w) where i and o are true, if the port is an input (output) port, and w contains the width of the port in bits. V defines the set of views the class consists of. A view represents the behavior of an instance of the class in a certain model. $V : string \mapsto string$ is a map from a name of a view to a string that describes the behavior in terms of the view. When modeling RISC processors, sensible views are VHDL, temporal logic, and Petri–nets. An instance tree at this level is called construction.
– $H_c = H_{c1}, \ldots, H_{cl}$ for some $l \in \mathbb{N}$ is defined as a set of hierarchies, each of them corresponding to a component and its parts. Specializations are already resolved on this level, therefore $\forall i < l : \text{is-}a_{ci} = \emptyset$.

– M_{sf} is a mapping relation from the specification level to the function level that associates a specification class C with an incomplete path from the root class of the function level to a class C':

$$M_{sf} \subseteq S_s \times S_f^*, \text{ where } f(C) = (c_1, \ldots, c_m = C') \Rightarrow \forall i, 1 < i < m \; \exists n, n':$$
$$\left(\text{is-a}^{-1} \cup \text{has-parts}\right)^n (c_{i-1}, c_i) \wedge \left(\text{is-a}^{-1} \cup \text{has-parts}\right)^{n'} (c_i, c_{i+1})$$

– M_{fc} is defined as a relation mapping classes in the function level to classes in the component level, $M_{fc} \subseteq S_f \times S_c$.

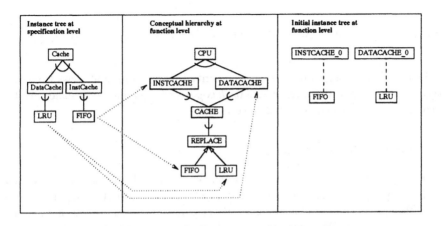

Fig. 5. From a specification to the function level

The reason for associating a sequence of function classes to a specification class in M_{sf} instead of a single one can be shown by a simple example from the domain of RISC processors: Suppose the designer specifies that he wants a separate data and instruction cache for his CPU and selects "last recently used" as replacement strategy for the data cache and "first in, first out" as the one for the instruction cache. Suppose further the function level of the domain model contains a class CACHE representing all kinds of caches. CACHE has a part that describes the replacement strategy. Specializations of this class are LRU and FIFO. Fig. 5 shows this situation. We see that is not sufficient to simply select a one function class for each instance present in the specification. The consequence would be that it could not be decided which strategy should be used for which cache. Since we want to be able to select function classes somewhere else in the hierarchy, we cannot simply use (LRU, INSTCACHE) $\cup$ (LRU, LRU) $\subseteq M_{sf}$.

Therefore we use the mapping relation described above to describe how an initial, incomplete tree of instances in the function level can be derived from an instance tree at the specification level.

2.3 Adding Inheritance to Our Model

In object–oriented frameworks, inheritance is a key concept to minimizing redundancy in class descriptions. The concept behind inheritance is that a class should pass on its properties to its specializations. The notion of overloading appertains to inheritance. If a class explicitly defines a property it inherits the inherited one is irrelevant for it and its specializations.

In our system, classes inherit all attributes, ports (if available), and the *has-parts* relation of their parents. Formally, inheritance could be defined by deriving an inheriting relation from a non–inheriting one by an inheritance closure:

Definition 5 (Inheritance Closure). In a hierarchy H based on a set S of classes, a relation R' is the *inheritance closure* of a relation $R : S \times X$ (with any finite set X) iff

- $R \subseteq R'$
- $C_p, C_c \in S \wedge is\text{-}a(C_p, C_c) \wedge R'' = \{(C_c, x) | x \in X \wedge R(C_p, x) \wedge \neg R(C_c, x)\} \implies R'' \subseteq R'$

Similarly to specializations, instances inherit attributes, ports, and views from their classes (in some sense they even inherit the *has-parts* relation since an instance tree has to correspond to its hierarchy like defined in Def. 3).

2.4 Designing Concrete Systems

After a domain is described using the model shown above, real systems can be designed. The first step of our design cycle is to specify a system. As a result of this step, an instance tree at the specification level is produced. By mapping all classes present in it onto the function level via the M_{sf} relation an initial, incomplete construction is derived from the specification.

A knowledge based configuration system expands this tree by adding instances according to H_f until it is complete in the sense of Def. 3. During this completion process the configuration system often has to decide which specialization of a class to use or how to fit parts together to build a complete system. The result of the configuration process is an instance tree T_f consisting of instances of function level classes. T_f represents one specific system. Model generators produce prototypes from the views in T_f. A more detailed description of system design using our approach can be found in [1].

3 Conclusion and Future Research

The approach we presented is characterized by the following features: An informal and intuitive specification, a fast design cycle of systems after a domain has been described, and several mechanisms to exploit the reuse of system components, together with the features common to most object–oriented models like a modularity and transparency — features that allow to understand a big model just by looking at the interface of each class in the model and the connections between the classes without having to worry about how each class is implemented. The major drawback of our approach is that before being able to design the first system the whole domain has to be represented. However, after a certain number of systems have been designed the number of instances used will exceed the number of classes described. After this point is reached the advantages of reuse will outweigh the costs of building a knowledge base.

During the first nine months of this project we have developed a partial function and component level for RISC processors with a 5-staged pipeline, a specification hierarchy for RISC instructions based on the MIPS and PowerPC families of processors, a model generator for VHDL, and an analysis tool for estimating the area required for a component and its parts. Our priorities during the next months will be the knowledge based configuration system itself, on a graphical user interface, and on the mapping from specification to function level. Another major part of our research will be extending our model by decomposing several RISC CPUs and adding the informations obtained by this process to the function level.

Our work is supported by the "Deutsche Forschungsgemeinschaft" under project VF 1298.

References

1. K. Agsteiner, D. Monjau, and S. Schulze. Object oriented high–level modeling of system components for the generation of VHDL. In *Proc. Europ. Design Automation Conf. EURO-DAC'95*, Brighton, Great Britain, September 18-22 1995.
2. K. Agsteiner, D. Monjau, and S. Schulze. Object oriented system level specification and synthesis of heterogeneous systems. In *Proc. EUROMICRO '95*, Como, Italy, September 4-7 1995.
3. D. Drusinsky and D. Harel. Using Statecharts for hardware description and synthesis. In *IEEE Transactions on Computer–Aided Design*, 1989.
4. W. Glunz, T. Rössel, T. Kruse, and D. Monjau. Integrating SDL and VHDL for system–level hardware design. In *Proc. Intl. Symposium on Computer Hardware Description Languages CHDL*, Ottawa, Canada, 1993.
5. H. Haugeneder, E. Lehmann, and P. Struß. Knowledge–based configuration of operating systems — problems in modeling the domain knowledge. In W. Brauer and B. Radig, editors, *Wissensbasierte Systeme*, number 112 in Informatik Fachberichte. Springer, Heidelberg, 1985.
6. H.-P. Juan, N. D. Holmes, S. Bakshi, and D. D. Gajski. Top-down modeling of RISC processors in VHDL. In *Proc. Europ. Design Automation Conf. EURO-DAC'93*, Hamburg, Germany, 1993.
7. S. Kahlert, J.-U. Knäbchen, and D. Monjau. Design and analysis of heterogeneous systems using graphically oriented methods: A case study. In *Proc. SASIMI'93*, Nara, Japan, 1993.
8. S. Mittal and F. Frayman. Towards a generic model of configuration tasks. In *Proc. Eleventh International Joint Conference on AI*, pages 1395–1401, Detroit, 1989.
9. S. Narayan and D. Gajski. Features supporting system–level specification in hdls. In *Proc. Europ. Design Automation Conf. EURO-DAC'93*, Hamburg, Germany, 1993.
10. SpeedChart, Inc. *speedCHART — User's Manual*, 1993.
11. F. Vahid, S. Narayan, and D. D. Gajski. SpecCharts: A language for system level specification and synthesis. In *Proc. Intl. Symposium on Computer Hardware Description Languages CHDL*, 1991.

Multifacetted, Object Oriented Modeling in the Transportation Domain [*]

Herbert Praehofer and Franz Pichler

Systems Theory and Information Engineering
Johannes Kepler University
A-4040 Linz, Austria

Abstract

Multimodal transport, i.e. transport which is accomplished by different transport means like truck and train, is a most important issue of the European transport policy. It offers a viable and efficient alternative to long distance road transport. However, due to its much more complex organizational needs compared to pure road transport, multimodal transport systems have to be designed with utmost care and its operation has to be well coordinated and managed. In this paper we discuss concepts and techniques evolved in systems theory based modeling and simulation research to provide a methodology for large scale transport system analysis and design. The methodology gains its power by integrating several distinct approaches, viz. multilevel, hierarchical modeling as developed by Mesarovic, multifacetted object oriented modeling as defined by Zeigler, and multiformalism, modular hierarchical systems theory based modeling formalisms.

1   Introduction

Multimodal transport, i.e. transport which is accomplished by different transport means like truck and train, is a most important issue of the European transport policy. It offers a viable and efficient alternative to long distance road transport. However, due to its much more complex organizational needs compared to pure road transport, multimodal transport systems have to be designed with utmost care and its operation has to be well coordinated and managed.

Transportation systems are in reality highly complex, heterogeneous objects. Therefore, modeling and analysis of transport systems requires careful attention to the methodology to be applied. As major difficulties in transport system design we identify the following:

- Transport systems are of extraordinary complexity with many different components which highly interact.
- The subsystems identified are of diverse character. Their investigation needs many different scientific disciplines and has to be performed from various perspectives and for various purposes.

---

[*] Work supported by SIEMENS AG, Munich, ZFE ST

- The data about the system and environment are derived from different types of observations by different procedures which are not necessarily compatible.
- The interaction of the components do not show any regularities and simplicities.
- Usually, in any decision situation in the design of a transport system, numerous or even an infinite number of alternatives have to be taken into account.
- As future economic and social developments have to be incorporated in the studies, the decisions derived are based on the uncertainties of such predictions.

To meet these difficulties, modeling of transportation systems cannot be subject to analytical methods like, linear programming, statistics, etc. alone. Modeling and analysis of transportation systems in a comprehensive way requires in addition a multidimensional, interdisciplinary modeling and simulation approach. To analyze transport systems in a comprehensive way, in particular considering its dynamic properties, one has to rely on computer simulation methods. Computer simulation has, as it is generally known, the following strength:

- it is generally applicable,
- it allows one to investigate quickly different scenarios,
- it can be applied in all stages of analysis and design,
- it can be applied without risk, and
- it allows to predict future states.

In the following we discuss concepts and techniques evolved in systems theory based modeling and simulation and knowledge-based system design research to provide a methodology for large scale transport system analysis and design. The methodology gains its power by integrating several distinct approaches, viz. multilevel, hierarchical modeling as developed by Mesarovic [2], multifacetted object oriented modeling as defined by Zeigler [13], and multiformalism, modular hierarchical systems theory based modeling formalisms [7, 6].

2 Multilevel, Hierarchical Modeling and Simulation

Developments during the second half of this century are characterized by the emergence of truly large organizations. The new challenges to science and research imposed by that fact has been accounted for by the development of a multilevel, hierarchical system theory by Mesarovic and Takahara [2, 4]. In their approach to systems theory they recognize that large organizations and systems, evade complete and detailed descriptions and have to be described by a set of interacting subsystems. Therefore, complex systems depict a multilevel, hierarchical structure, i.e. a vertical arrangement of interacting subsystems. The operation on any level is influenced directly from the higher levels, most often from the immediately superseding level. This influence reflects a priority of importance in the actions and goals of the higher levels and is called *intervention*. On the other side, the higher levels directly depend on the performance of the lower ones. As higher levels determine the actions of the lower levels, the performance of the lower level subsystems directly define the success of the higher ones.

The multistrata modeling approach as one special kind of multilevel modeling takes into account a complex system's multiplicities of behavioral aspects. The total system is described by a *set of models*, each concerned with the system as viewed from one particular perspective. Each of the representations at the different levels serves a given purpose. Important is that each level refers to the entire system and the difference between the levels is actually in terms, variables and concepts used to describe the system. Each representation has its individual laws and modes of operation. One such representation is called a *stratum* and the entire system a *multistrata* or a *stratified system*.

The selection of the individual strata to describe a system is not fixed for a particular system but depends upon the individual knowledge and interest of the modeler (problem solver). However, in most systems strata exist which appear as natural or inherent. This is especially true for the lower levels of abstractions. An observer from outside, easily would see the operational aspects of a transport system - how goods are transported - however it is much more difficult to recognize its decision making and management policy stratum.

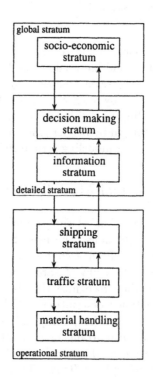

Fig. 1. Multistrata model of a transport system

In the following we give one possible stratification of transport system. As outlined above, the identification of the various strata to represent a system depends on the particular objectives and interests of the observer. Fig. 1 shows a transport system as a hierarchical arrangement of six strata. At the lowest level, in the *material handling stratum* the modeling goal is to describe how transport goods are handled, loaded and unloaded to various transport devices like containers, how containers are loaded on vehicles, and how the actual transport is carried out. This is a very detailed level of abstraction and, usually, will be employed to study the operation of loading transport devices or design transport terminals. As a next stratum we identify the *traffic stratum* where the transport system is described by the traffic carrying the transport. Here different vehicles with different mode of operation are represented. Their behavior is modeled as moving objects in traffic facilities (roads, railways, waterways). The stratum above the traffic stratum is what we called the *shipping stratum*. In this stratum the transport of goods is represented in terms of flow of goods shipped between different locations. These first three strata define the physical strata (operational strata) which together represent the physical manifestation of the system.

The stratum above the shipping stratum is the *information stratum*. It provides for the information infrastructure for a transport system. As a next stratum we identify the *decision making stratum*. Here decision are made how and where goods are shipped. This stratum heavily relies on the information stratum which provides for the information of the status of the transport system, in particular, about traffic facilities and transport devices available. Within the decision making stratum, usually we will identify a multilayer decision system. The model of the transport system provided by the information strata and the decision strata gives already detailed information for the detailed logistic to be used for managing the system on a command level (detailed stratum). As the highest stratum we use the *socio-economic stratum* (global stratum). In this stratum all the social, economic, and also ecological constraints are represented. In particular, it also defines the transport demands in terms of economic factors.

3   Levels of Resolution / Aggregation

A model for a given stratum can be developed in many different ways and in different degrees of detail. The choice in such a case depends primarily on the purpose for which the model is developed but also on the existing body of knowledge about the relevant phenomena and the type and amount of data available. Principal choices concern the level of decomposition of the model and the degree of aggregation of variables. The stratification of the transport system and the levels of aggregation/resolution for each stratum define an orthogonal relationship as shown in Fig. 2. Examples of different levels of resolution/aggregation are shown in detail for the traffic stratum and the socio-economic stratum. In the traffic stratum usually three major levels of resolution/aggregation are identified. In *macroscopic traffic models* traffic is represented as continuous flow in traffic channels. In *microscopic traffic models* the movements of individual vehi-

345

cles is described in detail. In *mesoscopic traffic modeling* which is located between
the two others, individual objects are identified as in microscopic level but its
dynamic is represented in terms of flow parameters as in macroscopic models.

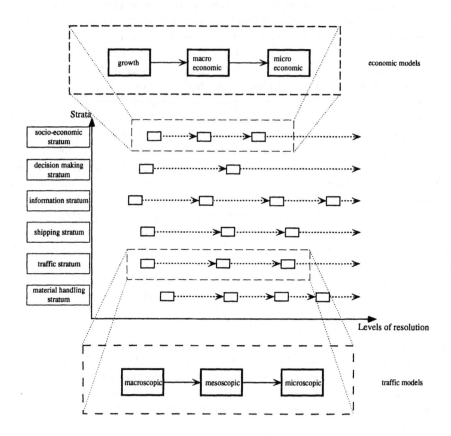

Fig. 2. Orthogonal diagram of strata hierarchy and aggregation/resolution levels

In the socio-economic stratum many types of levels of resolution/aggregation
can be imagined. First the stratum can be decomposed into various interacting
economic regions, e.g. individual countries. Then each region can be described
at different levels of aggregations. According to [3], possible level of aggregations
for an economy are the *growth*, the *macro*, and the *micro level*. On the growth
level the economy is modeled by one variable representing the gross regional
product. On the macro level the gross regional product is specified in terms of
capital formation and production function. On the micro level the production is
decomposed into various production sectors and intersectional demands in terms
of an input/output matrix.

The models at different levels of resolution and aggregation should not be stand-alone units but should interrelate. More abstract models should present as abstractions of more detailed ones. More concrete models should manifest as concretizations of the abstract one. The *system morphism* concepts as defined in system theory [12, 5] can provide a basis for formal treatment of interrelations of models of systems at different abstraction levels. The system morphism guarantees that state correspondence is preserved under state transitions and outputs for the base model and its abstraction. This is depicted in Fig. 3. Starting the base model in a state s_0 and its abstract model in a homomorphic state $\bar{s}_0 = H_S(s_0)$ and injecting an input sequence ω into the base and its corresponding version $\bar{\omega} = H_X(\omega)$ into the abstract model, then also the resulting state s_f and $\bar{s}_f$ correspond under H_S, i.e., $\bar{s}_f = H_S(s_f)$. Similarly, the output is preserved by an homomorphic map H_Y. If the diagram of Fig. 3 commutes , we speak of a *system homomorphism* (also *system dynamorphism*).

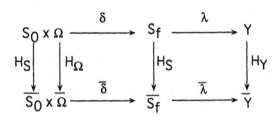

Fig. 3. System morphism guarantees that state and output correspondence is preserved under state transitions and outputs

Besides this exact system morphism, in practice frequently approximate system morphism are applied. Here not the exact matching of the states is required, but the state $\bar{s}_f$ and the homomorphic image of the state of the original system $H_S(s_f)$ are allowed to differ only within certain bounds ϵ, i.e., $d_{\bar{s}}(\bar{s}_f - H_S(s_f)) < \epsilon$ where $d_{\bar{s}}$ is a distance measure for states in the abstract model.

Abstraction can be built in several ways. The following basic ways to build abstractions are identified [13, 15]:

- Coarsening one or more state variable values,
- Aggregating several state variables into one state variable,
- Abstraction of the state transitions,
- Replacing deterministic behavior by stochastic behavior,
- Abstraction of the time base,
- Taking out part of the system's behavior and neglecting the rest, and
- Grouping of components.

Usually, when building an abstract model, several types of basic abstractions work together. Figure 4 gives an example of a multilevel abstraction of a

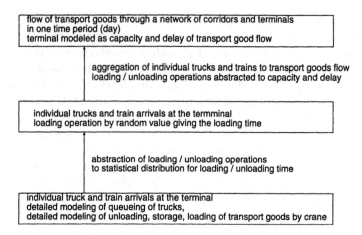

Fig. 4. Different levels of abstraction of a multimodal transport terminal.

operation of a transport train terminal. At the lowest level, the operations of the individual trucks and trains are modeled in detail. Such a model could be applied to study in detail the operation, layout, and the organization of a terminal. At a next higher abstraction level, the terminal is used as a component in a transport network. The loading and unloading operations are not modeled in detail but by a stochastic parameter giving the loading/unloading time. The statistical distribution for the stochastic parameter is derived from observations in the detail terminal model. The various state transitions for loading/unloading are abstracted to one state transition. Due to this coarse representation of the terminal operation, the state space can be coarsened significantly.

At the next level of abstraction a model is built which is applied as a component in a system modeling the flow of goods in a network of corridors and terminals. The terminal is represented as a node which delays arriving transport flows. Also it is characterized by a maximal capacity of transport flow it can handle. The abstraction is built from the model at the lower level by aggregating the individual trucks and trains to transport goods flow parameters. The loading and unloading operations are abstracted to continuous parameters representing the delay of the flow in the terminal and the capacity of the terminal.

In that way, abstract models should be built based on detailed models. However, we also envision components at different abstraction levels integrated in one simulation model. The system morphism concept allows one to substitute a model at a detailed level of abstraction by a model which is at a higher level of abstraction. It is always possible to derive a coarse model from a more detailed one. However, the opposite direction is usually not as simple. As morphism mappings usually are onto mappings from the set of detailed models to the sets of the abstracted models, unique inverse mappings do not exist. To accomplish this, additional assumptions have to be made or more knowledge has to be made available. Very often, however, help can be given by stochastic methods. This can be illustrated by conceiving a transport flow network with a detailed subsystem of a terminal. The transport flow variable which is input to the submodel at the detailed level has to broken up into a sequence of arrivals of individual trucks and trains. An exponential distribution with the value of the flow variable as mean arrival rate can be used to stochastically represent the interarrival times. However, if different types of trucks and trains have to be generated, more assumptions about distribution of types have to be made.

4 Multifacetted Modeling

Multifacetted modeling methodology as presented in [13] is an approach which recognizes the existence of multiplicities of objectives and models in the problem solving enterprise. A comprehensive model incorporating all the different strata and all the abstraction levels as shown in Fig. 2 certainly is beyond the complexity measures we can meet and can therefore not be considered to be built. Instead we can envisage a collection of partial models, each oriented to one or more objectives. In an objectives-driven methodology, the multiplicity of objectives result in multiplicity of models representing different aspects of the same real system. Only some aspects, the aspects of the real system relevant for the objectives in hand, may be incorporated into the model.

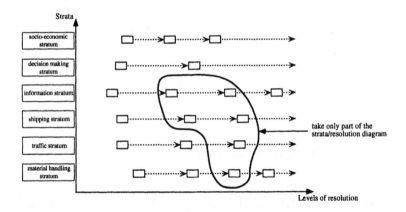

Fig. 5. Extract of orthogonal strata and aggregation diagram.

In context of our orthogonal diagram we understand a partial model as an extraction of only a very limited part of the strata hierarchy and abstraction levels as shown in Fig. 5. When the goal of an computer-aided environment is not the construction and usage of one single model for one single objective, but when a set of different models emerged from different objectives should be built and maintained as whole, new concepts and techniques have to be introduced. Zeigler summarized the concepts introduced for that purpose by the term *multifacetted modeling methodology* [13].

Management of the multiplicities of objectives and models calls for a systematization and organization of models. Models should show good decomposition and modularity to facilitate exchange and recycling of components. Models are conceived as embodying knowledge of the real system. Thus models should have some characteristics of knowledge - it should be transmittable from one person to another and open to modification, improvement and combination with other knowledge.

The organization of models is accomplished by a *model base* which is central to the modeling process. Fig. 6 depicts the modeling and simulation activities as an objective-driven process [13]. New objectives initiate the model construction which is based on knowledge available from the model base and also from the data base. The emerging model structures are immediately stored in the model base to facilitate reuse. Model construction is followed by simulation, validation of the model, and finally experimentation. This may result in the formulation of new, refined objectives which reinitiates the modeling and simulation cycle.

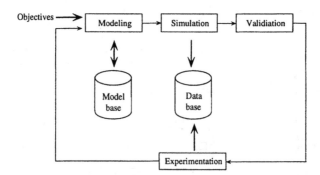

Fig. 6. Objectives-driven modeling process.

The heart of the multifacetted modeling methodology is the *system entity structure* [13] knowledge representation scheme. This knowledge representation scheme has its origins in the systems theory context and in artificial intelligence. Systems theory provides the concepts of decomposition and couplings while it does not provide a representation of taxonomic knowledge. This can be accomplished by the usage of the frame concept of artificial intelligence and the object oriented programming paradigm. The system entity structure incorporates these concepts to represent a system in its multiplicity of decomposition and possible variants. It is used to integrate the various models representing the different aspects of the real system and to represent all feasible configurations of a system design.

The system entity structure is represented by a tree-like graph with three types of nodes. An *entity* node represents a conceptual part of the real system which has been identified as a component in one or more decompositions. An entity may have several *aspect* nodes each denoting a possible decomposition of the entity and therefore may have several entities. An entity may have several *specialization* nodes each representing a classification of possible variants of the entity. Inheritance is defined for entity variants in the way that properties of general entities are inherited to their specializations. In that, the system entity structure is an advanced objected oriented concept, however, differs from other object oriented modeling paradigm as it recognizes the existence of different decomposition of entities and coupling constraints.

Fig. 7 sketches an example system entity structure of a transportation system. There are two different aspects, viz. the *technical aspect* an the *economic aspect*. In the technical aspect the system is decomposed into sets *road connections, terminals,* and *railway corridors* which decompose into individual road connections, terminals and corridors, respectively. The terminal here is again decomposed into *load/unloading stations, loading units, storage,* and *control.* For loading units three different types are identified, viz. *automated guided vehicles, crane,* and *stacker.* In the economic aspect the system is decomposed into main *economic regions* and each region is decomposed into a component modeling the *demand* and one modeling the *supply* of goods. Economic regions are then classified into *industrial, rural* and *mixed.*

The system entity structure only represents the static structures of the possible models. A *dynamic model base* contains the dynamic structures of the models in form of system specifications. In the next section basic modeling formalisms to describe dynamical systems are discussed. Together with a base of system entity structures, the dynamic model base forms a knowledge base representing static as well as dynamic knowledge about real systems.

This knowledge is organized that the entities in the system entity structure contain references to dynamic models in the model base. Several models at different levels of resolution may be connected with an entity. An entity also may have a dynamic model at a high level of abstraction, but also may be decomposed into several subcomponents, which then with their connected dynamic models represent the entity at a detailed level. The dynamic model connected with the entity is a homomorphic abstraction of the coupled model connected with the decomposition of the entity.

Employing a system entity structure / model base, the modeling process is described in a more elaborate way as follows: Driven by the objectives, the entity structure base is consulted to retrieve the static structure of a model which is appropriate for the objectives. This process is denoted *pruning* the entity structure [13, 10] and is accomplished as follows: First an entity is selected which represents the whole system which should be investigated. In the transportation example, this could be the transportation system or also only one particular terminal. From this starting point appropriate decompositions and variants are

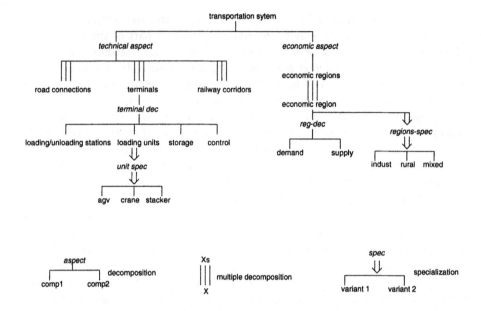

Fig. 7. System entity structure of a transportation system

selected until entities are reached which have connected dynamic models in the
model base with appropriate resolution to satisfy our objectives. Based on the
resulting static model structure, a hierarchical model is built by retrieving the
knowledge from the dynamical model base and coupling these models as given
by the coupling constraints. When no appropriate model can be found in the
entity structure / dynamic model base, a new model has to be built from scratch
which can be recycled by putting it into the entity structure / model base.

5 Modular, Hierarchical, Multiformalism Modeling and Simulation

5.1 Modular, Hierarchical Modeling and Simulation

The description of the transportation domain as a quasi-decomposable system
(see also [11]) strives for a modular, hierarchical object oriented modeling and
simulation methodology as promoted by systems theory based simulation research [14]. Simulation models are built by coupling together atomic building
blocks through their well defined input/output interface (modular modeling).
Coupled models set up in this way are again usable as components in a more
complex coupled model (hierarchical modeling).

The approach facilitates top-down design allowing to continually break up
the entire system into subsystems. And the approach also supports bottom-up

design. Modularity allows to set up bases of reusable building blocks which can be plugged into a system through the well defined input/output interface. In this way it is easy to set up and test different structure variants of a system.

5.2 Basic Modeling and Simulation Strategies

As outlined above, transportation systems can be described at different levels of abstractions with various levels of details, from different perspective, and for different purposes. For these different system descriptions, different system specification formalisms are provided. From the simulation point of view we identify three major types of simulation strategies, viz. continuous, discrete time, and discrete event simulation [12]:

Continuous simulation: In the transportation domain, continuous simulation is applicable in the higher levels of abstractions where major flows of material, energy, and information is considered. However, continuous simulation also is used at the lowest strata and levels of abstractions where continuous movements of objects should be studied in detail (e.g. in microscopic traffic simulation).

System Dynamics as introduced by Forrester [1] is a general strategy for modeling continuous systems with totally unknown laws and are preferable used in social-economic systems analysis. While the method can be used to construct models in a completely inductive manner, it will allow to incorporate in the models any physical insight that may exist. Inductive modeling also will be of major importance in the transport domain, in particular, in the socio-economic stratum. In System Dynamics, the model is specified as a set of level variables which denote the actual state variables. For these level variables the derivatives are specified in terms of inflow and outflow *rates* or *flows* which may depend on values of level, other rate variables, or some constant system parameters called *converters*. The relations of the different variables in a model is represented by so-called *structure diagrams*. Such a model is readily implementable as a set of first order differential equations.

Discrete time simulation: If the system is described through a next state function which defines the state at the next time step based on the current time and input, the methods of discrete time simulation are applied. Simulation execution is done stepwise. Often, discrete time models are morphisms of differential equation specified models. Examples of formal models of discrete time systems are difference equations, finite state machines or marked Petri-nets.

Macroscopic models of traffic flow dynamics can often be specified by discrete time difference equations. First the roads are subdivided into networks of segments (typically 250 to 500 m long). With respect to this spatial discretization for each segment i a difference equation specifies the traffic density $c_i(t + 1)$ for time $t + 1$ based on state values at time t by

$$c_j(t + 1) = c_j(t) + (\Delta T / \Delta_j)[q_{j-1} - q_j]_{(t)}$$

where q_{j-1} is the volume entering from the upstream segment, q_j is the volume leaving to the downstream segment, ΔT is the constant time interval of the difference equation, and Δ_j is the length of the segment j.

Discrete event simulation: In distinction to continuous simulation where state changes are smoothly, state changes in discrete event simulation are described to occur event-like from one particular value to the next. In that, the changes can occur at arbitrary time instances and do not occur in fixed steps in time. Simulation proceeds from one event to next omitting the times between events. Discrete event simulation has acquired a dominant role for system analysis in such diverse application areas like digital logic verification, flexible manufacturing system design, computer system design, communication systems design, queuing system analysis etc. In the transportation domain it has acquired an important role in many different areas, e.g. to analyze material handling systems in automated warehouses or to evaluate different storekeeping policies. Also in traffic simulation discrete event simulation is used at the medium and lower levels of abstractions (mesoscopic traffic simulation).

Due to the diversity of applications of discrete event simulation, many different modeling strategies - so-called *world views* - have emerged. The strategies are classified into three main categories. The *event scheduling* strategy emphasizes the prescheduling of events. The system's behavior is specified by a set of event routines which are scheduled to occur at particular times in the future. When such a time is reached the event has to occur and the event routine is executed leading to changes in states. In the *activity scanning* strategy the activation of event routines also can be determined in terms of *test predicates*. Only if the test is passed, the event routine is executed, otherwise the event is said to be due and has to wait until the predicate becomes true. The *process interaction* strategy integrates the former two. Additionally, it specifies the system by a set of interacting quasi-parallel process routines each of which describes the dynamic behavior of one component in the system. The *transaction flow* strategy is an important variation of the process interaction strategy where the process routines describe the flow of transactions through a static system.

The DEVS formalism as been introduced by Zeigler [12] as a system theoretic formalism for discrete event modeling. In that it is independent of any particular application and world view. Additionally it allows modular, hierarchical model construction as demanded by the multifacetted modeling approach. Because of its interdisciplinary character and its modular, hierarchical modeling capabilities we promote the DEVS-based approach to discrete event modeling.

The following example sketches the design of mesoscopic simulation model for integrated transport chains. The model shall serve as an example how DEVS-based simulation can be employed for the design of a information infrastructure in intermodal freight transport.

To handle the complexity and provide for easy changes in the design, the system is split into a hierarchy of components. In this example we only deal with the top level of the hierarchy. There are two major functional components:

the transport system itself and the information system. The first part represents the physical structure of the transport domain such as the road and traffic infrastructure, regions, hauliers and shippers, terminals etc. The second part is dedicated to the control of the system and will fulfill tasks like communication, route planing, dispatching, reservation etc. It will be structured according to the principles of multilayer decision systems.

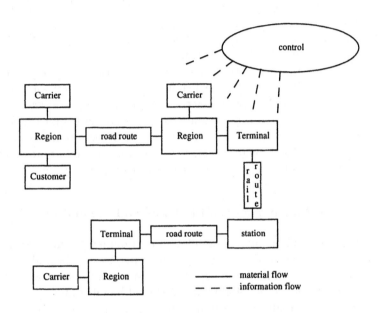

Fig. 8. Integrated transport chain model

The transport system consists of the following types of components: (compare with Fig. 8)

- customer: generate transport demands which include the source and destination region, the pick-up and expected delivery time.
- carrier (haulier, shipper): provides the containers and rolling stock for the transport and represents the source and destination of orders. The carrier receives the orders from the customer and is responsible for picking-up and delivering the freight.
- region: represents in a highly aggregated way a complex local road network such as a town and its suburban area or an industrial center. A region can be connected with carriers, railway terminals and roads. It is characterized by the current traffic density which effects the average driving time of trucks moving in the region. A second characteristic is the distance between all models connected to the region to calculate e.g. the driving time from a

road route to a carrier. A region can also be used as a node in the traffic network like highway crossings.

- road route: this is the element which connects two regions by a road. Its characteristics are the traffic density, which affects the average speed of trucks, and the length of the road. When the average speed reaches a specific lowest level, a signal is sent to the control to signal the traffic jam. The control tries to find alternative routes for trucks.
- railway station: a node in the rail network. It delegates all trains to the next rail route.
- railway station with shunting: a station with an additional shunting feature. Here cars are assembled to whole trains.
- terminal: it is a railway station also providing for the interface between the road and the rail. It will have a loading/unloading station and a storage place for containers. A parking place is required for empty waggons.
- rail-route: connects two railway stations. Since no individual traffic moves on a rail route, it is rather easier to control and observe than a comparable transport by trucks through a road route. A jam can only occur on railway stations, when trains have to wait for the next route to become free.

5.3 Combined Multiformalism Modeling and Simulation

In a comprehensive modeling and simulation environment, it must be possible to integrate models specified in different formalisms, to allow a multiformalism modeling and simulation methodology. This is even more desired when various subsystems at different levels of abstraction should be integrated.

The DEVS-based multiformalism methodology as introduced in [7] provides a basis for the integration of the various simulation types. It introduces a system specification formalism for combined modeling and shows how components of different types can be coupled in a modular hierarchical way into a *multiformalism network*.

6 Summary and Outlook

In this paper we have discussed approaches to support modeling and simulation of large-scale multimodal transportation systems. In particular we worked out that transportation systems have to be modeled as multilevel stratified system with various levels of resolution and abstraction. The various models can be built employing different modeling formalisms with different simulation strategies which have to be combined to a multiformalism modeling and simulation methodology. The organization of the different models can be accomplished by an object oriented knowledge representation scheme, most preferable the system entity structure knowledge representation scheme with the possibility to represent various decompositions and classification of entities. The system entity structure can also be used to organize the models at various levels of resolution.

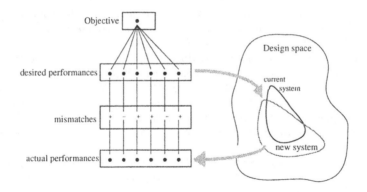

Fig. 9. Knowledge-based system design environment

The realization of a simulation-based decision support and design environment is underway [8, 9]. It is based on the DEVS-based multiformalism simulation methodology described in [7, 6]. As a final stage of the developments we envision an environment which should support the designer in all phases of his design in a generate and test manner (see Fig. 9). Several different types of knowledge have to cooperate to fulfill this. The design space is represented by the system entity structure and the dynamic model base. Additionally we will use a rule based approach for representing design constraints similar as in [10]. Design objectives manifest as desired performance variables. They should guide the selection of the design alternatives. Actual performances are computed by simulation and other means which then are compared to the desired performances. The eventual difference may initiate a new generate and test cycle.

References

1. J. W. Forrester. *Principles of Systems*. Wright-Allen Press, Cambridge, Mass., 1968.
2. M. Mesarovic, D. Macko, and Y. Takahara. *Theory of Hierarchical, Multilevel Systems*. Academic Press, New York, 1970.
3. M. Mesarovic and E. Pestel, editors. *Multilevel Computer Model of World Development System*. IIASA Symposium Proceedings, Laxenburg, Austria, 1974.
4. M. Mesarovic and Y. Takahara. *General Systems Theory: Mathematical Foundations*. Academic Press, New York, 1975.
5. L. Padulo and M.A. Arbib. *Systems Theory*. Saunders, Philadelphia, 1974.
6. F. Pichler and H. Schwaertzel, editors. *CAST Methods in Modelling*. Springer-Verlag, 1992.
7. H. Praehofer. *System Theoretic Foundations for Combined Discrete-Continuous System Simulation*. PhD thesis, Johannes Kepler University of Linz, Linz, Austria, 1991.

8. H. Praehofer, F. Auernig, and G. Reisinger. An environment for DEVS-based multiformalims simulation in Common Lisp / CLOS. *Discrete Event Dynamic Systems: Theory and Application*, 3(2):119–149, 1993.

9. H. Praehofer and G. Reisinger. Distributed simulation of DEVS-based multiformalism models. In *Proc. of AI, Simulation and Planning in High-Autonomy Systems*, pages 150–156, Gainesville FL, Dec 1994. IEEE/CS Press.

10. J. Rozenblit. *A conceptual Basis for Integrated, Model-Based System Design*. PhD thesis, Wayne State University, Detroit, Michigan, 1985.

11. H. A. Simon. The architecture of complexity. *Proc. Am. Philos. Soc.*, 106:467–482, 1962.

12. B. P. Zeigler. *Theory of Modelling and Simulation*. John Wiley, New York, 1976.

13. B. P. Zeigler. *Multifacetted Modelling and Discrete Event Simulation*. Academic Press, London, 1984.

14. B. P. Zeigler. *Object-Oriented Simulation with Hierarchical, Modular Models*. Academic Press, London, 1990.

15. B. P. Zeigler. A systems methodology for structuring families of models at multiple levels of abstraction. In *Proc. Variable Resolution Modeling Conference*, pages 52–101. RAND Publication CF–103–DARPA, Feb. 1993.

EaSy-Sim: A Tool Environment for the Design of Complex, Real-Time Systems

Chr. Schaffer, R.J. Raschhofer and A. Simma

Systems Theory and Information Engineering
Institute of Systems Science
Johannes Kepler University
Linz/Austria

Abstract. Up to now no tool is available on the market that allows functional design and performance analysis within the same environment. Mostly new models have to be built to do performance analysis. This approach is time consuming and erroneous. To overcome this awkward situation two tools, namely GEODE/SDL a typical design tool and SES/workbench a typical simulation tool were coupled. The resulting design and simulation environment will allow the designer to make multiple iterations between functional and performance validation, and therefore the quality of the system design will be improved. Additionally the risk not to meet e.g. some of the performance requirements will be reduced dramatically. [1]

1 Introduction

Whereas systems to be designed become more and more complex the tools being used for the design of these systems do not follow this tremendously fast trend. So the design of embedded real time systems is mostly done with the same tools used for non-real-time critical applications.

Therefore fulfilling e.g. all the performance requirements is very difficult, and very often it is not recognized that not all of them can be met until integrating the system. In that case some kind of reengineering - more often it is a despairing attempt to repair - is needed which will cause additional costs, and mostly results in a badly designed system [10]. To avoid this situation the designer needs an adequate design environment that allows him to check if the proposed design will meet all the performance requirements or not.

It is a well known problem that most of the design decisions made in the early phases of systems design will have a major impact to all of the subsequent design steps. Therefore this kind of performance simulation should be possible at any time in the systems life cycle, also at the very beginning.

The tools available on the market today can be categorized into two main classes, typical design tools and simulation tools. It is this clear distinction and the missing link between these tools, that makes it difficult to do e.g. performance

---

[1] EaSy-Sim is an outcome of the ESTEC Onboard Management System Behavioral Simulation (OMBSIM) study (ESTEC Contract No. 10430/93/NL/FM(SC)).

validation of a system designed with such a typical design tool. Mostly a new model of the system has to be built if the designer wants to determine the system performance. This approach is very time consuming and erroneous and therefore only a small number of iterations between design and performance simulation will be possible.

To overcome this unsatisfactory situation we decided to couple two commercial available tools. A detailed evaluation of multiple design and simulation tools has shown that GEODE/SDL [17], [18] and SES/workbench [13], [14] will be the best candidates for this coupled tool environment. The resulting tool environment was called EaSy-Sim (**Early System Sim**ulation) [8].

2 Considerations on Systems Design

Beside all the other aspects of systems engineering finding the best architecture is one of the most complicated tasks to be solved. Concentrating on embedded systems the designer has to find the best hardware-/software architecture fulfilling all the functional as well as all the nonfunctional requirements. He has to decide if e.g. some functionality should be realized by a program running on a microprocessor or by an FPGA (field programmable gate array). Multiple combinations are imaginable, but which one is really the best? Which solution shows the highest performance? Which is the cheapest? Can the used microprocessor fulfill the difficult timing requirements of our real time system?

By making a clear separation between functional behavior and the underlying architecture used to realize the functionality we will be able to find an answer to all of these questions. Therefore the question will be to find a more or less optimal mapping function m which maps the functional components F to architectural A ones (figure 1).

$$m : F \to A \tag{1}$$

Whereas F is relatively fixed (due to the functional requirements) A can be varied in most cases. Since the final architecture is not available we will use performance models (PM) to determine the impact of the used architecture.

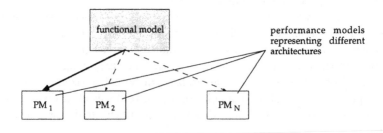

Fig. 1. Evaluation of different architectures

Although this approach is not new, e.g. [6] and [19] use a similar approach, there is no tool available which supports this mapping process. Therefore designers mostly will start with architectural design without having any performance figures available.

Figure 2 shows a small system where the designer uses performance models of communication channels (e.g. twisted pair and coax) to determine the communication media to be used. A result might be that twisted pair cannot be used because some real time constraints will be missed. Another system is shown in

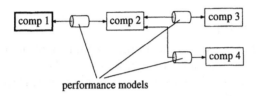

performance models

Fig. 2. System using channel models

figure 3. There the designer wants to know if comp2 should be realized as software running on the microprocessor, which could be the cheaper solution, or if it should be realized on the FPGA. It is quite obvious, if two components have to be realized on one single microprocessor there will be a competition for resources. Therefore it will be of interest for the designer how the overall temporal behavior of the system changes if two or more components are mapped to the microprocessor.

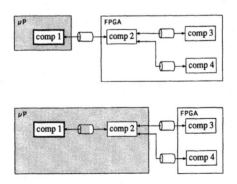

Fig. 3. Comparison of two different architectures

Another essential point in systems design is to model the environment of the system to be built. This model should help to understand the system, and to test the systems reaction if a specific input is fed into the system. The system inputs themselves can be split into two main categories, namely functional input and architectural input.

2.1 Functional Input

Functional inputs should be used to test the pure functional behavior of our system. These inputs might e.g. come from a user terminal or from the uplink channel of a satellite. Here the designer is interested how the system behaves if a specific input is fed into the system.

2.2 Architectural Input

Architectural inputs are used to model the inadequacy of the underlying architecture. This might be drop outs of a hardware unit, the overhead caused by the used operating system, or the bus error rate of a used communication media to mention only a few of them.

By making this clear distinction between functional and architectural input it is easy for the designer to investigate the influence of different architectures. To do this the functional inputs will be the same for all tests, only the architectural inputs will change according to the used architecture (figure 4).

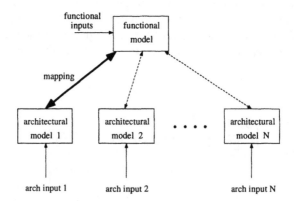

Fig. 4. Modeling the systems environment

3 Background on Tools

3.1 GEODE

GEODE is based on the formal specification and description language **SDL** which became a CCITT standard in 1988 [4]. SDL is mainly known within the telecommunications field [12], but might also be used for other systems where real-time behavior and interaction between system components plays a significant role. According to [2] the application area of SDL can be characterized as follows:

- **type of system:** real time, interactive, distributed;
- **type of information:** behavior and structure;
- **level of abstraction:** overview to detail;

3.1.1 The Language

3.1.1.1 Structuring Mechanisms

By using blocks and subblocks SDL allows a hierarchical decomposition of the system. Blocks allow the designer to have a "Black Box" view of the system. Channels used to define the coupling of the system are the medium to transport data from one block to another. The hierarchically decomposed system can be depicted in two different ways. One is the so called *Hierarchy View* (figure 5) where only the decomposition of the system is shown. If the designer is interested in the signals (data) to be exchanged between the blocks he has to use the so called *Interconnection View* (figure 6).

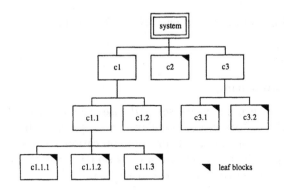

Fig. 5. Hierarchy View of a system

3.1.1.2 Systems Behavior

Whereas blocks and subblocks are used to show the static decomposition of the system, processes, which will be assigned as leaves to these blocks, will keep the SDL system alive. Each SDL process includes a behavioral description which is defined by an extended finite state machine (EFSM). Here EFSMs are used to avoid the state explosion problem. By including local variables less important information is hidden, and therefore the visible complexity is reduced dramatically [2]. Task nodes, as shown in figure 7 (e.g. command i:=i+1), are used to define tasks to be executed when transferring from one state to another. All the processes run in parallel, and it is possible to start, kill or instantiate them. Figure 6 shows two processes each including a simple EFSM.

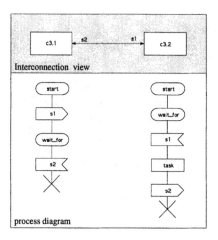

Fig. 6. Interconnection View and FSMs of a system

3.1.1.3 Communication

To communicate with other processes SDL uses signals. The SDL commands OUTPUT and INPUT are used to send/receive a signal to/from another SDL process. Beside these signals used for communication purposes, SDL uses so called timer signals. Timer signals are always sent back to the sending process indicating that a defined time-out has elapsed (figure 7).

3.1.1.4 Textual and Graphical representation of the system

SDL gives a choice of two different syntactic forms to be used when representing a system; a graphic representation, and a textual phrase representation (figure 7). Both represent the same SDL semantic and therefore they are equivalent [4].

3.1.1.5 Temporal behavior in SDL

As already mentioned above SDL offers only one simple mechanism to specify time, namely time-outs. Usually these time-outs are used in protocol applications

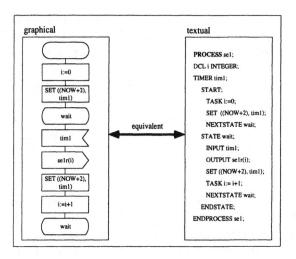

Fig. 7. Graphical and textual representation of the same FSM

where e.g. a sender has to wait a specified amount of time until a new signal can be sent. If no time-out is specified then it is assumed that the whole application will be executed in zero time units. This approach is very dangerous, because it is a fact that e.g. the calculation of a fast fourier transformation (FFT) will need some time. Depending on the used hardware we can imagine execution times between 10 minutes (PC) and 1ms (DSP) for a complex 1024 point FFT.

Again we can see that we have to distinguish between temporal behavior which is given due to the functional requirements (e.g. wait for the specified amount of time in the protocol application) and temporal behavior which is caused by the used hardware and software architecture. Typically in SDL only the first kind of temporal behavior is modeled, and therefore very often the simulation of an SDL model does not correspond to the execution of the model on the real target. It should be stressed that it is possible to model the architectural aspects in SDL as well, but then it is necessary to remove all these parts when generating code for the real target.

More details on SDL can be found in [4], [2], [16] and [15].

3.1.2 The Tool

GEODE in principle consists of three different parts which are the GEODE Editor, the GEODE Simulator and the GEODE Application Builder.

Editor : The graphics oriented editor will be used to create the SDL model and the associated message sequence charts (MSCs). Lexical and syntactic errors will be detected by the built in verification facility.

Simulator : Using the simulator the model can be animated and checked for deadlocks, livelocks, dynamic errors or unspecified reception of signals. By using predefined MSCs the designer can validate if the system behaves in the expected way or not.

Application Builder : Having fixed all errors the designer can proceed with generating target code by using the GEODE Application Builder which allows the generation of C code for a large number of real-time executives like UNIX, VRTX, pSOS+, MTOS, RTC, OSE and VxWorks.

3.2 SES/workbench

SES/workbench is a graphics oriented specification, design, modeling and simulation tool. It can be used to construct and evaluate proposed system designs, and to analyze the performance of the implemented system. By simply connecting predefined (resource management, transaction flow control, submodel management, miscellaneous) and user defined nodes the designer can build up his models. Simulation is possible in animated and batch mode. By tracing signals and gathering statistics the designer will get detailed knowledge about his system.

4   EaSy-Sim Coupling Principle

To overcome the problems mentioned in chapter 1 it was necessary to couple both tools. Coupling should be achieved in a way that,

- both tools are operatable in stand alone mode too. There should be no difference to the normal operation mode.
- coupling is possible at any time.
- user intervention is minimized as much as possible. Therefore the switch between coupled and stand alone simulation should be automated.
- standard SDL models can be used for coupled simulation.

Whereas the GEODE simulation environment is very encapsulated the application building environment allows multiple adaptations to the users need. By modifying the code generation library it was possible to realize the coupling of both tools. On the fact GEODE itself uses the inter process communication (IPC) mechanism of UNIX to exchange signals between SDL processes, we decided to use this concept too, to realize the signal exchange between GEODE and SES/workbench (figure 8).

Unfortunately both tools use a different timer concept. GEODE uses a real time kernel whereas SES/workbench uses simulation time. Because it was not possible to merge both event lists in an easy way the following concept was used to synchronize both tools: Each time SDL sets a new timer, the resulting timer signal is rerouted to an SES/workbench submodel including a simple delay node, which is set to the time defined by the timer. Thereby each SDL timer is handled by a delay node of SES/workbench. After SES/workbench has processed

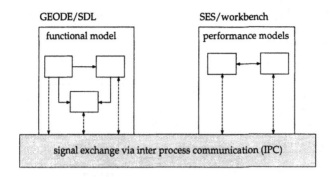

Fig. 8. Coupling of GEODE/SDL and SES/workbench

this delay the signal is sent back to GEODE. SDL itself does not recognize the difference because each time a timer is set the process will run into a wait state. There the process remains until the timer signal is received (figure 9).

5 Modeling Concepts

EaSy-Sim offers four different concepts to model the underlying architecture and the systems environment, namely

1. timer refinement,
2. channel refinement,
3. task refinement and
4. component exchange.

As shown in figure 8 these concepts are used to access the SES/workbench performance models. How to define this access is shown in chapter 6. In the following we want to show when and how to use these concepts.

5.1 Timer Refinement

As already mentioned, above all SDL time-outs are mapped automatically to SES/workbench when running EaSy-Sim in the coupled operation mode (figure 9). Therefore it is possible to use the statistical facilities of workbench to investigate the temporal behavior of a standard SDL model. If the designer is interested in a more detailed investigation it is also possible to reroute a timer signal to the specific predefined SES/workbench submodel.

5.2 Channel Refinement

Communication plays a significant role in systems design. To investigate e.g. the data rate on a channel EaSy-Sim allows to insert a performance model of a

GEODE/SDL   SES/workbench

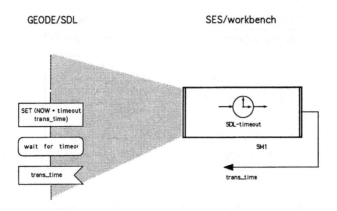

Fig. 9. Mapping of an SDL timer to SES/workbench

channel between two SDL components (figure 10). Therefore, each time a signal is sent to the other component it will be rerouted to the specified performance sub model. After the signal has passed through the channel model the signal

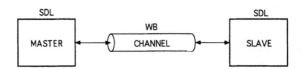

Fig. 10. Using a channel performance model

will be rerouted to the legal receiver of the signal. The performance model itself might be very simple, e.g. a delay, or very detailed including all the aspects of the real communication channel. Typical applications are:

data rate determination : The data rate between two components will be a significant design criteria for the realization of the channel. If the data rate is low a "slow" communication medium can be used and vice versa. Especially in systems consisting of many interacting components it is very difficult or even impossible to determine the data rate on the channels without simulation.

injection of transmission errors : When rerouting a signal to SES/workbench all the parameters associated with this signal can be accessed on the SES/workbench side. Therefore it is possible to change the values of parameters which can be interpreted as transmission errors. Also lost signals can be simulated. In that case the signal will be destroyed in the channel model.

performance model of the real channel : Transportation of data is always associated with transmission delay. When designing real-time applications the transmission delay might play a significant role. To model this delay a WB submodel can be used including just one single delay node. But it is also possible to use a very detailed performance model of e.g. a sophisticated data bus.

5.3 Task Refinement

This concept is probably the most important one, because it allows to model the influence of the used architecture to the execution time of a specific task. As we can see in figure 11 this aspect is modeled by the *wb_conn()* command. At the position this command can be found the process stops its execution and sends a signal to the WB environment. There this artificial signal can be used e.g. to model the needed calculation time (delay node) of this task or the access to a specific resource (resource node). Using resource nodes we can investigate e.g. the resulting temporal behavior of N processes using one single resource (operating system running on one single microprocessor). After having passed the WB sub

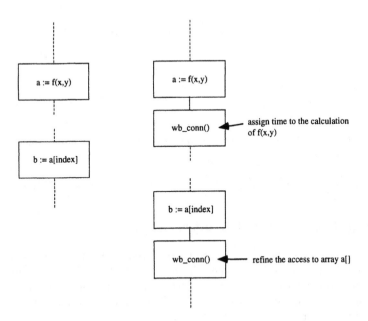

Fig. 11. Assign time to the execution of tasks

model the signal is sent back to the sending process which causes the process to proceed its execution. It is up to the designer to specify the granularity of

underlying architectural model. But in principle it is possible to assign time to each operation which needs time.

5.4 Component Exchange

As already mentioned above modeling the systems environment is a very critical aspect in systems design. Very often the input to our system can be described only by statistical distributions. Here it is desirable to use the powerful statistical features of SES/workbench. By defining an SDL process which will be replaced in the coupled simulation mode by the specified WB model it is possible to generate signals on the SES/workbench side, and to feed them into the SDL system. In the coupled version the behavior of this SDL process is reduced to its interface behavior. Therefore it only receives and forwards signals(figure 12). Another case of application will be the use of more detailed/abstract models of

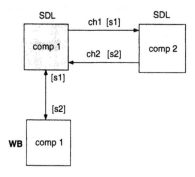

Fig. 12. Using component exchange to model e.g. the environment

an SDL process, which are available as reusable components in SES/workbench.

6 Definition of Signal Routes

To define where a specific signal has to be rerouted to the designer has to use the textual representation of SDL. There he has to insert a special comment which will be used during the translation process. The comment has to be written before the SDL command (OUTPUT, SET and TASK wb_conn()) which uses the signal to be rerouted. So the definition

```
/* WB_START
BATCH_1(,,channel_1,)
BATCH_2(,,channel_2,)
BATCH_3(,,new_channel,)
WB_END */
```
OUTPUT sig1(a,b,c) TO slave

represents a typical channel refinement. Here the signal *sig1* will be rerouted to WB sub model *channel_1* in batch run 1. Batch run 2 will reroute the signal to WB sub model *channel_2* and batch 3 will reroute the signal to WB sub model *new_channel*.

To use the component exchange mechanism the designer has to use the following construct:

```
/*WB_SDL_EX BATCH_2(WB_p1) */
PROCESS p1(1,1)
. . . . .
```

Here we define that SDL process p1 has to be exchanged by SES/workbench sub model *WB_p1*. This exchange should only take place in batch run 2.

The batch definitions allow the designer to define multiple mappings (scenarios) within the same model. So the model has to be compiled only once, and afterwards all the defined batch runs can be executed without having to recompile the system. Making the routing definitions within the SDL description of the model itself will support a good documentation because the model and the simulation scenarios build one unit. If the designer decides to generate final target code a script will remove all the overhead (wb_conn() commands etc.) automatically.

7 Modeling the Systems Environment

EaSy-Sim allows to define all the signals to be injected into the system in two different files. One file holds all the signals which belong to the functional part (injected into SDL), the other holds all the signals for the architectural part (injected into SES/workbench). In that way the approach shown in figure 4 will be supported. Files are used because they allow a very compact form of specification. More details on this can be found in [9].

8 Life Cycle

In the following we want to outline a possible design approach which can be used in conjunction with EaSy-Sim.

Logical Validation: By using the abstract data types (ADTs) of SDL, and the different analyzing techniques (dead-lock, live-lock etc.) of GEODE the designer will be able to detect logical errors in his system. Additionally he can use the message sequence charts (MSCs) to verify if the system behaves in the expected way or not.

Performance Validation : If the system behaves logically correct the designer can proceed with performance validation. Here he will define different architectural mappings to find the best architecture and to identify potential bottlenecks of the system. A result of this phase might also be that there is a logical error in the system. In that case the designer has to correct these errors in the SDL model and repeat the logical validation phase.

Generation of the target code : If the system fulfills all the functional and
nonfunctional requirements the designer can proceed with generating code
for the target platform.

It is quite obvious that there will be many iterations between logical and performance validation. As soon as there is an executable SDL model available we
can run our first performance validation, e.g. to observe the resulting data rates
on our communication channels.

In this paper unfortunately only the basic idea can be presented. A more
detailed approach can be found in [5].

9 Application Example

In the following a small data acquisition system will be demonstrated. The interconnection view (figure 13) shows two devices that are connected to a central
controller unit. The devices receive signals from two sensors which are part of
the systems environment. Sensor 1 and 2 should generate signals in a uniform
distributed time interval U[0..4]. The values generated by the sensors also should
follow a uniform distribution U[0..1]. These signals are read by the corresponding
devices. The devices themselves are polled by the controller unit in a regular time
interval of 3 (device1) and 5 (device2) time units. Additionally the controller has
to add the two polled sensor values, and forward the result to a visualization
unit.

To verify if the system behaves in the expected way, the coupled operation
mode of EaSy-Sim will be used. If we assume that channels cd1, cd2, d1c and d2c
are all realized by different realization technologies we might use four different
performance models. Figure 14 shows e.g. the population on these channels.
Additionally we can see the mean value of the interarrival times of the sensor
signals.

10 Summary and Conclusion

EaSy-Sim is a powerful design and simulation environment which supports the
designer in designing complex real time application. By using a formal language
(SDL) and a sophisticated simulation tool it is possible to do logical and performance validation within the same environment and without having to build new
models. The possibility to switch from stand alone to coupled operation mode
and vice versa at any time allows the designer to make multiple iterations, which
will increase the quality of the design.

Another advantage of EaSy-Sim is the possibility of multilevel simulation. By
using very detailed models the designer can put the focus to the interesting part
of the system. All the other parts can be represented by very abstract models.
This approach will increase simulation performance.

Currently EaSy-Sim is used to model the data management system of a
satellite. Here it turned out that the missing performance models are the main

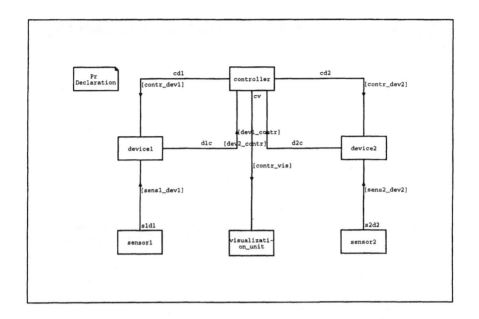

Fig. 13. Small data acquisition system (*Interconnection View*)

problem to be solved. But this seems to be a general problem when using new methods or tools.

Another still existing problem is the missing link to a hardware description language like VHDL. Due to the split of functional behavior and the underlying architecture EaSy-Sim supports design approaches as shown in [11]. Using such an approach the designer will be supported in finding good hardware and software partitions, and therefore it will be the right tool for HW/SW-codesign, because there this partitioning is one of the most essential problems [3]. By realizing an SDL to VHDL translator, some publications on this topic are available [1], [7] EaSy-Sim will cover the whole systems design life cycle.

Finally we would like to thank all the other project partners which are Mr. Rainer Gerlich (Dornier GmbH/Germany), Yankin Tanurhan and Thomas Stingl (FZI/Germany).

References

1. W. Glunz B. Lutter and F.J. Rammig. Using vhdl for simlation of sdl specifications. *Proceedings EURO-DAC/EURO-VHDL*, pages 630–635, September 1992.
2. Ferenc Belina, Dieter Hogrefe, and Amardeo Sarma. *SDL with Applications from Protocol Specifications*. Prentice Hall, 1991.
3. Klaus Buchenrieder and Jerzy W. Rozenblit. *Codesign: An Overview*, pages 1–15. IEEE PRESS Marketing, 1993.

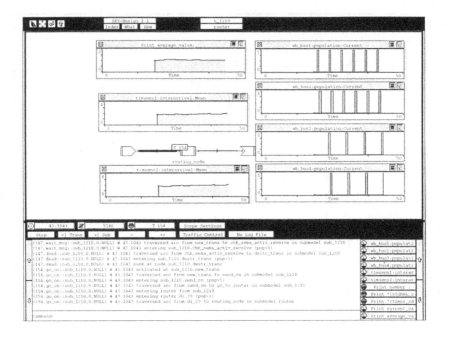

Fig. 14. Screen shot of SES/workbench

4. CCITT. *Functional Specification and Description Language (SDL), Z.100.* International Consultative Committee on Telegraphy and Telephony, Geneva, 1988.

5. R. Gerlich, Chr. Schaffer, V. Debus, and Y. Tanurhan. Easyvade: Validation of system design by behavioural simulation. ESTEC 3rd Workshop on Simulators for European Space Programmes. European Space Agency, November 1994.

6. Derek J. Hatley and Imtiaz A. Pirbhai. *Strategies for Real-Time System Specification.* Dorset House Publishing Co., Inc, New York, 1988.

7. Otto Pulkkinen and Klaus Kronfloef. *SDL-VHDL Integration,* chapter 10, pages 271–308. Wiley Series in Software Based Systems. John Wiley & Sons, 1993.

8. Chr. Schaffer. Software User Manual for EaSy-Add, August 1995. ESTEC Contract No. 10430/93/NL/FM(SC), Issue 4.

9. Chr. Schaffer. Software User Manual for Test Execution Environment, July 1995. ESTEC Contract No. 10430/93/NL/FM(SC), Issue 1.

10. Christoph Schaffer and Herbert Praehofer. On requirements for a cast-tool for complex, reactive system analysis, design and evaluation. In F.Pichler and R.Moreno Diaz, editors, *Computer Aided Systems Theory-EUROCAST 93,* number 763 in Lecture Notes in Computer Science. Springer Verlag, 1994.

11. Christoph Schaffer and Jerzy W. Rozenblit. Modular, hierarchical modeling concepts for support of heterogeneous systems design. In *1995 International Symposium and Workshop on Systems Engineering of Computer Based Systems,* pages 200–208. IEEE, March 1995.

12. D. Schefstrom and G. van den Broek, editors. *Tool Integration: Environments and Frameworks.* Wiley Series in Software Based Systems. John Wiley & Sons, 1993.

13. SES. SES/workbench - Reference Manual, February 1992. Release 2.1.

14. SES. SES/workbench - User's Manual, February 1992. Release 2.1.

15. K. Tarnay. *Protocol Specification and Testing*. Plenum Press, 1991.

16. Kenneth J. Turner, editor. *Using Formal Description Techniques: An Introduction to ESTELLE, LOTOS and SDL*. Wiley Series in Communication and Distributed Systems. John Wiley & Sons, 1993.

17. Verilog. GEODE An Introduction to SDL and MSC, October 1993. Document Reference: D/GEXX/LA/100/340.

18. Verilog. GEODE C Application Generators - Reference Manual, November 1993. Document Reference: D/GCXX/RA/211/344.

19. A. Wayne Wymore. *Model-Based Systems Engineering*. Systems Engineering Series. CRC Press, 1993.

Systems Level Specification and Modelling of Reactive Systems: Concepts, Methods, and Tools

Uwe Glässer

Heinz Nixdorf Institut, Universität-GH Paderborn, D-33098 Paderborn, Germany
glaesser@uni-paderborn.de

Abstract. As part of a comprehensive design concept for complex reactive systems we investigate the derivation of formal requirements and design specifications at systems level. We discuss the meaning of correctness with respect to the embedding of mathematical models into the physical world. A crucial aspect in our attempt to make the logic link between the application domain specific view and the formal view explicit is the concept of *evolving algebra* [13, 14]; it provides the formal basis of a specification methodology which has successfully been applied to a variety of specification and verification problems. We introduce an *evolving algebra abstract machine* as a conceptual framework for the development of tools for machine based analysis and execution of evolving algebra specifications.

1 Introduction

Reactive systems[1] cover a wide range of challenging applications of computer based information, communication, and control systems; this class, in particular, does also include various kinds of concurrent systems such as parallel, distributed, or real–time systems, which by their nature are *reactive* rather than *transformational*. Reactivity thereby becomes the predominating behavioural characteristic of a system: the purpose of a system run is not necessarily to compute a final result, but to maintain some ongoing interaction with the external system environment.

Since the embedding of a reactive system into a given environment may impose considerable functional requirements having a strong impact on the entire design, a precise interface specification should be considered as the starting point for the design process. The interface specification explicitly describes how the system is influenced by its environment. Such an approach corresponds to an *open system view*, which is in contrast to a closed world assumption (*closed system view*) where everything relevant is included in the system [10]. According to widely accepted principles of systems engineering, for instance, the concept of *model–based system design* as stated by Wayne Wymore in his book on model-based systems engineering [24]:

---

[1] We refer to the notion as defined by D. Harel and A. Pnueli in [16] and [22].

> *To design a system is to develop a model on the basis of which a real system can be built, developed, or deployed that will satisfy all its requirements.*

the functional system requirements should be specified as *complete, precise,* and *unambiguous* as possible. Such a behavioural description requires to have a well–defined *mathematical* model as rigorous formalization of the functional requirements. However, a formal basis alone does not guarantee that the model fulfills the requirements; even if the model has been proven to be correct[2] this does not necessarily mean that it really *fits* into the given environment, since the assumptions on which such proves are based may be incomplete or wrong. Practical experiences with applications of formal methods, like the "Production Cell" case study [20], have indeed shown that such mismatchings do frequently occur.

As part of a comprehensive design concept for complex reactive systems we investigate the derivation of formal requirements specifications from given informal system descriptions. More precisely, we are concerned with the formal definition of functional and timing requirements at the systems level. In our terminology which is based on the notion of *evolving algebra*, as described in the next section, the resulting mathematical models are called *ground models*.

The evolving algebra notation enables a specification style which makes the relationship between the informal description and the ground model explicit; this seems to be a crucial issue in any attempt at mathematical modeling of non-mathematical reality. A ground model should reflect our intuitive understanding of the intended system behaviour not only with the necessary completeness and precision, but also in a clear and understandable way. The ground model thus provides the logic link between the application domain specific view and the formal view.

After a brief introduction of the specification language in Section 2, we investigate the derivation of ground models in Section 3. To illustrate the concepts, Section 4 presents an example of specifying reactive system behaviour. In Section 5 we consider the development of tools for analysis and execution of specifications in a CAST context. Section 6 contains the conclusions.

2   Theoretical Foundations

The concept of *evolving algebra*[3] as defined by Yuri Gurevich in [13, 14] provides the formal basis of our specification methodology. Evolving algebras are *abstract*

---

[2] Correctness here can not have an absolute meaning (since there is no way to prove it), rather it means correctness with respect to certain assumptions about the physical world (as represented by the external environment).

[3] The term *algebra*, as we use it here, is characterized by the notion of *first-order structure* of classical logic. A regular first-order structure consists of *domains, functions,* and *relations*, while structures without relations are called *algebras* [12]. (Note that relations can also be expressed through their characteristic functions.)

machines specifying the *operational semantics* of algorithmic descriptions of discrete dynamic systems. An *EA* machine models the effect of simulated system operations by updating a global structure (representing the machine *state*) as defined by a finite set of transition rules (the *EA program*).

In contrast to classical formalisms, like Turing machines for instance, evolving algebras simulate the underlying system in a direct and essentially coding–free manner at a *natural* abstraction level—one step in a computation of the system is reflected by one step (or at most some few steps) in the *EA* computation. Depending on the granularity of abstract machine operations more concrete or more abstract specifications are obtained: *refinement* is expressed by substituting complex operations through several more detailed ones; *abstraction* is expressed by hiding operational details in complex operations. Due to the operational view and the familiar description style, *EA* specifications enable an intuitive understanding as 'pseudocode over abstract data.'[4]

Evolving algebras have been applied with considerable success to various problems in mathematical modelling of non–trivial architectures [5, 8, 9], languages [3, 4, 6], and protocols [15, 18] (for further references see also [2]). The basic concept of sequential evolving algebras is introduced in [13]. For a rigorous mathematical foundation of *sequential* and *distributed* evolving algebras we refer to [14].

2.1   Sequential Evolving Algebras

Static State Representations   For the user it is convenient to consider an *EA* machine $\mathcal{M}$ as consisting of an *EA* program and a first–order *many–sorted* structure representing the *initial* computation state of $\mathcal{M}$. Formally, such a heterogeneous structure is defined through a *static algebra* S_0 of the form[5]

$$S_0 = (D_1, \ldots, D_n; f_1, \ldots, f_m)$$

where the D_i identify the various *domains* of abstract data and the f_j denote *partial functions* over these domains. When a function f_j is applied to some argument $\bar{x}$ on which it is not defined, we expect that $f_j(\bar{x}) = undef$, where *undef* refers to a distinguished element not contained in any of the D_i.

Modelling Dynamic Behaviour   Computations are modeled by finite or infinite sequences of static algebras

$$S_0 \; S_1 \; S_2 \; \ldots$$

such that S_{i+1} is obtained from S_i by executing one step of the EA program. As all the relevant state information is encoded in the functions, a change from one state to the next state means that the functions have to be updated accordingly.

---

[4] This analogy was contributed by Egon Börger.
[5] Strictly speaking the D_i are all subsets of a single set, called the *superuniverse* [13].

More precisely, what has to be updated are the *interpretations* of functions[6].
This is expressed through basic *function updates* of the form

$$f(t_1, \ldots, t_k) := t_0$$

where the t_i's represent first–order *ground terms*[7] identifying elements in the
corresponding domains. The function update effectively changes the function
value which is associated with the *location l* to the new value $Val(t_0)$, where l is
uniquely determined through the pair $(f, \langle Val(t_1), \ldots, Val(t_k) \rangle)$.

Complex Update Operations Transition rules of *EA* programs structure complex
updates. They are built from the composition of *conditional, sequence*, and *declaration* constructs. More complex rules are obtained by nesting of simple rules.
Guarded transition rules have the elementary form

if *Cond* **then** *Updates*

where *Cond* (condition or guard) is a boolean valued first–order expression,
the truth of which triggers *simultaneous* execution of all update operations in
the finite set of *Updates*. Within each step of a computation all rules of the
EA program are inspected and the updates of those rules for which the guard
is true are executed simultaneously. The rules have to be constructed in such a
way that the guards imply *consistency* of updates; otherwise, the computation
stops as soon as two update operation attempt to assign different values to the
same location (to the same function at the same argument).

2.2 Distributed Evolving Algebras

A *distributed evolving algebra* comes as a finite set of sequential *EA* programs,
called *modules*, together with a finite set of concurrently operating *agents*. A
function *Mod* specifies the mapping of agents to modules. Operating independently, each agent runs its own copy of a module. Agents may communicate
with each other through the globally shared structure representing the current
state. For a detailed definition of the notion of *run* with respect to distributed
evolving algebras, we refer to [14].

3 Derivation of Ground Models

The embedding of our mathematical models into the physical world is established through ground models (as discussed in Section 1). Being aware of the
fact that there is no way to ensure the correctness of ground models other than
validating them by experimentation and inspection, their definition requires to

---

[6] Functions are treated as data structures which are subject to *local* modifications.
Note that the modifications do not affect the *signature*.

[7] *Ground terms* are terms without variables.

take special care. In a detailed investigation of this subject [7] Egon Börger convincingly argues that there are at least three basic requirements to be satisfied by a ground model: it must be *precise*, *abstract*, and it must have a *rigorous foundation*. Despite of the required formalization and precision, there are also other indispensable properties a ground model must apparently have in order to be understandable: *simplicity* and *conciseness*. For the significance of these properties it does not matter whether the ground model serves as requirements specification in the design of some new system, or it is used in 'reverse engineering' applications to model an already existing system.

The problem to establish a suitable ground model for a complex reactive system is obviously a challenging task of systems engineering. However, in a first attempt it may be hard to find a satisfying layer of abstraction and precision; thus, one usually starts with some informal description at hand trying to adopt this view to the ground model. In many engineering disciplines it is a common practise to formulate design problems in an operational style. For instance, the functions of a system are often specified by explaining their effect in terms of operations to be carried out[8]. In such a context the use of evolving algebras allows an incremental derivation of the ground model out of the informal description. It is then possible to construct the *EA* rules together with the signature of static state representations in a straightforward manner [1].

A special problem in the construction of the ground model is the definition of the interface to the real world. To attach the model to the real world, one usually needs to refer certain *non-mathematical entities* expressing conditions or assumptions about events outside the model. Within the ground model such entities may not yet have a precise meaning in a formal sense, rather they will be subject to further refinement steps at more concrete specification layers. They thus identify the 'loose ends' in the embedding of the mathematical model.

To cope with that problem, evolving algebras offer the concept of *external functions*. In contrast to *internal* functions which are modified by the *EA* program, external functions are controlled by the environment. This does not necessarily mean that external functions may change their values in an arbitrary manner. The declaration of external functions allows to restrict their behaviour through the definition of *integrity constraints*. As an example of the use of external functions consider the specification of real-time constraints in [15, 18]. Time is modeled through an external nullary function $CT : Real$ indicating the current time. A reasonable integrity constraint is that the value of CT increases monotonically.

4 A Specification Example

In this section we consider a non-trivial example of an *EA* based specification of reactive system behaviour to illustrate the role of ground models. The example is part of a semantic definition for the hardware description language VHDL [3].

---

[8] Technical instructions, manuals, etc. are typical examples.

Note that it is not really necessary to be familiar with VHDL for the purpose we use it here. The required details will be explained on the way.

The language VHDL'93, the current version of VHDL, is defined by the *IEEE VHDL'93 standard language reference manual (LRM)* [19] on the basis of an event–driven simulator specifying the effect of VHDL programs. Our behavioral specification is derived out of the informal description in the LRM in such a way that it faithfully reflects and supports the view given there. The resulting ground model defines an abstract VHDL'93 interpreter.

Modelling of Signal Behaviour Consider a VHDL hardware description as a flat set of asynchronously operating iterative *processes* which communicate with each other through *signals*. A process P writes on output signals and reads from input signals. However, P cannot immediately assign a value to a signal S. A signal assignment merely schedules a value *val*, desired at time t, into a sequence *driver*(P, S) consisting of pairs (val, t), so–called *transactions*.

The transactions of a driver, which are linearly ordered by their time components, form a *projected output waveform*. When the simulation time is increased, the simulator updates the drivers such that the following invariant on projected output waveforms holds: the time component of the *first* element is always less than or equal to the *current time* T_c; the time components of all other transactions are strictly greater than T_c. If the first element of the projected output waveform of some driver is updated in a given simulation cycle, then the driver is said to be *active*.

For signal assignments the VHDL standard defines a preemptive scheduling (LRM, page 117):

Updating a projected output waveform consists of the deletion of zero or more previously computed transactions (called old transactions) from the projected output waveform and the addition of the new transactions, as follows:

a) *All old transactions that are projected to occur at or after the time at which the earliest new transaction is projected to occur are deleted from the projected output waveform.*

b) *The new transactions are then appended to the projected output waveform in order to their projected occurrence.*

c) *All of the new transactions are marked.*

d) *An old transaction is marked if the time at which it is projected to occur is less than the time at which the first new transaction is projected to occur minus the pulse rejection limit.*

e) *For each remaining unmarked, old transaction, the old transaction is marked if it immediately precedes a marked transaction and its value component is the same as that of the marked transaction.*

f) *The transaction that determines the current value of the driver is marked.*

g) *All unmarked transactions (all of which are old transactions) are deleted from the projected output waveform.*

As an example of a signal assignment instruction we consider the *inertial delay* signal assignment[9], which may schedule several new transactions for the same signal S at once. The value components are given in the form of expressions $Expr_i$ (to be evaluated); time components $Time_i$ express the distance from the current time T_c:

$$S \Leftarrow \text{INERTIAL } Expr_1 \text{ AFTER } Time_1, \ldots, Expr_n \text{ AFTER } Time_n$$

The preemptive scheduling requires to delete all the old transactions from the projected output waveform which were scheduled for time points $\geq T_c + Time_1$. In our description we use a function $|_<: DRIVER \times TIME \rightarrow DRIVER$ such that $|_< (d, t)$ returns excactly those transactions in d which have a time component $< t$. In the special case, when a new value is scheduled for the current time T_c, i.e., when $Time_1 = 0$, the complete waveform of the driver gets relpaced by the waveform specified in the signal assignment.

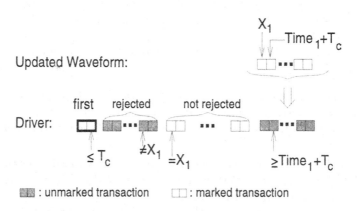

Fig. 1. Preemptive scheduling for inertial delay

The inertial delay instruction is specified below by means of a single *EA* rule. In order to concentrate on the essential behavioral characteristics of VHDL'93, we assume that the control flow of each individual process is determined by the environment through an external function *program_counter*. Within the *EA* rules the current *program_counter* value is referred in the form "*Process does* $\langle INSTRUCTION \rangle$."

---

[9] This is one of the most complex operations of VHDL.

INERTIAL DELAY

if *Process does*
$$\langle S \Leftarrow INERTIAL\ Expr_1\ AFTER\ Time_1, \ldots, Expr_n\ AFTER\ Time_n \rangle$$

thenif $Time_1 = 0$
  then $driver(Process, S) := Waveform$
    $active(driver(Process, S)) := true$
  else $driver(Process, S) :=$
    $first(driver(Process, S))^\wedge reject(driver', X_1)^\wedge Waveform$

  where $Waveform = \langle (X_1, Time_1'), \ldots, (X_n, Time_n') \rangle \wedge Time_j' = Time_j + T_c \wedge$
    $X_j = value(Expr_j) \wedge driver' = tail(driver(Process, S)\mid_< (Time_1 + T_c))$

The function *reject* is specified by:

  $reject(TransList, Val) \equiv$
    if $TransList = \langle \rangle \vee value(last(TransList)) \neq Val$
    then return $\langle \rangle$
    else return $reject(front(TransList, Val))^\wedge last(TransList)$

5   An EA-Based Design Environment.

From a pragmatic point of view a specification methodology is not really applicable to complex systems engineering and design tasks, especially not for industrial purposes, as long as there is no appropriate tool support [17]. In the specific context of reactive system design special requirements on tools are imposed by the reactive nature of the systems. Ch. Schaffer and H. Prähofer have investigated this aspect in [23] from a systems theory point of view. According to more general considerations of systems science and systems technology,e.g., as discussed in [21], CAST tools and environments should also provide the necessary support to relate complex systems specifications to given design constraints.

As a first step towards a comprehensive *EA* based specification and design environment, we discuss the realization of an *EA abstract machine (EAM)* as a conceptual framework for the development of *EA* tools. The *EAM* introduces an intermediate level of abstraction between the one on which evolving algebras are defined and the one which is appropriate for machine based analysis and execution of *EA* specifications; i.e., for implementing evolving algebras on real machines. Our formal definition of the *EAM* comes as an *EA* specification [11].

We define the *EAM* in a stepwise manner through a hierarchy of *abstract machine models* EAM_0, $EAM_1, \ldots$, where EAM_0 refers to the most abstract and EAM_{i+1} to some more concrete layer in the representation of a given *EA* program P. With each EAM_i, we associate a certain representation P_i of P and a corresponding transformation from EAM_i to EAM_{i+1}. Transformations between machine models EAM_i and EAM_{i+1} are carried out such that the related representations P_i, P_{i+1} are semantically equivalent preserving the semantics of the original program P. The formal definition of the *EAM* is considerably simplified by the fact that our machine models are uniformly expressed as *EA* specifications; this offers a natural way to leave certain aspects in the description of a machine model abstract while concentrating on constructive definitions for others.

The *EAM* design realizes a strict separation of concerns in the treatment of syntactical and semantical objects, i.e., in the representation of *signature* and the representation of *interpretations* of domains, functions, and rules. Within the *EAM* model the interpretations of user defined functions are uniformly represented through a single internal function *val*, which is a mapping from *locations* (see Section 2.1) to *values* (elements of the superuniverse). To update a user defined function at some location l, the corresponding value of the function *val* at argument l is modified. Such a uniform representation scheme offers a high degree of regularity, which is the basis for an efficient implementation of the current prototype of the *EAM*. For further details see [11].

6 Conclusions

Formal methods are a reasonable and vital means for specifying and verifying complex reactive systems. There is a great variety of different formal approaches; they all have their particular strengths, but also their limitations and weaknesses. However, mathematical precision alone does not meet the requirements of real–life engineering problems; at the same time, the models should also reflect the intuitive understanding of the problem in a clear and understandable way. The relationship between the formal model and the physical world must become obvious. This aspect is reflected by the notion of *ground models* in connection with *EA* based specifications. The simplicity of the method considerably simplifies the problem to establish the correctness of the ground model with respect to the assumptions on which it is based.

References

1. Ch. Beierle, E. Börger, I. Ðurđanović U. Glässer, and E. Riccobene. An evolving algebra solution to the steam-boiler control specification problem. Seminar on *Methods for Specification and Semantics* (Dagstuhl, June 1995), Report, 1995.
2. E. Börger. Annotated bibliography on evolving algebras. In E. Börger, editor, *Specification and Validation Methods*. Oxford University Press, 1995.
3. E. Börger, U. Glässer, and W. Mueller. Formal definition of an abstract VHDL'93 simulator by EA-machines. In C. Delgado Kloos and Peter T. Breuer, editors, *Semantics of VHDL*, volume 307 of *The Kluwer International Series in Engineering and Computer Science*. Kluwer Academic Publishers, 1995.
4. E. Börger and D. Rosenzweig. A mathematical definition of full Prolog. *Science of Computer Programming*, 1994.
5. E. Börger and D. Rosenzweig. The WAM – definition and compiler correctness. In L. C. Beierle and L. Plümer, editors, *Logic Programming: Formal Methods and Practical Applications*, Series in Computer Science and Artificial Intelligence. Elsevier Science B.V./North–Holland, 1995.

6. E. Börger, I. Đurđanović, and D. Rosenzweig. Occam: Specification and compiler correctness. Part I: The primary model. In E.-R. Olderog, editor, *Proc. of PRO-COMET'94 (IFIP Working Conference on Programming Concepts, Methods and Calculi)*, pages 489–508. North-Holland, 1994.

7. Egon Börger. Three pragmatic suggestions for making formal methods practical. Dipartimento di Informatica, Università di Pisa, Report, 1995.

8. Egon Börger, Giuseppe Del Castillo, Paola Glavan, and Dean Rosenzweig. Towards a mathematical specification of the APE100 architecture: The apese model. In B. Pehrson and I. Simon, editors, *Proc. of the IFIP 13th World Computer Congress 1994, Volume I: Technology and Foundations*, pages 396–401. Elsevier Science Publishers B. V., 1994.

9. Egon Börger and Uwe Glässer. A formal specification of the PVM architecture. In B. Pehrson and I. Simon, editors, *Proc. of the IFIP 13th World Computer Congress 1994, Volume I: Technology and Foundations*, pages 402–409. Elsevier Science Publishers B. V., 1994.

10. Manfred Broy, Frank Dederichs, Claus Dendorfer, Max Fuchs, Thomas F. Gritzner, and Rainer Weber. The design of distributed systems – an introduction to FO-CUS. Technical Report TUM-19202-2 (SFB-Bericht Nr. 342/2-2/92/A), Institut für Informatik, Technische Universität München, January 1993.

11. Igor Đurđanović and Uwe Glässer. An evolving algebra abstract machine. FB Mathematik & Informatik, Universität-GH Paderborn, Report, May 1995.

12. George Grätzer. *Universal Algebra*. Van Nostrand, 1968.

13. Yuri Gurevich. Evolving algebras – a tutorial introduction. *Bulletin of the EATCS*, (43):264–284, February 1991.

14. Yuri Gurevich. Evolving Algebra 1993: Lipari Guide. In E. Börger, editor, *Specification and Validation Methods*. Oxford University Press, 1995.

15. Yuri Gurevich, Jim Huggins, and Raghu Mani. The generalized railroad crossing problem: An evolving algebra based solution. CSE Technical Report CSE-TR-230-95, EECS Department, University of Michigan–Ann Arbor, 1995.

16. D. Harel and A. Pnueli. On the development of reactive systems. In Krzysztof R. Apt, editor, *Logics and Models of Concurrent Systems*, pages 477–498. Springer-Verlag, 1985.

17. Gerald J. Holzman. The theory and practice of a formal method: NewCoRe. In B. Pehrson and I. Simon, editors, *Proc. of the IFIP 13th World Computer Congress 1994, Volume I: Technology and Foundations*, pages 35–44. Elsevier Science Publishers B. V., 1994.

18. Jim Huggins. Kermit: Specification and verification. In E. Börger, editor, *Specification and Validation Methods*. Oxford University Press, 1995.

19. The Institute of Electrical and Electronics Engineering. *IEEE Standard VHDL Language Reference Manual—IEEE Std 1076-1993*, New York, NY, USA, 1994. Order Code SH16840.

20. T. Lindner C. Lewerentz, editor. *Formal Development of Reactive Systems*, volume 891 of *Lecture Notes in Computer Science*. Springer-Verlag, 1995.

21. Franz Pichler, Heinz Schwärtzel, and Roberto Moreno–Diaz. System Science and Systems Technology: From conceptual frameworks to applicable solutions. In *Proceedings of the Fourth International Workshop on Computer Aided Systems Technology (Ottawa, Ont., May 16-20)*, 1994.

22. A. Pnueli. Applications of temporal logic to the specification and verification of reactive systems: A survey of current trends. In J. W. de Bakker, W.-P. de Roever,

and G. Rozenberg, editors, *Current Trends in Concurrency—Overviews and Tutorials*, volume 224 of *Lecture Notes in Computer Science*, pages 510–584. Springer-Verlag, 1986.

23. Christoph Schaffer and Herbert Prähofer. On requirements for a CAST-tool for complex, reactive system analysis, design and evaluation. In F. Pichler and R. Moreno–Diaz, editors, *Computer Aided Systems Theory – EUROCAST'93*, volume 763 of *Lecture Notes in Computer Science*, pages 137–159. Springer-Verlag, 1994.

24. A. Wayne Wymore, editor. *Model–Based Systems Engineering: An Introduction to the Mathematical Theory of System Design*, chapter 1. Systems Engineering Series. CRC Press, 1993.

DEVS-Based Endomorphic Agents: Control Through Deliberative and Reactive Planning

Hamaidi Lyes, Patrick Bourseau and Gilles Muratet

Ecole Nationale Superieure de Chimie de Paris
UR Modelisation, Equipe Procedes Chimiques
11 rue P. M. Curie, 75231 Paris Cedex 05, FRANCE

Jerry M. Couretas and Bernard P. Zeigler

AI and Simulation Research Group
Department of Electrical and Computer Engineering
University of Arizona, Tucson, AZ 85721

Abstract. A DEVS-based Endomorphic Agent employs models of the environment and itself to achieve autonomy in various way. In this paper, we present a framework for an agent able to flexibly reprogram itself under changing objectives or constraints such as might be provided in a flexible manufacturing environment. We show how the agent is able to employ its DEVS-models to develop control schemes for given objectives and constraints. The schemes can then be revised as required when a change in the desired objectives or constraints occurrs. The systems model knowledge representation thus gives the agent greater flexibility and autonomy than is possible with purely rective planners or supervisory controllers.

1 Introduction

Designing autonomous agents is a difficult problem for artificial intelligence because they operate in dynamic environments in which sensing and perception is difficult, and can only be done with uncertainty. Yet, engineers have long been able to build automatic devices that function effectively for long periods in the physical world without human intervention. From the governors controlling steam engine speed to complex guidance systems, these devices work as well as they do because they have the means for changing their actions based on continuously sensed properties of their environment. We accept the control theory's central notion that continuous feedback is a necessary component for effective action.

Perhaps it is easier for control theorists than computer scientists to think about continuous feedback. Control theorists conceive of their mechanisms as composed of electrical circuits or other physical systems rather than as automata with discrete read-compute-write cycles. The basics notions of goal seeking servo-mechanisms include homeostasis, feedback, filtering, and stability. These are so essential to control in dynamic environments and also arise naturally when one builds control devices with electrical circuits. Circuits, by their nature, are continuously responsive to their inputs.

On the other hand, some of the central ideas of computer science including sequences, events, discrete actions, and subroutines seem incompatible with the notion of continuous feedback. For example, in conventional programming, when one program calls another the calling program is suspended until the called program returns control. This feature is awkward in applications in which the called program might encounter unexpected environmental circumstances. In such cases, the calling program can regain control through interrupts explicitly provided by the programmer.

Attempts to blend control theory and computer science have been made. For example, the work of Ramadge and Wonham [17] on discrete-event systems used the computer science notions of events, grammars, and discrete states to study the control of processes for which those ideas are appropriate. A recent book by Dean and Wellman [7] focuses on the overlap between control theory and artificial intelligence.

The various methods of planning and control differ substantially in how they allocate attention to monitoring and prediction. Moreover, the standard techniques employed in these two disciplines are based on distinct forms of process models. These methods draw on variant terminologies and seemingly divergent technical traditions. Nevertheless, at a fundamental level, planning and control address the same problem: choosing actions over time to influence a process based on some model of that process. Starting with this common perspective, planning and control can be viewed as complementary bodies of techniques. Each is effective in varying degrees over different classes of the same basic problem.

In the succeeding sections, we survey these two perspectives in preparation for the third section, where we will demonstrate the need of a hybrid approach integrating both planning and control.

2 The Delebirative Control

The predominant view of goal directed agent activity in AI is based upon the "Plan, then Execute" strategy of Ambros-Ingerson [4]. In this model, an action plan is synthesized in its entirety before an execution phase can begin. This is the phase in which the agents attempt to carry out the actions specified by the plan.

The deliberative processing view assumes that reasoning has largely supplanted reactive behavior commonly found in animals. Yet, no explanation is offered for how this conversion from reaction to reasoning might have occurred. Typically, models colored by this worldview begin their inquiry from the top, positing highly structured symbolic representation of knowledge that is manipulated according to rules of logic to produce behavior.

Planning for a task is seen as searching through a problem space for an appropriate sequence of operators to transform the initial state to a desired goal state. Only then is the plan executed. For the deliberative view, processing is decomposed into three main modules: perception, reasoning, and execution. First, the task is perceived according to the initial and goal states, then a solution is fully reasoned out using a search through the appropriate problem space. Finally, the computed actions are executed.

Because deliberative processing models plan by searching through problem spaces, they have been quite successful when applied to problems with the following features:

- The domain can be described with discrete states

- Tasks in the domain can be defined by an initial state and a goal state

- Given the current state and an operator, the next state can be uniquely determined

Deliberative control requires plan monitoring to check which actions achieved their expected results, and that the environment is unchanged relative to present planning. Should plan execution fail due to a necessary action never achieving its postcondition, then replanning is necessary.

A failure usually involves discarding all or most of the original plan, thus wasting a lot of the earlier planning effort. In addition, the most powerful and general planners developed with this approach, i.e. hierarchical and non-linear, are subject to combinatorial explosions as explained by Chapman [5]. These two problems result in the classical agent architecture being unsuitable for complex and/or dynamic domains. This is perhaps most clearly demonstrated by the fact that the archetypical planning domain is the blocks world. This contains relatively few objects and assumes that a single agent, controlling the robot arm, is the only entity capable of changing the environment.

3. The Reactive Control

Another control solution has recently been proposed, "reactive control"[1] [2] [3]. The basis of this approach is that real-time performance of agents embedded in a complex domain can be achieved by some form of direct mapping from a situation, i.e. particular environmental conditions, to action. This situation-action mapping needs to have near complete coverage of possible environmental situations to achieve prespecified goals. The advantage is that with a sufficiently well-designed mapping, the agent can react appropriately to sudden environment changes in a timely manner. The simplest example of this is a system that perceives its environment through external sensors, and uses this to index a look-up table of responses. This foregoes a time-consuming search process.

This initial outline may seem to imply that reactive control is essentially advocating behaviorism under a different name. While this may be the case of the most simplistic reactive systems, this charge cannot be laid against more sophisticated reactive controllers. Controllers of this kind allow for internal states, which represent such things as goals, beliefs, values, etc. Actions are then selected on the basis of internal states in conjunction with the external world state. Such systems therefore need not always select the same action in the same situation and their behavior is not fully contingent upon the environment.

The strength of purely behavior-based, or non-deliberative, architectures lies in their ability to identify and exploit local patterns of activity in their current surroundings. These responses are more or less hardwired in that they use no memory, predictive reasoning, and minimal state information to process a given set of environmental stimuli. Successful operations of this control method presupposes:

1. That the complete set of environmental stimuli required for unambiguously determining subsequent action sequences is always present and readily identifiable - in other words, that the agent activity can be strictly situationally determined.

2. That the agent has no global task constraints - for example, explicit temporal deadlines - which need to be reasoned about at run-time

3. The agent's goal or desire system is capable of being represented implicitly in the agent's structure according to a fixed, precompiled ranking scheme.

Although fairly complex behaviors can be carried out in a Markov environment, very often an agent cannot be assumed to have complete knowledge about the effects and/or costs of its own actions. Non-Markov situations are basically of two different types:

Hidden State Environment A hidden state is a part of the environmental situation that is not accessible to the agent, but is relevant to the effects and/or costs of the actions. If the environment includes hidden states, a reactive agent cannot choose an optimal action; for example, a reactive agent cannot decide an optimal movement to reach an object that it does not see.

Sequential Behavior Suppose that at time t an agent has to choose an action as a consequence to an action performed at time t_{-1}. A reactive agent can perform an optimal choice only if the action performed at time t-1 has some characteristic and observable effect at time t. That is, only if the agent can infer which action was performed at time t_{-1} by inspecting the environment at time t.

4 Why a Hybrid Approach?

Situationally determined behavior will succeed when there is sufficient local constraints in the agent's environment to determine actions that have no detrimental long-term effects. Only then will the agent be able to avoid representing alternative courses of action to determine which ones lead to dead ends, loops, local minima, or otherwise undesirable outcomes.

Many activities require knowledge which cannot found in its entirety. Difficult to obtain information includes those interactions involving other agents, which typically require making behavior predictions and reasoning about plans and goals. Another example is information requiring responses to events and actions which are either spatially or temporally beyond the agent's current sensory limits. These cannot be considered situationally determined as they often require knowledge about the agent's environment, which is not immediately available through perception. The common defining feature of such tasks, in effect, is that besides requiring reliable and robust local control to be carried out, they also possess a non-local or global structure which will need to be addressed by the agent.

Non-deliberative control techniques ensure fast responses to changing events is the environment. By virtue of being represented implicitly, in effect embedded in the agent's own structure or behavioral rule set, they do not enable the agent action choices to be influenced by deliberative reasoning. When goals are not represented explicitly, they cannot be changed dynamically and there is no way to reason about alternative plans. Moreover, without explicit goals, it is not clear how an agent will learn or improve its performance.

There are undoubtedly a number of real-world domains which are suitable for strictly non-deliberative agent control architectures. It is less likely whether there exist any realistic or non-trivial domains which are equally suited to purely deliberative agents. What is most likely, however, is that the majority of real world domains will require that intelligent autonomous agents be capable of a wide range of behaviors, including some basic non-deliberative ones such as perception driven reaction. This should also include more complex deliberative behaviors such as flexible task planning, strategic decision making, complex, i.e. time dependent and prioritized goal handling, or predictive reasoning about the beliefs and intentions of other agents.

Our position is that it is both desirable and feasible to combine deliberative and non-deliberative control. These functions can obtain effective, robust, and flexible behavior from autonomous agents operating in real time multi-agent environments. In particular, the research highlighted here is concerned with the design and implementation of an integrated agent control architecture. This is suited for controlling and coordinating the actions of autonomous agents embedded in a dynamic, multi-agent world. This architecture employs classical planning as a declarative problem-solving method integrated with situation-action rules. By integrating a high-level declarative planner with a reactive layer using situation-action rules, the architecture combines the flexibility of the former with the efficiency of the latter.

Recently, there have been efforts to develop a combined controller [9] [10] [15]. Due to the divided research between deliberative and reactive planning, the technology of the two fields has also been divided. We believe the major difficulty in trying to build a combined planner is integrating the different methods of each area.

5 The Overall Agent Architecture

Intelligent Control is a kind of feedback control that supervises the behavior of a plant to control the plant in desired objectives. It is assumed that the behavior of the plant is known. Thus the agent can deduce the current behavior of the plant from the observed output events. Then it compares the behavior with desired one and generates appropriate next control outputs.

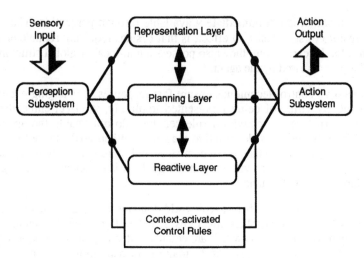

Fig. 1. The Overall agent architecture

To achieve realism, models of intelligent agents must represent not only decision making capabilities but also the models on which such capabilities are based. As a concrete illustration, consider modeling of air traffic control. The simulation model must contain representations of aircraft being controlled and the radar that detects them as well as of the human air traffic controllers. The latter model can represent not only the decision making employed by air traffic controllers, but also the models of the world built up from the radar data in the form of pictures. The controllers uses these to generate commands. The latter representation includes what Zeigler [19] calls look-a-head use of internal models to answer "what if" questions about planning such as "what would happen if this aircraft moved there?"

The controller is a generic engine, similar to an inference engine.

5.1 The DEVS Formalism

As explained by Zeigler [18], the Discrete Event System Specification(DEVS) is a formalism through which a system is specified. A system is defined as having a time base, inputs, states, outputs, and functions which determine the next states and the outputs resulting from the current state and input. Discrete event systems handle all of these elements of a model differently than continuous systems do. While continuous systems represent inputs as piecewise continuous functions of time, a discrete event system represents them at arbitrarily spaced moments. The key difference provided bye the DEVS formalism in is the easy specification it allows for defining discrete event system parameters.

The ideological underpinning to the DEVS formalism has three basic objects:

Real System The fundamental source of data, this can be an operating entity melded into a system to extract its contribution to the systems behavior, or it can be a proposed prototype.

Model A homomorphism of the real system, the model's behavior is the set of all possible data that can be generated by executing the model's instructions - the instructions define its structure.

Simulator This exercises the model's instructions to generate its behavior.

The basic objects of the system are made meaningful by two relations:

Modeling Relation This defines how well the model represents the system or entity being modeled. The modeling relation is valid if the model data and real system data agree in the domain of interest.

Simulation Relation This represents how well the simulator carries out the instructions of the model.

System or model data comes in the form of time segments. A time segment maps from intervals defined over a specified time base to values in the range of one or more variables.

A model's structure is expressed in a mathematical language called a formalism. The discrete event formalism focuses on variable value changes and generates piecewise constant time segments. An event is therefore an instantaneous change in a variable value.

DEVS basically defines how to generate new variable values and at what times the new values should be in effect. One thing to note is that the time intervals between events are variable - in discrete time systems, the time step is a fixed number.

Discrete Event System Specification:

In the DEVS formalism, one must specify:

- Basic models from which larger ones are built

- How these models are connected together in hierarchical fashion

We define basic models by the following structure:

$$M = (\ X, S, Y, d_{int}, d_{ext}, \lambda, ta\ )$$

X   the set of external input event types

S   the set of sequential states

δ_{int} the internal transition function dictating state transitions due to internal events

δ_{ext} the external transition function dictating state transitions due to external events

λ the output function generating external events at the output

ta the time advance function

A very useful aspect of the DEVS formalism is that a multi-component model can be expressed as a basic model. The allows the coupled model to then be incorporated into other multi-component models in a hierarchical fashion. This allows abstract behaviors to be encapsulated in a single coupled model, internally connected to interact and produce outputs corresponding to those of the real world model when stimulated with the same inputs.

5.2 The Internal DEVS-Based Representation

Like most real-world domains, a process plant is populated by multiple entities and so will often involve complex dynamics process. For an agent and, to be useful in such domains, a number of special skills are likely to be required. Among these are the ability to monitor the execution of one' own actions, the ability to reason about actions in futur, the ability to deal with actions which might (negatively) interfere with one another or with one's own goal, and the ability to form contingency plans to overcome such interference.

The potential gain from incorporating a internal modelling or endomorphic capabilities in an autonomous agent is that by making succesful predictions about entities activities the agent should be able to detect potential goal conflicts earlier on. This would enable it to make changes to its own plans in a more effective manner than if it were to wait for these conflicts to materialize. The space-time projections (in effect, knowledge-level simulations) thus created by the agent to detect any potential interference or goal conflicts among the modelled entities' anticipated/desired actions. Should any conflicts intra or inter-agent be identified, the agent will then have to determin how such conflicts might best be resolved, and also which entities will be responsible for carrying out these resolutions.

Kaelbling and Rosenschein [12] refer to "computer systems that sense and act on their environments" as embedded agents or situated automata. An ideal environment for the interoperation of these agents is DEVS [18]. It provides a means of specifying autonomous systems as consisting of time bases, inputs, states, outputs, next states and output functions given the current states and inputs. Given the inherent hierarchical and modular construction of DEVS, it is extensible to any system or control architecture desired.

We want to program agents to achieve various goals in their environment. These goals are specified in terms of the state vector components, embedded into the agent in the form of its internal transition function, dint. The agent can only tell whether or not it has achieved its goal through its sensory apparatus, or external transition function, dext. Therefore, we have to specify goals in terms of the agent's transition functions, which are its sensory mechanisms.

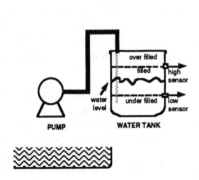

Fig. 2. The Tank-Pump example

Generating an initial agent operation plan is a two step process. First one takes a cross-product of the states of each system in the environment for which an agent response is required. Second, the agent is constructed to react to this environmental information through its external perception, δ_{ext}, and internal reasoning, δ_{int}. Figure 2 shows an example system. This system's agent is responsible for coordinating the filling of the tank using the water-pump.

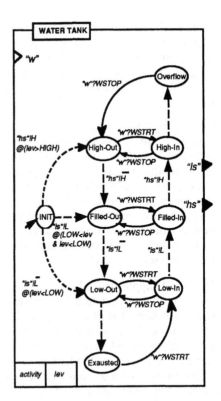

Fig. 3. The Tank State Diagram's

The tank and the pump states shown in Figure 2 are combined via cross-product to produce the overall system state transition diagram. From this the agent's responses are formed.

Sometimes an agent's actions do not have the effect anticipated by the agent's designer. Sometimes environmental dynamics, which are separate from the actions of the agent, change the world in unexpected and even helpful ways. These phenomena, of course, are the reason continuous feedback is required. When the world is not completely predictable, the agent need constantly check to see which, if any, of its goals and preconditions for actions are satisfied.

6 The Controller Architecture

Our position is that is it both desirable and feasible to combine deliberative and non-deliberative control functions to obtain effective, robust, and flexible behaviour from autonomous agents operating in real time multi-agent environment. In particular, the research highlighted here is concerned with the design and implementaion of an integrated agent control architecture, suitable for controlling and coordinating the actions of autonomous agents embedded in a dynamic, multi-agent world. This architecture employs a classical planning as a declarative problem-solving method integrated with situation-action rules as the compiled results of this planning. By integrating a high-level declarative planner with a reactive layer using situated-action rules, the architecture combines the flexebility of the former with the efficiency of the latter.

One possible architecture as illustrated in Figure 1 for a system integrating high-level planning and low-level control might consist of two components: a tactical component that determines what to do at the next instant, and a strategic component that attempts to mediate the behavior of the tactical component by imposing constraints on the behavior of the low-level systems. It is up to the tactical component to interpert the constraints provided by the strategic component so as to adjust the behavior of the low-level systems while at the same time maintaining real-time performance. To provide a label for the two kinds of control qnd identify the source for the corresponding mind sets, we call the first the planning level and the second the reactive level.

In many AI applications, Levesque and Brachman [16] point out a fundamental trade-off between representational power and computational tractability. Intelligent control is no exception. The different layers in our architecture occupy different positions of this trade-off. Thus, as one moves up through the different levels, flexibility increases but computational efficiency decreases. The first level is a very high-level specification system for planners. The second level is an interpreter for situation-action rules, which are automatically derived from the first level generated plans. Finally, the lowest level at which the system interacts with the world, either through sensors or via effectors.

DEVS'[18] internal and external transitions are the basic components of our proposed controller architecture. This is intended for use in domains which are neither entirely static, such as the traditional formulation of the blocks-world, nor entirely dynamic, such as video games. In the former, classical planners are sufficient, while in the latter only "pure" reactive controllers are useful. Instead, our architecture is intended for domains which have some dynamic elements, but in which the "peace of life" is not so frantic that the agent never has sufficient time to engage in classical planning.

6.1 The Planning Level

In the general planning framework, the robot is given a causal event model, the agent's internal representation of the external world, with a distinguished subset of events, called actions, deemed under the agent's control. In other words, the agent can directly establish the truth of actions, but can influence other events only indirectly through their causal relations to actions. The agent also has some objectives of describing desirable properties of controlled processes in terms of event patterns. Planning is the process of assembling basic actions into a composite plan, in the form of an object, designed to further these objectives.

An agent system architecture is made up of many components, as shown in Figure 1. The core component of an agent is a planner, the tool which find a sequence of actions to achieve the current objective of the operating procedure. In this section we present the design of our prototype planning system, based on the state graph planning paradigm. In this case the planner is the search engine which finds a path through the graph from the current state to a goal state.

The state graph planning paradigm appears to have been proposed independently by Ivanov et al [11] and Kinoshita [14]. In this approach problems are represented as a graph of the possible states of the planning domain (process plant). Directed arcs in the graph representing the use of an action to move from one state to another. Using this representation, the planner must find the path through the graph from the start node to the goal node.

State graph planning has many advantages. It does not require complex techniques to deal safety and valid sequencing operations. Planning time using this approach is bounded by a polynomial function on the number of arcs in the state graph. Most others planners have an exponential time complexity.

Ideally a planning engine should use a backward chaining search so that heuristics like means-end analysis can be used. AI planning research has shown that very efficient backward chaining planners can be created [6].

The tools surrounding the planner in the agent system architecture seems to require a forward chaining approach. For example, the natural way to verify the safety of an operating procedure is to simulate the effects of the plan step by step. If plans are created in order, from the first action to the last, then this natural safety cheking algorithm can be used. However, if the planner uses a backward chaining search, and especially if the planner uses a least commitment approach, then safety cheking become more complex. Other related problems, like ction synergy, are also harder to solve by the use of backward chaining.

Most of the current Operation Procedure Synthesis (OPS), kind of planner used in chemical plant control are based on forward chaining search strategy. However, these forward chaining planners are limited because of problems with planning time. So in our approch we use a forward planning tool with an advanced graph searching procedure using Genetics algorithm to overcome the planning time problem [13].

In our approach, an agent dynamically constructs, refines, and modifies plans for its actions. For example, given a goal to empty the tank, the agent might construct and follow the plan in Figure 4 (bold lines), which is the cross product of the tank-pump system shown in Figure 2. This plan is comparable to the sort of plan that might be generated and refined top-down by a traditional planning system. Unlike traditional planning control, we assume that planning occurs dynamically at run-time. The planning level preserves a key strength of the traditional planning model: it recognizes and implements the fact that an agent cannot be at the mercy of its sensors, but must be able to construct and follow a goal-oriented course of action. It focuses attention on activities that help it follow the goal-oriented plan it previously adopted.

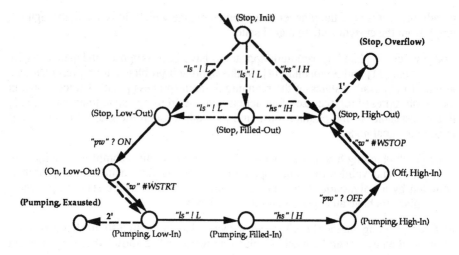

Fig. 4. A state graph representation of a plan

Usually more than one action is required to achieve a specified goal. The reasons for multiple actions are, first, that separate actions might be required to achieve different components of the goal. Second, some of the goal-achieving actions might not be executable in the agent's current environment. This necessitates the performance of enabling precedence actions. The situation-action rules result from this analysis; they constrain the actions that might be taken at any state to those that produce a state that is on the path to the goal.

Improving planner performance in real-time control requires raising the question of how the agent should decide its response when faced with a novel situation. In a potentially time-critical situation, three basic planning strategies are possible:

The first strategy, *Full-planning*, requires invoking the planner with the current situation description and the overall agent goal. This strategy is the most time-consuming of the three but delivers a plan from which the derived situation-action rules are guaranteed to achieve the goal in the optimal number of steps. Most classical planners implicitly use this strategy. It is more appropriate in cases where decision-making is not time-critical, i.e. for off-line planning or in static domains.

Partial Planning provides an alternative strategy of finding the situation-action rule for the goal whose situation description is "closest" to the actual situation. As a simple heuristic the "closest" might be defined as the rule whose situation description has the most states, or predicates, that are the same as the actual situation. This strategy should reduce planning time and the resultant situation-action rules will still advance the agents towards its goal. However, unlike full-planning, this strategy does not guarantee an optimal solution. The partial-planning strategy might be used in cases where time-criticality is a factor in problem solving but "instant" decisions are not needed. Thus, it seems suitable for moderately dynamic domains.

The final possibility is *Guess-an-Action*. Under this strategy, an action which is applicable in the current situation is selected at random and then executed. The guess-an-action strategy is the least expensive computationally. However, there is no guarantee that the selected action has utility in achieving the goal, and under certain circumstances it may even render the goal unachievable. This strategy is thus very similar to Drummond's [8] strategy of allowing the execution module to select actions directly from the plan net before full planning has been completed. The guess-an-action strategy is most useful for highly time-critical situations and is based on the principle that in emergencies it is better to make an "intelligent guess" about the action to perform rather doing nothing. It is thus suitable for highly dynamic domains, but at the cost of impaired agent performance in comparison to the other two methods.

Obviously, the previous basic strategies can be combined to form a more sophisticated hybrid strategy, namely "Guess-Then-Try-to-Plan." As in the guess-an-action strategy, a random action is selected. This action is then scheduled for execution but not actually executed. Partial planning is then begins but with the additional proviso that it can be interrupted and the scheduled action executed only if the available decision-making time is exceeded. This strategy can be generalized further, so that after partial-planning has been completed, and no need to act has been detected. Thus, the system may engage in full planning again with the proviso that this process may be interrupted. This strategy seems to offer an optimal compromise in the performance-decision speed trade-off and is thus appropriate to domains with any degree of dynamism.

6.2 The Reactive Level

The first-level generated plans are used as input by the second-level, which will convert them into situation-action rules. These rules can later be used to control the agent's activities without the need to resort to planning, unless an entirely novel situation is encountered. A situation-action rule for a goal at the second-level simply consists of a list of predicates describing the world, or situation, which is associated with a predicate describing the action to be performed. This all takes place in that world state so as to progress the agent towards achieving its goal.

The situation-action rules are derived in the following way:

1. The second-level receives from the first-level a plan of actions in the form of a record, of which actions are invoked to prove the goal. This set of actions is temporally ordered.

2. The description of the initial situation in the first-level specification is assigned as the "immediate situation." The first action in the ordering from the planner is similarly assigned the "immediate action."

3. The "immediate situation" is associated with the "immediate action." This then forms one situation-action rule for the goal.

4. The "immediate situation" is updated by simulating the effect of performing the "immediate action" in the "immediate situation," based on the simulation assumption of successful execution in a static environment. This simulation is achieved by a simulation loop on the internal agent representation of the real world.

5. We set the "immediate action" to the next action in the plan, if there is one, and we go to step 2. Otherwise, the procedure terminates.

It should be noted that the "immediate situation" used in the above outline is not intended to be an up-to-date description of the actual world state at the time of rule derivation. It is simply a projected world state description updated at each cycle of the derivation process. It is assumed that later execution will be problem-free.

It may happen that the agent finds itself in a state with no predefined situation-action rules. In that case it should activate the objective associated with the current state and ask the planner to construct a plan that addresses the new objective. The ability to act appropriately over a broad range of situations is an important measure of competence for agents controlling dynamic and unpredictable processes. It is also possible for an agent to find itself without predefined situation-action rules to serve any current plan or objective. In that case, it may attempt to perform actions whose outcome will either trigger plan-relevant-actions or evaluate the system to an objective-based-state.

In order to improve performance of the entire architecture, we provide other facilities to extend the knowledge of the agent prior to its actual embedding in the environment. The designer can "hard-wire" the agent with situation-actions rules which achieve goals in the anticipated situation. It anticipates situations that will be frequently encountered by the agent when it is actually in its world. Hence, the agent need not begin as a tabula rasa and be disadvantaged by initially having to spend all its time in plan generation. All the designer does is put these situation-action rules in the set of constraints.

The question of how much basic knowledge should be given to the agent is a matter for the designer's discretion. Obviously, the more "canned" plans the agent begins with, the better its initial performance will be. But, our intention is not that all problem-solving activity be done for the agent prior to its embedding. As a rough heuristic, the more dynamic the execution domain, the more pre-planning needed for acceptable agent performance.

7   Limitations and Future Work

The main limitation of this method arises because this architecture assumes planners to deliver only the simplest type of plan, namely linearized plans for single goals which allow only one action to be executed at a time. This raises to the reactive module to ensure that it can deal with more complicated plans. In particular how could it deal with conjunctive goals and parallel actions?

Another desirable generalization would be to allow for parallel actions in the reactive module. Parallel actions which do not interact are allowable; but those which do interact are not. Thus, consider a blocks-world using two robot arms. The reactive module could cope with each hand placing a block on the table simultaneously but could not deal with the held blocks being brought together together to form a stack. This is because in the latter case whether the bottom block's description was clear or not would depend on which operator effect template was invoked first.

Another issue that arises is that of deriving situation-action rules from the planner's generated plans. These are generally more applicable than for simply achieving the top-level agent goal. At the moment, all the situation-action rules created from a generated plan are indexed under the goal that was originally passed to the planner. They will therefore only be used if the system is faced with exactly the same top-level goal.

However, situation-actions rules are generally more applicable. For example, consider a plan to stack a on b by removing c from a, removing d from b, picking up a, and finally putting a on b. It is clear that this plan contains actions which achieves the subgoal of clearing a, the subgoal of clearing b, and the subgoal of moving a to b. Currently, however, all situation-actions rules derived from such a plan would be stored together under the banner of "Achieves-a-on-b." By decomposing this rule set into subgoals, the situation-action rules would become employable for different top-level goals and one avoids the redundant storage of the same rules for these different goals. This is a problem which could become particularly acute when conjunctive goals are stored.

A final shortcoming of the present implementation is that the situation-action rules that are the planner's reactive module are in a sense too specific. In the derivation of such rules, we take the entire state of the world before the action occurred as our situation.

However, certain facts are clearly irrelevant to the situation-action rule. Thus, as long a and b are clear, the question of whether c is clear or not is irrelevant to the rule for stacking a on b. We therefore need to restrict the information about the world that is used to build situation-action rules. Note, however, that finding the appropriate definition of irrelevance is not straightforward. In particular, an initial suggestion that the only relevant facts in the world are those that are explicitly referred to in the current action is unsatisfactory. For example, even though the assumption concerning picking up a only refers to whether a is clear and whether the hand is free, if the goal is stacking a on b, the question whether b is clear or not is clearly relevant: when b is not clear, picking up a is not a smart thing to do; one first wants to remove whatever is on top of b.

Finnaly and in order to appreciate the concepts of the proposed approach, an example of the modeling and control of an alchool plant unit where both non- intelligent devices (tank, pump, valves...) and intelligent entities called agent are coexistant, is under study. We try to apply to an illustrative example the differents concepts develloped within the DEVS-based endormophic agent approach. The results of this work will be published in comming publications.

8 Conclusion

We have presented a DEVS based architecture for the construction of autonomous agents functioning in dynamic domains. It employs classical planning as a declarative problem-solving method integrated with situation-action rules as the compiled results of this planning. We argue that the architecture provides the agent with the reactivity needed in time-critical situations. On the other hand, it is also flexible enough that it allows the designer to provide the agent with the basic knowledge necessary to function in the domain prior to its actual embedding.

References

1. P. Agre and D. Chapman, "Pengi: An implementation of a theory of activity" *AAAI*, pp. 268-272, 1987.

2. P. Agre and D. Chapman, "What are Plans for?" AI memo 1050, Department of Computer Science, MIT, 1988.

3. P. Agre, *The dynamic structure of everyday life*, Technical Report 1085, Dept. of Computer Science, MIT, 1988.

4. J.A. Ambros-Ingerson and S. Steel, "Integrating Planning, execution and monitoring" *AAAI*, Vol. 7, Pp. 83-88, 1988.

5. D. Chapman, "Planning for conjunctive goals" *Artificial Intelligence*, Vol. 32, Pp. 333-377, 1987.

6. K. Curie and A. Tate, "O-Plan: the open plan architecture" *Artificial Intelligence*, Vol. 52, Pp. 49-86, 1991.

7. T.L. Dean and M.P. Wellman, *Planning and Control*, Morgan Kaufmann Publishers, California, 1991.

8. M. Drummond and J. Bresina , "Planning for Control" *Proceedings of the 5th IEEE International Symposium on Intelligent Control*, Vol. 2, Pp. 657-62, 1990.

9. I.A. Ferguson, "On the Role of Device Modeling for Autonomous Agent Control" *AAAI workshop on Representing and Reasoning with Device Function*, July 1994.

10. B. Hayes-Roth, "Architectural foundations for real-time performance in intelligent agents" *Real-time Systems: The International Journal of Time-Critical Computing Systems*, vol. 2, Pp. 99-125, 1990.

11. V. A. Ivanov, V. V. Kafarov, V. L. Perov and A.A. Reznichenko, "On algorithmization of the start-up of chemical productions" *Computers Cybernetics*, Vol. 18, Pp. 104-110.

12. L.P. Kaelbling and S.J. Rosenschein, "Action and Planning in Embedded Agents" *Robotics and Autonomous Systems*, Vol. 6, Pp. 35-48, 1990.

13. Kim J., L. Hamaidi and B. P. Zeigler (1995). A planner for the manufacturing system using evolution strategies. To appear

14. A. Kinoshita, T. Umeda and E. O'Shima, "An algorithm for synthesisof operational sequences of chemical plants. *In 14th European Symposium on*

Computerized control and operation of chemical plants, Pp363-368, Vienna 1981.

15. J.J. Lee, W.D. Norris, and P.A. Fishwick, *An Object-Oriented Multimodel Design for integrating simulation and planning tasks*, Internal Report, University of Florida, 1993.

16. H.J. Levesque and R.J. Brachman, "A fundamental tradeoff in knowledge representation and reasoning" *Readings in Knowledge Representation*, ed. R.J. Brachman \& H.J. Levesque, Morgan Kaufmann, New York, 1985.

17. P.J.G. Ramadge and W.M. Wonham, "The Control of Discrete Event Systems" *Proceedings of the IEEE*, Vol. 77, No. 1, Pp. 81-98, 1989.

18. B.P. Zeigler, *Multifaceted Modelling and Discrete Event Simulation*, Academic Press, San Diego, 1984.

19. B.P. Zeigler, *Object Oriented Simulation with Hierarchical, Modular Models*, Academic Press, San Diego, 1990.

Software Processes, Work Flow and Work Cell Design - Separated by a Common Paradigm?*

Gerhard Chroust and Witold Jacak

System Engineering and Automation
Johannes Kepler University Linz, A 4040 Linz, Austria
email: chroust@sea.uni-linz.ac.at

Abstract. This paper discusses similarities of computer support in three areas: development of software, supporting the flow of work/documents in an office and the production of goods in a flexible work cell. All three areas obey the same underlying principle, i.e. defining a process and then interpreting the process by an enactment (interpretation) mechanism. In the paper elementary questions with respect to the similarity are raised and tentative answers given. The conclusion is that the use of the same paradigm is valid, that considerable difference have to be considered in its implementation.

1 The Process/Interpreter Paradigm

One of the fundamental ideas of automation is the separation of the WHAT ('what one wants to achieve') from the HOW ('how this is to be done').
In many instances the HOW can be standardized and largely left to a computer. The WHAT is then expressed in a so-called *process model* which is interpreted by an interpreter ('enacted' [10] [21]) similar to an interpreter for a programming language (Fig. 1). Once this paradigm is established the next step is usually the creation of an engineering environment which provides all necessary components to support the development process. A typical environment for software development is sketched in Fig. 1.

One recognizes the process engine as the central coordinator which provides access and guidance with respect to the process model, access to the development tools and the results. The tools themselves communicate via the Repository. The interrelationship between these individual components is shown in Fig. 2. This concept has been first implemented for software development [12] [23] [3] but gradually applied to the other areas, too:

software development In software development historically the emphasis was on tools (initially assemblers and compilers, later CASE-tools, [1] [20] [22]). The concept of a software process as an independent focus of concern followed later [29]. Now its importance is understood [27] [21], and the appearance of ISO-9000 and Humphrey's maturity model puts economic pressure on this

---

* This work is partially supported by the Austrian Founds zur Förderung der wissenschaftlichen Forschung, Project P09372-PHY (CADforCIM)

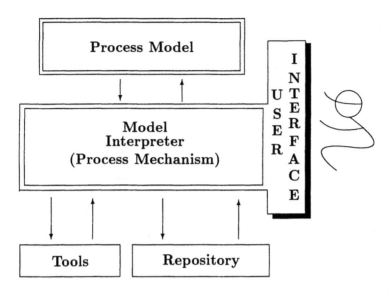

Fig. 1. Components of a SW Engineering Environment

area. The challenge is to define a *SOCIO-technical* process (development) to create a *socio-TECHNICAL* process (a program).

work cell design (Workcell) Automation of production processes has always been the backbone of industrialization. Today fully automatic intelligent work cells [5] [14] [15] exist, where machines, robots and transportation facilities produce goods, controlled by local and global programs loaded-down into each component of such a cell (Fig. 3). The design process for these programs is currently largely done in an ad-hoc, stand-alone fashion. In the last few years, however the idea of a process engineering environment and a development process guided by a process model has been accepted: We are involved in a *SOCIO-technical* process (design) creating a *socio-TECHNICAL* process (work cell programs).

work flow enactment In administrative work a different approach can be found: Administrative procedures and bureaucracy were always given special attention, even in archaic empires like Assyria [26] or Egypt [17]. Administration is mostly a human activity. The question of automatic enactment of the process was not a major issue. The challenge is to perform a *SOCIO-technical* process (design) to create another *SOCIO-technical* process (the office procedure).

Only in the last few years the support for the office has reached a certain level of attention. Computer Supported Cooperative Work (CSCW) [25] and in particular the support of flow of documents are under study: *work flow*.

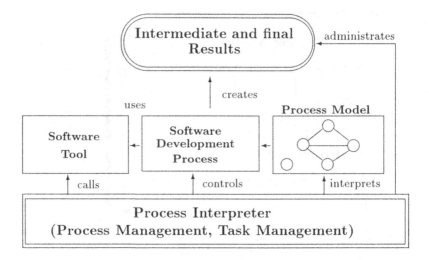

Fig. 2. Functional schema of a software development environment

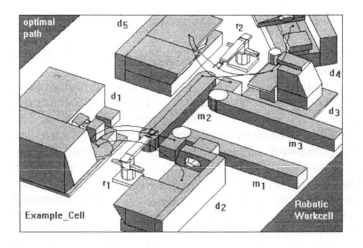

Fig. 3. Simulation model of a work cell

2 Separated by a common paradigm?

It is legitimate to ask, whether beyond the very basic concept, as shown in Fig. 1 and Fig. 2, three areas are supported by the same paradigms, concepts and tools, especially with respect to the process enactment mechanism. We therefore compare the three areas with respect to various properties (also [2] [4] [5]) Fig. 4.

When doing this comparison we take rather extreme positions with respect to the character of these environment, although we know that usually the differences are not so clear cut.

Meta-Levels: What level of product and process do we distinguish? shows the hierarchy of processes in each area, as seen from a developer's viewpoint. We see two product levels (target product, end product), two enactment levels (development process, product enactment) and a guidance level.

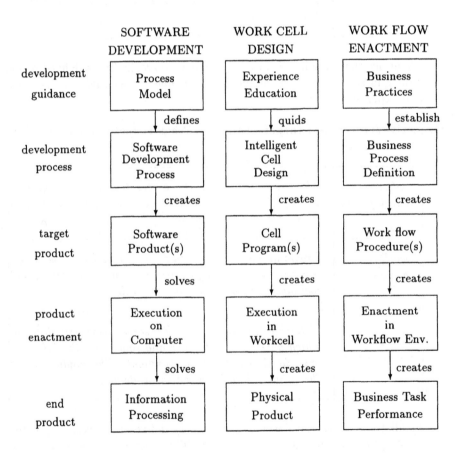

Fig. 4. Alternative Process Automation Areas

software development	The result is the description of a process (the 'program') which has to be enacted on a (usually different) machine.
work cell design	A largely heuristic engineering process is used to design the programs for the individual work cells (or work cell compounds).
workflow enactment	A given (administrative) process is enacted and controlled by computer, documents are routed to the enactors and the admissibility of performing the intended actions is controlled.

We notice that only in software development we really find a defined process model, in the other two areas the process is much more guided by heuristics and experience.

Objective/Outcome (Target product): What is the objective of process enactment?

software development	The objective is to create via accepted software engineering practices a computer system. This system is then run in the target environment.
work cell design	Programs for the individual components of a work cell are created. The design process includes simulation and loading-down to the actual work cell.
workflow enactment	The objective is to produce some document/decision which have some influence and impact on the 'life outside the development environment'. The application of the result is largely in the social domain.

In all three cases the development process defines a process template, a prescription how to execute the process. The prescriptiveness of the target product is different in the three considered areas: cell programs are fully coded and do not lend themselves to ambiguity, for work flow it is largely a prescription for humans as to their activities, software seems to be in the middle.

Objective/Outcome (end product): What is the purpose of the end product?

software development	The objective is to solve an information processing task, the solution of a real-world problem.
work cell design	The results are some real-world physical products.
workflow enactment	The produced document/decision influences the 'life outside the development environment'.

We notice that in the work cell design we completely change the medium between development and use. to some extent also in work flow. Software products stay basically on the same medium (computer) although they might change the platform.

Implications with respect to user creativity: How and where does human creativity get in ?

software development	Creativity is expended in defining the appropriate development process (methods!) and in designing the actual programs.
work cell design	The creativity is mostly spent in designing the interplay/interfaces between the programs/components of the work cell. The work cell programs themselves are rather standardized. The design process is iterative and loosely defined.
workflow enactment	Creativity is not an important issue, except when performing individual activities (decision making) on the level of product enactment. Business restructuring, however, will soon involve creativity in process definition.

For software the use of creativity (cf. also [6], [19]), is necessary both in defining the contents of the target product and also the actual steps in producing it. For work cells the individual components (robots and machines) are largely fixed as well as the sequence operations. Creativity is expended in finding optimal arrangements and minimal resources (energy, speed). For workflow the challenge is to simplify the procedures and to simplify the procedures without violating external constraints, cf. business process reengineering [9].

Human Interaction: What type of interactions expect humans when cooperating with the process?

software development	*The human partner considers himself mainly as a creative engineer, being either helped or straight-jacketed by process enactment, depending on the interface design.*
work cell design	*A similar frame of mind as in software development exists, but due to a liberal design process little straightjacket feeling arises.*
workflow enactment	*Users see themselves as officials following pre-established procedures, applying their creativity within individual activities.*

It seems that in this area major psychological differences can be detected: While in software engineering the 'creative artist' is still the accepted vision, the engineering aspect is predominant for work cell design. In the workflow context the aspect of conformity to established rules/procedures is prevalent.

Strictness/Liberality of Navigation: How strict a process is prescribed by the model?

software development	*'strict control of a liberal process'. [13].*
work cell design	*'liberal control of a liberal process'.*
workflow enactment	*'strict control of a strict process'.*

This discussion is strongly related to the discussion of creativity. Given the varying interaction with humans both when designing the target product and when applying it to create the end product, different navigation strategies are necessary.

Formally defined results: What predefined representation and structure is expected from the results? How much standardization is expected?

software development	Gradually the representation and contents of results is standardized and formalized (e.g. terminology [11], notation for diagrams etc.)
work cell design	At the design level little formalism exists. The cell programs, on the other hand, must be fully formalized.
workflow enactment	The external form of results is usually formalized. A strong standardization of interfaces is pushed by the Workflow Management Coalition [28].

The nature of work cells and computer interfaces requires considerable formalism. Once work flow systems (cf. [7] [8]) will become common place, their interfaces will also require more formalism than now, a tendency which reflects itself in work flow systems.

Documentability: How precisely does one have to document the performed steps in the process?

software development	The actually performed development process has only historical interest.
work cell design	Although the actually performed development process has only little importance, in order to reuse know-how, most of the information will be kept.
workflow enactment	The actual steps (even iterations) of the process have to be exactly recorded, failure to follow the process might invalidate the result on formal grounds.

Considerable differences exist in this area, largely due to legal restrictions for work flow execution.

Multiplicity of instantions: What orders of magnitude are envisioned as instances of the model's meta-results and meta-activities? How many instances of the whole process are expected?

software development	One starts with a few instances per meta-result (resp. meta-activity) but the number of instances grows 'in the middle', i.e. in the implementation phase, to be reduced to a few instances during integration ('the final product').
work cell design	Only a small number of instances per result exist, the development process is rather 'one-of-a-kind'.
workflow enactment	Work Flow is rather restricted to few 'folders' passing through the system.

Despite the fact that these differences are logically largely irrelevant, they have a considerable influence on the actual design of the support system (their quantitative layout). Access mechanisms, sort mechanisms, retrieval mechanism must take this into account.

Validation/Verification: How can the validity of the process be shown?

software development	Both with respect to the development process (methodology!) and the products the issue of correctness/validation is unresolved.
work cell design	Validation of the process is not an important issue, the validity/correctness of the work cell programs is established by simulation.
workflow enactment	Semantic/pragmatic validity of processes is an important issue, especially with respect to needed business restructuring (lean management!).

Especially with respect to software this is an important, but largely unresolved issue. Malfunctioning of embedded computer systems (atomic power plants!) may adversively affect human mankind. Malfunctioning of work cells can be largely contained locally. Work flow carries the hope that the involved human beings avoid disastrous results.

Process Restructuring: How important is it to restructure the process?

software development	*This is currently not an important issue, since industry is still concerned with defining the process initially.*
work cell design	*This is not an issue at all. After having performed the production, work cells are 'logically' dismantled and re-designed when needed again.*
workflow enactment	*This will soon become one of the major business problems.*

In software development and in work cell design the actual design process has little historical importance (cf. 'documentability') thus it can be changed without too much concern of previous processes.

Re-use: Can previous results be reused? Can results be built for re-use?

software development	*Reuse of partial products is a major issue (object orientation!). Re-use of development processes is still a research topic.*
work cell design	*Reuse of cell programs is partially implemented, reuse of design processes is not yet discussed.*
workflow enactment	*Reuse of business (sub)processes is very important and under discussion.*

Currently only in work cell the reuse of design information is well established, largely due to the relative stability of both robots and tooling machines (cf. [16]). In work flow the reuse in not discussed yet with the exception of standardized sub-procedure. For software-development the re-use of parts of end-product is fast becoming a major issue (cf. [18] [24]).

3 Summary

The apparent similarly of software development, work cell design and work flow enactment induce investigations about a common applicability of the process-definition/enactment paradigm. Transfer of know-how and cross-fertilization of ideas may result, hopefully preventing re-inventions of the wheel.

The paper identified a list of comparison criteria and tried to answer some of the resulting questions. Certain differences were identified, but it seems that there still is enough commonality to justify common research. Obviously more research is needed to answer these questions.

In the authors' opinion it still remains to be seen whether there are other areas of computer applications which also could be included into similar considerations. We believe that many more areas can draw profit from the model/interpreter paradigm and thus become candidates for further comparisons.

References

1. Balzert H.(ed.): CASE - Systeme und Werkzeuge.- B-I Wissenschaftsverlag 1989
2. Chroust G., Leymann F.: Anwendungsentwic und Büroautomation.- Preprints, GI Workshop Königswinter, May 1990.
3. Chroust G.: Software-Entwicklungsumgebungen - Synthese und Integration.- Informatik-Spektrum vol 15 (1992) no. 7, pp. 165-174
4. Chroust G., Leymann F.: Interpretable Process Models for Software Development and Administration.- Trappl R. (ed.): Cybernetics and Systems Research 92, Vienna, April 1992, World Scientific Singapore 1992, pp. 271-278
5. Chroust G., Jacak W.: Simulation in Process Engineering.- Rozenblit J. (ed.): AIS-93, 4th Conf. on AI, Simulation, and Planning in High Autonomy Systems, Tucson Sept. 1993, IEEE C/S Press pp. 232-237.
6. Chroust G.: Quality Implications of System Development Paradigms.- Lucas P. (ed.): Austrian Hungarian Seminar on Software Engineering.- Graz University of Technology, Inst. f. Software Technology, April 20-21, 1995
7. CTR (Computer Technology Research Corp.): Office Automation - Technologies for the 1990s.- Computer Technology Res. Corp., Charleston, SC 1990.
8. Hales K., Lavery M. (eds.): Workflow Management Software: the Business Opportunity.- OVUM Ltd. London 1991.
9. Hammer M., Champy J.: Business Reengineering - Die Radikalkur für das Unternehmen.- Campus Frankfurt/M, 3. Auflage, 1994
10. Hardt S.: Sprachunabhängige dynamische Ausführung von Vorgehensmodellen.- Dissertation, Kepler University Linz, 1994
11. Hesse W., Luft A.L., Keutgen H., Rombach H.D.: Ein Begriffssystem für die Softwaretechnik.- Informatik Spektrum vol. 7 (1984) No. 4, pp. 200-213
12. Huenke H. (ed.): Software Engineering Environments.- Proceedings, Lahnstein, BRD, 1980, North Holland 1981
13. Humphrey W.S.: Managing the Software Process.- Addison-Wesley Reading Mass. 1989
14. Jacak W., Rozenblit J.W.: Virtual Process Design Techniques for Intelligent Manufacturing.- Rozenblit J. (ed.): AIS-93, 4th Conf. on AI, Simulation, and Planning in High Autonomy Systems, Tucson Sept. 1993, IEEE C/S Press, p. 192-199.
15. Jacak W., Rozenblit J.W.: CAST Tools for Intelligent Control in Manufacturing Automation.- Moreno-Diaz R., Pichler F. (eds.): CAST-93, Lecture Notes in Computer Science No. 763, 1994, pp. 203-219
16. Jacak W.: Intelligent Robotic System: Design, Planning and Control.- Springer Verlag, 1995 (in print).
17. Klengel H.: Handel und Händler im alten Orient.- H. Böhlaus Nfg. Wien/Köln/Graz 1979
18. Matsumoto Y.: A Software Factory: An Overall Approach to Software Production.- Freeman P. (ed.): Tutorial: Software Reusability.- IEEE Computer Society, Order No. 750, 1986
19. Mittermeir R.: Creativity.- Lucas P. (ed.): Austrian Hungarian Seminar on Software Engineering.- Graz University of Technology, Inst. f. Software Technology, April 20-21, 1995

20. Ovum Ltd.: Ovum Evaluates: Case Products.- Ovum Ltd. Jan 1993
21. Schaefer W. (ed.): Software Process Technology - 4th European Workshop EWSPT'95 Noordwijkerhout, April 1995 Springer Lecture Notes No. 913, Springer Berlin-Heidelberg, 1995
22. Schulz. A.: CASE-Report 94.- GES-Edition, GESmbH, Im Vogelsang 14-16, D-7753 Allensbach, Spring 1993
23. Sommerville I. (ed.): Software Engineering Environments.- P. Peregrinus Ltd. London 1986
24. Tracz W.: Software Reuse Maxims.- Software Engineering Notes vol. 13 (1988), No. 4, pp. 28-31
25. Turner J., Kraut R. (eds.): CSCW-92, Sharing Perspectives.- Proc. Conf. on Computer-supported Cooperative Work, Oct.13-Nov.2, 1992 Toronto., ACM Press 1992
26. Walker C.B.F.: Cuneiform - Reading the Past.- British Museum Publ., London 1987
27. Warboys B.C. (ed.): Software Process Technology - 3rd European Workshop EWSPT'94 Villard-de-Lans Springer Lecture Notes No. 772, Springer Berlin-Heidelberg, 1994
28. Glossary - A Workflow Management Coalition Specification.- Workflow Management Coalition, Belgium Nov. 1994
29. Wileden J.C., Dowson M. (eds.): Internat. Workshop on the Software Process and Software Environments.- Software Eng. Notes vol. 11 (1986) No. 4, pp. 1-74

4 SPECIFIC APPLICATIONS

High-Performance Parallel Computing for Analyzing Urban Air Pollution

Achim Sydow, Thomas Lux, Ralf-Peter Schäfer

GMD FIRST, Rudower Chaussee 5, D-12489 Berlin, Germany

Abstract. The paper deals with results and experience of research work in the field of air pollution modelling and simulation. An air pollution simulation system consisting of models for meteorology, air pollutants transport and air chemistry is described. The computational aspects implementing numerical models as part of the simulation system are discussed with emphasis on parallel computing. An application example of the air pollution simulation system is presented.

1 Introduction

The modelling, and simulation of complex processes in the environment is a challenge for systems theory and informatics. The increasing environmental pollution destroys the ecological balance, continuously reduces the healthy biosphere, and diseases caused by civilization are a problem with growing importance. Thus the numerical modelling and simulation of man-made changes in the ecosystem is becoming increasingly important to government bodies and industries involved in environmental and health protection.

Complex multi-dimensional simulation models of environmental systems require modern high-performance computer systems being still within the budgets of small companies and local government. The quality of the numerical algorithm design (fast equation solvers) is of the same importance as the hardware. Parallel computers and parallel simulation software play a central role for future research in this field. There is also a need for the introduction of modern software engineering concepts, which allow the efficient use and servicing of complex simulation software packages.

2 The DYMOS System

An air pollution simulation system has been developed at GMD-FIRST [6] in order to support users in governmental administrations and industry in operative decision making as well as short to long-term regional planning. The components of the simulation system are (see Figure 1):

- parallelly implemented simulation models (meteorology, transport, air chemistry)
- data bases for model input and simulation results
- graphic user interface for spatial data visualization.

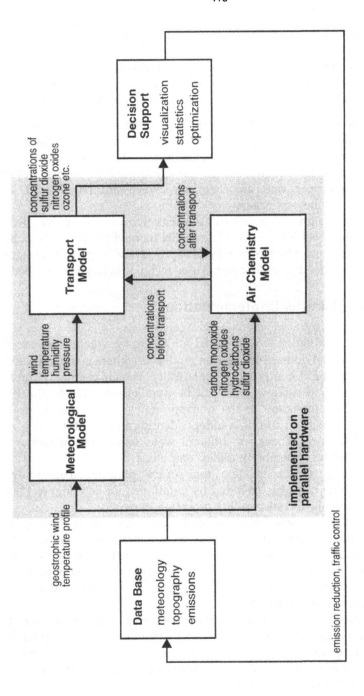

Fig. 1. Structure of the air pollution simulation system

The basis for simulating air pollution is the acquisition and selection of input data, and its storage in data bases. Three groups of data are necessary:
- topographical data (surface elevation and land utilization),
- meteorological (wind, vertical profiles of temperature, pressure, etc.),
- emission data (sources of industry, private households, and traffic).

Currently the decision support for users of the simulation system is limited to the 2D visualization of the simulation results obtained from scenario analyses. Future improvements will allow a 3D visualization, statistical analyses, and optimizations. The system kernel are the numerical models for meteorology, air pollutants transport, and air chemistry which are parallelized and implemented on parallel computers.

For the system design and parallel implementation various approaches of systems theory has been used. There is a model hierarchy (micro, meso, and macroscale models), and a hierarchy in parallel processing (host-worker design). For splitting the model domain decomposition techniques has been applied.

3 Aspects of Parallel Implementation

The air pollution simulation is well-suited for an implementation on parallel computers. The model domain of Eulerian models used here is represented by a 3D grid that can be decomposed geometrically. The air chemistry models coupled with Eulerian models must not be parallelized. Due to the high reaction speed in comparison to the transport rates of the substances the solution of the chemical equations is independently carried out in every grid box at every time step. There are different ways to implement sequential programs on distributed memory parallel computers:
- message-passing approach: Here the source program (commonly a FORTRAN code) must be extended by primitives for sending/receiving messages, initiating and suspending processes, etc.
- object-oriented approach: Here the application program is decomposed into appropriate objects by means of classes and inheritance, and subjected to methods. The advantages of this approach (better data abstraction, program maintenance, and use of inherent parallelism) must be weighted against the effort of object-oriented redesign of the models and program translation (e.g. from FORTRAN to C++).
- automatic parallelization: Here a special imperative language provides the user with a mean to logically specify data partitioning and mapping in a sequential program. From such an annotated program a special compiler automatically generates parallel distributed processes and the necessary data communication.

The air pollution simulation system developed at GMD FIRST has been already implemented on different parallel systems [4]. At the moment the work is concentrated to three platforms: MANNA, Parsytec PowerPC systems, and workstation clusters.

MANNA [1] is a parallel computer prototype developed at GMD FIRST and equipped with the special operating/run-time system PEACE [5]. On MANNA with PEACE user programs can be implemented as message-passing or object-oriented versions. In case of the message-passing approach the visible interface is a large subset of PVM (parallel virtual machine). Instead of PVM the use of PARMACS [2] or MPI is also possible.

On Parsytec PowerPC systems the functionality provided by the operating system PARIX eases the system implementation in form of a message-passing version. From PARIX the concept of virtual processors, the concept of virtual topologies (tree structure for host-worker-communication, mesh structure for worker-worker-communication), the synchronous communication, and the dynamic code loading is used. Fig. 2 shows the values of the execution time, speed-up, and parallel efficiency depending on the number of used processors on the GC/POWER PLUS with 8 nodes (16 processors) for a typical simulation. The simulated time horizon is 12 minutes, and the model domain consists of 2597 grid points.

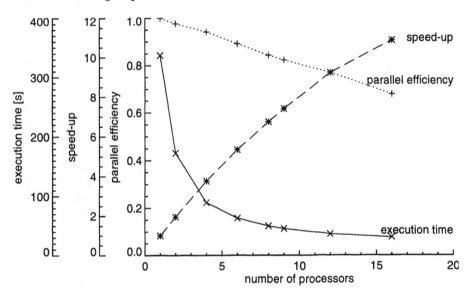

Fig. 2. Run-time measurements of a Parsytec PowerGC implementation

4 Application Example

On behalf of the environmental department of the state government of Berlin and the ministry for environment of the state Brandenburg summer smog analyses were carried out for a period in July 1994 [3]. The visualization of the simulation results shows a significant wide-area ozone trail on the lee-side of

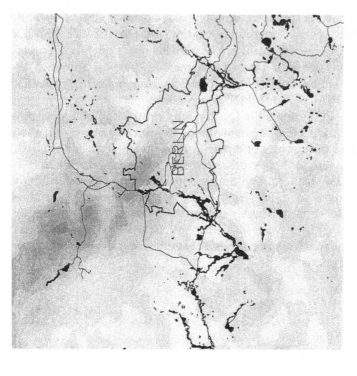
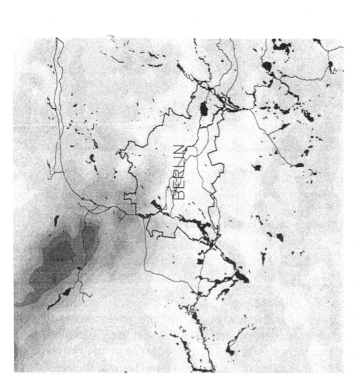

Fig.3. Simulated ozone concentration in μg/m³ in Berlin/Brandenburg on July 25, 1994 at 4 p.m. (left - standard case, right - scenario 1)

Berlin resulting from man-made emissions of ozone precursor substances in Berlin. This phenomenon could be confirmed by measurements. Scenario analyses were carried out to study the consequences of possible measures for emission reduction on the production of ozone. The success of a special measure under defined meteorological conditions could be evaluated. In Fig. 3 the simulated surface-near ozone concentration in $\mu g/m^3$ of the standard case and scenario 1 on July 25, 1994 at 4 p.m. is presented. Scenario 1 means:

- traffic ban for cars and trucks without emission-reduction technology like controlled catalysts.
- speed limit (90 km/h on highways, 80 km/h on normal roads outside of urban areas).
- reduction of emissions caused by private households by 5 %, industry by 15 %, point sources (e.g. power plants) by 10 %.

The horizontal extent of the model domain is about 100 km x 100 km. The horizontal grid resolution is 2 km x 2 km. The surface is relatively flat. The meteorological situation of the considered episode is characterized by a long-term high-pressure weather condition with strong solar radiation and high temperatures as well as a large mixing layer. The comparison between simulation results and measurements shows a relatively good correspondence of the location of the computed and measured ozone trail and its extent. The simulation runs confirm the existence of a significant ozone production mainly caused by the man-made emissions of precursor substances in Berlin. In most cases the maximum of the ozone concentration is reached in some distance from Berlin in the state of Brandenburg.

References

1   U. Brüning, W.K. Giloi, W. Schröder-Preikschat: Latency Hiding in Message-Passing Architectures. Proc. IPPS'94, IEEE-CS Press, 1994.

2   R. Calkin, R. Hempel, H.-C. Hoppe, P. Wypior: Portable programming with the PARMACS message passing library. Parallel Computing 20, 615-632 (1994)

3   P. Mieth, S. Unger, R.-P. Schäfer, M. Schmidt: Simulation der Ozon-produktion in Berlin und Brandenburg für den Zeitraum der FLUMOP-Meßkampagne. Editor: Senatsverwaltung für Stadtentwicklung und Umweltschutz, Berlin, 1995

4   M. Schmidt, R. Hänisch. Implementation of an air pollution transport model on parallel hardware. Proc. International Conference on Massively Parallel Processing, June 21 - 23, 1994, Delft, The Netherlands

5   W. Schröder-Preikschat. Logical Design of Parallel Operating Systems. Prentice-Hall, Englewood-Cliffs, NJ, 1994

6   A. Sydow, M. Schmidt, Th. Lux, R.-P. Schäfer, P. Mieth: Simulation of Air Pollutant Dispersion on Parallel Hardware. Simulation Practice and Theory 1, 57-64 (1993)

Performance Analysis of a Dual Robot System Using a Geometric Concurrency Model*

Elżbieta Roszkowska

Institute of Technical Cybernetics
Technical University of Wrocław, ul. Janiszewskiego 11/17, 50-372 Wrocław, Poland,
e-mail: ekr@ict.pwr.wroc.pl

Abstract. In the paper we consider a manufacturing cell in which two robots cyclically move along well-defined paths of the workspace area. The concurrent motion of the robots in the common workspace must comply with the physical motion constraints. This implies a necessity of delays which are difficult to predict because the robots progress independently without synchronisation for variable interval of times. Our objective is to develop a technique to formally analyse concurrent behaviour of the robots. In order to model the execution behaviour of the system we use a geometric concurrency model that represents synchronisation constraints in concurrent movement of the robots by the spatial arrangement of line segments in a two dimensional real coordinate system. The model is mapped next to a Diophantine equation and its solution applied in a numeric algorithm that determines the steady state of the system, i.e. the sequence and timing of global states the system passes through during its execution.

1 Introduction

Rapid advances in robotics technology over the past decade have made possible the use of a variety of autonomous and semiautonomous machines to perform strenuous and repetitive tasks in present days factories. Robots in particular have been used in performing diverse tasks like painting, welding, assembly, as well as transporting material between different locations within a work cell. The use of multiple robots in a common workspace can enhance the utilisation of robots, increase productivity and improve the versatility in handling different applications. However, in order to exploit this potential it is necessary to develop models that can predict the system performance and provide guidelines for the design of system parameters and operational control of the system.

Because of the inherent complexity of the concurrent movement problem of multiple robots most of the research conducted so far in this area has concentrated on simulation, e.g. [3, 4]. A simulation model enables detailed representation of robots dynamics and complex supervisory control. Thus predictions of performance made by the model are potentially very accurate. However, this

---

* This research was supported by KBN grant Design of Intelligent Robotics Systems Based on Knowledge Engineering

ability to capture the complexity of the system has disadvantages. Each simulation run can be lengthy, thus deterring the analyst from trying a wide range of parameter values. Because of the complexity of simulation model the time to develop and adequately validate it can be quite substantial.

An alternative way to gain information about the system performance is through formal analysis. It is impossible for analytical models to capture all the details of the system; there has to be a compromise between complexity of representation and ease of solution. Therefore one has to extract from the general problem of concurrent robots movement sufficiently simple, analytically tractable sub problem, whose analysis can be done exactly. However, once a solution of such an analytical model has been developed it can be subjected to the full power of tests of mathematical correctness and precise statements can be made about the validity of the solution for the given assumptions. The processes of model development and solution almost always lead to new insights into the system and suggest ways in which assumptions may be relaxed. Moreover, one can usually build on the exact analysis of simple concurrent models to obtain results applicable to more complex problems or produce valuable insights for further research along alternate paths.

In the paper we consider a manufacturing cell in which two robots move along well-defined paths of the workspace area. Each robot repeatedly performs some particular task, i.e. cyclically follows some specified path. The concurrent motion of the robots in the common workspace must comply with the physical constraints which allow the robots neither to occupy the same space area at the same time nor to pass or overtake each other while moving along the same edge of the path. This implies a necessity of delays which are difficult to predict because the robots progress independently without synchronisation for variable interval of times.

Our objective is to develop a technique to formally analyse concurrent behaviour of the robots. While performing their tasks the robots change their state. We assume that the state of the robot is represented by a pair of data carrying the information how far is the robot advanced in executing its task and which part of the workspace it occupies at the moment. The global state of the system is composed of the state of each individual robot. A global cyclic steady state is reached in the system if a finite sequence of global state transitions is repeated forever. We want to find the sequence and timing of global states the system passes through during its execution. In particular we would like to find answers to such questions as: Under what conditions, if any, the system reaches a steady state which does not require any waiting by any robot? How can the length of the steady state cycle be calculated?

In order to model the execution behaviour of the system considered we use the geometric concurrency model that represents synchronisation constraints in concurrent movement of the robots by the spatial arrangement of line segments in a two dimensional real coordinate system. Such models were applied by several authors for solving job-shop scheduling problem with two machines (e.g. [7, 6]) as well as for the analysis of dual computer processes systems [1, 2]. Following the concept there presented we show how the specification of the robots system can be mapped to the model. Then we map the model to a Diophantine equation (a linear equation whose coefficients and unknowns are integers), solve it and use the solutions to answer the problems stated above.

2 The geometric model of robots concurrent movement

We consider a dual robots system where each of the robots performs cyclically some specified task consisting of a sequence of operations executed in different points of their workspace. Since it is a common workspace for both of the robots, they constitute dynamic obstacles each to other. Obviously such a system requires some synchronisation of robots movements preventing the robots from attempting to reach the same place at the same time. To provide this we assume that the working space is divided into a finite number of sub spaces, (called further spaces), which are big enough to include within it's volume the whole arm of a robot. The movements of the robots R_1 and R_2 while executing their tasks can be thus specified as follows:

$$TR_1 = (p_{1,1}, t_{1,1}), (p_{1,2}, t_{1,2}), \ldots, (p_{1,n}, t_{1,n_1})$$
$$TR_2 = (p_{2,1}, t_{2,1}), (p_{2,2}, t_{2,2}), \ldots, (p_{2,n}, t_{2,n_2})$$
(1)

where TR_i stands for the technological route of the robot R_i, $i \in \{1, 2\}$, consisting of a sequence of pairs $(p_{i,j}, t_{i,j})$ that indicate the consecutive spaces $(p_{i,j})$, $j \in \{1, 2, \ldots, n_i\}$, crossed by R_i while executing its task, as well as the minimal times $t_{i,j}$ spent in each of the spaces.

It should be noted that the technological route may require any of the two robots to occupy a given space multiple times. This implies that we can not identify the robot's state, in the sense of its position, with the robot's state, in the sense of the realisation stage of the task it executes. In order to model the dynamics of the dual robots system we need both of these informations to describe a state of a robot. Thus, we distinguish n_1 (n_2) local states of robot R_1 (robot R_2, respectively), each of which tells us the stage of the process the robot executes and the space it occupies. The global state of such system is given by a pair of local states of the two robots.

The synchronisation protocol requires that only one robot can occupy any given space at a time. Each time one robot attempts to enter the space occupied by another one it has to be delayed until the latter one releases it by proceeding to the consecutive space in its route. Obviously, if the sets of spaces traversed by each of the robots were mutually disjoint, no delays would occur and it would be easy to calculate the state of each robot as a function of time. In order to include in our consideration the requirements of the synchronisation protocol we will employ a geometric concurrency model. The structure of such model will be explained on the basis of the following example.

Let us consider the flexible assembly cell given in Fig. 1. The cell consists of two robots R_1 and R_2, two conveyer systems, a tools magazine and a parts magazine. There are two types of assembly processes executed in the cell concurrently. Each conveyer is used to deliver one type of pallets, containing the base assembly component, to one of the robots. Each robot executes some specific assembly task, carried through repeatedly for each pallet of its conveyer stream. The accomplishment of the tasks requires the robots to change their tools in the tool magazine and to take parts, to be assembled into the base, from the parts magazine. The technological routes of the robots are given by:

$$TR_1 = (p_2, 2), (p_3, 3), (p_1, 3), (p_3, 2), (p_1, 2), (p_2, 2), (p_1, 2)$$
$$TR_2 = (p_2, 1), (p_3, 1), (p_4, 2), (p_2, 1), (p_3, 1), (p_4, 2)$$
$$(2)$$

where p_1, p_2, p_3, p_4, stand for the spaces corresponding to first robot assembly area, tools magazine area, parts magazine area and second robot assembly area, respectively.

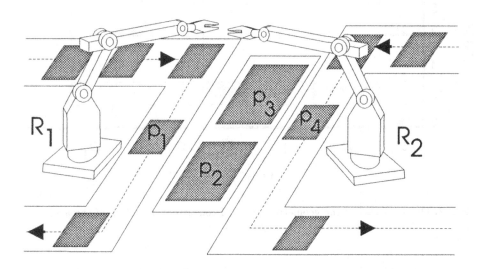

Fig. 1. Flexible assembly cell with two robots working partly in common workspace

The geometric model of robots concurrent operation is given in the framework of the Cartesian coordinate system (Fig. 2). The local states of robot R_1 are represented by the intervals along the x axis and the local states of robot R_2 are mapped to intervals along the y axis. The length of the interval is proportional to the minimal time the robot spends in the given state and it is labelled by the space the robot occupies in this state. A geometric view of the global state comes by drawing a set of vertical lines through each state boundary on the x axis and a set of horizontal lines through each state boundary on the y axis. The global states are the Cartesian product of the local states and they are represented by the rectangles in the x/y plane. Points within the rectangles represent partial execution of the global states. A rectangle whose vertical and horizontal sides are labelled by the same label represents a forbidden state, i.e. the state where both robots are in the same space at the same time. Such rectangles will be addressed further as obstacles; in the picture they are filled with grey colour.

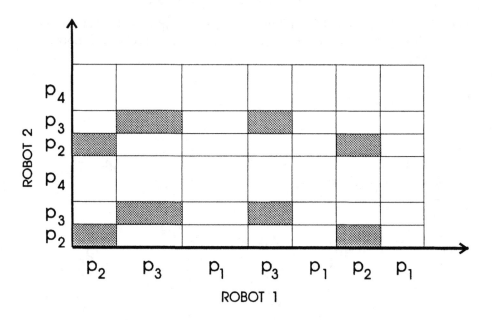

Fig. 2. One quadrant of the geometric model of concurrent operation of the assembly robots

The geometric implication of the fact that the robots execute their tasks cyclically is the partition of the plane into a set of equal sized quadrants (Fig.3) whose width and height correspond to the cycle times $C_x = 16$ of robot R_1 and $C_y = 8$ of robot R_2, respectively. The cycle time is understood here as the sum of the minimal times spent by the robot in each of its states, or equivalently, the time required by the robot for a single execution of its task in the absence of blocking.

The dynamic behaviour of the system is represented by a trajectory, i.e. the sequence and timing of the global state transitions. In the geometric model the trajectory is a sequence of segments that are either diagonal, parallel to the line $y = x$, or horizontal or vertical. A startpoint of the trajectory can be any point on the x or y axis in the interval $[0, C_x)$, $[0, C_y)$, respectively, depending on the initial condition, i.e. the time at which each process is started. Fig. 3 shows

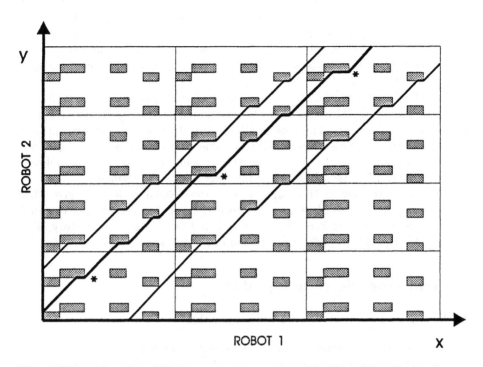

Fig. 3. The geometric model of concurrent operation of the assembly robots

the trajectory starting from point $(0,0)$, as well as two additional exemplary trajectories drawn from points $(10,0)$ (robot R_1 starts first) and $(0,6)$ (robot R_2 starts first).

The diagonal segments represent this part of the trajectory where the robots operate simultaneously. The trajectory changes its direction in case it hits a boundary of an obstacle. This corresponds to the event when one robot requires for its further movement the space occupied at the moment by the other robot. Then the trajectory goes horizontally (in case of robot R_1 blocking further movement of R_2) or vertically (in case of robot R_2 blocking further movement of R_1) until it reaches the endpoint of the obstacle edge. The blocking robot enters another space then and the delayed one can finally enter the space it has awaited. Both robots can proceed simultaneously again - the trajectory continues as a diagonal line until it intersects another obstacle.

Looking at Fig. 3 we can note that after an initial phase of a transient state each trajectory reaches its steady state where it becomes cyclic. This means that there exists a pair of integers (k^1, k^2) which make the following implication true for each point (x,y) of the steady state portion of the trajectory: if (x,y) belongs to the trajectory then the point (x',y') such that $x' = x + k^1 C_x$ and

$y' = y + k^2 C_y$ also belongs to the trajectory. In other words the two points are congruent. In the example considered $k^1 = 1$ and $k^2 = 2$. In the figure the portion of the trajectory corresponding to its first cycle is indicated by two asterisks. The first asterisk shows the border between transient and steady state trajectory fragments. The second asterisk is placed at the endpoint of the first cycle of the trajectory.

In order to calculate the cycle time of the trajectory (the global cycle time of the dual robot system) we sum up the times required by the trajectory to traverse its consecutive segments. The time length of vertical and horizontal segments are given by their projection on the y axis and y axis, respectively. Since the diagonal segments are parallel to the $y = x$ line, their x and y projections are equal and any of them can be taken to measure the time length of a segment.

The main problem of this paper can be thus stated as follows: given the parameters (cycle times C_x, C_y and coordinations of the obstacles) of the dual robot system geometric concurrency model find the system's trajectory. The solution to the problem will be considered in the following section.

3   Trajectory derivation problem

In the following consideration we will assume that:

a. The cycle times of robots are given by rational numbers.
b. Conflicts (if occur) are resolved in some deterministic pre-assumed way.
c. The system is deadlock free.

A trajectory of the system can be one of the following two types:

case 1 The trajectory never hits any obstacle, thus it is a diagonal line parallel to the line $y = x$.
case2 The trajectory hits some obstacles, thus it consists of diagonal and vertical and/or horizontal segments.

The assumptions taken provide that in both cases the trajectory is infinite, deterministic and cyclic.

In case 1 the global cycle of the system is given by the smallest number C such that $C = aC_x = bC_y$, where a and b are integers. The assumption (a) provides that this equation can always be satisfied.

In case 2 the trajectory hits at least one obstacle and moves further along its horizontal or vertical edge until it reaches the endpoint of the edge. It continues from there as a diagonal line until it hits another obstacle or intersects no obstacle any more. The latter means that the trajectory proceeds further as in case 1. In the former situation we note that each quadrant has the same layout of obstacles. It follows from the assumptions (b) and (c) that the trajectory is infinite and moves in a deterministic way. Thus for each edge (vertical or horizontal) of each obstacle there is a unique other obstacle and a unique point on one of its edges which the trajectory will hit next in the same or another quadrant. Since, however, the number of different obstacles in one quadrant is finite, given by some integer f, then the sequence of consecutively hit edges can not contain more then $2f$ different elements. Each edge hit next will be one of those that were hit before. Hence obviously, the trajectory is cyclic and the sequence of its segments lying within two edges of the same type constitutes one trajectory cycle.

It comes from the above discussion that a trajectory of a dual robot system can be derived from the parameters of its geometric model by going through the following algorithm.

Assume k is an element of K, where K is a set consisting of eastern (vertical) and southern (horizontal) edges of all obstacle types of the model. Denote by $TK = k_{i_1}, k_{i_2}, \ldots k_{i_v}$, $k_{i_v} \in K$, the sequence of edges consecutively hit by the trajectory in its one cycle.

1. Set the coordinates of the point p as equal to the initial state of the system. Set $i = 1$.
2. Repeat for all $k \in K$:
   (a) Assume there are no other edges in the model but k. Find out if the diagonal line going out of the point p intersects k. In case it does not go to step (c).
   (b) Find the quadrant containing the nearest intersection of k and calculate the parallel execution time of the robots $\overline{p, r_k}$ represented by the diagonal segment of the trajectory lying between the points p and r_k. Skip step (c).
   (c) Set $\overline{p, r_k} = \infty$.
3. If $\overline{p, r_k} = \infty$ for all $k \in K$ go to step 7.
4. Find the edge k_i hit by the trajectory going out diagonally from the point p by taking the minimum of $\overline{p, r_k}$ over all edges $k \in K$. If k_i has already occurred in TK, i.e. there exists $j < i$ such that $k_i = k_j$, go to step 8.
5. Calculate the length $\overline{r_{k_i}, q_{k_i}}$ of the horizontal or vertical (depending on what edge is k) segment of the trajectory lying between the point r_i and the endpoint q_i of the obstacle edge hit.
6. Set $i := i + 1$, $p := q_i$. Go to step 2.
7. The trajectory in it's steady state is a diagonal line going out of the point p. The global cycle of the system is given by the smallest number C such that $C = aC_x = bC_y$, where a and b are integers. End algorithm.
8. The trajectory in it's steady state is a cyclical repetition of the sequence of diagonal and vertical or horizontal segments (depending on the type of the edge hit by a given diagonal segment of the trajectory) given by the segments lying between the points r_{k_j}, q_{k_j} and $q_{k_j}, r_{k_{j+1}}$, respectively, where $j \in \{1, \ldots, i-1\}$. End algorithm.

The algorithm described presents a general line of conduct leading to determination of the steady state behaviour of the system. In order to make it complete it is necessary to determine analytical methods allowing to get the solutions required in points (a) and (b) of step 2 of the algorithm. In the following three sections we derive mathematical formulas being the explicit answers to these problems, i.e. stating the conditions of diagonal line and obstacle intersection, determining the quadrant containing the nearest intersection and giving the parallel execution time of the robots $\overline{p, r_k}$ represented by the diagonal segment of the trajectory lying between the points p and r_k.

4 Intersection conditions

With no loss of generality we can assume further that the robot cycle lengths C_x and C_y are given by two relatively prime numbers. If the condition is not satisfied originally, we can re-scale the model by dividing all time parameters by the greatest common divisor of C_x and C_y, providing thus its fulfilment.

Before deriving the intersection conditions let us consider first how the relative position of a diagonal line and a given point of the model quadrant varies in the consecutive quadrants the line intersects (Fig. 4).

Fig. 4(b) presents the projection of the diagonal line $y = x$ from Fig. 4(a) to the first row of the model quadrants obtained through the transformation given by : $x' = x$, $y' = y \; MOD \; C_y$. Fig. 4(c) results from projecting of the latter diagram to the first quadrant of the model according to the transformation: $x'' = x' \; MOD \; C_x$, $y'' = y'$. It is important to note that the diagram consists now of a finite number of segments. This reflects the fact that the line crosses the model in a cyclic way and the segments show all possible positions of the line within a quadrant. We are interested in the distance δ between the consecutive segments along the x or y axis.

The length of the global cycle C can be found as:

$$C = \min_{C'} \{ C' = kC_x = lC_y \, | \, k, l \in \{1, 2, \ldots\} \tag{3}$$

The distances δ is thus given by:

$$\delta = \frac{C_x}{C/C_y} \tag{4}$$

Since, however, we have assumed that C_x and C_y are relatively prime then

$$C = C_x C_y \tag{5}$$

hence

$$\delta = 1 \tag{6}$$

The result obtained lets us derive the conditions of the trajectory and the obstacles intersection. Figure 5. presents two quadrants placed nC_x and mC_y units along the x and y axes from each other. We are looking for the necessary and sufficient conditions for the diagonal line going out from point p (endpoint of the vertical edge of one of the obstacles) to intersect the segment ended with point q (the vertical edge of another obstacle). We assume that the coordinates of the points are given by (p_x, p_y) and (q_x, q_y), respectively. The length of the potentially intersected obstacle is given by l.

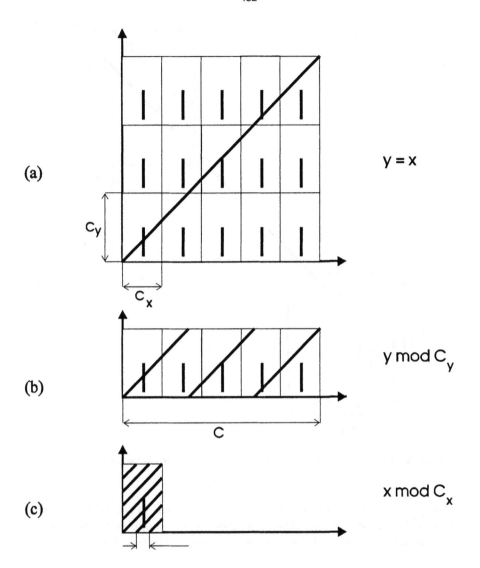

Fig. 4. Relative position of the obstacles and with respect to the trajectory in different quadrants of the geometric model

It can be easily derived from the geometry of the picture that the segment is intersected iff $L < \Delta \leq L + l$ and $L = p_y, q_y - (p_x, q_x$. As we know from our previous discussion that Δ can only be a multiple of δ and $\delta = 1$ then the intersection condition of the diagonal line going out from point p and the vertical edge of the obstacle ending with q takes the form of:

$$p_y - q_y - (p_x - q_x) < \Delta \leq p_y - q_y - (p_x - q_x) + l \qquad (7)$$

where $\Delta \in \{\ldots, -2, -1, 0, 1, 2, \ldots\}$.

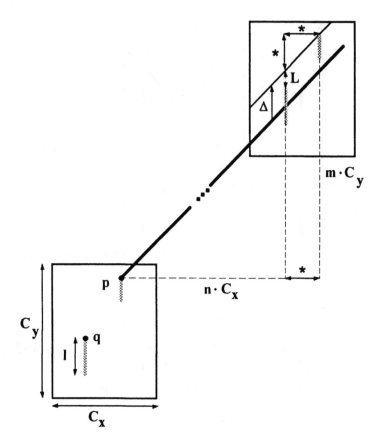

Fig. 5. Looking for the conditions of the trajectory and the obstacles intersection

A similar reasoning process can be conducted in case of the horizontal edge of an obstacle. If we assume that point q is the left endpoint of the edge we obtain the intersection conditions in the same form as stated above.

5 Finding the quadrant containing the nearest intersection

Let us come back to Figure 5. Let us assume that the quadrant containing the intersection of the diagonal line going out of the quadrant with the obstacle edge having the endpoint q is placed nC_x units to the left and mC_y units up from qr. In order to find the unknowns n and m we have to solve a Diophantine equation

$$C_x n - C_y m + \Delta = 0 \tag{8}$$

with constraints $L < \Delta < L + l$, where n, m, Δ are integers and L is defined in the previous section.

To solve the equation we employ the method applied in [1] and based on the results of [5]. The technique consists in solving the system of equations:

$$\begin{bmatrix} C_x & -C_y & 1 \\ t & s & 0 \\ C_x v & -C_y v & u \end{bmatrix} \begin{bmatrix} n \\ m \\ \Delta \end{bmatrix} = \begin{bmatrix} 0 \\ y \\ z \end{bmatrix} \qquad (9)$$

for integer t, s, u and v such that $C_x s + C_y t = 1$ and $u - v = 1$.
The general solution is:

$$\begin{aligned} n &= yC_y - s\Delta \\ m &= yC_x + t\Delta \end{aligned} \qquad (10)$$

Obviously there are an infinite number of particular solutions for m, n and Δ. We must choose an integer value for Δ in the interval $L < \Delta < L + l$ to obtain values of m and n representing the first obstacle edge intersected. We will determine the correct choice below, in the process of obtaining the parallel execution time of the robots $\overline{p, r_k}$ represented by the diagonal segment of the trajectory lying between the points p and r_k.

6 Finding the parallel execution time of the robots

The parallel execution time of the robots $\overline{p, r_k}$ is given by the length of the perpendicular projection onto the x or y axis of the diagonal trajectory segment between points p and r (see again Fig.5). Thus the projected trajectory length is simply the difference between the x (or the y) coordinates of point the intersection and the endpoint p of the edge of the obstacle hit earlier. The coordinates of the point p are known. As for the coordinates of the intersection point we take advantage from the facts that $r_x = q_x$ if the edge hit is vertical, and that $r_y = q_y$ if the edge hit is horizontal. Thus we use the x axis projection in first case and the y axis projection in the latter. This leads to the following formula:

$$\overline{p, r} = \begin{cases} \infty & \text{if no obstacle is intersected} \\ C_x n + q_x - p_x & \text{if the edge hit is vertical} \\ C_y m + q_y - p_y & \text{if the edge hit is horizontal} \end{cases} \qquad (11)$$

We can now eliminate m and n by substituting m and n determined in (9) into (10). We obtain thus:

$$\overline{p, r} = \begin{cases} \infty & \text{if no obstacle is intersected} \\ C_x(yC_y - s\Delta) + q_x - p_x & \text{if the edge hit is vertical} \\ C_y(yC_x + t\Delta) + q_y - p_y & \text{if the edge hit is horizontal} \end{cases} \qquad (12)$$

Taking advantage of the fact that $\overline{p, r} \geq 0$ we obtain:

$$y \geq \left\lceil \frac{s\Delta C_x + q_x - p_x}{C_x C_y} \right\rceil \text{ or } y \geq \left\lceil \frac{-t\Delta C_y + q_y - p_y}{C_x C_y} \right\rceil \qquad (13)$$

Using the fact that $\lceil -y \rceil = -\lfloor y \rfloor$ and substituting y into (11) we obtain the final form for the expression:

$$\overline{p,r} = \begin{cases} \infty & \text{if no obstacle is intersected} \\ C_x \left(C_y \left\lfloor \frac{s\Delta C_x + q_x - p_x}{C_x C_y} \right\rfloor - s\Delta \right) + p_x - q_x & \text{if the edge hit is vertical} \\ C_y \left(C_x \left\lfloor \frac{-t\Delta C_y + q_y - p_y}{C_x C_y} \right\rfloor + t\Delta \right) + p_y - q_y & \text{if the edge hit is horizontal} \end{cases}$$

$$(14)$$

The solution obtained can be directly applied in the calculations required to perform the steps 4 and 5 of the algorithm discussed in Section 3. Taking the minimum of $\overline{p,r_k}$ over all edges $k \in K$ we can determine thus the parallel execution time of the robot $\overline{p,r_{k_i}}$ corresponding to the diagonal segment of the trajectory between the endpoint p of the obstacle edge k_{i-1} and the nearest intersection point r_{k_i}, as well as the horizontal or vertical (depending on what edge is k_i) segment of the trajectory $\overline{r_{k_i}, q_{k_i}}$ lying between the point r_i and the endpoint q_i of the obstacle edge hit.

$$\overline{p,r_{k_i}} = \min_{k \in K} \min_{L < \Delta \leq L+1} (\overline{p,r_k})$$
$$\overline{r_{k_i}, q_{k_i}} = \Delta(p, k_i) - L(p, k_i)$$

$$(15)$$

The global cycle time of the system can be calculated now by summing up the times required by the trajectory to traverse its consecutive segments.

7 Conclusions

The objective of the paper was to present a formal technique of analysing concurrent behaviour of two robots operating in a common workspace. We assume that each of the robots repeatedly follows some specified path and that their motion must comply with the physical motion constraints. Our particular interest was to derive the formulas determining the sequence and timing of the global states the system passes through during its execution. In order to represent the behaviour of the system considered we used the geometric concurrency model, which we mapped next to a Diophantine equation. The formulas derived by solving the equation allowed us to calculate the consecutive segments of the trajectory describing the concurrent operation of the dual robots system. The drawback of the method is, however, the fact that the formulas obtained are not in close form because they require two minimisation's. Finding a closed form solution for these minimisation's appears to be difficult, thus in order to evaluate the minimums a numerical algorithm must be used.

A straightforward extension of these studies and the subject of our future research will concern extending the analysis to the models relaxing the assumptions taken, i.e. allowing a greater number of robots to cooperate in the common workspace, allowing some uncertainty in operations time specification, as well as including in the considerations the systems where deadlocks may occur.

References

1. Abrams, M.: Performance analysis of unconditionally synchronizing distributed computer programs using the geometric concurrency model. Technical Report TR–1696 (1986), Dep. of Comp. Sci., Uni. of Maryland
2. Abrams, M., Agrawala, A.K.: Exact performance analysis of two distributed processes with one synchronization point. Technical Report CS–TR–1844 (1987), Dep. of Comp. Sci., Uni. of Maryland
3. Baines, T.D., Harrison, D.K., Vitanov, V.I.: Introducing discrete event simulation into a production project engineering environment. Proc. of the 8th International Conference on System Engineering, Coventry Polytechnic, 12 September 1991, Coventry, U.K., 699–706
4. Banks, J., Carson, J.S.: Discrete-Event System Simulation. Prentice-Hall, Inc., Englewood Cliffs, NJ (1984)
5. Jones, B.W.: The Theory of Numbers. New York, Reinehart & Company, Inc., (1955), Ch. 2,3
6. Hardgrave, W.W., Nemhauser, G.L.: A geometric model and a graphical algorithm for a sequencing problem. Operations Research 11 (1963) 789–900
7. Szwarc, W.: Solution of the Ackers-Friedman scheduling problem. Operations Research 8 (1960) 782–788

Computer Aided Rule Extraction from Examples

Petr Vysoký and Zdeněk Pechal

Czech Technical University, Department of Control Engineering, Technická 2,
166 27 Praha 6, Czech Republic

Abstract. In this paper, a method for finding IF–THEN rules based on the information theoretic approach is submitted. The method utilizes an approach known as a General System Problem Solver (GSPS) and enables to find the rules from empirical data. Submitted method is useful in cases if human expert is able to control given process but is unable to formulate the rules explicitly.

1 Introduction

Fuzzy controllers ususally do not need a mathematical model of a controlled system. This fact is considered as their main advantage in practical applications. But this advantage is recompensated by nonexistence of exact methods for the design of fuzzy controllers.

In our contribution we will focus our attention on crucial part of the fuzzy controller, the rule base. The rule base usually consists of set of IF – THEN rules. The design of the rule base means to decompose the state space of the controller on appropriate number of cells and every cell assigned by relevant rule. There are in essence three possible approaches for the choice of relevant rules:

1. Linguistic approach
2. Identification
3. Template based methods

The first approach is widespread. Knowledge is in rule form acquainted from human expert. An experienced expert or skilled operator is interviewed and asked which rules he uses in a specific situation to obtain a successful decision.

The second direction, inspired by classic system theory and developments in neural networks, is based on the use of input output data of a known controller or system.

The third technique combines the use of expert knowledge and available data. An expert provides template linguistic values which are used to partition the input-output space. These template values are then used to define the potential for the fuzzy system model. Input-output data are then used to generate weights or probabilities associated with the importance of the potential rules. Any approach has some advantages and disadvantages. A successful operator is often not able to describe his decision processes satisfactorily. He is not able to formulate the rules explicitly. In some cases operator's decision depends on variables which are measurable indirectly. For instance decisions of an operator controlling biotechnological process depend on color and smell of the mixture in the reactor and these variables are manifested like concentrations of specific liquid and gaseous components [1]. From this point of view it is difficult to distinguish if all variables necessary for decision are available. Neural nets are a very powerful tool for learning rules and membership functions. But the limiting factor is the training set. We usually have no information on training set, if it is satisfactorily rich, if it contains all necessary states. Having the bad training set we obtain a bad controller.

We may add many other items to the list of problems connected with building the rule base. In order to solve these problems we must initially answer the question – do we have all information necessary for a decision? Do measured variables contain this information? And on the other hand, are all measured variables necessary? Maybe some of them are redundant and may be excluded. These questions concern the structure identification of the controlled system and the structure of the knowledge base. The structure identification is usually considered as a theoretical problem from general system theory. In this contribution we try to show, that it may have a very practical impact and that it can help to the effective building of rule base utilizing empirical data.

2 Assumptions

Let us consider initially, that we deal with a crisp system. We will show later, that results can be extended for fuzzy systems too. Let us assume, that the controller is a SISO or MISO system, where y is an output and x_i, are inputs or states. Values of the variables are elements of sets Y, X_i, $i = 1, 2, \ldots, n$. We assume, that all variables are sampled with optimal sampling frequency. The mentioned controller is hypothetical controller in the operator's mind. The x_i are variables observed by operator and y is operator's control action. Let us assume further that requisite (from the statistical point of view) amount of data is available. The data consist of values of all variables which need an expert or an operator for his decision process and the values of his decision. The variables can be nominal, ordinal or metric variables. The values of a variable can be truth values of some propositions, while the values of another variable can be real numbers obtained by some physical measurement. Let us assume further that requisite (from the statistical point of view) amount of data is available.

At first we will try to judge if measured variables carries all necessary information. Generally according to [2] the best controller is a state controller and it must be in a certain sense a model of the controlled system. For any state of the system a corresponding state of the controller has to exist. In the ideal deterministic case the output of the controller and all necessary states and inputs are connected by a deterministic functional relation. The strength of this relation is measurable by means of mean mutual information

$$T(Y : X_1, X_2, \ldots, X_n) = T(Y : X) = H(Y) + H(X) - H(X, Y) \qquad (1)$$

where $X = \{X_1, X_2, \ldots, X_n\}$ and $H(.)$ are Shannon's entropies. This information measures the strength of the relation from independence $(T(X : Y) = 0)$ through stochastic dependency of different strengths to deterministic functional relation, for which it obtain the maximum value

$$T(X : Y)_{\max} = \min[H(X), H(Y)] \ . \qquad (2)$$

For the same number of quantising levels of all variables we have

$$T(Y : X) = H(Y) = H(X) \ . \qquad (3)$$

Reaching this maximum we know, that the relation is deterministic and that all necessary variables are available. In other cases we can conclude, that the relation is stochastic or some necessary variable is missing. It leads to the common tenet: Try to find all variables which can maximize the considered information. Exclude any variable which does not carry additional information.

Table 1. Activity matrix of the controller

k	x_1	x_2	x_3	...	x_s	y
1	0,15	13,2	18,5	...	24,8	31,7
2	12,5	133	4,3	...	8,6	25,6
3	8,6	2,5	27,6	...	13,2	8,1
4	33,9	8,6	0,76		6,3	2,2
5	3,2	45,7	87,6		0,37	8,9
6	25,6	0,18	15,6		3,2	2,7
7	2,87	8,17	0,03	...	34,8	7,6

The missing states can be often reconstructed with help of delayed values of available variables. Description of the acceptable technique is the aim of the following paragraph.

3 Optimal Dimension of the State Space

Our task is now to distinguish which variables carry the necessary information and which delayed states of this variables can be considered as unmeasurable states. For this purpose we will utilize several techniques from a GSPS (General system problem solver) [3]. Let us consider, that we have measured data arranged into the table according to Table 1.

Columns corresponds with individual variables and rows contain values measured in specific sampling periods $1,2,\ldots,k$. This matrix is called activity matrix of our system. If the interpretation of all variables is available (number of quantisation levels, units for their measurements, domain of their possible values etc.) then both activity matrix and interpretation provide data system in Klir's terminology. To obtain a generative system – a mathematical relation among variables, which enables to generate the same data as in the activity matrix, variables carrying a maximum information for examined variable must be choosen. An actual value of an output variable is a generated element and actual or delayed values of relevant variables are generating elements. Generated element and generating elements are connected by the translation rule for instance as

$$y(k) = f(x_3(k-1), y(k-1), x_1(k), x_3(k)) \ . \tag{4}$$

The translation rule corresponds with a specific matrix called mask. Generally the mask is a matrix $v \times (d+1)$ where v is a number of variables, d is a depth of a memory.

The mask corresponding with translation rule (4) is on the Table 2.

Table 2. Example of the generative mask

x_1	x_2	x_3	...	x_v	y	
0	0	0	...	0	0	k-2
0	0	-1	...	0	-2	k-1
-3	0	-4	...	0	+1	k

The elements of a generative mask are zero, negative or positive, meaning "neutral element", "generating element" and "generated element" respectively, [4].

4 Search for Optimal Mask

There are different approaches how to find an optimal mask. Their overview is out of the frame of this paper. The new branch of the system theory – reconstructability analysis, was opened by solving this problem. The reader is referred to [5], [6].

In our case for simplicity the "classical" method [7] is applied. In principle the method is following. We start with an actual value of variable y and we find which actual or delayed value of any other variable in the mask carries maximum information for y. We find $\max T(Y : X_i)$, where $i = 1, 2, \ldots, v(d - 1)$. Let us imagine, that the maxima will be obtained for x_{i0}. Now we find maximum information carried by the pair x_{i0}, x_j, where $j = 1, 2, \ldots, v(d - 1)$, $j \neq i0$. We obtain x_{j0}. In the following step we find maximal information carried by the triplet x_{i0}, x_{j0}, x_k, for $k = 1, 2, \ldots, v(d - 1)$, $k \neq i0$, $k \neq j0$, etc.

In the ideal case the process is terminated if any subsequent variable does not carry additional information. In the real case, especially for dynamical systems the problem is not so simple. If for instance $y(k)$ depends on $y(k - 1)$, then $y(k - 1)$ depends on $y(k - 2)$ and $y(k - 2)$ carries some information for $y(k)$. We must examine, if $y(k - 2)$ carries some information for $y(k)$, excluding variability of $y(k - 1)$. It may be accomplished with help of conditional mean mutual information

$$T(Y(k) : Y(k-1), Y(k-2)) - T(Y(k) : Y(k-1)) = T(Y(k) : Y(k-2) \mid Y(k-1)) . \tag{5}$$

If $y(k - 2)$ is relevant with respect to $y(k)$, then conditional information (5) is zero. Due to the fact that we do not deal with entropies but with estimates of entropies we usually obtain small nonzero value. Now it is necessary to distinguish if this small value will be considered as zero or not. It leads to testing of hypothesis "both variables are independent" against alternative hypothesis "they are not independent". The modified χ^2 test may be utilized for this purpose. With help of (6) the mean mutual information may be transformed into variable with approximately χ^2 distribution.

$$\frac{2N}{\log_2 e} T(Y : X) \sim \chi^2(\alpha, \nu) \tag{6}$$

where N is the number of measured values, α is the significance level, ν is the degree of freedom.

The degrees of freedom for multidimensional conditional mean mutual information are computed with help of expansion on individual entropies. The degree of freedom for multidimensional entropy can be calculated as

$$H(X_1) \qquad \cdots \nu = -(j-1)$$
$$H(X_1, X_2) \qquad \cdots \nu = -(jk-1)$$
$$H(X_1, X_2, X_3) \cdots \nu = -(jkl-1)$$
$$\vdots$$

where j, k, l are numbers of quantizing levels for individual variables. More information on the practical application of the presented method is in [6], [7], [8].

Using this method we obtain an suboptimal mask [7]. Sometimes we obtain several equivalent masks. Choice among equivalent masks depends on experience of the designer and on prior informations. For instance on obstacles in the measurement of individual variables. Having the mask, we have all necessary variables or in other words we have dimensions of the controller state space.

5 Partition of the State Space

We still consider crisp variables. Using a fuzzy controller needs fuzzification of these crisp variables. It means that any value of any state variable is assigned by membership degrees into one or more fuzzy sets. In order to obtain a linguistic description of the state space (the rule base of the controller), it is necessary to decompose the whole state space on the individual cells and to stipulate a specific rule for any cell. The number and the volumes of these cells depend on the number and shape of the relevant membership functions.

There are different approaches for the choice of the number and the shape of relevant membership functions in common use. We may define membership functions apriori (popular triangular or trapezoidal membership functions). We may define only the desired number of fuzzy sets and estimate their membership functions with help of some clustering algorithm using available data. (Algorithms like ISODATA, fuzzy C-MEANS etc.). Or algorithms finding the "natural" number of clusters may be applied [9].

Let us note, that selected fuzzy sets have to satisfy a condition of ε-completnes. The union of their supports should cower the relevant universes in relation to some level set ε. This level corresponds with membership degree in crossover points of neighbor membership functions.(The level of the crossover point is usually choosen greater then 0.5). Crossover points coincide with boundaries between individual cells of the state space. Having crossover points, we have also the partition of the state space. Between crossover points (in the specific cell of the state space) a dominant rule always exists. From the point of view of the rules, the state space is partitioned on crisp areas. Probabilistic methods described in a foregoing text can be used without any modification for estimating dimensions of the state space.

In some cases the data available are fuzzy in their nature. Any value is accompanied by the membership degree of this value in one or more fuzzy sets. Having fuzzy data the method must be slightly modified. We try to estimate a probability of the fuzzy event now. For this extension, a few words about the probability of fuzzy events are necessary.

Let the standard probability space be (Ω, K, P). Here Ω is a sample space, K is the complete σ algebra of a subsets of the Ω, and P is a probability measure. Now let an ordinary event be $E \in K$. With the help of the characteristic function χ, the probability of the event E can be expressed as

$$P(E) = \int_\Omega \chi_E(\omega)\,dP \quad \text{where } \chi_E(\omega) = \begin{cases} 1 & \omega \in E, \\ 0 & \omega \notin E \end{cases}. \tag{7}$$

According to [10], the membership function $\mu(\omega)$ can be considered as an extension of the characteristic function. For the fuzzy event F, with the membership function $\mu_F(\omega)$ we obtain in this manner (7) in the form

$$P(F) = \int_\Omega \mu_F(\omega)dP \qquad \mu_F(\Omega) : \Omega \to (0,1). \tag{8}$$

If we have a discrete sample space $\Omega = \{\omega_1, \omega_2, \ldots, \omega_n\}$, then the probability will be:

$$P(F) = \sum_{i=1}^{n} \mu_F(\omega_i)P(\omega = \omega_i). \tag{9}$$

This is summation of the probabilities $P(\omega = \omega_i)$ multiplied by the degree to which ω_i belongs to the fuzzy event F. In realistic situations the probability is estimated by the category frequency of ω_i and we obtain the relative pseudofrequency of the event F as an estimate of the probability of the fuzzy event. We use the term pseudofrequencies because absolute frequencies as sums of the membership functions of the fuzzy event F, in ensemble of measured fuzzy data, are usually not integers. (Conventional absolute category frequencies of crisp events are integers, numbers of discrete objects belonging to a class). Let us consider a "fuzzy version of a histogram". On the universum, x, discrete fuzzy sets $X_1, X_2, \ldots, X_n$ are defined. Any fuzzy set, X_k, consists of discrete values $x_{k1}, x_{k2}, \ldots, x_{km}$ with relevant values of membership functions. The sum of all the membership degrees for all occurrences of the value x_{kj}, in an available ensemble of data, is the absolute pseudofrequency. Normalization with respect to a sum of all absolute pseudofrequencies provides a relative pseudofrequency as an estimate of the probability of a fuzzy event.

According to [11] it is also possible to use the χ^2 test for fuzzy data. Let us consider that $P(x)$ is assumed to be a theoretical probabilistic distribution. Let $\Pi(k)$ be

$$\Pi(k) = \int_x \mu_k(x)dP(x). \tag{10}$$

This is Zadeh's distribution induced by theoretical distribution $P(x)$ on the k-th fuzzy set with membership function $\mu_x(x)$, defined on universum x. $\Gamma(k)$ are experimental pseudofrequencies for the fuzzy sets $k = 1, 2, \ldots, m$ and n is the number of measurements.

In [11] it is proven that the statistics

$$\Gamma = 2 \sum_{k \in x}^{n} \gamma(k) \log[\gamma(k)/n\Pi(k)] \qquad (11)$$

has an approximate χ^2 distribution with $r - 1 = \nu$, where r is a cardinality of X. For $n \to \infty$ we can write

$$\sum_{k=1}^{n} \frac{[\gamma(k) - n\Pi(k)]^2}{n\Pi(k)} = \chi_\nu^2 \, . \qquad (12)$$

From these relations follows that there are no principal restrictions in the extension of the presented method for fuzzy data. We deal with pseudofrequencies instead of frequencies and we obtain estimates of probabilities as well as for crisp data.

6 The Extraction of the Rules

Now we have the state space of the controller partitioned on cells and we can assign appropriate outputs to individual cells and to form rules. Due to overlapping of neighbor fuzzy sets and due to uncertainties in measurement the assignment of the appropriate output to a specific cell is ambiguous. It is natural to select as a rule the most frequented coincidence between a specific cell and a specific output. It leads to the multidimensional histogram or histogram depicting the pseudofrequencies.

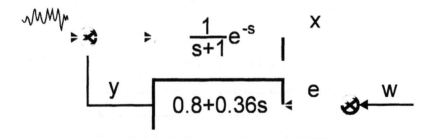

Fig. 1. A simple control system for demonstration of the method

The technique can be demonstrated with help of the following example. A simple control system according to Fig. 1 has been simulated.

A conventional PD controller has been used and the system was stimulated by the white noise. The sampled corresponding inputs and outputs of the controller have been stored. The data set consists of 200 samples of input and output. Analysis of the mask showed, that for $y(k)$ we need $e(k)$ and $e(k-1)$. The variables $y(k)$, $e(k)$ and $e(k) - e(k-1)$ were quantised into three levels. (assigned with linguistic terms "positive"=P, "zero"=Z, "negative"=N). Frequencies of coincidences among cells and output are in the Table 3.

Table 3. Frequencies of coincidences among cells and output values for estimation of the rules

		abs.	freq.		rule
e(k)	Δe(k)	N	Z	P	
N	N	18	0	0	P
N	Z	40	5	0	P
N	P	2	8	0	Z
Z	N	5	14	0	Z
Z	Z	0	34	3	Z
Z	P	0	6	9	Z
P	N	0	6	3	Z
P	Z	0	6	32	N
P	P	0	0	9	N

Choosing most frequented rule as a typical rule for specific cell of the state space, we obtain the following rule base – Table 4.

Table 4. Final form of the rule base

		Δe		
		N	Z	P
	N	P	P	Z
e	Z	Z	Z	Z
	P	Z	N	N

7 Conclusion

The method submitted enables to find the control rules if any controller exists which is able to control a given system. For instance if exists an expert who is able to control the given system, but is unable to formulate the rules explicitly. The method is important especially in situations where more complicated controllers are applied. For instance by the control of biotechnological processes connected with water purification. The method has little significance for the design of fuzzy PI, PD, PID controllers. This is the domain of template based methods.

Having all relevant variables after the structure identification, the neural nets approach may be used for determining the rules and the membership functions. Newertheless a simple method for the choice of rules on the base of their frequency (or pseudofrequency) provides information on statistical properties of the training set if it contains data corresponding with all necessary states. Using neural nets, these properties are usually not known, what leads sometimes to the erroneous results.

References

1. Flaus J.M., Cheruy A., Engasser J.M., Poch M., Sola C.: Estimation of the state and parameters in bioprocesses from indirect measurement. Proc. European control, conf. Grenoble, 1991, 1642–1647
2. Connant R.W., Ashby W.R.: Every good regulator of a system must be a model of that system, Int. J. Gen. Syst. 1970, vol. 1, 89–97
3. Klir G.J.: Architecture of system problem solving. Plenum Press, New York, 1985
4. Cellier F.E.: General system problem solving paradigm for qualitative modeling. In: Qualitative simulation, modeling and analysis, Fishwick P.A. and Luker P.A. eds., Springer, New York, 1991
5. Klir G.J., Way E.C.: Reconstructability analysis: Aims, results, open problems. System research, 1985, vol. 2., no. 2, 141–163
6. Connant R.C.: Extended dependency analysis of large systems. Part I-II. Int. J. Gen. Syst. 1988, vol. 14., no. 2., 97–141
7. Connant R.C.: Structural modeling using a simple information measure. Int. J. System Sci. 1980, vol. 11., no. 6., 721–730
8. Valdes-Perez R.E., Connant R.C.: Information loss due to data quantization in reconstructability analysis. Int. J. Gen. Syst. 1983, vol. 9., no. 4., 235–247
9. Yaeger R.R., Filev D.P.: Essentials of fuzzy modeling and control. J. Willey, New York, 1994
10. Zadeh L.A.: Probability measures of fuzzy events. J. Math. Anal. Appl. 1968, no. 23, 421–427
11. Gill M.A., Corral N., Cassals M.R.: The likelihood ratio test for goodness of fit with fuzzy experimantal observations. IEEE trans. SMC, 1989, vol. 19., no. 4., 771–779

Cast Methods for Generation of Non-Orthogonal Complete Transforms

J.C.Quevedo Losada, O.Bolivar Toledo, & R.Moreno Díaz jr.

Departament of Computer Science and Systems
University of Las Palmas de Gran Canaria.
Las Palmas. Canary Island. 35017.
Spain

1 Introduction

As well as neurophysiologists investigate what natural neuron receptive fields are and what they are doing, people working in picture processing and in general in artificial vision question about sizes of receptive fields and functions that should be performed on them by neuron like elements.

In non structured artifitial vision systems, what scientists and engineers seek is for kinds of complete transforms which provide for alternative descriptions of images that can be truncated for particular purposes, so that a much low number of degrees of freedom are to be handle. In that sense, after applying a whole set of standard transformations to pictures to obtain descriptors we were aware that the search for orthogonality in the descriptors functions was really a handicap inherited from the times that global transforms (like Fourier, Hadamard, Haar) had to be made almost by hand. But with modern computer techniques it was no clear that there was any advantage except for the insurance of independence, that is, insuring that the corresponding transform results were non redundant. We looked then for complete transforms, not necessarily orthonormal, but independent, so that the inverse transform, will exist.

The first interesting result is that the partition of the receptive field matter as much as the function performed on them [1][2]. Partition means that one is computing on the sensory data in parallel, though with overlapping.

The concept of Progressive Resolution Transform was introduced [3], in which it was emphasized that no matter what function it is performed, a vast class of partitions could be complete. That is, given an image (a "data field" in fact. because the image fills a data field in memory), then one can, and it is convenient, to separate receptive fields from functions, so that a data field partition can be, by itself, complete.

The next logical problem was one of tradeoff, wich is probably what happens in the retina, since the resolution of fibers is not necessarily preserved, and there is a multiple meaning coding, which in this terminology will mean that each fibre of the optic nerve sends information pertaining to more than one operation on the receptive field. Here the question was faced by stating of a theorem [4], that showed that for a family of L algebraic partitions, of the same lenght, the computation of M=N/L functional coefficients linearly indpendent in each partition provides for a complete description of the data field.

In this context, the next step is to consider the more general case, inspired by natural systems, in which the size of the receptive field is a variable, that is say the dimention of the partition established is not the same. This new case has been considered in this work and we have formulated a new theorem, based on the yuxtaposition of functionals linearly independents in each partition, which provide a systematic way to obtain complete transformations. As a powerfull tool to provide independent descriptors we have used the Newton Filters.

We have formulated the theory for one dimension and considering the transformation to be separable we have applied it to bidimentional images. At the same time we have investigated the existence of fast algorithms of computation.

Nature does not follow theorems exactly, but they provide us with a clear way to approach nature. On any case, the parallel computing structures which result, are both illuminating to understand natural systems and to build artificial ones.

2 Receptive Field-Functional Transformation

2.1 Partitions of Constant Length

Let us consider an unidimentional data field D(N) with resolution R, addressed by index i (i=1...N), and consider also a set of L independent partitions of the i addresses. This set can be represented by a binary matrix.

A class of partitions used in previous works corresponded to one level of a foveal transformation. For a receptive field of N places, the number of partitions generated of this type would be L=N-d+1, d being the length of the partition. The dimension of the corresponding matrix would be N*(N-d+1).

These partitions are not, a priori, complete, due to the fact, that in general L<N, although they are independent.

If we are looking for a complete representation, we have developed a theorem [5], which integrates the algebra and analysis of the data fields, stating that given an algebraic partition with certain restictions, the computation of a number $M = N/L$ of analytical descriptors, independent in eac' partition provide a complete and non redundant description of the data field.

The algebraic-analytical transformation, represented by a matrix $N*N$ is obtained by the "application" of each functional vector to each partition.

$$
\begin{bmatrix}
F11 & \cdots & F1d \\
F21 & \cdots & F2d \\
\cdot & & \cdot \\
\cdot & & \cdot \\
\cdot & & \cdot \\
Fm1 & \cdots & Fmd
\end{bmatrix}
\text{*}
\begin{bmatrix}
P11 & \cdots & P11 \\
P21 & \cdots & P21 \\
\cdot & & \cdot \\
\cdot & & \cdot \\
\cdot & & \cdot \\
Pn1 & \cdots & Pn1
\end{bmatrix}
= N
\begin{bmatrix}
\quad
\end{bmatrix}
\begin{matrix}
\} M_1 \\
\\
\} M_2 \\
\\
\} M_k
\end{matrix}
= M
$$

As we can see, groups of vectors M_1, M_2, ..., M_k have been generated, all of which have the same extension over the data field. In each group, the vectors are independent by construction. Likewise, the groups are independent among themselves since they correspond to independent partitions. Therefore, the N horizontal vectors are independent, thus the corresponding transformation is complete.

2.2 Partitions of Variable Length

We are now under adequate conditions to consider the most general case of variable length partitions, that is, those partitions in which the dimension of each subpartitions is not the same. In this new case, for a data field of N dimension $D(N)$, and a set of L partitions, we must compute a number $M = N/L$ of independent descriptors per partition, but now the indepency of functionals has to be guaranteed when they are applied to each of the columns, not to only just one.

For example, let us consider the partition:
Two independent functionals for the first column could be of Haar type:

$$F_1 = 1/8 \; (1\ 1\ 1\ 1\ 1\ 1\ 1\ 1)$$
$$F_2 = 1/8 \; (1\ 1\ 1\ 1\ -1\ -1\ -1\ -1)$$

It is easy to see that when they are applied to the second column, the numbers obtained are not only non independent, but the same.

$$\begin{bmatrix} 1 & 1 & 1 & 0 \\ 1 & 1 & 1 & 0 \\ 1 & 1 & 0 & 0 \\ 1 & 1 & 0 & 0 \\ 1 & 0 & 0 & 1 \\ 1 & 0 & 0 & 1 \\ 1 & 0 & 0 & 0 \\ 1 & 0 & 0 & 0 \end{bmatrix}$$

Nevertheless, focusing on the other limit case, if we select two independent functionals for the lower dimension column, for example those of weights:

$$(1,1)$$
$$(1,-1)$$

and two new functionals of the dimension corresponding to that of the larger column, are generated by juxtaposition, that is say:

$$F_1 = 1/8 \,(\, 1\ 1\ 1\ 1\ 1\ 1\ 1\ 1 \,)$$
$$F_2 = 1/8 \,(\, 1\ -1\ 1\ -1\ 1\ -1\ 1\ -1 \,)$$

it is easy to see that the generated numbers are now independent. The corresponding transformation matrix is:

$$\begin{bmatrix} 1 & 1 & 1 & 1 & 1 & 1 & 1 & 1 \\ 1 & -1 & 1 & -1 & 1 & -1 & 1 & -1 \\ 1 & 1 & 1 & 1 & 0 & 0 & 0 & 0 \\ 1 & -1 & 1 & -1 & 0 & 0 & 0 & 0 \\ 1 & 1 & 0 & 0 & 0 & 0 & 0 & 0 \\ 1 & -1 & 0 & 0 & 0 & 0 & 0 & 0 \\ 0 & 0 & 0 & 0 & 1 & 1 & 0 & 0 \\ 0 & 0 & 0 & 0 & 1 & -1 & 0 & 0 \end{bmatrix}$$

This transformation is similar to the detector contrast progressive resolution transformation, introduced by Candela in 1991 [3].

The solution founded in this example, has been made possible because the average number of functionals to be calculated per column of the partition, is equal or lower than the resolution of the column of lower dimension. So, obviously, it does not make sense to calculate three descriptors from the third and fourth column, of the partition which only have two addresses.

The above, lead us to formulate the following theorem:

THEOREM

Given a data field of N dimension, and an arbitrary partition of L columns, such that d_m is the dimension of the lower dimension column, with $d_m \geq N/L$, then a set of N/L independent functionals of d_m length, juxtaposed up until the column of larger dimension, provide a complete transformation.

It is easy to demostrate this theorem according what has been presented in the example shown previosly. In effect, let us consider the transformation matrix:

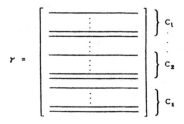

C_1 corresponds to the set of lower dimension, affected by the corresponding weights, which are independent by construction, while $C_2, C_3, \ldots C_1$. corresponds to the remaining columns, which will be independent by the additional condition of the independency of partitions, and/or by the extended functional used.

Limit Cases

In the developed previously transformation treatment, and from a completeness point of view, what remains to be considered are the situations where the dimension of the columns of lower dimension (d_m) is such that $d_m < N/L$. However, in this case, symmetry, which is one of the basic reasons for the separation of receptive field and function, is lost, in the sense that, depending on the partition length, we would need more or less vector coefficients. In this case, the utility of the separation carried out, becomes questionable, instead of considering the transformation matrix directly, with the condition of independency of its vectors. In other words, because we need a number $N' > N/L$ of weight vectors, which form the functional, the product $N'L$ needed, exceeds the initial number of freedom degrees and in order to avoid redundancies, the application of these vectors to columns must be carried out selectively.

However, some considerations can be carried out, which provide complete transform generation methods. According ↄ what has been pointed out previosly, the above situation correspond to partitions, where, on average, for reason of completness, it is essential to extract N/L independent descriptors, but certain corresponding columns can not provide then. This, could be due to the following:

1) Columns exist where it is possible to extract a number of descriptor higher than the average.

2) Addresses exist, which are lost from the data field, with data which cannot be retrieved by any function of the set of proccesors.

Case 1 correspond to a partition of the type considered above (where each one of the addresses is considered once) and case 2 always correspond to a situation of incompletness. This last one, is theoretical interesting with regard to reliability or performance security, as far as it corresponds to the problem of "scotomas" (local disappearance of data), against the "disfunction problem" (local disappearance of proccesors), corresponding this, in a limit situation, with the typical method, used in artificial vision, of cutt the number of descriptors, which is enough in a practical situation.

It is possible to extend the systematic way developed to generate complete transformation to that correspondieng to case 1.

As an illustration, let us consider the partition matrix:

$$\begin{bmatrix} 1 & 1 & 1 & 0 \\ 1 & 1 & 0 & 0 \\ 1 & 1 & 0 & 0 \\ 1 & 1 & 0 & 0 \\ 1 & 0 & 0 & 0 \\ 1 & 0 & 0 & 0 \\ 1 & 0 & 0 & 1 \\ 1 & 0 & 0 & 0 \end{bmatrix}$$

The number of descriptors per column must be $N/L=8/4=2$, in average. But columns third and fourth cannnot provide it, therefore columns first and second must provide the additional number in order to keep the average. Particularly, columns third and fourh can generate a unic descriptor each one, remaining 6 which must be distributed between columns one and two. Since the dimension of each one of then is equal or higher to the remainder average(6/3=2), theorem proposed above, is again applicable to this columns.

From the point of view of modern retinal theory, the above solution, do not seen, a priori, to be sustained, since this woud be equivalent to admit that gangilon cells, with extensive receptive fields, must carried out a proccess and codification function, greater than the carried out by cells with restricted receptive field. But, this would be so, only if completeness is required for the whole retina, which is a quostionable and even refutable argument, due to the fact that is the fovea (where the preccision is high) where are the cells of restricted receptive fields.

Newton Filters

In the present work, in addition to use the Haar and Hadamard transform to obtain linearly independent functional, we have also uses the Newton Filters [6] as a tool to generate functionals, since the set of vector generated by this Newton Filters of certain size, L, are lineal independent.

For example:

1.- L=2:

$$N_1 = N(A1) = (1,1)$$
$$N_2 = N(D1) = (1,-1)$$

2.- L=3:

$$N_1 = N(A2) = (1,2,1)$$
$$N_2 = N(A1,D1) = (1,0,-1)$$
$$N_3 = N(D2) = (1,-2,1)$$

3.- L=4:

$$N_1 = N(A3) = (1,3,3,1)$$
$$N_2 = N(A2,D1) = (1,1,-1,-1)$$
$$N_3 = N(A1,D2) = (1,-1,-1,1)$$
$$N_4 = N(D3) = (1,-3,3,-1)$$

From the above examples, we can generate the matrix which rows are the corresponding weight vectors of the Newton Filter. In this way, the Newton Filters of second ordes is:

$$\begin{bmatrix} 1 & 1 \\ 1 & -1 \end{bmatrix}$$

The third order is:

$$\begin{bmatrix} 1 & 2 & 1 \\ 1 & 0 & -1 \\ 1 & -2 & 1 \end{bmatrix}$$

and so on.

3 Practical Illustration

As a practical illustration, consider the case of an image of 256*256.

1) In this case, we have considered a partition of $L=128$ columns and Haar Functionals. In the figure we show in a) the original image; in b) c) and d) the image transformed with ordered different sorting of the partitions matrix.

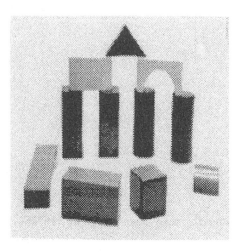

Figure a)

Figure b)

Figure c)

Figure d)

2) In this case, have considered a partition of L=64 columns and Hadamard Functional. In the figure we show in a) the original image; in b) the image transformed.

Figure a)

Figure b)

3) In this case, have considered a partition of L=128 columns and Newton Filters Functional. In the figure we show in a) the original image; in b) the image transformed.

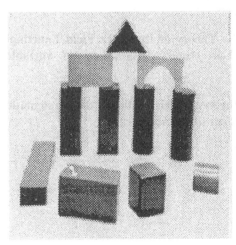

Figure a)

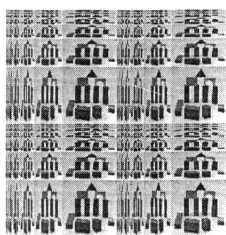

Figure b)

4) In this case, have considered a partition of L=64 columns and Newton Filters Functional. In the figure we show in a) the original image; in b) the image transformed.

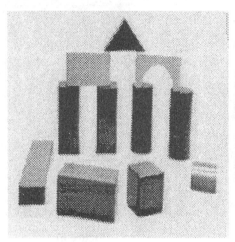 

Figure a)   Figure b)

4 Conclusions

1) We have studied in depth the Theory of Receptive Field Functinal Transformation, increasing their scope to situations of variable dimension partitions.

2) We have developped a theorem which allows the Systematic generation of Complete Transform in the above case.

References

[1] J.A.Muñoz Blanco, J.C. Quevedo Losada, O. Bolivar Toledo. "The role of Partitions and Functionals in Descriptor Computation for Data Receptive Fields". Computer Aided Systems. Theory-Eurocast´93 (Las Palmas, Spain. 1.993).

458

[2] J.C Quevedo Losada, J.A. Muñoz Blanco, O. Bolivar Toledo. "Variable Receptive Field System Transformation and its Applications to Visual Field". United Kingdom Systems Society Conference on Systems Thinking in Europe (1.991 :Huddersfield. England).

[3] S. Candela Solá. "Transformaciones de Campo Receptivo Variable en Proceso de Imágenes y Visión Artificial". Doctoral Thesis. 1988.

[4] O.Bolivar Toledo, S.Candela Solá & R.Moreno Díaz. "Complete Transforms and Their Incidence in Artificial Perception Systems Theory". Computer Aided Systems. Theory-Eurocast´91 (Krems, Austria, April 1.991).

[5] O. Bolivar Toledo. "Hacia una teoria de las Transformaciones en Campos Receptivos y Campos de Datos" Implicaciones en Teoría retinal y Proceso de Imágenes" Doctoral Thesis. 1990.

[6] R. Moreno Díaz, jr. "Computación Paralela y Distribuida:Relaciones Estructura-Función en Retinas. Redes de Newton, Transformadas de Hermite, Complitud, Cooperación y Óptimos". Doctoral Thesis. 1993.

Cast System Approach for Visual Inspection

Candela, S., Garcia, C., Alayon, F., and Muñoz, J.

Department of Informática y Sistemas.
Campus Universitario de Tafira
University of Las Palmas de Gran Canaria.
Las Palmas, Canary Islands, 35017 Spain
Fone +34 28 458753, Fax +34 28 458760. Email scandela@dfei.ulpgc.es

ABSTRACT: Begining with the concepts and techniques of Artificial Vision and Systems Theory, the main goal of this paper is the analysis and synthesis of a formal general model to be the base for the design of visual automatic inspection systems and its implementation and testing in a real case of fault detection using digital images acquired through a camera-computer chain.

KEYWORDS: Visual Inspection, Texture Changes, Artificial Vision, Fault Detection.

1. INTRODUCTION.

The main goal of this work is to analyze and to synthesize a general formal model, from artificial vision techniques and System Theory concepts, a CAST model [1], wich permits automatic visual inspection systems design, and to allow us to carry out and test a real case fault detection [2]. In this work we use natural leather from cow and pig, and the system input is composed of digitalized images acquired by a camera-computer.

There are two methodologies for automatic fault resolution, depending on the type of knowledge known on the faults [3]. If we have precise knowledge about them, then the detection process consists of searching for these faults, and do not need to analyze the material's texture. In a few cases we have this situation, and normally we must use tools for texture analysis.

We can found several mathematical models for texture analysis [4][5], (basically statistical or structural), but the automatic visual problem using texture analysis is not resolved in a general form. We have found two types of classification:

Deterministic- when the material's texture can be described by a deterministic function, it is a periodic texture, in this case the basic methods consist of finding deviations in a periodic texture.

Non deterministic- the texture is made by aleatory distributions of elements, therefore, the detection process is based on considering a fault as a break in the material's texture. It is in this case that we develop this work.

In non deterministic case, the fault detection problem is equivalent to detecting changes on uniform or periodic textures. These changes are local deviations in homogeneity [6], or strange elements which appear on the texture such as a crack or a tear. If we accept the previous hypothesis, the resolution of the problem consists of finding a set of properties which characterize the uniform texture, which are sensitive and wich change appreciably on fault zones or non homogeneous zones.

When we study the different catalog faulty leather, we observe that:

a) the fault has two origins, structural changes or tonality changes.

b) In similar faults, the intensities of the structural changes or the tonality changes are not the same in relation to all the good areas.

c) Good material presents soft structural and tonality changes.

From these observations, we can say that the fault detection systems need processes that detect sligth changes on material texture. The task of finding the optimal descriptors set, wich allows us to discriminate and separate a good area from a faulty area, is not easy, and requires us to set up several algorithms and to test and try them.

2. MAIN RESULTS.

We divide the work results into two classes: theoretical and practical. The theoretical model has the following characteristics:

1) It represents an alternative model to classical Artificial Vision with an inverted pyramid. It has a representation space larger than the input data space [7], and the number of degrees fredom of the problem expands.

2) The model does not use any information "a priori" from the object that we must study. It directly applies low level image processes and it does not need to learn processes from the material to be analyzed.

3) It has specified and defined all aspects related to local window size, descriptors set, and local homogeneity measure.

Other practical results related to theoretical ones are:

1) We have studied the influence of the work window size on the goodness of the descriptor wich we use in fault detection. We have developed a semiautomatic method to settle the optimal window size or kernel size in the convolution process. This point is not formally studied in automatic vision systems for fault detection.

2) We have proved and tested different techniques to characterize textures. These suggest that we propose a new diagnostic method wich works on difference space, compared to traditional methods which work on characteristic space. This is justified because the difference images are more stable when environmental conditions are changed by noise or light.

3) We have analyzed several distance functionals to measure the local homogeneity level. We propose low cost computational functionals and high sensitivity, which compute relative differences on each characteristic space [8]. These differences allow us to detect a large set of defaults by elemental decision rules.

4) The general model permits us to design and implement a particular automatic visual

system to study different materials: wood, leather, fabric, plastic, etc.

The model uses a facilitatory process in the preprocess layer [9]. This technique consists of multipling two local processes' outputs. It produces a non-linear high pass filter, when we apply it to fault texture. The fault intensity is increased, and the localization process fault is easier. This process can be implemented by a parallel net using elemental processors.

In fault detection literature [10][11][12][13][14] references are made to wood, fabrics but not to leather. We have camed out an exhaustive bibliographic search to find different fault detection techniques and we have tried and tested these techniques and the method proposed is for pig leather and cow leather.

3. PROBLEMS AND SOLUTIONS.

Integrating the vision system with a computer system.
We have designed a driver for the (IMAGIN VT100) vision board, and is integrated into the UNIX operating system.
Select a set of digitized images.
From the catalog fault leather, we select a set sample which we call VDF visual detectable fault.
Preprocess for picture improvement.
We use a facilitatory non linear high pass filter to make the fault stand out from the backgraund. This is based on a statistical process of computing local averages and variances.
Window setting.
We design a semiautomatic

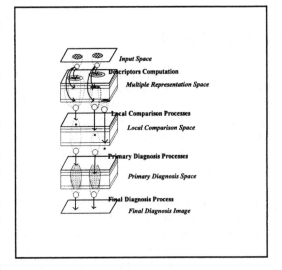

method for window setting, which it is based on a knowledge of the areas without faults, and studies the performance of the characteristics.
Descriptors Computation.
We implement and test several algorithms to obtain image descriptors. These programs use the following techniques:
Generalized Convolutions based on first and second order statistics[15][16].
Kernels sensitive to changes in frequencies of grey levels.
Kernels which emphasize topological properties[17].
Algorithmic kernels.
The histogram space as a descriptor-decision space.
Assessed Techniques.
Assessed Kernels.

Techniques based on Fourier Spectra[18][19].

Local comparison processes.

The local comparison processes are implemented with a rule inspired by lateral inhibition center-periphery.

Primary diagnosis.

This is based on a semiautomatic threshold, and the decision rule works on each image descriptor with a function multidescriptor.

Final diagnosis.

The input space for the final diagnosis is the output of the primary diagnosis volume. The process element computes a logical function within the primary diagnosis volume, to generate the output image or final dianosis image.

4. GENERAL CONCLUSION.

The difficulty in formalizing the problem of fault detection, (because of its fuzzy nature) force us to carry out a lot of testing with several parameters; after words we can heuristically find a descriptor set, that even when they are not optimal, at least they can solve our problem.

The model uses tools from artificial vision to detect faults, it has possibilities and it is suitable for industrial applications.

The system has technological advantages. Principally, it automatically carries out the control process, and it eliminates o reduces the expert's work. It is convenient, because repetitive and monotone work causes the expert's fatigue and it produces errors in the diagnosis. The subjective diagnosis from the expert is removed. It has other advantage of the economic type, when the expert is removed and the process cost is reduced.

The possible industrial sectors interested are those related to leather, wood, plastic, fabric, carpets, cars, in general, all industrial companies carrying out quality control and inspection by visual methods.

The results are directly applied in real industrial problem. Nevertheless, each particular application needs a particular definition prototype that can be adapted to a concrete problem.

Two topics are of interest for further research: fault classification methods; and the interaction with a robotic system. Normally, the quality control techniques based on an artificial vision system are integrated with a robotic subsystem. Therefore, the main system produces the diagnosis, handles the material, and sometimes it may need to move to areas of interest or problem areas.

ACKNOWLEDGMENTS The work presented in this paper has been partially supported under Proyect TAP92-0738 from CICYT Comisión Interministerial de Ciencia y Tecnología, and the catalog used belong to GUCCI (leather company).

5. EXAMPLES AND FIGURES.

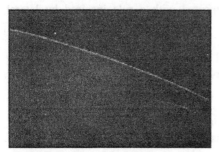

Fig. 1A Cow,Tear, 768x512x8

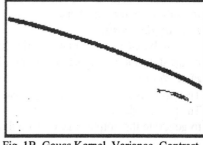

Fig. 1B Gauss Kernel, Variance, Contrast

Fig. 2A Cow, Wrinkle, Pricks, 768x512x8

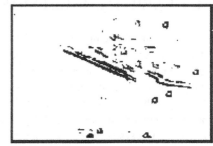

Fig. 2B Gauss Kernel, Variance, Contrast

Fig. 3A Pig, Backbone, 768x512x8

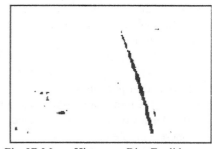

Fig. 3B Mean, Histogram Dist. Euclidea

Fig. 4A Pig, Scar, 768x512x8

Fig. 4B Mean, Histogram Dist.Euclidea

6. REFERENCES.

[1] Pichler, F. Computer Aided System Theory: A Framework for Interactive Method Banks. Cibernetics and Systems. 88. pp 731-736.The Netherlands 1988.

[2] Candela, S., Muñoz, J., Alayon, F., Garcia C. Un Sistema de Visión para la Detección de Defectos.Actas de Panel '92 p 240-247. Las Palmas de G. Canaria.1992. Universidad de Las Palmas de Gran Canaria

[3] Unser, M., Coulon, F. Detection of Defects by Texture Monitoring in Automatic Visual Inspection. Proceedings of The 2md International Conference on Robot Vision and Sensory Controls November 1982. Stuttgart, Germany.

[4] Muñoz Blanco, J. A."Jerarquización de estructuras de nivel bajo y medio para reconocimiento visual. Aplicaciones a texturas y formas. Tesis Doctoral. 1987.

[5] Wang, L.; and D. He. "Texture Classification Using Texture Spectrum". Pattern Recognition". 1990.

[6] Amelia C. Fong, Lionel M. Ni, Kwan Y. Wong "Fast Discrimination Between Homogeneous and Texture Regions".

[7] García, C. Estructuras de Representación Visual Múltiple. Aplicación a la Detección de Variaciones Locales en Texturas y a la Inspección Visual. Tesis Doctoral. 1995.

[8] Muñoz, J., Garcia, C., Alayon, F., Candela, S. Systems Concepts for Visual Texture Change Detection Strategy. Lecture Notes in Computer Science 763. pp 358-366. 1994.

[9] Candela, S., Garcia, C., Muñoz, J., Alayon, F. Facilitatory Process for Contrast Detection. Lecture Notes in Computer Science 720. pp 627-630. 1993.

[10] Borghesi, V. Cantoni, M. Diani."An Industrial Application of Texture Analysis".

[11] Conners, R. Identifying and Locating Surface Defects in Wood: Part of an Automated Lumber Processing System. IEEE Transactions on Pattern Analysis and Machine Intelligence, Vol.Pami-5, No 6, November 1983.

[12] Ade, F. "Application of principal component analisys to the inspection of industrial goods". Applications of Digital Image Processing, vol 397, pag 216-223, SPIE 1983.

[13] Siew, H., Hodgson, R. "Texture Measures for Carpet Wear Assesment". Transactions on Pattern Analisys and Machine Intelligence. vol 10,n1.IEEE Computer Society Press.1988.

[14] Neubauer, C. "Segmentation of Defects in Textile Fabric". International Conference on Pattern Recognition Proceeding. pp 688-691. IEEE Computer Society Press.1992.

[15] Haralick, R. Statistical and Structural Approaches to Texture. Procced ings of the IEEE, vol 67, no 5, May 1979.

[16] Calvin C. Gotlieb, Helbert E. Kreyszig."Texture Descriptors Based on Co-Ocurrences Matrices". Computer Vision, Graphics, and Image Processing. Academic Press, Inc. 1990.

[17] Rao, K., Ahmed, N. Orthogonal Transforms for Digital Signal Processing. IEEE International Conference on Acustics, Speech and Signal Processing P 136-40, 1976.

[18] D'Astous and M. E. Jernigan."Texture Discrimination Based On Detailed Measures Of Power Spectrum". IEEE. 1984.

[19] Eklundh, J. O."On The Use of Fourier Features for Texture Discrimination". Computer Graphics and Image Processing. 1979.

Finite Dimensional Generalized Baker Dynamical Systems for Cryptographic Applications

Franz Pichler and Josef Scharinger
Institute of Systems Science
Chair of Systems Theory and Information Engineering
Johannes Kepler University Linz, Austria
A - 4040 Linz

1   Introduction

In the past there have been several attempts to apply the field of deterministic chaos to cryptography. In this paper we propose for cryptographic applications to use maps as state transition function of a discrete dynamical system which leads to deterministic chaos. More specifically, we make use of generalized versions of the well-known baker transform, which are discrete and finite. Since they relate by group–theoretic representation to Bernoulli–shifts, we call them *Bernoulli permutations*.

The iteration of Bernoulli permutations on a set of data realizes a repeated "stretching" and "compressing" which has been compared by the "rolling" and "folding" in the work of a baker by mixing a dough. The knowledge of the importance of such operations for cryptography goes back to the fundamental paper of Claude Shannon ([8]), a fact which has been pointed out earlier in a paper by N.J.A. Sloane ([9]).

The results reported in this paper are based mainly on the PhD–thesis of the second author ([6]). A Technical Report of the first author formed the starting basis for it. This paper extends the results which have been reported in earlier papers ([10],[11]).

2   Baker Transform and its Generalization

2.1   Baker Transform T

The baker transform $T : [\,0\,,1\,)^2 \to [\,0\,,1\,)^2$ can be defined by

$$T(x,y) \quad := \quad \begin{cases} (2x, \frac{1}{2}y) & : \quad 0 \leq x < \frac{1}{2} \\ (2x - 1, \frac{1}{2}(y + 1)) & : \quad \frac{1}{2} \leq x < 1 \end{cases} \tag{1}$$

By T the left part $[\,0\,,\frac{1}{2}\,) \times [\,0\,,1\,)$ of $[\,0\,,1\,)^2$ is mapped by "stretching" and "folding" to the part $[\,0\,,1\,) \times [\,0\,,\frac{1}{2}\,)$. The right part $[\,\frac{1}{2}\,,1\,) \times [\,0\,,1\,)$ of $[\,0\,,1\,)^2$ is similar mapped to $[\,0\,,1\,) \times [\,\frac{1}{2}\,,1\,)$. The following properties of T are well-known in mathematics ([1],[2]).

1. T is invertible

2. If $(x, y) \in [0, 1)^2$ is represented as a both–side infinite sequence

$$s = \ldots, x_3, x_2, x_1 . y_1, y_2, y_3, \ldots$$

where

$$x = x_1 2^{-1} + x_2 2^{-1} + x_3 2^{-3} + \ldots$$
$$y = y_1 2^{-1} + y_2 2^{-1} + y_3 2^{-3} + \ldots$$

(chose for dyadic rational x, y the finite expansion) then T as defined by (1) has on s the effect of a left-shift that is:

$T(x, y)$ corresponds to the one–step–shift of s " to the left "

$$s \to 1 = \ldots x_2, x_1, y_1 . y_2, y_3, y_4, \ldots$$

3. the dynamical system T^* generated by T is mixing and ergodic.

2.2 Generalized baker transform T_π

For $\pi = (p_1, p_2, \ldots, p_k)$ with $0 < p_i < 1$ for $i = 1, 2, \ldots, k$ and $p_1 + p_2 + \ldots + p_k = 1$ the generalized baker transform $T_\pi : [0, 1)^2 \to [0, 1)^2$ is defined by

$$T_\pi(x, y) = \left(\frac{1}{p_s}(x - F_s), p_s y + F_s \right) \tag{2}$$

for $(x, y) \in [F_s, F_s + p_s)$ where $F_1 := 0$ and $F_s := p_1 + p_2 + \ldots + p_{s-1}$ for $s = 2, \ldots, k$.

The "probabilities" $p_1, p_2, \ldots, p_k$ of π partition the unit square $[0, 1)^2$ into k vertical strips; the numbers $F_1, F_2, \ldots, F_k$ represent the initial x–coordinates of these strips (compare with figure 1).

Application of T_π on $[0, 1)^2$ maps the vertical strip $[F_s, F_s + p_s) \times [0, 1)$ into the horizontal strip $[0, 1) \times [F_s, F_s + p_s)$. x–values of the strip are stretched by the factor $\frac{1}{p_s}$; y–values of the strip are compressed by p_s (compare with figure 2).

It can be proven, that T_π has similar mathematical properties as the baker transform T. As a specific property, it should be mentioned that T_π can also be realized by Bernoulli–shift operations.

3 Bernoulli Permutations

3.1 Definition

By $\mathbb{N}_0^n$ we denote the subset $\mathbb{N}_0^n := \{0, 1, 2, \ldots, n - 1\}$ of integers. With δ we denote a list of non-negative integers $\delta = (n_1, n_2, \ldots, n_k)$ with the following properties

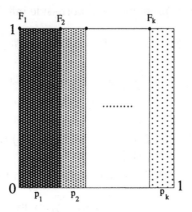

Fig. 1. vertical partitions of the unit square

E

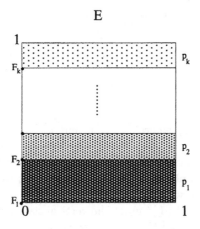

1. $n_1 + n_2 + \ldots + n_k = n$

2. each number n_s $(s = 1, 2, \ldots, k)$ divides n; $n_s | n$.

Let Δ denote the set of all lists δ which have the properties 1. and 2. Our goal is to define a transformation $T_{n,\delta} : \mathbb{N}_0^n \times \mathbb{N}_0^n \to \mathbb{N}_0^n \times \mathbb{N}_0^n$ which is a discrete and finite version of the generalized baker transform T_π. This is the case if we define $T_{n,\delta}$ as follows:

Let the numbers q_s $(s = 1, 2, \ldots, k)$ be defined by $q_s = \frac{n}{n_s}$. Then

$$T_{n,\delta}(x,y) \quad := \quad \left(q_s(x - N_s) + y \bmod q_s, \frac{1}{q_s}(y - y \bmod q_s) + N_s \right) \quad (3)$$

for $(x,y) \in [N_s, N_s + n_s) \times \mathbb{N}_0^n$ where $N_1 := 0$ and $N_s := n_1 + \ldots + n_{s-1}$ for $s = 2, \ldots, k$.

It is easy to prove, that $T_{n,\delta}$ maps in $\mathbb{N}_0^n \times \mathbb{N}_0^n$ the vertical "strips" $[N_s, N_s + n_s) \times \mathbb{N}_0^n$ $(s = 1, 2, \ldots, k)$ into the corresponding horizontal "strips" $\mathbb{N}_0^n \times [N_s, N_s + n_s)$.

It can be shown that $T_{n,\delta}$ is a bijective map. The inverse $T_{n,\delta}^{-1}$ is given by

$$T_{n,\delta}^{-1}(x,y) \quad = \quad \left(\frac{1}{q_s}(x - x \bmod q_s) + N_s, q_s(y - N_s) + x \bmod q_s \right) \quad (4)$$

for $(x,y) \in (\mathbb{N}_0^n \times [N_s, N_s + n_s)$ where $N_1 := 0$ and $N_s := n_1 + n_2 + \ldots + n_{s-1}$ for $s = 2, \ldots, k$.

For any chosen list $\delta = (n_1, n_2, \ldots, n_k)$ we will call $T_{n,\delta}$ a *Bernoulli permutation*.

In analogy to T and T_π respectively, a Bernoulli permutation $T_{n,\delta}$ can also be realized by Bernoulli-shift operations.

3.2 Size of Δ

For our application of Bernoulli permutations in Cryptography it is important to determine for a given n the number c_n of possible permutations, that is, to determine the cardinality of the set Δ consisting of all valid lists δ. According to our earlier definition of δ, we have to determine the number of lists $(n_1, n_2, \ldots, n_k)$ where each component n_s $(s = 1, 2, \ldots, k)$ divides n, $n_s = n$ is excluded and $n_1 + n_2 + \ldots + n_k = n$.

This constitutes a well-known problem in combinatorics (e.g. compare [4]). For the solutions we chose a reported method which is based on formal power series expansion which allows to compute the number c_n recursively ([12],[6], [10]).

Table 1 shows the number $c_n = \text{card } \Delta$ for some n which are powers of 2.

4 Representation by Bernoulli–shifts

Let Z_{q_s} denote the cyclic group of order q_s. If we chose $m_s := \lceil \log_{q_s} n_s \rceil + 1$ then every number $x \in \mathbb{N}_0^{n_s}$ has uniquely a q_s–adic representation:

$$x \quad = \quad x_0 + x_1 q_s + x_2 q_s^2 + \ldots + x_{m_s-2} q_s^{m_s-2} \quad (5)$$

where the coefficients x_i $(i = 0, 1, \ldots, m - 2)$ are from Z_{q_s}. For $y \in \mathbb{N}_0^n$ we have the q_s–adic representation

n	c_n	n	c_n
1	1	128	10^{31}
2	2	256	10^{63}
4	5	512	10^{126}
8	55	1 024	10^{252}
16	5 271	2 048	10^{505}
32	47 350 055	4 096	10^{1001}
64	10^{15}	8 192	10^{2023}

Table 1. number c_n of valid lists δ for some n which are powers of 2

$$y \;=\; y_0 + y_1 q_s + y_2 q_s^2 + \ldots + y_{v-1} q_s^{v_s-1} \tag{6}$$

where $v_s := \lceil \log_{q_s} n \rceil$. Since $n = n_s q_s$ we have $\log_{q_s} n = \log_{q_s} n_s + 1$ and consequently $v_s = m_s$. Let $Z_{q_s}^{2m_s}$ denote the $2m_s$–fold direct product of Z_{q_s}. The pair $(x,y) \in N_0^{n_s} \times N_0^n$ has in $Z_{q_s}^{2m_s}$ using (5) and (6) a representation

$$s \;=\; (x_0, x_1, \ldots, x_{m_s-2}, 0.y_{m_s-1}, y_{m_s-2}, \ldots, y_2, y_1, y_0) \tag{7}$$

The result of the cyclic Bernoulli–shift $s' = s \to 1$ of s is given by

$$s' \;=\; (y_0, x_0, x_1, \ldots, x_{m_s-2}.0, y_{m_s-1}, \ldots, y_2, y_1) \tag{8}$$

Interpretation of s on the effect in $N_0^n \times N_0^n$ shows that by the Bernoulli–shift as defined by (8) is compatible with expression (3) for the definition of $T_{n,\delta}$.

We see that the mapping of $(x,y) \in [N_s, N_s + n_s) \times N_0^n$ as defined by (3) has in the group $Z_{q_s}^{2m_s}$ a corresponding representation which is generated by a cyclic shift on the coordinate set $\{0,1,2,\ldots,2m_s - 1\}$ of indices, referring to the component groups Z_{q_s} of $Z_{q_s}^{2m}$.

5 Bernoulli–Product Cipher

In the following we outline the principal construction to realize a secret key ciphering system of block–type by means of Bernoulli permutations. Let us assume that the plain text is already encoded such that it is represented by a function M of the form

$$M : N_0^n \times N_0^n \to A \quad,$$

where A is the alphabet of M with $A := GF(q)$ for some $q = p^m$. Let M be called for our purposes a "message". In signal processing we would call M also a discrete and finite 2D–signal or an "image".

Each Bernoulli permutation $T_{n,\delta}$ on $N_0^n \times N_0^n$ induces in the set of messages M a related functions P_δ by

$$P_\delta(M)(x,y) \;:=\; M\left(T_{n,\delta}(x,y)\right) \tag{9}$$

for all $(x, y) \in \mathbb{N}_0^n \times \mathbb{N}_0^n$.

For $k = 1, 2, \ldots$ we denote with $P_{\delta,k}$ the k–fold composition of P_δ, which is given by

$$P_{\delta,k} \quad := \quad \underbrace{P_\delta \circ P_\delta \circ \cdots \circ P_\delta}_{k \quad \text{times}} \tag{10}$$

As an example we show in Figure 3 the application of $P_{\delta,k}$ for $k = 3, 6$ and 9 to a message M (image "test saw–tooth"). In this example we have chosen $n = 180$ and $\delta = (45, 90, 45)$.

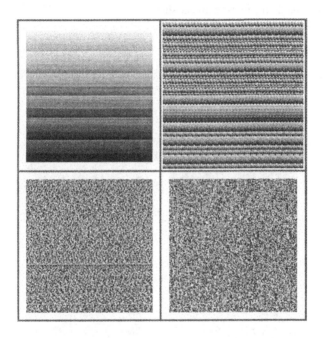

Fig. 3. Application of $P_{\delta,k}$ on a message M (image "test saw–tooth") for $k = 3, 6, 9$

A function $P_{\delta,k}$ as defined in (9) does, when applied to a message M, not change the histogram of the different values of M ("grey level histogram").

For cryptography applications we have to supplement the function $P_{\delta,k}$ by a function S which "smoothes" the histogram of any message M. There are many ways to construct such a function S. Let us discuss two of them:

- Let S be realized by an appropriate chosen MLFSR ("maximum length linear feedback shift register") over $A = GF(q)$ which is fed by taking M row by row as an input–stream. It outputs a scrambled stream which is put together row by row to form the result $S(M) : \mathbb{N}_0^n \times \mathbb{N}_0^n \to A$.

– A second example to realize S by a MLFSR is to use the MLFSR as a pseudo–random–generator and to scramble M by mixing it row by row in a kind of stream–cipher operation with the pseudo–random sequence of the MLFSR.

In both examples we have to assume that the MLFSR is initialized at a certain state $q \neq 0$. If necessary this scrambling operation can be repeated k–times.

Figure 4 is showing the results of the first method which uses a MLFSR of length 2 as an I/O–machine for scrambling the message M and repeats this operation 2– and 4–times. As message M the constant $M = 0$ (image "black square") is chosen. For S realized by repeating the MLFSR I/O operation 4– times also the resulting histogram is shown.

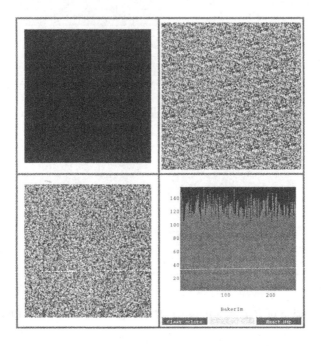

Fig. 4. Results of the application of a repeated I/O operation ($k = 2, 4$) of a MLFSR to a message M (image "black square") and related histogram for $k = 4$

We are now prepared to construct an encryption operation which has a product architecture. Let $N \in \mathbb{N}$ denote the number of "rounds" and let $(k_1, k_2, \ldots, k_N)$ be a list consisting of numbers $k_i \in \mathbb{N}$ for $i = 1, 2, 3, \ldots N$. We define the encryption operation E_δ associated with $(k_1, k_2, \ldots, k_N)$ for messages $M : \mathbb{N}_0^n \times \mathbb{N}_0^n \rightarrow A$ and chosen key $\delta \in \Delta$ by

$$E_\delta \quad := \quad P_{\delta, k_1} \circ S \circ P_{\delta, k_2} \circ S \circ \cdots \circ P_{\delta, k_N} \circ S \tag{11}$$

From table 1 we can see that the cardinality of the "key–space" Δ is for large n sufficiently large to block key exhaustion attacks.

Figure 5 shows the result of the operation E_δ on a message M for $n = 256$, $\delta = (128, 64, 32, 16, 8, 4, 2, 1, 1)$ and $N = 8$ where all k_i $(i = 1, 2, , \ldots, 8)$ are chosen as $k_i = 1$. In this example S is realized by a row by row convolution operation realized by a MLFSR over $GF(256)$ of length 2. The figure shows the message M (image "country road") and the related histogram. The second row shows the encrypted message $E_\delta(M)$ and the associated histogram.

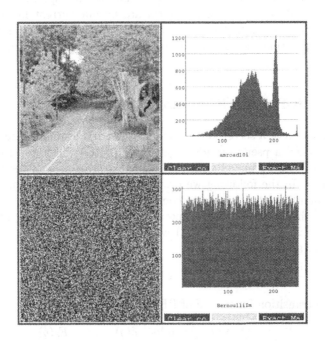

Fig. 5. Encryption of M (image "country road") with associated histograms

The deciphering operation D_δ which corresponds to E_δ is given in a straight forward manner by

$$D_\delta \quad := \quad S^{-1} \circ P_{\delta,k_N}^{-1} \circ \cdots S^{-1} \circ P_{\delta,k_2}^{-1} \circ S^{-1} \circ P_{\delta,k_1}^{-1} \tag{12}$$

Both, determination of S^{-1} of S and the determination of $P_{\delta,k}^{-1}$ for $P_{\delta,k}$ can be done with little computational effort. In the case of our first example for realizing S by a MLFSR we can use the inverse machine MLFSR^{-1} for S^{-1}; in the second example we can use the same MLFSR as a pseudo–random generator to realize S^{-1}.

The determination of $P_{\delta,k}$ is comparable easy to perform since the inversion of P_δ means in group–theoretical terms, to apply the inverse Bernoulli shift operation in $\mathbb{Z}_{q_s}^{2m_s}$ which maps an element s which is given by

$$s \;=\; (x_0, x_1, \ldots, x_{m_s-2}, 0, y_{m_s-1}, y_{m_s-2}, \ldots, y_2, y_1, y_0)$$

to $s' =: 1 \leftarrow s$, that is

$$s \;=\; (x_1, \ldots, x_{m_s-2}, 0, y_{m_s-1}, y_{m_s-2}, \ldots, y_2, y_1, y_0, x_0)$$

with the family $(E_\delta, D_\delta)_{\delta \in \Delta}$ as given by (11) and (12) we have developed a block cipher system in product form, which is mainly based on the concept of Bernoulli permutations. We call such a system a *Bernoulli product cipher*.

Bernoulli product ciphers of this form are by our current knowledge new in the field of cryptology. Since they can be effectively implemented in hard– or software and since they are open for customization they give promise of practical application.

6   Bernoulli Pseudo Random Generators

For the realization of a secret key system on the basis of the concept of stream ciphering we need a pseudo random generator (PRG) which generates a "key stream" (KS) — to be mixed with the plain text stream — of certain cryptographic quality. In the following we propose — and this is straight forward — to use a Bernoulli product cipher to construct a PRG.

We define the pseudo random generator PRG as the following autonomous finite state machine $PRG = (Q, \delta, \lambda)$ where Q denotes the state set, which is given by set of all functions

$$q : \mathbb{N}_0^n \times \mathbb{N}_0^n \to A \tag{13}$$

The state transition function δ of PRG is determined by

$$\delta \;:\; Q \to Q \quad \text{given by} \quad \delta(q) \;:=\; E_\delta(q) \tag{14}$$

The output function λ is the identity map on Q, that is

$$\lambda \;:\; Q \to Q \quad \text{given by} \quad \lambda(q) \;:=\; q \;.$$

If we start the PRG at time 0 at state q_0 it will generate as an output the sequence

$$\lambda^*(q_0) \;=\; (q_0, E_\delta(q_0), E_\delta^2(q_0), \ldots)$$

The following properties of KS are required in cryptography:

1. KS has to have a long primitive period

2. KS has to be statistically "nice", what means that it has to be strongly similar to a pure random sequence

3. The knowledge of a finite piece $(q_t, q_{t+1}, \ldots, q_{t+l-1})$ of length l ($t = 0, 1, 2, \ldots$) should not allow to determine the initial parameters of the PRG

The fulfillment of (1) essentially depends on the periodicity property of the substitution operation S which we employ in E_δ. The use of MLFSRs to construct S makes this possible. (2) depends on the statistical property of P_{δ,k_i} $(i = 1, 2, \ldots N)$ and the statistical property of S. Both considered individually are statistically "nice". It is not to expect that their combination degenerates to become statistically "weak". The property (3) — which means in automata-theoretic terms that the PRG is not identifiable in its structure and initial state — depends on the complexity of finding a solution x of the equation

$$P_{\delta,k}(x) \quad = \quad b \tag{15}$$

for a given $b \in Q$ and unknown list $\delta \in \Delta$. The solution of the problem (15) is known to be computational hard for a $k = \lceil \log_2 n \rceil$ where n is chosen large enough.

7 Harmonic Analysis of Bernoulli shifts

Bernoulli shift representations are — interpreted on the space $\mathbb{N}_0^n \times \mathbb{N}_0^n$ — highly nonlinear. However they have certain properties with respect to their spectral representation in the context of the mathematical theory of abstract harmonic analysis. In [5] it has been shown how the (classical) baker transform (and related Bernoulli shift operation on the dyadic group $\mathbb{D}$) can be investigated by Walsh–Fourier analysis. It can be proven that the baker transform preserves Walsh functions; by the baker transform T Walsh functions are transformed into Walsh functions again. This result allows to investigate "signals" x and the related "output signal" $T(x) = y$ in the spectral domain.

However it has been shown in [5] that the spectral operator $\hat{T}$ corresponding to T, defines also a kind of a baker transform ("discrete baker transform"). Therefor the solution of the equation $\hat{T}(\hat{x}) = \hat{y}$, where $\hat{x}, \hat{y}$ denotes the Walsh–Fourier–Spectra of x and y, respectively, needs for getting a solution the same computational effort as the original given equation $T(x) = y$. Therefor Walsh–Fourier analysis does not establish an operational calculus for the baker transform.

In the case of the discrete generalized baker transform a similar result can be achieved. There the Abelian group under discussion is given by $\mathbb{Z}_{q_s}^{2m_s}$ where the numbers q_s and m_s depend for an element $x \in \mathbb{N}_0^n$ on the interval $[N_s, N_s + n_s)$ for which $x \in [N_s, N_s + n_s)$ is valid.

In that case the character functions of the group $\mathbb{Z}_{q_s}^{2m_s}$, that are the discrete Chrestenson functions of order q_s can be used to analyze the part of the signal which has its domain of definition on $[N_s, N_s + n_s)$ by Chrestenson–Fourier analysis. By the fact that Bernoulli permutations preserve on these domains Chrestenson functions similar results as in the case of Walsh–Fourier analysis can be expected ([6]).

However for a given x the related number n_s and therefor also the number q_s and m_s can only be derived by knowing the used key δ. Therefor the knowledge of the order q_s of the Chrestenson function and the dimension $2m_s$ of the related group $\mathbb{Z}_{q_s}^{2m_s}$ generally is not available.

Further investigations on the applicability of results of abstract harmonic analysis for the cryptanalysis of Bernoulli permutations and Bernoulli cipher systems are currently under consideration.

8 Summary and Conclusion

The paper presents a method to construct by means of the Bernoulli permutation $T_{n,\delta}$ a symmetric product cipher and a pseudo random generator for use in cryptography. The parameter $\delta = (n_1, n_2, \ldots, n_k)$ of $T_{n,\delta}$ is used as a component of the cipher–key. We were able to show that a q_s–adic representation of $(x, y) \in \mathbb{N}_0^n \times \mathbb{N}_0^n$ where $q_s \cdot n_s = n$ for $s = 1, 2, \ldots k$ allows to represent $T_{n,\delta}$ by cyclic Bernoulli–shifts in the finite groups $Z_{q_s}^{2m}$ where $m = \lceil \log_{q_s} n \rceil$. The known "nice" mathematical properties of dynamical systems which are generated by Bernoulli–shifts suggest that properly designed cipher systems based on Bernoulli permutations have a high crypt–analytic quality. Furthermore, the implementation of Bernoulli permutations can be done very effectively in software. Possible fast hardware implementations are currently investigated.

Although some research on the cryptanalytic properties of "Bernoulli–Ciphers" (let us suggest this name for all ciphering systems based on Bernoulli permutations) has been done in [6]; further investigations seem to be necessary. The same is true for the development of architectures and algorithms to implement Bernoulli–Ciphers effectively in hardware or software. It is known that Bernoulli shifts realize special dynamical systems called K–flows (K stands for the name of the famous Russian mathematician *A.N. Kolmogorov*). This suggests to base further investigations and extensions on the available mathematical theory of K–flows.

Another possibility of extension is to use shifts defined on continued fraction expansion of numbers. Currently it is not known to us whether such dynamical systems are also special K–flows.

The research of Josef Scharinger got financial support from Austria by "FWF-Project S0 70001 MAT Task 1" (Mathematical methods in digital image processing and applications), which is acknowledged.

References

1. V.I. Arnold, A. Avez. *Ergodic Problems of Classical Mechanics*. W.A. Benjamin, New York 1968.
2. Jürgen Moser. *Stable and Random Motions in Dynamical Systems*. Princeton University Press, Princeton 1973.
3. Paul Shields. *The Theory of Bernoulli Shifts*. The University of Chicago Press, Chicago 1973.
4. M. Jeger. *Einführung in die Kombinatorik I, II*. Klett, Stuttgart 1973.

5. F. Pichler. *Realisierung der Λ-Transformation von Prigogine mittels dyadischer Faltungsoperatoren.* Österreichische Studiengesellschaft für Kybernetrik. Wien, Schottengasse 3, ISBN 385206-127-X. Dezember 1992. (52 pages)

6. J. Scharinger. *Experimentelle harmonische Analyse von Bäcker–dynamischen 2D–Systemen und ihre Anwendung in der Kryptographie, Dissertation (Informatik).* Institut für Systemwissenschaften, Universität Linz, September 1994. (174 pages, will be published)

7. S. Wolfram. *Cryptography with Cellular Automata.* Advances in Cryptology–CRYPTO '85 Proceedings, Berlin: Springer Verlag, 1986, pp. 429–432.

8. C.E. Shannon. *Communication theory of secrecy systems.* Bell Syst.Tech.J., 28,pp. 656–715.

9. N.J.A. Sloane. *Encrypting by Random Permutations.* in: Cryptography. Proceedings Burg Feuerstein, 1982 (ed. T. Beth). Lecture Notes in Computer Science, Berlin 1983, pp. 71–128.

10. J. Scharinger, F. Pichler. *Bernoulli Chiffren.* Elektrotechnik und Informationstechnik, 111. Jg. (1994) 11, pp. 576–582.

11. F. Pichler, J. Scharinger. *Ciphering by Bernoulli–Shifts in finite abelian Groups.* 1994. In: Contributions to General Algebra, Proc. of the Linz–Conference, June 2–5, 1994. (eds. H.K. Kaiser, W.B. Müller, G.F. Pilz), Hölder–Pichler–Tempsky Verlag (Austria) and B.G. Teubner, Stuttgart (Germany) (in print)

12. J. Scharinger. *Verschlüsselung mit Bernoulli–Systemen.* Institute of Systems Science, University Linz, internal technical report, July 22, 1993 (21 pages)

Introduction of the Aristotle's Final Causation in CAST Concept and Method of Incursion and Hyperincursion

Daniel M. Dubois

Université de Liège -Institut de Mathématique
15 Avenue des Tilleuls, B-4000 Liège, Belgium

Abstract. This paper will analyse the concept and method of incursion and hyperincursion firstly applied to the Fractal Machine, an hyperincursive cellular automata with sequential computations where time plays a central role. This computation is incursive, for inclusive recursion, in the sense that an automaton is computed at the future time t+1 in function of its neighbour automata at the present and/or past time steps but also at the future time t+1. The hyperincursion is an incursion when several values can be generated at each time step. The incursive systems may be transformed to recursive ones. But the incursive inputs, defined at the future time step, cannot always be transformed to recursive inputs. This is possible by self-reference. A self-reference Fractal Machine gives rise to A non deterministic hyperincursive field rises in a self-reference Fractal Machine. This can be related to the Final Cause of Aristotle. Simulations will show the generation of fractal patterns from incursive equations with interference effects like holography. The incursion is also a tool to control systems. The Pearl-Verhulst chaotic map will be considered. Incursive stabilisation of the numerical instabilities of discrete linear and non-linear oscillators based on Lotka-Volterra equation systems will be simulated. Finally the incursive discrete diffusion equation is considered.

1 Introduction

CAST, the Computer Aided Systems Theory proposed by F Pichler, deals with the applications of Systems Theory in modern engineering. Systems Theory supplements the field of applied mathematics with the introduction of concepts and methods which have been responsible for critical advances in the art of modelling and control. Computer Aided Systems are based on recursion where the present state of systems is function of its preceding states so that the future is always a result of the past.

This paper deals with an extension of the recursion by the concept of incursion and hyperincursion defined by the author [4,5,6,7,8,9,10,11,12] from his Fractal Machine, a new type of Cellular Automata, where time plays a central role. The design of the model of any discrete system is based on incursion relations where past, present and future states variables are mixed in such a way that they define an indivisible wholeness invariant. Most incursive relations can be transformed in different sets of recursive algorithms for computation. In the same way, the hyperincursion is an extension of the hyper recursion in which several different solutions can be generated at each time step. By the hyperincursion, the Fractal Machine could compute beyond the theoretical limits of the Turing Machine [15,16].

Holistic properties of the hyperincursion are related to the Golden Ratio with the Fibonacci Series and the Fractal Golden Matrix [16]. An incursive method was developed for the inverse problem, the Newton-Raphson method and an application in robotics [14]. Control by incursion was applied to feedback systems [17]. Chaotic recursions can be synchronised by incursion [16]. An incursive control of linear, non-linear and chaotic systems was proposed [1] and applied to the control of an electrical engine [2]. The hyperincursive discrete Lotka-Volterra equations have orbital stability and show the emergence of chaos [3,5]. By linearisation of this non-linear system, hyperincursive discrete harmonic oscillator equations give stable oscillations and discrete solutions [1]. A general theory of stability by incursion of discrete equations systems was developed with applications to the control of the numerical instabilities of the difference equations of the Lotka-Volterra differential equations as well as the control of the fractal chaos in the Pearl-Verhulst equation [14]. The incursion harmonic oscillator shows eigenvalues and wave packet like in quantum mechanics. Backward and forward velocities are defined in this incursion harmonic oscillator. A connection is made between incursion and relativity as well as the electromagnetic field. The foundation of a hyperincursive discrete mechanics was proposed in relation to the quantum mechanics [16,14].

This paper will show that "incursion", that is an inclusive or implicit recursion where the present state of a system is also a function of its future states, looks like time feedforward or feed-in-time. The anticipatory property of incursion is an incremental final cause which could be related to the Aristotelian Final Causation. It is interesting to notice that Cybernetics was initiated in 1943 with the basic paper "Behaviour, Purpose and Teleology" by A. Rosenblueth, N. Wiener and J. Bigelow. They introduced the feedback paradigm, based on recursive processes, to give a finality to systems. So, I think that CAST and Cybernetics lack a conceptual tool and a method for formalising such anticipation in systems.

The concept and method of incursion and hyperincursion will be analyse from this point of view with applications to the Fractal Machine, a cellular automata, the Pearl-Verhulst chaotic map, the discrete Lotka-Volterra equation system, the harmonic oscillator and the diffusion equation.

Classically cellular automata are computed in a recursive way with parallel iterations. The Fractal Machine is a cellular automata with incursive sequential computations. This computation is incursive, for inclusive recursion, in the sense that an automaton is computed at the future time $t+1$ in function of its neighbour automata at the present and/or past time steps but also at the future time $t+1$. The boundary conditions must be defined at the future time step. The incursion becomes an hyperincursion when several future values can be generated at each time step. The incursion and hyperincursion are related to the Final Cause of Aristotle. Several different incursive equations are given with their numerical simulation on computer. Fractal patterns emerges from these equations. In a three-dimensional equation it is shown that an initial picture multiplies through whole the network with interference effects like holography. The incursion is also a tool to control systems. Incursive control of the Pearl-Verhulst chaotic map will be considered. Incursive stabilisation of the numerical instabilities of discrete linear and non-linear oscillators based on Lotka-Volterra equation systems will be simulated. Finally it will be shown that the implicit recursion applied to diffusion equation is related to the Fractal Machine.

2 Incursion and Aristotle's Final Causation

Aristotle identified four explicit categories of causation: 1. Material cause; 2. Formal cause; 3. Efficient cause; 4. Final cause. Robert Rosen [22] asks why a certain Newtonian mechanical system is in the state (phase) [x(t) (position), v(t) (velocity)]. First, Aristotle's "material cause" corresponds to the initial conditions of the system [x(0), v(0)] at time t=0. Second, the current cause at the present time is the set of constraints which convey to the system an "identity", allowing it to go by recursion from the given initial phase to the latter phase, which corresponds to what Aristotle called formal cause. Third, what we call inputs or boundary conditions are the impressed forces by the environment, called efficient cause by Aristotle. As pointed out by Robert Rosen, the first three of Aristotle's causal categories are tacit in the Newtonian formalism: "*the introduction of a notion of final cause into the Newtonian picture would amount to allowing a future state or future environment to affect change of state in the present, and this would be incompatible with the whole Newtonian picture. This is one of the main reasons that the concept of Aristotelian finality is considered incompatible with modern science. In modern physics, Aristotelian ideas of causality are confused with determinism, which is quite different. ... That is, determinism is merely a mathematical statement of functional dependence or linkage. As Russel points out, such mathematical relations, in themselves, carry no hint as to which of their variables are dependent and which are independent.*" . The final cause could impress the present state of evolving systems, which seems a key phenomenon in engineering and biological systems. Indeed, anticipation, viewed as an Aristotelian final cause, is of great importance to explain the dynamics of systems. The founders of Cybernetics, Rosenblueth, Wiener and Bigelow [23] introduced the concept of purpose and teleology to feedback systems. An interesting analysis of the Final Causation was made by Ernst von Glasersfeld [28]. Causality is related to recursion and is defined for sequential events. If x(t) represents a variable at time t, a causal rule $x(t+1)=f(x(t))$ gives the successive states of the variable x at the successive time steps t, t+1,t+2,... from the recursive function f(x(t)), starting with an initial state x(0) at time t=0. Defined like this, the system has no degrees of freedom: it is completely determined by the function and the initial condition. No new things can happen for such a system: its future is completely determined by its past. How to detect a change of value of a variable x(t)? In measuring two successive values at its past time t-1 and present time t (the unit of the time interval is arbitrary), by the backward derivative, $D_b(x(t)) = x(t) - x(t-1)$, gives incursive equations [1]. Indeed, it is impossible to measure the value of a variable at a future time t+1 at the current time t. The change of the value of any variable x(t) at the present time step t to another value at the future time step t+1 is performed by an action defined by the forward derivative, $D_f(x(t)) = x(t+1) - x(t)$, which gives recursive equations [1]. Indeed, it is impossible to change the already instantiated past and present values of any variable, only the future value at time t+1 step can be changed. If a change occurs by an action during the time interval (t, t+1), the forward derivative $D_f(x(t))$ at time t will become the backward derivative $D_b(x(t+1)) = D_f(x(t))$ which can then be measured. It must be pointed out that classical mathematical analysis deals with derivatives defined for a time interval dt tending to zero, so the backward and the forward derivatives are identical for derivable continuous systems. But the majority of systems are discrete. So any dynamical system can be defined at any time step t by the backward derivative $D_b(x(t))$ and the forward derivative $D_f(x(t))$. The forward derivative is related to the formal causation of Aristotle and the backward derivative, to the final causation, because the incursive equation system take into account variables at the future time step t+1 to compute them at this future time step. Final causation is a potential causation because it is not yet realised. Let us remark that we defined here an incremental final causation, changing at each time step. The principle of finality or teleonomy defined classically deals with a goal like in control theory, that is to say a final value of a variable. Anticipation seems to be the rule for engineering and living systems: how can we justify the fact that the mathematical models of such systems are feedback based on recursive processes depending only on past events? The anticipative nature of evolving systems is difficult to conceptualise and to model because the computational paradigm is essentially based on recursive processes.

The concept and method of incursion and hyperincursion could meet the Final Causation. Now let us present some typical incursive and hyperincursive systems.

3 The Hyperincursive Field of the Fractal Machine

Classically, a one-dimensional network of cellular automata is represented by a vector of automata states, each automaton state having an integer numerical value at the initial time t=0. A set of rules defines how the states change at every clock time. See Wolfram for a general survey [29]. A simple rule consists of replacing the value of each automaton by the sum modulo 2, for example, of itself and its left neighbour at each clock time. Figure 1a shows a one-dimensional network of cellular automata giving rise to the Sierpinski napkin which is a self-similar fractal structure.

	n=0 1 2 3 4 5 6 7 8	n=0 1 2 3 4 5 6 7 8
t=0	0 1 0 0 0 0 0 0 0	0 1 0 0 0 0 0 0 0
t=1	0 1 1 0 0 0 0 0 0	0 1 1 1 1 1 1 1 1
t=2	0 1 0 1 0 0 0 0 0	0 1 0 1 0 1 0 1 0
t=3	0 1 1 1 1 0 0 0 0	0 1 1 0 0 1 1 0 0
t=4	0 1 0 0 0 1 0 0 0	0 1 0 0 0 1 0 0 0
t=5	0 1 1 0 0 1 1 0 0	0 1 1 1 1 0 0 0 0
t=6	0 1 0 1 0 1 0 1 0	0 1 0 1 0 0 0 0 0
t=7	0 1 1 1 1 1 1 1 1	0 1 1 0 0 0 0 0 0
t=8	0 1 0 0 0 0 0 0 0	0 1 0 0 0 0 0 0 0

Figure 1a-b: Recursive Sierpinski napkin and incursive Sierpinski napkin

The recursive model of this network is

$$X(n,t+1)=(X(n,t)+X(n-1,t)) \bmod 2 \quad \text{with } t=0,1,2,... \text{ and } n=1,2,..., \qquad (1)$$

with initial conditions $X(n,0)$ and boundary conditions $X(0,t)$. The *recursion* consists of the computation of the future value of the variable from the values of these variables at present and/or past times. So, the present and the past always determine the future.

The computation in the Fractal Machine is based on what I called INCURSION [5,7] for "INclusive or implicit reCURSION". An incursive relation is defined by: $X(t+1)=f(...,X(t+1),X(t),X(t-1),...,p)$ which consists in the computation of the values of the vector $X(t+1)$ at time t+1 from the values $X(t-i)$ at time t-i, i=1,2,..., the value $X(t)$ at time t and the value $X(t+j)$ at time t+j, j=1,2,....in function of a command vector p. This incursive relation is not trivial because future values of the variable vector at time steps t+1, t+2, ... must be known to compute them at the time step t+1. In the same way, an extension of the hyper recursion is defined by HYPERINCURSION, when multiple solutions are generated at each time step,. Sometimes incursion will be used as a generic word for both concepts. Let us show some typical examples.

Starting from the recursive equation (1), the following incursive relation is defined

$$X(n,t+1)=(X(n,t)+X(n-1,t+1)) \bmod N \qquad \text{with n=1,2,...,8, and t=0,1,2,...,7} \quad (2)$$

where $X(n,t)$ is the automaton state at position n and time t. The modulo N with N=2 is XOR. The computation of eq. (2), given at Figure 1b, gives rise to a time reverse Sierpinski napkin [10,11]. This fractal Sierpinski triangles napkin is at the origin of the name of the Fractal Machine [5,11 p. 197]. A survey on the definition and properties of fractals can be found in Mandelbrot [19].

If it is natural to consider the successive time steps t in the increasing order, it is also necessary to consider the successive computations in the increasing order of the number n of automata which can be considered as an internal time. Explicitly it is possible to define two times: an external time and an internal time. The duration of the external time is the sum of the sequential computational internal times. For n=1, the future inputs $X(0, t+1)$ must be defined at each time step in view of computing the automata $X(n, t+1)$ as a final cause which controls the dynamics of the system.

In transforming this incursive equation (2) in a quasi recursive equation system

$$X(0,t+1)= \textit{external inputs} = \textit{final causation} \qquad (2')$$
$$X(1,t+1)=(X(1,t)+X(0,t+1)) \bmod N$$
$$X(2,t+1)=(X(2,t)+X(1,t)+X(0,t+1)) \bmod N$$
$$X(3,t+1)=(X(3,t)+X(2,t)+X(1,t)+X(0,t+1)) \bmod N$$
$$...$$
$$X(8,t+1)=(X(7,t)+X(6,t)+ ... +X(1,t)+X(0,t+1)) \bmod N$$

it is explicitly seen that the external inputs must be defined in the future time like a final causation which controls completely all the automata at the same time step in a holistic way. Indeed the inputs $X(0,t+1)$ are present in each automata at the same external time.

It is impossible to transform external inputs defined in the future time t+1 to inputs defined in the present time t. In this, we can say that we are dealing with a strict incursive system. Thus the final causation is really the 4th causation which must be taken into account in systems modelling as Aristotle had proposed. It seems also impossible to construct a real working engineering system where real working external future inputs would control its current present state. But it is possible to define internal future inputs in considering self-reference systems.

For example, in taking the following initial conditions $X(n,0)=0$ and boundary conditions $X(0,t+1)=X(8,t+1)$

	n=0	1	2	3	4	5	6	7	8		0	1	2	3	4	5	6	7	8
t=0	0	0	0	0	0	0	0	0	0		0	0	0	0	0	0	0	0	0
t=1	1	1	1	1	1	1	1	1	1		0	0	0	0	0	0	0	0	0
t=2	0	1	0	1	0	1	0	1	0		1	1	1	1	1	1	1	1	1

it is shown that there are two solutions at each time step. Indeed if $X(0,1)=1$ then $X(8,1)=1$ and if $X(0,1)=0$ then $X(8,1)=0$. Thus this is an hyperincursive system because we have two different solutions at each time step. Moreover in some cases, contradiction can appears. For example, starting with the following different initial conditions at time $t=0$

	n=0	1	2	3	4	5	6	7	8		0	1	2	3	4	5	6	7	8
t=0	0	1	0	0	0	0	0	0	0		0	1	0	0	0	0	0	0	0
t=1	1	0	0	0	0	0	0	0	0		0	1	1	1	1	1	1	1	1

in taking $X(0,1)=1$ then $X(8,1)=0$ and if $X(0,1)=0$ then $X(8,1)=1$. This case could be resolved in deciding that $X(0,t+1)=1-X(8,t+1)$, then the first example will give a contradiction. The Fractal Machine can become non deterministic or non algorithmic, what I suggest to call an HYPERINCURSIVE FIELD where uncertainty (indecidability) or contradiction (exclusion principle) occur. This sefl-reference system is autopoietic as defined by Varela [25]. It will be shown in the last section that the incursive diffusion equation can be algorithmically deterministic with a self-reference for the inputs defined at future time.

Let us consider numerical simulations on computer of a few incursive composition rules. Figures 2a-b give the simulation of the incursive rule given by eq. (2) for N=2 and N=3, the initial conditions and boundary conditions are the same as in Figures 1a-b.
Remark: With parallel iterations, classically it is necessary to memorise the preceding time step of the automata and the order in which the iterations are made is without importance. With incursive iterations, the current automata is sufficient.

Fig. 3a-b show an other Sierpinski napkin and a fractal pattern from the incursive relation

$$X(n,t+1)=(X(n-1,t-1)+X(n-2,t+1)) \bmod 2 \qquad (3)$$

with two different initial conditions, the first with all automata at 1 and the second with automata at 1 for each multiple of 11 of the number n.

The incursive relation depending on 3 automata generates a square fractal in Fig. 4a

$$X(n,t+1)=(X(n,t)+X(n-1,t+1)+X(n-1,t)) \bmod 3 \qquad (4)$$

Fig. 4b shows a pentagon fractal given by the incursive equation with 4 automata

$$X(n,t+1)=(X(n,t)+X(n-1,t+1)+X(n-1,t-1)+X(n-2,t)) \bmod 2 \qquad (5)$$

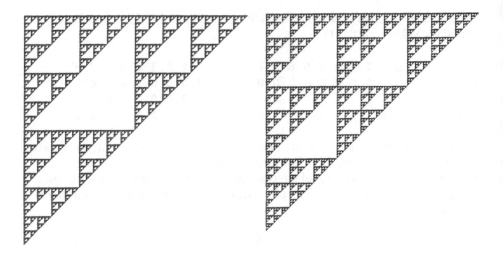

Figures 2a-b: Simulation of hyperincursive equation (2) with N=2 and 3.

Figures 3a-b: Simulation of hyperincursive equation (3).

A three-dimensional frame of automata X(i,j,t) is built with the hyperincursive relation

$$X(i,j,t+1) = [X(i-1,j,t+1)-X(i,j,t)+X(i,j-1,t+1)+X(i-1,j-1,t+1)] \bmod 2 \qquad (6)$$

where X(i,j,t) is the state of an automaton at time t, i the line index, j the column index of a node. Each successive state of the nodes x(i,j,t+1) is computed from the left to the right, line by line. The initial conditions X(i,j,0) is given by the picture of a chaos diagram as an example. The boundary conditions are zero.

The Fig. 5a-b-c-d-e give successively the initial condition, the pattern at the different times t=16, t=32, t=48 and t=64. The process continues until t=256 for which the initial picture reappears. The process is inversible in changing the order of the computations.

The basic evolution of the system is the multiplication of the initial picture through the whole frame with order/chaos transitions (the chaos transitions are obtained for odd time steps and not shown in the figures, see [5,6] for examples) and then their fusion by interferences. The process is fractal by its self-similarity and looks like holography. With other composition rules, similar holographic effects happen [5,6].

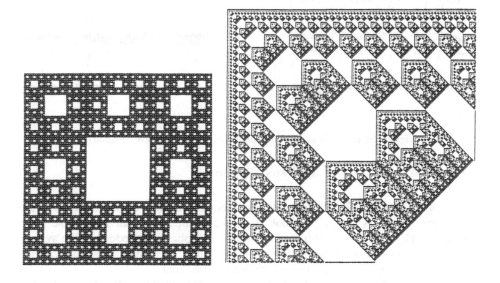

Figures 4a-b: Simulation of hyperincursive equation (4) giving a square fractal and simulation of equation (5) showing a pentagon fractal.

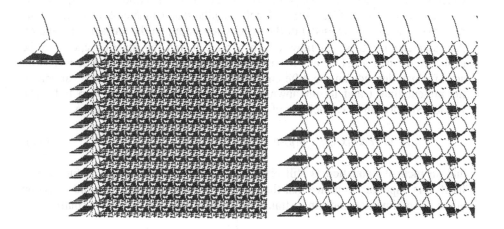

Figures 5a-b-c: Simulation of hyperincursive equation (6). The initial condition is given by the left picture.

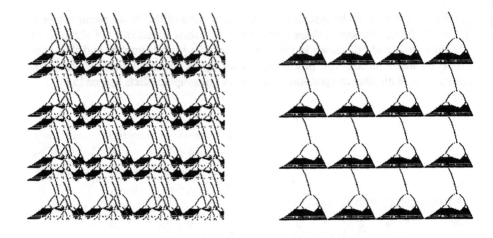

Figures 5d-e: Continuation of the simulation of hyperincursive equation (6).

4 Incursive Control of a Chaos System

The control theory deals with an explicit set-point or reference signal for directing an artificial system. A control without an explicit set-point signal is possible with incursion [1,2,5,14,17]. This incursive control is implicitly embedded in the system model and the goal is defined by the stability regimes. Incursive control can change an unstable regime to a stable one which becomes the goal.

Let us consider the incursive control of a system represented by a discrete equation:

$$u(t) = ur + c(x).(x(t) - x(t+dt)) \qquad (7a)$$
$$x(t+dt) = f(x(t), \mu) + b.u(t) \qquad (7b)$$

where u(t) is the incursive control function [1,2], ur is a function of the explicit set-point or reference signal r(t) of the variable, x(t) the state variable of the system, f the recursive function of the model of the system depending on the variable x(t) and on the parameter μ, b is generally known parameter and the function c(x) is to be explicitly defined. First of all, let us remark that the incursive control u(t) is an action which depends on the difference between the known value of the variable at the present time t and its unknown value at the next future time step t+dt. The variable x(t+dt) can be explicitly replaced in the control function as follows:

$$u(t) = ur + c(x).(x(t) - f(x(t), \mu) - b.u(t)) \qquad (7a')$$

and an incursive equation is still obtained because the control u(t) is function of itself. It is important to notice that the incursive control takes into account its action at the future time step and can be transformed to the following recursive control:

$$u(t) = (ur + c(x).(x(t) - f(x(t), \mu)))/(1 + c(x).b) \qquad (7a'')$$

The control of a chaotic system is the most difficult problem in the non-linear control theory. Let us consider the most well-known fractal chaos system [20] which is the Pearl-Verhulst [21,26] recursive map: $x(t+1)=4.\mu.x(t).(1- x(t))$, where the parameter μ and the variable x are defined in the unit interval. This non-linear system is sensitive to the initial conditions and shows a deterministic chaos. The incursive control function u(t) of the chaotic system without set-point signal is defined by:

$$u(t)= \ddot{}(c.(x(t)- \mu_e.x(t).(1-x(t))).x(t))/(1+c.b.x(t)) \tag{8a}$$
$$x(t+1) = 4.\mu.x(t).(1- x(t))+b.u(t) \tag{8b}$$
$$\mu_e=(x(t+1)-b.u(t))/(1-x(t)) \tag{8c}$$

where the parameter $4.\mu$ is estimated by μ_e and $c=\mu_e/b$. The figures 6a-b give the simulation of the eqs. (8) without and with incursive control, in function of μ.

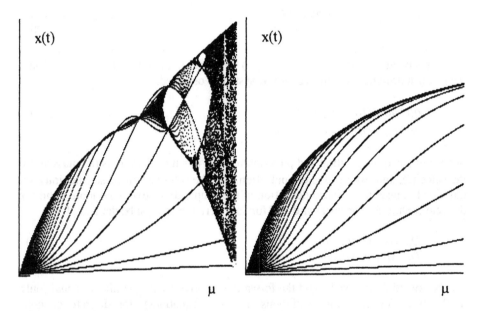

Figures 6a-b: Simulations of the chaotic system without and with the incursive control; the iterates of the variable x(t) are given in function of the parameter μ.

Indeed, with the incursive control, the Pearl-Verhulst equation is given by the incursive equation [5]: $x(t+1) = 4.\mu.x(t).(1- x(t+1))$ which can be transformed in the following recursive logistic one [5]: $x(t+1) = 4.\mu.x(t)/(1+4.\mu.x(t))$, the solution of which being the non zero fixed point: $x^*=1-1/(4.\mu)$ for $1/4<\mu<1$. The original equation shows an unstable solution for $x=1-1/(4.\mu)$ for $3/4<\mu<1$, that is in the bifurcation and chaos zones. Thus the incursive control transforms an unstable state of the system in a stable one. The set-point value of the variable is thus given implicitly by the unstable point which becomes stable by the incursive control. When the controlled system reaches its fixed point $x(t)=x(t+1)$, so $u(t)=0$, its solution is a solution of the original equation [17].

5 Hyperincursive Discrete Equation Systems

In computer science, the discretisation of differential equations systems gives sometimes numerical instabilities which can be controlled by defining incursive discretisation. Let us first consider the non-linear model of the discretised Lotka-Volterra equations:

$$X(t+dt) = X(t) + dt.[a.X(t) - b.X(t).Y(t)] \qquad (9a)$$
$$Y(t+dt) = Y(t) + dt.[-c.Y(t) + d.X(t).Y(t)] \qquad (9b)$$

where t is a discrete time with steps dt, and a,b,c,d are the parameters.

Analytical solutions exist only for small oscillations from the steady state $X_0 = c/d$ and $Y_0 = a/b$, which are identical to a harmonic linear oscillator. In taking $X = X_0 + x$ and $Y = Y_0 + y$, when x and y are small, the linearisation of these equations gives

$$x(t+dt) = x(t) - dt.(bc/d).y(t) \qquad (9a')$$
$$y(t+dt) = y(t) + dt.(ad/b).x(t) \qquad (9b')$$

With the change in variables q(t)=x(t), p(t)=-y(t) and in taking bc/d=1/m and ω^2=ac, the linear harmonic oscillator equations system is obtained:

$$q(t+dt) - q(t) = dt.p(t)/m \qquad (10a)$$
$$p(t+dt) - p(t) = - dt.m.\omega^2.q(t) \qquad (10b)$$

in defining by q the position and p the momentum (p=m.v where m is the mass and v the velocity), and where ω is the pulsation. But the solutions all these equations are unstable because the classical definition of the simple derivative is no more valid for discrete equations. The backward and forward derivatives must be defined [1,14]

$$D_b=(x(t)-x(t-dt))/dt \qquad (11a)$$
$$D_f=(x(t+dt)-x(t))/dt \qquad (11b)$$

The backward derivative D_f and the forward derivative D_f are not always equal (only at the limit for dt=0 for continuous derivable equations); for discrete or non-derivable continuous equations like in fractal equations systems, two derivatives must be defined. The second derivative is now defined as D_bD_f or D_fD_b, that is the successive applications of the forward and the backward derivatives.

Different incursive discrete equations systems exist to control the oscillations of these non-linear and linear discrete equations.

The iterative values of X(t+dt) of the first equation (9a) can be propagated to the second equation (9b), in an incursive way, as proposed by the author [1,3,5,6],

$$X(t+dt) = X(t) + dt.[a.X(t) - b.X(t).Y(t)] \qquad (12a)$$
$$Y(t+dt) = Y(t) + dt.[-c.Y(t) + d.X(t+dt).Y(t)] \qquad (12b)$$

The simulation in the phase space (X,Y) given in Figure 7 shows an orbital stability with a chaos zone for large distance from the stationary point.

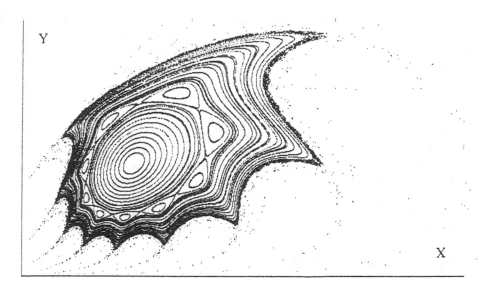

Figure 7: Simulation of hyperincursive discrete Lotka-Volterra equations 14.

The linearised incursive Lotka-Volterra equations give the incursive harmonic oscillator [1]

$$q(t+dt) = q(t) + dt.p(t)/m \qquad \text{or} \qquad D_f(q(t)) = p(t)/m \qquad (13a)$$
$$p(t+dt) = p(t) - dt.m.\omega^2.q(t+dt) \qquad \text{or} \qquad D_b(p(t)) = - m.\omega^2.q(t) \qquad (13b)$$

The incursive harmonic oscillator is thus defined by the forward derivative of the position and the backward derivative of the momentum. At low pulsation, the simulation gives the classical harmonic oscillator, whereas at a higher pulsation the iterates of the position and the momentum are complex.
A second incursive Lotka-Volterra equations can be defined [5,6]

$$Y(t+dt) = Y(t) + dt.[-c.Y(t) + d.X(t).Y(t)] \qquad (14a)$$
$$X(t+dt) = X(t) + dt.[a.X(t) - b.X(t).Y(t+dt)] \qquad (14b)$$

where now we propagate the value of $Y(t+dt)$ in the equation of $X(t+dt)$.
The linearisation of these equations gives a second incursive harmonic oscillator [1]

$$q(t+dt) = q(t) + dt.p(t+dt)/m \qquad \text{or} \qquad D_b(q(t))=p(t)/m \qquad (15a)$$
$$p(t+dt) = p(t) - dt.m.\omega^2.q(t) \qquad \text{or} \qquad D_f(p(t))=- m.\omega^2.q(t) \qquad (15b)$$

The second incursive harmonic oscillator is given by the backward derivative of the position and the forward derivative of the momentum.

Remark: The two hyperincursive harmonic oscillators systems 13 and 15 are time reverse of each other. In replacing dt by - dt in eqs. 13, eqs. 15 are obtained [1]. In replacing p of the first equation in the second, both systems give the classical discrete harmonic oscillator equation depending only on the position q

$$q(t+dt) - 2q(t) + q(t-dt) = - \, dt^2.\omega^2.q(t) \tag{16}$$

So the two hyperincursive systems 13 and 15 give the forward and the backward solutions of the same discrete harmonic oscillator system 16. There is an uncertainty to know the position and the momentum of a particle, but it is possible to only know its position at different times, like in quantum mechanics. Hyperincursive discrete equation systems give richer information than differential equation systems [1].

A general theory of stability by incursion was developed by Dubois & Resconi [14], which demonstrates the incursive stabilisation of linear and non-linear systems.

6 Incursive Discrete Diffusion Equation

Let us consider the one dimension diffusion equation

$$\partial x(s,t)/\partial t = a.x(s,t) + v. \, \partial x(s,t)/\partial s + D.\partial^2 x(s,t)/\partial s^2 \tag{17}$$

With a forward time derivative $\partial x(s,t)/\partial t$ given by $x(s,t+1) - x(s,t)$, the discrete diffusion equation gives unstable solution for integer parameters. But, in defining a diffusion difference equation modulo N, with a=v=0, D=1 and dt=ds=1, the following "digital" diffusion equation gives fractal pattern shown in figure 8a

$$x(s,t+1) = [- x(s,t) + x(s+1,t) + x(s-1,t)] \, mod \, N \tag{18a}$$

The term "digital" was proposed by Konrad Zuse [30] for discretised differential equation systems. With a=1, v=0, D=1 and dt=ds=1, the following digital equation gives the Sierpinski fractal pattern given in Fig. 8b

$$x(s,t+1) = [x(s+1,t) + x(s-1,t)] \, mod \, N \tag{18b}$$

```
       s= 01234567...              01234567...

t=0       00000000100000000        00000000100000000
t=1       00000001110000000        00000001010000000
          00000010101000000        00000010001000000
          00000110101100000        00000101010100000
          00001000100010000        00001000000010000
          00011101110111000        00010100000101000
          00101000100010100        00100010001000100
          01101101110110110        01010101010101010
          10000000100000001        10000000000000001
```

Figure 8a-b: Generation of fractal patterns with N=2.

To avoid numerical instabilities, let us use the implicit finite difference method (see Scheid [24]) in considering the backward time derivative: $\partial x(s,t)/\partial t$ given by $x(s,t) - x(s,t-1)$. The implicit diffusion equation is then given by incursive equations

$$x(s,t+1) = x(s,t) + D.[x(s-1,t+1)-2.x(s,t+1)+x(s+1,t+1)] \qquad (19)$$

or $\quad x(s,t+1)=x(s,t)/[1+2.D]+ [D/[1+2.D]][x(s-1,t+1)+x(s+1,t+1)] \qquad (20)$

To compute the value of $x(s,t+1)$, we must know the value of $x(s-1,t+1)$ as in the Fractal Machine, but also $x(s+1,t+1)$.

$$[1+2.D].x(1,t+1)-D.[x(0,t+1)+x(2,t+1)]=x(1,t) \qquad (21)$$
$$[1+2.D].x(2,t+1)-D.[x(1,t+1)+x(3,t+1)]= x(2,t)$$
$$[1+2.D].x(3,t+1)-D.[x(2,t+1)+x(4,t+1)]= x(3,t)$$
$$...$$
$$[1+2.D].x(S,t+1)-D.[x(S-1,t+1)+x(S+1,t+1)]= x(S,t)$$

that is to say with the matrix form $A.x(t+1)=x(t)$. It looks like the Fractal Machine where each iterate $x(s,t+1)$ is propagated to its two space adjacent iterates $x(s-1,t+1)$ and $x(s+1,t+1)$. In the Fractal Machine, the iterates are only propagated in one direction. In inverting the matrix A, we obtain a recursive system $x(t+1)=A^{-1}.x(t)$. In the literature, this procedure is called "implicit recursion" which justifies the name of "incursion for inclusive or implicit recursion" I proposed. Indeed, it is the inclusion of each iterate in the others which defines them in a self-reference way. In taking periodic boundary conditions $x(0,t+1)=x(S,t+1)$ and $x(S+1,t+1)=x(1,t+1)$, the system defines itself the values of the boundaries. For example, with a constant diffusion $D=1$ and $S=3$, we obtain, in inverting the matrix A,

$$x(1,t+1)=x(1,t)/2+x(2,t)/4+x(3,t)/4 \qquad (22)$$
$$x(2,t+1)=x(2,t)/2+x(3,t)/4+x(1,t)/4$$
$$x(3,t+1)=x(3,t)/2+x(1,t)/4+x(2,t)/4$$

s=	1	2	3
t=0	1	0	0
t=1	½	¼	¼
t=2	6/16	5/16	5/16
t=3	22/64	21/64	21/64

Figure 9: Simulation of equation system 22

the simulation in Figure 9 shows that the convergence is very rapid, a few time steps. I think that this example is a good one to explain "holistic" properties of self-reference system as autopoietical systems as defined by Varela [25]. Each automaton at time $t+1$ is related to itself at the preceding time t and at the future time $t+1$ and to its direct space adjacent neighbours at the future time $t+1$. Due to the self-reference of each automaton with its neighbours, it is possible to compute a new transformed recursive system where now each automaton is computed in function of itself only at the preceding time step but in function of all the automata of the system at the preceding time.

This is really an important result which shows that an incursive holistic non-local property comes from local interaction dealing with a recurive system depending on future states.

With boundary conditions as external inputs $x(0,t+1)$ and $x(4,t+1)$, the system becomes

$$x(1,t+1)=[8.[x(1,t)+x(0,t+1)]+3.x(2,t)+[x(3,t)+x(4,t+1)]]/21 \qquad (23)$$
$$x(2,t+1)=[3.x(2,t)+9.[x(3,t)+x(4,t+1)]+3.[x(1,t)+x(0,t+1)]]/21$$
$$x(3,t+1)=[[x(3,t)+x(4,t+1)]+3.[x(1,t)+x(0,t+1)]+8.x(2,t)]/21$$

We remark that the inputs are defined at the future time $t+1$ and they are present in the three equations. This can be related to the Aristotelian Final Cause. It means that the inputs at the boundaries are transmitted instantaneously, that is to say during the time step 1, to each automata, and that their effect are immediate because it is the same time step that the equations are computed. Why this phenomenon? As the movement equations are defined in the future time by the backward derivative, the inversion of the matrix A has the effect of mixing all the automata together at the present time t (and the inputs at the future time $t+1$) to compute their future values at time $t+1$. The inversion of the matrix A transforms a non-local incursive system to a local incursive system, that is to say a folding of each automaton to the other ones from the future time $t+1$ to the present time t.

Remark: the digital diffusion equation modulo N, in considering again the backward time derivative and the advective derivative $\partial x(s,t)/\partial s=(x(s+ds,t)-x(s-ds,t))/2ds$, with a=1, v=-1, D=1/2 and dt=ds=1is the incursive equation of the Fractal Machine

$$x(s,t+1) = [x(s,t) + x(s-1,t+1)] \bmod N \qquad (24)$$

It is possible to suppress the modulo in adding non-linear terms. For example, the modulo 2 can be realised by the following non-linear incursive equation

$$x(s,t+1) = x(s,t) + x(s-1,t+1) - 2.x(s,t).x(s-1,t+1) \qquad (25)$$
$$\text{or} \qquad x(s,t+1) = 2.[x(s,t) + x(s-1,t+1)].[1 - [x(s,t) + x(s-1,t+1)]/2] \qquad (26)$$

which always digital solutions 0 or 1. This last equation is similar to the Pearl-Verhulst map, in taking $x(s-1,t+1)=x(s,t)$,

$$x(s,t+1)=4.x(s,t).(1 - x(s,t)) \qquad (27)$$

the simulation of which with real numbers giving rise to fractal chaos. So, a bridge is made between diffusion equation, Pearl-Verhulst map and the Fractal Machine.

7 Conclusion

This paper deals with the concept and method of incursion and hyperincursion to model and control linear, non-linear and chaos discrete systems. These are an extension of recursive processes where the computation of future time steps only depends on present and past steps. With incursion and hyperincursion, future time steps can be introduced to compute these future steps. Hyperincursion is an incursion when several future values can be generated at each time step. These can be interpreted as an incremental anticipation similar to the Aristotelian Final Causation. They are related to the definition of backward and forward time derivatives. It was shown that chaos modelled by Pearl-Verhulst map can be controlled by incursion. The discretisation of differential equation systems can show unstable numerical solutions. The method of incursion is a powerful tool for modelling discrete systems. With the Fractal Machine, it is explicitly seen that the external inputs must be defined in the future time like a final causation which controls completely all the automata at the same time step in a holistic way. Indeed the inputs are present in each automata at the same external time. It is impossible to transform external inputs defined in the future time t+1 to inputs defined in the present time t. In this, we can say that we are dealing with a strict incursive system. Thus the final causation is really the 4th causation which must be taken into account in systems modelling as Aristotle had proposed. It seems also impossible to construct a real working engineering system where real working external future inputs would control its current present state. But it is possible to define internal future inputs in considering self-reference systems. The Fractal Machine can become non deterministic or non algorithmic, what I suggest to call an HYPERINCURSIVE FIELD where uncertainty (indecidability) or contradiction (exclusion principle) occur. This self-reference system is autopoietic. It was shown in the last section that the incursive diffusion equation can be algorithmically deterministic with a self-reference for the inputs defined at future time by space periodic conditions. As the movement equations are defined in the future time by the backward derivative, the recursive transformation has the effect of mixing all the automata together at the present time t in view of computing their future values at time t+1. The transformation of a non-local incursive system to a local recursive system leads to a folding of each automaton to the other ones from the future time to the present time.

References

1. D. M. Dubois: Total Incursive Control of Linear, Non-linear and Chaotic systems. in G. Lasker (ed.): Advances in Computer Cybernetics. Int. Inst. for Advanced Studies in Syst. Res. and Cybernetics, vol. II, 167-171 (1995)

2. D. M. Dubois: Contrôle-commande incursif d'un système chaotique. Bull. de l'A.I.LG, n°6-7, 11-12 (1994)

3. D. M. Dubois: Hyperincursivity: inclusive recursivity without time arrow. Proceedings of the 13th International Congress on Cybernetics, Namur, 152-156 (1992)

4. D. M. Dubois: The fractal machine: the wholeness of the memory chaos. Proceedings of the 13th International Congress on Cybernetics, Namur, 147-151 (1992)

5. D. M. Dubois: The Fractal Machine. Presses Universitaires de Liège 1992

6. D. M. Dubois: The hyperincursive fractal machine as a quantum holographic brain. Communication & Cognition -Artificial Intelligence 9-4, 335-372 (1992)

7. D. M. Dubois (editor): Designing new Intelligent Machines (COMETT European Symposium, Liège April 1992). Communication & Cognition -Artificial Intelligence, .9-4 (1992), sequel 10-1-2 (1993)

8. D. M. Dubois: Mathematical fundamentals of the fractal theory of artificial intelligence. Invited paper in New Mathematical tools in artificial intelligence. Communication & Cognition - Artificial Intelligence, 8-1, 5-48 (1991)

9. D. M. Dubois: Fractal Algorithms for holographic Memory of inversible neural Networks. Invited paper in Issues in Connectionism: part II. Communication & Cognition Artificial Intelligence, 8-2, 137-189 (1991)

10. D. M. Dubois: Self-Organisation of fractal objects in XOR rule-based multilayer Networks. In EC2 (ed.): Neural Networks & their Applications, Neuro-Nîmes 90, Proceedings of the third International Workshop, 555-557 (1990)

11. D. M. Dubois: Le Labyrinthe de L'intelligence: de l'intelligence naturelle à l'intelligence fractale. Academia (Louvain-la-Neuve) 1990, 321 p., 2ème édition, InterEditions (Paris)/Academia 1990, 331 p., 2ème tirage, 1991

12. D. M. Dubois: Un modèle fractal des systèmes intelligents. In AFCET France (ed.): Actes du 1er Congrès Européen de Systémique, Tome II, 665-674, 1989

13. D. M. Dubois, G. Resconi: Hyperincursivity: a new mathematical theory. Presses Universitaires de Liège 1992

14. D. M. Dubois, G. Resconi: Advanced Research in Incursion Theory applied to Ecology, Physics and Engineering. COMETT European Lecture Notes in Incursion. Edited by A.I.Lg., Association des Ingénieurs de l'Université de Liège, D/1995/3603/01, 1995

15. D. M. Dubois, G. Resconi: Hyperincursive Fractal Machine beyond the Turing Machine. In Lasker (ed.): Advances in Cognitive Engineering and Knowledge-based Systems. Int. Inst. for Adv. Studies in Syst. Res. and Cybernetics, 212-216 (1994)

16. D. M. Dubois, G. Resconi: Introduction to hyperincursion with applications to computer science, quantum mechanics and fractal processes. Communication & Cognition - Artificial Intelligence, vol. 10, N°1-2, 109-148 (1993)

17. D. M. Dubois, G. Resconi: Holistic Control by Incursion of Feedback Systems, Fractal Chaos and Numerical Instabilities. In R. Trappl (ed.): Cybernetics and Systems'94. World Scientific, 71-78 (1994)

18. A. J. Lotka: Elements of Physical Biology. William and Wilkins, Baltimore 1925

19. B. Mandelbrot: The Fractal Geometry of Nature. Freeman, San Francisco 1983

20. R. M. May: Simple mathematical models with very complicated dynamics. Nature 261, 459-467 (1976)

21. R. Pearl: Studies in human biology. William and Wilkins, Baltimore 1924

22. R. Rosen: Causal Structures in Brains and Machines, Int. J. Gen. Syst. 12, 107-126 (1986)

23. A. Rosenblueth, N. Wiener, J. Bigelow: Behavior, purpose and teleology. Philosophy of Science, 10, 18-24 (1943)

24. F. Scheid: Theory and Problems of Numerical Analysis. McGraw-Hill Inc. 1986

25. F. Varela: Autonomie et connaissance. Seuil 1989

26. P. F. Verhulst: Nuov. Mem. Acad. Royale, Bruxelles, 18, 1, 1845 & 20,1, 1847

27. V. Volterra: Leçon sur la théorie mathématique de la lutte pour la vie. Gauthier-Villars 1931

28. E. von Glasersfeld: Teleology and the Concepts of Causation. In: G. Van de Vijver (ed.): Sel-organizing and Complex Systems. Philosophica 1990, 46, pp. 17-43

29. S. Wolfram (ed.): Theory and Application of Cellular Automata. World Scientific, Singapore/Teanek, N. Y. 1986

30. K. Zuse: The Computing Universe. International Journal of Theoretical Physics, 21, 6/7, 589-600 (1982)

A Semantic Logic for CAST Related to Zuse, Deutsch and McCulloch and Pitts Computing Principles

Daniel M. DUBOIS

Institut de Mathématique, Université de Liège
Avenue des Tilleuls 15, B-4000 LIEGE, Belgium

Abstract. The goal of CAST research and development is to provide modelling tools for formal systems design in the field of information and systems engineering. This paper deals with such modelling tools for formal systems related to Zuse, Deutsch and McCulloch and Pitts computing principles. The semantic logic of such systems can be exhibited in replacing the differential equations by digital cellular automata. K. Zuse proposed such a method for representing physical systems by a computing space. I show that the digital wave equation exhibits waves by digital particles with interference effects. The logical table of the wave equation shows the conservation of the parity related to exclusive OR. The Fractal Machine proposed by the author deals with a cellular automata based on incursion, an inclusive recursion, with exclusive OR. In this machine, the superimposition of states is related to the Deutsch quantum computer. Finally, it is shown that the exclusive OR can be modelled by a fractal non-linear equation and a new method to design digital equations is proposed to create McCulloch and Pitts formal neurons.

1 Introduction

The newly established field of Computer Aided Systems Theory, CAST, was initiated by F. Pichler. CAST methods in modelling for the design of intelligent machines were proposed in the book edited by Pichler and Schärtzel [32]. The goal of CAST research and development is to provide modelling tools for formal systems design in the field of information and systems engineering. A fundamental problem in computer-based engineering systems deals with the duality of continuous versus discrete systems. Engineers have been compelled to penetrate beneath the grosser level of the continuous to that of the basic discrete structure of change. "For such an analysis, and indeed for the study of discontinuous but systematic sequential changes in general, the differential equation is replaced by the Finite Difference Equation, and its detailed examination and mastery is therefore now of first importance" [25].

This paper deals with the semantic information of systems which is embedded in their mathematical representation by differential equations. The semantic logic of such systems can be exhibited in replacing the differential equations by digital cellular automata as proposed by the inventor of the computer Konrad Zuse [5,46,45]. In cellular automata, for example the Life Game of Conway [24], the states of the automata play both the role of data that give rise to the patterns and the role of operators that govern the behaviour of the automata. Cellular automata can be considered as computing devices [42,43].

Konrad ZUSE [44,46,48] has explored possible new avenues of future research in proposing the paradigm of computing space (Rechnender Raum) as a cellular automata. Konrad Zuse is convinced that massively parallel processors working in complex networks could simulate formal models of physical systems. For example, Konrad ZUSE considered a fluid mechanical system in replacing the differential equation system by total finite difference equations which he called digital equations. These digital equations constitute a computing space where digital particles propagate as in cellular automata. These digital particles take integer values. In fact any engineering systems can be viewed as Zuse's computing space.

With this Zuse's paradigm, I show that a digital wave equation, obtained by finite difference of the classical wave differential equation, gives solutions with digital particles. These particles shows interference effects and behave like waves, as in quantum mechanics. In considering backward and forward time derivatives, hyperincursive equation systems are deduced from the digital wave equation. An uncertainty in the amplitude and velocity of the wave is simulated. Moreover these variables show time contraction properties as in relativity. The logical table of the digital wave equation shows the conservation of the parity related to exclusive OR.
The hyperincursive Fractal Machine proposed by the author [7,8,9,10,12,13,14,15] is a cellular automata ruled by exclusive OR, XOR. The Fractal Machine is beyond the Turing Machine [17,19,21]. As pointed out by Hasslacher [22], there are theoretical limits to the Universal Turing Machine. He proposed that an extension of the Turing Machine would be a fractal machine.

In the framework of the Turing Machine, there is a separation between the data and the operators: a transformation function is defined as a truth table which is separated from the data, the data never change the function. Classical algorithmic programmes deal with only syntactic information, that is to say without semantic and pragmatic information. In looking in a computer programme, all the orders (instructions and commands) are data for the computer. The data flow through the computer without influence of these data to the orders. An other proposition for an extension of the Turing Machine is the Universal Quantum Computer as proposed by D. Deutsch [2] after the Church-Turing principle. The Deutsch machine is also related to XOR.

Artificial Intelligence deals with non-algorithmic programmes where data steer their runs. In this case data play the role of orders, that is to say operators, and then we can speak of semantic/pragmatic information. Expert Systems and Neural Networks deal with data-driven programmes. For example, McCulloch and Pitts proposed in 1943 the concept of formal neuron [30,33]. This is a very important paradigm because they were able to extract the logic of the electrobiochemical nervous system, in initiating the now well established Threshold Logic. It is interesting to notice that the XOR plays a particular role in the Threshold logic. It is not possible to realise XOR or any Parity Problem with only one single McCulloch and Pitts formal neuron. I have shown that a non-linear fractal neuron can model XOR [11,13,14]. From this, a Non-linear Threshold Logic was proposed [18,20]. This paper will show a new method to design non-linear formal neurons by digital equations and to create, from them, a network of McCulloch and Pitts neural network with hidden neurons. These digital equations give the semantic logic of dynamic Boolean Tables.

2 Digital Wave Equation Related to Zuse Computing Space

Let us consider the one dimension wave equation

(1) $\partial^2 x(s,t)/\partial t^2 = c^2 \partial^2 x(s,t)/\partial s^2$

where $x(s,t)$ is the value of the wave at position s at time t, and c the velocity.
The differential equation 1 can be replaced by the finite difference equation [e g 36]

(2) $x(s,t+dt)-2.x(s,t)+x(s,t-dt) = c^2.dt^2.[x(s+ds,t)-2.x(s,t)+x(s-ds,t)]/ds^2$

In physics, the velocity of light is limited by $c = 300,000$ km/sec and the constants of Planck are given by the smallest space length $ds_p = 10^{-35}$ cm and the smallest time duration $dt_p = 10^{-44}$ sec. In taking them as units in the wave equation, $ds = 1$, $dt = 1$ and $c = 1$, the following digital wave equation is obtained

(3) $x(s,t+dt)-2.x(s,t)+x(s,t-1) = x(s+1,t)-2.x(s,t)+x(s-1,t)$

We can write the digital wave equation as

(4) $D_{t,f} x(s,t) - D_{t,b} x(s,t) = D_{s,f} x(s,t) - D_{s,b} x(s,t)$

where

(5) $D_{t,f} x(s,t) = x(s,t+1) - x(s,t)$
(6) $D_{t,b} x(s,t) = x(s,t) - x(s,t-1)$

are the forward and backward time derivatives, and

(7) $D_{s,f} x(s,t) = x(s+1,t) - x(s,t)$
(8) $D_{s,b} x(s,t) = x(s,t) - x(s-1,t)$

the forward and backward space derivatives which can be interpreted as the measure and the action [1,4]. It means that the difference of the time action and the measure is equal to the difference of the space action and measure. We can also write

(9) $D_{s,f} - D_{t,f} = D_{s,b} - D_{t,b}$

where the difference of the space and time actions is equal to the difference of the space and time measures. These are related to a conservation law.
In cancelling the terms $x(s,t)$, equation 3 becomes

(10) $x(s,t+1) + x(s,t-1) = x(s+1,t) + x(s-1,t)$

where the term $x(s,t)$ can be cancelled in both members of the relation. It is only true when $ds/dt = c$. This means that the sum of the value of the wave at position s at two different times $t+1$ and $t-1$ is equal to the sum of the values of the wave at time t at two different positions $s+1$ and $s-1$. The time and the space play the same role.

This digital wave equation 10 is a cellular automata which can be computed from

(11) $x(s,t+1) = - x(s,t-1) + x(s+1,t) + x(s-1,t)$

where the wave at position s at the future time t+1 is equal to the sum of the waves at the adjacent positions at the present time t minus itself at the preceding time t-1.
Let us show that the digital wave equation 11 is similar to the Computing Space defined by Zuse [46,47,48]. Indeed a purely digital solution exists in considering the following figure 1a with initial conditions given by the first two lines at time 0 and 1

```
s=0  1  2  3  4  5  6  7  8  9  10        1  2  3  4  5  6  7  8  9  10

t=0   0  0  0  0  0  0  0  0  0  0  0        0  0  0  X  0  0  Y  0  0  0
t=1   0  0  0  0  0  1  0  0  0  0  0        0  0  X  0  X  Y  0  Y  0  0
      0  0  0  0  1  0  1  0  0  0  0        0  X  0  X  Y  X  Y  0  Y  0
      0  0  0  1  0  1  0  1  0  0  0        X  0  X  Y  X  Y  X  Y  0  Y
      0  0  1  0  1  0  1  0  1  0  0        Y  X  Y  X  Y  X  Y  X  Y  X
      0  1  0  1  0  1  0  1  0  1  0
      1  0  1  0  1  0  1  0  1  0  1
```

Figures 1a-b:(a) A digital solution of the digital wave equation 11.
(b) Two independent networks can be defined.

The periodicity 2 of an automaton at each time step corresponds to the periodicity 2 of all the automata at the same time step. Two independent waves X and Y can be defined in two independent space networks as shown in Figure 1b.

Let us consider the digital wave equation with other particular initial conditions given at t=0 and t=1. The figure 2 shows that the wave is now a digital particle which reflects on the boundary, in taking the boundary conditions $x(-1,t) = x(+1,t)$

```
        s=-1  0  1  2  3  4  5  6  7

t=0      0  0  0  0  0  1  0  0  0
t=1      0  0  0  0  1  0  0  0  0
         0  0  0  1  0  0  0  0  0
         1  0  1  0  0  0  0  0  0
         0  2  0  0  0  0  0  0  0
         1  0  1  0  0  0  0  0  0
         0  0  0  1  0  0  0  0  0
         0  0  0  0  1  0  0  0  0
         0  0  0  0  0  1  0  0  0
```

Figures 2: A digital solution of equation 11 where a digital particle reflects on the boundary.

It is really important to notice that the wave is represented by a digital particle. This could be related to the wave-particle duality in quantum mechanics.

Now what happens when two particles meet?

```
s= 0 1 2 3 4 5 6 7 8          s= 0 1 2 3 4 5 6 7 8

t=0    0 0 0 1 0 0 0 0 2          0 0 1 0 0 0 0 0 2
t=1    0 0 0 0 1 0 0 2 0          0 0 0 1 0 0 0 2 0
       0 0 0 0 0 1 2 0 0          0 0 0 0 1 0 2 0 0
       0 0 0 0 0 2 1 0 0          0 0 0 0 0 3 0 0 0
       0 0 0 0 2 0 0 1 0          0 0 0 0 2 0 1 0 0
       0 0 2 0 0 0 0 0 1          0 0 0 2 0 0 0 1 0
```

Figures 3a-b: (a) Two digital particles cross without interaction because there are on two different networks; (b) Two particles only interact on the same network

Figure 3a shows that two particles cross without interaction because they are in the two different networks. From two particles in the same network, surprisingly the two particles interact as shown in figure 3b. There is an addition of the two particles because they have the same space phase. I obtain a case of what Zuse called "space phase" [44]. Zuse thinks that space phase could explain non-locality.

Remark: when the wave equation in taken in two or three space dimensions, there is only one network. For example, in 2-D, with $dt=ds1=ds2=1$, where s1 and s2 are the space variables, the term $x(s1,s2,t)$ is present

(12) $x(s1,s2,t+1)=-x(s1,s2,t-1)-2.x(s1,s2,t)+x(s1+1,s2,t)+x(s1-1,s2,t)$
              $+x(s1,s2+1,t)+x(s1,s2-1,t)$

From eq. 1 the position and the velocity of the wave can be described by the system

(13) $\partial x(s,t)/\partial t = v(s,t)$
         $\partial v(s,t)/\partial t = c^2.\partial^2 x(s,t)/\partial s^2$

It means that the second time derivative is split to two time derivatives. In view of satisfying the conservation law and the stability of the solutions, it is necessary to consider backward and forward time derivatives. It is shown elsewhere that these derivatives are related to incursion and hyperincursion [3,4, 17]. Incursion was defined by the author [6,7,8,10] as an inclusive recursion, and hyperincursion is a multivalued incursion. So in taking the forward derivative for x and the backward derivative for v, a first hyperincursive equation system is obtained

(14) $x(s,t+dt)-x(s,t)=dt.v(s,t)$
         $v(s,t)-v(s,t-dt)=dt. c^2.[x(s+ds,t)-2.x(s,t)+x(s-ds,t)]/ds^2$

or

(15) $x(s,t+dt)=x(s,t)+dt.v(s,t)$
         $v(s,t+dt)=v(s,t)+dt. c^2.[x(s+ds,t)-2.x(s,t)+x(s-ds,t)]/ds^2+$
              $dt^2. c^2.[v(s+ds,t)-2.v(s,t)+v(s-ds,t)]/ds^2$

and it is seen that the velocity at position s at time t+dt is the classical term plus an incursive term given by the diffusion of the velocity multiply by dt.

In taking dt=ds=c=1, eq. 15 becomes

(16) $x(s,t+1)=x(s,t)+v(s,t)$
        $v(s,t+1)=v(s,t)+x(s+1,t+1)-2.x(s,1)+x(s-1,t+1)$

and the term $x(s,t)$ doesn't disappear. The second equation is incursive because the variable $v(s,t+1)$ is computed in function of $x(s+1,t+1)$ and $x(s-1,t+1)$ defined at the same future time step t+1. The following figures 4a-b show a computation corresponding to the previous case. Let us remark that we must compute three successive steps of x for computing a velocity step. The variable x is the amplitude of the wave. We can interpret x as a transversal position

```
s= 0 1 2 3 4 5 6 7 8 9     0 1 2 3 4 5 6 7 8 9

t=0   0 0 0 1 0 0 0 0 0 0   0 0 0-1 1 0 0 0 0 0
t=1   0 0 0 0 1 0 0 0 0 0   0 0 0 0-1 1 0 0 0 0
      0 0 0 0 0 1 0 0 0 0   0 0 0 0 0-1 1 0 0 0
      0 0 0 0 0 0 1 0 0 0   0 0 0 0 0 0-1 1 0 0
      0 0 0 0 0 0 0 1 0 0   0 0 0 0 0 0 0-1 1 0
      0 0 0 0 0 0 0 0 1 0   0 0 0 0 0 0 0 0-1 1
```

Figures 4a-b: A solution of eqs. 16: (a) Digital particle $x(s,t)$; (b) Digital velocity $v(s,t)$

Let us remark that the velocity is not space determined. Two successive automata are necessary to define it. For the same position s and time t, a particle which has an amplitude $x(s,t)=1$ corresponds to a velocity $v(s,t) = -1$ and an adjacent forward velocity $v(s+1,t)=+1$. The mean value of the velocities is zero, but the two opposite velocities are spatially separated. It looks like two operators. An annihilation operator with -1 and a creation operator with +1. The incursion was made in taking the backward derivative for the velocity. Let us remark that there is no more two independent networks because the term $x(s,t)$ is present in eq. 16. The two following figures 5a-b give the solution with initial conditions interaction between two wave particles as previous (fig. 3a)

```
s= 0 1 2 3 4 5 6 7 8      0 1 2 3 4 5 6 7 8

t=0   0 0 0 1 0 0 0 0 2    0 0 0-1 1 0 0 2-2
t=1   0 0 0 0 1 0 0 2 0    0 0 0 0-1 1 2-2 0
      0 0 0 0 0 1 2 0 0    0 0 0 0 0 1 1-1 0 0
      0 0 0 0 0 2 1 0 0    0 0 0 0 2-2-1 1 0
      0 0 0 0 2 0 0 1 0    0 0 0 2-2 0 0-1 1
      0 0 0 2 0 0 0 0 1    0 0 2-2 0 0 0 0-1
```

Figures 5a-b: A solution of eqs. 16 in taking two digital particles as if fig. 3a
(a) Digital particle $x(s,t)$; (b) Digital velocity $v(s,t)$

In this case we observe that the two amplitudes $x(s,t)$ do not interact directly, but the velocities of the two particles interact. These are no more independent.

There is a new property when we like to know simultaneously two variables instead of one. In fact, when the wave equation is discretised, the term x(s,t) disappears, but if the discretisation is performed with two separate equations, the term x(s,t) must be taken explicitly into account.

The second hyperincursive equations with the backward derivative for the amplitude and the forward derivative for the velocity, with dt=ds=c=1, are given by

(17)   v(s,t+1)=v(s,t)+x(s+1,t)-2.x(s,t)+x(s-1,t)
          x(s,t+1)= x(s,t)+v(s,t+1)

we obtain the dual or complementary result where the evolution of x(s,t) is the same but the velocity field is different. Indeed, we compute first the velocity and then the amplitude. Let us notice that the computation can be made now completely sequentially. Each value v(s,t+1) from x and v at the preceding time is sufficient to compute the new x(s,t+1) from the computed velocity and the preceding amplitude as shown in the two following figures

```
s=  0 1 2 3 4 5 6 7 8 9        0 1 2 3 4 5 6 7 8 9

t=0    0 0 0 1 0 0 0 0 0 0      0 0-1 1 0 0 0 0 0 0
t=1    0 0 0 0 1 0 0 0 0 0      0 0 0-1 1 0 0 0 0 0
       0 0 0 0 0 1 0 0 0 0      0 0 0 0-1 1 0 0 0 0
       0 0 0 0 0 0 1 0 0 0      0 0 0 0 0-1 1 0 0 0
       0 0 0 0 0 0 0 1 0 0      0 0 0 0 0 0-1 1 0 0
       0 0 0 0 0 0 0 0 1 0      0 0 0 0 0 0 0-1 1 0
```

Figures 6a-b: A solution of eqs. 17: (a) Digital particle x(s,t); (b) Digital velocity v(s,t)

Now, for a value x(s,t)=1 corresponds a value v(s,t)=1 at the same space-time and a value v(s-1,t) = - 1. It is the same velocity field as in the other incursion but with a time delay of dt=1, corresponding to the time step. Knowing perfectly the amplitude x(s,t)=1, the two hyperincursive solutions give two opposite values for the velocity, v(s,t)=+1 and v(s,t)=-1, that is to say a maximum of uncertainty in total similarity with the Heisenberg Uncertainty Principle in Quantum Mechanics.

Surprisingly some properties seem related to the Relativity Theory. Indeed, starting with initial conditions x(s+ds,0)=x(s-ds,0)=v(s+ds,0)=v(s-ds,0)=0, eq. 15 becomes

(18)   x(s,t+dt)=x(s,t)+dt.v(s,t)
          v(s,t+dt)= v(s,t)-2.dt. c².x(s,t)/ds²-2.dt.dt. c².v(s,t)/ds²

which is similar to the hyperincursive harmonic oscillator [4] with a frequency equal to $(\omega.dt)^2 = 2.c^2./v_c^2$ where $v_c = ds/dt$

(19)   x(s,t+dt)=x(s,t)+dt.v(s,t)
          v(s,t+dt)= v(s,t).[1- $\omega^2.dt^2$] -dt.ω^2.x(s,t)

and we can interpret the incursive term as a contraction of the velocity [3,4].

In taking the other incursive equation, we obtain a contraction of the amplitude. So the digitalisation of the equations give rise to relativistic effects in parallel with quantum effects. We can give an interpretation of the quantum relativistic effect in saying that it is not possible to determine if it is the amplitude or the velocity which gives rise to a contraction. The lonely certitude is to say that one of these variables will contract, but we do not know which one. In having a difference of dt between the two velocity fields, and knowing that the velocity of light is c, we can say that the uncertainty is related to c.dt, that is to say the constant length of Plank $ds_p = 10^{-35}$ cm, the smallest duration being $dt_p = 10^{-44}$ sec. The wave is perhaps the superposition of these two solutions? It is interesting to notice that the two hyperincursive equations are the reverse of each other [1,4]. Indeed, in replacing dt by - dt in the first hyperincursive system, we obtain the second hyperincursive system. But it is not possible to know which one goes to the future? Perhaps it is necessary to consider that both forward and backward waves work together. The resulting wave would have a double front for propagating.

It is interesting to build a multi-valued table from the digital equation

x(s-1,t)	x(s,t-1)	x(s+1,t)	x(s,t+1)
0	0	0	0
1	1	0	0
0	1	1	0
1	0	1	2
1	1	1	1
1	0	0	1
0	0	1	1
0	1	0	-1

This table shows the conservation of the parity between the output x(s,t+1) and the set of inputs. This is an important property of elementary particles in physics. The parity is related to exclusive OR, XOR. Let us now consider the Fractal Machine in relation to the Quantum computer of Deutsch which are based on XOR.

3 The Fractal Machine Related to Deutsch Quantum Computer

In a recent paper about Quantum Computers, Jean-Paul Delahaye [1] gives some arguments about the weakness of the reference model of the computer which is the Turing Machine. A generalisation of the Turing Machine was proposed by David Deutsch [2] after a question of Feynman [23], defining a quantum model of computation based on superposition of states and interference waves. Feynman asked if a classical computer could always simulate a quantum physics process in a reasonable time. If a quantum machine could be constructed [26], it would be more powerful than the Turing Machine. Delahaye gives a simple example based on exclusive OR to explain that the information obtained from superimposed states is useful even if this information is only partial. The power of a quantum computer would be to compute in a parallel way the exclusive OR. Algorithms for a Quantum Machine are already proposed for the factoring problem [37]. Let us give a very simple case of computation of superimposed states from the Fractal Machine.

The description of the Fractal Machine is given elsewhere in details [3,8]. Recall just the main principle in view of demonstrating the computation of superimposed states.

Classically, a one-dimensional network of cellular automata is represented by a vector of automata states, each automaton state having an integer numerical value at the initial time t=0. A set of rules defines how the states change at every clock time [eg 42]. A simple rule consists of replacing the value of each automaton by the sum modulo 2, for example, of itself and its left neighbour at each clock time. Figure 7a shows a one-dimensional network of cellular automata giving rise to the Sierpinski napkin which is a self-similar fractal structure. Properties of fractals can be found in Mandelbrot [27].

	n=0 1 2 3 4 5 6 7 8	n=0 1 2 3 4 5 6 7 8
t=0	0 1 0 0 0 0 0 0 0	0 1 0 0 0 0 0 0 0
t=1	0 1 1 0 0 0 0 0 0	0 1 1 1 1 1 1 1 1
t=2	0 1 0 1 0 0 0 0 0	0 1 0 1 0 1 0 1 0
t=3	0 1 1 1 1 0 0 0 0	0 1 1 0 0 1 1 0 0
t=4	0 1 0 0 0 1 0 0 0	0 1 0 0 0 1 0 0 0
t=5	0 1 1 0 0 1 1 0 0	0 1 1 1 1 0 0 0 0
t=6	0 1 0 1 0 1 0 1 0	0 1 0 1 0 0 0 0 0
t=7	0 1 1 1 1 1 1 1 1	0 1 1 0 0 0 0 0 0
t=8	0 1 0 0 0 0 0 0 0	0 1 0 0 0 0 0 0 0

Figure 7a-b: Recursive Sierpinski napkin and incursive Sierpinski napkin

The recursive model of this network is

(20) $X(n,t+1) = (X(n,t) + X(n-1,t)) \bmod 2$ with t=0,1,2,... and n=1,2,...,

with initial conditions $X(n,0)$ and boundary conditions $X(0,t)$. The recursion consists of the computation of the future value of the variable from the values of these variables at present time.

The computation in the Fractal Machine is based on incursion [8] for "INclusive or implicit reCURSION". Hyperincursion is an incursion when several values can be generated, as an extension of hyper recursion [6,10,19].

Starting from the recursive equation (20), the following incursive relation is defined

(21) $X(n,t+1) = (X(n,t) + X(n-1,t+1)) \bmod 2$ with n=1,2,...,8, and t=0,1,2,...,7

where $X(n,t)$ is the automaton state at position n and time t. The modulo 2 is exclusive OR, XOR. The computation of eq. (21), given at Figure 7b, gives rise to a time reverse Sierpinski napkin.

It was shown that incursion and hyperincursion is related to Aristotle's Final Causation [3,34,41] and to the purpose and teleology in cybernetics [35]. The Fractal Machine gives rise to an hyperincursive field [3] related to self-reference system [38]. Indeed the future boundary conditions $X(0,t+1)$ can be defined by self-reference. This is also related to cosmological models [28].

Let us define the initial conditions of two strings $S1(n,0)$ and $S2(n,t)$ and a third string $S3(n,0) = S1(n,0)$ XOR $S2(n,0)$ by the XOR superimposition of the two first strings. In applying the incursive equation 21 to the three strings, the figure 8 shows that the third string is the XOR superimposition of the two iterates of the two first strings at each iteration.

	$S_1(n,t)$	$S_2(n,t)$	$S_3(n,t)$
n=	12345678	12345678	12345678
t=0	10000111	00010111	10010000
t=1	11111010	00011010	11100000
t=2	10101100	00010011	10111111
t=3	11001000	00011101	11010101
t=4	10001111	00010110	10011001
t=5	11110101	00011011	11101110
t=6	10100110	00010010	10110100
t=7	11000100	00011100	11011000
t=8	10000111	00010111	10010000

Figure 8: Incursive generation of three digital strings S1, S2 and S3 by eq. 21. The initial conditions of the third string S3 is given by XOR of the initial conditions of S1 and S2.

We see that the composition rule for the third string is applied to the two other superimposed strings, and at each step, the output is given by a superimposed state of the two strings, i.e. a mixed state. This means that the output of this machine is given by the mixing of variables which are not separated as $S_1(n,t+1)$ and $S_2(n,t+1)$. Without knowing one of the two strings S_1 or S_2, it is impossible to obtain the values of the two outputs. It is possible to represent XOR Boolean Table or the modulo 2 of equation 21 by a digital non-linear equation (see below). In knowing only $S_3(n,0)$ at initial conditions with the boundary conditions $S_3(0,t+1)$, the incursive non-linear digital eq. 21 for $S3(n,t)$ is given by

(22) $\quad S_3(n,t+1)=S_3(n,t) + S_3(n-1,t+1)-2.S_3(n,t).S_3(n-1,t+1)$
(23) $\quad S_1(n,t) + S_2(n,t) - 2\ S_1(n,t).S_2(n,t)= S_3(n,t)$

If only one string is known, what is the information in this string about the two others ? Considering that the symbols represent a truth table, i.e. TRUE $= 1$ and FALSE $= 0$, we can know partial information about the two other strings.
If $S_3(n,t)=0$ then $S_1(n,t)=S_2(n,t)$: $S_1(n,t)=$ 0 or 1 and $S_2(n,t)=$ 0 or 1.
If $S_3(n,t)=1$ then $S_1(n,t)=1-S_2(n,t)$ and $S_1(n,t)$: $S_1(n,t)=$ 0 or 1 and $S_2(n,t)=$ 1 or 0.
At a given position in one string, a 0 means that the values of the symbols in the two other strings are identical and a 1 means that the values of the symbols in the two other strings are different, but we do not know their values. We have incomplete information. This reminds us of the uncertainty principle in quantum mechanics.

Let us now consider the digital equation 23 related to the Threshold Logic of McCulloch and Pitts formal neuron for XOR.

4 Digital Equation Related to the McCulloch-Pitts Threshold Logic

The Threshold Logic was initiated by the pioneer work of McCulloch and Pitts for modelling formal neurons at a logic level. But, one single McCulloch & Pitts neuron is not able to learn the parity of binary patterns. For example, a few neurons are necessary to learn the truth table of the exclusive OR, i. e. the parity of two inputs.
I have proposed non-linear fractal neurons as digital equations for modelling Boolean Tables [11,13,14,18,20]. They can be split into a set of McCulloch and Pitts neurons where the weights are always either an activation weight +1 or an inhibition weight -1. The fractal property of the neurons permits to reduce the original Boolean table to a new simpler ortho-normal Boolean table. The fractality of the neurons unfolds the apparent disorder of the original table to an ordered table. Each neuron is in competition with the others related to an exclusion principle. It seems that the competition between neurons is a shift in the paradigm of the co-operative approach of neural networks.
An application is fully developed for the exclusive OR, XOR table. In linking the outputs of these neurons to their inputs, it is shown that surprisingly we obtain the finite difference equations of the competition between the neurons similar to the equations of Volterra for competing species. An exclusion principle is present in competing species: only one survives depending on initial conditions.
Let us consider the general Boolean Table with two inputs x1 and x2 and one output y

x_1	x_2	y
0	0	y_1
0	1	y_2
1	0	y_3
1	1	y_4

An algebraic non-linear logic can be based on

$$(24) \qquad y=(1-x_1).(1-x_2).y_1+(1-x_1).x_2.y_2+x_1.(1-x_2).y_3+x_1.x_2.y_4$$

which is the general non-linear logic equation for the 16 Boolean Tables, that is to say all the combinations of the outputs $y = (y_1, y_2, y_3, y_4)$. It is sufficient to only consider the cases in the Boolean Table for which the outputs are 1, because each term is multiply by an output. For the exclusive OR, XOR, the outputs 1 are $y_2=1$ and $y_3=1$, so the equation is

$$(25) \qquad y=(1-x_1).x_2+(1-x_2).x_1=x_1+x_2-2.x_1.x_2$$

It was shown by Dubois and Resconi [20] that this non-linear equation is the Heaviside Fixed Function. The McCulloch and Pitts formal neuron given by

$$(26) \qquad y=\Gamma(w_1.x_1+w_2.x_2+...-\theta)$$

where $\Gamma(x)$ is the Heaviside function which is equal to 1 if and only if $x>0$, w_i are the weights and θ the threshold.

Indeed, we have

(27) $y = (1-x_1).x_2+(1-x_2).x_1 = x_1+x_2-2.x_1.x_2 = \Gamma(x_1+x_2-2.x_1.x_2)$

The AND Boolean Logic, given by a product as $y=x_1.x_2... x_n$, is given by

(28) $y=\Gamma(x_1+x_2+x_3+...+x_n-(n-1))$

where all the weights are equal to 1 and the threshold is equal to the number of inputs minus 1. So hidden neurons can be created from each non-linear term. For example, let us create two hidden neurons y_1 and y_2 from the two non-linear terms of the non-linear equation of XOR, and an output neuron y which is the simple sum of these hidden neurons

        $y_1=(1-x_1).x_2=\Gamma(1-x_1+x_2-1)=\Gamma(x_2-x_1)$
(29) $y_2=(1-x_2).x_1=\Gamma(x_1-x_2)$
        $y=\Gamma(y_1+y_2)$

It can be easily demonstrated that it is possible to build any Boolean Table with McCulloch & Pitts neurons, the weights of which being equal to +1 and -1.

The polynomial equation of the neuron [11,13,14] in function of the sum of the inputs (x_1+x_2):

(30) $y=2.(x_1+x_2)[1-(x_1+x_2)/2]$

two hidden neurons can be defined, in knowing that $x^2 = x$ in Boolean system,

        $y_1=2x_1(1-(x_1+x_2)/2)=x_1(1-x_2)$
(31) $y_2=2x_2(1-(x_1+x_2)/2)=x_2(1-x_1)$
        $y=y_1+y_2$

The Boolean table with the hidden variables is

x_1	x_2	y_1	y_2	y
0	0	0	0	0
0	1	0	1	1
1	0	1	0	1
1	1	0	0	0

The two inputs x_1 and x_2 are transformed to two hidden variables y_1 and y_2 which are mutually exclusive vectors $y_1.y_2=0$. The role of these hidden variables is to fold the input values so that $x_1=x_2=1$ folds to $x_1=x_2=0$. With the hidden variables, there is an exclusion principle: the two variables cannot be equal to one together.
This is due to the fractal property of the equations of these hidden variables.

For example $y_1=x_1.(1-x_2)$ is zero, that is to say false, when the two inputs are equal, that is to say false-false or true-true; it is one, that is to say true, when the two inputs are different, that is false-true or true-false.

This could represent a semantic logic, because there is no ambiguity on the meaning of the hidden variables which represent the concepts of *equality* and *difference*. A first level of a hierarchy of hidden variables is built on the input variables. With more complex Boolean Tables, many semantic levels could be built, in the same way.

Digital equations can be built from Boolean Tables. Indeed, let us consider a feedback between the these hidden neurons and the input neurons in defining $x_1(t)=x_1$, $x_2(t)=x_2$ and $x_1(t+1)=y_1$, $x_2(t+1)=y_2$, two digital non-linear equations can be built

$$(32) \quad x_1(t+1)-x_1(t)=x_1(t)(1-x_1(t))-x_1(t).x_2(t)$$
$$x_2(t+1)-x_2(t)=x_2(t)(1-x_2(t))-x_1(t).x_2(t)$$

which is a digital equation system of the difference equations of Volterra [40] for two competing species x_1 and x_2

$$(33) \quad dx_1/dt=x_1-x_1x_2-x_1^2$$
$$dx_2/dt=x_2-x_1x_2-x_2^2$$

where the square of the variables are saturation of the growth rate. In defining the sum $y = x_1 +x_2$

$$(34) \quad dy/dt=y(1-y)$$

it is seen that the sum is only function of itself. This is the Pearl-Verhulst equation [31,39]. In replacing this differential equation by finite difference equation

$$(35) \quad y(t+dt) = y(t)+dt.y(t).(1-y(t))$$

is similar to the Pearl-Verhulst map studied by May [29] which gives rise to chaos. Indeed, for dt varying from -1 to 3, one obtains a fixed point, the direct cascade and then the fractal chaos. This dynamic system is a representation of XOR where the Boolean variables are now real variables. This is an extension of the Boolean Logic similar to a fuzzy or chaos logic. Numerical simulations of eqs. 33 show a chaotic behaviour where the two populations can survive contrary to the classical case.

5 Conclusion

This paper has explored possible new avenues of future research and development of tools for the application of systems and computer-based engineering systems. Formal methods for modelling of computer systems of different kinds are proposed.

Any systems theory deals with a semantic logic, corresponding to a meaning in the mind of the CAST engineer, which can be represented by mathematical equations. A fundamental problem is the duality of continuous versus discrete system equations.

Any Computer-based Engineering Systems deal with two basic aspects: measures as data and actions as operators. In fact, the actions can be viewed as data, and data can be viewed as operators. When an engineer conceptualise such systems, hardware or software, he must formalise in a syntactic programme his semantic solution of the problem to be resolved. In the CAST, CAD and CAM chain, we can say that the CAD-CAM systems programmes are designed in a syntactic framework even if some programmes are non-algorithmic. The big new issue with the paradigm of CAST, Computer Aided Systems Theory and Technology pioneered by Franz Pichler, is to create syntactic representations of the semantic ideas of the engineer for formal specification of computer systems at any level. The CAST tools must be considered as generators of syntactic information from semantic/pragmatic information. The meaning of a problem to be resolved deals with semantic data in the mind of the engineer. The engineer is able very often to formalise his semantic ideas with syntactic information given by orders, gates for hardware and instructions/commands for software. The big question is to know if an algorithmic CAST tool will be sufficiently powerful to transform the semantic information in the mind of the engineer to a syntactic information in the CAST tool. The string of characters is constituted of operators represented by data and the meaning is constituted of data which play the role of operators. In conclusion the purpose of CAST tools could be the transformation of data-based operators to operator-based data.

This paper is an attempt to integrate Zuse, Deutsch and McCulloch and Pitts computing principles by providing a common conceptual basis. The semantic logic of such systems can be exhibited in replacing the differential equations by digital cellular automata. K. Zuse proposed such a method for representing physical systems by a computing space. I show that the digital wave equation exhibits waves by digital particles with interference effects. The logical table of the wave equation shows the conservation of the parity related to exclusive OR. The Fractal Machine proposed by the author deals with a cellular automata based on incursion, an inclusive recursion, with exclusive OR. In this machine, the superimposition of states is related to the Deutsch quantum computer. Finally, it is shown that the exclusive OR can be modelled by a fractal non-linear equation and a new method to design digital equations is proposed to create McCulloch and Pitts formal neurons.

Acknowledgement: I would like to warmly thank Professor Dr. Ir. Konrad Zuse for many fascinating discussions at Hünfeld about his computing space (Rechnender Raum) and discrete mathematics.

References

1. J. P. Delahaye: Les ordinateurs quantiques. Pour la SCIENCE (French edition of Scientific American), 100-104, Mars 1995

2. D. Deutsch: Quantum Theory, the Church-Turing Principles and the Universal Quantum computer. Proc. R. Soc., London, A 400, 97-117 (1985)

3. D. M. Dubois: Introduction of the Aristtle's Final Causation in CAST: Concept and Method of Incursion and Hyperincursion. In F. Pichler (ed.): EUROCAST'95. Lecture Notes in Computer Science. Springer-Verlag 1996

4. D. M. Dubois: Total Incursive Control of Linear, Non-linear and Chaotic systems. in G. Lasker (ed.): Advances in Computer Cybernetics. Int. Inst. for Advanced Studies in Syst. Res. and Cybernetics, vol. II, 167-171 (1995)

5. D. M. Dubois: Les idées, toujours d'actualité, de l'inventeur du premier ordinateur, le Dr. Ir. K. ZUSE. In: Actes du Colloque International, Histoire de l'Informatique, Sophia Antipolis 13-15 octobre 1993, France: édité par l'Institut de Recherche en Informatique et en Automatique, 20 p. (1993)

6. D. M. Dubois: Hyperincursivity: inclusive recursivity without time arrow. In: Association Internationale de Cybernétique (éditeur): 13th International Congress on Cybernetics, Namur, 152-156 (1992)

7. D. M. Dubois: The fractal machine: the wholeness of the memory chaos. In: Association Internationale de Cybernétique (éditeur): 13th International Congress on Cybernetics, Namur, 147-151 (1992)

8. D. M. Dubois: The Fractal Machine. Presses Universitaires de Liège 1992

9. D. M. Dubois: The hyperincursive fractal machine as a quantum holographic brain. Communication & Cognition -Artificial Intelligence 9-4, 335-372 (1992)

10. D. M. Dubois (editor): Designing new Intelligent Machines (COMETT European Symposium, Liège April 1992). Communication & Cognition -Artificial Intelligence, .9-4 (1992), sequel 10-1-2 (1993)

11. D. M. Dubois: Mathematical fundamentals of the fractal theory of artificial intelligence. Invited paper in New Mathematical tools in artificial intelligence. Communication & Cognition - Artificial Intelligence, 8-1, 5-48 (1991)

12. D. M. Dubois: Fractal Algorithms for holographic Memory of inversible neural Networks. Invited paper in Issues in Connectionism: part II. Communication & Cognition Artificial Intelligence, 8-2, 137-189 (1991)

13. D. M. Dubois: Self-Organisation of fractal objects in XOR rule-based multilayer Networks. In EC2 (ed.): Neural Networks & their Applications, Neuro-Nîmes 90, Proceedings of the third International Workshop, 555-557 (1990)

14. D. M. Dubois: Le Labyrinthe de L'intelligence: de l'intelligence naturelle à l'intelligence fractale. Academia (Louvain-la-Neuve) 1990, 321 p., 2ème édition, InterEditions (Paris)/Academia 1990, 331 p., 2ème tirage, 1991

15. D. M. Dubois: Un modèle fractal des systèmes intelligents. In AFCET France (ed.): Actes du 1er Congrès Européen de Systémique, Tome II, 665-674, 1989

16. D. M. Dubois, G. Resconi: Hyperincursivity: a new mathematical theory. Presses Universitaires de Liège 1992

17. D. M. Dubois, G. Resconi: Advanced Research in Incursion Theory applied to Ecology, Physics and Engineering. COMETT European Lecture Notes in Incursion. Edited by A.I.Lg., Association des Ingénieurs de l'Université de Liège, D/1995/3603/01, 1995

18. D. M. Dubois, G. Resconi: Advanced Research in Non-linear Threshold Logic Applied to Pattern Recognition. COMETT European Lecture Notes in Threshold Logic. Edited by AILg, Association des Ingénieurs sortis de l'Université de Liège, D/1995/3603/02, 1995

19. D. M. Dubois, G. Resconi: Hyperincursive Fractal Machine beyond the Turing Machine. In Lasker (ed.): Advances in Cognitive Engineering and Knowledge-based Systems. Int. Inst. for Adv. Studies in Syst. Res. and Cybernetics, 212-216 (1994)

20. D. M. Dubois, G. Resconi: Mathematical Foundation of a Non-linear Threshold Logic: a New Paradigm for the Technology of Neural Machines. ACADEMIE ROYALE DE BELGIQUE, Bulletin de la Classe des Sciences, 6ème série, Tome IV, 1-6, 91-122 (1993)

21. D. M. Dubois, G. Resconi: Introduction to hyperincursion with applications to computer science, quantum mechanics and fractal processes. Communication & Cognition - Artificial Intelligence, vol. 10, N°1-2, 109-148 (1993)

22. B. Hasslacher: Beyond the Turing Machine. In R. Herken (ed.): The Universal Turing Machine. A Half-Century Survey. Oxford University Press, Oxford, 1988, pp. 417-431

23. R. Feynman: Simulating Physics with Computers. International Journal of Theoretical Physics 21, 6-7, 467-488 (1982)

24. M. Gardner: Mathematical Games on Cellular Automata, Self-reproduction, the Garden of Eden and the Game Life. Scientific American, 112-117, February 1971

25. H. Levy, F. Lessman: Finite Difference Equations. Pitman, London 1959

26. S. Lloyd: A Potentially Realizable Quantum Computer. Science 261, pp. 1569-1571 (1993) and 263, p. 695 (1994)

27. B. Mandelbrot: The Fractal Geometry of Nature. Freeman, San Francisco 1983

28. P. Marcer, D. M. Dubois: An outline model of cosmological evolution. In: Association Internationale de Cybernétique (éditeur): 13th International Congress on Cybernetics, Namur 1992, pp. 157-160

29. R. M. May: Simple mathematical models with very complicated dynamics. Nature 261, 459-467 (1976)

30. W. S. McCulloch, W. Pitts. Bulletin of Mathematical Biophysics 5:115-133 (1943)

31. R. Pearl: Studies in human biology. William and Wilkins, Baltimore 1924

32. F. Pichler, H. Scwärtzel (Eds.): CAST Methods in Modelling: Computer Aide Systems Theory for the Design of Intelligent Machines. Springer-Verlag 1992

33. W. Pitts, W. S. McCulloch. Bulletin of Mathematical Biophysics 9:127-147 (1947)

34. R. Rosen: Causal Structures in Brains and Machines, Int. J. Gen. Syst. 12, 107-126 (1986)

35. A. Rosenblueth, N. Wiener, J. Bigelow: Behavior, purpose and teleology. Philosophy of Science, 10, 18-24 (1943)

36. F. Scheid: Theory and Problems of Numerical Analysis. McGraw-Hill Inc. 1986

37. P. W. P. Shor: Algorithms for Quantum Computation: Discrete Log and Factoring. In: Conference on Foundations of Computer Science, November 1994

38. F. Varela: Autonomie et connaissance. Seuil 1989

39. P. F. Verhulst: Nuov. Mem. Acad. Royale, Bruxelles, 18, 1, 1845 & 20,1, 1847

40. V. Volterra: Leçon sur la théorie mathématique de la lutte pour la vie. Gauthier-Villars 1931

41. E. von Glasersfeld: Teleology and the Concepts of Causation. In: G. Van de Vijver (ed.): Sel-organizing and Complex Systems. Philosophica 1990, 46, pp. 17-43

42. G. Weisbuch: Dynamique des systèmes complexes: une introduction aux réseaux d'automates. InterEditions/Editions du CNRS 1989

43. S. Wolfram (ed.): Theory and Application of Cellular Automata. World Scientific, Singapore/Teanek, N. Y. 1986

44. K. Zuse K: Discrete Mathematics and Rechnender Raum (Computing Space) - Part 1 - Cellular Structured Space (Rechnender Raum) and Physical Phenomena - Part 2 - Konrad-Zuse-Zentrm für Informationstechnik, Berlin, Technical Report TR 94-10, 1994

45. K. Zuse: The Computer - My Life. Springer-Verlag 1993, 245 p.

46. K. Zuse: The Computing Universe. International Journal of Theoretical Physics, 21, 6/7, 589-600 (1982)

47. K. Zuse: Ansätze einer Theorie des Netzautomaten. Nova Acta Leopoldina, Halle, Saale, West Germany 43, 220 (1975)

48. K. Zuse: Rechnender Raum. Schriften zur Datenverarbeitung, Band 1, Friedrich Vieweg und Sohn, Braunschweig, West Germany 1969, 70 p.

Validation of a Model of an AGVs Scheduling Heuristic Using Radio-Taxi Data

J. Barahona da Fonseca

UNL/FCT/DEP. ELECTRICAL ENGINEERING
QUINTA DA TORRE
2825 MONTE DA CAPARICA
PORTUGAL

Abstract. In this paper it is tried to present the methodology of design, implementation, experimentation and validation used in the development of an autonomous guided vehicle (AGV) network simulator. This work arises in the context of the design of AGVs networks. The optimal solution of the problems associated to the management of an AGVs network is very heavy computationally. In common practice are used heuristics that don't guarantee the optimal solution. The main motivation of this work was to find an answer to the question:
Given an AGVs network, a computational power and a criteria of evaluation of the performance, which are the scheduling heuristic and the length of the list of tasks that give the best performance?
The answer to this question was found through the simulation of four Scheduling Heuristics over the same AGVs Network- FIFO, Closer First, Closer First with Timeouts and Mixed. FIFO had the best fit with radio-taxi data. To implement these scheduling heuristics it was developed a Simulator of AGVs Networks over the package PC-Model. The results obtained were validated through the comparison of the simulation results with the data acquired in a radio-taxis central. This comparison is legitimated by the existence of an quasi-isomorphic relationship between some aspects of an AGVs Network and some characteristics of a radio-taxis network. The area of validation of simulators is an area where there are not standard techniques and where research development is needed. By the validation of a simulator It is meant the estimation of its confidence degree. The confidence degree of a simulator is defined as the probability of making a correct decision in consequence of the use of the simulator. The formulation of the validation problem is made through hypothesis testing. The confidence degree of a simulator is expressed in terms of the probabilities of type I and II errors. Given the limitations of some of statistical tests, the validation of a simulator included the application of tests similar to the Turing tests. A radio-taxis network proved to provide a satisfactory model validation for an AGVs network using a set of indicator variables.

1 Introduction

The detailed simulation of an industrial environment implies the implementation of the whole scheduling both of the production system and the AGVs Network, in case such a transportation network exist. This type of representation involves the simultaneous solution of two NP-Complete problems. French (1982) has shown that the scheduling of the production (m jobs over n machines) is a NP-Complete problem [5] and Meng et al (1989) have demonstrated that the scheduling of tasks executed by AGVs is also NP-Complete [6]. Due to the limitations of the computational environment we used we did choose to not implement the production scheduling. The modelling of the production was made through a set of random generators of AGV demands. These generators of demands were implemented by the workstations. This choice led us to difficulties in the definition of the optimal solution since the classical theory of scheduling is not valid in this case[5]. In this context, the characterization of the scheduling heuristics in terms of the distance to optimal solution is out of the scope of the methods used in our approach. We centred the study of the scheduling heuristics in the comparative analysis based on the performance measures:

a. mean distance traveled by task,

b. mean waiting time for an AGV.

The mean distance traveled by task was used as a performance measure because when its value decreases the costs due to energy consumption and maintenance of the AGVs network also decrease. In the following sections we describe respectively the (a) methods, (b) the approach followed in the Design, Implementation and Experimentation of the AGVs network simulator, (c) validation procedure and its application and (d) the main results and conclusions as well as the possible evolution of this study.

2 Methods

Simulation methods were used in the study of an AGVs network due to the complexity of mathematical analysis which would be required[7,8]. Our work was centred in the solution of the problem of scheduling of tasks executed by AGVs. We may consider the model of our simulator as distributed since the various sub-problems (scheduling, routing and solution of collisions) were solved separately by intelligent autonomous agents [9,10]. We adopted a low level approach in which to every entity we associated a simulation object. The AGVs and other objects hadn't any decision power. Intelligent autonomous agents were implemented by heuristics. With this distributed approximation the optimal solution couldn't be obtained since the heuristics don't guarantee optimal solutions for each of the sub-problems. On the other hand the drawback of the centralized solution consists in the need of using a heavy computational power to obtain the optimal solution in real time tasks [6,11,12]. Given that the heuristics that solve each of the sub-problems can be formulated as a set of rules, the techniques of distributed artificial intelligence have a broad application in the project of AGVs networks simulators [9,13,14,15,16,17,18].

The problem of validation of simulators of observable systems [23,24,25,26] has rare references in the literature [19,20,21,22]. The problem of validation of simulators of non-observable systems is only referred by some authors [24]. We developed and implemented a methodology of validation of simulators of non-observable systems. This validation methodology rests in the putative attribution of a relation of isomorphism between a network of AGVs and a network of radio-taxis. This isomorphic relation legitimates the comparison of the results of the simulation of a network of AGVs with the data acquired in the records of a radio-taxis centre. We find here the main goal of our work namely the validation of a simulator. The problems of validation of simulators belong to an area in which still there isn't a consensus and a great effort of investigation is still going on [23,24,25,26]. In [23] the problem of the validation of a simulator is approached according with a theoretical point of view in which more attention is given to statistical processing. Balci and Sargent (1981) proposed a multivariate statistical test for estimating the confidence degree of a simulator [25]. We didn't use this test because its applicability requires a normal distribution for all the characterization variables. It was used the chi-square test to compare each pair of characterization variables. The result of the most unfavorable test was taken as an indicator of the confidence degree.

3 Design, Implementation and Experimentation of the AGVs Networks Simulator

In this section we describe the simulator of networks of AGVs developed over the environment PC-Model [35]. The limitations of this computational environment forced us to not try the simultaneous solution of the problems of production scheduling and scheduling of the AGVs. We made the option of not reproducing in detail the production process. As an alternative we developed a stochastic approach to the industrial production environment. We considered each workstation as a random generator of requests of AGVs. In this approach we found difficulties in the definition of the optimal solution once the results of the classic scheduling theory [5] aren't applicable. Therefore the solutions we obtained were not compared with the optimal solution. We made relative comparisons between four distinct scheduling heuristics of AGV tasks. As performance indicators were used the *mean distance traveled by task* and the *mean waiting time for an AGV.*

3.1 Computational Model

It was used a distributed approximation. The problem of management of the network of AGVs was partitioned in three independent sub-problems:

a.   Scheduling of the tasks executed by the AGVs,

b.   Routing of the AGVs,

c.   Solution of collisions between AGVs.

The scheduling heuristic attribute the tasks to the AGVs. When it is attributed a task to an AGV it is inserted in the last position of the list of tasks. In parallel the heuristic of routing makes the decision about which will be the next node for those AGVs that at that moment stay at a node. The heuristic of routing does also contribute to the solution of collisions problem. The computational model of the simulator of networks of AGVs was developed following the principle of isomorphism in the simulation [1,2,3,4]. Given the same situations (chosen attributes which characterize the relevant aspects of the physical system) the objects of simulation must react in the same way as the physical entities that they represent. All the states of the physical system must have a equivalent representation in the model. The computational model of the simulator of networks of AGVs is constituted by *inert objects, live objects and intelligent autonomous agents*. In figure 1 we present the main relations between the various elements of the computational model.

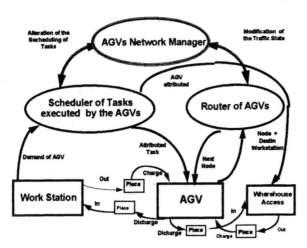

Fig. 1. The ellipses represent the intelligent agents and the rectangles represent live objects.

By *inert objects* we mean the objects that don't move along the AGVs network. The *inert objects* form a set to which belong the *nodes* and *lines between nodes*. By *live objects* we mean the objects that move around the AGVs network but haven't any type of decision power. To the set of *live objects* belong the *AGVs, workstations, warehouses accesses and pieces*. The *intelligent agents* include the *heuristics of scheduling, routing and solution of collisions*. Each intelligent agent is formed by a routine that is always running and monitoring the state of the network of AGVs with the aim of finding any *live object* waiting 'new orders'. The description of the *intelligent agents* is done through the definition of the algorithm or heuristic that implement them.

3.2 Implementation of the Computational Model

In the development of the simulator of AGVs networks we used exclusively the simulation package PC-Model [35]. This package has the characteristics of being oriented to the graphical animation and of being based in concurrent processes. Each live object and intelligent agent was implemented by a concurrent process. The interaction of the live objects and between the live objects and intelligent agents is translated into a communication problem between concurrent processes.

3.3 Experimentation with the Simulator

The simulations that we developed were oriented to obtain an answer to the fundamental question that motivated this work. In these simulations we used a network of AGVs with 8 workstations, 4 warehouse accesses, 24 nodes, 36 lines and 4 AGVs. In figure 2 we present this network.

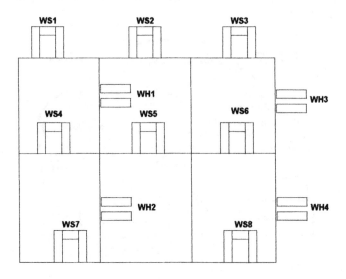

Fig. 2. Each pair of rectangles represents a warehouse access and each triple represents a workstation

The network presents a maximum connectivity of 4, a minimum connectivity of 2 and a mean connectivity of 3. We preserved a not minimal degree of connectivity once the performance of the heuristic of routing and solution of collisions decreases with the decrease of the connectivity. With the increase of connectivity the probability of arising collisions and deadlock situations decreases and the obtained trajectories approximated the optimum ones. In figure 3 we show the result of a comparative analysis of the evolution of the *mean distance traveled by task* with the *length of the list of tasks* associated to each of the four scheduling heuristics. The minimum value was obtained for the heuristic 'Nearer First' for a length of the list of tasks of 2.

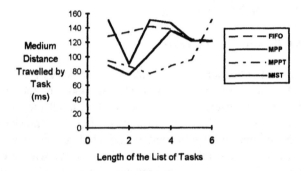

Fig. 3. The mean distance is calculated above all the executed tasks.

The heuristic 'Nearer First with Time-outs' is the one that presents lower values of the *mean waiting time for an AGV* for a value of the length of the list of tasks of 3. In figure 4 we present a comparative analysis in terms of the *mean waiting time for an AGV*.

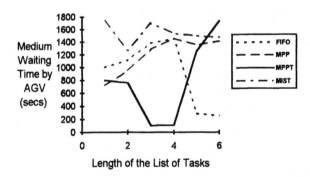

Fig. 4. It wasn't implemented any mechanism of given up of calls for AGVs.

4 Statistical Validation of the Simulator of AGVs Networks

The final result of the statistical validation is the confidence degree of the simulator. This confidence degree express the probability of adequate applicability of the results presented in the previous section to a real AGVs network. We define the null hypothesis as the no adjustment of the computational model of the simulator of AGVs networks to the computational model of a simulator of a radio-taxis network as we didn't have available any real AGVs network. We test the null hypothesis comparing the distributions of the number of services and tasks associated to the characterization variables of the AGVs network and of the radio-taxis network. We calculate the probability of errors of type I through the application of the test of chi-square.

4.1 Isomorphism Relation AGVs-Taxis

The methodology of validation of the simulator of the AGVs network is based in the isomorphic relation between the computational model of the simulator of a AGVs network and the computational model of the simulator of a radio-taxis network. The existence of this isomorphic relation is translated into the correspondence one-to-one between the objects and intelligent autonomous agents of the two universes and in the similarity of their behaviors. We will now analyze this isomorphic relation. Comparing the computational model of the simulator of a AGVs network, see figure 2, with the computational model of a simulator of radio-taxis network, see figure 5, the following correspondences can be established :

- Manager of the AGVs network-Manager of the Radio taxis network,

- Scheduler of tasks executed by the AGVs- Radio taxis Central Operator,

- Router of AGVs- taxi driver,

- Workstation-Commercial/Services zone,

- Warehouse access-Residential/Leisure zone,

- Piece-Person,

- AGV-Taxi,

- Task-Service,

- Node-Crossing.

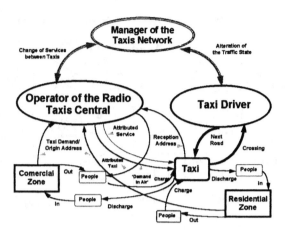

Fig. 5. The behavior of the radio radio-taxis central operator is described by the regulations of the central.

These correspondences are translated into the similarity of behavior of the objects and intelligent autonomous agents of the AGVs network and radio-taxis network.

4.2 Data Acquisition in a Radio-Taxis Central

The data sample resulted from the records of the communications with the radio-taxis central during four Fridays. We have chosen the Fridays because those are the higher demand days. Taxis were in a charge situation in those days and we also considered AGVs in a charge situation. This data sample consists of about 500 services. We selected the charge situation since to an economic project of an AGVs network corresponds a network totally explored. When the AGVs network is in a charge situation there are no free AGVs. The management of free AGVs is a difficult problem that we didn't explore in this work.

4.3 Adjustment and calibration of the simulator

To calibrate the simulator we obtained the equivalent AGVs network. In figure 6 we present the equivalent AGVs network obtained from the acquired data. The calibration of the active simulator consists in the adjustment of the topologic and dynamic parameters of the simulated network and equivalent network.

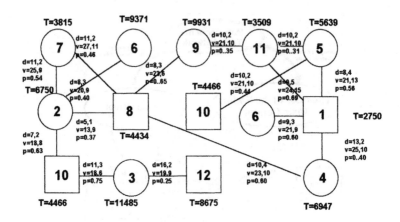

Fig. 6. To simplify the equivalent AGVs network the nodes 6 and 10 are duplicated.

In figure 7 we present the AGVs network that resulted from the calibration and adjustment of the initially proposed model (see figure 2).

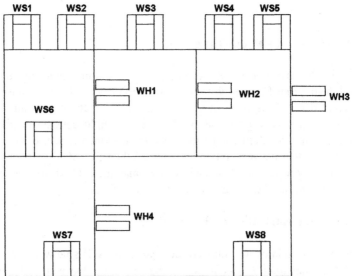

Fig. 7. The differences between the distances of pares of workstations are compensated through the velocity of the AGVs.

4.4 Statistical Evaluation

Once obtained the distributions of the number of tasks by interval of the characterization variable over a universe of 500 tasks, these distributions are compared with the distributions of the number of services by interval of the correspondent characterization variable. We applied the test of chi-square to each pair of distributions. We considered the confidence degree as the most unfavorable, that is, 75%.

5 Discussion and Conclusions

The main result of this work can be written as:"Given an AGVs network and a computational power, exists a scheduling heuristic and a length of the task list which maximize the performance of the scheduling heuristic in terms of a measure of performance". The distributed approximation to the implementation of simulators is a recent topic of research [17,18,30,31,32]. We didn't find any reference on simulators of AGVs networks using the distributed approximation. One of the advantages that result from the use of a distributed model consists in the greater facility of his implementation over a distributed computational environment [9,10]. Since the problem of management of an AGVs network is very heavy computationally the implementation of a high quality simulator of networks of AGVs justifies the use of multiprocessing [1,2,3,4]. The assumption of an isomorphic relation justifies that the results of the simulation of one of universes (network of AGVs) can be compared with the acquired data in the other universe (network of radio-taxis). Thus the heuristics applied in one of the universes can be identically applied in the isomorphic universe. We show that the heuristic 'first in first out' ('FIFO') in AGVs is very similar to the protocol of attribution of services to radio-taxis [34]. Conversely the existence of a isomorphism relation between a network of AGVs and a network of radio-taxis allows that the *results obtained in the investigation of methods of solution of the problems of the AGVs network can be identically applied in the management of a radio-taxis network.*

We conclude that the developed simulator is a good simulator but it still needs a lot of work to improve its confidence degree. We are now developing a new version above a network of transputers in concurrent C++.

7. REFERENCES

[1] J. Barahona da Fonseca, *Simulation of Scheduling Heuristics in an AGVs Network*, Lisboa: IST, 1990.

[2] J. Barahona da Fonseca, *Final Report- Medida F- Formação Profissional de Investigadores para Inserção nas Empresas- Transporte Automático de Materiais.* Lisboa: IST, 31 de Outubro de 1991.

[3] J. Barahona da Fonseca, "Design, Analysis and Simulation of de Scheduling Heuristics in an AGVs Network," *3.as Jornadas Nacionais de Projecto, Planeamento e Produção Assistidos por Computador*, 4 a 6 de Dezembro de 1991.

[4] J. Barahona da Fonseca, *Project, Implementation and Validation of a AGVs Networks Simulator*, Tese de Mestrado, Lisboa: IST, Janeiro 1994.

[5] S. French, *Sequencing and Scheduling: An Introduction to the Mathematics of the Job-Shop.* London: Ellis Horwood Limited, 1982.

[6] A. C.-C. Meng, Y. F. Choong and M. Sullivan, "Scheduling and Path Planning of Multiple Robots in a Factory," *Applications of Artificial Intelligence VII, SPIE,* vol. 1095, pp. 394-404, 1989.

[7] J. Lee, "Evaluation of Automated Guided Vehicle Systems by Simulation," *Proc. 12th Annual Conf. on Comp. and Industrial Engineering,* 1990.

[8] D. D. Grossman, "Traffic Control of Multiple Robot Vehicles," *IEEE Journal of Robotics and Automation,* Vol. 4, No. 5, October, 1988.

[9] A. H. Bond and L. Gasser, *Readings In Distributed Artificial Intelligence.* New York: Morgan Kaufmann Publishers, Inc., 1988.

[10] M. Kamel and A. Syed, "Strategies for problem decomposition in multiagent planning," *Robotics and Manufacturing: Recent Trends in Research, Education and Applications,* 1991.

[11] C. L. Chen, C. S. Lee and C. D. McGillem, "Task Assignment and Load Balancing of Autonomous Vehicles in a Flexible Manufacturing System," *IEEE Journal of Robotics and Automation,* Vol. RA-3, No. 6, December, 1987.

[12] L. Magdalena et al., "Collision Free Path Generation in a FMS with Multiple Autonomous Vehicles," *Proc. INCOM,* 1989.

[13] J. Liebowitz and P. Lightfoot, "Expert scheduling systems: survey and preliminary design concepts," *Applied Artificial Intelligence,* N.1, pp. 261-283, 1987.

[14] J. R. Slagle and H. Hamburger, "An expert system for a resource allocation problem," *Communications of the ACM,* vol. 28, No. 9, pp. 994-1004, September 1985.

[15] M. A. Wing and G. Rzevski, "The use of Artificial Intelligence Techniques in AGV Systems," *5th Int. Conf. Automated Guided Vehicle Systems,* pp. 183-194, October 1987.

[16] T. C. Goodhead, C. N. Nwufoh and M. Stevens, "AGV control using an intelligent environment approach," *Proc. 6th Int. Conf. Automated Guided Vehicle Systems,* pp. 241-251, October 1988.

[17] C. Tsatsoulis, "A Review of Artificial Intelligence in Simulation," *SIGART Bulletin,* Vol. 2, N. 1, 1992.

[18] B. Chaib-draa, R. Mandiau and P. Millot, "Distributed Artificial Intelligence: an annotated bibliography," *SIGART Bulletin,* Vol. 3, N. 3, 1992.

[19] T. Araki, "Flexible *AGV* System Simulator," *Proc. 5th Int. Automated Guided Vehicle Systems,* pp. 77-86, Oct. 1987.

[20] V. B. Norman, T. A. Norman and K. Farnsworth, "Rule-based simulation of AGV systems," *Proc. 5th Int. Conf. Automated Guided Vehicle Systems,* 1987.

[21] J. Banks, "The simulation of material handling systems," *Simulation,* vol. 55, No.5, pp. 261-270, Nov. 1990.

[22] A. Carrie, *Simulation of Manufacturing Systems,* London: John Wiley & Sons, 1988.

[23] V. Deslandres and H. Pierreval, "An expert system prototype assisting the statistical validation of simulation models," *Simulation,* vol. 56, No. 2, pp. 79-90, Feb 91.

[24] J. W. Schmidt, *Model Validation.* Blacksburg: Dep. Industrial Engineering and Operations Research, Virginia Polytechnic Institute and State University, 1983.

[25] D. A. Balci and R. G. Sargent, "A Methodology for Cost-Risk Analysis in the Statistical Validation of Simulation Models," *Communications of the ACM.,* April 1981, Vol. 24, N. 11, pp. 190-197.

[26] I. D. Greig, "Validation, statistical testing, and the decision to model," *Simulation,* August 1979.

[27] M. R. Spiegel, *Estatística.* New York: McGraw-Hill, 1971.

[28] B. W. Lindgren, *Statistical Theory.* New York: Macmillan Publishing Co., Inc., 1976.

[29] L. W. Schruben, "Establishing the credibility of simulations," *Simulation,*March 1980, pp. 101-105.

[30] V. K. Madisetti, J. C. Walrand and D. G. Messerschmitt, "Asynchronous Algorithms for the Parallel Simulation of Event-Driven Dynamical Systems," *ACM Transactions on Modeling and Computer Simulation,* Vol. 1, N. 3, July 1991, pp. 244-274.

[31] R. Bagrodia, K. M. Chandy and W. T. Liao, "A unifying framework for Distributed Simulation," *ACM Transactions on Modeling and Computer Simulation,* Vol. 1, N. 4, October 1991, pp. 348-385.

[32] P. Konas and P.-C. Yew, "Parallel Discret Event Simulation on Shared-Memory Multiprocessors," *Simulation,* Vol. 1, N. 5, April 1991, pp. 134-148.

[33] M. P. P. Sousa, *Concurrent and Object Oriented Languages.* Covilhã: Universidade da Beira Interior, 1993.

[34] Autocoope, *Regulations of the Radio Radio-taxis Central,* Lisboa, 1989.

[35] D. A. White, "PCModel and PCModel/GAF- Screen Oriented Modeling," *Proc. 1986 Winter Simulation Conf.,* pp. 164-167.

Training Simulator for Garoña Nuclear Power Plant

Francisco Bustío, Pedro Corcuera, Eduardo Mora

Department of Applied Mathematics and Computer Sciences
University of Cantabria
Avda. de los Castros s/n. 39005 Santander. SPAIN

Fax: 34-42-282190

Abstract. The training of Nuclear Power Plant Operators is the utmost importance for the proper running of Plants, with the strictest of security conditions. Given the specific characteristics of this type of energy, the training of operators can be carried out only by means of simulators.

All Nuclear Power Plants have access to accurate simulation programs which are used for other purposes. This paper describes the development of a training simulator using one of these codes.

Firstly, the modifications carried out on the simulation code to make it interactive and its operating mode are described.

Then, the graphic and multimedia capacities allotted to the user interface are detailed.

Finally, reference is made to lines of work currently being developed, such as the acquisition and representation under the same environment, of plant data in real time and the connection with expert systems.

Description

TS-G (**Training Simulator for Garoña plant**) is an interactive graphic representation system which enables all kinds of accidents and operator actions to be simulated in real time.

TS-G is a tool which, because of its interactivity characteristics, is particularly suitable for the training of plant operators, teaching of new staff and analysis of accidents occurred, although it can also be used for other purposes. The Dataviews graphic interface design software with an adapted version of the MAAP simulation code has been used in the development of the system.

This simulator has been designed for general use, although it has been customized to fit the parameters and characteristics of the current layout of the Santa Maria de Garoña Nuclear Power Plant.

Background

TS-G was initiated as part of a Research and Development project jointly undertaken by NUCLENOR S.A. and the Department of Applied Mathematics and Computer Science of The University of Cantabria. This project's aims are to study, analyze and develop information science techniques for the control and simulation of the systems which make up a Nuclear Power Plant (NPP), particularly in the fields of Neutronics and Thermohydraulics, with specific application to the Santa Maria de Garoña Nuclear Power Plant.

It was necessary, therefore, to provide an analytic tool capable of simulating malfunctions which affect the running of a NPP, as well as probable temporary adjustments and hypothetical accident sequences. This tool was to have several important applications in the running and the security of the power plant, as well as in the training of operators.

Since codes capable of simulating the running of a NPP have long been available, the first stage was to develop a series of applications which, by incorporating graphic capacities, would enable a faster interpretation of the results of the simulations obtained by these codes. These applications were designed in such a way that real plant events could also be studied and even compared with the simulations.

With the experience acquired from these developments, it was decided to commence the development of a training simulator which, whilst maintaining and improving the previously mentioned graphic characteristics, would facilitate an interactive link to the adopted simulation code.

Project Aims

In order to be sure that the simulation codes truly correspond to reality, it is necessary to constantly evaluate its models by comparing the simulated events with real plant data, which leads to the adjustment of parameters.

The initial aim of the project was to compile real and simulated events for risk analysis, the study of systems behavior and the revision of operating procedures.

These operations, whilst they may be enhanced by interactive simulation, can largely be dealt with by non-interactive applications such as those developed initially.

Another important purpose of the simulation of NPPs is to be found in the area of education, both in teaching and in the training of operators. In order to adequately fulfill this latter objective, it is essential to dispose of a simulator with an interactive capacity. In this way, the operators can manipulate the controls in a manner similar to that which they would use in the plant, and can thus be trained to respond to any anomalous situation.

To give the TS-G greater flexibility and a greater likeness to the reality of the everyday running of the plant, a user interface was built.

Simulation Code

In order to choose the most appropriate code to build the interactive simulator, the TRAC (Transient Reactor Analysis Code) [5] and MAAP (Modular Accident Analysis Program) [4] codes were studied in depth. Their structures, modelization capacities, the variables that they use, accuracy and speed of calculation, the capability for interactive use, etc. were all studied.

As a consequence, it was considered that the MAAP code was the most suitable for the development of the software. It should be pointed out that while the MAAP code offered the best characteristics for use in the simulator, it had to be appropriately adapted in order to function interactively.

Software Used for Development

In order to develop the interface, the Dataviews software was chosen, principally for its orientation towards instrumentation engineering and process control. Moreover, this software uses the graphics standard X-Window [3] and runs under the operating system UNIX.

Furthermore, the machines in which it is installed do not need to be particularly powerful; low priced work-stations and/or high level personal computers are enough.

The Training Simulator

The TS-G screens make up a user environment and, in them, the power plant's systems are represented by objects whose dynamic properties are associated to the events and variables which determine their performance. At the beginning of each session a routine creates the connections between these properties and the variables and events of the MAAP code, thus making way for interactive communication. The interface also incorporates event control routines allowing the user's actions to be registered (see fig.1).

The simulator is designed in such a way that several users can interact simultaneously on the process. At the moment, it consists of six monitors assigned both to control and to visualize systems. The instructor, who is the person in charge of provoking anomalies during the training exercises for operators, disposes of a console from which he can interact in real time. Meanwhile, by means of five other consoles, the operator can undertake control operations, resolving the conflictive situations provoked by the instructor.

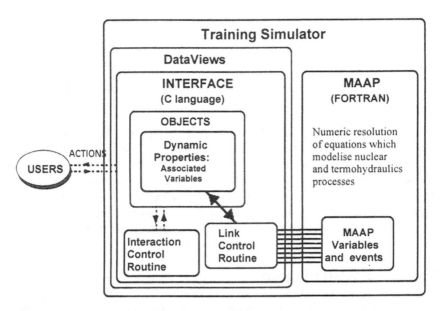

Fig. 1. Internal Functional Operation.

The TS-G layout (see fig 2.), currently in operation, consists of the following hardware:

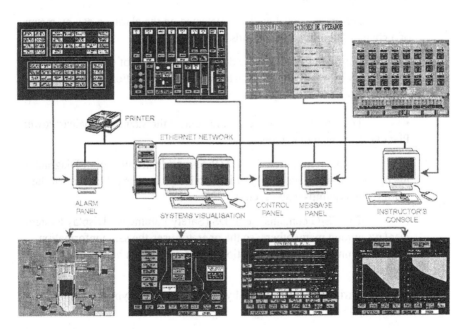

Fig. 2. The TS-G layout.

A Hewlett Packard series 9000/712 workstation.

Six X11 terminals to visualize different systems, one of them for use as the instructor´s post.

One laser printer for printing graphics of the evolution of the desired variables during or at the end of each session.

An additional capacity already incorporated into the simulator is the possibility of visualizing the real time plant data by making use of the data acquisition system installed in Santa María de Garoña NPP. This means that the same screens developed for the TS-G have been used, saving effort. This capacity can be achieved from any computer post at NUCLENOR or even the University of Cantabria. In this process, a microwave radiolink is used to overcome the problem of the 140 km. which separate the University of Cantabria from the NPP.

Training Simulator Features

When working in a training session, the simulator enables several operations to be carried out. With the aim of clarifying its possibilities some of these are as follows:

- The INSTRUCTOR can initiate malfunctions and/or accidents using his control panel.

- The emergency signals are detected on the alarm screen by means of a change of color and/or sounds.

- During the simulation, a detailed description of events can be observed by means of messages which describe the actions of the operator and the responses of the system itself.

- The operator can observe and control the status of Nuclear Power Plant systems using the mouse.

- Using an imported P & ID (Pipes and Instrumentation Diagrams), the operator has the possibility of interactively changing the status of the components (pumps, valves, etc.).

- The TS-G contains the SPDS (Safety Parameters Display System) displays among many others, so the operator uses the same information during training and during operation. The displays can be customized as needed.

- Variables are displayed by means of several types of graphics and/or digits with color changes.

- By means of X-Y graphics values can be identified both inside and outside of admissible regions.

Work in Progress

Furthermore, work is already being carried out on the incorporation of an expert system. This expert system will enable real time plant data to be taken and processed in order to generate a MAAP input file. This input file will contain the accident sequence which the expert system has arrived at. The expert system will also contain all the Emergency Operation Procedures (EOP's) in such a way that the transient evolution reflects the actions that the operator should take.

A global schema of the system can be seen in figure 3.

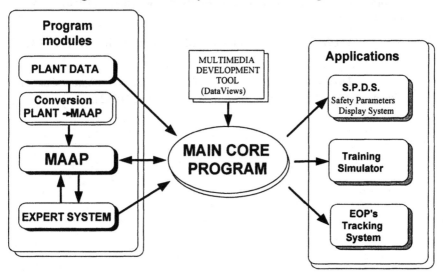

Fig. 3. Final schema of the system.

Conclusions

This paper describes the building of a training simulator using the methodology proposed in Bustío and others [1], [2].

The development achieved is applicable both in the simulation of other types of Nuclear Power Plants and in a wide variety of industrial processes in which the user interface needs to be particularly friendly. This has been achieved by following the current trends in "software reusability".

References

1.   F. A. Bustío, P. A. Corcuera, J. A. García, E. Mora. *Multimedia Environments: Designs for Simulation.* Cybernetics and Systems 25, 63-71 (1994).

2.   Meyer, B. *Object Oriented Software Construction.* Prentice-Hall (1988).

3.   Quercia, Valerie, and Tim O'Reilly. *X Window System User's Guide vol. 3.* Sebastopol, CA. O'Reilly & Associates (1988). ISBN 0-937175-36-6.

4.   *MAAP - 3.0 B Computer Code Manual.* EPRI NP-7071-CCML (Nov 1990).

5.   *TRAC-BF1/MOD1: An advanced Best-Estimate Computer Program fro BWR Accident Analysis.* User's Guide (1992).

Supervisory Control and Data Acquisition System for the Gas Flow Networks

Ryszard Klempous, Barbara Łysakowska, Jan Nikodem

Institute of Technical Cybernetics, Wrocław Technical University,
27 Wybrzeże Wyspiańskiego Str. 50-372 Wrocław, POLAND

Abstract. In this paper is proposed a complex acquisition system with data measurement and control that makes it possible to simulate methods of usage of the control of non-linear flow networks. The system consists of three hierarchical levels: a strategy level with supervisory centre, a tactical level with dispatcher centres, and a control level with local remote controllers. An approach of data received from a pipeline network using a radio communication link rapidly accelerates the simulation process of gas flow in the network. It provides very effective monitoring for dispatcher centres of the network's actual states and co-ordinates the local controllers work.

1 Introduction

The flow networks are distribution systems consisting of pumping stations, consumers and flow accumulation points, connected together by means of a pipeline network , which ensure the demanded amount of flow transportation from the sources to the receivers.

The medium flow principles at these networks are defined by three physical laws concerned with flow dynamics [1].

First, *the state equation* establishing the relationship between the substance pressure (head) P and its density ρ, can be written as

$$P = \alpha \, T \, \rho, \qquad \alpha \in \mathbf{R}_{+} \qquad (1)$$

where T is the temperature of the substance.

The next equation expresses *the law of substance conservation* [8]. If we consider the flow at a particular point of a pipeline, the velocity of the density abatement results in the divergence of the mass velocity vector

$$div(pV) = -\frac{\partial p}{\partial t} , \qquad (2)$$

where div - the divergence of a vector,

V - the molecules velocity vector.

Finally , the third equation is based on *Newton's law of a motion.* If one considers the variations of the vector (V) resulting in force activity, one obtains the following partial differential equations [1]

$$p\left[\frac{\partial V}{\partial t}+(V\,\nabla)V\right]=\nabla P-p\nabla\varphi\ ,\qquad\qquad(3)$$

where: P - pressure (head) vector,

φ - the potential of external field,

∇ - the nabla operator.

In the last equation, the left side describes the molecules acceleration vector. On the right side is denoted respectively the forces related to pressure within a pipeline and the external potential field.

Although equations (1)-(3) fully describe the flow in the closed distribution networks during the non-stationary forced flow of a compressible substance, because of their degree of complexity they are not useful for numerical calculations [5]. Below is presented a short description of a more helpful model of the flow in a closed distribution network.

2 The Closed Flow Network Modelling

Based on the equations (1)-(3) together with some simplifying assumptions that follow from an engineering practice (and at the same time ensure the appropriate relationship between the physical phenomena and their model [4]), one obtains the following equations;

Kirchhoff's first law which defines material continuity at nodes in the following form

$$A\,y-q=0\,,\qquad\qquad(4)$$

where:

$q\in R^{w}$ - the vector of the flow from network nodes,

$A_{[wxm]}$ - the incidence matrix,

$y\in R^{m}$ - the vector of the flow on network arcs.

Kirchhoff's second law:

$$Bx=0\ ,\qquad\qquad(5)$$

where

$B_{[(m-w+1)xm]}$ - the loop matrix,

$x \in R^m$ - the vector of head differences between two ends of an arc.

It has been shown [4] that, in hydrodynamics, mathematical confirmation of Newton's law (3) is accomplished with the help of Bernoulli's theorem (for one dimensional steady state flow) and Hanzen-William's law [9]. Concerning the gas pipelines network, the rules of gas flow in a pipe, related to Newton's equation (3), are described using Herming's formula and Redlich-Kwong 's law [2].

So, as a generalisation the third equation can be written as follows

$$f(x,y) = O . \tag{6}$$

Moreover, for convenience, the vector of network nodes relative potentials $\pi \in R^m$ is introduced in the following way;

$$\pi = Cx + 1\pi_0 \tag{7}$$

where $1 = (1,1,...,1)^T$

        π_0 - is an arbitrary chosen pressure at the reference node,

        $C_{[wxm]}$ - is a matrix whose entries are -1,0,+1.

In [3] was shown the iterative method of solving the non-linear system equations (4)-(7), based on a modified version of Cross's method [4]. This method applies the accelerating procedures and takes into account flow accumulation phenomena in a pipeline network. The essence of that method is the iterative assignment of successive approximations of the node potentials vector p components. The paper [7] shows that, having real pressure values occurring at chosen network points, it is basically possible to accelerate obtaining the solution by using the algorithm convergence increasing. The task of operative network control needs such high pressure levels in the pumping station to ensure proper flow in the network and, at the same time, guarantee the consumers the demanded quantity of flow with suitable pressure.

Furthermore, the network distribution management needs the knowledge of its actual state, defined explicitly by the node potential π. The important role for the network management is also the possibility of the prediction of its states. This is possible with the help of the simulation method presented above, which is also based on the values of actual node potential π.

Due to the varying topographical conditions the pumping stations and flow accumulation points are located in, the control of the flow in the network is also variant. The additional pieces of information concerning node potentials and flow quantities coming to the receivers, being the feedback information of the control process, should also be picked up from the area of network localisation. Therefore, the communication between the dispatcher centre and each node of the pipelines network becomes extremely important from the network flow control point of view. The knowledge of node potentials at chosen network points increases the simulation algorithm convergence, additionally assuring full correspondence of the given solutions with the real network flow state. The communication with the pumping stations gives the dispatcher the opportunity to define the control strategy at each pumping station, whereas the communication with the receivers gives the feedback information of the control process.

3 The Architecture of Proposed System

The system consists of three subsystems representing the hierarchical structure of the proposed solution:

— a supervisory centre monitoring the actual state of a distribution system and coordinating the dispatcher's centre work,
— dispatcher centres monitoring the control and coordinating the local controllers work,
— local microprocessor controllers carrying out data acquisition and control in accordance with decisions from the dispatcher centre.

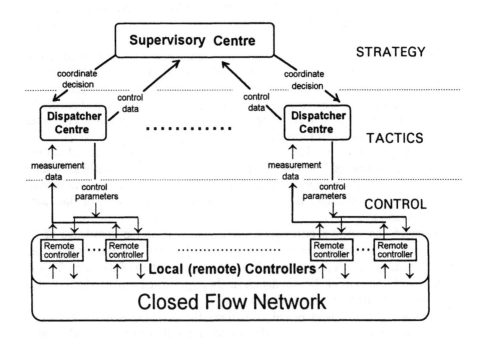

Fig.1. The hierarchical structure of the supervisory control and data acquisition system

Each level in such a structure can carry out different functions. At the highest level a strategy is defined, at the second level - tactics, and at the lowest level the closed flow network control decisions are carried out. The separation of levels also makes possible the performance and compression of information used at a given level and transferred onto adjoining levels. Each level receives the pieces of information about the flow and heads in the network , that are transferred to actual level from the nearest lower level (the lowest level gets the information directly from sensors installed on a pipeline or a node). Moreover, the functions carried out on a given level are parametrised, and the actual values of these parameters are given from the nearest higher level (on the highest level the values of these parameters are defined by a supervisor, determining the system control strategy).

The Supervisory Centre is in fact the central monitoring and coordination centre which has to provide accurate and update information. Its general task is system monitoring, and only in emergency situations (for instance supply deficiency, i.e. an imbalance between receivers' demands and pumping stations efficiency) does it take over the actual task of the system work coordination. While settling the distribution system work on the highest level, the supervisor defines the tasks for each dispatcher centre.

The level of dispatcher centre is responsible for the proper operation of the distribution system providing demanded flow from sources to consumers. On this level, it is a fully closed-loop automated control system which is not only capable of providing accurate real-time information of flow distribution parameters at each remote control point, but is also capable of controlling the pressure and flow characteristics at desired levels without the necessity of manual intervention. Knowing the actual state of the flow in the pipeline network and measurement data, the dispatcher can define control parameters for subordinated controllers. While working with the detectors set on a pipeline in the network, the controllers control the flow in the system based on parameters transferred from the dispatcher centres.

4 The Communication System

In the proposed solution two communication subsystems are assigned:

— between the supervisory centre and dispatcher's centres, this being a typical communication link serving to update information transmission concerning the actual state of the process,
— between dispatcher's centres and remote controllers, this being a telemetric link for on-line control and measurement data transmission.

Both of the above-mentioned communication subsystems have different possibilities for their technical realisation [6], resulting from different tasks of data communication. The proposed solutions are as follows:

- wireline data communication, using a leased telephone line for direct data transmission between Supervisory and Dispatcher Centres (our intended system is the Microwave Link Satellite Communication).
- wireless radio telemetry system that would be a valuable asset in streamlining operations, reducing recurring costs and improving remote service.

The communication between Dispatcher Centres and remote controllers is the crucial point for the whole distribution system, and the proposed customer-owned radio network for data communication provides a number of benefits. A reliable communication system for data transfer and control is available when needed, even during emergencies, and critical communications requirements are not controlled by a third party (telephone company), placing the control of the system in the customer's hands.

The proposed solution relies on packet-radio network application under the AX.25 standard based on the CCITT X.25 orders. The AX.25 protocol meets ISO Standard 3309,4335, and 6255 High Level Data Link Control (HDLC). The communication subsystem realised in agreement with the AX.25 standard assures the transmission of digital data both between the remote controllers and the Dispatcher Centres and at the same time between each of Dispatcher Centres and the Supervisory Centre.

Every station consists of a microprocessor controller and a transceiver with an antenna. The microprocessor controller consists of the following elements:

- a microprocessor MS-01 block supervising the controller work ,
- a TNC-2 node controller.

The node controller includes two main components - the microprocessor AX.25 protocol controller and the modem. The TNC-2 node controller is connected from the one side with the microprocessor MS-01 block, and from the other side with the transceiver.

The controller ensures information acquisition from the station where it is installed and on the other hand, while controlling the TNC2 node controller work, it ensures the communication with other network nodes. The transmitted data is grouped in packets including correctness data control word (CDC). In case of errors occurring in data received at the station, it claims the packed retransmission, and this can be repeated many times. In that way the system ensures the correction of errors which occurred during the data transmission. Each station has its own unique address on the network. The typical functions of a packet-radio communication system use a unique radio band (the simplex transmission), but collisions can occur when a band of two or more stations is accessed at the same time. One of the functions of the node controller is detecting and avoiding of such collisions, so that on a unique radio band many stations could work together.

The TNC-2 node controller works in the following modes:

- stations addressing, connecting, data transmitting and disconnecting,
- detecting of transmission errors and their automatic correction,

- determining access conflicts to the common transmission medium (radio band),
- converting a digital signal to an analogue signal and vice-versa by means of modem function,
- digipeater, i. e. a digital transmitter working in automatic mode.

The connection can be initiated by either of the communication participants. The following rules for establishing connections exist::

- normal mode: the connections are initiated by the Supervisory or Dispatcher Centres with a given repeated interval of a call-tone,
- emergency mode: the connection is initiated by other communication participants in any situation when it is necessary.

In the case of telephone communication the transmission range is limited by the accessibility of the public switched telephone network. With the radio communication technique the situation is different. Using transmitter just of a few watts power, a good receiver and a proper antenna installation, the range of UKF band available is basically equal to the optical horizon. So, it depends mainly on the height of the antenna installation. In the case of a necessary connection between the stations not being within the range of a direct connection, the digital transmitter should be used. The node controller can serve also as a digital transmitter. That means the controller intercepts transmission from one node and retransmitts it automatically to another one .
Therefore, if two stations are not at their radio range, they can use the retransmission capability of the other stations or retransmitters. This is illustrated below.

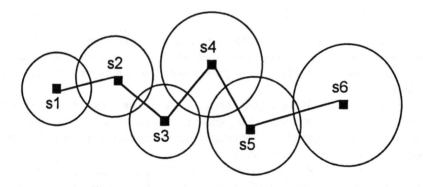

Fig. 2. The communication between s_1 and s_6 stations using s_2 ,..,s_5 digipeaters

Worth mentioning is the possibility of fixing the node controller at a point with a high terrain position and ranging over some large area. In that case the node controller serves as a digital transmitter with the possibility of communication between areas not being at a mutual radio range. The possibility of the retransmitting stations usage is very attractive in mountainous terrain. That situation is illustrated below.

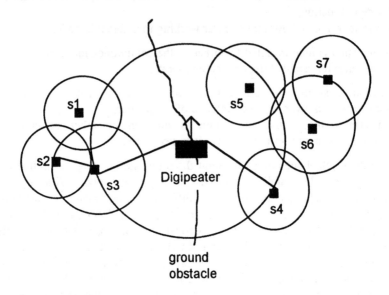

Fig. 3. The communication between s_3 and s_4 stations using a digipeater

5 Conclusions

The packet radio link ensures reliable and efficient communication over variety of line links (leased line, dial-up line, fiber, etc.). As regard the cost of most communication scheme solutions, the packet radio link is not very expensive; this includes maintenance.

The application of the ISO compliant protocol AX. 25 ensures secure and efficient transfer of large packets of data. Using data transmission rates up to 9600 bps, this kind of transmission permits full programming and diagnostic transfers from any location within the distributed system.

Using the intelligent Remote Terminal Units (RTU) the system provides a cost effective solution for most applications in distributed systems of Supervisory Control and Data Acquisition (SCADA) located on a wide area. The solution of RTU proposed here ensures the automatic alarms signal and gives remote diagnostics of these problems' origins.

The proposed SCADA system involves dispatchers to the computer aided decision making process in flow control of the gas or water distribution networks. So, the system can serve as a base of on-line automatic control using conventional or trunked radio links at these networks.

References

1. R.B. Feynmann,et al. : The Feynmann lectures on physics. Reading, MA: Addison-Wesley 1963.
2. F. Herming, Grundlangen und Praxis der Durchflussmessung. Dusseldorf: VDI Verlag 1967.
3. R. Klempous et al.: Simulation model of high pressure gas pipeline networks.In: Systems Analysis and Simulation. Berlin: Akademie Verlag 1988.
4. R. Klempous et al.: Simulation algorithm for non-linear network model with substance accumulation. In: 5-th International Congress of JCCAM. Leuven, Belgium , July 25-30, 1994.
5. J. Kralik et al.: Modelling the dynamics of flow in gas pipelines. In: IEEE Trans. on Systems, Man and Cybernetics, SMC 14(4), pp.586-596 (1984).
6. Motorola: Application note on data over radio. Schaumburg, IL 1994.
7. J. Nikodem, J. Ulasiewicz: Steady state flow optimisation in non-linear gas network based on the modified Cross's method. In: Journal of Gas, Water and Environment Engineering, JGWEE 8-9, Warszawa 1989.
8. A.J. Osiadacz: Simulation and analysis of gas networks. London: E.&F. Spon 1987.
9. U. Shamir: Optimisation in water distribution systems engineering. In: M. Avriel & R.S. Dembo (eds.): Engineering Optimisation, Mathematical Programming Studies 11. Amsterdam: North Holland 1979, pp.65-84.

Index of Authors

Springer-Verlag
and the Environment

We at Springer-Verlag firmly believe that an international science publisher has a special obligation to the environment, and our corporate policies consistently reflect this conviction.

We also expect our business partners – paper mills, printers, packaging manufacturers, etc. – to commit themselves to using environmentally friendly materials and production processes.

The paper in this book is made from low- or no-chlorine pulp and is acid free, in conformance with international standards for paper permanency.

Lecture Notes in Computer Science

For information about Vols. 1–954

please contact your bookseller or Springer-Verlag